British Qualifications 2016

46TH EDITION

A Complete Guide to Professional, Vocational & Academic Qualifications in the United Kingdom

KoganPage

LONDON PHILADELPHIA NEW DELHI

Publisher's note

Every possible effort has been made to ensure that the information contained in this book is accurate at the time of going to press, and the publishers and authors cannot accept responsibility for any errors or omissions, however caused. No responsibility for loss or damage occasioned to any person acting, or refraining from action, as a result of the material in this publication can be accepted by the editor, the publisher or any of the authors.

First published in Great Britain in 1966

Forty-sixth edition published in Great Britain and the United States in 2016 by Kogan Page Limited

2nd Floor, 45 Gee Street	1518 Walnut Street, Suite 1100	4737/23 Ansari Road
London EC1V 3RS	Philadelphia PA 19102	Daryaganj
United Kingdom	USA	New Delhi 110002
www.koganpage.com		India

© Kogan Page, 2016

British Library Cataloguing-in-Publication Data

A CIP record for this book is available from the British Library.

ISBN 978 0 7494 7480 5
E-ISBN 978 0 7494 7481 2
ISSN 0141-5972

Typeset by AMA DataSet Ltd, Preston
Print production managed by Jellyfish
Printed and bound by CPI Group (UK) Ltd, Croydon, CR0 4YY

PUBLISHER'S NOTE

This 46th edition of *British Qualifications* has been considerably revised and updated to reflect the many changes in degree, diploma and certificate courses and to take account of legislative reforms affecting the structure of higher and further education over the past year.

The editor and compilers are most grateful to the academic registrars and the secretaries of the many bodies they have contacted for information and advice. Without their cooperation, the revision and updating of *British Qualifications* would not have been possible.

CONTENTS

Contents

Contents

Contents

Contents

REFERENCES

Association of MBAs (AMBA) (annual) *AMBA – Financial Times Guide to Business Schools*, AMBA, London

Committee of Vice-Chancellors and Principals (CVCP) (annual) *University Entrance: The official guide*, CVCP, London

Department for Education and Skills (DfES) (2003) *The Future of Higher Education*, The Stationery Office, London [online] http://www.dfes.gov.uk/hegateway/strategy/hestrategy/foreword.shtml

DfES (2004) *Five-Year Strategy for Children and Learners*, DfES, London

Qualifications and Curriculum Authority (QCA) (2004) *New Thinking for Reform: A framework for achievement*, QCA, London (July)

HOW TO USE THIS BOOK

You may find these notes helpful when using the book.

Part 1 presents an overview of the further and higher educational systems currently in operation in the United Kingdom, including a discussion of the major reforms that have taken place over the past year and their impact.

Part 2 takes a look at the teaching establishments whose qualifications are listed in Part 4 of the book, offering an explanation of the different types of institution, their place in the overall system and the levels of qualification that they award.

Part 3 presents a detailed description of vocational qualifications awarded by many of the professional associations included in Part 5, including an explanation of validating, examining and awarding bodies.

Part 4 is a directory of qualifications awarded by universities in the United Kingdom (ordered by university name). There is a brief introduction detailing admission to degree courses, degree structure and the various categories of degree available.

Part 5 is a directory of qualifications awarded by professional, trade and specialist associations in the United Kingdom (ordered by profession / discipline), including certificates, diplomas, NVQs and SVQs. A short introduction explains the functions of professional associations and how to gain membership.

Part 6 describes various bodies involved in the accreditation of colleges in the independent sector of further and higher education.

Part 7 is a list of study associations and learned societies.

Also included (at the beginning of the book) is a list of all abbreviations and designatory letters used throughout *British Qualifications*.

INDEX OF ABBREVIATIONS AND DESIGNATORY LETTERS

ACP	Association of Computer Professionals
ACPM	Associate of the Confederation of Professional Management
ACPP	Associate of the College of Pharmacy Practice
ACT	Associate of the College of Teachers
ACYW	Associate of the Community and Youth Work Association
ADCE	Advanced Diploma in Childcare and Education
ADCM	Archbishop of Canterbury's Diploma in Church Music
AdDipEd	Advanced Diploma in Education
ADI	Approved Driving Instructor
AECI	Association Member of the Institute of Employment Consultants
AEWVH	Association for the Education and Welfare of the Visually Handicapped
AFA	Associate of the Faculty of Actuaries
AFA	Associate of the Institute of Financial Accountants
AFBPsS	Associate Fellow of the British Psychological Society
AFCI	Associate of the Faculty of Commerce and Industry Ltd
AffBMA	Affiliate of the Business Management Association
AffIManf	Affiliate of the Institute of Manufacturing
AffIMI	Affiliate of the Institute of the Motor Industry
AffIMS	Affiliate of the Institute of Management Specialists
AffInstM	Affiliate of the Meat Training Council
AffIP	Affiliate of the Institute of Plumbing
AffProfBTM	Affiliate of Professional Business and Technical Management
AFIMA	Associate Fellow of the Institute of Mathematics and its Applications
AFISOL	Aerodrome Flight Information Service Officer's Licence
AFPC	Advanced Financial Planning Certificate
AFRCSEd	Associate Fellow of Royal College of Surgeons of Edinburgh
AGCL	Associate of the Guild of Cleaners and Launderers
AGI	Associate of the Greek Institute
AGSM	Associate of the Guildhall School of Music and Drama
AHCIMA	Associate of the Hotel and Catering International Management Association
AHFS	Associate of the Council of Health Fitness and Sports Therapists
AHRIM	Associate of the Institute of Health Record Information and Management
AIA	Associate of the Institute of Actuaries
AIA	Association of International Accountants
AIAgrE	Associate of the Institution of Agricultural Engineers
AIAT	Associate of the Institute of Asphalt Technology
AIBCM	Associate of the Institute of British Carriage and Automobile Manufacturers
AIBMS	Associate of the Institute of Biomedical Science
AICB	Associate of the Institute of Certified Book-Keepers
AIChor	Associate of the Benesh Institute of Choreology
AICHT	Associate of the International Council of Holistic Therapists
AICM(Cert)	Associate Member of the Institute of Credit Management
AICS	Associate of the Institution of Chartered Shipbrokers
AICSc	Associate of the Institute of Consumer Sciences Incorporating Home Economics
AIDTA	Associate of the International Dance Teachers' Association
AIE	Associate of the Institute of Electrolysis
AIEM	Associate of the Institute of Executives and Managers
AIExpE	Associate of the Institute of Explosive Engineers
AIFA	Associate of the Institute of Field Archaeologists
AIFBQ	Associate of the International Faculty of Business Qualifications
AIFireE	Associate of the Institution of Fire Engineers
AIFP	Associate of the British International Freight Association

AIGD	Associate of the Institute of Grocery Distribution
AIHort	Associate Member of the Institute of Horticulture
AIIMR	Associate of the Institute of Investment Management and Research
AIIRSM	Associate of the International Institute of Risk and Safety Management
AIL	Associate of the Institute of Linguists
AILAM	Associate of the Institute of Leisure and Amenity Management
AIMBM	Associate of the Institute of Maintenance and Building Management
AIMC	Associate of the Institute of Management Consultancy
AIMgt	Associate of the Institute of Management
AIMIS	Associate of the Institute for the Management of Information Systems
AIMM	Associate of the Institute of Massage and Movement
AInstAM	Associate of the Institute of Administrative Management
AInstBA	Associate of the Institute of Business Administration
AInstBCA	Associate of the Institute of Burial and Cremation Administration
AInstBM	Associate of the Institute of Builders' Merchants
AInstCM	Associate of the Institute of Commercial Management
AInstM	Associate of the Meat Training Council
AInstPkg	Associate of the Institute of Packaging
AInstPM	Associate of the Institute of Professional Managers and Administrators
AInstSMM	Associate of the Institute of Sales and Marketing Management
AInstTA	Associate of the Institute of Transport Administration
AInstTT	Associate Member of the Institute of Travel and Tourism
AIOC	Associate of the Institute of Carpenters
AIOFMS	Associate of the Institute of Financial and Management Studies
AIP	Associate of the Institute of Plumbing
AIQA	Associate of the Institute of Quality Assurance
AIS	Accredited Imaging Scientist
AISOB	Associate of the Incorporated Society of Organ Builders
AISTD	Associate of the Imperial Society of Teachers of Dancing
AISTDDip	Associate Diploma of the Imperial Society of Teachers of Dancing
AITSA	Associate of the Institute of Trading Standards Administration
AIVehE	Associate of the Institute of Vehicle Engineers
AIWSc	Associate Member of the Institute of Wood Science
ALCM	Associate of the London College of Music
ALI	Associate of the Landscape Institute
ALS	Associate of the Linnean Society of London
AMA	Associate of the Museums Association
AMABE	Associate Member of the Association of Business Executives
AMAE	Associate Member of the Academy of Experts
AMASI	Associate Member of the Architecture and Surveying Institute
AMBA	Association of MBAs
AMBA	Non-Teacher Associate Member of the British (Theatrical) Arts
AMBCS	Associate Member of the British Computer Society
AMBII	Associate Member of the British Institute of Innkeeping
AmCAM	Associate of the Communication Advertising and Marketing Education Foundation
AMCT	Associate of the Association of Corporate Treasurers
AMCTHCM	Associate Member of the Confederation of Tourism, Hotel and Catering Management
AMI	Association Montessori Internationale
AMIA	Affiliated Member of the Association of International Accountants
AMIAgrE	Associate Member of the Institution of Agricultural Engineers
AMIAP	Associate Member of the Institution of Analysts and Programmers

AMIAT	Associate Member of the Institute of Asphalt Technology
AMIBC	Associate Member of the Institute of Building Control
AMIBCM	Associate Member of the Institute of British Carriage and Automobile Manufacturers
AMIBE	Associate Member of the Institution of British Engineers
AMIBF	Associate Member of the Institute of British Foundrymen
AMICE	Associate Member of the Institution of Civil Engineers
AMIChemE	Associate Member of the Institution of Chemical Engineers
AMIED	Associate Member of the Institution of Engineering Designers
AMIEE	Associate Member of the Institution of Electrical Engineers
AMIEx	Associate Member of the Institute of Export
AMIHIE	Associate Member of the Institute of Highway Incorporated Engineers
AMIHT	Associate Member of the Institution of Highways and Transportation
AMIIE	Associate Member of the Institution of Incorporated Engineers
AMIIExE	Associate Member of the Institution of Incorporated Executive Engineers
AMIIHTM	Associate Member of the International Institute of Hospitality Tourism & Management
AMIISE	Associate Member of the International Institute of Social Economics
AMIM	Associate Member of the Institute of Materials
AMIManf	Member of the Institute of Manufacturing
AMIMechE	Associate Member of the Institution of Mechanical Engineers
AMIMechIE	Associate Member of the Institution of Mechanical Incorporated Engineers
AMIMI	Associate Member of the Institute of the Motor Industry
AMIMinE	Associate of the Institute of Mining Engineers
AMIMM	Associate Member of the Institution of Mining and Metallurgy
AMIMS	Associate Member of the Institute of Management Specialists
AMInstAEA	Associate Member of the Institute of Automotive Engineer Assessors
AMInstBE	Associate Member of the Institution of British Engineers
AMInstE	Associate Member of the Institute of Energy
AMInstR	Associate Member of the Institute of Refrigeration
AMInstTA	Associate Member of the Institute of Transport Administration
AMIPlantE	Associate Member of the Institution of Plant Engineers
AMIPR	Associate Member of the Institute of Public Relations
AMIPRE	Associate Member of the Incorporated Practitioners in Radio and Electronics
AMIQ	Associate Member of the Institute of Quarrying
AMIQA	Associate Member of the Institute of Quality Assurance
AMIRTE	Associate Member of the Institute of Road Transport Engineers
AMISM	Associate Member of the Institute for Supervision & Management
AMIStrutE	Associate Member of the Institution of Structural Engineers
AMITD	Associate Member of the Institute of Training and Development
AMIVehE	Associate Member of the Institute of Vehicle Engineers
AMNI	Associate Member of the Nautical Institute
AMPA	Associate Member of the Master Photographers Association
AMProfBTM	Associate Member of Professional Business and Technical Management
AMRAeS	Associate Member of the Royal Aeronautical Society
AMRSH	Associate Member of the Royal Society for the Promotion of Health
AMS	Associate of the Institute of Management Services
AMS(Aff)	Affiliate of the Association of Medical Secretaries, Practice Managers, Administrators and Receptionists
AMSE	Associate Member of the Society of Engineers (Inc)
AMSPAR	Association of Medical Secretaries, Practice Managers, Administrators and Receptionists

AMusEd	Associate Diploma in Music Education
AMusLCM	Associate in Music of the London College of Music
AMusTCL	Associate in Music of Trinity College of Music
AMWES	Associate Member of the Women's Engineering Society
ANAEA	Associate of the National Association of Estate Agents
ANCA	Advanced National Certificate in Agriculture
AOP	Association of Photographers
AOR	Association of Reflexologists
APA	Accreditation of Prior Experience
APC	Assessment of Professional Competence
APCS	Associate of the Property Consultants Society
APMI	Associate of the Pensions Management Institute
APMP	Association for Project Management Professional
AQA	Assessment & Qualifications Alliance
ARAD	Associate of the Royal Academy of Dancing
ARAM	Associate of the Royal Academy of Music
ARB	Architects Registration Board
ARCM	Associate of Royal College of Music
ARCO	Associate of the Royal College of Organists
ARCS	Associate of the Royal College of Science
AREC	Associate of the Recruitment and Employment Confederation
ARELS	Association of Recognised English Language Services
ARELS-FELCO	Association of Recognised English Language Teaching Establishments in Britain
ARIBA	Associate of the Royal Institute of British Architects
ARICS	Associate of the Royal Institution of Chartered Surveyors
ARIPHH	Associate of the Royal Institute of Public Health and Hygiene
ARPS	Associate of the Royal Photographic Society
ARSC	Associate of the Royal Society of Chemistry
ARSCM	Associate of the Royal School of Church Music
ARSM	Associate of the Royal School of Mines
AS	Advanced Supplementary level
ASCA	Associate of the Institute of Company Accountants
ASCT	Associate of the Society of Claims Technicians
ASDC	Associate of the Society of Dyers and Colourists
ASE	Associate of the Society of Engineers (Inc)
ASI	Ambulance Service Institute
ASI	Architecture and Surveying Institute
ASIAffil	Affiliate of the Ambulance Service Institute
ASIS	Accredited Senior Imaging Scientist
ASLC	Advanced Secretarial Language Certificate
ASMA	Associate of the Society of Sales Management Administrators Ltd
ASNN	Associate of the Society of Nursery Nursing
AssCI	Associate of the Institute of Commerce
AssociateCIPD	Associate of the Chartered Institute of Personnel and Development
AssociateIEEE	Associate of the Institution of Electrical and Electronics Engineers Incorporated
AssociateIIE	Associate of the Institution of Incorporated Engineers
AssocIMechIE	Associate of the Institution of Mechanical Incorporated Engineers
AssocIPD	Associate of the Institute of Personnel & Development
AssocIPHE	Associate of the Institution of Public Health Engineers
AssocMIWM	Associate Member of the Institute of Wastes Management
AssocTechIIE	Associate Technician of the Institution of Incorporated Engineers
ASTA	Associate of the Swimming Teachers' Association

ASVA	Associate of the Incorporated Society of Valuers and Auctioneers
ATC	Art Teacher's Certificate
ATCL	Associate of Trinity College of Music
ATCLicence	Air Traffic Controller's Licence
ATCLTESOL	Associate Diploma in the Teaching of English to Speakers of Other Languages, Trinity College
ATD	Art Teacher's Diploma
ATI	Associate of the Textile Industry
ATII	Associate of the Chartered Institute of Taxation
ATPL	Airline Transport Pilot's Licence
ATSC	Associate of the Oil and Colour Chemists' Association
ATSC	Associate in the Technology of Surface Coatings
ATT	Association of Taxation Technicians
ATT	Member of the Association of Taxation Technicians
ATTA	Association of Therapy Teachers Associate
ATTF	Association of Therapy Teachers Fellow
ATTM	Association of Therapy Teachers Member
AWeldI	Associate of the Welding Institute
BA	Bachelor of Arts
BA(Econ)	Bachelor of Arts in Economics & Social Studies
BA(Ed)	Bachelor of Arts (Education)
BA(Lan)	Bachelor of Languages
BA(Law)	Bachelor of Arts in Law
BA(Music)	Bachelor of Music
BABTAC	British Association of Beauty Therapy and Cosmetology Ltd
BAC	British Accreditation Council for Independent Further and Higher Education
BAC	British Association for Counselling
BAcc	Bachelor of Accountancy
BACP	British Association for Counselling Psychotherapy
BADA	British Antique Dealers' Association
BADN	British Association of Dental Nurses
BAE	British Association of Electrolysists Ltd
BAGMA	British Agricultural and Garden Machinery Association
BAgr	Bachelor of Agriculture
BAO	Bachelor of Obstetrics
BAP	British Association of Psychotherapists
BArch	Bachelor of Architecture
BASELT	British Association in State English Language Teaching
BBO	British Ballet Organisation
BChD	Bachelor of Dental Surgery
BChir	Bachelor of Surgery
BCL	Bachelor of Civil Law
BCom	Bachelor of Commerce
BCombStuds	Bachelor of Combined Studies
BComm	Bachelor of Communications
BCS	Bachelor of Combined Studies
BCS	British Computer Society
BD	Bachelor of Divinity
BDA	British Dietetic Association
BDes	Bachelor of Design
BDS	Bachelor of Dental Surgery
BEconSc	Bachelor of Economics

BECTU	Broadcasting, Entertainment, Cinematograph and Theatre Union
BEd	Bachelor of Education
BEng	Bachelor of Engineering
BEng and Man	Bachelor of Mechanical Engineering, Manufacture and Management
BER	Board for Engineers' Regulation
BFA	Bachelor of Fine Arts
BFin	Bachelor of Finance
BHA	British Hypnotherapy Association
BHI	British Horological Institute Ltd
BHS	British Horse Society
BHSAI	British Horse Society's Assistant Instructor's Certificate
BHSI	British Horse Society's Instructor's Certificate
BHSII	British Horse Society's Intermediate Instructor's Certificate
BHSIntSM	British Horse Society's Intermediate Stable Manager's Certificate
BHSSM	British Horse Society's Stable Manager's Certificate
BIA	Beauty Industry Authority
BIAT	British Institute of Architectural Technologists
BIBA	Bachelor of International Business Administration
BIE	British Institute of Embalmers
BIFA	British International Freight Association
BIPP	British Institute of Professional Photography
BIS	British Interplanetary Society
BKSTS	British Kinematograph Sound and Television Society
BLD	Bachelor of Landscape Design
BLE	Bachelor of Land Economy
BLEng	Bi-Lingual Engineer
BLib	Bachelor of Librarianship
BLing	Bachelor of Linguistics
BLitt	Bachelor of Letters
BLS	Bachelor of Library Studies
BM	Bachelor of Medicine
BMA	British Medical Association
BM, BCh	Conjoint degree of Bachelor of Medicine, Bachelor of Surgery
BM, BS	Conjoint degree of Bachelor of Medicine, Bachelor of Surgery
BMedBiol	Bachelor of Medical Biology
BMedSci	Bachelor of Medical Sciences
BMedSci(Speech)	Bachelor of Medical Sciences (Speech)
BMet	Bachelor of Metallurgy
BMid	Bachelor of Midwifery
BMidwif	Bachelor of Midwifery
BMSc	Bachelor of Medical Sciences
BMus	Bachelor of Music
BN	Bachelor of Nursing
BNNursing	Bachelor of Nursing, Nursing Studies
BNSc	Bachelor of Nursing
BNurs	Bachelor of Nursing
BOptom	Bachelor of Optometry
BPA	Bachelor of Performing Arts
BPharm	Bachelor of Pharmacy
BPhil	Bachelor of Philosophy
BPhil(Ed)	Bachelor of Philosophy (Education)
BPL	Bachelor of Planning

BSc	Bachelor of Science
BSc(Archit)	Bachelor of Science (Architecture)
BSc(DentSci)	Bachelor of Science in Dental Science
BSc(Econ)	Bachelor of Science in Economics
BSc(MedSci)	Bachelor of Science (Medical Science)
BSc(Social Science)	Bachelor of Science (Social Science)
BSc(Town & Regional Planning)	Bachelor of Science (Town & Regional Planning)
BSc(VetSc)	Bachelor of Science (Veterinary Science)
BScAgr	Bachelor of Science in Agriculture
BScEng	Bachelor of Science in Engineering
BScFor	Bachelor of Science in Forestry
BScTech	Bachelor of Technical Science
BSocSc	Bachelor of Social Science
BSSc	Bachelor of Social Science
BSSG	Member of the British Society of Scientific Glassblowers
BTEC	Business and Technology Education Council
BTech	Bachelor of Technology
BTechEd	Bachelor of Technological Education
BTEC HC	Business and Technology Education Council Higher Certificate
BTEC HD	Business and Technology Education Council Higher Diploma
BTEC HNC	Business and Technology Education Council Higher National Certificate
BTEC HND	Business and Technology Education Council Higher National Diploma
BTechS	Bachelor of Technology Studies
BTh	Bachelor of Theology
BTheol	Bachelor of Theology
BTP	Bachelor of Town Planning
BVC	Bar Vocational Course
BVetMed	Bachelor of Veterinary Medicine
BVMS	Bachelor of Veterinary Medicine
BVM&S	Bachelor of Veterinary Medicine
BVSc	Bachelor of Veterinary Science
C&G	City and Guilds
CA	Member of the Institute of Chartered Accountants of Scotland
CAA	Civil Aviation Authority
CABE	Companion of the Association of Business Executives
CACHE	Council for Awards in Children's Care and Education
CAE	Certificated Automotive Engineer
CAE	Companion of the Academy of Experts
CAM	Communication Advertising and Marketing Education Foundation
CAS	Certification of Accountancy Studies
CASS	Certificate of Applied Social Studies
CAT	Certificate for Accounting Technicians
CAT	College of Advanced Technology
CATS	Postgraduate Qualification by Credit Accumulation and Transfer
CBA	Companion of the British (Theatrical) Arts
CBAE	Companion of the British Academy of Experts
CBIM	Companion of the British Institute of Management
CBiol	Chartered Biologist
CBLC	Certificate in Business Language Competence
CBSSG	Craft Member of the British Society of Scientific Glassblowers
CCETSW	Central Council for Education and Training in Social Work

CChem	Chartered Chemist
CCol	Chartered Colourist
CCST	Certificate of Completion of Specialist Training
CDBA	Certified Doctor of Business Administration
CDipAF	Certified Diploma in Accounting and Finance
CEE	Extended European Command Endorsement
CeFA	Certificate for Financial Advisers
CEM	Certificate in Executive Management
CeMAP	Certificate in Mortgage Advice and Practice
CEng	Chartered Engineer
CertAMed	Certificate in Aviation Medicine
CertArb	Certificate in Arboriculture
CertBibKnowl	Certificate of Bible Knowledge
CertCIH	Chartered Institute of Housing recognised Housing Qualification
CertCM	Certificate of Cash Management
CertDesRCA	Certificate of Designer of the Royal College of Art
CertEd	Certificate in Education
CertEPK	Certificate of Essential Pensions Knowledge
CertHE	Certificate of Higher Education
CertHSAP	Certificate in Health Services Administration Practice
CertHSM	Certificate in Health Services Management
CertMFS	Certificate in the Marketing of Financial Services
CertOccHyg	Certificate in Operational Competence in Comprehensive Occupational Hygiene
CertRP	Certificate in Recruitment Practice
CertTEL	Certificate in the Teaching of European Languages
CertTESOL	Certificate of Teaching of English to Speakers of Other Languages
CertTEYL	Certificate of Teaching of English to Young Learners
CertYCW	Certificate in Youth and Community Work
CETHV	Certificate of Education in Training as Health Visitor
CEYA	Council for Early Years Awards
CFS	Certificate in Financial Services
CFSP	Certificate in Financial Services Practice
CGeol	Chartered Geologist
CGLI	City & Guilds of London Institute
CHARM	Centre for Hazard and Risk Management
ChB	Bachelor of Surgery
CHD	Choral-Training Diploma
ChM	Master of Surgery
CHP	Certificate in Hypnosis and Psychology
CHRIM	Certified Member of the Institute of Health Record Information and Management
CIAgrE	Companion of the Institution of Agricultural Engineers
CIArb	Chartered Institute of Arbitrators
CIB	Chartered Institute of Bankers
CIBM	Corporate Member of the Institute of Builders' Merchants
CIBS	Chartered Institute of Bankers in Scotland
CIBSE	Chartered Institution of Building Services Engineers
CIC	Construction Industry Council
CIEx	Companion of the Institute of Export
CIFE	Conference for Independent Further Education
CIH	Chartered Institute of Housing
CII	Chartered Insurance Institute
CILA	Chartered Institute of Loss Adjusters

CILIP	Chartered Institute of Library and Information Professionals
CIM	Chartered Institute of Marketing
CIMA	Chartered Institute of Management Accountants
CIMediE	Companion of the Institution of Mechanical Engineers
CIMgt	Companion of the Institute of Management
CIOB	Chartered Institute of Building
CIP	Certificate of Institute Practice
CIPD	Chartered Institute of Personnel and Development
CIPFA	Chartered Institute of Public Finance & Accounting
CIPS	Chartered Institute of Purchasing and Supply
CISOB	Counsellor of the Incorporated Society of Organ Builders
CIT	Certificate in Information Technology
CIWEM	Chartered Institution of Water and Environmental Management
CL(ABDO)	Diploma in Contact Lens Practice of the Association of British Dispensing Opticians
CLAC	Commercial Language Assistant Certificate
CLAIT	Computer Literacy & Information Technology
CLC	Council for Licensed Conveyancers
CLE	Limited European Command Endorsement
ClinPsyD	Doctorate in Clinical Psychology
CMA	Certificate in Management Accountancy
CMathFIMA	Fellow of the Institute of Mathematics and its Applications
CMBA	Certified Master of Business Administration
CMBHI	Craft Member of the British Horological Institute
CMC	Certified Management Consultants
CMet	Chartered Meteorologist
CMIWSc	Certified Member of the Institute of Wood Science
CMS	Certificate in Management Studies
CNAA	Council for National Academic Awards
COA	Certificate of Accreditation
COBC	Certificate of Basic Competence
CoEA	Certificate of Educational Achievement
COES	Certificate of Educational Studies
CofE	Church of England
CofS	Church of Scotland
CompBCS	Companion of the British Computer Society
CompIAP	Companion of the Institution of Analysts and Programmers
CompIEE	Companion of the Institution of Electrical Engineers
CompIGasE	Companion of the Institution of Gas Engineers
CompIManf	Companion of the Institute of Manufacturing
CompIMS	Companion of the Institute of Management Specialists
CompIP	Companion of the Institute of Plumbing
CorporateIRRV	Corporate Member of the Institute of Revenues, Rating and Valuation
COSCA	Confederation of Scottish Counselling Agencies
CPA	Chartered Patent Agents
CPC	Certificate of Professional Competence, the Institute of Transport Administration
CPD	Continuing Professional Development
CPE	Common Professional Exam
CPEA	Certificate of Practice in Estate Agency
CPFA	Member of Chartered Institute of Public Finance and Accountancy
CPhys	Chartered Physicist of the Institute of Physics
CPIM	Certificate in Production and Inventory Management

CPL	Commercial Pilot's Licence
CPM	Certified Professional Manager
CPP	Certificate of Pre-school Practice
CPR	Chartered Professional Review
CProfBTM	Companion of Professional Business and Technical Management
CPS	Certificate in Pastoral Studies and Applied Theology
CPSC	Certificate of Proficiency in Survival Craft
CPsychol	Chartered Psychologist, British Psychological Society
CPT	Continuing Professional Training
CPVE	Certificate of Pre-Vocational Training
CRAeS	Companion of the Royal Aeronautical Society
CRAH	Central Register of Advanced Hypnotherapists
CRCW	Church Related Community Workers
CRNCM	Companion of the Royal Northern College of Music
CSCT	Central School for Counselling Training
CSD	Chartered Society of Designers
CSE	Certificate of Secondary Education
CSM	Certificate in Safety Management
CSMGSM	Certificate in Stage Management (Guildhall School of Music and Drama)
CStat	Chartered Statistician
CSYS	Certificate of Sixth Year Studies
CTABRSM	Certificate of Teaching of the Associated Board of the Royal School of Music
CTextATI	Associate of the Textile Institute
CTextFTI	Fellow of the Textile Institute
CTHCM	Confederation of Tourism, Hotel and Catering Management
CVA	Certificated Value Analyst
CVM	Certificated Value Manager
CVT	Certified Vehicle Technologist
DA	Diploma in Anaesthetics
DAdmin	Doctor of Administration
DAES	Diploma in Advanced Educational Studies
DArch	Doctor of Architecture
DAvMed	Diploma in Aviation Medicine
DBA	Doctor of Business Administration
DBE	Diploma in Business Engineering
DBO	Diploma of the British Orthoptic Society
DBS	Diploma in Business Studies
DCC	Diploma of Chelsea College
DCDH	Diploma in Child Dental Health
DCE	Dangerous Cargo Endorsements
DCE	Diploma in Childcare and Education
DCG	Diploma in Careers Guidance
DCH	Diploma in Child Health
DChD	Diploma of Dental Surgery
DChM	Diploma in Chiropodial Medicine, Institute of Chiropodists and Podiatrists
DCHT	Diploma in Community Health in Tropical Countries
DCL	Doctor of Civil Law
DCLF	Diploma in Contact Lens Fitting
DClinPsych	Doctor of Clinical Psychiatry
DCLP	Diploma in Contact Lens Practice
DCR(R)or(T)	Diploma of the College of Radiographers
DD	Doctor of Divinity

DDH(Birm)	Diploma in Dental Health, University of Birmingham
DDOrthRCPSGlas	Diploma in Dental Orthopaedics of the Royal College of Physicians and Surgeons of Glasgow
DDPHRCS(Eng)	Diploma in Dental Public Health, Royal College of Surgeons of England
DDS	Doctor of Dental Surgery
DDSc	Doctor of Dental Science
DEBA	Diploma in European Business Administration
DEdPsy	Doctor of Educational Psychiatry
DEM	Diploma in Executive Management
DEng	Doctor of Engineering
DES	Department of Education and Science (now the Department for Education)
DETR	Department of the Environment, Transport and the Regions
DFin	Doctor of Finance
DFSM	Diploma in Financial Services Management
DGA	Diamond Member of the Gemmological Association and Gem Testing Laboratory of Great Britain
DGDPRCSEng	Diploma in General Dental Practice, Royal College of Surgeons of England
DGM	Diploma in Geriatric Medicine
DGO	Diploma in Obstetrics and Gynaecology
DHC	Doctorate in Healthcare
DHE	Diploma in Horticulture, Royal Botanic Garden, Edinburgh
DHMSA	Diploma in the History of Medicine, Society of Apothecaries of London
DHP	Diploma in Hypnosis and Psychotherapy
DIA	Diploma of Industrial Administration
DIB	Diploma in International Business
DIC	Diploma of Membership of Imperial College of Science and Technology, University of London
DIH	Diploma in Industrial Health
DipABRSM	Diploma of the Associated Board of the Royal Schools of Music
DipAD	Diploma in Art and Design
DipAdvHYP	Diploma in Advanced Hypnotherapy
DipAE	Diploma in Adult Education
DipAgrComm	Diploma in Agricultural Communication
DipArb	Diploma in Arbitration
DipArb	Diploma in Arboriculture
DipArch	Diploma in Architecture
DipASE(CofP)	Graduate Level Specialist Diploma in Advanced Study in Education, College of Preceptors
DipASSc	Diploma in Arts and Social Sciences
DipAT	Diploma in Accounting Technology
DipAvMed	Diploma in Aviation Medicine
DipBA	Diploma in Business Administration
DipBldgCons	Diploma in Building Conservation
DipBMA	Diploma in Business Management
DipCAM	Diploma in the Communication Advertising and Marketing Education Foundation
DipCD	Diploma in Community Development
DipCHM	Diploma in Choir Training, Royal College of Organists
DipClinPath	Diploma in Clinical Pathology
DipCOT	Diploma of the College of Occupational Therapists
DipCP	Diploma of the College of Teachers
DipCT	Diploma in Corporate Treasury Management
DipDerm	Diploma in Dermatology

DipEd	Diploma in Education
DipEF	Diploma in Executive Finance
DipEH	Diploma in Environmental Health
DipEM	Diploma in Environmental Management
DipEMA	Diploma in Executive and Management Accountancy
DipEngLit	Diploma in English Literature
DipFD	Diploma in Funeral Directing, National Association of Funeral Directors
DipFS	Diploma in Financial Services
DipGAI	Diploma of the Guild of Architectural Ironmongers
DipGrTrans	Diploma in Greek Translation
DipGSM	Diploma of the Guildhall School of Music and Drama
DipHE	Diploma of Higher Education
DipHS	Diploma of the Heraldry Society
DipIEB	Diploma of the International Employee Benefits
DipISW	Diploma of the Institute of Social Welfare
DipLE	Diploma in Land Economy
DipLP	Diploma in Legal Practice
DipM	Postgraduate Diploma in Marketing
DipMedAc	Diploma in Medical Acupuncture
DipMetEng	Diploma in Meteorological Engineering
DipMFS	Diploma in the Marketing of Financial Services
DipMth	Diploma in Music Therapy
DipOccH	Diploma in Occupational Health
DipOccHyg	Diploma of Professional Competence in Comprehensive Occupational Hygiene
DipPDTC	Diploma in Professional Dancers Teaching Course
DipPharmMed	Diploma in Pharmaceutical Medicine
DipPhil	Diploma in Philosophy
DipProjMan	Diploma in Project Management
DipPropInv	Diploma in Property Investment
DipRAM	Diploma of the Royal Academy of Music
DipRCM	Diploma of the Royal College of Music
DipRMS	Diploma of the Royal Microscopical Society
DipSc	Diploma in Science
DipSM	Diploma in Safety Management
DipSurv	Diploma in Surveying
DipSW	Diploma in Social Work
DipTCL	Diploma of the Trinity College of Music, London
DipTCR	Diploma in Organ Teaching
DipTESOL	Diploma in Teaching of English to Speakers of Other Languages
DipTHP	Diploma in Therapeutic Hypnosis and Psychotherapy
DipTM	Diploma in Training Management, Institute of Personnel and Development
DipTransIoL	Diploma in Translation, Institute of Linguists
DipUniv	Diploma of the University
DipVen	Diploma in Venereology, Society of Apothecaries of London
DipWCF	Diploma of the Worshipful Company of Farriers
DIS	Diploma in Industrial Studies
DLang	Doctor of Language
DLit(t)	Doctor of Letters or Literature
DLO	Diploma of Laryngology and Otology
DLORCSEng	Diploma in Laryngology and Otology, Royal College of Surgeons of England
DLP	Diploma in Legal Practice
DM	Doctor of Medicine

DMedRehab	Diploma in Medical Rehabilitation
DMedSc	Doctor in Medical Science
DMet	Doctor of Metallurgy
DMJ(Clin) or DMJ(Path)	Diploma in Medical Jurisprudence (Clinical or Pathological), Society of Apothecaries of London
DMRD	Diploma in Medical Radio-Diagnosis
DMRT	Diploma in Radiotherapy
DMS	Diploma in Management Studies
DMU	Diploma in Medical Ultrasound
DMus	Doctor of Music
DMusCantuar	Archbishop of Canterbury's Doctorate in Music
DNSc	Doctor in Nursing Science
DO	Diploma in Ophthalmology
DO	Diploma in Osteopathy
DocEdPsy	Doctorate in Educational Psychology
DOpt	Diploma in Ophthalmic Optics
DOrth	Diploma in Orthoptics
DOrthRCSEdin	Diploma in Orthodontics, Royal College of Surgeons of Edinburgh
DOrthRCSEng	Diplomate in Orthodontics, Royal College of Surgeons of England
DP	Diploma in Psychotherapy
DPA	Diploma in Public Administration
DpBact	Diploma in Bacteriology
DPD(Dund)	Diploma in Public Dentistry, University of Dundee
DPH	Diploma in Public Health
DPharm	Diploma in Pharmacy
DPhil	Diploma in Philosophy
DPHRCSEng	Diploma in Dental Public Health, Royal College of Surgeons of England
DPM	Diploma in Psychological Medicine
DPodM	Diploma in Podiatric Medicine
DProf	Doctor of Professional Studies
DPS	Diploma in Professional Studies
DPSE	Diploma in Pastoral Studies and Applied Theology
DPsychol	Doctor of Psychology
DrAc	Doctor of Acupuncture
Dr(RCA)	Doctor of the Royal College of Art
DRCOG	Diploma of the Royal College of Obstetricians and Gynaecologists
DRDRCSEd	Diploma in Restorative Dentistry, Royal College of Surgeons of Edinburgh
DRE	Diploma in Remedial Electrolysis, Institute of Electrolysis
DRI	Diploma in Radionuclide Imaging
DRSAMD	Diploma in the Royal Scottish Academy of Music and Drama
DSA	Diploma in Secretarial Administration
DSc	Doctor of Science
DSc(Econ)	Doctor of Science (Economics) or in Economics
DSc(Eng)	Doctor of Science (Engineering)
DSc(Social)	Doctor of Science in the Social Sciences
DScEcon	Doctor in the Faculty of Economics and Social Studies
DSCh(Ox)	Diploma in Surgical Chiropody (Oxon), Oxford School of Chiropody and Podiatry
DScTech	Doctor of Technical Science
DSocSc	Doctor of Social Science
DSSc	Doctor of Social Science
DSTA	Diploma Member of the Swimming Teachers' Association
DTCD	Diploma in Tuberculosis and Chest Diseases

DTech	Doctor of Technology
DTI	Department of Trade and Industry
DTMH	Diploma in Tropical Medicine and Hygiene
DTM&H	Diploma in Tropical Medicine and Hygiene
DTp	Department of Transport
DUniv	Doctor of the University
DVetMed	Doctor of Veterinary Medicine
DVM	Doctor of Veterinary Medicine
DVM&S	Doctor of Veterinary Medicine and Surgery
DVS	Doctor of Veterinary Surgery
DVSc	Doctor of Veterinary Science
ECBL	European Certification Board for Logistics
ECDL	European Computer Driving Licence
ECG	Executive Group Committees (of the Board for Engineers Registration)
EDBA	Executive Diploma in Business Accounting
EdD	Doctor of Education
EDH	Efficient Deck Hand
EdPsyD	Doctor of Educational Psychology
EEAC	European Executive Assistant Certificate
EFB	English for Business
EFL	English as a Foreign Language
EHO	Environmental Health Officer
EIS	Educational Institute of Scotland
EITB	Engineering Industry Training Board
EMBA	European Master of Business Administration
EMBS	European Master of Business Sciences
EMFEC	East Midland Further Education Council
EN	Enrolled Nurse
EN(G)	Enrolled Nurse (General)
EN(M)	Enrolled Nurse (Mental)
EN(MH)	Enrolled Nurse (Mental Handicap)
ENB	English National Board
EngC	Engineering Council
EngD	Doctor of Engineering
EngTech	Engineering Technician
ENS	Electronic Navigational System
ESD	Executive Secretary's Diploma
ESOL	English for Speakers of Other Languages
ESSTL	Engineering Services Training Trust Ltd
EurIng	European Engineer
EuroBiol	European Biologist
FABE	Fellow of the Association of Business Executives
FACB	Fellow of the Association of Certified Bookkeepers
FACP	Fellow of the Association of Computer Professionals
FAE	Fellow of the Academy of Experts
FAFC	Fellow of the Association of Financial Controllers and Administrators
FAIA	Fellow of the Association of International Accountants
FAMS	Fellow of the Association of Medical Secretaries, Practice Managers, Administrators and Receptionists
FAPM	Fellow of the Association for Project Management
FASI	Fellow of the Ambulance Service Institute
FASI	Fellow of the Architecture and Surveying Institute

FASP	Fellow of the Association of Sales Personnel
FBA	Fellow of the British Academy
FBA	Fellow of the British (Theatrical) Arts
FBCS	Fellow of the British Computer Society
FBDO	Fellow of the Association of British Dispensing Opticians
FBDO(Hons)	Fellow of the Association of British Dispensing Opticians with Honours Diploma
FBDO(Hons)CL	Fellow of the Association of British Dispensing Opticians with Honours Diploma and Diploma in Contact Lens Practice
FBEI	Fellow of the Institution of Body Engineers
FBEng	Fellow of the Association of Building Engineers
FBHA	Fellow of the British Hypnotherapy Association
FBHI	Fellow of the British Horological Institute
FBHS	Fellow of the British Horse Society
FBID	Fellow of the British Institute of Interior Design
FBIDST	Fellow of the British Institute of Dental and Surgical Technologists
FBIE	Fellow of the British Institute of Embalmers
FBIPP	Fellow of the British Institute of Professional Photography
FBIS	Fellow of the British Interplanetary Society
FBMA	Fellow of the Business Management Association
FBPsS	Fellow of the British Psychological Society
FCA	Fellow of the Institute of Chartered Accountants in England and Wales
FCAM	Fellow of the Communication Advertising and Marketing Education Foundation
FCB	Fellow of the British Association of Communicators in Business Ltd
FCBSI	Fellow of the Chartered Building Societies Institute
FCCA	Fellow of the Association of Chartered Certified Accountants
FCEA	Fellow of the Institute of Cost and Executive Accountants
FCGI	Fellowship, City & Guilds
FChS	Fellow of the Society of Chiropodists and Podiatrists
FCI	Faculty of Commerce and Industry
FCI	Fellow of the Institute of Commerce
FCIArb	Fellow of the Chartered Institute of Arbitrators
FCIB	Fellow of the Chartered Institute of Bankers
FCIBS	Fellow of the Chartered Institute of Bankers in Scotland
FCIBSE	Fellow of the Chartered Institute of Building Services Engineers
FCIH	Fellow of the Chartered Institute of Housing
FCII	Fellow of the Chartered Insurance Institute
FCIJ	Fellow of the Chartered Institute of Journalists
FCILA	Fellow of the Chartered Institute of Loss Adjusters
FCIM	Fellow of the Chartered Institute of Marketing
FCIOB	Fellow of the Chartered Institute of Building
FCIPD	Fellow of the Chartered Institute of Personnel and Development
FCIPS	Fellow of the Chartered Institute of Purchasing and Supply
FCIS	Fellow of the Institute of Chartered Secretaries and Administrators
FCIT	Fellow of the Chartered Institute of Transport
FCLIP	Chartered Fellow of CILIP
FCLS	First Certificate for Legal Secretaries
FCMA	Fellow of the Chartered Institute of Management Accountants
FCMA	Fellow of the Institute of Cost and Management Accountants
FCMC	Fellow Grade Certified Management Consultants
FCOphth	Fellow of the College of Ophthalmology
FCOptom	Fellow of the College of Optometrists
FCoT	Ordinary Fellow of the College of Teachers

FCPM	Fellow of the Confederation of Professional Management
FCPP	Fellow of the College of Pharmacy Practice
FCSP	Fellow of the Chartered Society of Physiotherapy
FCT	Fellow of the Association of Corporate Treasurers
FCoT	Fellow of the College of Teachers
FCTHCM	Fellow of the Confederation of Tourism, Hotel and Catering Management
FCYW	Fellow of the Community and Youth Work Association
FDSRCPSGlas	Fellow in Dental Surgery of the Royal College of Surgeons of Glasgow
FDSRCSEd	Fellow in Dental Surgery of the Royal College of Physicians and Surgeons of Edinburgh
FDSRCSEng	Fellow in Dental Surgery of the Royal College of Surgeons of England
FE	Further Education
FEANI	Fédération Européene d'Associations Nationales d'Ingénieurs
FECI	Fellow of the Institute of Employment Consultants
FEFC	Further Education Funding Council
FEIS	Fellow of the Educational Institute of Scotland
FFA	Fellow of the Faculty of Actuaries
FFA	Fellow of the Institute of Financial Accountants
FFARCSEng	Fellow of the Faculty of Anaesthetists of the Royal College of Surgeons in England
FFARCSIrel	Fellow of the Faculty of Anaesthetists of the Royal College of Surgeons in Ireland
FFAS	Fellow of the Faculty of Architects and Surveyors (Architects)
FFCA	Fellow of the Association of Financial Controllers and Administrators
FFCI	Fellow of the Faculty of Commerce and Industry
FFCS	Fellow of the Faculty of Secretaries
FFHom	Fellow of the Faculty of Homeopathy
FFPHM	Fellow of the Faculty of Public Health Medicine, Royal College of Physicians of London and Edinburgh and Royal College of Physicians and Surgeons of Glasgow
FFPHMIrel	Fellow of the Faculty of Public Health Medicine, Royal College of Physicians of Ireland
FFRRCSIrel	Fellow of the Faculty of Radiologists, Royal College of Surgeons in Ireland
FFS	Fellow of the Faculty of Architects and Surveyors (Surveyors)
FGA	Fellow of the Gemmological Association and Gem Testing Laboratory of Great Britain
FGCL	Fellow of the Guild of Cleaners and Launderers
FGI	Fellow of the Greek Institute
FGSM	Fellow of the Guildhall School of Music and Drama
FHCIMA	Fellow of the Hotel and Catering International Management Association
FHFS	Fellow of the Council of Health, Fitness and Sports Therapists
FHG	Fellow of the Institute of Heraldic and Genealogical Studies
FHRIM	Fellow of the Institute of Health Record Information and Management
FHS	Fellow of the Heraldry Society
FHSM	Fellow of the Institute of Health Services Management
FHT	Federation of Holistic Therapies
FIA	Fellow of the Institute of Actuaries
FIAB	Fellow of the International Association of Book-keepers
FIAEA	Fellow of the Institute of Automotive Engineer Assessors
FIAgrE	Fellow of the Institution of Agricultural Engineers
FIAP	Fellow of the Institution of Analysts and Programmers
FIAT	Fellow of the Institute of Asphalt Technology
FIBA	Fellow of the Institution of Business Agents
FIBC	Fellow of the Institute of Building Control

FIBCM	Fellow of the Institute of British Carriage and Automobile Manufacturers
FIBCO	Fellow of the Institute of Building Control Officers
FIBE	Fellow of the Institution of British Engineers
FIBF	Fellow of the Institute of British Foundrymen
FIBiol	Fellow of the Institute of Biology
FIBM	Fellow of the Institute of Builders' Merchants
FIBMS	Fellow of the Institute of Biomedical Science
FIBMS	Fellow of the Institute of Medical Laboratory Sciences
FICA	Fellow of the Institute of Company Accountants
FICB	Fellow of the Institute of Certified Book-Keepers
FICE	Fellow of the Institution of Civil Engineers
FIChemE	Fellow of the Institution of Chemical Engineers
FIChor	Fellow of the Benesh Institute of Choreology
FICHT	Fellow of the International Council of Holistic Therapies
FICM	Fellow of the Institute of Credit Management
FICorr	Fellow of the Institute of Corrosion
FICS	Fellow of the Institute of Chartered Shipbrokers
FICW	Fellow of the Institute of Clerks of Works of Great Britain Incorporated
FIDTA	Fellow of the International Dance Teachers' Association
FIED	Fellow of the Institution of Engineering Designers
FIEE	Fellow of the Institution of Electrical Engineers
FIEM	Fellow of the Institute of Executives and Managers
FIEx	Fellow of the Institute of Export
FIExpE	Fellow of the Institute of Explosives Engineers
FIFBQ	Fellow of the International Faculty of Business Qualifications
FIFireE	Fellow of the Institution of Fire Engineers
FIFM	Fellow of the Institute of Fisheries Management
FIFST	Fellow of the Institute of Food Science and Technology
FIGasE	Fellow of the Institution of Gas Engineers
FIGD	Fellow of the Institute of Grocery Distribution
FIGeol	Fellow of the Institute of Geologists
FIHEc	Fellow of the Institute of Home Economics Ltd
FIHIE	Fellow of the Institute of Highway Incorporated Engineers
FIHort	Fellow of the Institute of Horticulture
FIHT	Fellow of the Institution of Highways and Transportation
FIIE	Fellow of the Institution of Incorporated Engineers
FIIHTM	Fellow of the International Institute of Hospitality Tourism & Management
FIIM	Fellow of the International Institute of Management
FIIMR	Fellow of the Institute of Investment Management and Research
FIIRSM	Fellow of the International Institute of Risk and Safety Management
FIISE	Fellow of the International Institute of Social Economics
FIISec	Fellow of the International Institute of Security
FIL	Fellow of the Institute of Linguists
FILAM	Fellow of the Institute of Leisure and Amenity Management
FILT	Fellow of the Institute of Logistics and Transport
FIM	Fellow of the Institute of Materials
FIMA	Fellow of the Institute of Mathematics and its Applications
FIManf	Fellow of the Institute of Manufacturing
FIMarE	Fellow of the Institute of Marine Engineers
FIMatM	Fellow of the Institute of Materials Management
FIMBM	Fellow of the Institute of Maintenance and Building Management
FIMechE	Fellow of the Institute of Mechanical Engineers

FIMechIE	Fellow of the Institute of Mechanical Incorporated Engineers
FIMF	Fellow of the Institute of Metal Finishing
FIMgt	Fellow of the Institute of Management
FIMI	Fellow of the Institute of the Motor Industry
FIMIS	Fellow of the Institute for the Management of Information Systems
FIMM	Fellow of the Institute of Massage and Movement
FIMM	Fellow of the Institution of Mining and Metallurgy
FIMM	International Federation of Manual Medicine
FIMS	Fellow of the Institute of Management Specialists
FIMunE	Fellow of the Institution of Municipal Engineers
FInstAEA	Fellow of the Institute of Automotive Engineer Assessors
FInstAM	Fellow of the Institute of Administrative Management
FInstBA	Fellow of the Institute of Business Administration
FInstBCA	Fellow of the Institute of Burial and Cremation Administration
FInstBM	Fellow of the Institute of Builders' Merchants
FInstBRM	Fellow of the Institute of Baths and Recreation Management
FInstCh	Fellow of the Institute of Chiropodists
FInstCM	Fellow of the Institute of Commercial Management
FInstD	Fellow of the Institute of Directors
FInstE	Fellow of the Institute of Energy
FInstLEx	Fellow of the Institute of Legal Executives
FInstMC	Fellow of the Institute of Measurement and Control
FInstNDT	Fellow of the British Institute of Non-Destructive Testing
FInstP	Fellow of the Institute of Physics
FInstPet	Fellow of the Institute of Petroleum
FInstPkg	Fellow of the Institute of Packaging
FInstPM	Fellow of the Institute of Professional Managers and Administrators
FInstPS	Fellow of the Institute of Purchasing and Supply
FInstR	Fellow of the Institute of Refrigeration
FInstSMM	Fellow of the Institute of Sales and Marketing Management
FInstTA	Fellow of the Institute of Transport Administration
FInstTT	Fellow of the Institute of Travel and Tourism
FInstWM	Fellow of the Institute of Wastes Management
FInstWM	Fellowship of the Institute of Wastes Management
FIntMC	Fellow of International Management Centre
FIOC	Fellow of the Institute of Carpenters
FIOM	Fellow of the Institute of Operations Management
FIOP	Fellow of the Institute of Plumbing
FIOP	Fellow of the Institute of Printing
FIOSH	Fellow of the Institution of Occupational Safety and Health
FIPA	Fellow of the Institute of Practitioners in Advertising
FIPD	Fellow of the Institute of Personnel Development
FIPI	Fellow of the Institute of Professional Investigators
FIPlantE	Fellow of the Institution of Plant Engineers
FIPR	Fellow of the Institute of Public Relations
FIQ	Fellow of the Institute of Quarrying
FIQA	Fellow of the Institute of Quality Assurance
FIR	Fellow of the Institute of Population Registration
FIRSE	Fellow of the Institution of Railway Signal Engineers
FIRTE	Fellow of the Institute of Road Transport Engineers
FIS	Fellow of the Institute of Statisticians
FISM	Fellow of the Institute for Supervision & Management

FISOB	Fellow of the Incorporated Society of Organ Builders
FISTC	Fellow of the Institute of Scientific and Technical Communicators
FISTD	Fellow of the Imperial Society of Teachers of Dancing
FIStrucE	Fellow of the Institution of Structural Engineers
FISW	Fellow of the Institute of Social Welfare
FIT	Foundation Insurance Test
FITD	Fellow of the Institute of Training and Development
FITSA	Fellow of the Institute of Trading Standards Administration
FIVehE	Fellow of the Institute of Vehicle Engineers
FIWM	Fellow of the Institute of Wastes Management
FLAW	Foreign Languages at Work
FLCM	Fellow of the London College of Music
FLCSP	Fellow of the London and Counties Society of Physiologists
FLI	Fellow of the Landscape Institute
FLIC	Foreign Languages for Industry and Commerce
FLS	Fellow of the Linnean Society of London
FMA	Fellow of the Museums Association
FMAAT	Fellow Member of the Association of Accounting Technicians
FMPA	Fellow of the Master Photographers Association
FMR	Fellow of the Association of Health Care Information and Medical Records Officers
FMS	Fellow of the Institute of Management Services
FMusEd	Fellowship in Music Education
FN	Fellow of the Nautical Society
FNAEA	Fellow of the National Association of Estate Agents
FNAEAHon	Honoured Fellow of the National Association of Estate Agents
FNCP	Fellow of the National Council of Psychotherapists
FNI	Fellow of the Nautical Institute
FNIMH	Fellow of the National Institute of Medical Herbalists
FPC	Financial Planning Certificate
FPC	Foundation for Psychotherapy and Counselling
FPCS	Fellow of the Property Consultants Society
FPMI	Fellow of the Pensions Management Institute
FPodS	Fellow of the Surgical Faculty of the College of Podiatrists
FProfBTM	Fellow of Professional Business and Technical Management
FRAeS	Fellow of the Royal Aeronautical Society
FRAS	Fellow of the Royal Astronomical Society
FRCA	Fellow of the Royal College of Anaesthetists
FRCGP	Fellow of the Royal College of General Practitioners
FRCM	Fellow of the Royal College of Music
FRCO	Fellow of the Royal College of Organists
FRCO(CHM)	Fellow of the Royal College of Organists (Choir-training Diploma)
FRCOG	Fellow of the Royal College of Obstetricians and Gynaecologists
FRCP	Fellow of the Royal College of Physicians of London
FRCPath	Fellow of the Royal College of Pathologists
FRCPEdin	Fellow of the Royal College of Physicians of Edinburgh
FRCPsych	Fellow of the Royal College of Psychiatrists
FRCR	Fellow of the Royal College of Radiologists
FRCS(Irel)	Fellow of the Royal College of Surgeons in Ireland
FRCSEd	Fellow of the Royal College of Surgeons of Edinburgh
FRCSEd(C/TH)	Fellow of the Royal College of Surgeons of Edinburgh, specialising in Cardiothoracic Surgery

FRCSEd(Orth)	Fellow of the Royal College of Surgeons of Edinburgh, specialising in Orthopaedic Surgery
FRCSEd(SN)	Fellow of the Royal College of Surgeons of Edinburgh, specialising in Surgical Neurology
FRCSEng	Fellow of the Royal College of Surgeons of England
FRCSEng(Oto)	Fellow of the Royal College of Surgeons of England, with Otolaryngology
FRCSGlasg	Fellow of the Royal College of Physicians and Surgeons of Glasgow
FRCVS	Fellow of the Royal College of Veterinary Surgeons
FREC	Fellow of the Recruitment and Employment Confederation
FRHS	Fellow of the Royal Horticultural Society
FRIBA	Fellow of the Royal Institute of British Architects
FRICS	Fellow of the Royal Institution of Chartered Surveyors
FRIN	Fellow of the Royal Institute of Navigation
FRINA	Fellow of the Royal Institution of Naval Architects
FRIPHH	Fellow of the Royal Institution of Public Health and Hygiene
FRNCM	Fellow of the Royal Northern College of Music
FRPharmS	Fellow of the Royal Pharmaceutical Society of Great Britain
FRPS	Fellow of the Royal Photographic Society
FRS	Fellow of the Royal Society
FRSC	Fellow of the Royal Society of Chemistry
FRSCM	Fellow of the Royal School of Church Music
FRSH	Fellow of the Royal Society for the Promotion of Health
FRTPI	Fellow of the Royal Town Planning Institute
FSAPP	Fellow of the Society of Advanced Psychotherapy Practitioners
FSBP	Fellow of the Society of Business Practitioners
FSBT	Fellow of the Society of Teachers in Business Education
FSCT	Fellow of the Society of Claims Technicians
FSDC	Fellow of the Society of Dyers and Colourists
FSE	Fellow of the Society of Engineers (Inc)
FSElec	Fellow of the Society of Electroscience
FSG	Fellow of the Society of Genealogists
FSG(Hon)	Honorary Fellow of the Society of Genealogists
FSGT	Fellow of the Society of Glass Technology
FSIAD	Fellow of the Society of Industrial Artists and Designers
FSMA	Fellow of the Society of Martial Arts
FSMA	Fellow of the Society of Sales Management Administrators Ltd
FSNN	Fellow of the Society of Nursery Nursing
FSS	Fellow of the Royal Statistical Society
FSSCh	Fellow of the British Chiropody and Podiatry Association
FSSF	Fellow of the Society of Shoe Fitters
FSTA	Fellow of the Swimming Teachers' Association
FSVA	Fellow of the Incorporated Society of Valuers and Auctioneers
FTCL	Fellow of the Trinity College of Music
FTI	Fellow of the Textile Institute
FTII	Fellow of the Chartered Institute of Taxation
FTSC	Fellow of the Oil and Colour Chemists' Association
FTSC	Fellow in the Technology of Surface Coatings
FWeldI	Fellow of the Welding Institute
FYDA	Associate Fellowship of the Youth Development Association
GAGTL	Gemmological Association and Gem Testing Laboratory of Great Britain
GAI	Guild of Architectural Ironmongers
GASI	Graduate Member of the Ambulance Service Institute

GBSM	Graduate of the Birmingham School of Music
GCE	General Certificate of Education
GCE A	General Certificate of Education Advanced Level
GCE O	General Certificate of Education Ordinary Level
GCGI	Graduateship, City & Guilds
GCL	Guild of Cleaners and Launderers
GCSE	General Certificate of Secondary Education
GDC	General Dental Council
GIBCM	Graduate of the Institute of British Carriage and Automobile Manufacturers
GIBiol	Graduate of the Institute of Biology
GIEM	Graduate of the Institute of Executives and Managers
GIMA	Graduate of the Institute of Mathematics and its Applications
GIMI	Graduate of the Institute of the Motor Industry
GInstP	Graduate of the Institute of Physics
GIntMC	Graduate of the International Management Centre
GIS	Graduate Imaging Scientist
GLCM	Graduate Diploma of the London College of Music
GMAT	Graduate Management Admissions Test
GMC	General Medical Council
GMDSS	Global Maritime Distress & Safety System
GMInstM	Graduate Member of the Meat Training Council
GMus	Graduate Diploma in Music
GMusRNCM	Graduate in Music of the Royal Northern College of Music
GNSM	Graduate of the Northern School of Music
GNVQ	General National Vocational Qualifications
GradAES	Graduate of the Royal Aeronautical Society
GradBEng	Graduate Member of the Association of Building Engineers
GradBHI	Graduate of the British Horological Institute
GradDip	Graduate Diploma
GradIAP	Graduate of the Institution of Analysts and Programmers
GradIBE	Graduate of the Institution of British Engineers
GradIElecIE	Graduate of the Institution of Electrical and Electronics Incorporated Engineers
GradIIE	Graduate of the Institution of Incorporated Engineers
GradIISec	Graduate of the International Institute of Security
GradIManf	Graduate of the Institute Manufacturing
GradIMF	Graduate of the Institute of Metal Finishing
GradIMS	Graduate of the Institute of Management Specialists
GradInstNDT	Graduate of the British Institute of Non-Destructive Testing
GradInstP	Graduate of the Institute of Physics
GradInstPS	Graduate of the Institute of Purchasing and Supply
GradIOP	Graduate of the Institute of Printing
GradIPD	Graduate of the Institute of Personnel and Development
GradIS	Graduate of the Institute of Statisticians
GradISCA	Graduate of the Institute of Chartered Secretaries and Administrators
GradMechE	Graduate of the Institution of Mechanical Engineers
GradMIWM	Graduate Member of the Institute of Wastes Management
GradRNCM	Graduate of the Royal Northern College of Music
GradRSC	Graduate of the Royal Society of Chemistry
GradSMA	Graduate of the Society of Martial Arts
GradStat	Graduate Statistician
GraduateCIPD	Graduate of the Chartered Institute of Personnel and Development
GraduateIEIE	Graduate of the Institution of Electrical and Electronics Incorporated Engineers

GradWeldI	Graduate of the Welding Institute
GRC	General Readers Certificate
GRC	Grade Related Criteria
GRIC	Graduate Membership of the Royal Institute of Chemistry
GRSC	Graduate of the Royal Society of Chemistry
GRSM	Graduate Diploma of the Royal Manchester School of Music
GRSM(Hons)	Graduate of the Royal Schools of Music
GSMA	Graduate of the Society of Sales Management Administrators Ltd
GSNN	Graduate of the Society of Nursery Nursing
GTC	General Teaching Council
HABIA	Hairdressing and Beauty Industry Authority
HC	Higher Certificate
HCIMA	Hotel and Catering International Management Association
HD	Higher Diploma
HDCR (R) or (T)	Higher Award in Radiodiagnosis or Radiotherapy, College of Radiographers
HEFCE	Higher Education Funding Council for England
HFInstE	Honorary Fellow of the Institute of Energy
HNC	Higher National Certificate
HND	Higher National Diploma
HonASTA	Honorary Associate of the Swimming Teachers' Association
HonDrRCA	Honorary Doctorate of the Royal College of Art
HonFAE	Honorary Fellow of the Academy of Experts
HonFBID	Honorary Fellow of the British Institute of Interior Design
HonFBIPP	Honorary Fellow of the British Institute of Professional Photography
HonFCP	Charter Fellow of the College of Preceptors
HonFEIS	Honorary Fellow of the Educational Institute of Scotland
HonFHCIMA	Honorary Fellow of the Hotel, Catering and Institutional Management Association
HonFHS	Honorary Fellow of the Heraldry Society
HonFIEE	Honorary Fellow of the Institution of Electrical Engineers
HonFIExpE	Honorary Fellow of the Institute of Explosives Engineers
HonFIGasE	Honorary Fellow of the Institution of Gas Engineers
HonFIMarE	Honorary Fellow of the Institute of Marine Engineers
HonFIMechE	Honorary Fellow of the Institution of Mechanical Engineers
HonFIMM	Honorary Fellow of the Institution of Mining and Metallurgy
HonFInstE	Honorary Fellow of the Institute of Energy
HonFInstMC	Honorary Fellow of the Institute of Measurement and Control
HonFInstNDT	Honorary Fellow of the British Institute of Non-Destructive Testing
HonFIQA	Honorary Fellow of the Institute of Quality Assurance
HonFIRSE	Honorary Fellow of the Institution of Railway Signal Engineers
HonFIRTE	Honorary Fellow of the Institute of Road Transport Engineers
HonFPRI	Honorary Fellow of the Plastics and Rubber Institute
HonFRIN	Honorary Fellow of the Royal Institute of Navigation
HonFRINA	Honorary Fellow of the Royal Institution of Naval Architects
HonFRPS	Honorary Fellow of the Royal Photographic Society
HonFSE	Honorary Fellow of the Society of Engineers (Inc)
HonFSGT	Honorary Fellow of the Society of Glass Technology
HonFWeldI	Honorary Fellow of the Welding Institute
HonGSM	Honorary Member of the Guildhall School of Music and Drama
HonMIFM	Honorary Member of the Institute of Fisheries Management
HonMInstNDT	Honorary Member of the British Institute of Non-Destructive Testing
HonMRIN	Honorary Member of the Royal Institute of Navigation
HonMWES	Honorary Member of the Women's Engineering Society

HonRAM	Honorary Member of the Royal Academy of Music
HonRCM	Honorary Member of the Royal College of Music
HonRNCM	Honorary Member of the Royal Northern College of Music
HonRSCM	Honorary Member of the Royal School of Church Music
HSC	Higher School Certificate
HSE	Health & Safety Executive
HTB	Hairdressing Training Board
HTC	Higher Technical Certificate
IAAP	International Association for Analytic Psychology
IAB	International Association of Book-Keepers
IABC	International Association of Business Computing
IAC	Investment Advice Certificate
IAgrE	Institution of Agricultural Engineers
IAP	Institution of Analysts and Programmers
IAQ	Investment Administration Qualification
IAT	Institute of Asphalt Technology
IBA	Institute of Business Administration
IBC	Institute of Building Control
IBE	Institution of British Engineers
IBF	Institute of British Foundrymen
IBMS	Institute of Biomedical Science
ICAEW	Institute of Chartered Accountants in England and Wales
ICAI	Institute of Chartered Accountants in Ireland
ICAS	Institute of Chartered Accountants of Scotland
ICB	Institute of Certified Book-Keepers
ICE	Institution of Civil Engineers
ICEA	Institute of Cost and Executive Accountants
ICG	Institute of Careers Guidance
IChemE	Institution of Chemical Engineers
ICIOB	Incorporated Member of the Chartered Institute of Building
ICM	Institute of Commercial Management
ICM	Institute of Complementary Medicine
ICM	Institute of Credit Management
ICMQ	International Capital Markets Qualification
ICSA	Institute of Chartered Secretaries and Administrators
ICSF	Intermediate Certificate of the Society of Floristry
IDA	Improvement and Development Agency
IDTA	International Dance Teachers' Association Ltd
IED	Institution of Engineering Designers
IEE	Institution of Electrical Engineers
IEM	Institute of Executives and Managers
IEng	Incorporated Engineer
IETTL	Insulation and Environmental Training Trust Ltd
IEx	Institute of Export
IExpE	Institute of Explosives Engineers
IFA	Institute of Field Archaeologists
IFA	Institute of Financial Accountants
IFA	Insurance Foundation Certificate
IFBQ	International Faculty of Business Qualifications
IFM	Institute of Fisheries Management
IFST	Institute of Food Science and Technology (UK)
IHBC	International Health & Beauty Council

IHIE	Institute of Highway Incorporated Engineers
IHort	Institute of Horticulture
IHT	Institute of Highways and Transportation
IIA	Institute of Internal Auditors
IIE	Institution of Incorporated Engineers
IIExE	Institution of Incorporated Executive Engineers
IIHHT	International Institute of Health & Holistic Therapies
IIHTM	International Institute of Hospitality Tourism & Management
IIRSM	International Institute of Risk and Safety Management
ILAM	Institute of Leisure and Amenity Management
ILE	Institution of Lighting Engineers
ILEX	Institute of Legal Executives
ILT	Institute of Logistics and Transport
IMarE	Institute of Marine Engineers
IMBM	Institute of Maintenance and Building Management
IMC	Institute of Management Consultancy
IMechE	Institution of Mechanical Engineers
IMF	Institute of Metal Finishing
IMI	Institute of the Motor Industry
IMIBC	Incorporated Member of the Institute of Building Control
IMInstAEA	Incorporated Member of the Institute of Automotive Engineer Assessors
IMIS	Institute for the Management of Information Systems
IMM	Institution of Mining and Metallurgy
IMS	Institute of Management Specialists
IncMWeldI	Incorporated Member of the Welding Institute
InstAEA	Institute of Automotive Engineer Assessors
InstAM	Institute of Administrative Management
InstBCA	Institute of Burial and Cremation Administration
InstE	Institute of Energy
InstPet	Institute of Petroleum
IOB	Institute of Brewing
IOC	Institute of Carpenters
IoD	Institute of Directors
IOM	Institute of Operations Management
IOP	Institute of Packaging
IOSH	Institution of Occupational Safety and Health
IOTA	Institute of Transport Administration
IPA	Institute of Practitioners in Advertising
IPD	Initial Professional Development
IPD	Institute of Personnel and Development
IPFA	Member of the Chartered Institute of Public Finance and Accountancy
IPlantE	Institution of Plant Engineers
IPR	Incorporated Professional Review
IPR	Institute of Public Relations
IPSM	Institute of Public Service Management
IQ	Institute of Quarrying
IQA	Institute of Quality Assurance
IRMT	International Register of Massage Therapists
IRRV	Corporate Member of the Institute of Revenues, Rating and Valuation
IRRV	Institute of Revenues, Rating and Valuation
IRSE	Institution of Railway Signal Engineers
IRTE	Institute of Road Transport Engineers

ISEB	Information Systems Examinations Board
ISM	Incorporated Society of Musicians
ISM	Institute for Supervision & Management
ISMM	Institute of Sales and Marketing Management
ISRM	Institute of Sport and Recreation Management
ISTD	Imperial Society of Teachers of Dancing
IStructE	Institution of Structural Engineers
ITEC	International Therapy Examination Council
ITIL	IT Infrastructure Library
ITSA	Institute of Trading Standards Administration
IVehE	Institute of the Vehicle Engineers
IVM	Institute of Value Management
IWSc	Institute of Wood Science
JEB	Joint Examination Board
JET	Jewellery, Education and Training
JP	Justice of the Peace
LA	Library Association
LABAC	Licentiate Member of the Association of Business and Administrative Computing
LAE	Licentiate Automotive Engineer
LAEx	Legal Accounts Executive
LAMDA	London Academy of Music and Dramatic Art
LAMRTPI	Legal Associate Member of the Royal Town Planning Institute
LASI	Licentiate of the Ambulance Service Institute
LASI	Licentiate of the Architecture and Surveying Institute
LBEI	Licentiate of the Institution of Body Engineers
LBIDST	Licentiate of the British Institute of Dental and Surgical Technologists
LBIPP	Licentiate of the British Institute of Professional Photography
LCCI	London Chamber of Commerce and Industry
LCCIEB	London Chamber of Commerce and Industry Examinations Board
LCEA	Licentiate of the Association of Cost and Executive Accountants
LCFI	Licentiate of CFI International (Clothing and Footwear Institute)
LCGI	Licentiate, City & Guilds
LCIBSE	Licentiate of the Chartered Institution of Building Services Engineers
LCP	Licentiate of the College of Preceptors
LCSP	London and Counties Society of Physiologists
LCSP(Assoc)	Associate of the London and Counties Society of Physiologists
LCSP(BTh)	Member of the London and Counties Society of Physiologists (Beauty Therapy)
LCSP(Chir)	Member of the London and Counties Society of Physiologists (Chiropody)
LCSP(Phys)	Member of the London and Counties Society of Physiologists (Physical and Manipulative Therapy)
LCT	Licentiate of the College of Teachers
LDS	Licentiate in Dental Surgery
LDSRCPSGlas	Licentiate in Dental Surgery of the Royal College of Physicians and Surgeons of Glasgow
LDSRCSEd	Licentiate in Dental Surgery of the Royal College of Surgeons of Edinburgh
LDSRCSEng	Licentiate in Dental Surgery of the Royal College of Surgeons of England
LFA	Licentiate of the Institute of Financial Accountants
LFCI	Licentiate of the Faculty of Commerce and Industry
LFCS	Licentiate of the Faculty of Secretaries
LFS	Licentiate of the Faculty of Architects and Surveyors (Surveyors)
LGCL	Licentiate of the Guild of Cleaners and Launderers
LGSM	Licentiate of the Guildhall School of Music and Drama

LHCIMA	Licentiate of the Hotel and Catering International Management Association
LHG	Licentiate of the Institute of Heraldic and Genealogical Studies
LI	Landscape Institute
LicentiateCIPD	Licentiate of the Chartered Institute of Personnel and Development
LicIPD	Licentiate of the Institute of Personnel & Development
LicIQA	Licentiate of the Institute of Quality Assurance
LICW	Licentiate of the Institute of Clerks of Works of Great Britain Incorporated
LIDPM	Licentiate of the Institute of Data Processing Management
LIEM	Licentiate of the Institute of Executives and Managers
LIIST	Licentiate of the International Institute of Sports Therapy
LILAM	Licentiate of the Institute of Leisure and Amenity Management
LIM	Licentiate of the Institute of Materials
LIMA	Licentiate of the Institute of Mathematics and its Applications
LIMF	Licentiate of the Institute of Metal Finishing
LIMIS	Licentiate of the Institute for the Management of Information Systems
LInstBCA	Licentiate of the Institute of Burial and Cremation Administration
LInstBM	Licentiate of the Institute of Builders' Merchants
LIOC	Licentiate of the Institute of Carpenters
LIR	Licentiate of the Institute of Population Registration
LISTD	Licentiate of the Imperial Society of Teachers of Dancing
LISTD(Dip)	Licentiate Diploma of the Imperial Society of Teachers of Dancing
LittD	Doctor of Letters
LIWM	Licentiate of the Institute of Wastes Management
LLB	Bachelor of Law
LLCM	Performers Diploma of Licentiateship in Speech, Drama and Public Speaking
LLCM(TD)	Licentiate of the London College of Music and Media (Teachers' Diploma)
LLD	Doctor of Law
LLM	Master of Law
LM	Licentiate in Midwifery
LMIFM	Licentiate Member of the Institute of Fisheries Management
LMInstE	Licentiate Member of the Institute of Energy
LMPA	Licentiate Member of the Master Photographers Association
LMRTPI	Legal Member of the Royal Town Planning Institute
LMSSALond	Licentiate in Medicine, Surgery and Obstetrics & Gynaecology, Society of Apothecaries of London
LMusEd	Licentiate Diploma in Music Education
LMusLCM	Licentiate in Music of the London College of Music
LMusTCL	Licentiate in Music, Trinity College of Music
LNCP	Licentiate of the National Council of Psychotherapists
LPC	Legal Practice Course
LRAD	Licentiate of the Royal Academy of Dancing
LRAM	Licentiate of the Royal Academy of Music
LRCPEdin	Conjoint Diplomas Licentiate of the Royal College of Physicians of Edinburgh
LRCPSGlasg	Conjoint Diplomas Licentiate of the Royal College of Physicians and Surgeons of Glasgow
LRCSEdin	Conjoint Diplomas Licentiate of the Royal College of Surgeons of Edinburgh
LRCSEng	Licentiate of the Royal College of Surgeons in England
LRPS	Licentiate of the Royal Photographic Society
LRSC	Licentiate of the Royal Society of Chemistry
LRSM	Licentiate Diploma of the Royal Schools of Music
LSBP	Licentiate of the Society of Business Practitioners
LSCP(Assoc)	Associate of the London and Counties Society of Physiologists

LTCL	Licentiate of Trinity College of Music
LTh	Licentiate in Theology
LTI	Licentiate of the Textile Industry
LTSC	Licentiate of the Oil and Colour Chemists' Association
LVT	Licentiate Vehicle Technologist
MA	Master of Arts
MA(Architectural)	Master of Arts (Architectural Studies)
MA(Econ)	Master of Arts in Economic and Social Studies
MA(Ed)	Master of Arts in Education
MA(LD)	Master of Arts (Landscape Design)
MA(MUS)	Master of Arts (Music)
MA(RCA)	Master of Arts, Royal College of Art
MA(SocSci)	Master of Arts (Social Science)
MA(Theol)	Master of Arts in Theology
MAAT	Member of the Association of Accounting Technicians
MABAC	Member of the Association of Business and Administrative Computing
MABE	Member of the Association of Business Executives
MAcc	Master of Accountancy
MACP	Member of the Association of Computer Professionals
MAE	Member of the Academy of Experts
MAgr	Master of Agriculture
MAgrSc	Master of Agricultural Science
MAMS	Member of the Association of Medical Secretaries, Practice Managers, Administrators and Receptionists
MAMSA	Managing & Marketing Sales Association Examination Board
MAnimSc	Master of Animal Science
MAO	Master of Obstetrics
MAP	Membership by Assessment of Performance
MAPM	Member of the Association for Project Management
MAppSci	Master of Applied Science
MAQ	Mortgage Advice Qualification
MArAd	Master of Archive Administration
MArb	Master of Arboriculture
MArch	Master of Architecture
MArt/RCA	Master of Arts, Royal College of Art
MasFCI	Master of the Faculty of Commerce and Industry
MASHAM	Management and Administration of Safety and Health at Mines
MASI	Member of the Architecture and Surveying Institute
MBA	Master of Business Administration
MBAE	Member of the British Association of Electrolysists
MB, BCh	Conjoint Degree of Bachelor of Medicine, Bachelor of Surgery
MB, BChir	Conjoint Degree of Bachelor of Medicine, Bachelor of Surgery
MB, BS	Conjoint Degree of Bachelor of Medicine, Bachelor of Surgery
MB, ChB	Conjoint Degree of Bachelor of Medicine, Bachelor of Surgery
MBChA	Member of the British Chiropody and Podiatry Association
MBCO	Member of the British College of Ophthalmic Opticians
MBCS	Member of the British Computer Society
MBEng	Member of the Association of Building Engineers
MBHA	Member of the British Hypnotherapy Association
MBHI	Member of the British Horological Institute
MBIAT	Member of the British Institute of Architectural Technologists
MBID	Member of the British Institute of Interior Design

MBIE	Member of the British Institute of Embalmers
MBII	Member of the British Institute of Innkeeping
MBioc	Master of Biochemistry
MBKS	Member of the British Kinematograph, Sound and Television Society
MBM	Master of Business Management
MBMA	Member of the Business Management Association
MBSc	Master in Business Science
MBSSG	Master of the British Society of Scientific Glassblowers
MCAM	Member of the Communication Advertising and Marketing Education Foundation
MCB	Mastership in Clinical Biochemistry
MCB	Member of the British Association of Communicators in Business
MCBDip	Member of the British Association of Communicators in Business who hold the Association's Certificate and Diploma
MCC	Master of Community Care
MCCDRCS(Eng)	Member of the Royal College of Surgeons of England, Clinical Community Dentistry
MCD	Master of Civic Design
MCDH	Master of Community Dental Health
MCGI	Membership, City & Guilds
MCGPIrel	Member of the Irish College of General Practitioners
MCh	Master of Surgery
MChD	Master of Dental Surgery
MChem	Master of Chemistry
MChemA	Master of Chemical Analysis
MChemPhys	Master of Chemical Physics
MChemPST	Master of Chemistry Polymer Science and Technology
MChir	Master of Surgery
MChOrth	Master of Orthopaedic Surgery
MChS	Member of the Society of Chiropodists and Podiatrists
MCIArb	Member of the Chartered Institute of Arbitrators
MCIBS	Member of the Chartered Institute of Bankers in Scotland
MCIBSE	Member of the Chartered Institution of Building Services Engineers
MCIH	Corporate Member of the Chartered Institute of Housing
MCIJ	Member of the Chartered Institute of Journalists
MCIM	Member of the Chartered Institute of Marketing
MCIOB	Member of the Chartered Institute of Building
MCIPD	Member of the Chartered Institute of Personnel and Development
MCIPS	Member of the Chartered Institute of Purchasing and Supply
MCIT	Member of the Chartered Institute of Transport
MCIWEM	Member of the Chartered Institution of Water and Environmental Management
MCLIP	Chartered Member of CILIP
MCom	Master of Commerce
MCommH	Master of Community Health
MComp	Master of Computer Science
MCOptom	Member of the College of Optometrists
MCoT	Member of the College of Teachers
MCPM	Member of the Confederation of Professional Management
MCPP	Member of the College of Pharmacy Practice
MCQ	Multiple Choice Question paper
MCSD	Member of the Chartered Society of Designers
MCSP	Member of the Chartered Society of Physiotherapy
MCT	Member of the Association of Corporate Treasurers

MCTHCM	Member of the Confederation of Tourism, Hotel and Catering Management
MCYW	Member of the Community and Youth Work Association
MD	Doctor of Medicine
MDA	Master of Defence Administration
MD; ChM	Conjoint Doctorate in Medicine, Doctorate in Surgery
MDCR	Management Diploma of the College of Radiographers
MDent	Master of Dental Science
MDes	Master of Design
MDes(RCA)	Master of Design, Royal College of Art
MDORCPSGlas	Membership of Dental Orthopaedics, Royal College of Physicians and Surgeons of Glasgow
MDra	Master of Drama
MDS	Master of Dental Surgery
MDSc	Master of Dental Science
MEBA	Master of European Business Administration
MECI	Member of the Institute of Employment Consultants
MEd	Master of Education
MEd(EdPsych)	Master of Education (Educational Psychology)
MEdStud	Master of Educational Studies
MEng	Master of Engineering
MEnv	Master of Environmental Studies
MEnvSci	Master of Environmental Science
MESc	Master of Earth Sciences
MFA	Master of Fine Art
MFC	Mastership in Food Control
MFCM	Member of the Faculty of Community Medicine
MFDO	Member of the Faculty of Dispensing Opticians
MFDS	Member of the Faculty of Dental Surgery
MFGDPEng	Membership in General Dental Practice, Royal College of Surgeons of England
MFHom	Member of the Faculty of Homeopathy
MFM	Master of Forensic Medicine
MFPHM	Member of the Faculty of Public Health Medicine, Royal College of Physicians of London and Edinburgh and Royal College of Physicians and Surgeons of Glasgow
MFPHMIrel	Member of the Faculty of Public Health Medicine, Royal College of Physicians of Ireland
MFTCom	Member of the Faculty of Teachers in Commerce
MGDSRCSEd	Membership in General Dental Surgery, Royal College of Surgeons of Edinburgh
MGDSRCSEng	Membership in General Dental Surgery, Royal College of Surgeons of England
MGeog	Master of Geography
MGeol	Master of Geology
MGeophys	Master of Geophysical Sciences
MHCIMA	Member of the Hotel and Catering International Management Association
MHM	Master of Health Management
MHort(RHS)	Master of Horticulture, Royal Horticultural Society
MHSM	Member of the Institute of Health Services Management
MIAB	Member of the International Association of Book-keepers
MIAEA	Member of the Institute of Automotive Engineer Assessors
MIAgrE	Member of the Institution of Agricultural Engineers
MIAP	Member of the Institution of Analysts and Programmers
MIAT	Member of the Institute of Asphalt Technology
MIBC	Member of the Institute of Building Control

MIBCM	Member of the Institute British Carriage and Automobile Manufacturers
MIBCO	Member of the Institution of Building Control Officers
MIBE	Member of the Institution of British Engineers
MIBF	Member of the Institute of British Foundrymen
MIBiol	Member of the Institute of Biology
MIBM	Member of the Institute of Builders' Merchants
MICB	Member of the Institute of Certified Book-Keepers
MICE	Member of the Institute of Civil Engineers
MIChemE	Member of the Institution of Chemical Engineers
MICHT	Member of the International Council for Holistic Therapies
MICM	Member of the Institute of Credit Management
MICM(Grad)	Graduate Member of the Institute of Credit Management
MICorr	Member of the Institute of Corrosion
MICS	Member of the Institute of Chartered Shipbrokers
MICSc	Corporate Member of the Institute of Consumer Sciences Incorporating Home Economics
MICW	Member of the Institute of Clerks of Works of Great Britain Incorporated
MIDTA	Member of the International Dance Teachers' Association
MIED	Member of the Institution of Engineering Designers
MIEE	Member of the Institution of Electrical Engineers
MIEM	Member of the Institute of Executives and Managers
MIEx	Member of the Institute of Export
MIEx(Grad)	Graduate Member of the Institute of Export
MIExpE	Member of the Institute of Explosives Engineers
MIFA	Member of the Institute of Field Archaeologists
MIFireE	Member of the Institution of Fire Engineers
MIFM	Registered Member of the Institute of Fisheries Management
MIFST	Member of the Institute of Food Science and Technology
MIGasE	Member of the Institution of Gas Engineers
MIGD	Member of the Institute of Grocery Distribution
MIHEc	Member of the Institute of Home Economics
MIHIE	Member of the Institute of Highway Incorporated Engineers
MIHM	Member of the Institute of Healthcare Management
MIHort	Member of the Institute of Horticulture
MIHT	Member of the Institution of Highways and Transportation
MIIA	Member of the Institute of Internal Auditors
MIIE	Member of the Institution of Incorporated Engineers
MIIExE	Member of the Institution of Incorporated Executive Engineers
MIIHTM	Member of the International Institute of Hospitality Tourism & Management
MIIM	Member of the Institute of Industrial Managers
MIIM	Member of the International Institute of Management
MIIRSM	Member of the International Institute of Risk and Safety Management
MIISE	Member of the International Institute of Social Economics
MIISec	Member of the International Institute of Security
MIL	Member of the Institute of Linguists
MILAM	Member of the Institute of Leisure and Amenity Management
MILT	Member of the Institute of Logistics and Transport
MIM	Professional Member of the Institute of Materials
MIMA	Member of the Institute of Mathematics and its Applications
MIManf	Member of the Institute of Manufacturing
MIMarE	Member of the Institute of Marine Engineers
MIMatM	Member of the Institute of Materials Management

MIMBM	Member of the Institute of Maintenance and Building Management
MIMC	Member of the Institute of Management Consultancy
MIMechE	Member of the Institution of Mechanical Engineers
MIMechIE	Member of the Institution of Mechanical Incorporated Engineers
MIMF	Member of the Institute of Metal Finishing
MIMI	Member of the Institute of the Motor Industry
MIMinE	Member of the Institution of Mining Engineers
MIMIS	Member of the Institute for the Management of Information Systems
MIMM	Member of the Institute of Massage and Movement
MIMM	Member of the Institution of Mining and Metallurgy
MIMS	Member of the Institute of Management Specialists
MInstAEA	Member of the Institute of Automotive Engineer Assessors
MInstAM	Member of the Institute of Administrative Management
MInstBA	Member of the Institute of Business Administration
MInstBCA	Member of the Institute of Burial and Cremation Administration
MInstBE	Member of the Institution of British Engineers
MInstBM	Member of the Institute of Builders' Merchants
MInstCF	Master Fitter of the National Institute of Carpet and Floorlayers
MInstChP	Member of the Institute of Chiropodists & Podiatrists
MInstCM	Member of the Institute of Commercial Management
MInstD	Member of the Institute of Directors
MInstE	Member of the Institute of Energy
MInstLEx	Member of the Institute of Legal Executives
MInstMC	Member of the Institute of Measurement and Control
MInstNDT	Member of the British Institute of Non-Destructive Testing
MInstP	Member of the Institute of Physics
MInstPet	Member of the Institute of Petroleum
MInstPkg	Member of the Institute of Packaging
MInstPkg(Dip)	Diploma Member of the Institute of Packaging
MInstPM	Member of the Institute of Professional Managers and Administrators
MInstPS	Corporate Member of the Institute of Purchasing and Supply
MInstPSA	Member of the Institute of Public Service Administrators
MInstR	Member of the Institute of Refrigeration
MInstSMM	Member of the Institute of Sales and Marketing Management
MInstTA	Member of the Institute of Transport Administration
MInstTT	Full Member of the Institute of Travel and Tourism
MInstWM	Member of the Institute of Wastes Management
MIOC	Member of the Institute of Carpenters
MIOFMS	Member of the Institute of Financial and Management Studies
MIOM	Member of the Institute of Operations Management
MIOP	Member of the Institute of Printing
MIOSH	Member of the Institution of Occupational Safety and Health
MIP	Member of the Institute of Plumbing
MIPA	Member of the Institute of Practitioners in Advertising
MIPD	Member of the Institute of Personnel and Development
MIPI	Member of the Institute of Professional Investigators
MIPlantE	Member of the Institution of Plant Engineers
MIPR	Member of the Institute of Public Relations
MIPRE	Member of the Incorporated Practitioners in Radio & Electronics
MIQ	Member of the Institute of Quarrying
MIQA	Member of the Institute of Quality Assurance
MIR	Member of the Institute of Population Registration

MIRRV	Member of the Institute of Revenue, Rating and Valuation
MIRSE	Member of the Institution of Railway Signal Engineers
MIRTE	Member of the Institute of Road Transport Engineering
MISM	Member of the Institute for Supervision & Management
MISOB	Member of the Incorporated Society of Organ Builders
MISTC	Member of the Institute of Scientific and Technical Communicators
MIStrucE	Member of the Institution of Structural Engineers
MISW	Member of the Institute of Social Welfare
MITAI	Member of the Institute of Traffic Accident Investigators
MITSA	Member of the Institute of Trading Standards Administration
MIVehE	Member of the Institute of Vehicle Engineers
MIWM	Member of the Institute of Wastes Management
MIWPC	Member of the Institute of Water Pollution Control
MJur	Master of Jurisprudence
MLA	Master of Landscape Architecture
MLang	Master of Languages
MLangEng	Master of Language Engineering
MLD	Master of Landscape Design
MLE	Master of Land Economy
MLI	Member of the Landscape Institute
MLing	Master of Languages
MLitt	Master of Letters
MLPM	Master of Landscape Planning and Management
MLS	Master of Library Science
MM	Master of Midwifery
MMA	Master of Management and Administration
MMAS	Master of Minimal Access Surgery
MMath	Master of Mathematics
MMedE	Master of Medical Education
MMedSci	Master of Medical Science
MMet	Master of Metallurgy
MML	Master of Modern Languages
MMS	Member of the Institute of Management Services
MMSc	Master of Medical Sciences
MMus	Master of Music
MMus(Comp)	Master of Music (Composition)
MMus(Perf)	Master of Music (Performance)
MMus, RCM	Master of Music, Royal College of Music
MMusArt	Master of Musical Arts
MN	Master of Nursing
MNAEA	Member of the National Association of Estate Agents
MNatSc	Master of Natural Science
MNCP	Member of the National Council of Psychotherapists
MNeuro	Master of Neuroscience
MNI	Member of the Nautical Institute
MNIMH	Member of the National Institute of Medical Herbalists
MNRHP	Full Member of the National Register of Hypnotherapists and Psychotherapists
MNRHP(Eqv)	Full Member (Equivalent) of the National Register of Hypnotherapists and Psychotherapists
MNTB	Merchant Navy Training Board
MObstG	Master of Obstetrics and Gynaecology
MOptom	Master of Optometry

MOrthRCSEng	Membership in Orthodontics, Royal College of Surgeons of England
MPA	Master of Public Administration
MPaedDenRCSEng	Membership in Paediatric Dentistry, Royal College of Surgeons of England
MPC	Master of Palliative Care
MPH	Master of Public Health
MPharm	Master of Pharmacy
MPharmSci	Master of Pharmaceutical Science
MPhil	Master of Philosophy
MPhil(Eng)	Master of Philosophy in Engineering
MPhys	Master of Physics
MPhysGeog	Master of Physical Geography
MPlan	Master of Planning
MPPS	Master of Public Policy Studies
MPRI	Member of the Plastics and Rubber Institute
MProf	Master of Professional Studies
MProfBTM	Member of the Professional Business and Technical Management
MPS	Member of the Pharmaceutical Society of Northern Ireland
MPsychMed	Master of Psychological Medicine
MPsychol	Master of Psychology
MQB	Mining Qualifications Board
MRad	Master of Radiology
MRad; MRad(D)	Master of Radiology (Radiodiagnosis) or (Radiotherapy)
MRAeS	Member of the Royal Aeronautical Society
MRCGP	Member of the Royal College of General Practitioners
MRCOG	Member of the Royal College of Obstetricians and Gynaecologists
MRCP	Member of the Royal College of Physicians of London
MRCP(UK)	Member of the Royal College of Physicians of the United Kingdom
MRCPath	Member of the Royal College of Pathologists
MRCPEdin	Member of the Royal College of Physicians of Edinburgh (superceded by MRCP(UK))
MRCPGlasg	Member of the Royal College of Physicians of Glasgow (superceded by MRCP(UK))
MRCPIrel	Member of the Royal College of Physicians of Ireland
MRCPsych	Member of the Royal College of Psychiatrists
MRCSEd	Member of the Royal College of Surgeons of Edinburgh
MRCSEng	Member of the Royal College of Surgeons of England
MRCVS	Member of the Royal College of Veterinary Surgeons
MRDRCS	Membership in Restorative Dentistry, Royal College of Surgeons of England
MREC	Member of the Recruitment and Employment Confederation
MREHIS	Member of the Royal Environmental Health Institute of Scotland
MRes	Master of Research
MRIN	Member of the Royal Institute of Navigation
MRINA	Member of the Royal Institution of Naval Architects
MRIPHH	Member of the Royal Institute of Public Health and Hygiene
MRPharmS	Member of the Pharmaceutical Society of Great Britain
MRSC	Member of the Royal Society of Chemistry
MRSH	Member of the Royal Society for the Promotion of Health
MRSS	Member of the Royal Statistical Society
MRTPI	Member of the Royal Town Planning Institute
MS	Master of Surgery
MSA	Marine Safety Agency
MSAPP	Member of the Society of Advanced Psychotherapy Practitioners

MSBP	Member of the Society of Business Practitioners
MSBT	Member of the Society of Teachers in Business Education
MSc	Master of Science
MSc(Econ)	Master of Science in Economics
MSc(Ed)	Master of Science in Education
MSc(Eng)	Master of Science in Engineering
MSc(Entr)	Master of Entrepreneurship
MSc(Mgt)	Master of Science in Management
MScD	Master of Dental Science
MScEcon	Master in Faculty of Economic and Social Studies
MSCi	Master of Natural Sciences
MScTech	Master of Technical Science
MSE	Member of Society of Engineers (Inc)
MSF	Member of the SMAE Institute
MSFA	Advanced Financial Planning Certificate
MSIAD	Member of the Society of Industrial Artists and Designers
MSMA	Member of the Society of Martial Arts
MSocSc	Master of Social Science
MSSc	Master of Social Science
MSSc	Master of Surgical Science
MSSCh	Member of the British Chiropody and Podiatry Association
MSSF	Member of the Society of Shoe Fitters
MSt	Master of Studies
MSTA	Member of the Swimming Teachers' Association
MSTI	Certificate of Insurance Work
MSurgDentRCSEng	Membership in Surgical Dentistry, Royal College of Surgeons of England
MSW	Master of Social Work
MTCP	Master of Town and Country Planning
MTD	Master of Transport Design
MTech	Master of Technology
MTh	Master of Theology
MTheol	Master of Theology
MTP	Master of Town Planning
MTPI	Master of Town Planning
MTropMed	Master of Tropical Medicine
MTropPaediatrics	Master of Tropical Paediatrics
MUniv	Master of University (Honorary)
MURP	Master of Urban and Regional Planning
MusB	Bachelor of Music
MusD	Doctor of Music
MVC	Management Verification Consortium
MVM	Master of Veterinary Medicine
MVSc	Master of Veterinary Science
MWeldI	Member of the Welding Institute
MWES	Member of the Women's Engineering Society
MYD	Member of the Youth Development Association
NACOS	National Approval Council for Security Systems
NAEA	National Association of Estate Agents
NAG	National Association of Goldsmiths
NAMCW	National Association for Maternal and Child Welfare
NC	National Certificate
NCA	National Certificate in Agriculture

NCC	National Computing Centre
NCC	Navigational Control Course
NCDT	National Council for Drama Training
NCTJ	National Council for the Training of Journalists
NCVQ	National Council for Vocational Qualifications
ND	Diploma in Naturopathy
NDD	National Diploma in Design
NDF	National Diploma in Forestry
NDH	National Diploma in Horticulture
NDSF	National Diploma of the Society of Floristry
NDT	National Diploma in the Science and Practice of Turfculture and Sports Ground Management
NEBOSH	National Examination Board in Occupational Safety and Health
NEBS	National Examining Board for Supervision & Management
NFTS	National Film and Television School
NICCEA	Northern Ireland Council for the Curriculum, Examinations and Assessment
NID	National Intermediate Diploma
NIM	Northern Institute of Massage
NNEB	National Nursery Examination Board
NRHP	National Register of Hypnotherapists and Psychotherapists
NRHP(Affil)	Affiliate of the National Register of Hypnotherapists and Psychotherapists
NRHP(Assoc)	Associate of the National Register of Hypnotherapists and Psychotherapists
N-SHAP	National School of Hypnosis and Psychotherapy
NTTG	National Textile Training Group
NUJ	National Union of Journalists
NVQ	National Vocational Qualifications
NWRAC	North Western Regional Advisory Council for Further Education
OCR	Oxford, Cambridge & RSA Examinations
ODLQC	Open & Distance Learning Quality Council, formerly CACC, Council for Accreditation of Correspondence Colleges
ONC	Ordinary National Certificate
OND	Ordinary National Diploma
OSCE	Objective Structured Clinical Exam
PBTM	Professional Business and Technical Management
PCN	Personnel Certification in Non-Destructive Testing Ltd
PDP	Professional Development Programme
PESD	Private and Executive Secretary's Diploma, London Chamber of Commerce and Industry
PgC	Postgraduate Certificate
PGCE	Postgraduate Certificate in Education
PGCert	Postgraduate Certificate
PgD	Postgraduate Diploma
PGDip	Postgraduate Diploma
PGDip(Comp)	Postgraduate Diploma in Composition
PGDip(LCM)	Postgraduate Diploma of the London College of Music
PGDip(Perf)	Postgraduate Diploma in Performance
PGDip(RCM)	Postgraduate Diploma of the Royal College of Music
PGDipMin	Postgraduate Diploma in Ministry
PGDipMus	Postgraduate Diploma in Music
PhD	Doctor of Philosophy
PhD(RCA)	Doctor of Philosophy (Royal College of Art)
PIC	Professional Investment Certificate

PIFA	Practitioner of the Institute of Field Archaeologists
PIIA	Practitioner of the Institute of Internal Auditors
PInstNDT	Practitioner of the British Institute of Non-Destructive Testing
PJDip	Professional Jewellers' Diploma
PJGemDip	Professional Jewellers' Gemstone Diploma
PJManDip	Professional Jewellers' Management Diploma
PJValDip	Professional Jewellers' Valuation Diploma
PPL	Private Pilot's Licence
PPRNCM	Professional Performance Diploma of the Royal Northern College of Music
PQS	Professional Qualification Structure
PQSW	Post-Qualifying Award in Social Work
PRCA	Public Relations Consultants Association
PSC	Private Secretary's Certificate
PSD	Private Secretary's Diploma
PTA	Pianoforte Tuners' Association
PVM	Professional in Value Management
QC	Queen's Counsel
QCA	Qualifications and Curriculum Authority
QCG	Qualification in Careers Guidance
QDR	Qualified Dispute Resolver
QICA	Qualification in Computer Auditing
QIS	Qualified Imaging Scientist
QPA	Qualification in Pensions Administration
QPSPA	Qualification in Public Sector Pensions Administration
RA	Royal Academician
RAD	Royal Academy of Dancing
RADA	Royal Academy of Dramatic Art
RAM	Royal Academy of Music
RANA	Royal Animal Nursing Auxiliary
RAS	Royal Astronomical Society
RBS	Royal Ballet School
RC	Roman Catholic
RCM	Royal College of Midwives
RCN	Royal College of Nursing
RCSLT	Royal College of Speech and Language Therapists
RCVS	Royal College of Veterinary Surgeons
REA	Regional Examining Body
REC	Recruitment and Employment Confederation
Ret'dABID	Retired Associate of the British Institute of Interior Design
Ret'dFBID	Retired Fellow of the British Institute of Interior Design
Ret'dMBID	Retired Member of the British Institute of Interior Design
RGN	Registered General Nurse
RHS	Royal Horticultural Society
RHV	Registered Health Visitor
RIBA	Royal Institute of British Architects
RICS	Royal Institution of Chartered Surveyors
RINA	Royal Institution of Naval Architects
RJDip	Diploma for Retail Jewellers
RJGemDip	National Association of Goldsmiths Gemstone Diploma
RM	Registered Midwife
RMN	Registered Mental Nurse
RMS	Royal Microscopical Society

RNMH	Registered Nurse for the Mentally Handicapped
RP	Registered Plumber
RPS	Royal Photographic Society
RSA	Royal Society of Arts
RSBEI	Registered Student of the Institution of Body Engineers
RSC	Royal Society of Chemistry
RSCN	Registered Sick Children's Nurse
RSP	Registered Safety Practitioner
RTO	Recognised Training Organisation
RTPI	Royal Town Planning Institute
SA	Salvation Army Management
SBP	Society of Business Practitioners
SCAA	School Curriculum and Assessment Authority
ScD	Doctor of Science
SCE	Scottish Certificate of Education
SCLS	Second Certificate for Legal Secretaries
SCMT	Ship Captain's Medical Training
SCOTVEC	Scottish Vocational Education Council
SCPL	Senior Commercial Pilot's Licence
SE	Society of Engineers
SEE	Society of Environmental Engineers
SEFIC	Spoken English for Industry and Commerce
SenAWeldI	Senior Associate of the Welding Institute
SEng	Qualified Sales Engineer
SenMWeldI	Senior Member of the Welding Institute
SF	Society of Floristry Ltd
SFA	Securities and Futures Authority
SFInstE	Senior Fellow of the Institute of Energy
SG	Society of Genealogists
SGT	Society of Glass Technology
SHNC	Scottish Higher National Certificate
SHND	Scottish Higher National Diploma
SIEDip	Securities Industry Examination Diploma
SInstPet	Student of the Institute of Petroleum
SITO	Security Industry Training Organisation Ltd
SLC	Secretarial Language Certificate
SLD	Secretarial Language Diploma
SNC	Scottish National Certificate
SND	Scottish National Diploma
SNNEB	Scottish Nursery Nurses Examination Board
SPA	Screen Printing Association
SPRINT	Sport Play and Recreation Industries National Training Executive
SQA	Scottish Qualifications Authority
SRD	State Registered Dietician
SRN	State Registered Nurse
SSC	Secretarial Studies Certificate, London Chamber of Commerce and Industry
STA	Specialist Teacher Assistant (CACHE)
STA	Swimming Teachers' Association
STAT	Society of Teachers of the Alexander Technique
StudentIEE	Student of the Institution of Electrical Engineers
StudentIIE	Student of the Institution of Incorporated Engineers
StudentIMechE	Student of the Institution of Mechanical Engineers

StudIAP	Student of the Institution of Analysts and Programmers
StudIManf	Student Member of the Institute of Manufacturing
StudIMS	Student of the Institute of Management Specialists
StudProfBTM	Student of the Professional Business and Technical Management
StudSE	Student of the Society of Engineers (Inc)
StudSElec	Student of the Society of Electroscience
StudWeldI	Student of the Welding Institute
SVQ	Scottish Vocational Qualification
TC	Technician Certificate
TCA	Technician in Costing and Accounting
TCA	Technician of the Institute of Cost and Executive Accountants
TCert	Teacher's Certificate
TD	Technician Diploma
TDCR	Teacher's Diploma of the College of Radiographers
TechICorr	Technician of the Institute of Corrosion
TechMIWM	Technician Member of the Institute of Wastes Management
TechRICS	Technical Surveyor of the Royal Institution of Chartered Surveyors
TechRMS	Technological Qualification in Microscopy, Royal Microscopical Society
TechRTPI	Technical Member of the Royal Town Planning Institute
TechSP	Technician Safety Practitioner
TechWeldI	Technician of the Welding Institute
TEMOL	Training in Energy Management through Open Learning
TI	Textile Institute
TIMBM	Technician of the Institute of Maintenance and Building Management
TMBA	Teacher Member of the British (Theatrical) Arts
TnIMBM	Technicians of the Institute of Maintenance and Building Management
TOEFL	Test of English as a Foreign Language
TPP	Test of Professional Practice
TVM	Trainer in Value Management
UCAS	Universities and Colleges Admissions Service
UCL	University College London
UEB	United Examining Board
UKCC	United Kingdom Central Council
UKCP	United Kingdom Council for Psychotherapy
UMIST	University of Manchester Institute of Science and Technology
URC	United Reformed Church
VetMB	Bachelor of Veterinary Medicine
VTCT	Vocational Training Charitable Trust
WCMD	Welsh College of Music and Drama
WES	Women's Engineering Society
WJEC	Welsh Joint Education Committee
WMAC	West Midlands Advisory Council for Further Education
WSA	West of Scotland Agricultural College
YHAFHE	Yorkshire and Humberside Association for Further and Higher Education
ZSL	Zoological Society of London

Part 1

Introduction

Since its first publication in 1970, *British Qualifications* has charted a number of fundamental changes in further and higher education provision in the UK. Major advances in technology and more flexible delivery and attendance patterns have created different types of learning opportunity, encouraging an ever more diverse student population to access education at all levels. The range of subjects delivered has grown beyond all recognition. New areas of research have been established and developed into major subject specialisms. Employers and professional bodies have collaborated to develop subject areas aligned to changing industry requirements. Flexibility and choice are the hallmarks of today's system, and anyone new to higher education may well be bewildered by the sheer variety of degree pathways available. The capacity to combine and mix modules and subjects has in fact grown beyond anything that could have been imagined in 1970.

Traditional boundaries between academic and vocational pathways continue to break down, and today most degrees have a vocational slant. Extended industry and professional placements, sponsored research projects, practitioner input and field-based assignments are common features in many degrees, and provide an important link into practice at the early stages of learning. Overall, in 20 years universities have doubled in size and the responsibilities they have taken on have expanded considerably. Collaboration between further education (FE) and higher education (HE) institutions has enabled a substantial amount of HE-level provision to be delivered in FE institutions. Clear progression routes have been established for some time. Considerable breadth of provision is now available in FE: not only has the sector grown to accommodate sub-degree provision, it has also continued to deliver a wide range of pre- and post-18 vocational qualifications, which include technical, occupational and professional awards.

Today, certain types of external qualification cross the boundaries between further and higher education. Several higher education institutions (HEIs) — particularly those that gained university status in the 1990s and in 2005 — deliver advanced professional qualifications and higher national diplomas or certificates from awarding bodies like Edexcel, OCR and SQA. At the same time there has been a significant shift towards FE's involvement in delivery of these types of qualification, and a greater input from private sector colleges.

EDUCATION REFORM

The Higher Education Act 2004 introduced in 2006/07 brought new student support and tuition fee arrangements. Following the Browne Review of 2010, universities are able to charge full-time UK and EU undergraduate students up to £9,000 a year as part of a reorganization of HE funding and student finance. You will find further authoritative, official information about universities and colleges in the UK at the Unistats website: http://unistats.direct.gov.uk/. The Unistats website enables you to compare data and information on UK university and college courses, as well as providing useful information on cost and financial support. Information on student finance and how to apply for it can be found at www.direct.gov.uk and this site also give information about university and higher education courses.

As well as implementing reforms, the further and higher education sectors contribute to UK economic performance and the delivery of the government's policies on HE. As part of this shared responsibility a great deal of effort is being made to increase access to and participation in education, particularly among individuals who have not had much involvement in the past. The general availability of modular study programmes and related credit recognition of units, and greater use of ICT and e-learning resources, have done a lot to create more flexible methods of delivery and attendance requirements in further and higher education.

Foundation degrees

Foundation degrees (FDs) were established to give people the intermediate technical and professional skills that are in demand from employers, and to provide more flexible and accessible ways of studying. They are a higher-level qualification awarded by universities. The qualification can be 'built up' from a range of relevant learning experiences, to allow for extremely flexible and adaptable qualifications that can be 'tailored' by employers to support their workforce and business development needs. They offer opportunities for employment and career advancement. Progression routes include links with associated professional qualifications and/or direct entry to the final year of a relevant Honours-level degree. FDs are offered by universities, colleges and other providers.

The first FDs in 2001 were studied by 4,000 students. In 2010, there were just over 99,700 enrolled on FDs. There are now hundreds of FD courses available, both full- and part-time.

- Information about FDs can be found on the UCAS website: http://fd.ucas.com/Foundation Degree/About.aspx
- Information, advice and guidance resources for work-based learners and their advisers are hosted by unionlearn at www.unionlearn.org.uk/higher-learning-work
- fdf e-learning resources that support the delivery of work-based higher education in sectors such as retail, travel and low carbon energy are available at www.workforcedevelopment.fdf.ac.uk
- The Higher Education Academy hosts publications produced by fdf so that they remain available to the higher education community at www.heacademy.ac.uk/fdf

Policy and regulation

The UK and Scottish parliaments and the Welsh and Northern Ireland assemblies set national priorities for further and higher education. Policy development, planning and implementation rest with the government departments responsible for each national education brief – the Department for Business, Innovation and Skills (BIS website: www.gov.uk/government/organisations/department-for-business-innovation-skills), the Department for Employment and Learning Northern Ireland (DELNI website: www.delni.gov.uk), the Scottish Government (www.scotland.gov.uk), and The Department for Education and Skills (DfES website: http://gov.wales/topics/education andskills/) in Wales.

In England, delivery of FE is subject to external audit and public reporting by the Office for Standards in Education, Children's Services and Schools (Ofsted website: www.gov.uk/government/organisations/ofsed).

In Scotland, the Scottish Funding Council (SFC website: www.sfc.ac.uk) is the national, strategic body that is responsible for funding teaching and learning provision, research and other activities in Scotland's 27 colleges and 19 universities and higher education institutes. Inspection is carried out by Education Scotland (www.educationscotland.gov.uk/inspectionandreview).

DfES is responsible for planning, funding and promotion of all post-16 education in Wales. Estyn (the Welsh-language acronym for Her Majesty's Inspectorate for Education and Training in Wales, website: www.estyn.gov.uk) is the appointed authority for audit of the quality of provision and related areas.

The Department for Employment and Learning (DELNI) is responsible for planning and funding of further education provision in Northern Ireland. The Education and Training Inspectorate (ETI) on behalf of the Department (www.delni.gov.uk, www.etini.gov.uk) undertakes inspection and audit.

QUALITY ASSURANCE

A degree of convergence exists in the quality assurance of qualifications at level 3 and below. England, Wales and Northern Ireland share a common qualifications system, and the regulators in each country (listed below) work together in regulating qualifications for use across the three countries. Scotland has a separate qualifications system, although there is close correlation across all four countries, particularly in the area of vocational qualifications.

The following four bodies are responsible for the accreditation and standards of external qualifications and for curriculum and assessment for ages 3–16:

- *England*: Office of the Qualifications and Examinations Regulator (Ofqual website: www.gov. uk/government/organisations/ofqual);
- *Northern Ireland*: Council for Curriculum, Examinations and Assessment (CCEA* website: www.rewardinglearning.org.uk/);
- *Scotland*: Scottish Qualifications Authority (SQA** website: www.sqa.org.uk);
- *Wales*: Department for Education and Skills (DfESwales website: http://gov.wales/topics/ educationandskills/).

*CCEA is also an Awarding Body for qualifications in Northern Ireland, offering a diverse range of qualifications, such as GCSEs, including the new GCSE Double Award specifications in vocational subjects, GCE A and AS levels, Entry Level Qualifications, and Graded Objectives in Modern Languages.

**SQA is also an Awarding Body that develops and validates SQA-branded qualifications including National Qualifications (Access, Intermediate, Higher and Advanced Higher Levels, Skills for Work, National Progression Awards and National Certificates), Higher National Certificates and Diplomas, Scottish Vocational Qualifications, Modern Apprenticeships and Scottish Professional Development Awards. The SQA also award Functional Skills qualifications and qualifications under the Qualifications and Credit Framework.

In HE the responsibility for standards and quality rests firmly with each institution. All institutions work with the independent Quality Assurance Agency for Higher Education (QAA) for England, Northern Ireland, Scotland and Wales. Institutional audits and subject-level reviews have been undertaken by QAA since 2001. It publishes its findings on its website (www.qaa.ac.uk) as publicly accessible information; see www.qaa.ac.uk

Given the current scale and diversity of degree provision in the HE sector, there has been a need to clarify what can reasonably be expected from undergraduate and postgraduate programmes. QAA has responded to this requirement and developed the Quality Code for HE providers (www.qaa.ac. uk/assuring-standards-and-quality/the-quality-code), and subject benchmark statements indicating the expected standards of degrees across a range of subjects.

QUALIFICATION FRAMEWORKS

In further response to the breadth and diversity of qualifications available, a number of national qualification frameworks have been introduced. The framework concept is closely associated with greater transparency and comparability between types of qualification, particularly between those that were traditionally classified as academic or vocational. Common characteristics of all frameworks include universal adoption and understanding of qualification titles, and national tariffs of credits that recognize relevant levels of achievement.

Figure 1.1 Framework for Higher Education Qualifications in England, Wales and Northern Ireland (*Source*: http://ofqual.gov.uk/help-and-advice/comparing-qualifications)

The framework for Higher Education Qualifications in England, Wales and Northern Ireland (FHEQ) applies to degrees, diplomas, certificates and other academic awards by higher education providers (see Figure 1.1).

The Scottish Credit and Qualification Framework (SCQF) was developed by SQA, the Scottish Executive, QAA (Scottish Office) and Universities for Scotland. It provides an overview of all levels of national and higher qualifications provision in Scotland (see Figure 1.2). Further information and the database of courses can be found at http://scqf.org.uk

The Qualifications and Credit Framework (QCF) (find information at: www.accredited qualifications.org.uk/qualifications-and-credit-framework-qcf.html) is the framework for recognizing and accrediting qualifications in England, Wales and Northern Ireland. It is intended to make the system and qualifications offered far more relevant to the needs of employers, with more flexibility for learners. Every unit and qualification in the framework has a credit value (where one credit roughly equals 10 hours) and a level from Entry level to level 8.

There are three types of qualification in the QCF:

Awards: 1–12 credits;
Certificates: 13–36 credits;
Diplomas: 37 credits or more.

This means that each qualification title contains the level (from Entry to level 8), the size (Award/Certificate/Diploma) and the details of the content of the qualification. Ofqual regulates the framework, and more information can be found at http://ofqual.gov.uk/qualifications-and-assessments/qualification-frameworks/ and http://register.ofqual.gov.uk/, which is a searchable database of qualifications and organizations.

If qualifications do not meet the rules of the Qualifications and Credit Framework they are developed to fit the National Qualifications Framework (NQF), which gives an indication of the

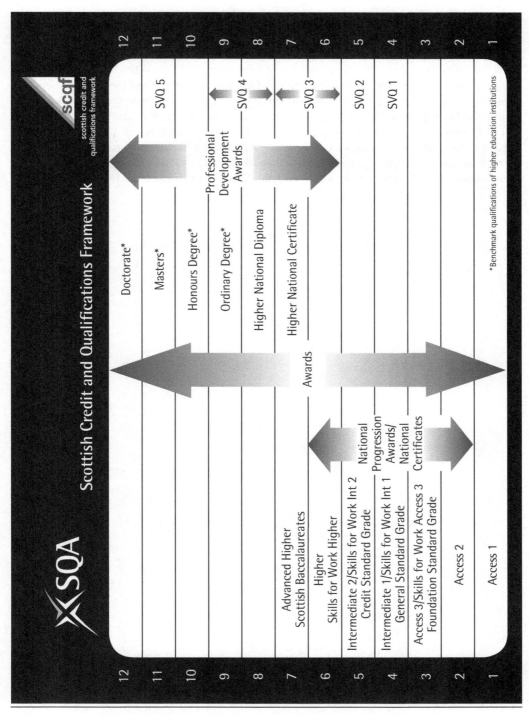

Figure 1.2 Framework for Higher Education Qualifications in Scotland
(*Source*: www.sqa.org.uk/sqa/4595.html)

relative demand of different qualifications. Qualifications in the NQF are grouped together according to their difficulty.

However, in 2015 Ofqual announced that following consultation, they have decided to withdraw the rules for the qualifications and credit framework (QCF) and the NVQ qualifications. They are now consulting on new, simpler rules which will replace parts of the QCF. In the meantime, the current rules and regulations will still apply. Visit their website www.gov.uk/government/collections/qualifications-and-credit-framework-requirements for more information.

The European Qualifications Framework (EQF) compares the level of qualifications across Europe to make it easier for employers and educational establishments to compare their value. More information can be found at: www.accreditedqualifications.org.uk/european-qualifications-framework-eqf.html and the website of the European Commission: https://ec.europa.eu/ploteus/en

Part 2

Teaching Establishments

INTRODUCTION

The statutory responsibility for the provision of education in the United Kingdom lies with the Department for Education (www.gov.uk) and the Department for Business, Innovation and Skills (BIS) in England, the Welsh Assembly Government's Department for Education and Skills (DfES), the Education Department of the Scottish Government and the Department of Education and Department for Employment and Learning in Northern Ireland.

In the United Kingdom the statutory system of public education has three progressive stages: primary education (up to the age of 11 or 12), secondary education (up to age 16), and further education (post-16).

The Education and Skills Act 2008 introduced a new requirement that all young people in England must continue in education or training at least part-time until they are 18 years old, and this applies to any person born on or after 1 September 1997 (see www.gov.uk/know-when-you-can-leave-school). The website www.ucas.com/ucas/after-gcses gives useful information on the options available and the government website www.gov.uk/further-education-courses also gives information on courses and funding.

This section briefly describes further and higher provision and the main types of institution.

FURTHER AND HIGHER EDUCATION

'Higher education' (HE) is a term that broadly defines any course of study leading to a qualification at level 4 and above in the Qualifications and Credit Framework (QCF)/National Qualifications Framework (NQF) for England, Wales and Northern Ireland, and level 6 and above in the Scottish Credit and Qualifications Framework.

HE incorporates study towards a wide range of qualifications including Foundation, undergraduate and postgraduate degrees, certificates and diplomas awarded by individual universities and other higher education institutions (HEIs) with degree-awarding powers. It can also include study towards general, technical or occupationally-related diplomas and certificates awarded by the large unitary awarding bodies. Unitary awarding bodies are characterized by their breadth of provision, from NVQs and BTEC courses and A levels through to qualifications at level 5 and above in the national frameworks.

The other category that can be characterized as HE includes post-experience education above level 4 (and level 7 in Scotland). This includes qualifications available from awarding bodies that represent a particular sector, occupation or technical/craft area, and professional institutions that are also approved as awarding bodies.

HE can take place in universities and HE colleges (which continue to provide the majority of undergraduate and postgraduate courses). It can also take place in colleges of further education (FE). A significant number of colleges deliver parts of, and in some cases entire, Foundation and undergraduate degree courses in agreement with a selected university partner that is responsible for quality assurance and final awards.

In general terms, FE is available for students who are over the age of 16 and still in full-time education, and for adults aged 19 and over. FE provision includes GCSEs, A levels and other types of general and vocational qualifications below level 4 (and level 6 in Scotland) in the National Qualifications Frameworks.

All qualifications are awarded by approved external awarding bodies that include AQA, City & Guilds, Edexcel, LCCI, OCR, OCN and SQA in Scotland. This also includes qualifications below level 4 (level 6 in Scotland) that have a craft or technical focus or are related to an occupation/ sector. At the time of writing, readers who want to find out more about approved qualifications below level 4 will find The Register of Regulated Qualifications website informative (http:// register.ofqual.gov.uk). It contains details of all regulated qualifications in England (Ofqual), Wales (Welsh Government) and Northern Ireland (Ofqual and CCEA).

FURTHER AND HIGHER EDUCATION INSTITUTIONS

England and Wales

There is a wide range of further and higher education establishments, including colleges with various titles. There are also a number of independent specialist establishments, like secretarial and correspondence colleges.

In 2015 there were 161 universities and colleges that were allowed to award degrees. All institutions that are recognized as having degree-awarding powers in the UK can be found on the government website (www.gov.uk/check-a-university-is-officially-recognised/recognised-bodies).

There were also over 600 colleges and other institutions that could not award degrees themselves, but provided courses leading to UK degrees. Institutions offering courses leading to a degree from a recognized body can be found at www.gov.uk/check-a-university-is-officially-recognised/listed-bodies. For general information on UK degrees visit www.gov.uk/ recognised-uk-degrees.

Courses include those for first and second degrees, certain graduate-equivalent qualifications, and the examinations of the principal professional associations. These institutions also provide courses leading to important qualifications below degree level, such as Foundation degrees, Higher National Diplomas and Certificates, and Diplomas of Higher Education. Most FE colleges specialize in providing courses that lead to qualifications below degree level, such as A levels and BTEC qualifications. Some offer degree courses, including in many cases Foundation degrees.

Students aged 16–18 who have been ordinarily resident in the UK for three years and European Economic Area nationals normally have the right to attend a full-time course without paying tuition fees. More detailed information on tuition fees for international students can be found at www.ukcisa.org.uk. Colleges are free to determine fee levels for students who do not qualify for 'home fees'.

Further Education choices can be searched on http://fechoices.skillsfundingagency.bis.gov.uk/ Pages/home.aspx and also http://findfe.com. The 2015 figures show there were 348 FE colleges in England (of which 94 were sixth-form colleges) 19 in Wales, 40 in Scotland and 6 in Northern Ireland.

Scotland

There are 40 FE colleges in Scotland that provide a broad mix of courses, many awarded by the Scottish Qualifications Authority (SQA). Most HE courses at or near degree level and beyond are provided by the 18 universities/HE institutions and The Open University in Scotland (www.universities-scotland.ac.uk; www.studyinscotland.org). These institutions offer a range of vocationally-oriented courses ranging from science, engineering and computing to health care, art and design, music and drama, and teacher training, as well as the more traditional 'academic' courses. The Scottish Funding Council funds all the universities and HE institutions in Scotland.

Northern Ireland

Responsibility for the FE sector in Northern Ireland rests with the Department for Employment and Learning (DELNI) which directly funds colleges. There are six further and higher education colleges, offering a wide range of vocational and non-vocational courses for both full- and part-time students. Details can be found at www.anic.ac.uk

Queen's University Belfast and the University of Ulster receive Quality-related Research (QR) funding from the Department for Employment and Learning, Northern Ireland. Many of the courses in both universities are designed to suit the needs of industry, commerce and the professions. Agricultural, horticultural and food colleges in Northern Ireland are administered through the Department of Agriculture and Rural Development (DARD, website: www.dardni.gov.uk), which offers a range of further and higher education courses at the College of Agriculture, Food and Rural Enterprise (CAFRE, website: www.cafre.ac.uk).

UNIVERSITIES AND HE COLLEGES

Universities are self-governing bodies, largely financed by the government through the Higher Education Funding Councils in the UK. They generally derive their rights and privileges from Royal Charter or Act of Parliament, and any amendment of their charters or statutes is made by the Crown acting through the Privy Council on the application of the universities themselves. The universities alone decide what degrees they award and the conditions on which they are awarded; they alone decide which students to admit and which staff to appoint. However, government policies have started to influence admission criteria, particularly in terms of widening access and participation in HE. Student fees set by universities are also subject to strict guidelines set by the government.

The Higher Education Funding Council (www.hefce.ac.uk) funds HE, research and related activities in English HE institutions and FE colleges. In 2015–16 it funded 132 HE institutions (including University Campus Suffolk, established and validated by the Universities of East Anglia and Essex) and 212 FE colleges.

Institutions receiving funding from Higher Education Funding Council for England

The schools and institutes of the University of London which receive funds directly from the HEFCE are marked *.

Anglia Ruskin University; Aston University; University of Bath; Bath Spa University; University of Bedfordshire; Birkbeck, University of London*; University of Birmingham; Birmingham City University; University College Birmingham; Bishop Grosseteste University; University of Bolton; Arts University Bournemouth; Bournemouth University; University of Bradford; University of Brighton; University of Bristol; Brunel University; Buckinghamshire New University; University of Cambridge; Institute of Cancer Research*; Canterbury Christ Church University; University of Central Lancashire; University of Chester; University of Chichester; City University, London; Conservatoire for Dance and Drama; Courtauld Institute of Art*; Coventry University; Cranfield University; University for the Creative Arts; University of Cumbria; De Montfort University; University of Derby; Durham University; University of East Anglia; University of East London; Edge Hill University; University of Essex; University of Exeter; Falmouth University; University of Gloucestershire; Goldsmiths, University of London*; University of Greenwich; Guildhall School of Music and Drama; Harper Adams University; University of Hertfordshire; Heythrop College, University of London*; University of Huddersfield; University of Hull; Imperial College London; Keele University; University of Kent; King's College London*; Kingston University; Lancaster University; University of Leeds; Leeds College of Art; Leeds Beckett University; Leeds Trinity University; University of Leicester; University of Lincoln; University of Liverpool; Liverpool Hope University; Liverpool Institute for Performing Arts; Liverpool John Moores University; Liverpool School of Tropical Medicine; University of the Arts, London; London Business School*; London School of Economics and Political Science*; London School of Hygiene and Tropical Medicine*; London Metropolitan University; London South Bank University; Loughborough University; University of Manchester; Manchester Metropolitan University; Middlesex University, London; National Film and Television School; Newcastle University; Newman University; University of Northampton; Northumbria University; Newcastle; Norwich University of the Arts; University of Nottingham; Nottingham Trent University; The Open University; University of Oxford; Oxford Brookes University; Plymouth University; Plymouth College of Art; University of Portsmouth; Queen Mary, University of London*; Ravensbourne; University of Reading; Roehampton University; Rose Bruford College; Royal Academy of Music*; Royal Agricultural University; Royal Central School of Speech and Drama*; Royal College of Art; Royal College of Music; Royal Holloway, University of London*; Royal Northern College of Music; Royal Veterinary College*; St George's, University of London*; University of St Mark and St John; St Mary's University, Twickenham; University of Salford; University of Sheffield; Sheffield Hallam University; SOAS, University of London*; University of Southampton; Southampton Solent University; Staffordshire University; University of Sunderland; University of Surrey; University of Sussex; Teesside University; Trinity Laban Conservatoire of Music and Dance; UCL (including UCL Institute of Education)*; University of Warwick; University of the West of England, Bristol; University of West London; University of Westminster; University of Winchester; University of Wolverhampton; University of Worcester; Writtle College; University of York; York St John University.

(*Source*: Higher Education Funding Council for England)

Universities receiving funding from the Department for Employment and Learning in Northern Ireland

Queen's University Belfast; University of Ulster.

(*Source*: Higher Education Funding Council for England)

Higher Education Institutions receiving funding from the Scottish Funding Council

University of Aberdeen; University of Abertay Dundee; University of Dundee; Edinburgh Napier University; University of Edinburgh; Glasgow Caledonian University; Glasgow School of Art; University of Glasgow; Heriot-Watt University; The Open University in Scotland; Queen Margaret University; Robert Gordon University; Royal Conservatoire of Scotland; SRUC; University of St Andrews; University of Stirling; University of Strathclyde; University of the Highlands and Islands; University of the West of Scotland. They also fund 25 colleges.

(*Source*: Scottish Funding Council, www.sfc.ac.uk/funding/funding.aspx)

Institutions receiving funding from the Higher Education Funding Council for Wales

Aberystwyth University; Bangor University; Cardiff University; Cardiff Metropolitan University (formerly UWIC); Glyndwr University; The Open University in Wales; Swansea University; University of South Wales; University of Wales Trinity Saint David.

(*Source*: Higher Education Funding Council for Wales, www.hefew.ac.uk)

OTHER HE ORGANIZATIONS

There are a number of other organizations involved in shaping the HE sector. You can find a full list of these organizations on the Universities UK website: www.universitiesuk.ac.uk

Part 3

Qualifications

Qualifications

INTRODUCTION

Definition of Common Terms

A number of terms are commonly used as synonyms for qualifications, for example 'examinations' and 'courses'. This can hide important differences of meaning and lead to confusion and misunderstanding. In some contexts it may be important to make these differences explicit to guard against exaggerating or diminishing the level of achievement, which is an essential core of the concept of qualification. It is especially important to clarify the difference in meaning between 'examination', 'course' and 'qualification'.

Examination

An examination is a formal test or assessment. It can focus on one or more of the following: knowledge, understanding, skill or competence. An examination may be set as a written test, an oral test, an aural and oral test (e.g. a foreign language test) or a practical test. In the past, most forms of external assessment in FE were based on a model of examination dominated by the psychometric model, designed to discriminate between individuals – normative referencing – and took the form of written tests. There was considerable variation in different kinds of written examination, including essays, question and answer, and 'multiple response'. Today, largely as a result of the introduction of National Vocational Qualifications (NVQs), the purpose and format of many examinations have been reappraised, and criterion-referenced examinations that focus on achievement (and in the case of NVQs, competence) are increasingly common. Many forms of assessment are now an integral part of the learning process, with a formative as well as a summative function rather than a separate, terminal, summative function.

Course

A course implies an ordered sequence of teaching or learning over a period of time. A course is governed by regulations or requirements, frequently imposed by an external awarding body and sometimes by the institution providing the course. An important distinguishing feature between different courses is the length of time allocated to study: it can vary from a few days to several years. Some courses offer a terminal award on the basis of course completion, and these courses are set for a given period of time. Other 'set period' courses may prescribe examinations; these can include continuous assessment, terminal testing or a combination of both. In other courses, the programme of study may be accomplished at a faster or slower rate; such courses normally enjoin continuous assessment or a terminal examination, or both. Many courses require attendance at an institution, while distance learning, correspondence courses, and various forms of flexible-learning courses are usually free of these requirements, although some may require occasional attendance for residential components or face-to-face tutoring. A successful examination result usually confers a qualification or an award.

Qualification

A qualification is normally a certificated endorsement, from a recognized awarding body, that a level or quality of accomplishment has been achieved by an individual. Qualifications are usually conferred on successful completion of an examination, although not all examinations necessarily offer qualifications. An examination may offer an award that is a part-qualification. For example, an NVQ candidate may acquire a unit of competence that is a part-qualification building towards a full statement of competence – an NVQ. A first-year student on an HND course may be required to pass all first-year examinations to be permitted to continue into the second year: in a sense that student is 'qualified' to continue the course but no qualification is awarded. Some award-bearing examinations may be fully recognized and certificated qualifications in themselves (e.g. a BTEC HNC) but only part-qualifications for a profession (e.g. chartered engineer).

Apparent anomalies do exist. Some professional bodies and trade associations award qualifications that are recognized within the profession or association but are not obtained by examination. They are usually awarded on the basis of experience, and payment of a fee, and denote membership or acceptance. When the body also offers an examination route to the same qualification, successful examinees are usually known as 'graduate members'.

There are a number of accreditation authorities that approve qualifications. There are also many specialist and general validating, examining and awarding bodies that are responsible for the design and assessment of qualifications.

ACCREDITING REGULATORY BODIES

England

Sector Skills Councils

Federation for Industry Sector Skills and Standards (FISSS)
Tel: 0300 303 4444 E-mail: info@fisss.org Website: www.fisss.org
The Federation for Industry Sector Skills and Standards, is an organization that supports the network of licensed UK Sector Skills Councils (SSCs). These are employer-led, independent organizations that cover specific work sectors across the UK (currently accounting for approximately 90 per cent of the UK workforce). With the influence granted by licences from the governments of England, Scotland, Wales and Northern Ireland, and with private and public funding, this independent network engages with the education and training supply-side such as universities, colleges, funders and qualifications bodies to increase productivity at all levels in the workforce. There are 22 Sector Skills Councils and 5 Sector Skills Bodies who work with over 550,000 employers to define skills needs and skills standards in their industry. There are also 16 National Skills Academies. Details of the Sector Skills Councils are listed in the following table.

Table 3.1

The Building Futures Group *Sector:* Facilities Management, Housing, Property, Cleaning and Parking Tel: 0207 9209632 E-mail: info@thebuildingfuturesgroup.com Website: www.thebuildingfuturesgroup.com	**Construction Skills** *Sector:* Construction Tel: 0344 994 4400 E-mail: call.centre@cskills.org Website: www.cskills.org
Cogent skills *Sector:* Science industries Tel: 01925 515 200 E-mail: info@cogentskills.com Website: www.cogentskills.com	**Creative & Cultural Skills** *Sector:* Craft, cultural heritage, design, literature, music, performing and visual arts Tel: 020 7015 1800 E-mail: info@ccskills.org.uk Website: www.ccskills.org.uk

continued

Table 3.1 *Continued*

Creative Skillset
Sector: TV, film, radio, interactive media, animation, computer games, facilities, photo imaging, publishing, advertising and fashion and textiles
Tel: 020 7713 9800
E-mail: info@creativeskillset.org
Website: www.creativeskillset.org

Energy & Utility Skills
Sector: Gas, power, waste management and water industries
Tel: 0845 077 9922
E-mail: enquiries@euskills.co.uk
Website: www.euskills.co.uk

ecITB
Sector: Engineering
Tel: 01923 260000
E-mail: ecitb@ecitb.org.uk
Website: www.ecitb.org.uk

Financial Skills Partnership
Sector: Finance, accountancy and financial services
Tel: 0114 261 5800
E-mail: info@financialskillspartnership.org.uk
Website:
www.financialskillspartnership.org.uk

IMI The Institute of the Motor Industry
Sector: Retail motor industry
Tel: 01992 519039
E-mail: comms@theimi.org.uk
Website: www.theimi.org.uk

Improve Ltd
Sector: Food and drink manufacturing and associated supply chains
Tel: 0845 644 0448
E-mail: info@improveltd.co.uk
Website: www.improveltd.co.uk

Lantra
Sector: Land management and production, animal health and welfare and environmental industries
Tel: 024 7669 6996
E-mail: connect@lantra.co.uk
Website: www.lantra.co.uk

People 1st
Sector: Hospitality, leisure, passenger transport, travel and tourism and retail
Tel: 020 3074 1222
E-mail: info@people1st.co.uk
Website: www.people1st.co.uk

Proskills
Sector: Printing, mineral extraction and processing, health and safety and process and manufacturing of furniture, glass, ceramics, coatings and paper
Tel: 01235 833 844
E-mail: info@proskills.co.uk
Website: www.proskills.co.uk

SEMTA
Sector: Science, engineering and manufacturing technologies
Tel: 0845 643 9001
E-mail: customerservices@semta.org.uk
Website: www.semta.org.uk

Skills Active
Sector: Sport, fitness, outdoors, playwork, caravans and hair and beauty
Tel: 0207 840 1900
E-mail: skills@skillsactive.com
Website: www.skillsactive.com

Skills for Care & Development
Sector: Social care, children, early years and young people's workforces in the UK
Tel: 01133 241 1240
E-mail:
sscinfo@skillsforcareanddevelopment.org.uk
Website:
www.skillsforcareanddevelopment.org.uk

continued

Table 3.1   *Continued*

Skills CFA	**Skills for Security**
Sector: Business and administration, customer service, enterprise and business support, human resources and recruitment, industrial relations, leadership and management, marketing and sales Tel: 020 7091 9620 E-mail: info@skillscfa.org Website: www.skillscfa.org	*Sector:* Security Tel: 01905 744000 E-mail: info@skillsforsecurity.org.uk Website: www.skillsforsecurity.org.uk

Skills CFA

Sector: Business and administration, customer service, enterprise and business support, human resources and recruitment, industrial relations, leadership and management, marketing and sales
Tel: 020 7091 9620
E-mail: info@skillscfa.org
Website: www.skillscfa.org

Skills for Health

Sector: UK Health
Tel: 0117 922 1155
E-mail: office@skillsforhealth.org.uk
Website: www.skillsforhealth.org.uk

Skills for Justice

Sector: Community Justice, Courts Services, Custodial Care, Fire and Rescue, Forensic Science, Policing and Law Enforcement and Prosecution Services
Tel: 0114 261 1499
E-mail: info@skillsforjustice.com
Website: www.skillsforjustice.com

Skills for Security

Sector: Security
Tel: 01905 744000
E-mail: info@skillsforsecurity.org.uk
Website: www.skillsforsecurity.org.uk

Summit Skills

Sector: Building Services Engineering
Tel: 0207 313 4890
E-mail: enquiries@summitskills.org.uk
Website: www.summitskills.org.uk

Tech Partnership

Sector: Software, internet and web, IT services, telecommunications and business change
Tel: 020 7963 8920
E-mail: info@e-skills.com
Website: www.e-skills.com

In October 2013, in response to the Richard Review of Apprenticeships (2012), the government set out its plans to reform Apprenticeships in England by replacing the existing Apprenticeship frameworks with employer-defined standards, putting employers in control and giving them a high degree of freedom to develop these standards to best meet the needs of their occupations and sectors. To support this reform, they established Trailblazers – groups led by employers and professional bodies – to develop the first of these new Apprenticeship standards.

The Government plan to introduce new standards for all occupations by 2017. A number of new Apprenticeship standards have already been government approved with the number growing all the time. Information on the new standards can be found at www.apprenticeships.org.uk/standards. The Federation for Industry Sector Skills and Standards is developing a series of practical tools and guides for employers and employer-led partnerships to support the development of a new Apprenticeship standard and the detail of the implementation requirements which go with it - assessment, training and governance. The Federation currently manages the following certification systems for apprenticeships: ACE (England), ACW (Wales), MA Online v1 (Scotland) and MA Online v2 (Scotland).

The National College for Teaching and Leadership

The National College for Teaching and Leadership (NCTL) is part of the Department for Education and is involved in the exam administration function. The NCTL can be found at www.gov.uk/nctl, General enquiries, Ministerial and Public Communications Division, Department for Education, Piccadilly Gate, Store Street, Manchester, M1 2WD; Tel: 0370 000

2288. Information about the administration of exams can be found at www.gov.uk/exams-administration-information-for-exam-centres. The Department for Education is also a useful source of information, www.gov.uk/government/organisations/department-for-education.

Standards and Testing Agency (STA)

The Standards and Testing Agency is responsible for the development and delivery of all statutory assessments from early years to the end of Key Stage 3; National Curriculum assessments helpline: 0300 303 3013; E-mail: assessments@education.gov.uk; Website: www.gov.uk/sta.

Ofqual: Office of Qualifications and Examinations Regulation

Contact details for Ofqual are: Ofqual, Spring Place, Herald Avenue, Coventry, CV5 6UB; Tel: 0300 303 3344; Helpline: 0300 303 3346; E-mail: public.enquiries@ofqual.gov.uk; Website: www.ofqual.gov.uk
Northern Ireland office: Ofqual, 2nd Floor, Glendinning House, 6 Murray Street, Belfast, BT1 6DN; Tel: 028 9033 0706.

Ofqual is the regulator of qualifications, examinations and tests in England and a wide range of vocational qualifications in both England and Northern Ireland. Ofqual also regulates the National Curriculum Assessments in England. It monitors organizations that deliver qualifications and assessments as set out in the Apprenticeship, Skills, Children and Learning Act (2009) and Education Act (2011). Ofqual's role is to ensure all learners get the results they deserve, standards are maintained, and qualifications are correctly valued and understood, now and in the future.

Ofqual is accountable to parliament rather than to government ministers and advises the Government on qualifications and assessment based on their research into these areas.

Scotland

Scottish Qualifications Authority (SQA)

Customer Contact Centre, Tel: 0345 279 1000; Fax: 0345 213 5000; E-mail: customer@sqa.org.uk; Website: www.sqa.org.uk

The Scottish Qualifications Authority (SQA) is the national accreditation and awarding body in Scotland. It is an executive non-departmental public body (NDPB) sponsored by the Scottish Government's Learning Directorate and is fully committed to working with other organizations, agencies and institutions in Scotland to help meet the Scottish Government's National Outcomes, strategies, policies and priorities.

SQA works in partnership with schools, colleges, universities and industry to provide high-quality, flexible and relevant qualifications and assessments, embedding industry standards where appropriate. It strives to ensure that SQA qualifications are inclusive and accessible to all, that they provide clear progression pathways, facilitate lifelong learning and recognize candidate achievement. The National Qualifications have been designed to meet the aims, purposes and values of Curriculum for Excellence.

People take SQA qualifications at all stages of their lives – at school, at college, at work and in their leisure time. There are qualifications at all levels of attainment. SQA is responsible for three main types of qualification: units, courses and group awards. Most SQA-awarded qualifications are made up of a combination of units, which can also be used in their own right. Each unit represents approximately 40 hours of teaching with additional study. Units are achieved by passing an assessment.

National Courses

There are seven levels of National Courses – National 1–5, Higher, and Advanced Higher and there are at present four Scottish Baccalaureates which are awarded at Pass and Distinction.

National Courses are designed to develop skills and knowledge in a specific subject area as well as skills for learning, skills for life and skills for work. Achieving a National Course shows that a learner has demonstrated the specified knowledge and skills in a particular subject at the defined national standard. Some of the new Awards cover work from across different subject areas, are shorter than traditional Courses and recognize success at different levels of difficulty, meaning they are suitable for young people of all abilities.

New Higher National Courses

New Higher Courses provide progression from National 5 and lead on to Advanced Higher and are designed to develop skills and knowledge in a specific subject area. Offered by colleges, some universities and many other training centres, Higher National Certificates (HNCs) and Higher National Diplomas (HNDs) are specially designed to meet the needs of employers. HNCs are made up of 96 SCQF credit points and usually take one year to complete; HNDs are made up of 240 SCQF credit points and usually take two years to complete.

New Advanced Higher National Courses

New Advanced Higher awards are designed to meet the aims, purposes and values of Curriculum for Excellence, and provide progression from Higher Courses. These courses, which are designed to develop skills and knowledge in a specific subject area, are usually made up of three National Units and an external assessment – normally an examination or project. Advanced Highers tend to be taken in the sixth year at school or college by students who have normally passed Highers.

Skills for Work

There are also Skills for Work Courses from National 3 to National 5. These are vocational courses for pupils in third and fourth year of secondary school and above. Normally pupils following the Skills for Work courses will spend some of their time at a local college or another training provider or with an employer. The courses are intended to provide progression pathways to further education, training and employment.

Skills for Work courses, National 3, 4 and 5 and Higher are designed to develop skills and knowledge in a broad vocational area, as well as an understanding of: the workplace skills and attitudes for employability, Core Skills, and other transferable skills. They involve a strong element of learning through involvement in practical activities which are directly related to a particular vocational area. National 3 is usually made up of three 40-hour units and National 4, 5 and Higher are usually made up of four 40-hour units.

Other SQA Courses

National Qualification Group Awards – National Certificates (NCs), Higher National Certificates and Diplomas (HNCs and HNDs) and National Progression Awards (NPAs) – are designed to be taken at college; Scottish Vocational Qualifications (SVQs), Professional Development Awards (PDAs), QCF (Qualifications and Credit Framework) registered Awards, Certificates and Diplomas and Functional Skills, and Customized Awards are designed for the workplace. A private company or training provider must become an 'approved centre' to deliver SQA qualifications, or work in partnership with a college or training provider. SQA also offer Modern Apprenticeships.

SQA Qualifications

Higher National Certificates (HNCs) and **Higher National Diplomas** (HNDs) are developed by SQA in partnership with FE colleges, universities, and industry and commerce. They are credible, flexible qualifications that are designed to deliver skills and knowledge to meet the needs of today's businesses. Some HNCs allow direct entry into the second year of a degree programme, and some HNDs allow direct entry to the third year. Higher National qualifications can also give you the knowledge and understanding required for Scottish Vocational Qualifications (SVQs).

National Progression Awards (NPAs) are designed to assess a defined set of skills and knowledge in specialist vocational areas. They are mainly used by colleges for short programmes of study.

National Certificates are primarily aimed at 16–18-year olds and adults in full-time education. They prepare candidates for employment or further study by developing a range of knowledge and skills.

Scottish Vocational Qualifications (SVQs) are based on job competence, and recognize the skills and knowledge people need in employment. SVQs can be attained in most occupations and are available for all types and levels of job. They are primarily delivered to candidates in full-time employment and in the workplace.

Professional Development Awards (PDAs) are qualifications for people who are already in a career and who wish to extend or broaden their skills. In some cases they are designed for people wishing to enter employment. PDAs can be taken at college or the workplace.

Customized Awards are specially designed vocational qualifications at any level to meet an organization's need for skills and expertise and provide recognition and development opportunities for individuals. They can also help a company meet regulatory requirements and demonstrate the competence of its employees to external parties.

Scottish Credit and Qualifications Framework

The SQA is a partner in a 'credit' system called the Scottish Credit and Qualifications Framework (SCQF), which sets out the Scottish qualifications and how they relate to one another by making clear the credit value of each type of qualification available in Scotland. The framework has 12 levels, from Level 1 for very basic education to Level 12 for doctoral degrees.

More information about SQA and its qualifications can be found at its website: www.sqa.org.uk

Validating, examining and awarding bodies/organizations

A large number of external bodies provide qualifications recognized by accrediting and regulatory bodies. Not all qualifications are available across the entire FE sector: some colleges specialize in particular vocational areas while others are involved in more general adult education provision.

The Federation of Awarding Bodies (FAB) is a trade federation and membership organization for vocational awarding bodies. At the time of writing there are nearly 120 Ofqual-recognized awarding bodies that are full members of FAB. It also has associate members. Find more information at www.awarding.org.uk.

It is important to contact the examining or awarding bodies directly to find which colleges deliver the qualifications desired. However, most colleges deliver courses leading to qualifications awarded by the sample selection of organizations listed below.

ABC Awards

Robins Wood House, Robins Wood Road, Aspley, Nottingham NG8 3NH; Tel: 0115 854 1616; Fax: 0115 854 1617; e-mail: centresupport@abcawards.co.uk; website: www.abcawards.co.uk

ABC Awards is a vocational awarding organization with accredited QCF qualifications in all sectors. It is a registered charity and part of the EMFEC Group. ABC has a portfolio of over 650 Ofqual regulated qualifications, covers 12 industry sectors and is designed for all ages and abilities post-14. ABC Awards' qualifications give learners the skills they need to find employment, progress within education and training or enhance their skills within their current job roles.

AQA

Stag Hill House, Guildford, Surrey GU2 7XJ; Tel: 0800 197 7162; Fax: 01483 300 152; Exams Office Support e-mail: eos@aqa.org.uk; website: www.aqa.org.uk

AQA is an independent education charity and the largest of the exam boards, currently setting and marking the papers for around half of all GCSEs and A-levels in England, Wales and Northern Ireland. AQA qualifications are internationally recognized and are taught in around 30 countries around the world. As an awarding body AQA offers a broad range of academic qualifications for 14–19-year olds including GCEs, GCSEs, AQA iGCSEs, the Extended Project Qualification and the AQA Baccalaureate.

ASDAN

Wainbrook House, Hudds Vale Road, St George, Bristol BS5 7HY; Tel: 0117 941 1126; e-mail: info@asdan.org.uk; website: www.asdan.org.uk

ASDAN is a curriculum development organization and awarding body, offering programmes and qualifications that explicitly grow skills for learning, for employment and for life. ASDAN is established as a registered charity for the 'advancement of education, by providing opportunities for all learners to develop their personal and social attributes and levels of achievement through ASDAN awards and resources, and the relief of poverty, where poverty inhibits such opportunities for learners'.

ASDAN qualifications contribute towards school/college performance measures and Ofsted requirements. ASDAN offers a range of nationally approved qualifications based around the development of personal, social and employability skills:

- Entry 1, 2 and 3 (Access) qualifications meet the needs of learners working below GCSE (Intermediate) level
- Levels 1 and 2 (Intermediate) qualifications are comparable to GCSEs
- Level 3 (Higher) qualifications are A/AS-level comparable
- Level 4 accreditation represents a Certificate of Higher Education

Ofqual, DfES, CCEA and the Secretary of State approve ASDAN qualifications for pre- and post-16 provision. ASDAN qualifications sit within the National Qualifications Framework

(NQF) or Qualifications and Credit Framework (QCF), and some have approval within the SCQF in Scotland. ASDAN also offers a wide choice of activity-based curriculum programmes that can be used in a variety of educational settings with learners working at a range of levels, offering imaginative ways of developing, recording and certificating young people's personal achievements. Through Customised Accreditation ASDAN also accredits programmes that are already being offered or has been written by another organization.

The following ASDAN qualifications are available:
- Qualifications in Personal Progress: Entry 1
- Personal and Social Development (PSD): Entry 1–3, Levels 1 and 2
- Employability: Entry 2 to Level 3
- Diplomas in Life Skills: Entry 1–3
- Event Volunteering Qualifications (CVQ): Entry 3 to Level 3
- Wider Key Skills: Levels 1–4
- Certificate of Personal Effectiveness (CoPE): Levels 1–3
- Award of Personal Effectiveness (AoPE) Levels 1–3

City & Guilds

1 Giltspur Street, London EC1A 9DD; Tel: Customers: 0844 543 0000, Main switchboard: 0207 294 2468; e-mail: centresupport@cityandguilds.com; website: www.cityandguilds.com

City & Guilds is a leading vocational educational organization, offering hundreds of work-related qualifications worldwide. City & Guilds' qualifications, which span from basic skills to the highest level of professional achievement, are delivered in more than 10,000 training centres across the world.

With over 130 years of experience, City & Guilds offers a wide range of vocational qualifications, apprenticeships and traineeships from agriculture to engineering; hairdressing to health and social care; IT to tourism; and photography to catering. They are developed with the help of industry experts and are workplace-relevant, so these qualifications equip people for doing a real job – benefiting them and their employer.

City & Guilds qualifications develop both knowledge and practical skills. They are available at nine levels, from Entry Level to Level 8, and are suitable for anyone, whether they are beginners or advanced in their career or area of study. Assessment is based on any combination of examination, projects or coursework. The organizations that offer City & Guilds qualifications include schools, colleges, training organizations, companies and adult education institutes. Depending on the organization, it is possible to study full time, part time or through distance learning.

City and Guilds offer the following qualifications: National Vocational Qualifications (NVQs) and Scottish Vocational Qualifications (SVQs), Functional Skills, Core Skills and Essential Skills, International Vocational Qualifications (IVQs), Single Subject Qualifications, International English Qualifications (IEQs), Institute of Leadership and Management (ILM) qualifications, Professional Recognition Awards, Tech Levels, TechBac, Apprenticeships and Traineeships.

Pearson (Edexcel, BTEC, EDI and LCCI)

190 High Holborn, London WC1V 7BH; Tel: 0845 618 0440; website: https://qualifications. pearson.com

Edexcel, of Pearson Education Limited, is the UK's largest awarding organization, offering academic and vocational qualifications and testing to schools, colleges, employers and other places of learning in the UK and internationally. Edexcel academic qualifications include GCSE, GCE (A level) and International GCSE (Edexcel Certificate for UK state schools). Edexcel vocational qualifications include NVQ and BTEC from entry level to Higher National Diplomas.

Pearson acquired EDI, a leading provider of education and training qualifications and assessment services and the EDI qualifications have been rebranded as Pearson material. The qualifications selected from EDI have been redeveloped or reaccredited to be delivered through Pearson's brands including: Pearson Edexcel, Pearson BTEC and Pearson LCCI.

LCCI International Qualifications are widely used in South East Asia and over 100 countries around the world. LCCI International Qualifications, vocational qualifications available as single subjects or diplomas, cover the key areas of business, language and teaching.

NCFE

Q6, Quorum Business Park, Benton Lane, Newcastle upon Tyne NE12 8BT; Tel: 0191 239 8000; e-mail: service@ncfe.org.uk; website: www.ncfe.org.uk

NCFE is a national awarding organization and registered educational charity. It currently offers over 500 nationally accredited qualifications from Entry level up to and including level 4 as well as NVQs, Functional Skills, Apprenticeships and Traineeships. Further qualifications are constantly in development. The NCFE website has a qualifications finder search facility: www.ncfe.org.uk/ qualification-search

OCR

1 Hills Road, Cambridge CB1 2EU; Fax: 01223 552627;
14–19 qualifications: Tel: 01223 553998; e-mail: general.qualifications@ocr.org.uk;
Post-19 qualifications: Tel: 02476 851 509; e-mail: vocational.qualifications@ocr.org.uk;
website: www.ocr.org.uk

OCR is a leading UK awarding body, committed to providing qualifications that engage learners of all ages at school, college, in work or through part-time learning programmes to achieve their full potential. It offers a wide range of general and vocational qualifications, from GCSEs, A levels and Diplomas to OCR Nationals, NVQs and specialist qualifications. You can find a full index of OCR qualifications at: www.ocr.org.uk/qualifications/index.aspx

WJEC

245 Western Avenue, Cardiff CF5 2YX; Tel: 029 2026 5000; e-mail: info@wjec.co.uk;
website: www.wjec.co.uk

A registered charity with members from the 22 local authorities in Wales, WJEC is a leading awarding organization providing assessment, training and educational resources in England,

Wales, Northern Ireland and elsewhere; WJEC CBAC Ltd is a company limited by guarantee, registered in England and Wales. WJEC offers the following major qualifications: GCSE; Entry Level (EL) and Advanced (A)/Advanced Supplementary (AS) levels and the Welsh Baccalaureate, which is available at different levels and incorporates GCSEs, A Levels and NVQs. In addition, WJEC provides Essential Skills Wales, Project and Extended Project, Pathways QCF, Principal Learning and Wider Key Skills qualifications. The reformed GCSE and GCE qualifications in England will be provided via Eduqas, the new brand from WJEC (www.eduqas.co.uk).

Part 4

Qualifications Awarded or Validated by Universities

ADMISSION TO DEGREE COURSES

Higher Education Institutions (HEIs)

Most institutions have a general requirement for admission to a degree course; special requirements may be in force for particular courses. Requirements are usually expressed in terms of subjects passed at GCE A level and the Higher Grade of the SCE. The universities have a clearing house to handle applications for university courses – UCAS: www.ucas.com.

All intending students who live in the UK may obtain information on application procedures from their schools or colleges, or directly from UCAS. The scheme covers all universities and all medical schools. UCAS also has specialist services: the UCAS Teacher Training www.ucas.com/ucas-teacher-training, the UK Postgraduate Application and Statistical Service (UKPASS – www.ukpass.ac.uk) and the Conservatoires UK Admissions Service (CUKAS – www.cukas.ac.uk). HEIs have specific schemes to encourage access and participation in higher education. These can include partnerships with further education colleges that run access to higher education courses.

The Open University

For admission to most first-degree courses, no formal educational qualifications are necessary. However, students who have successfully completed one or more years of full-time study at the higher education level (or its equivalent in part-time study) may be eligible for exemption from some credit requirements of the BA degree. The Open University handles its own admissions.

Business schools

The degrees awarded by the various university business schools are postgraduate and therefore normally require an Honours degree as part of their entrance qualification.

AWARDS

The awards made by the universities may be separated into the following categories: first degrees; higher degrees; honorary degrees; first diplomas and certificates; higher diplomas and certificates.

First degrees

Nomenclature

Various names are given to first degrees at British universities. At most universities the first degree in Arts is the BA (Bachelor of Arts) and the first degree in Science is the BSc (Bachelor of Science), but at the universities of Oxford and Cambridge and at several new universities, the BA is the first degree gained by students in both arts and science. In Scotland the first arts degree at three of the four old universities is Master of Arts (MA). There are numerous variations on the bachelor theme, eg BSc (Econ) (Bachelor of Science in Economics), BCom (Bachelor of Commerce), BSocSc (Bachelor of Social Science), BEng (Bachelor of Engineering) and BTech (Bachelor of Technology). The first award in medicine is the joint degrees of MB, ChB (Bachelor of Medicine, Bachelor of Surgery), the designatory letters of which vary from university to university.

Structure of courses

First-degree courses vary considerably in structure, not only between one university and another but also between faculties in a single university. The degree examination is usually in two sections, Part I coming after one or two years of the course and Part II, 'finals', at the end of the course. The first-degree system at some Scottish universities differs substantially from that in English and Welsh universities (see below).

Bachelor degrees

These degrees, sometimes known as 'ordinary' or 'first' degrees, lead to qualifications such as Bachelor of Arts (BA), Bachelor of Science (BSc) or Bachelor of Medicine (MB). Each university decides the form and content of its own degree examinations. These vary from university to university.

The first-degree structure in all British universities is based on the honours degree. Successful candidates in honours degree examinations are placed in different classes according to their performance, first class being the highest. The other classes given vary from university to university, but the classification most often used is: Class I; Class II (Division 1); Class II (Division 2); Class III. Most graduates who go on to higher academic qualifications and those entering, for example, the higher grades in the Civil Service or research, normally have a good class honours degree.

You can find out more about recognized UK degrees at the Government website: www.gov.uk/recognised-uk-degrees.

Number of subjects studied

Excluding medicine and dentistry, the broad subject areas are Arts (or Humanities), Social Science, Pure Science and Applied Science. Most students study one main subject selected from one of these areas. It is possible to distinguish many types of degree course according to the number of subjects studied; these types are a variation on three main categories:

1. Honours course in one to three subjects with or without examinable subsidiary subjects.
2. Pass or ordinary courses in one to three subjects with or without examinable subsidiary subjects.
3. Common studies for pass and Honours in one to three subjects, with or without examinable subsidiary subjects.

Length of degree course

First-degree courses may be preceded by a preliminary year, from which students with the appropriate entry qualifications may be exempted. At most universities Honours and pass courses in arts, social science, pure and applied science last three or four years, but courses in architecture, dentistry and veterinary medicine usually last five years, and complete qualifying courses in medicine up to six years. Courses in fine arts and pharmacy may last four years; four-year courses exist mainly in double Honours schools, especially when they involve foreign languages and a period of study abroad, and in the technological universities where some courses include a period of integrated industrial training (sandwich courses).

The Scottish first degree

Undergraduate Honours degrees in Scotland are usually four years in duration and are structured to ensure a great deal of flexibility during the first two years of study. Most students only confirm their major in the final two years of study, which usually allows the student to choose a variety of subjects. This is different from the English system of undergraduate education, which is normally three years in duration and is more specialized from the beginning. After three years study students can gain a Bachelor or Ordinary degree or obtain the Honours degree by studying for a further year.

The Medicine and Veterinary Medicine degrees and MA Fine Art degree all take five years. In several science and engineering subjects there are opportunities to study for a five-year MChem, MChemPhys, MEng or MPhys degree. These degrees entail in-depth study, often with a research focus, but are undergraduate degrees and not equivalent to postgraduate Master's.

Aegrotat degrees

Candidates who have followed a course for a degree but have been prevented from taking the examinations by illness may be awarded a degree certificate indicating that they were likely to have obtained the degree had they taken the examinations.

Higher degrees

These comprise:

- some Bachelor's degrees: BPhil, BLitt, etc;
- Master's degrees: MA, MSc, etc;
- Doctor of Philosophy: PhD or DPhil;
- Higher Doctorates: DLitt, DSc, etc.

At Oxford and Cambridge the degree of MA is conferred on any BA of the university without any further course of study or examination after a specified number of years and on payment of a fee.

Candidates for a Master's degree at other universities (and at some for the degrees of BPhil, BLitt and BD, which are of equivalent standing) are normally required to have a first degree, although it need not have been obtained in the same university. Master's degrees are taken after one or two years' full-time study. The PhD requires at least two or more – usually three – years of full-time study.

In some universities and faculties students may be selected for a PhD course after an initial year's study or research common to both a PhD and a Master's degree. Candidates for a Master's degree are required either to prepare a thesis for presentation to examiners, who may afterwards question candidates on it orally, or to take written examination papers; they may be required to do both. All PhD students present a thesis; some may be required to take an examination paper as well. MPhil, MSc and similar degrees are usually awarded at the end of a one- or two-year course in a specific topic on the results of a written examination or a thesis. Higher doctorates are designated on a faculty basis, eg DLitt (Doctor of Letters) and DSc (Doctor of Science). Candidates are usually required to have at least a Master's degree of the awarding university. Senior doctorates are conferred on more mature and established people, usually on the basis of published contributions to knowledge.

Foundation degrees

Foundation degrees were established to give people the intermediate technical and professional skills that are in demand from employers and to provide more flexible and accessible ways of studying. Increasing opportunities for employment and career advancement are priorities; Foundation degree content and assessment are therefore designed in consultation with employers. Additional progression routes include links with associated professional qualifications and/or direct entry to the final year of a relevant Honours-level degree. Provision is available across a range of FE colleges and a number of HEIs.

Honorary degrees

Most universities confer honorary degrees on people of distinction in academic and public life, and on others who have rendered service to the university or to the local community. Normally degrees awarded are at least Foundation level.

Diplomas and certificates of higher education

Courses for first diplomas and certificates are relatively simple in structure; they usually reach a level lower than that required for the award of a degree. There is usually a carefully defined course in a specialized or vocational subject, lasting one or two years, followed by all candidates. Most courses are full time.

Postgraduate diplomas and certificates

Diplomas (eg in public health, social administration, medicine and technology) are awarded either on a full-time or, less often, part-time basis according to the subject and the university. Candidates must usually be graduates or hold equivalent qualifications. Diplomas are awarded after formal courses of instruction and success in written examinations. A Certificate or Diploma in Education is awarded to graduates training to become teachers after one year's full-time study and teaching practice.

Postgraduate courses

A number of courses for graduates or people with equivalent qualifications are offered in FE establishments. They include short specialist courses in management and business studies and secretarial courses for graduates.

Business schools

A Master of Business Administration (MBA) is an internationally recognized postgraduate qualification intended to prepare individuals for middle to senior general managerial positions. Most programmes contain as their core a number of subjects considered essential for understanding the operations of any enterprise. These are: accounting and finance, operations management, business policy, economics, human resource management, marketing, information systems and strategic planning.

Unlike any other Master's programme, the MBA is not only postgraduate, it is also strongly post-experience. A minimum of three years' (often more) work experience at an appropriate level of responsibility is generally expected of applicants. The requirement for a first degree (or equivalent) is sometimes waived for those holding an impressive track record of over five years at managerial level. Approximately one-third of MBA students have an engineering or information technology background. Many undertake the qualification to facilitate change from technical or specialist positions to more general ones.

The MBA was conceived originally in the United States at the beginning of the 20th century. Introduced in the United Kingdom in the late 1960s, it did not grow in popularity until the late 1980s. The popularity of this degree in the United Kingdom can be seen in the rapid expansion in the number of providers.

The Association of MBAs (AMBA) operates a system of accreditation. The accreditation process, which is internationally recognized for all MBA, DBA and Master's in Business and Management (MBM) programmes, measures individual MBA programmes against specific accreditation criteria.

Further information, including a list of accredited MBA programmes, can be obtained from the Association of MBAs, 25 Hosier Lane, London EC1A 9LQ; Tel: 020 7246 2686; e-mail: info@mbaworld.com; website: www.mbaworld.com.

The Association of Business Schools (ABS)

3rd Floor, 40 Queen Street, London, EC4R 1DD; Tel; 020 7236 7678, website: www.associationof businessschools.org.

The ABS is the representative body for management and business education and all the United Kingdom's leading business schools. The ABS works broadly in three main areas: policy development, promotion and representation, and training and development. The ABS is able to provide general information about the wide range of courses and programmes provided by the United Kingdom's business schools.

First awards

- **BA, BEd, BEng, LLB, BSc:** with 1st Class, 2nd Class (Divisions 1 and 2), 3rd Class Honours or Pass; or unclassified with or without Distinction.
- **MEng:** awarded to students who successfully complete a course of study that is longer and more demanding than the BEng first degree course in engineering.
- **GMus (Graduate Diploma in Music):** awarded to those students who complete three years' approved full-time study (or equivalent) in music and who demonstrate competence in musical performance.
- **DipHE (Diploma of Higher Education):** equivalent in standard and often similar in content to the first two years of an Honours degree course.
- **Certificates of Higher Education:** equivalent to the first year of an Honours degree course.

Higher awards

- **MA, MBA, MEd, MSc:** for successful completion of an approved postgraduate course of study of 48 weeks' duration (or the part-time equivalent).
- **MPhil, PhD:** for successful completion of approved programmes of supervised research.
- **DSc, DLitt, DTech:** for original and important contributions to knowledge and/or its applications.
- **Postgraduate Diploma:** awarded for the successful completion of an approved postgraduate course of study of 25 weeks' duration (or the part-time equivalent).
- **Postgraduate Certificate:** awarded for the successful completion of postgraduate/post-experience

courses of 15 weeks' duration (or the part-time equivalent).
- **Postgraduate Certificate in Education (PGCE):** awarded on completion of a one-year full-time course; candidates must be British graduates or hold another recognized qualification.
- **Diploma in Professional Studies:** available in the fields of education and nursing, health visiting, midwifery and sports coaching. Students normally hold an initial professional qualification. A minimum of two years' experience is normally expected.

UNIVERSITY OF ABERDEEN
www.abdn.ac.uk

College of Arts and Social Sciences: www.abdn.ac.uk/about/social-sciences/php

Aberdeen Business School; www.abdn.ac.uk/business

accounting, economics, finance, real estate, management, accounting & finance, applied economics, international business management, management consultancy, marketing management, energy management, energy economics, petroleum economics, property evaluation, finance & real estate/management, MBA programmes, MBA/HRM; MA(Hons), MBA, MRes, MSc, MPhil, PGCert, PhD

School of Divinity, History & Philosophy; www.abdn.ac.uk/sdhp

divinity, religious studies, theology, divinity, history of art, history, philosophy, Christian and religious studies, biblical studies, church history, ministry studies, ministry, leadership and management, theological ethics, systematic theology, ancient Greek, Islamic studies, art and business, medieval and early modern studies, Scandinavian studies, modern history, practical theology; BD, BTh, DMin, LicTh, MA(Hons), MLitt, MTh, PGDip, PhD, DPS, PGCert, ProfDoc

School of Education; www.abdn.ac.uk/education

education, childhood practice, professional development, teaching qualification further education,

counselling skills, autism and learning, inclusive practice, pastoral care, guidance and pupil support, person-centred counselling, enhanced professional practice, community learning and development, studies in mindfulness, early years, Streap: Gaelic medium education, leadership in professional contexts, leadership in professional contexts (incorporating the standard for headship), professional learning and development (primary), teaching qualification further education, social and educational research; BA(Hons), BEd(Hons), MEd, MPhil, MRes, MSc, BMus(Hons), PGCert, PGDE, PGDip, PhD, EdD

School of Language & Literature; www.abdn.ac.uk/sll

Celtic and Anglo-Saxon studies, English, film and visual culture, French and Francophone studies, Gaelic studies, German studies, Hispanic studies, language and linguistics, literature in a world context, professional communication, TESOL, translation studies, Celtic & Anglo-Saxon studies, creative writing, English literary studies, Irish and Scottish literature, literature, science and medicine, migration and postcolonial studies, the novel, visual culture; MA, MA(Designated), MA(Hons), MLitt, PhD

School of Law; www.abdn.ac.uk/law

law, law with English law/Spanish law/French law/German law/Belgian law, law with options in French language/German language/Spanish language/Gaelic language/music, energy law, oil & gas law /with professional skills, energy and environmental law, international law, public international law, private international law, international law and international relations, international law and strategic studies, criminal justice, human rights, criminal justice & human rights; LlB(Hons), LlM, MPhil, PhD

School of Social Science; www.abdn.ac.uk/ socsci

anthropology of religion, energy policy, global conflict & peace processes, international relations & international law, people & the environment, politics & international relations, international law, social anthropology, religion & society, Europolitics & society, globalisation, international security, Latin American studies, sex, gender & violence, museum studies, post conflict justice, radicalisation & resistance, refugee & displacement studies, religion & society, sex, gender & violence, sociology, strategic studies; MA(Hons), MA, MLitt, MPhil, MRes, MSc, PGDip, PhD

College of Life Sciences and Medicine; www.abdn.ac.uk/clsm

applied health science, environment & biological, medical bioscience, medical education, medical physics & clinicology, pharmacology, psychology; MSc, MRes, PGCert

School of Biological Sciences; www.abdn.ac.uk/biologicalsci

biology, biological sciences, zoology, marine biology, conservation biology, ecology, ecological & environmental ecology, environmental science/microbiology, animal, marine & fisheries ecology, forestry, soil science; BSc, MSci

School of Medical Science; www.abdn.ac.uk/sms

biochemistry, biomedical sciences, biotechnology, exercise and health science, genetics, genetics (immunology), human embryology & developmental biology, immunology, immunology & pharmacology, microbiology, molecular biology, neuroscience with psychology, pharmacology, physiology, sports & exercise science; BSc(Hons), MSc, MPhil, PGDip/ Cert, PhD/MD, MRes, MSci

School of Medicine & Dentistry; www.abdn.ac.uk/medicine-dentistry

dentistry, health science/studies, medicine, primary care, rural health, chronic disability, epidemiology, immunology, psychiatry, respiratory, musculoskeletal, obstetrics & gynaecology, primary care, urology, epidemiology, health economics, health psychology, medical statistics, public health nutrition; MBChB, BDS, PGDip

School of Psychology; www.abdn.ac.uk/ psychology

psychology, social/cognition, perception & attention, behavioural studies; BSc(Hons), MA, MRes, MSc, PhD

Rowett Institute of Nutrition and Health Studies; www.abdn.ac.uk/rowett

impacts on human health

CLSM Graduate School; www.abdn.ac.uk/ clsm/graduate

research methods for health by online learning, health psychology, economics of health, global health and management, health economics, human nutrition, public health research, applied marine & fisheries ecology, ecology & environmental sustainability, environmental science, forestry, soil science, biobusiness and medical sciences, clinical pharmacology, drug discovery, drug discovery and development, genetics, immunology, microbiology, stratified medicine and pharmacological innovation, research methods for health by online learning, medical education, medical research skills, physician associate studies, clinical pharmacology, drug discovery, drug discovery and development, medical imaging, medical physics, stratified medicine and pharmacological innovation, health psychology, psychology; BDS, BSc(Hons), MA, MBChB, MMedSci, MPhil, MSc, PhD, PGDip/Cert, MD, MRes

College of Physical Sciences; www.abdn.ac.uk/about/physical-sciences.php

School of Engineering; www.abdn.ac.uk/ engineering

chemical engineering, civil/structural engineering, electrical & electronic engineering, mechanical engineering, project management, reservoir engineering, safety engineering, renewable energy engineering, subsea engineering, oil & gas structural engineering, petroleum engineering, safety & reliability engineering for oil & gas; BEng(Hons), EngD, MEng, MSc, PhD

School of Geosciences; www.abdn.ac.uk/ geosciences

archaeology, geography, geology and petroleum geology, geoscience, geoscience and geography, geology and physics, geology and archaeology,

archaeology of the north, GIS, geophysics, land economy (rural surveying), hydrocarbon exploration, integrated petroleum geoscience, oil & gas enterprise management, petrophysics and formation evaluation; BSc, MA, MSc, PhD, MLE

Dept of Archaeology; www.abdn.ac.uk/ archaeology

archaeology, with Celtic civilization/history/geography, archaeology of the north; BSc(Hons), MA(Hons), MPhil, PhD, MSc

Dept of Geography & the Environment; www.abdn.ac.uk/geography

geography, physical/human geography, geographical information systems(GIS), marine & coastal resource management, urban/rural planning, rural surveying/ change, sustainable rural development, transport geography, environmental management/hydrology, land economy, (rural surveying), partnership management; BSc(Hons), MA, MSc, PGDip, PhD, MRes

Dept of Geology & Petroleum Geology; www.abdn.ac.uk/geology

oil & gas enterprise management, geology, geology & archaeology/geoscience/physics/petroleum geology, integrated petroleum geoscience; BSc(Hons), MA(Hons), MRes, MSc, PGDip/Cert, PhD, MGeol

School of Natural & Computing Sciences; www.abdn.ac.uk/ncs

Chemistry; www.abdn.ac.uk/ncs/chemistry

chemistry, biochemistry, environmental/ analytical chemistry, chemistry, oil & gas chemistry, jt degrees; BSc(Hons), MChem, MSc, PGDip, PhD

Computing; www.abdn.ac.uk/ncs/computing

computing (with numerous joint degrees), computing science, informatics, software project management, information systems/ & data management, information technology, oil & gas computing, software entrepreneurship; BSc(Hons), MA(Hons), MSc/PGDip, MSci, PhD, PGDip, MPhil, MEng

Institute of Mathematics; www.abdn.ac.uk/ncs/mathematics

mathematics (with numerous jt degrees), applied mathematics, statistics, topology of high dimension manifolds; BSc(Hons), MA(Hons), MSc, PhD, MPhil

Physics; www.abdn.ac.uk/ncs/physics

physical sciences, physics (with numerous jt degrees), physics education, physics with chemistry/geology/philosophy/engineering/mathematics; BSc(Hons), MSc(Hons), PhD

UNIVERSITY OF ABERTAY, DUNDEE
www.abertay.ac.uk

School of Arts, Media & Computer Games; www.abertay.ac.uk/studying/schools/amg

computer arts, game design & production management, computer game applications development/ technology, games development, creative sound production; BA(Hons), BSc(Hons), DipHE, MProf, MSc/PGDip

School of Science, Engineering & Technology; www.abertay.ac.uk/studying/schools/set

biomedical science, civil engineering, computing/& networks, ethical hacking, food & consumer science, food, nutrition & health, forensic sciences, medical biotechnology, energy, water & environmental management, ethical hacking & computer security, food & drink innovation; BSc(Hons), MSc, DipHE, PGDip, MProf

Dundee Business School; www.abertay.ac.uk/studying/schools/dbs

accounting with finance, finance & business, oil and gas accounting, finance, oil and gas finance, business administration, business studies, finance & business, business administration, energy industry economics, energy industry management, finance, law, European/business law, management, European economy & management, HRM, corporate finance, energy and petroleum, marketing and sports development, biotechnology; BA(Hons), GradCert, LlB(Hons), BBA(Hons), MBA, MSc, PGDip

The School of Social & Health Sciences; www.abertay.ac.uk/studying/schools/shs

Psychology; forensic psychobiology, psychology/& counselling
Sociology; sociology, criminological studies, media, culture/& society, social science

Nursing and Counselling; cognitive behavioural therapy, counselling skills/studies, nursing (mental health nursing)

CPD Sport and Exercise Sciences; performance golf, sport and exercise – leading to named routes/science, physical activity & health, sports coaching/development, strength & conditioning, sport & management/psychology; BA(Hons), BSc(Hons), GradCert, MSc, PGDip/Cert

ABERYSTWYTH UNIVERSITY
www.aber.ac.uk

School of Art; www.aber.ac.uk/en/art
art, art history, fine art, creative arts; BA(Hons), MA, MPhil, PhD

Institute of Biological, Environmental & Rural Sciences; www.aber.ac.uk/en/ibers
agriculture, animal science/zoology, biochemistry, biology, conservation/countryside management, environmental bioscience & ecology, microbiology, equine science, food & water security, genetics, livestock science, marine & freshwater biology/systems, microbiology, green biotechnology & innovation management, managing the environment – environmental sustainability/bioenergy & environmental change/habitat restoration & conservation, sport & exercise science; BSc(Hons), MPhil, MSc, PhD

Dept of Computer Science; www.aber.ac.uk/en/cs
computer science/& AI, AI & robotics, computer graphics vision and games, internet computing & systems administration, business information technology, software engineering, space science & robotics, intelligent autonomous systems, intelligent systems, ICT & computer science, statistics for computational biology; BEng, BSc(Hons), HND, MEng, MSc, PhD, MRes

School of Education & Lifelong Learning; www.aber.ac.uk/en/sell
childhood studies, lifelong learning, education, PGCE secondary education (English, drama, geography, ICT & modern languages), Welsh for adults; BA(Hons), BSc(Hons), MPhil, PGCE, PGDip, PhD

Dept of English & Creative Writing; www.aber.ac.uk/en/english
creative writing, English literature, literary/classical studies, American literature, 18th century writing & romanticism, post modernist writing & Welsh writing in English; BA(Hons), MA, PhD

Dept of European Languages; www.aber.ac.uk/en/eurolangs
French, German, Italian, European culture, Romance languages, modern languages with business & management, numerous post-graduate modules, Spanish; BA(Hons), MA, PhD

Institute of Geography & Earth Sciences; www.aber.ac.uk/en/iges
geography, physical geography, human geography, environmental earth science, environmental science, computer science /physical geography, education / human geography, French/human geography, human geography/joint degrees, economics with human geography/environmental earth studies, physical geography/ education/ statistics/mathematics, environmental change, impact and adaptation, environmental monitoring and analysis, food and water security, geography and earth sciences, landscape and territory, practising human geography, GIS, river system dynamics and management;
BSc(Hons), MPhil, MRes, MSc, PhD, BA(Hons), MA, PGCE

Dept of History & Welsh History; www.aber.ac.uk/en/history
film and TV studies /Welsh history, historical and archival studies, history/English literature/film and TV studies/fine art/mathematics/ Spanish/Welsh history, human geography/history, Welsh history, international politics/economic and social history, museum and gallery studies, politics/economic and social history/history/Welsh history, Welsh history/drama and theatre studies/English literature/French/Spanish, international politics/economic and social history/history, politics/history, early modern British isles, eighteenth century Britain, history of Wales, media history, medieval Britain & Europe, modern British history, modern European history, modern history, the history of popular culture, history, medieval Britain & Europe, history; BA(Hons), MA, PhD, MPhil, NQPG

Dept of Information Studies; www.aber.ac.uk/en/dis

information and library studies, archive administration, digital curation, digital information services, information and library studies, information management and leadership, international archives, records and information management, management of library and information services, information management;

BA(Hons), BSc(Econ), Dip/Cert, MPhil, MSc(Econ), PhD, MA(Econ), Dip, MSc, MPhil

Dept of International Politics; www.aber.ac.uk/en/interpol

European studies/politics, international politics/& strategic studies/international history/military history/intelligence studies/third world, intelligence & strategic studies, international history/strategic studies/third world/military history/security studies, political studies, critical international politics, food & water security, intelligence studies, intelligence and strategic studies, international politics of the internet, international relations, international security studies, politics, media and performance, strategic studies, Welsh politics and society; BSc(Econ), MA, MSc, MSc(Econ), PhD

Dept of Law and Criminology; www.aber.ac.uk/en/law-criminology

law, business law, criminal law, criminology with applied psychology/law, European law, human rights, law with criminology, criminology & criminal/international justice, climate change & human rights, democracy, human security & international law, information technology law, international commercial law and the environment/human rights/ criminology of armed conflict, internet commerce & law, human rights & development/humanitarian law, psychology with criminology, rights, gender & international law; BA(Hons), BSc(Econ), LlB, LlM, MSc, PhD

School of Management and Business; www.aber.ac.uk/en/smb

accounting & finance, digital marketing, enterprise & innovation management, green biotechnology & innovation management, international finance/& accounting/banking, management – corporate leadership/digital business finance/marketing/project management, tourism management with French/ German, marketing, international business management, management and digital business, management and finance, management and marketing, management and project management, management and tourism management; BSc(Econ), MBA, MSc(Econ), PhD

Dept of Mathematics www.aber.ac.uk/en/ maths

applied mathematics, pure mathematics/& statistics, statistics/for computational biolgy

Dept of Physics; www.aber.ac.uk/en/ physics

physics, planetary and space physics, space science & robotics, mathematical & theoretical physics, astrophysics, robotics; BSc(Hons), MMath, MPhys, PhD

Dept of Psychology; www.aber.ac.uk/en/ psychology

psychology/& criminology, psycho-oncology, exercise and health psychology, psycholinguistics, language and thinking, group processes and social identity, music psychology

BSc(Econ), BSc(Hons), MPhil, PhD

Dept of Sport & Exercise Science; www.aber.ac.uk/en/sport-exercise

sport & exercise science, exercise & health sciences, human performance in sport and exercise contexts, physical activity in ageing, rehabilitation and health; BSc(Hons), PhD

Dept of Theatre, Film & Television Studies; www.aber.ac.uk/en/tfts

drama & theatre studies, documentary, film/& television studies, media & communication, practising performance, scenography/theatre design, scriptwriting, TV studies & digital culture, Welsh medium courses, politics, media & performance; BA(Hons), MA, MPhil, PhD

Dept of Welsh; www.aber.ac.uk/en/ cymraeg

Celtic studies, Irish, professional Welsh, Welsh, medieval Welsh literature, literature & history of Wales; BA(Hons), MA

ANGLIA RUSKIN UNIVERSITY
www.anglia.ac.uk

Faculty of Arts, Law and Social Sciences: www.anglia.ac.uk/en/home/faculties/ alss.html

Dept of English, Communication, Film & Media; www.anglia.ac.uk/ruskin/en/ home/faculties/alss/deps/english_media

English Language and English Language Teaching, English Language and Linguistics, English Language Studies (for non-native speakers of English), English Literature, Film Studies/& Media Studies, International Business English, Journalism, Media Studies Sports Journalism, Writing & English Literature/Film Studies, Applied Linguistics and TESOL, Creative Writing, Intercultural Communication, Publishing, TESOL and Materials Development
Applied Linguistics and TESOL (Teaching English to Speakers of Other Languages), English Language and Intercultural Communication; BA(Hons), MPhil, PhD, DProf

Anglia Law School; ww.anglia.ac.uk/ ruskin/en/home/faculties/alss/deps/law

international business/commercial law, law, legal practice, medical law & ethics; BA(Hons), LlB, LlD, LlM, PGDip, MPhil, PhD, PGDip, ProfDoc

Cambridge School of Art; www.anglia.ac.uk/ruskin/en/home/ faculties/alss/deps/csoa

animation, children's book illustration & book arts, computer games art, fashion/interior design, film & TV production, fine art, illustration, photography, printmaking, graphic design & typography, computer games development; BA(Hons), FdA, MA, MFA

Dept of Humanities & Social Sciences; www.anglia.ac.uk/ruskin/en/home/ faculties/alss/deps/hss

archaeology & landscape history, criminology, forensic science, history, English, English literature, international relations, philosophy, psychosocial studies, public service, sociology, transnational crime; BA(Hons), FdA, MPhil, PhD

Dept of Music & Performing Arts; www.anglia.ac.uk/ruskin/en/home/ faculties/alss/deps/music

creative music technology, drama/& English literature/film studies, music/drama therapy, performing arts, pop music, music, theory & performance; BA(Hons), FdADip, MA, MPhil, PhD

Lord Ashcroft International Business School; www.anglia.ac.uk/ruskin/en/ home/faculties/aibs

accounting and finance, accounting and financial management, business administration, business and finance, business and HRM, business economics, business management, business management and finance, business management and leadership, charity and social enterprise management, finance and economics, international business management, law, leading business change, leading business development, management, marketing, professional practice in international trade, tourism management, finance, leadership & management, business administration (MBA), project management, supply chain management; BA(Hons), BSc(Hons), LlB, UnivDip, MA, MBA, MSc, CertHE, FdA, PGDip

Faculty of Health, Social Care & Education; www.anglia.ac.uk/ruskin/ en/home/faculties/fhsce

acute care (top-up), children and young people, community specialist practitioner (district nursing), counselling (child and young person), early childhood professional studies, early years, playwork and education, early years professional practice, education and childhood studies, education studies, education, international nursing studies, management of social and affordable housing, mental health, midwifery, nursing – adult, nursing – child, nursing – mental health, paediatric intensive care nursing, palliative care, primary and community care, social policy, social work, special and intensive care of the newborn, specialist community public health nursing (health visiting or school nursing), advanced midwifery practice, children and young people, community specialist practitioner (district nursing), early childhood education, education, international nursing studies, international social welfare and social policy, social work, specialist community public health nursing (health visiting or school nursing), adult critical care nursing, cardiac care, critical care, educational leadership and management, emergency care, family therapy and systemic practice, international social welfare and social policy, learning and teaching (higher education), military veterans and families studies, specialist community public health nursing (health visiting or school nursing); BSc(Hons), FdSc, FdA, Cert HE, Dip HE, MSc, MA, DipPGCE, PGDip/Cert, BA(Hons), Dips Grad Cert, Professional Practice, MBA

Faculty of Science and Technology;
www.anglia.ac.uk/ruskin/en/home/
faculties/fst

Dept of Engineering & Built Environment; www.anglia.ac.uk/ruskin/en/home/ faculties/fst/departments/eng_builtenv

architecture/technology, building surveying, civil engineering, conservation of buildings, construction/ project management, engineering management, integrated/engineering, environmental planning, manufacturing systems, mechanical engineering, motorsport engineering, project management, quantity surveying, town planning, urban design; BSc(Hons), BEng, FdSc, MSc, PGCert, PGDip, FdSc, GradCert

Dept of Computing & Technology; www.anglia.ac.uk/ruskin/en/home/ faculties/fst/departments/comptech

audio music technology, business information systems, computer gaming technology/science, computing & information systems, electronics, information & computer technology, information systems management, mobile telecommunications, telecommunications multimedia, network infrastructure & security/security, electronic & electrical engineering, information & communication technology; BEng(Hons), BSc(Hons), MBA, FdSc, MSc

Dept of Vision and Hearing Sciences; www.anglia.ac.uk/ruskin/en/home/ departments/vision_hearing

ophthalmic dispensing, optometry, hearing aid technology/audiology; BOptom(Hons), BSc(Hons), FdSc, UnivCert

Dept of Psychology; www.anglia.ac.uk/ ruskin/en/home/faculties/fst/ departments/psychology

psychology, cognitive neuroscience, abnormal & clinical psychology, clinical child psychology, cognitive & clinical neuroscience, psychology & criminology, formulations in clinical psychology; BSc(Hons), MSc, MPhil, PhD

Dept of Life Sciences; www.anglia.ac.uk/ ruskin/en/home/faculties/fst/ departments/lifesciences

animal behaviour/applications for conservation, bioscience, biotechnology, biodiversity & conservation, biomedical sciences, crime & investigative studies, forensic science, sports coaching & PE/ science, sport & exercise science, applied wildlife conservation, sustainability, zoology; BSc(Hons), FdSc, MSc, PGDip

Degrees validated by Anglia Ruskin University offered at:

COLCHESTER INSTITUTE
www.colchester.ac.uk

counselling studies, 3D design and craft, management of hospitality, management of sport, music education, musical theatre, photography, popular music, technical theatre, music education, construction management (commercial management/site management), IT systems and applications, education (further education and skills sector), business administration, construction, person-centred counselling, business administration, construction management, creative performance (acting), early years, health and social care, management, management of hospitality, management of sport/ musical theatre, photography, business administration, project management, reflective practice and leadership, business environment, management, education (further education and skills sector); CertHE, BSc(Hons), BA(Hons), CertEd, DipHE, MBA, MA, FD

ASHRIDGE
www.ashridge.ac.uk

executive MBA, management, executive coaching, advanced coaching & organisation development supervision, sustainability & responsibility, organisational change, leadership; Doc Orgn Change, ExecMBA, MBA, MSc, Masters, PGCert

ASTON UNIVERSITY
www.aston.ac.uk

Aston Business School; www1.aston.ac.uk/aston-business-school

accounting for management, business economics & management, business & marketing analytics, business computing & IT, finance, HRM/ & business, international business & management/economics, marketing, law/with management, international commercial law, national business & modern languages, business and psychology/ mathematics, mathematics with economics, sociology and business, politics and business, international relations and business, public policy, business and management, business and education management; accounting & finance, business & management, economics, entrepreneurship & international business, information systems & business analysis, international business, investment analysis, marketing management, market research & consultancy, organisational behaviour, social responsibility & sustainability, strategic marketing management, strategy & international business, supply chain management, work psychology & business; BSc(Hons), DBA, LlB, LlM, MBA, PhD, FD

School of Engineering and Applied Science; www1.aston.ac.uk/eas

Chemical Engineering & Applied Chemistry; www1.aston.ac.uk/eas/about-eas/academic-groups/ceac

applied/biological chemistry, chemical engineering, chemistry, professional engineering; BEng, MEng, MChem

Computer Science; www1.aston.ac.uk/eas/about-eas/academic-groups/computer-science

computing science/& mathematics, computing for business, multimedia computing, IT project management, software engineering, professional engineering; BSc, MSc

Electrical, Electronic & Power Engineering; www1.aston.ac.uk/eas/about-eas/academic-groups/electronic-engineering/

communications engineering, data communications networks, electronic & electrical engineering, electrical & electronic engineering/computer science, telecommunications systems, professional engineering; BEng, MEng, MSc

Engineering Systems & Management; www1.aston.ac.uk/eas/about-eas/academic-groups/esm

construction project management, engineering management, industrial enterprise management, supply chain management, professional engineering, logistics management, transport management; BSc, MSc, FD

Mathematics; www1.aston.ac.uk/eas/about-eas/academic-groups/mathematics

mathematics, mathematics with computing/business/economics, mathematics of complex systems; BSc, MSc

Mechanical Engineering & Design; www1.aston.ac.uk/eas/about-eas/academic-groups/med

electromechanical engineering, mechanical engineering/modelling, design engineering, transport product design, product design/enterprise/innovation, professional engineering, transport product design, industrial product design, product design & management; BEng, MEng, MSc

School of Life and Health Sciences; www1.aston.ac.uk/lhs

Audiology; hearing aid audiology, healthcare science (audiology)

Biology; human biology, biological sciences, cell & molecular biology, microbiology, biomedical science, clinical health, biomedical engineering
Optometry; ophthalmic science, optomology
Pharmacy; pharmaceutics, pharmacology, pharmacokinetics, drug delivery, molecular pharmaceutics, occupational toxicology, pharmacy
Psychology; psychology, cognitive neuroscience, health psychology, psychology & business/sociology; BSc(Hons), GradDip, FD, MPharm, MRes, MSc, PGCert/Dip, PhD, M/DOptom, Dip, Sci, PharmD, MBiol

School of Languages and Social Sciences: www1.aston.ac.uk/lss

Modern Languages
French, German, Spanish, translation studies, international business & modern languages studies, TESOL, applied linguistics, translation in European context, English language with French/German/Spanish, sociology with Spanish/French, international relations/politics/business with French/German/Spanish, Arabic/Chinese

English Language
English language, number of joint honours degrees with English language, English language with international relations/psychology/social policy/sociology/French/German/Spanish, modern languages with QTS/English language/sociology/international politics/international relations

Politics & International Relations
international relations with politics/business/social policy/sociology, politics with business/economics/English language/social policy/sociology, international politics with French/German/Spanish/Arabic/Chinese, international relations with French /German/Spanish

Sociology & Public Policy
sociology & French/German/Spanish/business/social policy/international relations/politics/psychology, social policy, politics/English language, international relations & social policy/English language, social policy & politics, public policy & business management

Business Combinations
international business & French/German/Spanish/business & sociology/international relations/politics/economics, business management & public policy

Taught postgraduate
TESOL, translation studies, translation in a European context, the EU/multilevel governance & international relations/global governance, EU & international relations, Europe & the world, governance & international politics, social research/public policy & social change, sociology, TESOL, TESP, TEYL, ELT EMT; BA(Hons), BSc(Hons), MA, MPhil, MRes, MSc, PhD

BANGOR UNIVERSITY
www.bangor.ac.uk

College of Arts and Humanities; www.bangor.ac.uk/cah

Creative Studies & Media; www.bangor.ac.uk/creative_industries
creative and professional writing, creative studies, creative studies and English language/Italian, creative writing and media studies, English language with film studies, English literature with journalism/theatre and performance, film studies, film studies with theatre, French with journalism/media studies, German with creative writing, history with film studies/journalism, journalism and English language/media studies, media studies, media studies and English, media studies with French/German/Italian/Spanish/theatre, music and creative writing/film studies filmmaking: concept to screen, international media management; BA(Hons), MA, MRes, MSc, PhD/MPhil

English; www.bangor.ac.uk/english
British and Irish literatures, creative and professional writing, English language with creative writing/English literature, English literature/and creative writing/Italian/creative writing/English language/journalism/songwriting/theatre and performance, law with English literature, linguistics with English literature, media studies and English; Arthurian literature, creative writing, English literature, literatures of Wales, medieval studies; BA(Hons), MA/Diploma, PhD/MPhil

History, Welsh History & Archaeology; www.bangor.ac.uk/history

archaeology, heritage, archaeology and history, history, history and economics/Italian, history with archaeology, history with film studies/journalism, medieval and early modern history, modern and contemporary history, social policy and philosophy & religion and history/Welsh history, Welsh history with archaeology, Celtic, archaeology, history, medieval studies, the Celts, Welsh history; BA(Hons), MA/PGDip

School of Linguistics & English Language; www.bangor.ac.uk/linguistics

English language, English language with creative writing/English literature/ film studies/media studies, English literature with English language, international English language, linguistics, linguistics with English literature/English language, numerous joint degrees, bilingualism, cognitive linguistics, linguistics; BA(Hons), MA, PhD, MPhil, MSc

School of Modern Languages & Cultures; www.bangor.ac.uk/ml

French, German, Italian, Spanish, in joint degrees with European law, accounting, banking, business studies, creative studies, criminology & criminal justice, economics, English literature, journalism, creative writing, marketing, media studies, psychology, linguistics, management, sport science, philosophy & religion, music, history; joint degrees between French, German, Italian, Spanish, history and Italian; European languages and cultures, translation studies; LlB(Hons), BA(Hons), BSc(Hons), MA, MPhil

School of Music; www.bangor.ac.uk/music

music, music technology/electronics, composition, electroacoustics, early music, 20/21st century music, performance, sonic arts, composition, numerous joint degrees; BA, BMus, BSc, MA, PGDip/Cert, MMus/Dip

School of Philosophy & Religion; www.bangor.ac.uk/spar

philosophy & religion, study of religion, theology, numerous joint degrees; BA, MA, MTh

School of Welsh; www.bangor.ac.uk/ysgolygymraeg

details of courses provided in Welsh language; Welsh, Welsh with creative writing/journalism/theatre studies and the media, creative Welsh with popular music, the Celt, Welsh /Celtic studies; MA,

MA/Diploma, MPhil/PhD, BA(Hons), BD, BMus, Dip, MMus, MTh, PGDip, PhD, MSc

College of Business, Social Sciences & Law: www.bangor.ac.uk/cbss

Bangor Business School; www.bangor.ac.uk/business

accounting, banking/& finance, business/studies/economics, chartered finance, consumer psychology, international banking & development finance, economics, environmental management, finance, financial economics, law, marketing, administration, ICT, management/& finance, social authority law, Islamic banking, information management; BA, BSc(Hons), MA, MSc, MBA, MPhil, PhD

School of Social Sciences; www.bangor.ac.uk/so

childhood studies and social policy, criminology & criminal justice/and Italian, cymdeithaseg a pholisi cymdeithasol (sociology and social policy), health & social care and social policy/social care, social policy and criminology & criminal justice/economics/history/history, sociology, sociology and economics/social policy, social studies, criminology and law, social work, comparative criminology and criminal justice, criminology and sociology, language policy and planning, social research and social policy; BA(Hons), MA/PGDip/Cert, PhD, MPhil, MARes

School of Law; www.bangor.ac.uk/law

(European) law with French/German/Italian/Spanish, business and law, English law and French law, law, law with accounting and finance, law with business studies/contemporary Chinese studies/ criminology law with English literature/ professional English/ social policy, law with Welsh, international intellectual property law, international law, international law – specialising in European law/ global trade law, international criminal law and international human rights law, law and banking, law and criminology, law of the sea, maritime law, public procurement law and strategy, international commercial and business law, law, criminology and law, law and management; BA(Hons), MBA, DBA, HND, LlB, LlM(Res/Dip), MA, MSc, MPhil, PGDip, PhD

School of Education and Lifelong Learning: www.bangor.ac.uk/addysyg

childhood studies, design & technology secondary education with QTS, education studies, product design, secondary education, early childhood & learning support studies, primary education, PGCE primary/secondary, preparing to teach; BA Cert, Dipl, FdA, EdD, MA, MEd, MPhil, PhD

Academic Development Unit; www.bangor.ac.uk/adu

Welsh for adults; PGCertHE, BSc(Hons), EdMed, FdA, MA, MEd, MMusD, MPhil, MTh, PGCE, PhD

College of Natural Sciences; www.bangor.ac.uk/cns

CNS School of Biological Sciences; www.bangor.ac.uk/biology

biology, biology with biotechnology, marine biology and zoology, zoology, zoology with animal behaviour (animal behaviour)/(climate change), zoology with conservation, zoology with evolution, zoology with herpetology/ marine zoology, molecular biology with biotechnology, wetland science and conservation/pollution control; ecology, natural sciences BSc(Hons), Dipl, MA, MBiol, MPhil, MRes, MSc, MZool, PhD

School of Environment, Natural Resources, & Geography; www.bangor.ac.uk/senrgy

txt]applied terrestrial and marine ecology, environmental conservation, environmental management, environmental science, geography, agroforestry, conservation and land management, environmental and business management, environmental forestry, forestry and environmental management, sustainable forest and nature management, food security in the changing environment, tropical/forestry BA(Hons), BSc(Hons), MA, MBA, MPhil, MSc, PhD, MEnvSci

School of Ocean Sciences; www.bangor.ac.uk/sos

applied marine biology, coastal geography, computing and oceanography, geological oceanography, marine biology/and oceanography/ zoology, marine environmental studies, marine vertebrate zoology, marine biology, marine science, ocean science, physical oceanography, applied marine geoscience, physical oceanography, marine biology, marine environmental protection BSc(Hons), MMBiol, MMSci, MOcean, MPhil, MSc, PhD

Welsh Institute for Natural Resources; www.bangor.ac.uk/winr

College of Health & Behavioural Sciences; www.bangor.ac.uk/cohabs

School of Healthcare Sciences; www.bangor.ac.uk/healthcaresciences

adv clinical practice, health studies/science, critical care, diagnostic imaging, health & social care leadership, implementing evidence in health & social care, midwifery, nursing, public health & health promotion, diagnostic radiography, risk management in health & social care; BN(Hons), BSc(Hons), BMidw, DipHE, GradCert/Dip, MPhil, PhD

School of Medical Sciences; www.bangor.ac.uk/sms

medical sciences/biology, biomedical science, behavioural neurology and neuropsychiatry, clinical sciences, medical molecular biology with genetics, clinical and functional brain imaging, medical education practice; MSc, PGDip/Cert(HE), BMedSci, BSc, PhD

School of Psychology; www.bangor.ac.uk/psychology

psychology, child & language development, clinical & health psychology/neuropsychology, consumer psychology with business, mindfulness-based approaches, foundations of clinical neuropsychology/psychology, neuroimaging, psychology & childhood studies/criminology & criminal justice/English language/linguistics/social policy/sociology, applied behaviour analysis, behavioural neurology & neuropsychiatry; BSc(Hons), BA(Hons) MSc, PhD, MRes, MA, PGDip/Cert, MPsych, DClinPsych

School of Sport, Health & Exercise Science; www.bangor.ac.uk/sport

sport science (PE/outdoor activities), sport, health & exercise science/& PE, applied exercise science, applied sport & exercise physiology/psychology, applied sport science & outdoor activities, exercise physiology, exercise rehabilitation, exercise, behaviour change & disease prevention; BSc(Hons), MPhil, MSc, PhD, MRes, MA

Institute of Medical & Social Care Research; www.bangor.ac.uk/imscar

ageing & dementia studies, health economics, health services research; PhD, MPhil, MSc

College of Physical and Applied Sciences; www.bangor.ac.uk/copas

School of Chemistry; www.bangor.ac.uk/chemistry

analytical chemistry, chemistry, environmental/marine chemistry; BSc, MChem, MSc, MRes, PGDip, PhD, MPhil

School of Electronic Engineering; www.bangor.ac.uk/eng

Computer systems engineering, control and instrumentation engineering, critical safety engineering, electronic engineering, electronic engineering and music, broadband and optical communications, nanotechnology and microfabrication, electronic engineering (bio-electronics/micromachining/ microwave devices/ nanotechnology, optical communications/optoelectronics/organic electronics/polymer electronics/VLSL design; BEng(Hons), BSc(Hons), MEng(Hons), MSc, PhD

School of Computer Science; www.bangor.ac.uk/cs

computer science for business/with AI/security/ vision/visualisation, computer information systems/ with business, creative technologies, information & communications technology, computing & oceanography, advanced visualization, virtual environments and computer animation
BA(Hons), BEng(Hons), MEng(Hons), MPhil, MRes, MSc, PhD

UNIVERSITY COLLEGE, BARNSLEY
www.hud.ac.uk/barnsley

interdisciplinary art & design, construction & project management, early years, teacher training, lifelong learning, education & professional development, digital film & visual effects, film production, animation, music, music production & sound recording, mechanical/electrical/electronic engineering technology, popular music & promotion, teacher training; CertEd, PGCE, BA(Hons), BSc(Hons), MA/PGDip/ PGCert

UNIVERSITY OF BATH
www.bath.ac.uk

Faculty of Engineering and Design: www.bath.ac.uk/engineering

Architecture & Civil Engineering; www.bath.ac.uk/ace

architectural engineering: environmental design, architecture, civil engineering, conservation of historic buildings, architectural engineering (facade engineering/innovative structural engineering), professional practice, modern building design; BEng, BSc, EngD, MArch, MEng, MPhil, MSc, PGCert, PhD

Chemical Engineering; www.bath.ac.uk/chem-eng

chemical engineering, biochemical engineering, sustainable chemical technologies, integrated environmental management; BEng, EngD, MEng, MPhil, MSc, PhD

Electronic & Electrical Engineering; www.bath.ac.uk/elec-eng

electronic & communication engineering, electrical & electronic/electrical power engineering, computer systems engineering, electrical power engineering, mechatronics, space science & technology, wireless systems; BEng, EngD, MEng, MPhil, MSc, PhD

Mechanical Engineering; www.bath.ac.uk/mech-eng

aerospace/automotive engineering, engineering design, mechanical engineering, manufacture & management, mechatronics, innovation & technology management, adv design & innovation; EngD, MEng, MPhil, MSc, PhD

Faculty of Humanities and Social Science: *www.bath.ac.uk/hss*

Dept of Economics; www.bath.ac.uk/economics

economics/& finance/politics/mathematics, international money & banking, economics; BSc(Hons), MPhil, MRes, PhD

Dept of Education; www.bath.ac.uk/education

education, international education & globalisation, education with psychology, TESOL; BA(Hons), EdD, FdSc, MA, MPhil, MRes, PGCE, PhD, ProfPGCE

Dept of Politics, Languages & International Studies; www.bath.ac.uk/polis

European politics, contemporary European studies, international relations/studies, interpreting, politics/ & economics/international relations, translating, international security, international management & modern languages, language & politics, politics & international relations, professional language skills, modern languages & European Studies; BA(Hons), BSc(Hons), MA, MPhil, PGDip, PhD

Dept of Psychology; www.bath.ac.uk/psychology

psychology, health psychology, clinical psychology, environment, energy & resilience; BSc(Hons), MPhil, MSc, PhD, MRes, DCin Psych

Dept for Health; www.bath.ac.uk/health

health, primary care, sport & exercise science/ medicine, sports physiotherapy, health practice, health & wellbeing; BSc, MPhil, MRes, MSc, PhD, ProfDoc, MD, MS, MSci

Dept of Social & Policy Science; www.bath.ac.uk/sps

sociology, social science, social policy, international development/public policy analysis, wellbeing in public policy & international development, social work & applied social studies; BSc(Hons), MSc, MRes, MPhil, PhD

Faculty of Science; *www.bath.ac.uk/science*

Dept of Biology & Biochemistry; www.bath.ac.uk/bio-sci

biology, biochemistry, biomedical sciences, biosciences, molecular & cellular biology, developmental biology, evolutionary & population biology, medical bioscience, molecular plant science, molecular microbiology, biotechnology & enterprise; BSc(Hons), MPhil, MRes, PhD

Dept of Chemistry; www.bath.ac.uk/chemistry

chemistry/for drug discovery, management, education; BSc(Hons), MChem, MSci, PhD

Dept of Computer Science; www.bath.ac.uk/comp-sci

computer science/with maths/business, software systems, digital entertainment systems, human-computer interaction; BSc(Hons), EngD, MComp, MSc, PhD

Dept of Mathematics; www.bath.ac.uk/math-sci

mathematical sciences, mathematics, modern applics of mathematics, statistics, mathematical biology; BSc(Hons), MMath, MSc, PhD

Dept of Natural Sciences; www.bath.ac.uk/nat-sci

multidisciplinary studies include biology, chemistry, pharmacology, physics, mathematics; BSc(Hons), MSci

Dept of Pharmacy & Pharmacology; www.bath.ac.uk/pharmacy

clinical pharmaceutical practice, pharmacology, pharmacy, advanced & specialist healthcare practice, pharmaceutical prescribing, medicinal chemistry, medicine management pharmacy; MPharm, MPharmacol, PhD, CPD

Dept of Physics; www.bath.ac.uk/physics

physics, mathematics/astrophysics and physics, physics/with computing, nanoscience, photonics; BSc, MSc, MPhil, MPhys, PhD

School of Management: *www.bath.ac.uk/management*

accounting/& finance, business administration, international management & languages, management/ marketing, advanced management practice, entrepreneurship & management, finance, finance with banking, finance with risk management, HRM & consulting, innovation & technology management, international management, management, marketing, sustainability & management; BSc(Hons), DBA, EngD, MBA, MPhil, MRes, MSc, PhD

BATH SPA UNIVERSITY
www.bathspa.ac.uk

Bath School of Art & Design: www.artbathspa.com

design ceramics, contemporary arts practice, fashion design, fine art, creative arts, 3D design/idea material objects, photography & digital media, visual communication, graphic communication, textile design for fashion & interiors, curatorial practice, design/fashion & textiles, integrating fashion design, fashion portfolio; BA(Hons), FdA, MFA, MA, MPhil, PhD

School of Education; www.bathspa.ac.uk/schools/education

early years/education/primary teaching pathway/workbased, education/studies, counselling & psychotherapy, education leadership & management, education studies/international, early years initial teacher training, professional practice in HE, specific learning difficulties/dyslexia, initial teacher education, teaching assistants, PGCE (primary (3–11)/middle years (7–14)/secondary (11–16); range of subjects), TESOL, international education & global citizenship; FD, GradCert, MA/MTeach, PGCE, PGCert/Dip

School of Humanities & Cultural Industries; www.bathspa.ac.uk/schools/humanities-and-cultural-industries

arts management, creative media practice/writing/arts, creative computing/technology & management/technologies & enterprise, feature film-making, film & screen studies, media communications, music production, English literature, literature, landscape & environment, heritage/ management, publishing, scriptwriting, religion, philosophy & ethics, film & TV production, travel & nature writing, writing for young people; BA(Hons), MPhil, PhD, MA

Music & the Performing Arts; www.bathspampa.com

commercial music, contemporary circus, creative arts, creative music technology, musical theatre, dance, drama, acting, music, composition, performance Shakespeare, songwriting, creative & media technology, performance, performing arts, theatre production/for young audiences, pop; BA(Hons), FdA, FdMus, MA, PhD

School of Society, Enterprise & Environment; www.bathspa.ac.uk/schools/society-enterprise-and-environment

accounting, biology, global development & sustainability, business & management, geography, HRM, counselling, environmental science, food & nutrition, GIS, health studies, tourism management, psychology, sociology; BA(Hons), BSc(Hons), MPhil, MSc, PhD, FDA, DipHE, Fd

UNIVERSITY OF BEDFORDSHIRE
www.beds.ac.uk

Faculty of Creative Arts, Technologies & Science; www.beds.ac.uk/departments/cats

Bedfordshire Institute of Media, Arts & Performance; www.beds.ac.uk/departments/bim

Art & Design

advertising design, animation, art and design, fashion design, fine art, graphic design, illustration, interior architecture, interior design, photography and video art

Biological and Biomedical Sciences

biological science, biomedical science, forensic science, biomedical engineering, biotechnology, pharmacology, environmental management; BSc(Hons), FdSc, MSc, PGCert, PGDip, MPhil, PhD

Computing and Engineering

artificial intelligence & robotics, business information systems, computer games development, computer networking, computer science, computer science and robotics, computer science and software engineering, computer security and forensics, computer systems engineering, computing and mathematics, electronic engineering, information systems, interactive digital technologies, software engineering, telecommunications and network engineering; BSc(Hons), FdSc, MSc, BEng, MPhil, PhD

Journalism and Communications

broadcast journalism, creative writing, creative writing & journalism, journalism, journalism and PR, magazine journalism, media communications, media and PR, sport journalism; BA(Hons), FdA, MA, MRes, PhD, PGCert

Media Arts and Production

interactive digital technologies, media performance, media production, media production (moving image/new media/radio/script writing), music technology, TV production

Creative and Performing Arts

dance and professional practice, English studies, English and theatre studies; BA(Hons), FdA, MA, MRes, PhD, PGCert

The Faculty offers postgraduate courses in Art & Design, Biological & Biomedical Sciences, Computing & Engineering

Faculty of Health and Social Sciences; www.beds.ac.uk/departments/healthsciences

Nursing, Midwifery & Health

sport and exercise rehabilitation, public health, nursing, midwifery and health; nursing studies, advanced nursing studies BA(Hons), BSc(Hons), MSc

Psychology

health psychology, psychology, psychology and criminology, psychology, counselling and therapies, forensic psychology, health psychology, psychological approaches to health and management; BA(Hons), BSc(Hons), MSc

Social Sciences

applied social studies, child and adolescent studies, criminology/and sociology, health and social care, BA(Hons), BSc(Hons)

Sports Therapy

sports therapy; BA(Hons), BSc

Dept of Clinical Education & Leadership;

Medical and Dental Education

medical education, medical education leadership, dental education, medical simulation, dental law and ethics; MSc, PGCert/Dip

Post qualifying health

advanced nursing studies, hospitals and health, services management, specialist community public health nursing (health/school nursing), specialist practitioner community district nursing; MSc/PGCert/Dip, MBA

Healthcare

short courses on health-related issues

Public Health

public health; MSc, PGCert/Dip, MBA

Dept of Applied Social Studies; www.beds.ac.uk/departments/appliedsocialstudies

sociology, criminology, criminology and sociology, preparing for social welfare, early years studies, applied social studies, social work (work based), youth and community work, health and social care, child and family studies/ adolescent studies, social work, children, families and community health applied social work practice: children and families, applied social work practice: leadership & management, applied social work practice: education, childhood and youth: applied perspectives, criminology, family and systemic psychotherapy, intermediate child focused systemic practice, intermediate systemic practice with families and couples, international social work and social development, professional social work practice, social work, systemic leadership and organisational development BSc(Hons), FdA, FdSc, MSc, ProfDoc, PGCert/Dip, MA, MSocWkPract

Dept of Healthcare Practice

assistant practitioner, operating department practice, nursing with registered nurse (adult/child/mental health), midwifery; Fd, DipHE, BSc(Hons)

Div of Psychology; www.beds.ac.uk/departments/psychology

applied/health psychology, counselling and therapies, criminal behaviour, psychology, psychology & crime/criminal behaviour/criminology/education, psychology, counselling & therapies, coaching psychology, forensic psychology, health psychology, psychological approaches to health & management, cognitive behavioural therapy, adv psychological research methods; BSc(Hons), BA(Hons), CertHE, FdA, MSc, PhD

Div of Sports Therapy; www.beds.ac.uk/departments/spoth

sports therapy/& exercise rehabilitation, physical exercise for sport & exercise rehabilitation; BSc(Hons), PGDip/Cert, Fd, MSc

Institute for Health Research; www.beds.ac.uk/research/ihr

psychological approach to health & management, public health; MSc, PhD, MPhil

Institute of Applied Social Research; www.beds.ac.uk/research/iasr

applied social studies, psychology, Europerspectives, leadership; ProfDoc, MA

University of Bedfordshire Business School; www.beds.ac.uk/departments/ubbs

Accounting and Finance

accounting, accounting and finance, accounting with management, business economics, International finance and banking, investment and finance

Law

law international commercial and dispute resolution law

Business, Management and HRM

beauty therapy and spa management, decision modelling/E-business/finance/marketing/project management, international business, international business with languages;
business pre-masters, business and management, business information systems, business web analytics and management, engineering business management, Executive MBA – (healthcare), finance and business management, HRM, information systems and business management, international business and management, international HRM, logistics and supply chain management, management, MBA (marketing/finance/Information technology management/i(international management practice/hospital and health services management)/HRM/engineering management/brand management/international hospitality management, project management

Marketing, Tourism and Hospitality

advertising and marketing communications, event management, hospitality and tourism management, marketing, PR, PR in practice; international tourism management, marketing and business management, marketing communications, tourism and events management; BA(Hons), BSc(Hons), MBA, DBA, FdA, LlB, LlM, MA, MSc, PGCert, LLM

Faculty of Education, Sport & Tourism; www.beds.ac.uk/departments/es

Dept of English Language & Communication

international foundation /premasters courses in business, computing, engineering, certificate in English language teaching, English language and linguistics, applied linguistics TEFL, ELT management

Dept of Teacher Education

PE (secondary), primary education (with QTS), Key Stage 2/3 mathematics, primary early years, primary with English/mathematics/modern community languages, primary with special educational needs & disabilities, secondary computer science & IT, secondary English/maths/modern languages/PE/science with biology/secondary science with chemistry/physics

Dept of Educational Studies

education studies, early years education, childhood and youth studies, special needs and inclusive education, behavioural issues in schools, difficulties literacy development and dyslexia, education, education (leadership and management), education (national award for special educational needs coordination), education (special educational needs), education studies (international), special educational needs, inclusion and disability, strategic leadership and management education

Dept of Sport Science & Physical Activity

football studies, health, nutrition and exercise, sport and exercise science, sport and physical education, sport development and management, sport science and coaching, sport science and personal training, sports studies, sport science and physical education, sports therapy, clinical exercise physiology, community sport management, physical activity, nutrition and health promotion, physical education and sport pedagogy, sport development management sports performance
PGCE, BA(Hons), BEd(Hons), MA, MSc, PGCert/Dip, FdA, PGCSMT, Univ Adv Cert, QTS, FdA

THE QUEEN'S UNIVERSITY OF BELFAST
www.qub.ac.uk

School of Biological Sciences; www.qub.ac.uk/schools/ schoolofbiologicalsciences

agricultural technology, adv food safety, animal behaviour & welfare, biological sciences, biochemistry & welfare, communication/strategy management/ training & development/for rural business, environmental biology, ecological management & conservation biology, leadership for sustainable/rural development, microbiology, molecular biology & biotechnology, food quality/safety & biotechnology, safety & nutrition, land use & environmental management, marine biology, zoology
BSc(Hons), MSc, PGDip, PhD, MPhil

School of Chemistry and Chemical Engineering; www.ch.qub.ac.uk

chemistry, medicinal chemistry, chemical engineering, chemical biology, chemical research, pharmaceutical analysis, process engineering, professional studies; BSc(Hons), MSci, BEng, MEng, MSc, PGDip, PhD

School of Creative Arts; www.qub.ac.uk/ schools/SchoolofCreativeArts

music, music technology, composition, drama, English, sonic arts, film studies, film & visual studies, arts management, musicology, Irish traditional; BA, MA, BMus, BSc, MPhil, PhD

School of Education; www.qub.ac.uk/ schools/schoolofeducation

behavioural analysis, applied autism spectrum disorders, children's rights, educational studies/ research, inclusion, initial teacher education (PGCE in wide range of secondary education subjects), educational leadership, inclusion/education & special education needs, professional development, TESOL, quantitative methods in educational research; AdvCertEd, DASE, EdD, MA, MEd, MSc, MSSc, PGCE, PGDip/Cert, UnivCert, BA(Hons)

School of Electronics, Electrical Engineering and Computer Science; www.qub.ac.uk/schools/eeecs

business IT, computing and IT, computer games design & development, computer science, cyber security, educational multimedia, electrical & electronic engineering, electronics, telecommunications, software/development & electronic systems engineering, software engineering/development, software electronics systems engineering, wireless communications, smart grids for electrical power systems; BEng, BSc, MEng, MSc, MPhil, PhD

School of English; www.qub.ac.uk/schools/ SchoolofEnglish

broadcast literacy, creative writing, English, English literature & linguistics, Irish literature, pathways and programmes, English literary studies, poetry: creativity and criticism; BA(Hons), MA, PhD

School of Geography, Archaeology and Palaeoecology; www.qub.ac.uk/schools/ gap

archaeology (inc jt degrees), professional archaeology, dating & chronology, environmental change, geography, heritage science, human geography & society, social space & culture, archaeology-palaeoecology, archaeology, palaeoecology & geography, geography; BA(Hons), BSc(Hons), MSc, PhD, PGDip/Cert

School of History and Anthropology; www.qub.ac.uk/schools/ SchoolofHistoryandAnthropology

history, history & theology, ethnomusicology, English & history/social anthropology, history & social anthropology/modern languages/philosophy/politics/sociology, Irish/local history/studies, social anthropology, anthropology; BA(Hons), GradDip, MA, MPhil, PhD

School of Law; www.law.qub.ac.uk

law/with politics, business & human rights law, common & civil law, corporate governance, environmental law/& sustainable development, human rights law & criminal justice, legal science, criminology, law & international commerce/governance, human rights law; LlB, LlM, MSSc, MLSc, PGDip, MPhil, PhD, JD

School of Modern Languages; www.qub.ac.uk/schools/ SchoolofModernLanguages

French/German/Irish & Celtic/ Spanish & Portuguese studies, interpreting, translation, Irish translation, Irish – medium film & production, jt degrees offered; BA(Hons), MA, PhD

Queen's University Management School; www.qub.ac.uk/schools/ QueensUniversityManagementSchool

accounting/& finance, actuarial science & risk management, business information technology, organisation & business economics/computational finance & trading, marketing, politics, philosophy & economics, marketing & investment management, executive/ international MBAs; BSc(Hons), MSc, MScs, MBA, PhD, MSSc

School of Mathematics and Physics; www.qub.ac.uk/schools/ SchoolofMathematicsandPhysics

mathematics, physics, plasma physics, materials science, pure & applied mathematics, applied physics; BSc(Hons), GradDip, MSc, MSci, PhD

School of Mechanical and Aerospace Engineering; www.qub.ac.uk/schools/ SchoolofMechanicaland AerospaceEngineering

adv/aerospace engineering, adv/mechanical engineering, product design engineering; BEng, MEng, MSc, PhD

School of Medicine, Dentistry and Biomedical Sciences; www.qub.ac.uk/ schools/mdbs

medicine, biomedical science, clinical education, clinical anatomy, dentistry, surgery, bioinformatics and computational genomics, translational medicine, public health, clinical education, mental health; BCh, BAO, BSc(Hons), BDS, DAO, MB, MD, MSc, MPH, PGDip/Cert

School of Nursing and Midwifery; www.qub.ac.uk/schools/ SchoolofNursingandMidwifery

nursing – adult/children's/learning disability/mental health, midwifery sciences, caring for children & young people with complex health needs, continuing professional development, clinical practice, neonatal studies, non-medical prescribing, health studies and health & clinical studies, specialist practice in nursing, professional studies in midwifery, enhanced/ neonatal studies, trauma studies, advanced professional practice, advanced professional & clinical practice, caring for children and young people with complex health needs, nursing practice, midwifery practice, nursing practice with advanced clinical assessment; BSc(Hons), Diploma, MPhil, PhD, DNursingPractice

School of Pharmacy; www.qub.ac.uk/ schools/SchoolofPharmacy

adv pharmaceutical practice, clinical pharmacy, community pharmacy, non medical prescribing, pharmaceutical science/biotechnology, pharmacist prescribing, pharmacy practice; MPharm, MSc, PGCert/Dip, MPhil

School of Planning, Architecture and Civil Engineering; www.qub.ac.uk/schools/ SchoolofPlanningArchitectureand CivilEngineering

architecture, adv concrete technology, civil engineering, construction & project management, durability of structures, environmental engineering/planning, environmental & civil engineering, European planning, planning with regeneration, professional practice, spatial regeneration, urban & rural design, structural engineering with architecture, sustainable practice in the built environment; BSc(Hons), MSc, MArch, MPhil, PhD, PGDip/Cert, MPlan

School of Politics, International Studies and Philosophy; www.qub.ac.uk/schools/ SchoolofPoliticsInternationalStudies andPhilosophy

comparative ethnic conflict, international relations, Irish politics, politics, legislative studies & practice, philosophy, politics & economics, international politics & conflict studies, violence, terrorism and security; BA(Hons), LlB, MA, MRes, MPhil, PhD

School of Psychology; www.psych.qub.ac.uk

atypical child development, psychology, educational child & adolescent psychology, medical ethics & law, moral, legal & political philosophy, political psychology, politics, applied/clinical psychology, psychology of childhood; BSc(Hons), MSc, DocClinPsych, PhD DocEducational

School of Sociology, Social Policy and Social Work; www.qub.ac.uk/schools/ SchoolofSociologySocialPolicySocialWork

applied social studies, criminology, childhood studies, social work, social policy, social research methods, sociology, youth justice; BA(Hons), BSW, MA, MSc, DChild, MRes

UNIVERSITY OF BIRMINGHAM
www.bham.ac.uk

*College of Arts and Law;
www.birmingham.ac.uk/schools/
historycultures/departments/caha/
index.aspx*

Birmingham Law School;
www.birmingham.ac.uk/schools/law/index.aspx

law, international law and globalisation, law with business studies/criminology/French law/German law, LlB for graduates; international law, ethics and politics, international law: crime, justice & human rights, commercial law, international commercial law, criminal law & justice; GradDip, LlB, LlM, MPhil/MJur/PhD

English, Drama and American & Canadian Studies; www.birmingham.ac.uk/schools/edacs/index.aspx

American & Canadian literature & culture, applied linguistics, business & American studies, English, corpus linguistics, film/& creative writing, directing & dramaturgy, playwriting, drama & theatre arts, English language/literature, gender studies, literature/culture & modernity, literary linguistics, medieval studies, Shakespeare studies, Shakespeare & theatre/in education, TEFL/TEST, transatlantic studies, translation studies, literature & film, film & TV; BA(Hons), BSc(Hons), MPhil, PhD, MA, MRes

School of History and Cultures;
www.birmingham.ac.uk/schools/historycultures/index.aspx

anthropology and political science/African studies/classical literature and civilisation, ancient history, classics, classical literature and civilisation, archaeology and ancient history, anthropology, English and classical literature & civilisation, classical literature & civilisation and philosophy, archaeology & ancient history and history, anthropology and classical literature and civilisation, war studies, history, ancient and medieval history, history and French studies/geography/ political science, history & theology and religion/ history of art/English/Russian studies/Hispanic studies/education/American and Canadian studies/German studies/archaeology & ancient history/philosophy

air power: history, theory and practice, British first world war studies, contemporary history, global history, history of warfare, holocaust and genocide, medieval studies, military history, modern British studies, renaissance, reformation and early modern studies, social research (economic and social history), West Midlands history

Africa and development, African studies, Caribbean literature

antiquity (Byzantine studies/European archaeology/archaeology/landscape archaeology), antiquity (ancient history/classical archaeology/classics/late antiquity/ roman history and archaeology), humanities, byzantine studies, modern east Mediterranean history, modern Greek studies, Ottoman studies, Greek archaeology, ancient history, late antiquity, archaeology, Egyptology, classics, cuneiform and ancient near eastern studies, world heritage studies, international heritage management, international heritage management by distance learning; BA(Hons), MA, MPhil, PGDip, PhD/Dip/Cert, MRes

School of Languages, Cultures, Art History and Music; www.birmingham.ac.uk/schools/lcahm/index.aspx

modern languages, film studies, English literature, European studies, French, gender studies, German, Hispanic, Italian, translation studies, Japanese, Mandarin, Russian & E European studies, history, history of art, music, composition, early music editing/performance, critical musicology, instrumental/vocal composition, performance/practice, electroacoustic composition, British music, choral conducting; BA, MA, BMus, MPhil, PhD

The School of Philosophy, Theology and Religion; www.birmingham.ac.uk/schools/ptr/index.aspx

global ethics, international law, ethics & politics, evangelical & charismatic studies, health bioethics & law, holocaust & genocide, Islamic studies, philosophy, philosophy of language and linguistics/of mind & cognition/of religion and ethics/health & happiness, pentecostal & charismatic studies, politics, religion & philosophy/culture, religion, politics & society, theology & religion, human rights & values, Sikh studies; BA(Hons), BMus, MA, MPhil, PhD, MRes, Dip/Cert, BD, MDiv, DPT D

School of Chemistry;
www.birmingham.ac.uk/schools/chemistry/index.aspx

chemical biology & biochemical imaging, chemistry/with pharmacology/business management, chemical biology, biomedical engineering; BSc, MSci, MSc, PhD/MPhil

School of Chemical Engineering;
www.birmingham.ac.uk/schools/chemical-engineering/index.aspx

adv/chemical engineering, biochemical engineering, efficient fossil energy technologies, energy engineering, food safety, hygiene & management, industrial project management, food quality & health; BEng, MEng, Masters/MSc/Diploma/PG Certificate

School of Civil Engineering;
www.birmingham.ac.uk/schools/civil-engineering/index.aspx

civil engineering/& energy engineering, civil engineering & management, civil & railway engineering, geotechnical engineering & management/international experience/international study, railway systems engineering & integration, railway risk & safety management, construction management, structural engineering & practice; BEng, MEng, Masters/MSC/Diploma/Certificate, PhD

School of Computer Science;
www.cs.bham.ac.uk

artificial intelligence, adv/computer science, computer science & business management/software engineering, computer security, electronic, electrical computer engineering, natural computation, human/computer interaction, cognitive robotics & psychology, mathematics & computer science, robotics; BSc, MEng, MSc, MRes, PhD, MSci

School of Electronic, Electrical and Computer Engineering;
www.birmingham.ac.uk/schools/eece/index.aspx

communications engineering & networks, electrical engineering & business management, electrical & energy/electronic engineering, electrical power systems, electromagnetic sensor networks, electrical & railway engineering, electronic transportation systems & infrastructure, RF & microwave engineering, computer systems engineering, RF & satellite engineering, electronic & computer engineering, embedded systems, industrial experience; BEng, MEng, MSc, MRes, PhD

School of Mathematics;
www.birmingham.ac.uk/schools/mathematics/index.aspx

mathematics, mathematics & computer science/sports science/music/philosophy/business management pure/applied mathematics, mathematics/with engineering, operational research, statistics, theoretical physics & applied mathematics, computer science, management mathematics, mathematic modelling, financial engineering, OR, statistics & econometrics, statistics; BA, BSc, MSci, MSc, MRes, PhD

School of Mechanical Engineering;
www.birmingham.ac.uk/schools/mechanical-engineering/index.aspx

adv/mechanical/automotive engineering, engineering/project/operations management; BEng, MEng, Masters/MSc, PhD/MSc

School of Metallurgy and Materials;
www.birmingham.ac.uk/schools/metallurgy-materials/index.aspx

biomaterials, materials/for sustainable energy technologies, materials science & technology/engineering/business management, metallurgy, biomaterials, mechanical & materials engineering, science & engineering of materials, materials engineering/& energy engineering/industrial experience, metallurgy & materials, nuclear engineering, nuclear science & engineering, sports & materials science; BSc, BEng, MEng, MRes, PhD/MSc

School of Physics and Astronomy;
www.birmingham.ac.uk/schools/physics/index.aspx

physics, physics & astrophysics/technology of nuclear reactors/nanoscale physics/particle physics & cosmology, nuclear engineering/science & materials, theoretical physics, & applied mathematics, physics & technology of nuclear reactors, nuclear decommissioning & waste management; BEng, BNatSci, BSc(Hons), DEng, MEng, MPhil, MRes, MSc, MSci, PGDip/Cert, PhD

College of Life and Environmental Sciences; www.birmingham.ac.uk/university/colleges/les/index.aspx

School of Biosciences;
www.birmingham.ac.uk/schools/biosciences/index.aspx

biochemistry/with biotechnology, biological sciences, biochemistry (genetics), bioscience with management, molecular & cellular biology, medical biochemistry, biological sciences (biotechnology/ environmental biology/genetics/microbiology/plant biology/zoology), human biology, natural sciences, toxicology, zoology, medical biology, microbiology & infection, molecular mechanistic toxology/biotechnology; BSc, MSci, MSc, MPhil, PhD

School of Geography, Earth and Environmental Sciences; www.birmingham.ac.uk/schools/gees/ index.aspx

geography (jt degrees), geology/& physical geography, applied & petroleum micropalaeontology, environmental geology, environmental & biological nanoscience, air pollution management & control, human geography (res), hydrogeology, environmental science/health, nuclear decommissioning & waste management, public & environmental health science, safety & the environment, palaeobiology & palaeoenvironment, planning & social policy, public & environmental health science, river environments their management, science of occupational health, spatial planning & business management, geography & urban & regional planning/studies, planning & economics, urban & regional studies, urban regeneration & renewal; BA, BSc/MSci, MSci, MSc, MRes

School of Psychology; www.birmingham.ac.uk/schools/ psychology/index.aspx

psychology, clinical criminology/psychology, cognitive robotics & computational neuroscience, cognitive behaviour therapy, forensic/clinical psychology, neuroscience, psychological practice/res, rational emotional behaviour therapy; BSc, MSci, MSc/Dip/Cert, ForClinPsyD, PhD

School of Sport, Exercise and Rehabilitation Sciences; www.birmingham.ac.uk/schools/ sport-exercise/index.aspx

adv practice, adv manipulative physiotherapy, clinical health management, exercise & sport medicine (football), health studies/research, sport & exercise sciences, sports science/& materials/mathematics, sport PE/coaching, coaching science, PE & sport pedagogy, sport policy & management, golf coaching, applied golf management studies physiotherapy, professional golf studies, sport policy, business & management; BSc(Hons), MPhil, MRes, MSc, PhD, FdSc, PGDip, PGCert

College of Medical and Dental Sciences; www.birmingham.ac.uk/university/ colleges/mds/index.aspx

The Five Schools of the College are: Cancer Sciences, Clinical & Experimental Medicine, Dentistry, Health & Population Sciences, Immunity & Infection

anaesthesia, adv general dental practice, biomedical/ materials science/research integrated & translational, cancer sciences, clinical & experimental medicine, clinical primary & community care, clinical neuropsychiatry/science/health research, clinical & primary healthcare, clinical oncology, dental hygiene & therapy, dental surgery, dentistry, diabetes & obesity, functional & clinical anatomy, genomic medicine, health sciences, healthcare, health economics & econometrics, ethics & the law, history of medicine, international health, inflammation, forensic mental health, immunity & infection, immunology & immunotherapy, medical science, medicine, surgery, musculoskeletal ageing & health, neuroscience, nursing, occupational health, pharmacy, pharmaceutics, pharmaceutical enterprise, physician studies, psychological medicine, physiotherapy, public health (health technical assessment/SEAL), science of occupational health, safety & the environment, trauma science, urology; BDS, BMedSci, BSc(Hons), BNurs, DDS, MBChB, MD, MPharm, DPharm, MEd, MSc, MRes, PGDip/Cert, MPH

College of Social Sciences; www.birmingham.ac.uk/university/ colleges/socsci/index.aspx

Birmingham Business School; www.birmingham.ac.uk/schools/business/ index.aspx

accounting and finance, accountancy, economics, money, banking and finance, mathematical economics and statistics, economics with language, money, banking and finance with language, geography and economics, economics and political science, policy, politics and economics, planning and economics, business management, business management with communications, international business with communications, business management with marketing, international business, money, banking and finance, money, banking and finance with modern language, mathematical economics and statistics, business administration, financial economics, development economics, economics, environmental and natural resource economics, international economics, international money and banking, mathematical finance, money, banking and finance, management, HRM, international business, management, management: entrepreneurship & innovation, management: strategy, international marketing, marketing, marketing communications, strategic marketing and consulting, MBA; international business, global banking and finance, strategy and procurement management; BSc(Hons), Dip, MSc, MBA, DBA, MPhil, PhD, PGCert, PGDip, UCert

School of Education; www.birmingham.ac.uk/schools/ education/index.aspx

autism (adults), autism (children), autism spectrum disorders (webautism), bilingualism in education, education for health professionals, education of learners with multisensory impairment (deafblindness), inclusion and special educational needs, international studies in education, language, literacies and dyslexia, management of special education in developing countries, school improvement and educational leadership, severe, profound and multiple learning difficulties, special educational needs coordination, special educational needs and disabilities, teachers of children with hearing impairment, TEFL, teacher training, early years, primary, secondary subject courses, QTS, visual impairment; AdvCert, BA(Hons), BPhil, ChildPsyD, EdD, EdPsychD, MEd, MPhil, PGCE, PGCert/Dip, PhD, PGDE, CertHE

School of Government and Society; www.birmingham.ac.uk/schools/ government-society/index.aspx

society & economics, international relations with French/German/Spanish, political economy, political science, sociology, international relations with economics/political science/Russian studies, political science with African studies/anthropology/economics/history/sociology/social policy/philosophy, sociology & social policy/philosophy/education/political science, international relations with political science/

economics, political science with philosophy/social policy/sociology, political economy, political science & sociology, politics, development management, aid management, human resources and development management, public economic management and finance, international development, conflict, security and development, governance and statebuilding, international political economy and development, poverty, inequality and development, public administration, international development, conflict, security and development, poverty, inequality and development, public administration and development, global cooperation and security, international studies in education (education and development), Africa and development, social research; BA(Hons), BSc(Hons), PGDipGDipGCert, MA, MEd, AdvCert, MPhil, MSc, PhD, MPA

The School of Social Policy (The Health Services Management Centre; Institute of Applied Social Studies); www.birmingham.ac.uk/schools/social-policy/index.aspx

policy, politics and economics, social work, social policy, social policy: crime, policing and community justice/ health and social care/ housing and communities, policy, politics and economic, social policy and criminology/ sociology, political science/planning and social policy, mental health and deafness, health care policy and management, leadership for health services improvement, healthcare commissioning, migration, superdiversity and policy, policy into practice, policy into practice with integrated placement, social policy, social research (social policy/ social work and professional practice), leadership and management for social work/ social care, social work with children, young people, their families and carer, specialist social work with adults, social research; BA(Hons), MA, MSc, PGDip, SocScD, PhD

Degrees validated at the University of Birmingham offered at:

SCHOOL OF EDUCATION, SELLY OAK
www.education.bham.ac.uk

applied golf management studies, autism, bilingualism in education, childhood, culture & education, dyslexia studies, education for health professionals, English language and literature in education, educational psychology, hearing impairment, inclusion &

special educational needs, international studies in education, IT & education, leaders & leadership in education, learning & learning contexts, learning difficulties/ multisensory impairment, sports coaching, teacher training – primary courses, early years, general primary/secondary subject courses (English, geography, history & citizenship, mathematics, modern foreign languages, PE, professional development, RE, biology, chemistry, physics), TEFL, visual impairment; AppEd, BA, ChildPsyD, EdPsychD, MPhil, PhD, PGCE

UNIVERSITY COLLEGE BIRMINGHAM
www.ucb.ac.uk

digital marketing, international tourism business management, international adventure travel management, sport and fitness studies, sports injury prevention & management, applied food and nutrition, food development and innovation; BA(Hons), BSc(Hons), FdA Dip HE, FdSc, MA, MSc, PGCE, PGDip/Cert

BIRMINGHAM CITY UNIVERSITY
www.bcu.ac.uk

Faculty of Arts, Design & Media; www.bcu.ac.uk/arts-design-and-media

School of Art
art and design, fine art, arts and education, arts and project management, arts practice and education, contemporary curatorial practice, history of art and design, media art philosophy practice, queer studies in arts and culture

Drama & Acting
acting, acting (the British tradition), applied performance (community and education), creative drama (adults), professional voice practice

Architecture
architecture, architectural practice, landscape architecture

School of Fashion, Textiles & 3D design; http:/ www.bcu.ac.uk/fashion-textiles-and-3d-design
3D design: 3D designer maker, design and visualisation, design innovation management, design management, fashion accessory design, fashion business and promotion, fashion accessories, fashion communication, fashion design with garment technology, fashion management, fashion media management, fashion promotion, fashion retail management, fashion styling, furniture and lifestyle products, interior design, product design, surface design, textile design, textile design (constructed textiles/embroidery), printed textiles and surface design, textile design (retail management), textile management; BA(Hons), MA, PGDip/Cert

School of Jewellery; www.bcu.ac.uk/jewellery
gemmology and jewellery studies, horology, jewellery and silversmithing – design for industry, jewellery and silversmithing, jewellery design and related products, gemmology and jewellery studies; BA(Hons), BSc(Hons)

Birmingham Conservatoire;http:/ www.bcu.ac.uk/conservatoire
jazz, music composition, instrumental performance, jazz (performance or composition), jazz performance, jazz studies; BA(Hons), BTEC, Cert/DipHE, MA, MPhil, PGCert/Dip, PhD, BMus, MMus, MFA, MArch, FD

School of Visual Communication
theatre, performance and event design, visual communication, visual communication – film and animation/graphic communication/illustration/photography; BA(Hons), MA

Faculty of Business, Law & Social Sciences; www.bcu.ac.uk/business-law-and-social-sciences

Birmingham City Business School; www.bcu.ac.uk/business-school
accountancy, accountancy and business, accountancy and finance, arts and project management, audit management and consultancy, business, business (professional practice), business administration, business and economics, business and finance, business and HRM, business and management, business and marketing, data analytics and management, design innovation management, economics and finance, executive MBA (internal audit and risk), fashion

59

management, global media management (advertising industry), global media management (the news business), HRM internal audit practice, internal auditing and management, international business, international finance, international HRM, international marketing, leadership and management practice, luxury brand management, luxury jewellery management, luxury product management, management and finance, management and international business, management and marketing, marketing, marketing (professional practice), marketing, advertising and PR, Master of Business Administration International, multi-unit leadership and strategy, textile management; BA(Hons), MBA, DBA, HND, MPhil, MSc, PhD, MA, PGDip

The School of Law; www.bcu.ac.uk/law
international business, international human rights, law, legal studies/practice, law with American legal studies/business law/criminology, legal practice, oil & gas management; Grad Dip, MPhil, PhD, LlB(Hons), LlM, PGDip/Cert, LPC, MSc

School of Social Sciences; www.bcu.ac.uk/socialsciences
conductive education, criminology, criminology and security studies, criminology, policing and investigation, forensic psychology, integrative psychotherapy, psychology/with sociology, public sociology, social sciences; BA(Hons), BSc(Hons), CertHE, FDA, MA, MPhil, MSc, PGCert/Dip, PhD

Faculty of Health Education & Life Sciences; www.bcu.ac.uk/

School of Allied & Public Health Professions
advanced healthcare, advanced practice, community health nursing specialist practitioner, diagnostic radiography, dimensions in healthcare, habilitation work – working with children and young people, health and social care, medical ultrasound, mental health – approved mental health practitioner, mental health studies, operating department practice, pain management, paramedic science, professional studies in health and social care, public health, radiography, radiotherapy, rehabilitation work (visual impairment), specialist community public health nurse, speech and language therapy; BSc(Hons), DipHE, FdA, MPhil, MSc, PGDip/Cert, PQ, PhD

School of Education; www.bcu.ac.uk/school-of-education
children & integrated professional care, conductive education, education, early childhood/education

studies, early years, education for academic purposes, international education, post compulsory education & training, primary & early years education, secondary design & technique: food & textiles, teaching & learning/education leadership, global education, studies, mathematics with secondary education & QTS, secondary art & design/drama/education/mathematics/music/chemistry, physics, primary education with QTS, subject enhancement in mathematics; BA(Hons), FD, MPhil, PGCert/Dip, PGCE, PhD, MTL, EdD

School of Life Sciences; www.bcu.ac.uk/life-sciences
bio-informatics, cell biology, clinical physiology, food science, microbiology, sport and exercise science, sports coaching and development, sport, health and physical activity; BSc(Hons)

School of Defence Healthcare Education; www.bcu.ac.uk/defence-healthcare-education
defence healthcare studies; BSc(Hons)

School of Nursing, Midwifery & Social Work; www.bcu.ac.uk/nursing-midwifery-and-social-work
midwifery, nursing – adult/child/learning disability/mental health, dimensions in healthcare, mental health studies, advanced healthcare, advanced practice, community health nursing specialist practitioner, dimensions in healthcare, habilitation work – working with children and young people, health and social care, medical ultrasound, pain management, numerous additional pathways; BSc(Hons), MSc, PGDip/Cert

Faculty of Performance, Media & English; www.bcu.ac.uk/pme

Birmingham Conservatoire; www.bcu.ac.uk/conservatoire
music, performance & pedagogy, composition, conducting, jazz (performance), professional performance/specialism, music technology, musicology, orchestral/instrumental performance, pop music, vocal performance; AdvPGDip, BMus(Hons), MA, MMus, MPhil, PhD

Birmingham School of Media; www.bcu.ac.uk/media
international/broadcast/online journalism, creative industries & cultural policy, interactive entertainment (digital art/marketing/games development), film

distribution & marketing, freelance photography/ media, event & exhibition management, film futures, video games development, media photography, music industry (PR/radio/TV/online), radio & audio production, TV production, screen studies, social media, video games; BA(Hons), PGDip, MA, MPhil, PhD

Birmingham School of Acting; www.bsa.bcu.ac.uk

acting/British tradition, physical theatre, professional voice practice, stage management, applied performance (community & education); BA(Hons), MPhil, PhD, MA, MFA

School of English; www.bcu.ac.uk/English

English, creative writing, drama, English language/ literature/linguistics, writing, philosophy; BA(Hons), Dip, MA, MPhil, PhD

Faculty of Technology, Engineering & the Environment; www.bcu.ac.uk/tee

Digital Media Technology; digital broadcast technology, film production technology, film technology & visual effects, music technology, sound engineering & production; BSc(Hons), MSc, PhD

Computing, Telecommunications & Networks

business information technology/computing/intelligence, cyber security, computer networks, computer science/games technology, computer data networks/ & security, data analytics & management, enterprise/ information systems management, computing, electronic engineering (microelectronics/telecommunication/foundation), financial mathematics, forensic computing, information & communication technology, mathematics, statistics; BSc(Hons), BEng, MEng, MSc, PGDip/Cert, foundation telecommunication & networks

Built Environment

architectural technology, building surveying, built environment, civil engineering, construction management, construction project management, environmental & spatial planning, environmental sustainability (design & construction), integrated design & construction, planning environmental development, quantity surveying, real estate/management; BSc(Hons), BEng/MEng, MSc, PGDip/Cert

Engineering, Design & Manufacturing Systems

automotive calibration & control/engineering, electronic engineering, mechanical engineering, international logistics & supply chain management, motorsports engineering, enterprise information systems/ systems management, international/project management/integration, quality management, computing/& telecommunications & networks, oil & gas management; BSc(Hons), FdSc, MSc, MPhil, PGCert/Dip, BEng, MEng, PhD

BISHOP GROSSETESTE UNIVERSITY
www.bgc.ac.uk

archaeology, counselling, drama, early childhood studies, education studies, history, mathematics, primary education with QTS, primary psychology, special educational needs & sport, theology & ethics, community archaeology, education, English literature, heritage education, social and cultural history, theology & religious studies, PGCE (primary/secondary), theology & ethics in society; BA(Hons), FdA, GradDip, MA, PhD, EdD, PGCE

BLACKBURN COLLEGE
www.blackburn.ac.uk

Vocation qualifications (BTEC, City & Guilds etc) Accounting & Finance; accounting, business accounting, financial services, Business, Retail & Management; retail management, business studies, business with HRM, retail management, management studiesCatering & Hospitality; hospitality management, hospitality management (events management) Childcare & Young People; positive practice with children & young people, early childhood studies, Computing;computing (software development/

networking & forensics/software development) Construction; construction sustainable design/project management/building surveyingCreative Arts; photographic media, contemporary textiles, contemporary fashion, contemporary design for interiors, graphic design, fine art (integrated media), graphic communication, illustration and animation, photographic media, contemporary textiles, contemporary design for interiors, contemporary fashionEducation, Coaching & Teaching; education and training, teaching & learning support (primary), coaching & mentoring, education studies, PGCE (education & training)Engineering; mechanical engineering, robotics & mechatronics, electrical and electronic engineering Health, Social Care & Counselling; social care, disability studies (inclusive practice), counselling, disability studies (inclusive practice), applied psychology (counselling & health) Justice;

criminology & criminal justice, criminologyLaw; paralegal studies, lawPublic Services; public service management, public service management (uniformed services/housing), fire & rescue service management, community policing & justice management, public service managementSocial Science & Humanities; English language & literary studies, history & politics/sociology/English language/literary studies, sociology & English language/literary studies, politics & English language/literary studies, social scienceSports, Fitness & Wellbeing; health & personal training, community coaching & sports development, sports coaching & performance, professional practice/in complementary therapiesBA(Hons, Ord), BEng(Hons, Ord), BSc(Hons, Ord), DMS (validated externally), FDA/Sc, LlB (validated by Lancaster), LlB, LlM, MBA, MSc, EDMS, CertEd

BOURNEMOUTH UNIVERSITY
www.bournemouth.ac.uk

Faculty of Science & Technology; schools-and-faculty/faculty-science-technology

Department of Archaeology, Anthropology & Forensic Science
archaeological, anthropological & forensic sciences, archaeology, archaeology & anthropology, forensic investigation, forensic science; Post Grad Degrees: applied sciences by research, biological anthropology, forensic archaeology, forensic osteology, forensic toxicology by research, archaeological practice, maritime archaeology, osteoarchaeology

Department of Computing & Informatics
business information technology, computer networks, computing, forensic computing & security, information technology management, software engineering, computing with networking; Post Grad degrees; applied data analytics, computer games technology, cyber security and human factors, information technology, enterprise information systems

Department of Creative Technology
games technology, games programming, music & audio technology, music & sound production technology; Post Grad Degrees: computer games technology, digital music & audio production

Department of Design & Engineering
design engineering, industrial design, product design, engineering, engineering (electronic design/manufacturing management/mechanical design); Post Grad Degrees: mechanical engineering design, engineering project management, industrial design, product design

Department of Life & Environmental Sciences
biological sciences, ecology & wildlife conservation, environmental science; Post Grad degrees: biodiversity conservation, biological anthropology, green economy

Department of Psychology
psychology; Post Grad Degrees: foundations of clinical psychology, clinical & developmental neuropsychology
All departments conduct applied sciences by research BSc(Hons), BA(Hons), MSc, PhD, FDEng, FdSc, MRes, BEng(Hons), MEng(Hons)

The Business School; www.business.bournemouth.ac.uk
Accounting and Finance; acounting & business/finance/law/taxation, economics, finance and business/economics

Business & Management; business studies, business studies with economics/enterprise/finance/HRM/law, business studies with marketing/operations and project management, international business studies/ & management

Law; law, law with economics/& taxation, business law, entertainment law

Postgraduate; Management; the Bournemouth MBA, consumer behaviour, innovation management & entrepreneurship, international management, marketing management, management with HRD, project management, professional development (HRM/loss adjusting)

Finance; corporate governance, finance, international accounting, economics & finance/finance/investment finance/risk management & finance/taxation & finance

Law; law/CPE, international commercial law, intellectual property, international tax law, public international law, legal practice course intellectual property; BA(Hons), LlB(Hons), BSc(Hons), LlM, MA, MBA, MPhil, MSc, PhD, PGCert, Grad Dip-LAw/CPE, MBA

School of Design, Engineering & Computing; www.dec.bournemouth.ac.uk

applied data analytics, business/computing, computer networks, design engineering, engineering project management, sustainable/product design/management, mechanical design engineering, mechanical design, industrial/product design, manufacturing management, business/information technology, computing networks, computing & security, engineering, enterprise information systems, games programming/technology, music & audio/sound production technology, computer games technology, psychology, clinical psychology, lifespan neuropsychology, computing, information technology management, software engineering/product design, forensic computing & security, digital media/music & audio production/technology; BA(Hons), BSc(Hons), FD, BEng, MEng, MA, MPhil, MSc, PhD

School of Health and Social Care; www.bournemouth.ac.uk/hsc

Health Sciences; nutrition, clinical exercise science, Social Studies; social work, sociology, sociology and anthropology/criminology/social policy

Health Professions; adult/children's and young people's/ mental health nursing, midwifery, occupational therapy, paramedic science, physiotherapy, operating department practice

Post Grad courses; public health, social care, social work, adult/ children and young people's/ mental health nursing (with professional registration), public health nurse – health visiting, advanced practice, advanced practice child and family social work/ vulnerable adults), advanced mental health practice, applied dementia studies, advanced nurse practitioner, leading and developing services; AdvDip, BA(Hons), BSc(Hons), DipHE, FdA, FdSc, MPhil, PGDip/Cert, PhD, MA, MSc, Dr Prof Practice

The Media School; www.media.bournemouth.ac.uk

Computer Animation; computer animation arts, software development for animation, games and effects, computer visualisation and animation

Advertising, Marketing & PR; advertising, marketing, marketing communications, politics, public relations

Journalism & Communication; communication and media, multimedia journalism, English

Media Production; digital media design, history, radio, scriptwriting for film and TV, TV production, media production, film production and cinematography, photography, global media practice

Post Graduate Degrees; Animation; 3D computer animation, computer animation and visual effects, computer games art, digital effects

Advertising, Marketing & Communications; advertising, corporate communications, international political communication

Journalism and Communication; adaptation, journalism studies, literary media, media and communication, multimedia journalism

Media Production; cinematography for film and TV, directing film and TV, media arts practice, post production editing, producing film and TV, production design/sound design for film and TV, radio production, scriptwriting

Excellence in Media Practice; creative and media education

BA(Hons), BSc(Hons), FdA, MA, MBA, MPhil, MSc, PhD, DProfD

School of Tourism; www.bournemouth.ac.uk/tourism

events management/marketing, events & leisure marketing, hospitality/hotel & food service management, international hospitality & tourism management, park management, retail management & marketing, sports development & coaching science/management, sustainable tourism planning, sports psychology & coaching science, sustainable tourism planning, tourism management & marketing/planning, tourism & hospitality; FDA, FDSc, BA(Hons), BSc(Hons), MA, MSc, PhD

UNIVERSITY OF BRADFORD
www.bradford.ac.uk

School of Engineering & Informatics
www.brad.ac.uk/ei

Computing; business computing, computational mathematics, computer science for games, computer science, ICT with business/ marketing, ICT, intelligent systems and robotics, software engineering

Postgrad Courses; advanced computer science, computing, computing by research, cyber security, mobile applications, multidisciplinary computing, networks and performance engineering, software engineering

Electrical & Electronic Engineering; electronic and electrical engineering, electronic, telecommunications and internet engineering, electrical and electronic engineering

Postgrad Courses; electrical and electronic engineering, personal, mobile and satellite communications, telecommunications engineering & entrepreneurship

Engineering; Mechanical & Automotive Engineering; mechanical engineering, mechanical and automotive engineering

Postgraduate; automotive engineering, mechanical engineering, medical engineering, information technology management, manufacturing management

Civil Engineering; civil and structural engineering

Postgraduate; civil and structural engineering

Chemical Engineering; chemical engineering

Postgraduate; chemical and petroleum engineering

Medical & Healthcare Engineering; clinical technology, medical engineering, healthcare science – clinical engineering

Media Design & Technology;

Film and Media; digital media, digital film and television production, film studies, photography for digital media, media studies, media studies with cinematics/television, media technology and production

Postgraduate; digital arts and media, digital filmmaking, film studies, media studies, music video creation, professional media practice, media production and entrepreneurship

Games, Animation and Visual Effects; computer animation and visual effects, computer animation, graphics for games, interactive systems and video games design

Postgraduate; advanced computer animation and visual effects, computer animation and visual effects, creative technology by research, visual computing, visual effects post-production

Design; product design, web design and technology, web design and technology

Postgraduate; web technologies

BEng(Hons), BSc(Hons), BA(Hons), FD, MEng, MPhil, MSc, PhD

School of Health Studies; www.brad.ac.uk/acad/health

acute & critical care, adult/child/mental health, nursing, dementia/studies/& older people, diversity management, health/wellbeing & social care, leadership & management in children's/social care, long term conditions, mental health, mentorship, clinical education and practice development, midwifery, reproductive & child health, occupational therapy, physiotherapy, public health & well being, public health nursing, diagnostic radiography, sport rehabilitation, practitioners with a special interest

AdvDip, BSc(Hons), CertHE, DipHE, FD, MSc, MPhil, PGDip/Cert, PhD

School of Life Sciences; www.brad.ac.uk/acad/lifesci

archaeological sciences, archaeology, biomedical science, chemistry, chemistry for analysis/drug discovery/forensic sciences/medicines development, chemistry with pharmaceutical & forensic science, clinical sciences, forensic & medical sciences, forensic archaeology & anthropology, forensic science, foundation in clinical sciences/medicine, healthcare science (life sciences), integrated science, optometry, pharmacy, biomedical science, cancer pharmacology, cancer drug discovery, clinical pharmacy, drug toxicology & safety pharmacology, human osteology and palaeopathology analytical sciences, pharmaceutical technology, archaeology, archaeological prospection/sciences, forensic archaeology & crime scene investigation, human osteology & palaeopathology; BSc(Hons), MPhil, PhD, MChem, MPharm, CertHE, MSc, MSci(Hons)

The School of Management (inc Law); www.brad.ac.uk/acad/management

business studies & law, accounting & finance, law, financial planning, HRM, marketing; Masters; applied management & enterprise, applied management & sustainability, finance, finance accounting & management, HRM, international marketing, international business & management, management, marketing & management, strategic marketing, sustainable operations & management, law; BA(Hons), BSc(Hons), DBA, LlB, LlM, GradDip(-Law), MBA, MRes, PhD, MSc, PGCert/Dip

The School of Social and International Studies; www.brad.ac.uk/acad/ssis

Economics; economics, business economics, financial economics, economics and international economics, economics with international relations, economics with development studies, economics with marketing, economics and history; PostGrad; economics, financial economics

International Development; Post Grad; development and project planning, economics and finance for development, human and organisational capacity building, international development management, project planning and management, public administration

Peace Studies; development and peace studies, international relations and security studies, history and politics, politics, peace studies; PostGrad;African peace and conflict studies, applied dual-use biosecurity education, conflict resolution, conflict, security and development, international politics and security studies, peace studies, peace, conflict and development

Psychology; psychology, psychology with counselling; Postgrad; psychology, sociology & criminology, sociology and psychology, sociology, applied criminal justice studies, psychology and crime, social sciences and management, criminal justice, human trafficking and contemporary slavery, PostGrad; ethnic diversity and community cohesion, family change, behaviour and policy, identity and the self Social Work and Social Care: social work, working with children, young people and families; Post Grad; social work; BA(Hons), BSc(Hons), MA, MPhil, PhD, PGDip, MPA

Degrees validated by University of Bradford offered at:

BRADFORD COLLEGE
www.bradfordcollege.ac.uk

film, photography, law (accountancy /marketing/ social), law and legal practice, legal integration, primary education with QTS, teaching and learning in the primary phase) with QTS, PGCE primary: primary (general), primary (French), PGCE secondary KS2/3, 11–16) science, physics, physics with mathematics, chemistry, mathematics, English, citizenship; design (food technology), post compulsory education, teaching 14–19 & adults, education and training in-service, initial teacher education, social care & community practice: childhood & youth studies, social care & community practice: health & social care, counselling and psychology in community settings, health and social welfare, social work, youth and community development, computer networks and systems support, computing, computing and information systems, computing and systems development, games and digital media, internet applications, contact lenses, ophthalmic dispensing; BSc(Hons), CertHE, DipHE, BA(Hons), LlB(Hons), BEngTechMA, MEd, PGDipCert, MSc, PGCE, FD, LawPGDip, LlM

UNIVERSITY OF BRIGHTON
www.brighton.ac.uk

College of Arts & Humanities; www.arts.brighton.ac.uk

Architecture & Interiors; architecture, interior architecture/design, architecture & urban design, arts & cultural research

Design; 3D design & craft, craft, sustainable design English Language Teacher Education; TESOL, English language teaching, TESOL with HCT
Literature; English literature & media studies, history, literature & culture, English literature, English

language & English literature, media & English literature, creative writing
Fashion & Textile Design; fashion/communication with business studies, textiles with business studies
Fine Art Practices; art & design by independent practice, digital media arts, sequential design/illustration, fine art, fine art (painting/printmaking/sculpture/critical practice), moving images, sequential design/illustration, performance & visual practice
Fine Art Performance, Music, Theatre Dance; theatre performance, visual art, music & visual art, performance & visual performance
History of Art & Design; fashion & dress history, history of decorative arts & crafts, history of decorative art & craft, history of design/art & design, museum & heritage studies, fashion & dress culture, visual culture, philosophy, politics & art, arts & cultural research, history of design & material culture
Humanities: History, Philosophy, Culture & Politics; politics, philosophy & ethics, globalisation, history, humanities/politics, craft & human rights, cultural & craft theory, politics/literature & culture, humanities, war, history & politics, applied ethics, culture & cultural theory, cultural history, memory & identity, arts & cultural research, literary culture, philosophy, politics & art
Language & Linguistics; English language, English language & linguistics, arts & cultural research, linguistics, English literature & language/media, philosophy of language
Media; media and English literature, film and screen studies, TV and digital media production, English literature and media studies, environment and media studies, media, industry and innovation, multimedia broadcast journalism, media studies, English language and media, digital film, broadcast media, TV production, arts and cultural research, creative media
Photography, Moving Image & Sound; photography, digital music & sound arts, moving image, film & screen studies arts & cultural research; BA(Hons), FdSA, Grad Dip, MA, MDes, MFA, MPhil, MRes, PGDip/Cert, PhD, MArch

College of Social Sciences

School of Education; www.brighton.ac.uk/educa
initial teacher training; primary and secondary; school direct or troops to teachers, further education and training, early years teachers programme, education, education (partnerships for learning), early childhood education and care, media studies

and education, education and English literature, computing and education, education and sociology/mathematics/human biology/environmental biology, early childhood practice, professional studies in learning and development, supporting learning 5–11 years/11–19 years, working with children and young people, youth work, adult learning and development, professional studies in learning and development, professional development, education leadership and management, mathematics for secondary school teachers, one-to-one learning relationships, primary mathematics specialist teacher programme, science education for primary and secondary school teachers, strategies for working with autistic learners, strategies for working with dyslexic learners, professional education studies, education (leadership and management/international education/higher education/mathematics education/early childhood), BA(Hons), BSc(Hons), MSc, MA, FdA, CertEd, PGCert/Dip, QTS, PGCE, EdD, MPhil, PhD

School of Sport & Service Management; www.brighton.ac.uk/sasm
hospitality, international hospitality management, retail management, retail marketing, journalism, sport journalism, sport and exercise science, sport and fitness, applied exercise physiology, applied sport physiology, sport coaching/and development, sport studies, sport business management, sport and international development, sport and media, sport and society, sport and social anthropology, physical education, international travel management, international tourism management with travel business, tourism and international development, tourism and social anthropology, PE with QTS degree/ PGCE, dance (secondary) PGCE; BA(Hons), BSc(Hons), FdA, MA, MSc, PhD, PGCert/Dip

Centre for Learning and Teaching; www.brighton.ac.uk/clt
higher education, learning & teaching in HE; MA, PGCE

School of Applied Social Science; www.brighton.ac.uk/sass
applied psychology/& criminology/sociology, applied social science, approved mental health practice, criminology & social policy/sociology/substance misuse interventions/social justice, community psychology, psychotherapy, mental health, approved mental health practice, politics, sociology, social policy, social work, public admin, social policy,

sociology, adv/social work, social science, sociology & social policy, substance misuse, humanistic/psychodynamic therapeutic counselling; BA(Hons), MA, MPhil, MSc, PGDip/Cert, PhD, MPA, FD, Prof Doc, BSc(Hons), MRes

Brighton Business School; www.brighton.ac.uk/bbs

accounting & finance, business & business management, business, business accounting & finance, business & business management, business with economics/finance/HRM/marketing, business management, business management with economics/finance/HRM/marketing, business with enterprise, international business, economics and finance, finance & investment, business management with economics/finance, marketing, international management/retail management, logistics & supply chain management, management, management (entrepreneurship/HR/innovation/knowledge management), retail management, change management, managing change and innovation, management (leadership for clinicians), general management, MBA, international management, MBA, knowledge & innovation management, MBA, leadership, economics & finance/finance & investment, Postgrad Diploma in Law, Common Professional Examination, CPE, marketing, marketing (branding & communication/digital marketing/international marketing/social marketing); ACCA, BA(Hons), LlB, MBA, MSc, PGCert/Dip, CPE, BSc(Hons)

College of Life, Health & Physical Science; www.brighton.ac.uk/scieng

School of Computing, Engineering & Mathematics; www.brighton.ac.uk/cem

business computer/information systems, computer science/games, computing systems & communication/networking, computing, creative computing, data analytics, digital media/production/development, digital games production, European computing, internet/computing, software engineering, computing, information systems, internet & distributed systems, electrical/ & electronic engineering/computing engineering, software engineering, automotive/electronic engineering, mathematics/with business/finance, aeronautical engineering, mechanical/& manufacturing engineering, product innovation & design, product design/ technology, sports/sustainable product design, user experience design;

BSc(Hons), FdSc, MA, MComp, MPhil, MSc, PGDip/Cert, MEng, BEng

School of Environment and Technology; www.brighton.ac.uk/set

architectural technology, building surveying, construction management, project management for construction, town planning, civil engineering/with environmental engineering/construction management, environmental sciences/media studies, GIS/& sustainability of the built environment/environmental management, water & environmental management, geography, physical geography & geology, geography & archaeology/geoinformatics, earth & ocean science, geology; BA/BSc(Hons), BEng(Hons), BSc(Hons), FdSc, FdEng, MEng, MPhil, PGDip/Cert, PhD

School of Pharmacy and Biomolecular Sciences; www.brighton.ac.uk/pharmacy

biomedical/biological sciences, bioscience, cellular science, chemistry, clinical/general pharmacy practice, pharmacology, ecology, industrial pharmaceutical studies, blood science, infection science, chemical sciences, pharmaceutical & chemical biomedical science, supplementary prescribing for pharmacists; BSc(Hons), MSc, MPharm(Hons), MPhil, MRes, PGDip, PhD

Brighton and Sussex Medical School; www.bsms.ac.uk

anaesthesia and perioperative medicine, cardiology, dementia studies, global health, leadership & commissioning, medical education, medical research, medical toxicology, psychiatry, public health, trauma and orthopaedic; BMBS, MD, MPhil, MSc, PGDip/Cert, PhD

School of Health Science; https:/www.brighton.ac.uk/about-us/contact-us/academic-departments/school-of-health-sciences.aspx

adult nursing, child nursing, or mental health nursing, midwifery, paramedic practice, acute clinical practice, community specialist practice, health studies, nurse practitioner, professional practice, specialist community public health nursing, health and social care practice, physiotherapy and management, neuromusculoskeletal physiotherapy, sports injury management, clinical research, podiatry, occupational therapy, occupational therapy and education/management, clinical research

UNIVERSITY OF BRISTOL
www.bris.ac.uk

Faculty of Arts; www.bris.ac.uk/arts

School of Arts

archaeology/& anthropology, film and television, film and English, film & modern European language, theatre & film; music, music and French/German/Italian, philosophy, English and philosophy, mathematics and philosophy, philosophy and economics/modern European language/politics/theology/physics/sociology, theatre and performance studies, theatre and English/film/modern European language

School of Humanities

ancient history, classics, classical studies, English, English literature and community engagement, English and classical studies/philosophy/film/theatre, history, history of art, history of art and modern European language, religion and theology, theology and sociology, philosophy and theology

School of Modern Languages

modern languages; Czech: Czech and modern European language, French: Czech/film & French, French & modern European language/history of art/law/music/philosophy/politics/theatre and French; German: German & Czech/film & modern European language/ history of art/law/music/philosophy/politics/theatre, Italian; Italian & Czech/film & modern European language/history of art/law/music/philosophy/politics/theatre, Portuguese; Portuguese & Czech/film & modern European language/history of art/law/ philosophy/politics/theatre; Russian: Russian & Czech/modern European language/philosophy/politics; Spanish: Hispanic Studies, Spanish & Czech/film & modern European language/ film/history of art/politics/theatre

Master Programmes in the Faculty of Arts

archaeology, Chinese-English translation, classical reception, composition of music for film and television, English literature, European literatures, film and TV production, film and television studies, history, history of art: histories and interpretations, logic and philosophy of mathematics, modern languages, music, philosophy, philosophy, philosophy and history of science, philosophy and law, religion, translation

BA(Hons), BSc(Hons), LlB, MA, MLitt, MPhil, PGDip, PhD

Faculty of Engineering; www.bris.ac.uk/engineering

Dept of Aerospace Engineering; www.bris.ac.uk/aerospace

integrated aerospace systems design, aeronautical engineering, advanced composites

Dept of Civil Engineering; www.bris.ac.uk/civilengineering

civil engineering, water & environmental management

Dept of Computer Science; www.cs.bris.ac.uk

computer science/& electronic/mathematics, adv computing (internet technologies with security/machine learning & data mining & high performance computing/creative technologies), adv microelectronic systems engineering

Dept of Electrical and Electronic Engineering; www.bris.ac.uk/eeng

optical communications/image & video communications & signals processing, communication networks & signal processing, computer science & electronics, electrical & electronic engineering, electronics & communication engineering, microelectronics & systems, wireless communication systems & signal processing, adv microelectronic & systems engineering, biomedical engineering

Dept of Engineering Mathematics; www.enm.bris.ac.uk

complexity sciences, systems engineering, adv engineering robotics & autonomous systems, neural dynamics, engineering mathematics

Dept of Mechanical Engineering; www.bris.ac.uk/mecheng

mechanical engineering, adv mechanical engineering, engineering design

BSc(Hons), BEng, EngD, PGCert, MEng, MSc, PhD

Faculty of Medical and Veterinary Science; www.bris.ac.uk/mvs

Dept of Biochemistry; www.bris.ac.uk/biochemistry

biochemistry/with molecular biology & biotechnology, biophysics & molecular life sciences, medical biochemistry, biomedical sciences

Dept of Cellular and Molecular Medicine; www.bris.ac.uk/cellmolmed

cancer biology and immunology, cellular and molecular medicine, medical microbiology, pathology and microbiology, virology and immunology, biomedical sciences research

Bristol Veterinary School; www.bris.ac.uk/vetscience
animal behaviour & welfare science, meat science & technology, veterinary nursing & bioveterinary science, veterinary science, global wildlife health & conservation, animal welfare & behaviour & rehab

Dept of Physiology & Pharmacology; www.bris.ac.uk/phys-pharm
biomedical science research, systems/neuroscience, pharmacology, physiological science; BSc(Hons), BVSc, MD, MSc, MSci, PhD

Faculty of Medicine and Dentistry; www.bris.ac.uk/fmd

medicine, surgery, child medicine, dentistry, dental implantology/hygiene/therapy, molecular neuroscience, orthodontics, palliative medicine, reproduction & development, stem cells and regeneration, teaching & learning for health professionals, translational cardiovascular medicine, health science research; MB, BDS, BSc(Hons), ChB, ChM, BDS, Diploma, DPDS, MClinDent, MD, MMedEd, MSci, PhD, DipDent

Faculty of Science; www.bris.ac.uk/science

School of Biological Sciences; www.bris.ac.uk/biology
biology, botany, geology, zoology, palaeontology & evolution, palaeobiology, research biological sciences

School of Chemistry; www.chm.bris.ac.uk
chemistry, chemical physics, inorganic & materials chemistry, organic & biological chemistry, physical & theoretical chemistry, chemical synthesis

School of Earth Sciences; www.bris.ac.uk/earthsciences
environmental geoscience, geology/& biology, geophysics, palaeobiology, volcanology, palaeontology & evolution, earth sciences

Dept of Experimental Psychology; www.psychology.psy.bris.ac.uk
biological psychology, clinical neuroscience, clinical/applied neuropsychology, psychology, neuropsychological studies, experimental psychology

School of Geographical Sciences; www.ggy.bris.ac.uk
geography, human/physical geography, human geography, society & space, geographical science, environmental policy & management, climate change science & policy, quantitative research

Dept of Mathematics; www.maths.bris.ac.uk
applied/pure mathematics, mathematics, mathematics & philosophy/physics/statistics/computer science, statistics & probability, statistics, mathematical science, applied/pure mathematics

Dept of Physics; www.bris.ac.uk/physics
astrophysics, physics, mathematics and physics, nanoscience & functional nanomaterial particle physics, physics/& philosophy, theoretical physics; BSc(Hons), DSc, LlB, MRes, MSci, MSc, PhD, UGCert

Faculty of Social Science and Law; www.bris.ac.uk/fss

Graduate School of Education; www.bris.ac.uk/education
education, psychology of education, education management, policy and international development, leadership and policy, learning, technology and society, mathematics education, neuroscience and education, psychology of education, science education, special and inclusive education, teaching and learning, neuroscience & education, PGCE/School Direct/Teach First TESOL, educational leadership, educational research

School for Policy Studies; www.bristol.ac.uk/sps
social policy, social policy with management/quantitative research methods, social policy and politics/sociology, childhood studies, childhood studies with management/quantitative research methods, global health, disability studies: inclusive theory and research, nutrition, physical activity and public health, public policy, policy research, social work research, social work, advanced social work with children and families

School of Economics, Finance & Management; www.bristol.ac.uk/efm
accounting, finance, management, econometrics, economics, public policy, investment, strategy, change & leadership, economics & mathematics/politics/philosophy, macro/micro economics

School of Law; www.bris.ac.uk/law
law, law and French/ German, socio-legal studies, adv studies legal system

School of Sociology, Politics & International Studies; www.bristol.ac.uk/spais

sociology & politics/quantitative research methods/ politics/social policy/philosophy/theology, politics & international relations/sociology/quantitative research methods/economics/philosophy/social policy/modern languages, identities, ethnicity & multiculturalism, social & cultural theory, European governance, gender, international relations, international security, development & security, E Asian development & global economy, international development

School of Geographical Sciences; www.bris.ac.uk/geography

geography, human geography, physical geography, geography with quantitative research methods, society & space, environmental policy & management, climate change science & policy, geographical sciences

BA(Hons), BSc(Hons), DSocSci, EdD, LlB, LlD, LlM, MEd, MPhil, MSc, MSci, PGCE, PhD, Dip, MEd, DEdPsY

UNIVERSITY OF THE WEST OF ENGLAND, BRISTOL
www.uwe.ac.uk

Faculty of Business & Law; www.uwe.ac.uk/bl

Bristol Business School; www.uwe.ac.uk/bbs

accounting & finance, accounting & financial management, business (team enterprise), business & events management/HRM/law/management, business enterprise, business management (leadership, change & organisations/practice), business management & economics, business studies, business management with accounting & finance/economics/marketing/events management, economics, events management, finance, international business, banking & finance, finance, global trade, leadership & media production management, marketing/communications, HRM, international HRM/management/ tourism management, professional accounting/management, project management, tourism management; BA(Hons), BSc(Hons), MA, MBA, MSc, PhD, MBA, PGDip/Cert, LlM

Bristol Law School; www1.uwe.ac.uk/bl/bls

adv legal practice, commercial law, environmental law & sustainable development, European & international law, international banking & financial/trade law/economic law, global trade, law, bar professional training, legal practice, law & psychology; LlB, LlM, PhD, PGDip

Faculty of Arts, Creative Industries & Education; www.uwe.ac.uk/cahe

Dept of Arts & Cultural Industries; http:/www1.uwe.ac.uk/cahe/arts.aspx

creative media design, drama/ and acting/creative writing, English, English language and linguistics/ English, language/history/journalism/writing, history, history with heritage, literature and film studies, media culture and practice – social media and cultural practice, writing for the cultural industries, linguistics, philosophy and politics; Post Grad; English and drama, European studies, film studies, history, linguistics; BA(Hons), FdA, MA, MPhil, PhD

Dept of Art & Design; www1.uwe.ac.uk/cahe/artanddesign

drawing and print, fashion, fashion communication, fine arts, graphic design, illustration, interior design, art, media and design by project, curating, design, fine art, graphic arts, multi-disciplinary printmaking; BA(Hons), MA, PGDip/Cert, MFA

Dept of Film & Journalism; www1.uwe.ac.uk/cahe/film and journalism

animation, filmmaking, journalism, journalism and PR, media and journalism, photography, documentary and features; BA(Hons), MA, PGDip/Cert

Dept of Education; www1.uwe.ac.uk/cahe/edu

early childhood, early years, education, education in professional practice, education in virtual world, initial teacher education, primary/early years, primary education, PGCE primary – early years (3–7)/ 5–11/education & training, secondary/post-16/post compulsory education & training, training, educational support, inclusive practice, lifelong learning, learning & skills, secondary initial teacher education in art & design/design & technology/history/mathematics with business studies/modern languages/physics with mathematics/chemistry/physics/English/geography, post-compulsory education; ASR, BA(Hons), CertEd, DipHE, MA, MPhil, MSc, PGCert/Dip, PhD, FD, MEd, EdD

Faculty of Environment and Technology; www.uwe.ac.uk/et

Dept of Computer Science & Creative Technologies; www.uwe.ac.uk/et/cst
applied computing, broadcast audio & music technology, business analytics, computer science for games & security, computer systems integration, computing, creative music technology, data science, digital media, enterprise computing, forensic computing & security, games technology, IT management for business, information & library management, information management/technology, mobile technology, software development for business, software engineering; BSc(Hons), MSc, MPhil, PhD, PGDip/Cert, FdSc

Dept of Architecture & the Built Environment; www.uwe.ac.uk/et/cp
architecture, architectural engineering & management, architectural technology & design, architecture & environmental engineering/planning, building information modelling, building services engineering, interior design, international construction law, quantity surveying & commercial management, building surveying/information modelling, construction/project management/product design/management, product design technology, professional practice & management in architecture, property development & planning/investment & management, real estate finance & investment/management, residential property; FDA, BA(Hons), BSc(Hons), MSc, MPhil, PhD, BEng(Hons), MArch, GradDip

Dept of Engineering Design & Mathematics; www.uwe.ac.uk/et/edm
aerospace engineering/manufacture/with pilot studies, automation & computer vision, automotive engineering, creative product design, electrical & electronic engineering, electronic & computer engineering, engineering/management, engineering operations & improvement, electronics & communications, embedded systems & wireless networks, mathematics, mechanical engineering, product design technology, professional engineering, robotics, statistics; BEng, MEng, BSc(Hons), MPhil, PhD

Dept of Geography & Environmental Management; www.uwe.acf.uk/et/gem
civil & environment engineering, geography, applied GIS, civil/& environmental engineering, environmental conservation/management, river & coastal engineering, sustainable development in practice, traffic engineering, transport engineering/ & planning, uniformed & public services, urban/& rural planning; BA(Hons), BSc(Hons), PGradDip, MPhil, PhD, FdSc

Dept of Planning & Architecture; www.uwe.ac.uk/et/pa
architecture & planning, architectural technology & design, environment engineering, geography, interior architecture, town & country planning, spatial/transport planning, urban design/planning; BA(Hons), BSc(Hons), BArch, MA, MSc, MPlan, MPhil, PhD

Faculty of Health & Life Sciences; www.uwe.ac.uk/hls

Dept of Allied Health Professions; www.uwe.ac.uk/hls/ahp
diagnostic imaging, applied/paramedic science, health professions, physiotherapy, health professions, occupational therapy, radiotherapy & oncology, medical ultrasound, nuclear medicine, physical activity & community health, sports therapy & rehabilitation; FdSc, BSc(Hons), MSc, PGDip/Cert, MPhil, PhD

Dept of Biological, Biomedical & Analytical Sciences; www.uwe.ac.uk/hls/as
adv forensic analysis, biological science, environmental health/science, forensic science, healthcare science (life sciences/physiological sciences), integrated wildlife conservation, biosensing technologies, premedical science, practical science communication, wildlife & conservation science/in practice; FdSc, BSc(Hons), MSc, MRes, ProfDoc, PGCert/Dip, MPhil, PhD, CertHE

Dept of Health & Social Sciences; www.uwe.ac.uk/hls/hass
criminology/& criminal justice/sociology/psychology, counselling/occupational psychology, environmental health, European philosophy, psychology/& health, integrated professional development (social work), philosophy, public health, social work/with adults, health/communication psychology, politics &

international relations, professional development, psychology with criminology/law/sociology, social work studies/with adults, sociology, specialist community public health/& environmental health, occupational psychology, professional development (practical skills/therapeutic education/psycho-social studies/social work), public health, public health (specialist community public health nursing), sport & exercise science, music therapy; FdA, BSc(Hons), BA(Hons), MSc, PGDip/Cert, GradDip, MPhil, PhD

Dept of Nursing & Midwifery; www.uwe.ac.uk/hls/nm

care management in the community, health and social care practice, midwifery, nursing (adult nursing/children's nursing/learning disabilities nursing/mental health nursing), professional studies, specialist practice, advanced practice, health and social care; FdSc, BSc(Hons), MSc, PGDip/Cert, ProfDoc, MPhil, PhD

Dept of Psychology; www.uwe.ac.uk/hls/psychology

psychology, psychology & criminology/law/sociology, psychological therapy (cognitive behaviour/relational psychotherapy), counselling psychology, occupational psychology, psychological; BA(Hons), BSc(Hons), MSc, DPS, ProfDoc, MPhil, PhD

Hartpury College (Associate Faculty); www.hartpury.ac.uk

animal behaviour & veterinary science/welfare, animal science management, equine performance & rehabilitation/behaviour & welfare/science, coaching science, PE & school sport, physiology, sport management/studies/injury management/business management/coaching performance/therapy, professional development (coaching science), sport & exercise nutrition, sport conditioning & injury management, sport management (equine/golf), equine veterinary nursing, veterinary nursing/science; BA(Hons), BSc(Hons), FdSc, FdA, MA, MSc, PGDip/Cert

BRUNEL UNIVERSITY
www.brunel.ac.uk

College of Business, Arts and Social Sciences; www.brunel.ac.uk/cbass

Department of Arts and Humanities; www.brunel.ac.uk/cbass/arts-humanities

composition, creative writing, English and film and TV studies, English, English with creative writing, music, performance, sonic arts, theatre and creative writing/English, theatre and film and TV studies, theatre: postgraduate: contemporary performance, creative writing/the novel, experimental music

Brunel Business School; www.brunel.ac.uk/cbass/bbs

business and management (accounting/marketing), business and management, international business, business administration, accounting and business management, applied corporate brand management, business intelligence and social media, global supply chain management, HRM, human resources and employment relations, international business, management, marketing; BSc, MSc, MBA, PhD

Dept of Economics & Finance; www.brunel.ac.uk/cbasse/economics-finance

economics and accounting, economics and business finance/management, economics, finance and accounting, politics and economics

Postgraduate; banking and finance, business finance, finance and accounting, finance and investment; BSc, MSc, PhD

Politics, History and the Brunel Law School; www.brunel.ac.uk/cbasse/politics-history-law

history, international politics, law, law with criminal justice/international arbitration & commercial law/professional placement, politics and economics/history/ sociology, politics

Postgraduate; law, intellectual property law, intelligence and security studies, international commercial law, international financial regulation and corporate law, international human rights law, international intellectual property law, international relations, law, military history, public affairs and lobbying; BA, BSc, LlB, LlM, PGCert, MSc, GradDip, CPE, PGCert, PhD, MPhil

Dept of Education; www.brunel.ac.uk/cbasse/education

education, teaching (MAT), PGCE (PGCert) primary education (5–11 years)/computer science and information and communications technology, PGCE (PGCert) secondary education (English/mathematics/physical education/physics with mathematics/science with biology/science with chemistry/science with physics) with recommendation for QTS; BA, MA, PhD

Department of Social Sciences, Media and Communications; www.brunel.ac.uk/cbasse/social-sciences-me

anthropology/ and sociology, communication and media studies, English/ and film and TV studies, games design/ and creative writing/ film and television studies, journalism, sociology/ and media studies, theatre and film and television studies Postgraduate; anthropology of childhood, youth and education, anthropology of international development and humanitarian assistance, digital games theory and design, documentary practice, international journalism, media and communications, media and public relations, medical anthropology, psychological and psychiatric anthropology, social and cultural research, social anthropology; BA, MA, MSc, MRes, PhD

College of Engineering, Design & Physical Sciences; www.brunel.ac.uk/cedps

Department of Computer Science; www.brunel.ac.uk/cedps/computer-science

business computing (ebusiness)/human computer interaction/social media, business computing computer science (artificial intelligence/digital media and games/network computing/software engineering), computer science, information systems, computing and mathematics

Department of Design; www.brunel.ac.uk/cedps/design

industrial design and technology, product design, product design engineering

Department of Electronics and Computer Engineering; www.brunel.ac.uk/cedps/electronics-computing

computer systems engineering (networks/software), computer systems engineering digital design, electrical engineering with renewable energy systems, electronic and communications engineering, electronic and computer engineering, electronic and electrical engineering, engineering, professional development, visual effects and motion graphics

Department of Mathematics; www.brunel.ac.uk/cedps/mathematics

financial mathematics, information systems, computing and mathematics, professional development, mathematics and statistics with management mathematics, mathematics with computer science

Department of Mechanical, Aerospace and Civil Engineering; www.brunel.ac.uk/cedps/mechanical-aerospace

aerospace engineering, automotive engineering, aviation engineering, aviation engineering with pilot studies, civil engineering, civil engineering/with sustainability, engineering, professional development, mechanical and energy engineering, mechanical engineering, mechanical engineering, mechanical engineering with aeronautics/ automotive design, motorsport engineering

Postgraduate; advanced electronic and electrical engineering, advanced engineering design, advanced instrumentation and smart systems, advanced manufacturing systems, advanced mechanical engineering, advanced multimedia design and 3D technologies, aerospace engineering, automotive and motorsport engineering, bioengineering, biomedical genetics and tissue engineering, biomedical, biomechanics and bioelectronics engineering, building services engineering management, building services engineering, building services engineering with sustainable energy, business systems integration (with sap technology), computer communication networks, data science and analytics, design and branding strategy, design strategy and innovation, digital design and branding, digital service design, distributed computing systems engineering, embedded systems (multimedia communications), embedded systems (signal processing), engineering management, financial mathematics, information systems management, integrated product design, oil and gas engineering, project and infrastructure management renewable energy engineering, structural engineering, structural integrity, sustainable electrical power, sustainable energy – technologies and management, water engineering, wireless communication systems

BA(Hons), BEng, BSc(Hons), EngD, MEng, MPhil, MSc, PhD, MMath, FdSc, MA, PGDip/Cert

College of Health and Life Sciences; *www.brunel.ac.uk/chls*

Dept of Clinical Sciences; www.brunel.ac.uk/chls/clinical sciences

occupational therapy, physiotherapy, social work, specialist community public health nursing, specialist social work (adults) (children and families),
Postgraduate; ageing studies, children, youth and international development, health information for clinical management, neurorehabilitation, occupational therapy, physiotherapy, public health and health promotion, social work, specialist community public health nursing, public health
BSc, BA, MA, PGCert, DPh, Ph

Dept of Life Sciences; www.brunel.ac.uk/ chls-life-sciences

biomedical sciences (biochemistry)/genetics/human health/biomedical sciences (immunology), biomedical sciences, PE and youth sport, psychology and anthropology/sociology, psychology, sport, health and exercise sciences (coaching/human performance/ sport development), sport, health and exercise sciences/with business
Postgraduate; ageing studies, children, youth and international development, climate change impacts and sustainability, cross-cultural psychology, environmental science – legislation and management/ pollution and monitoring, evolutionary psychology, functional neuroimaging, health information for clinical management, molecular medicine and cancer research, molecular medicine, neurorehabilitation, occupational therapy, physiotherapy, psychoanalysis and contemporary society, psychological sciences, psychology, health and behaviour, public health and health promotion, social work, social work, specialist community public health nursing, sport and exercise psychology, sport, health and exercise sciences (human performance/sport psychology), sport, health and exercise sciences, sustainability, entrepreneurship and design, toxicology and risk assessment; BSc, MSc, MA, BA, PGDip/Cert, PhD

University Specialist Research Institutes offer postgraduate degree opportunities

UNIVERSITY OF BUCKINGHAM
www.buckingham.ac.uk

Buckingham Business School; www.buckingham.ac.uk/business

business and management, marketing, accounting and financial management, business enterprise
Postgrad; MBA, accounting and finance, finance and investment, management in a service economy, management in a global service economy, continuous improvement in public services, lean enterprise; BSc(Econ)(Hons), BSc(Hons), CMS, MBA, MSc/ Diploma

School of Humanities; *www.buckingham.ac.uk/humanities*

Department of Art History and Heritage Studies; www.buckingham.ac.uk/art-history

art history and heritage management/English literature/French/history/journalism/Spanish
Postgraduate; decorative arts and historic interiors, history of art: Renaissance to modernism; BA(Hons), MA

School of Education; www.buckingham.ac.uk/education

Teacher's Standards: primary/secondary PGCE with QTS, educational leadership, middle leadership; MEd, BA(Hons), MPhil, DPhil, PGCert, CML

Dept of Economics & International Studies; www.buckingham.ac.uk/economics-international

Politics, Security & International Studies; international relations/politics with applied computing/ economics/English language studies/French/journalism/Spanish, international studies, politics and economics/history/ applied computing/English language studies/French/journalism/Spanish, economics and law, international affairs and diplomacy, global affairs, security and intelligence studies, global affairs and diplomacy, security, intelligence and diplomacy economics and international studies
Economics; business economics, economics, economics with applied computing/English language studies/French/history/journalism/politics/ Spanish, economics, business and law

Postgraduate; economics; BA(Hons), BSc(Econ)Hons, DPhil, MA, MPhil, MSc

Dept of Modern Foreign Languages; www.buckingham.ac.uk/mfl

French/Spanish as minor subject with business and management/economics/English literature/business studies/journalism/law/marketing/psychology/marketing, range of languages taught for part of joint degrees; BA(Hons), BSc(Hons), LlB(Hons)

Dept of English; www.buckingham.ac.uk/english

English language/literature, communication & media studies, media, journalism, biography, English studies for teaching/journalism/with media communication, English literature with English literature studies/French/history/journalism/psychology/Spanish, journalism with communication studies/English literature/French/Spanish/English language studies; BA(Hons), MA

London Programmes; www.buckingham.ac.uk/london

archaeology, Stonehenge a landscape, international affairs & diplomacy, biography, decorative arts & historic interiors, history of art renaissance to modernism, modern war studies, contemporary military history, military history, human rights, history; MA

Buckingham Law School; www.buckingham.ac.uk/law

law, international and commercial law; LlB, LLM, MPhil, DPhil, PGDip

Medical School; www.buckingham.ac.uk/medicine

PG medical school, general internal medicine, clinical science; Clinical MD, MBChB, MSc, BDS

School of Science; www.buckingham.ac.uk/science

Dept of Applied Computing; www.buckingham.ac.uk/applied computing

computing and software entrepreneurship/accounting and finance/ business and management/communication studies/economics
Postgraduate; computing, innovative computing, applied computing; BSc(Hons), MSc, MPhil, PhD, GradDip/Cert

Dept of Psychology; www.buckingham.ac.uk/psychology

psychology/with applied computing, media communications/business & management/Spanish/French/English literature/marketing; BSc(Hons), MPhil, MSc, PhD

Clore Laboratory; www.buckingham.ac.uk/clore

diabetes, obesity & metabolic research, molecular genetics, biochemistry, biochemical informatics, nutrition, dermatology; DPhil, MPhil, MSc

---

BUCKINGHAMSHIRE NEW UNIVERSITY
www.bucks.ac.uk

Art & Design

art & design/practice, art design & media, fashion design, graphic arts, illustration, internal spatial design, kitchen design, product design, furniture design & make, conservation of furniture & decorative arts, textile & surface design; BA(Hons), MA, FDA, Dip

Business & Management

advanced management & digital communications, accounting/business & finance, business & HRM/marketing, business management/law, marketing, business management, HRM, international accounting finance/business, PR & marketing communications, football business & marketing/media, sport business management, leadership & management, sport business retailing & marketing/coaching/media, MBAs; BA(Hons), MA, BSc(Hons), LlB(Hons), FDA, PGDip, MBA

Children & Young People

childhood & adolescent studies, child protection & adult safeguarding, early years practice, assistant practitioner (childcare/maternity & newborn), practice development (early years/primary education/working with children & young people), nursing (children), primary education, professional practice (early years); BSc(Hons), FDA, MSc

Computer Technology & New Media

computing & web development, software engineering, computing, games development, independent games production, technology enhanced learning; BA(Hons), BSc(Hons), FDSc, MSc

Education

education, early years practice, learning & teaching in HE, primary education, professional practice (primary education & education/working with children & young people), children & adolescence, working with children & young people; BA(Hons), MA, FDA, ProfDoc, PGCert

Furniture

art & design practice, furniture: design & make, conservation of furniture & decorative arts; BA(Hons), MA, FDA

Health & Nursing

specialist community public health nursing, community health care nursing (district nursing), professional practice (healthcare) psychotherapeutic approaches in mental health, health and social care, professional practice (integrated health and social care), advanced practice, professional practice (integrated health and social care), independent and supplementary nurse prescribing, professional practice (cancer and palliative care), professional practice (working with children and young people), health care practice (cardiac care), professional practice (critical care), professional practice (cardiothoracic care), professional practice, professional practice (policing), professional practice (renal care/respiratory care/cardiac care), sport, exercise and health, specialist community public health nursing, assistant practitioner (longer term care and care of older people), professional practice (primary education and education), renal care, professional practice (cancer care/early years) assistant practitioner (immediate critical and peri-operative care), professional practice (palliative care), assistant practitioner (child care), nursing (adult), nursing studies, assistant practitioner (acute rehabilitation), professional practice (mental health), nursing (mental health), professional practice (healthcare), assistant practitioner (maternity and newborn), professional practice (working with children and young people/child/dementia care/vascular care/peri-operative care/emergency and unscheduled care/renal care), assistant practitioner (mental health), healthcare practice,

enhanced consultation skills, enhanced paramedic skills, operating department practice, working with children and young people, nursing (adult/children's/mental health); BSc(Hons), MSc, FDSc, PGCert/Dip, DipHE, MPhil, PhD

Law

law, business law, international commercial law, sport business & business law; LlB, LlM

Media, Dance & Performance

dance & fitness, performance, musical theatre, performance arts (film/TV/stage); BA(Hons), MA, FDA

Media Production

animation & visual effects, audio & music production, film & TV production, creative writing for publication, 3D animation; BA(Hons), FDA

Music & Event Management

music & live/event management, music business & brand marketing, music management & artist development, studio production, music performance management, event & festival sustainability management, event & festival management, stadium & event management; BA(Hons), MA, FDA

Performance & Dance

professional dance, development, dance and fitness, performing arts, performing arts (film, TV and stage), dance and performance; BA(Hons), MA

Psychology

sports psychology, criminological psychology, psychology, applied positive psychology, sports psychology, criminological psychology, psychology and sociology/criminology, criminological psychology, mental health and educational practice, psychosocial interventions, cognitive behavioural therapy, applied positive psychology; BSc(Hons), MSc, GradDip

Security & Resilience

security management, organisational resilience, security consultancy, protective security management, crowd safety management; BA(Hons), MSc, FDA

Social Science & Policing

criminology and sociology, police studies and criminal justice, social work, criminology, criminology, communities and disorder, behavioural sciences, cognitive behavioural therapy, mental health and educational practice, health and social care, psychology, applied positive psychology, animal welfare & behaviour, police studies with criminological psychology/criminal investigation, policing; BSc(Hons), MSc, FDSc, FDA, PGDip

Social Work

child & adolescent studies, child protection & adult safeguarding, health & social care, social innovation, social work; BSc(Hons), MSc, FDA, PGDip, ProfDoc

Sport & Fitness

exercise, health and fitness management, sports coaching and performance, health exercise and well-being, health rehabilitation and exercise, sports psychology, sport, exercise and health, coaching science, sport management and officiating, sports business and sports law, sports business and coaching, sports business, retailing and merchandising, stadium and events management, football business and marketing, football business and finance, international football business, football business and media, sport business management, sports business and coaching, sports development and coaching, sports marketing, sport and exercise science BA(Hons), MSc, FDA, BSc(Hons), FDSc

Travel & Aviation

airline and airport management, air transport with commercial pilot training, international tourism management with air travel, international travel and tourism management, air transport with private pilot training; BSc(Hons), BA(Hons)

UNIVERSITY OF CAMBRIDGE
www.cam.ac.uk

Arts and Humanities; www.csah.cam.ac.uk

Faculty of Architecture and History of Art; www.aha.cam.ac.uk

architecture/and urban design/practice, professional practice, interdisciplinary design in the built environment, British architecture, building history, history of art, medieval art & architecture, Renaissance art & architecture, sustainable building, conflict in the city, 20th-century art & theory, western & non-western cultural exchange; BA, MPhil, MSt, PhD

Faculty of Asian & Middle Eastern Studies; www.ames.cam.ac.uk

Chinese studies, Hebrew and Semitic studies, Japanese studies, Korean studies, Arabic & Persian studies, East Asia, Middle Eastern/Southern Asia studies, Assyriology, Egyptology, Indian studies; BA, MPhil, PhD

Faculty of Classics; www.classics.cam.ac.uk

classics & Latin literature, history, philology and linguistics, philosophy, Greek & Roman studies, Greek and Latin literature, philosophy, philology and linguistics; BA, MPhil, PGCE, PhD

Faculty of Divinity; www.divinity.cam.ac.uk

biblical studies, history of Christianity, Jewish, early Christian studies, history of Christianity, religious studies, late antiquity, Old Testament/New Testament Christian theology, systematic theology, religious studies, the philosophy of religion, world religions/ Christianity, ministry, patristics, scriptural language; BA, MPhil, PhD, PGDip

Faculty of English; www.english.cam.ac.uk

American literature, Anglo-Saxon, Norse & Celtic, English & applied linguistics, medieval/English literature studies, European languages & literatures, English studies: criticism & culture/18th-century & romantic studies/medieval & renaissance literature, literary theory, middle English, modern & contemporary literature; BA, MLitt, MPhil, PhD

Faculty of Modern and Medieval Languages; www.mml.cam.ac.uk/

French, German & Dutch, Italian, Spanish & Portuguese, European literature, theoretical & applied/ linguistics, modern Greek, neo-Latin, Polish, Russian studies, screen & media cultures, Slavonic studies, Ukrainian, European & comparative literatures & cultures; BA, MPhil, PhD

Faculty of Music; www.mus.cam.ac.uk

ethnomusicology, music studies, music/with education studies, analysis, jazz & pop music, performance studies, recitals, tonal compositions & analysis & repertoire, musical composition, choral studies, Western classical tradition, cultural musicology, ethnomusicology, historical musicology, music and science, music before 1600, nineteenth-century music, opera studies, performance studies, popular and media music, theory and analysis; BA, MPhil, PhD, MMusD

Faculty of Philosophy; www.phil.cam.ac

ethics, experimental psychology, history of philosophy, logic, metaphysics, philosophy of science, political philosophy, aesthetics, mathematical logic, ancient philosophy; BA, MPhil, PhD, MLitt

Humanities & Social Sciences; www.cshss.cam.ac.uk

Faculty of Human, Social & Political Science

Dept of Archaeology and Anthropology; www.hsps.cam.ac.uk

archaeological heritage & museum/science, Aegean prehistory, archaeology, archaeology of the Americas, biological anthropology, Egyptian archaeology, Egyptology, Assyriology, European prehistory, human evolutionary studies, medieval archaeology/Britain, Mesopotamian studies, palaeolithic & mesolithic archaeology, social anthropology, south Asian archaeology; BA, MPhil, PhD

Dept of Politics & International Relations; www.hsps.cam.ac.uk

politics/and international relations/sociology, public policy; MPhil, PhD

Dept of Sociology; www.sociology/cam.ac.uk

sociology, social theory, economic and political sociology, media, culture and new technologies, gender, reproduction and family life, public health and biomedicine; MA, MPhil, PhD

Centre of Latin American Studies; www.latin-america.cam.ac.uk

Latin American studies; MPhil, PhD

Centre of African Studies; www.africa.cam.ac.uk

African studies; MPhil

Centre of South Asian Studies

modern South Asian studies; MPhil

Dept of Social Sciences

Centre of Development studies; www.devstudies.cam.ac.uk

development studies; MPhil, PhD

Centre for Family Research; www.cfr.cam.ac.uk

bioethics & the family, early social development & the family, genetics, health & families, non-traditional families, parent, children & family relationships, psychotherapeutics, social & cognitive development & the family, genetics, health and the family; MPhil, PhD

The Psychometrics Centre; www.psychometrics.cam.ac.uk

MPhil, PhD

Faculty of Economics; www.econ.cam.ac.uk

asset pricing, behavioural economics, economic theory, finance & economics, microeconomics, quantitative methods, microeconomics, macroeconomics, macroeconometrics, economics, economics research; BA, Adv Diploma, MPhil, PhD

Faculty of Education; www.educ.cam.ac.uk

philosophy, psychology, sociology or history of education, children and literature, creativity and thinking, educational inclusion and diversity, PGCE in early primary, primary, secondary subject specialities in: art, classics, design and technology, English, geography, history, mathematics, modern languages, music, science with biology, chemistry or physics, religious studies educational research, arts culture and education, critical approaches to children's literature, educational leadership and school improvement, mathematics education, perspectives on inclusive and special education, politics, development and democratic education, psychology and education, research in second language, education, researching practice, science teacher researchers and practitioners; BA, MEd, PGCE, PGDip/Cert, PhD, MPhil

Faculty of History; www.hist.cam.ac.uk

American history, British/early modern history, economic, social & cultural history, mid/European history, modern European history, ancient & medieval history, political thought & intellectual history, world history, modern British history, early modern history, modern European history, world history; BA, MPhil, PhD

History and Philosophy of Science; www.hps.cam.ac.uk

general philosophy of science, history of ancient and medieval science, technology and medicine, history of early modern science, history of modern science, technology and medicine, history, philosophy and sociology of the life sciences, history, philosophy and sociology of the physical and mathematical sciences, history, philosophy and sociology of the social and psychological sciences, history, philosophy and sociology of medicine, ethics and politics of science, history and methodology of history, philosophy and sociology of science, technology and medicine; BA, MPhil, PhD

Faculty of Law; www.law.cam.ac.uk

criminological research, criminology, international law, law, legal studies, civil law, communication law, European law, large range of legal topics at

Master level; BA, Diploma, LLD, LLM, MLitt, MPhil, PhD, MCL

Institute of Criminology; www.crim.cam.ac.uk
applied/criminology, penology/& management, police management; MPhil, MSt, PhD

Dept of Land Economy; www.landecon.cam.ac.uk
land economy, planning, growth & regeneration, real estate finance, environmental policy, environment, law & economics; BA, MPhil, PhD

School of Biological Sciences; www.cam.ac.uk/sbs

Faculty of Biology; www.cam.ac.uk

Biochemistry; www.bio.cam.ac.uk
biology of cells, biological science, computational biology, systems biology, evolution & behaviour, biochemistry & molecular biology

Psychology; www.psych.cam.ac.uk
psychology & human behaviour, experimental psychology, social & developmental psychology, neuropsychology, psychology by research, psychology & behavioural science, natural science

Genetics; www.gen.cam.ac.uk
mathematical biology, molecules in medical science, cells & developmental biology, genetics, ecology, systems biology, biology of cells

Centre for Family Research; www.cfr.cam.ac.uk
early social development & the family, non-traditional families, genetics, health and family, bioethics & the family, social development & the family

Pathology; www.path.cam.ac.uk
graduate clinical course in medicine

Pharmacology; www.pha.ca.ac.uk
pharmacology, medicinal chemistry, design/use of medicine

Physiology, Development & Neuroscience; www.pdn.cam.ac.uk
biological & biomedical sciences, physiology, neuroscience, neurobiology, developmental biology, stem cell biology, ageing, integrative biology

Plant Science; www/pplant.cam.ac.uk
bioenergy, cell biology and development, crop improvement and protection, epidemiology, ecology and evolution, systems biology, mathematical modelling, plant science, cell & developmental biology, ecology, plant & microbiological science, biology of cells

Zoology; www.zoo.cam.ac.uk
animal biology, cell & developmental biology, ecology, zoology, neurobiology/science, molecular

biology, infection & immunology, mathematical genomics & medicine; BA, MPhil, PhD

Faculty of Veterinary Medicine

Department of Veterinary Medicine; www.vet.cam.ac.uk
Clinical Course: veterinary science, preclinical course; MPhil, VetMB

Wellcome Trust Centre for Stem Cell Research; www.cscr.cam.ac.uk
stem cell biology, mammalian stem cells; PhD

Wellcome Trust/Cancer Research UK Gurdon InstituteTechnology; www.gurdon.cam.ac.uk
cellular & molecular biology, developmental, cell & cancer biology; PhD

School of Technology; www.tech.ac.uk

Faculty of Engineering; www.eng.cam.ac.uk
aerospace and aerothermal engineering, bioengineering, civil, structural and environmental engineering, electrical and electronic engineering, electrical and information sciences, energy, sustainability and the environment, information and computer engineering, instrumentation and control, mechanical engineering, manufacturing engineering, chemical engineering, management studies, energy, fluid mechanics & turbomechanics, materials design, civil, structural and environmental engineering, construction engineering, geotechnology & environmental structures, interdisciplinary design/future interaction and/ for the built environment, engineering sustainability, engineering for sustainable development, applied mechanics, manufacture & management, industrial systems, practice & management, gas turbine aerodynamics, graphene technology, information engineering, engineering for life sciences, turbomachines, energy & fluid mechanics, electrical engineering, energy technologies, mechanics, materials & design, manufacture & management, manufacturing engineering, nuclear engineering, sustainable development, production processes, integrated photonic & electronic systems, ultra precision; BA(Hons), MEng, MPhil, PhD

Faculty of Business & Management (Judge Business School); www.jbs.cam.ac.uk
Exec MBA; corporate finance, accounting, management practice, operations management, marketing, management of technology & innovation, innovation

strategy & organisation management science & operations, professional practice, entrepreneurship; management, technology policy, entrepreneurship, general management & leadership, programme of achievement, strategy, innovation, people & management, finance & accounting, marketing, operations management, professional service firms; MBA, MFin, MPhil, PhD, PGDip

Faculty of Computer Science & Technology; www.cl.cam.ac.uk

adv/computer science, AI, computer architecture, computer science, digital technology, graphics & integrated action, natural language & information, network architecture, internet user interface, forensic signal analysis, language processing, embedded systems, programming logic & semantics, security, systems research; BA, MPhil, PhD

Department of Chemical Engineering & Biotechnology; www.ceb.cam.ac.uk

advanced/ chemical engineering, biotechnology, innovation, materials, measurement, metrology, bioscientific enterprise, modelling, processes, sensor technology & enterprise; BA/MEng, MPhil, PhD

Cambridge Programme for Sustainability Leadership; www.cpi.cam.ac.uk

sustainability, health & care, innovation, sustainable business/leadership/value chains; MSt, PGCert

School of Physical Sciences; www.physci.cam.ac.uk

Faculty of Earth Sciences & Geography; www.physci.cam.ac.uk

Dept of Earth Sciences; www.esc.cam.ac.uk

earth sciences, environmental science, palaeontology, geological sciences, climate change & earth-ocean atmosphere systems, geodynamics, geophysics & tectonics, petrology, igneous, metamorphic & volcanic studies, minerals science, seismology, geophysics, oceanography, sedimentology, tectonics, minerals physics/science, palaeobiology, volcanology, petrology; BA, MPhil, PhD

Dept of Geography; www.geog.cam.ac.uk

geography, earth's atmosphere, glacial environments, globalisation, volcanology, physical geography, polar studies, environmental science/economy, conservation & ecology, hurricanes, coastal geomorphology, future of Africa, conservation leadership, geographies of labour and work, political geographies of violence, the human geography of the Arctic regions, political ecology in the global south, modelling

earth's atmosphere, biogeography, quaternary environments, political geographies of post-colonialism, environment & development/economy, glaciology, multidisciplinary gender studies; BA, MPhil, PhD

Faculty of Mathematics; www.maths.cam.ac.uk

Dept of Applied Mathematics & Theoretical Physics; www.physci.cam.ac.uk/about the school/dampt

mathematical science, applied mathematics, statistical science, theoretical physics, computational biology, quantum mechanics, relativity, fluid dynamics, numerical analysis

Dept of Pure Mathematics & Mathematical Statistics

pure mathematics & mathematical statistics, statistical science; BA, MPhil, PhD, MMath, MAdvStud, MASt

Faculty of Physics & Chemistry; www.cam.ac.uk/physchemfaculty

Institute of Astronomy; www.ast.cam.ac.uk

cosmology and fundamental physics, galaxies and active galactic nuclei, instrumentation, surveys and projects, milky way and local group stars, star formation and exoplanets, stars and stellar evolution, X-ray astrophysics, theoretical & observational astronomy, astrophysics

Dept of Chemistry; www.ch.cam.ac.uk

physical, theoretical, organic, inorganic biochemistry, synthesis, materials chemistry, chemistry, theoretical modelling & information

Dept of Material Science & Metallurgy; www.physci.cam.ac.uk/abouttheschool/materialsscience

materials science, metals, alloys, ceramics, polymers, semiconducting/magnetic/superconducting/ferroelectric/biomedical materials, composites, micro & nanotechnology enterprises, device materials, electron microscopy, materials chemistry, medical & pharmaceutical materials, structural materials, clean energy & sustainability, nuclear energy

Dept of Physics; www.phy.cam.ac.uk

experimental & theoretical physics, astrophysics, scientific computing, nanoscience & technology, atomic/high energy/quantum & condensed matter/thin film magnetism, scientific computing, astrophysics, atomic, mesoscopic and optical physics, biological and soft systems, high energy physics, nanophotonics, optoelectronics, microelectronics, quantum matter, quantum sensors, scientific computing, semiconductor physics, structure and dynamics, surfaces, microstructure and fracture, theory of condensed matter, thin film magnetism; BA, MPhil, MSci, PhD, MASt, MSC, EngD

School of Clinical Medicine;
www.medschl.cam.ac.uk

Dept of Clinical Biochemistry (Metabolic Research Laboratories);
www.clbc.cam.ac.uk
biomedical research, diabetes, molecular cell biology of membrane traffic pathways, obesity & other related endocrine and metabolic disorders; PhD

Dept of Clinical Neurosciences (Cambridge Centre for Brain Repair; Neurology Unit; Neurosurgery; Wolfson Brain Imaging Centre);
www.neurosciences.medschl.am.ac.uk
brain repair, neurology, neurosurgery, brain imaging; MB/PhD

Dept of Haematology;
www.haem.cam.ac.uk
transfusion medicine diagnostics development, structural medicine & thrombosis, haematopoiesis & leukaemia; PhD

Dept of Medical Genetics;
www.cimr.cam.ac.uk/medgen
cancer genetics, genetics of developmental disorders/inflammatory disorders and juvenile diabetes, genetic components of neurological disease, including cellular mechanisms of neurodegeneration and developmental biology of neural cell development and repair, genes contributing to X-linked disease, particularly intellectual disability, renal genetics, autoimmune liver disease, disorders of genomic imprinting; BChir, MB, MD, PhD

Dept of Medicine; www.med.cam.ac.uk
anaesthesia, clinical pharmacology, renal research
Obstetrics & Gynaecology
Oncology
Paediatrics
Psychiatry
brain mapping, developmental psychiatry
Public Health & Primary Care
general practice & primary care research, clinical gerentology
Radiology
Surgery
orthopaedic research

CAMBRIDGE INTERNATIONAL COLLEGE
www.cambridgecollege.ac.uk

early childhood education and care, human services, management studies, managerial accounting, multidisciplinary studies, psychology educational leadership, autism specialist, autism/behaviour analyst, early childhood teacher, elementary teacher, ESL, general science, health/family & consumer sciences, interdisciplinary studies, library teacher, mathematics, school administration, school nurse education, teacher of students with moderate disabilities, applied behaviour analysis, teaching social justice; BA, MA, EdD, Doctor degrees, Master degrees management counselling, psychology, mental health counselling, psychological studies, school adjustment & mental health counselling, school guidance counselling, early childhood education and care, human services management studies, managerial accounting, multidisciplinary studies, psychology

---

CANTERBURY CHRIST CHURCH UNIVERSITY
www.canterbury.ac.uk

Faculty of Arts and Humanities;
www.canterbury.ac.uk/arts-humanities

Humanities
American Studies; The CIA and the Soviet bloc, memory and history conference, elite power investigation, Archaeology; European prehistory, The Roman world, medieval Europe; gender and sexuality in past societies, warfare and violence in past societies, excavation, survey and geomatics, laboratory techniques, computer applications, landscapes and environment, human remains, politics & ethics of archaeology, artefact analysis, Creative and Professional Writing; writing comes alive, prose fiction, creative writing; English; History; British

81

history, English history, English social and economic history, early modern kentish history, English urban history, women's history and gender, Northern Ireland conflict, concepts of national identity, British foreign policy since the 1930's, Anglo-American relations since the 1930s, post-war international history, 20th century France; European labour and social movements; history of communism, political, social and ecclesiastical history; Religion, Philosophy and Ethics; theology

School of Language Studies and Applied Linguistics; www.canterbury.ac.uk/arts-humanities/english-language-studies

language teacher education, applied linguistics, general English, English language and communication, French, general English, TESOL; BA(Hons), MA, MPhil, PhD

Media, Art & Design; www.canterbury.ac.uk/arts-humanities/MediaArtAndDesign/home

broadcast & interactive TV, digital media, film, radio & TV studies, multimedia journalism/design, journalism, graphic design, web design, fine & applied arts, film & digital video production, media & communication, cultural studies, PR, media marketing, photography, media, art & design

Music & Performing Arts; www.canterbury.ac.uk/arts-humanities/music/departmenthome/Home

arts & media management, music, commercial/music production, creative arts, creative music technology, dance education, drama, performing arts, music industry management, access to music, theatre performance; BA, BSc, MA, MPhil, PhD, PGDip, FD, MMus

Faculty of Education; *www.canterbury.ac.uk/education*

supporting children's learning, childhood studies, counselling, coaching and mentoring, early childhood studies, early years, early years leadership, education and learning, education and professional training, education studies, education: global and international education studies, learning and teaching, mathematics with secondary education, PE and physical activity/ sport & exercise science, primary education, social pedagogy, special educational needs and inclusion studies, supporting young people, youth work Postgraduate; learning and teaching, primary mathematics specialist teacher, primary physical education, career management, early childhood education, education (specialist pathways), global and international education, myth, cosmology and the sacred, professional learning and education, transformational leadership, teaching and learning, research guidance & support; primary education, (7–11 part-time/progression route/mathematics specialism), PGCE primary with mathematics, PGCE primary, PGCE modular primary, PGCE 7–14/11–18/14–19/post compulsory, School Direct, subject knowledge enhancement; BA, MA, GradDip/Cert, FdA, BSc, DipHE, EdD, PGCert/Dip, BA(Hons), BSc(Hons), PGCE, EYPS, FDA, MA, MPhil/PhD, UnivDip

Faculty of Health and Social Care; *www.canterbury.ac.uk/health/home*

Department of Allied Health Professions; www.canterbury.ac.uk/health/allied-health-professions

advanced/occupational therapy, clinical reporting/imaging, diagnostic radiography, interprofessional health & social care, medical imaging, musculoskeletal ultrasound, operating dept practice, ophthalmic dispensing, paramedic science (range of post-graduate programmes), speech & language therapy

Centre for Health and Social Care Research; www.canterbury.ac.uk/health/health-social-care-research mental health, health & well-being, public health

Dept of Health, Well-being & the Family; www.canterbury.ac.uk/health

health & social care, approved mental health practitioner, midwifery, advanced practice (adult acute nursing, cancer care, community nursing, child nursing, clinical practice (children & young people/mental health/neonatal care/psychosocial care/public health), mental health practice/nursing, interprofessional health & social care (health promotion & public health), dance movement psychotherapy, social work

Department of Nursing and Applied Clinical Studies; www.canterbury.ac.uk/health/nursing-applied-clinical-studies

health & social care, nursing studies, advanced practice (adult acute nursing, cancer care, community nursing, child nursing, midwifery, mental health nursing, end of life care, public health nursing and occupational therapy), cardiology, clinical reporting, interprofessional health & social care (health promotion & public health), MBA in leadership &

management in health medical imaging, minimally invasive surgery, practice development & innovation, speech & language therapy, dance movement psychotherapy, social work, interprofessional practice, clinical practice, applied health social care studies, specialist practice community public health nursing, optical dispensing studies

Sidney De Haan Research Centre; www.canterbury.ac.uk/research/centre/SDHR

singing & mental health, singing & dementia projects, arts & health; BA(Hons), BSc(Hons), FD, EdD, MPhil, PhD, MA, MSc

Faculty of Health and Wellbeing; www.canterbury.ac.uk/healthandwellbeing

ophthalmic dispensing, adult nursing, child nursing, mental health nursing, diagnostic radiography – midwifery, occupational therapy, paramedic science, social work, operating department practice
Postgraduate; cardiology, clinical reporting, public health, leadership and management in health care, medical imaging, minimally invasive surgery (general surgery, gynaecology, orthopaedics, urology), practice development and innovation, speech and language therapy, dance movement psychotherapy, social work, mental health and approved mental health professional practice, otorhinolaryngology, health and wellbeing, applied practice (health & social care); BA(Hons), BSc(Hons), FD, PGDip/Cert, MBA, MCh, MA, MPhil, PhD

Faculty of Social and Applied Sciences; www.canterbury.ac.uk/social-applied-science

Dept of Psychology, Politics & Sociology; www.canterbury.ac.uk/social-applied-sciences/aspd

psychology, social psychology, sport & exercise psychology, cognitive behavioural therapy, clinical psychology, environment, European politics, society & sustainability, international relations, politics & governance, global politics, politics, professional practice, psychological perspectives, sociology; BA/BSc, MSc, MPhil, PhD, DClinPsych

Faculty of Business and Management; www.canterbury.ac.uk/business-management

The Christchurch Business School; www.canterbury.ac.uk/business-management/business-school

accounting & management, accounting, advertising, business studies, education/healthcare leadership & management, economics, entrepreneurship, finance, HRM, investment & wealth management, digital marketing, hotel management, international business, PR, media & marketing, business management (logistics/retail), shared services; BSc, BA, MSc, MA, Exec MBA, PGCert/Dip, MPhil, PhD

School of Law, Criminal Justice and Computing; www.canterbury.ac.uk/social-and-applied-sciences/law-criminal-justice-and-computing

applied criminology, business information systems, computing, forensic investigation, information technology, law, policing, web technology
Postgrad: computing, criminology and criminal justice, cybercrime forensics, forensic computing, policing and criminal justice, policing, criminal justice; BSc(Hons), BA/BSc, MSc, FD, LlB, MA, LPC

School of Human & Life Sciences; http://www.canterbury.ac.uk/social-and-applied-sciences/human-and-life-sciences/human-and-life-sciences.aspx

PE & psychology (sport and exercise), sport and exercise psychology, sport and exercise science, sport coaching science; ecology and conservation, environment, society and sustainability, events management, geography, tourism and leisure studies, tourism management, sport and leisure management; animal science, biosciences, environmental biology, environmental science, integrated science, plant science, science foundation; Postgrad biological sciences, geography, sport and exercise science

Centre for Sport, Physical Education & Activity Research; www.canterbury.ac.uk/SPEAR

Olympic & Paralympic research, physical education & activity in schools, sport, physical activity & health; BA/BSc, MBA, MSc, MA, Adv Dip, Grad Cert, PGDip, FD, DipHE, MPhil, PhD, MRes(Ed)

CARDIFF UNIVERSITY
www.cs.cardiff.ac.uk

College of Arts, Humanities & Social Sciences; *www.cardiff.ac.uk/ahss*

Cardiff Business School; www.business.cardiff.ac.uk

accounting, accounting with finance/modern languages, accounting & economics/management, finance & management, business management, business management (HR, international management/logistics & operations/marketing/modern languages), business & finance/with French/German/Spanish, business economics/ with modern languages, economics, economics /& finance/management/modern foreign languages, business studies & Japanese, banking & finance

Cardiff/Media/Executive MBA

Postgrad; accounting & finance, finance, economics, financial economics, international economics, banking & finance, HRM, international management/HRM, international transport, lean systems, logistic & operations management, marine policy, business strategy & entrepreneurship, strategic marketing BSc(Hons), BSc(Econ), MSc, MBA, MPA, PhD, Dip

Cardiff School of Planning & Geography; www.cardiff.ac.uk/cplan

human geography/& planning, city & regional planning, ecocities, food, space & society, geography, policy & practice, international planning & development, spatial policy & planning, sustainability, planning & environmental policy, transport & planning, urban & regional development, urban design, planning practice, European spatial planning, environmental policies & regional development, environmental planning; BSc, MSc, MA, PGCert, PhD

School of English, Communication & Philosophy; www.cardiff.ac.uk/encap

applied linguistics, creative writing, critical & cultural theory, analytic & modern European philosophy, English language/literature, ethics & social policy, forensic linguistics, language & communication studies, philosophy; BA, Dip, MA/Dip, MPhil, PhD

School of History, Archaeology & Religion; www.cardiff.ac.uk/share

Ancient history; archaeology and ancient history, ancient and medieval history, ancient history and other subjects (joint degrees)

Postgrad; ancient history, history and archaeology of the Greek and Roman world, ancient and medieval warfare, late antique and Byzantine studies

History; econ modern history and politics, history with Welsh history, ancient and medieval history, archaeology and medieval history, Postgrad; history, Welsh history, history of the Crusades, medieval British studies, ancient and medieval

Religious & Theological studies; Postgrad; religious studies, Indian religions/myth, narrative and theory/diplo Islam in contemporary Britain, myth/diplo in theology, chaplaincy studies/military route

Archaeology, archaeology & ancient history, archaeology & medieval history, archaeology and other subjects, conservation of objects in museums and archaeology; Postgrad; archaeology, prehistoric Britain, early medieval society and culture or European Neolithic, early Celtic studies, history and archaeology of the Greek and Roman world, professional conservation, conservation practice, care of collections, archaeology, conservation; BA, BSc, BScEcon, MA, MPhil, MSc, PhD

Cardiff School of Journalism, Media and Cultural Studies; www.cardiff.ac.uk/jomec

media, journalism and culture, journalism/media and communications, journalism and Welsh, journalism, media and English literature/sociology, journalism, media and sociology

Postgrad; broadcast journalism, computational journalism, digital media and society, international journalism, international PR and global communications management, magazine journalism, media management, newspaper journalism, political communication, science, media and communication, journalism, media and cultural studies; BA, MA, MPhil, MSc, PhD, PGDip

Cardiff Law School; www.law.cf.ac.uk

law, law & criminology/politics/sociology/French/German/Welsh, cannon law, European legal studies, governance & devolution, law & governance of the EU, legal & political aspects of international affairs, human rights law, legal aspects of medical practice, international commercial law, social care law, shipping law; LlB, LlM, MPhil, PhD

Cardiff Centre for Lifelong Learning; www.cardiff.ac.uk/learn

languages, business & management, computer studies, science & environment, social studies, humanities, law & politics

School of Modern Languages; www.cardiff.ac.uk/modern-languages

French, German, Italian, Spanish, Japanese, translation studies, European studies, area studies, culture & identity, history & memory, language & translation studies, literature & visual culture; BA, MA, MPhil, PhD

Cardiff School of Music; www.cardiff.ac.uk/music

music, music & English literature/French/German/Italian/Welsh/history/mathematics/physics, religious studies, composition, ethnomusicology, musicology, music, culture & politics, performance; BA, BMus, BSc, MMus, MA, PhD

Dept of Politics & International Relations; www.cardiff.ac.uk/politics=international relations-relat

politics, politics & international relations/economics/French/German/Italian/Spanish/law/modern history/philosophy/religious studies/sociology/Welsh, European studies, European governance & public policy, international relations, politics & public policy, social science research (European & international studies/Eurogovernance & public policy), Welsh government & politics; BA, BScEcon, MA, MScEcon, PGDip, PhD

School of Social Sciences; www.cardiff.ac.uk/socsci

criminology, science, media & communication, social policy/work, sociology, sociology & public policy, childhood & youth, crime, human & social sciences, safety & justice, skills & work development, social analytics, social science research; BA, BSc, DHS, DSW, MSc

School of Welsh; www.cardiff.ac.uk/welsh

Welsh, Welsh & ancient history/archaeology/education/English literature/English language/French/German/history/Italian/music/[philosophy/politics/religious studies/mathematics/sociology/Spanish, early Celtic studies, medieval British studies, Welsh & Celtic studies, Welsh & law; BA, LlB, MA, PhD

College of Biomedicine, Health & Life Sciences; www.cardiff.ac.uk/ahss

School of Biosciences; www.cardiff.ac.uk/bios

biochemistry, biology, biomedical science – anatomy/neuroscience/physiology, biotechnology, ecology, dental hygiene/therapy, biophotonics, genetics, microbiology, medicine, medical pharmacology, molecular biology tissue engineering, zoology; BSc(Hons), MRes, MSc, PhD

School of Dentistry; www.cardiff.ac.uk/denti

dentistry, dental surgery, clinical dentistry, conscious dental sedation, dental therapy & hygiene, implantology, orthodontics, tissue engineering; BDS, BSc(Hons), MClinDent, MD, MPhil, MSc, PhD

School of Healthcare Sciences; www.cardiff.ac.uk/healthcare-science

adult/children's nursing, diagnostic radiography and imaging, mental health nursing, midwifery, occupational therapy, operating department practice, physiotherapy, radiotherapy and oncology, advanced practice

advanced clinical practice, clinical photography, healthcare science, image appreciation, managing care in perioperative practice, neuromusculoskeletal physiotherapy, occupational therapy, radiographic reporting, radiography, specialist community public health nursing, sport & exercise physiotherapy, surgical care practice; CertHE, DipHE, MSc, MPhil, PGDip/Cert, PhD

School of Medicine; www.medicine.cf.ac.uk

advanced surgical practice, bioinformatics, critical care, diabetes, medicine, medical pharmacology, medical toxicology, occupational health pain management, palliative medicine/care, practical dermatology, therapeutics, psychiatry, primary care/and public health, wound healing and tissue repair, anaesthetics, intensive care & pain medicine, dermatology, genetic counselling, geriatric medicine, palliative medicine/care, pharmacology, therapeutics and toxicology, psychological medicine, child health, ultrasound (medical, obstetric and/or gynaecological); MBBCh, MD, MPH, MPhil, MSc/PGCert/Dip, PhD

School of Optometry and Vision Sciences; www.cardiff.ac.uk/optom

clinical optometry, optometry, eye care governance; BSc, MSc, MPhil, PGCert, PhD

Cardiff School of Pharmacy and Pharmaceutical Sciences

clinical pharmacy, clinical research, pharmacy, clinical practice, independent prescribing (community & healthcare, international pharmacological health economics; Dipl, MPharm, MPhil, MSc, PhD

School of Psychology; www.cardiff.ac.uk, psych

psychology, clinical/educational psychology, neuroimaging methods & applications, cognitive & behavioural therapies, with professional placement social science research methods; BSc, DEdPsych, DClinPsych, DradDip, PhD

College of Physical Sciences & Engineering; www.cardiff.ac.uk/pse

Welsh School of Architecture; www.cardiff.ac.uk/archi

architecture, architecture/& urban design, architectural professional studies, environmental design, sustainable energy & environment, building performance modelling, vertical studio, sustainable megabuilding/design/building construction, theory & practice of sustainable design; BSc, DipProfStuds, MA, MArch, MPhil, PhD, MSc

Cardiff School of Chemistry; www.cardiff.ac.uk/chemy

chemistry, chemical biology, chemistry with physics/industrial experience, catalytic science, inorganic/physical organic chemistry; BSc, MChem, MPhil, PhD

Cardiff School of Computer Science & Informatics; www.cs.cardiff.ac.uk

adv/computer science with high performance computing/security & forensics, business information systems, applied/software engineering, information security & privacy, strategic information systems, visual computing, computing & mathematics/IT management, computational journalism; BSc, MSc, PhD

School of Earth and Ocean Sciences; www.cardiff.ac.uk/earth

applied/environmental geology, environmental geoscience/hydrogeology, exploration & resource geology, geology, marine geology, earth & environmental science; BSc, MEnv, MPhil, MSc, PhD

Cardiff School of Engineering; www.cardiff.ac.uk/engin

architectural/civil/environmental/clinical engineering, civil & geoenvironmental engineering, community engineering & entrepreneurship, electrical & electronic/communications engineering, electrical energy systems, electronic & geoenvironmental/integrated engineering, adv/mechanical engineering, medical/orthopaedic engineering, orthopaedic engineering, structural engineering, sustainable energy & environment, hydroenvironmental engineering, wireless and microwave communications engineering, professional practice; BEng, EngD, MEng, MPhil, MSc, PhD

Cardiff School of Mathematics; www.cardiff.ac.uk/maths

mathematics, mathematics & its applications, mathematics, operational research & applied statistics, applied statistics & risk, operational research; BSc, MSc, MMath, MPhil, PhD

School of Physics & Astronomy; www.astro.cardiff.ac.uk

physics, astronomy, astrophysics, biophotonics, theoretical & computational physics, physics with mathematics/music; BSc, MPhil, MPhys, PhD

CARDIFF METROPOLITAN UNIVERSITY
www.cardiffmet.ac.uk

Cardiff School of Art & Design; www.csad.cardiffmet.uwic.ac.uk

advanced/product design, architectural design & technology, artist designer maker, art & design/ceramics, design, fine art, textiles, graphic communication, illustration, product design; BA(Hons), BSc, FD, MA, MFA, MPhil, MSc, MDes, PGCert/Dip, PhD

Cardiff School of Education; www3.cardiffmet.ac.uk/English/education

Dept of Humanities; www3.cardiffmet.ac.uk/English/education/humanities

creative writing and contemporary media, early childhood studies and literacy, educational studies and drama/ early childhood studies/English/literacy/ sport & physical activity/Welsh, drama and contemporary media/creative writing/ literacy, English & contemporary media/creative writing/drama, TESOL and educational studies/English/literacy; Postgrad; creative writing, English, English & creative writing; BA(Hons), MA, PGCert/Dip, PGCE

Dept of Professional Development; www3.cardiffmet.ac.uk/English/education/profdevelopment

education, youth & community work, managing community practice PGCE PCET, preparing to teach/ in the PCET sector, ECDL; BA, MA, PGD

Dept of Teacher Education & Training

PGCE (primary, secondary), secondary music/Welsh; BA(Hons), PGCE

Cardiff School of Health Sciences; www3.cardiffmet.ac.uk/English/health

Centre for Applied Social Sciences; www3.cardiffmet.ac.uk/English/health/ass

health & social care, housing: policy & practice/ supported housing, youth & community, management in the community professions, health & social science res, social science, postqual/social work; BA, BSc, FdSc, GradCert, GradDip, MRes, MSc, PGCert, PGDip

Dept of Biomedical Science; www3.cardiffmet.ac.uk/English/StudyAtUWIC/Courses/Pages/CareerBiomedical

biomedical science, complementary healthcare, dental technology, environmental health, food production management, food science & technology, health sciences, social sciences, health & social care healthcare science, housing: policy & practice/supported housing, human nutrition & dietetics, podiatry, psychology, public health nutrition, social work, speech and language therapy, sports biomedicine & nutrition; Postgrad; advanced dietetic practice, advanced practice, applied public health, biomedical science, clinical research methods, dental technology, dietetics, food safety management, food science & technology, food technology for industry, forensic psychology, health and social science, health psychology, musculoskeletal studies, occupational health, safety & wellbeing; BSc(Hons), MSc, MRes DForenSc, CertHE, DipHE, PGDip/Cert, Dip

Department of Applied Community Sciences; www.cardiffmet.ac.uk/health/Pages/Departments.aspx

Health and Social Care; social sciences, health & social care; Environmental Health, health sciences, applied public health, occupational health, safety & wellbeing; Housing; housing: policy & practice, housing: supported housing, Social Work; social work; Dip, BSc(Hons), MSc, FD, PGDip/Cert

Dept of Healthcare & Food

Dept of Complementary Therapies; www3.cardiffmet.ac.uk/English/health/cct
Complementary Healthcare; complementary healthcare; BSc[Hons], Dip/CertHE
Centre for Dental Technology; www3.cardiffmet.ac.uk/English/health/cdt
dental technology; BSc, FdSc, MSc, PGCert, PGDip
Dept of Nutrition & Dietetics; www3.cardiffmet.ac.uk/English/health/ndfs
human nutrition & dietetics, public health nutrition, advanced dietetic practice, dietetics; BSc(Hons), MSc, PGD
Dept of Food Science
food science & technology, food production management, food technology for industry, food safety management; BSc(Hons), MSc, PGD, PGC
Dept of Applied Psychology; www3.cardiffmet.ac.uk/English/health/cp
forensic/health psychology, psychology, clinical research, health & social science research; BSc, FdSc, MSc, PGDip, MRes, FdSc
Speech & Language Therapy; www3.cardiffmet.ac.uk/English/health/cslt
speech & language therapy; BSc(Hons)
Podiatry; www3.cardiffmet.ac.uk/English/health/wcps
musculoskeletal studies, podiatry, adv/therapeutic footware; BSc, MSc, PGCert, PGDip

Cardiff School of Management; www3.cardiffmet.ac.uk/English/management

accounting, accounting & finance, business & management studies, business & management studies with finance/HRM/information systems management/international business management/law/marketing, business economics, business information systems, business information systems with multimedia/networks, computing, economics, events management, events marketing management, international business administration, international business management, international economics & finance, international hospitality & events management, tourism management, international hospitality management, international hospitality marketing management, international tourism & events management, international tourism management, international tourism marketing management, marketing management, software engineering, software engineering with data security/multimedia/networking/software programming; Postgrad; computing, events project management, executive, finance, finance & information management, financial management, HRM, information & communication technology management, international business management, international hospitality and tourism management, international business, marketing, business administration (MBA), mobile technologies, product development management, sustainable leadership, 20twenty leadership, technology project management; BSc(Hons), BSc(Econ), BA(Hons), MSc, LlM, PGCert/Dip, MBA, FdA

Cardiff School of Sport; www3.cardiffmet.ac.uk/English/sport

applied sports psychology, dance, sport performance analysis, physical activity & health, sports coaching/development, sport & exercise/ medicine/physical education/science, sport management & leadership, applied sport psychology, sport, body & society, sports studies, sport conditioning rehabilitation & massage, sport management & leadership, strengthening & conditioning; BA(Hons), BSc(Hons), MA, MSc, PGDip/Cert

UNIVERSITY OF CENTRAL LANCASHIRE
www.uclan.ac.uk

School of Art, Design & Performance; www.uclan.ac.uk/schools/adp

acting, advertising, animation, antiques, arts health, art & design, fashion brand management/promotion, creative business management/thinking, dance & somatic well-being, performance, & teaching, fine art/studio practice/site & archive, consumer product design, design, digital design for fashion/graphics, Eastern/fashion design, drawing & image making, fashion promotion with styling promotion/design, fashion shaping/design/entrepreneurship, fashion & lifestyle brand studies/brand promotion/with photography/journalism/lifestyle promotion, fine art site & archive interventions, games design, graphics design, children's books/illustration, interior design, journalism, music production & management, music production/theatre/practice, performance, photography, product design, surface pattern & textiles, textiles, toy design, transdisciplinary design; BA(Hons), MA, MBA, MPhil, PGCert/Dip, PhD, UniCert

The Grenfell-Baines School of Architecture, Construction & the Environment; www.uclan.ac.uk/schools/architecture

architecture, architectural technology, building conservation & regeneration, building services & sustainable engineering, building/quantity surveying, construction law/& dispute resolution, construction/project management, facilities management, energy/& environmental management, project management, geography, carbon & resources management sustainable waste management, urban design, urban environmental management; BSc(Hons), BA(Hons), FdSc, PGDip/Cert, MSc, BEng(Hons), MArch

School of Computing, Engineering & Physical Sciences; www.uclan.ac.uk/schools/computing_engineering_physical

Computing: computing, computer aided engineering, computer games development, computer network technology, computing, forensic computing, IT systems, multimedia & mobile development, software engineering

Engineering: aerospace engineering, architectural engineering, building services systems, robotics engineering, digital computing/signal & image processing, electronic engineering, computer-aided engineering, fire engineering, interaction design, motorsports/engineering, mechanical/maintenance engineering, renewable energy engineering, nuclear engineering, nuclear project management & control, nuclear safety/& security/case authorship/& safeguards, nuclear law & regulation, robotics engineering

Physics & Mathematics: applied physics, mathematics, physics, astrophysics, astronomy, physics & astrophysics; BSc(Hons), BEng(Hons), MPhys, MSc, FdSc, MPhil, PhD, FDEng, MEng(Hons)

School of Education and Social Sciences; www.uclan.ac.uk/schools/education_social_sciences

community leadership, education (mathematics: numeracy), volunteering and safety management, philosophy and politics, education and psychology, professional practice in education, history and politics, religion, culture and society, health and social studies for bilingual workers, education and training, faith leadership, politics and social policy, sociology, teaching mathematics: numeracy, criminology and criminal justice/sociology, education and religion in society, teaching learning and assessment, intermediate, education and sociology, sociology and psychology, public services, history, equality and diversity in the workplace, community research and mental health, education and sociology, equality and community leadership, PGCE, education (education and training), community leadership, philosophy, education and history, sociology and psychology, volunteering and community action, deaf studies and education, children, schools and families, history, global security and justice, British sign language /an introduction/English interpreting and translation/& deaf studies/English interpreting and translation/and communication studies, education, history and politics, deaf studies and education, education with languages, children, schools and families, education and professional studies, politics and social policy, public history, mentoring in the community, religion, culture and society, international relations, contemporary practice with children and young people; BA(Hons), BSc(Hons), MA, MSc, PGCert/Dip, DipHE, UnivCert, PGCE, AdvCert, ProfDoc, MEd, EdD, PGCE, AdvCert, FdA, CertEd, UnivAdvCert

School of Forensic & investigative Sciences; www.uclan.ac.uk/schools/forensic.investigative

forensic science/ and anthropology/ chemical analysis/ molecular biology/criminal investigation, fire safety engineering, oil and gas safety engineering, fire safety (management/engineering) policing and criminal investigation, archaeology/and anthropology, chemistry, fire and leadership studies, fire

engineering, healthcare science, biomedical science, chemistry, neuroscience; Postgraduate; fire investigation, forensic science, forensic and conservation genetics, DNA profiling, fire scene investigation, synthetic organic chemistry, criminal investigation, fire and rescue service management, counter terrorism, financial investigation, instrumental analysis, fire safety, engineering, cybercrime investigation, document analysis, forensic toxicology, forensic anthropology; BA(Hons), MEng, BEng, MChem, BSc(Hons), FdSc, MPhil, PhD, PGDip/Cert, MSc, MSci

School of Health; www.uclan.ac.uk/schools/school of health

applied public health/improvement, advanced practice/health & social care, applied public health protection, advanced stroke practice, nursing (mental health/child/adolescent/adult), community specialist practitioner, conflict & violence minimisation, counselling for depression/& psychotherapy, enhanced clinical practice, evidence-based practice, caring for dementia, enhanced clinical practice, health research methods/informatics, herbal medicine, homeopathy, improving health & wellbeing, integrative psychotherapy, nurse practitioner, paramedic practice, neonatal practice, operating dept practice, philosophy & mental health, primary care/mental health practice, health informatics, integrated healthcare, personality disorder, psychotherapy, psychosocial mental health care, sexual health studies, therapeutic work with children & adolescents, professional practice, midwifery, specialist community public health visiting, safeguarding in international context, strategy for clinical trials; BA(Hons), BSc(Hons), MA, MPhil, PGDip/Cert, PhD

School of Journalism and Media Communication; www.uclan.ac.uk/schools/journalism

journalism (international, magazine, visual, broadcast, sport), journalism & English language, film production, film & media studies, screenwriting with film, TV & radio, TV production, scriptwriting, digital visual effects, media management/technology/innovation/production, photography, publishing, self/publishing, TV production, web design & development; BSc(Hons), BA(Hons), MA, MPhil, PGDip, PGCert, PhD

Lancashire Business School; www.uclan.ac.uk/schools/lbs

Accounting and Finance/investment/management

business studies, business studies (accounting and finance/business information systems/marketing/ enterprise), business administration, business and management/ marketing, business (foundation year entry), international business/and management, Postgrad; business management, international business and management, management online

Administration Management, business and management, international business and management, global business management, professional practice; Postgraduate; business administration (MBA), business management, international business and management, management, management studies, leadership in policing

PR and Marketing, Postgrad; international applied communication, marketing and public relations, strategic communication

Retail Management (buying, fashion, marketing)

Economics; economics, business economics

Business Studies (logistics and supply chain), Postgraduate; logistics and supply chain management, oil and gas operations management

Business Studies (HRM), Postgraduate; HRM/D, HRM

BA(Hons), BA/BSc, MBA, DBA, MA, MSc, PGDip/ Cert, FdA, PGCert

Lancashire Law School; www.uclan.ac.uk/ schools/lancashire_law_school

law, advanced legal practice, applied policy science, law with criminology/psychology/human rights/ business/management/international studies, law & international security, construction law & dispute resolution, international criminal justice & security law, law, law with mediation, nuclear law & regulation, policing & criminal investigation, senior status, legal practice; BA(Hons), BA/BSc, LlB, LLM, MA, MPhil, PGDip/Cert, ProfDoc

School of Languages and International Studies; www.uclan.ac.uk/schools/ languages_and_international

English literature, English language/literature and creative writing/literature, English language, business management and Chinese, English for international corporate/business communication, modern languages (Arabic, French, German, Japanese or Spanish) for international business, Arabic language and studies, academic English, international business communication with a modern foreign language, TESOL Asia Pacific studies, Postgraduate; interpreting and translation, TESOL with applied linguistics,

intercultural business communication, emotions, credibility and deception; BA(Hons), MPhil, PhD

School of Medicine & Dentistry; www.uclan.ac.uk/schools/medicine

medical education, medical science, medicine, surgery, musculoskeletal practice in primary care, general practice, dermatology in primary care, nonfacial aesthetics for healthcare professionals; dentistry, orthodontic therapy, clinical dental technology studies, cosmetic dentistry, clinical periodontology, dental studies (dental care professions), endontology, dental implantology, oral surgery, prosthdontics; BDS, CertHE, MSc, PGDip/Cert, AdCert, MB, BS, BSc(Hons)

School of Pharmacy and Biomedical Sciences; www.uclan.ac.uk/schools/ pharmacy

biomedical sciences, pharmaceutics, biological sciences, healthcare science, pharmacy, physiology & pharmaceutics, cancer biology & therapy, clinical pharmacy practice, industrial pharmacology; BSc(Hons), MPharm, MSc, PGDip/Cert, PhD

School of Psychology; www.uclan.ac.uk/ schools/psychology

psychology, psychology & criminology/education/ psychotherapy, forensic psychology, psychology of child development, law with psychology, sport & exercise psychology, health psychology, neuroscience, neuropsychology, psychology conversion, sociology & psychology; BSc(Hons), GradDip, MSc

School of Social Work; www.uclan.ac.uk/ health/schools/school_of_social_work

children, young people & their service, community & social care contemporary practice with children & young people, safeguarding children, sociology, social policy/work, specialist childcare/adults practice, social policy & sociology, professional development & practice, mental health practice, international community development; BA(Hons), MA, PGCert

School of Sport, Tourism and the Outdoors; www.uclan.ac.uk/management/ssto

exercise and fitness management, nutrition and exercise sciences (human nutrition/personal fitness training), sport and exercise physiology, sport and exercise science, sport science, strength and conditioning, physiotherapy, sport therapy, sports studies, sports business management, outdoor leadership, adventure sports/coaching, sports coaching and development, event management, hospitality and event management, international hospitality management, international tourism management, management in events, management in hospitality, management in tourism, food safety management, hazard analysis critical control point, nutrition and food sciences, sport and exercise biomechanics,, sport and exercise science, strength and conditioning, sport and exercise physiology, PE and school sport, sport marketing & business management, elite coaching practice, elite performance, sports coaching, international festivals and event management/ tourism management, international heritage and attraction management, international heritage and event management, international hospitality & event/tourism management, tourism and attraction management; BSc(Hons), BA(Hons), MSc, PGDip/Cert, FDA, FDSc, ProfDoc

---

UNIVERSITY OF CHESTER
www.chester.ac.uk

Faculty of Life Sciences; www.chester.ac.uk/faculties#A

Dept of Biological Sciences; www.chester.ac.uk/biology
animal behaviour/welfare, animal/zoo management, biomedical sciences, biology, wildlife conservation & ecology, forensic biology/ecology, healthcare sciences, mortuary science; BSc, MSc, PhD

Chester Centre for Research into Sport & Society
sociology of sport & exercise; MSc, PhD

Research in Clinical Science & Nutrition
cardiovascular health & rehabilitation, diabetes, exercise & nutrition science, weight management, human nutrition, neuromuscular therapy, nutrition & dietetics, public health nutrition, clinical science & nutrition; MPhil, MSc, PhD

Sport & Community Engagement
sport development, sports coaching; BSc, BA

Sport & Exercise Science
sport & exercise science, sport science, sociology of sport & exercise sciences; BA, BSc, MSc

Faculty of Science & Engineering; www.chesterac.uk/faculties/science-engineering

Dept of Computer Science and Information Systems
computer science, cyber security, games development, software engineering; Postgraduate; computer networks, computer science, information systems, programme and project management, project engineering, teaching of computer science in schools; FD, BSc(Hons), MPhil, PhD, MRes, PGCert

Dept of Mathematics; www.chester.ac.uk/maths
mathematics, applied statistics, applied mathematics, computational applied mathematics; BSc, MSc, MRes, PGCert, PhD

Dept of Chemical Engineering
chemical engineering; BEng, MEng(Hons)

Dept of Electronic & Electrical Engineering
electronic & electrical engineering; BEng, MEng(Hons)

Dept of Mechanical Engineering
mechanical engineering; BEng, MEng(Hons)

Dept of Natural Science
natural science; BSc

New Technology Initiatives
programming & project management; MSci

Faculty of Arts & Media; www.chester.ac.uk/faculties#B

Dept of Art & Design; www.chester.ac.uk/art & design
fine art, graphic design, design & fine art, photography; BA(Hons), MSc, MA

Dept of Media; www.chester.ac.uk/media
advertising, commercial music production, digital photography, journalism studies, radio/TV production, film studies, music/ sports/journalism, media studies; BA(Hons), MA, PGCert/Dip

Dept of Performing Arts; www.chester.ac.uk/departments/performing-arts
drama, dance & music, pop music, performance practice, music & performing arts; BA(Hons), MA

Chester Centre for Research in Arts & Media
art & design, drama, dance & music, media performance

University of Chester Business School; www.chester.ac.uk/bell
accounting & finance, hospitality management, business studies, international business, business management/& entrepreneurship, accounting & finance, events management, marketing, tourism management, marketing & PR, management, management with information systems, international business/finance/HRM, events management/marketing/marketing communications & PR, sustainability for community & business; Chester Masters, BA(Hons), BA/BSc, FdA, MBA, MPhil, PhD, MBA, DProfStuds, MSc, DBA

Centre for Work Related Studies; Professional Development Unit; Work Based Learning Office; www.chester.ac.uk/ pdu
work-based & integrated studies; FD, BA, MA

Faculty of Education & Children's Services; www.chester.ac.uk/education
education studies, early childhood studies, working with children, young people and families, supporting learning with children and young people, youth work teacher education: primary and early years – primary, childhood and youth professional studies, PGCE primary/early years/secondary, primary PE specialist, school direct initial teacher education, qualified teacher status (QTS), creativity and education for the professions, dyslexia research and practice, educational leadership, e teaching and learning, inclusion and marginalisation, school-based continuing professional development, coaching and mentoring, education, special educational needs; BA(Hons), BEd, EdD, FdA, MA, MEd, PGCE, MATL

Faculty of Health and Social Care; www.chester.ac.uk/health
midwifery, nursing, health & social care/commissioning, children, community health studies, advanced practice, applied palliative care, mental health practice, art therapy, communicable diseases, education for post graduate medical practice, oncology, endodontology, health improvement & well-being, health & social care, healthcare management, occupational health, oncology, applied mental health practice, global health, intercultural multi-method therapy, maternal & women's reproductive health, non-medical prescribing, palliative end of life care, professional education/studies/nursing, public health, restorative dentistry, specialist community public health nursing, specialist practice community, paediatrics; FdSc, BA(Hons), BSc(Hons), MA, MSc, PGCert, PhD, DPH, DProf, MPhil, PhD

Faculty of Humanities; www.chester.ac.uk/faculties#F

English; www.chester.ac.uk/english
creative writing, English/ language/literature, 19th-century literature and culture, modern & contemporary fiction, writing & publishing fiction; BA, MA, PhD, MPhil

History and Archaeology; www.chester.ac.uk/departments/history-archaeology
history, American, British, Irish, world history, military history, archaeology, archaeology of death & memory/heritage history; BA(Hons), MA, MPhil, PhD, MRes

Dept of Modern Languages; www.chester.ac.uk/languages
European languages & global cultures, French, German & Spanish, Chinese studies, modern languages; BA(Hons), MA, MRes, PGCert/Dip

Theology & Religious Studies; chester.ac.uk/trs
religious studies, theology, practical & contextual theology, theology, media, & communication; BA(Hons), BTh, DipHE, FdA, PhD, MA, MPhil, MTh

Faculty of Social Sciences; www.chester.ac.uk/faculties#G

Geography and Development Studies; www.chester.ac.uk/geography
geography, international development studies, natural hazard/environmental management, regeneration for practitioners, sustainability for community & business; BA(Hons), BSc(Hons), MA, MSc, PhD, PGCert

Dept of Psychology; www.chester.ac.uk/ psychology
psychology, cognitive & behavioural approaches, cognitive behavioural therapy, family & child psychology, clinical supervision; BA(Hons), BSc(Hons), PGCert, PhD, MPhil, MSc

**Dept of Social & Political Science;
www.chester.ac.uk/scc**
criminology, sociology, politics, economics, international relations; BA, BSc, MA, MSc, PGCert

Dept of Social Work
social work, applied mental health practice, health & social care; BA(Hons), MA, PGDip

Law School; www.chester.ac.uk/law
law/& business/criminology/politics, contemporary legal studies; LlB, LlM

UNIVERSITY OF CHICHESTER
www.chiuni.ac.uk

UG qualifications: early childhood studies, physical education in the primary years IES, event management and finance, business studies/ media and cultural studies with international English studies, graphic design, Postgraduate; contemporary dance, cultural history, performance: theatre or theatre collectives, TESOL, theatre – performance making, social work, performance: dance, choral studies, fine art, international business; BA(Hons), BSc(Hons), FD, GradDip/Cert, MA, PGCE, MSc, MSW, PhD, MEd, BMus

CITY UNIVERSITY LONDON
www.city.ac.uk

*School of of Arts & Social Sciences;
www.city.ac.uk/arts_and-social_science*

Department of Culture & Creative Industries
cultural & creative industries, audiovisual translation and popular culture, creative writing (non-fiction/ novels/ playwriting and screenwriting), creative writing and publishing, culture, policy and management, international publishing, publishing

Department of Economics
economics, economics with accounting, financial economics, behavioural economics, business economics, international business economics, development economics, economic evaluation in healthcare economics, financial economics, health economics

Department of International Politics
international political economy, international politics, international politics and sociology, diplomacy and foreign policy, global political economy, international politics, international politics and human rights

Department of Journalism
journalism, broadcast journalism, television/financial/interactive/international/investigative/magazine/ newspaper/science journalism, journalism, media and globalisation

Department of Music
music

Department of Psychology
psychology, sociology with psychology, behavioural economics, counselling psychology, counselling psychology, clinical, social and cognitive neuroscience, health psychology/psychology and health, organisational psychology

Department of Sociology
criminology, criminology and sociology, international politics and sociology, media, communication and sociology, sociology, sociology with psychology, criminology and criminal justice, food policy, international communications and development, media and communications

Centre for Language Studies; BSc(Hons), BA(Hons), BMus(Hons) GradDip/Cert, MA, MSc, PhD, ProfDoc

*Cass Business School;
www.cass.city.ac.uk*

Faculty of Actuarial Science and Insurance; www.cass.city.ac.uk/faculty-of-actuarial-science-and-insurance
actuarial management, actuarial science; BSc(Hons), MSc, Dip, PhD, MPhil

Faculty of Finance; www.cass.city.ac.uk/facfin

accounting/& finance, business studies, investment & financial risk management, banking & international finance, business studies, corporate finance, insurance & risk management, international accounting & finance, finance & investment, investment management, financial mathematics, management, mathematical trading & finance, quantitative analysis, real estate, shipping, supply chain & energy, charity accounts, charity marketing & fund-raising, voluntary sector management; BSc, MSc, PGDip

Faculty of Management; www.cass.city.ac.uk/facmana

corporate governance, information & knowledge management, management, marketing, organisational behaviour & HR, international Asian HRM & business, HRM operations & supply chain management, management in the charity sector, management, strategy, entrepreneurship; BSc(Hons), MBA, MEb, MPhil, MSc, PGDip, PhD

School of Engineering and Mathematical Sciences; www.city.ac.uk/mathematics-computing-science-engineering

Department of Civil Engineering; www.city.ac.uk/department-civil-engineering

civil engineering, cvil engineering with architecture, analysis & design of structures, civil engineering structures, construction management, professional engineering; BEng(Hons), MEng(Hons), MSc, FD, MPhil, PhD

Department of Electrical & Electronic Engineering; www.city.ac.uk/department-electrical-electronic-engineering

biomedical engineering/with healthcare technical management, telecommunication, computer systems engineering, electrical & electronic engineering, engineering with management & entrepreneurship, project management, finance & risk, renewable energy & power systems management, systems & control engineering, telecommunications & networks; BEng(Hons), MEng(Hons), MSc

Department of Mathematics; www.city.ac.uk/department-mathematics

mathematical science, mathematical sciences with computer science/finance & economics/statistics/finance, decision sciences; BSc(Hons), MMaths, MSc, MPhil

Department of Mechanical Engineering & Aeronautics; www.city.ac.uk/department-mechanical-engineering-aeronautics

aeronautical engineering, air transport engineering, automotive & motorsports engineering, energy engineering, mechanical air safety management, air transport management, aircraft maintenance management, energy & environmental technology & economics, mechanical engineering, transport systems, strategy & management, maritime operations & management in Greece; BEng(Hons), MEng(Hons), MSc, MPhil, PhD

School of Informatics

Department of Computer Science; www.city.ac.uk/department-computer-science

business computing systems, computer science/with games technology/cyber security, advanced computer science, business systems analysis & design, computer games technology, data science, e-business systems, health informatics, human-centred systems, management of information security & risk, information systems & technology, innovation, creativity & leadership, software engineering; BSc(Hons), MSc, MA, MInvo, PhD, MPhil, MSci

Department of Library & Information Science; www.city.ac.uk/department-library-information-science

information science, library science, library & information science; MSc, MA, MPhil, PhD

School of Health Sciences; www.city.ac.uk/health

speech & language science, nursing (adult/child/mental health), optometry, radiography (diagnostic imaging/radiotherapy & oncology), speech & language therapy, nursing studies, primary care (practice nursing)

PGrad qualifications, midwifery, nursing (adult/child/mental health), public health (school nursing, health visiting & district nursing), speech & language therapy, advanced practice in health & social care (adult mental health/child & adolescent mental health/ health long term conditions & long term care/midwifery/advanced nursing/ophthalmic nursing/clinical optometry/radiotherapy, clinical optometry, clinical research, health management, health policy, health services research, speech, language & communication, needs in schools: advanced practice, medical ultrasound, public health, radiography (computed tomography, medical magnetic resonance & radiotherapy), ophthalmic dispensing; FD, BSc(Hons), MSc, DipHE, PGDip, MPhil, PhD, Grad Dip, MRes, Cert

The City Law School; www.city.ac.uk/law

law, city litigation & dispute resolution, int banking & finance/commercial/competition/business law, maritime law (Greece), international energy law &

regulation, international human rights, criminal litigation, EU commercial/ law, innovation, civil litigation & dispute resolution, innovation, creativity & leadership, legal practice, professional advocacy, public international law, bar professional training; LlB, LlM, MPhil, PhD, MJur, Grad Dip, MInnov[a]Degrees validated by City University offered at:

GUILDHALL SCHOOL OF MUSIC & DRAMA
www.gsmd.ac.uk

acting, training actors (voice or movement), design realisation, music, music composition, music therapy, conducting, performance, singing, electronic music, range of musical instruments, technical theatre arts, stage management, basic philosophy & the arts,

video design for live performance, collective theatre production design; BA(Hons), BMus, MA, MMA/DMA, MMP, MMus, DMus, MPerf, PGDip, MPhil, PhD

REGENTS UNIVERSITY LONDON
www.regents.ac.uk

REGENTS UNIVERSITY LONDON

European Business School London, Regent's American College London, Regent's Business School London, Regent's Institute of Languages & Culture, Regent's School of Psychotherapy & Psychology, Regent's School of Drama, Film & Media, Regent's School of Fashion & Design

Numerous degree and diploma courses in the following subject areas: management and human resources, economics, accounting and finance, fashion and design, film, drama and acting, media, marketing, communications, PR and events, politics, international relations and social sciences, psychology and psychotherapy; BA(Hons), BSc(Hons), MA, MSc, DCounsPsy, DPsy, PGDip

---

THE NORDOFF-ROBBINS MUSIC THERAPY CENTRE
www.nordoff-robbins.org.uk

music therapy, music, health, society; MMusTherapy, PGDip, MPhil, PhD, DPsych

---

TRINITY LABAN CONSERVATOIRE OF MUSIC & DANCE
www.labantrinity.ac.uk

choreography, dance, dance/performance/science, contemporary dance, dance: the body in performance, music, musical theatre performance, jazz composition, music in education & performance, performance science, composition, the teaching

musician, musicians in education, piano & organ, strings, vocal studies, wind, brass, percussion, creative practice, dance; PGCE, BA(Hons), BMusMA, MPhil, MSc, PGDip, PhD

COVENTRY UNIVERSITY
www.coventry.ac.uk

Faculty of Business, Environment and Society; www.coventry.ac.uk/faculties-and-schools/faculty-of- business-environment-and-society

Coventry Business School

accounting & finance/for international business/ financial management, business/financial economics, accountancy, finance & investment, finance, accounting & financial management, banking & finance, investment management, & international economics & trade, economics, accountancy, business & HRM/finance, international HRM, HRM, investment management, international business/ economics/management, European business management, business management/administration, management of global development & comparative law, sports management/marketing & events management, international events & hospitality, international sports management/marketing, digital marketing, management, marketing/management, strategic/international marketing, advertising & marketing; BA(Hons), MA, MSc, MBA, PGCert/Dip, PhD

Department of English and Languages

English & creative writing/journalism/TEFL, Spanish & TEFL/English, English language teaching (ELT), French, Spanish, languages for business, TEFL; BA(Hons), MA

Coventry Law School

commercial law, business law, international corporate governance, international law, international business law, law, international corporate governance; LLB(Hons), LLM

Geography, Environment & Disaster Management

international disaster management/& emergency planning, emergency planning & management, environmental management, food security management, geography/& natural hazards, international disaster management, oil & gas management, oil, gas & energy management, petroleum & environmental technology; BA(Hons), BSc(Hons), MSc, PGDip, PGCert

International Studies and Social Science

commercial/business law, diplomacy, law & global change, history, international law, international relations/business, conflict reconciliation skills, maritime security, peace & conflict studies, peacebuilding, politics/& history, sociology/& criminology/& psychology, terrorism, international crime & global security; BA(Hons), LLB(Hons), MA, PGCert

Faculty of Engineering & Aeronautics; www.coventry.ac.uk/faculties-and-schools/faculty-of- engineering-and aeronautics

Department of Computer Science

computer science, computing, business information technology, hacking & network security, games technology, multimedia computing, informatics, data science & computational intelligence, software development, network computing, forensic science, computer hardware & software engineering; BSc(Hons), MSc, PhD

Department of Civil Engineering, Architecture & Building

civil engineering, architecture, architectural technology, interior design, graphic design, construction management, building services engineering, building surveying, construction management, civil & structural engineering; BSc(Hons), BEng(Hons), MEng, MDes, BA(Hons)

Department of Mathematics & Physics

mathematics, mathematics & theoretical physics/ statistics, aspects of causality in general relativity; BSc(Hons), MA/MSc, PhD

Department of Mechanical, Automotive & Manufacturing Engineering

automotive engineering, mechanical engineering, motorsport engineering, manufacturing engineering, engineering, international/ engineering business management, general engineering, metrology
Postgraduate; automotive engineering, mechanical engineering, control engineering, European/ systems and control, engineering business management, engineering management, engineering project management, manufacturing engineering; BEng(Hons), MEng, MSc, BSc(Hons), FD

Department of Aerospace, Electrical & Electronic Engineering

aerospace engineering/technology/systems engineering, electrical engineering, electronic engineering, electrical & electronic engineering; BEng(Hons), MEng, MSc

Faculty of Health & Life Sciences; www.coventry.ac.uk/faculties-and-schools/faculty-of-health-and-life-sciences

Department of Social, Therapeutic & Counselling Studies

leadership & management, occupational therapy, neurological occupational therapy, occupational psychology, social work & community studies, advanced professional practice in social work, youth work, childhood & youth studies, health & social work & welfare; BSc(Hons), MSc, MA

Department of Applied Sciences & Health

biological science, sports & exercise science, children & families, dietetics, health & lifestyle, physiotherapy, environmental health, food & nutrition, food security management, exercise, nutrition & health, biomolecular sport science, social & therapeutic horticulture; BSc(Hons), MSc

Department of Psychology and Behavioural Sciences

psychology, clinical psychology, forensic investigations, criminology; BSc(Hons), PhD

Coventry School of Art & Design; www.coventry.ac.uk/faculties-and-schools/coventry-school-of-art-and-design

art & design, fine art, illustration, graphic design, illustration & graphics, automotive/& transport design, contemporary arts practice, interior/product design, international product design, design & transport, contemporary arts practice, theatre & professional practice, music technology, illustration & animation, photography, music performance/composition, dance, music, media production, digital media & culture, multimedia computing, digital marketing, communication, culture & media, global media & communication, journalism & media, film & visual culture, English/& journalism, 21st century media print, photography, advertising & marketing, applied communications, automotive/health/specialist/global journalism; FD, BA(Hons), MDes, BDes, MSc

CRANFIELD UNIVERSITY
www.cranfield.ac.uk

School of Aerospace, Transport Systems and Manufacturing

Aerospace; aerodynamics, aerospace dynamics, aerospace materials, aircraft engineering, airport planning and management, air transport management (executive), airworthiness, astronautics and space engineering, autonomous vehicle dynamics and control, computational and software techniques in engineering, computational fluid dynamics, computer aided engineering, flight dynamics, gas turbine technology, military aerospace and airworthiness, power, propulsion and the environment, rotating machinery, engineering and management, safety and accident investigation – air transport/marine transport/rail transport, safety and human factors in aviation, software engineering for technical computing, through-life system sustainment

Transport Systems; advanced motorsport engineering, aerodynamics, aerospace dynamics, airport planning and management (executive), air transport management (executive), airworthiness, autonomous vehicle dynamics and control, safety and accident investigation – air transport/marine transport/ rail transport, safety and human factors in aviation, through-life system sustainment

Manufacturing; integrated vehicle health management, operations excellence, through-life system sustainment, advanced materials, aerospace manufacturing, aerospace materials, applied nanotechnology, cost engineering, design, strategy and leadership, design and innovation for sustainability, engineering and management of manufacturing systems, global product development and management, innovation and creativity in industry, knowledge management for innovation, management and information systems, manufacturing consultancy, manufacturing technology and management, operations excellence, sustainable manufacturing, through-life system sustainment, ultra precision technologies, welding engineering

integrated vehicle health management, operations excellence, through-life system sustainment; EngD, MSc, MDes, PhD, PGCert/Dip

School of Energy, Environmental Technology and Agrifood

Environmental Technology; community water and sanitation, design, strategy and leadership, design and innovation for sustainability, economics for natural resource and environmental management, energy from waste, environmental engineering, environmental informatics, environmental management for business, environmental risk management, environmental water management, environment and public policy, food chain systems, geographical information management, innovation and creativity in industry, integrated landscape ecology, land reclamation and restoration, offshore and ocean technology with subsea engineering, renewable energy technology, waste and resource management, water and wastewater engineering

Agrifood; future food sustainability; MSc, MDes, MPhil, PhD, PGCert/Dip

Cranfield School of Management; www.cranfield.ac.uk/som

executive MBA/ (defence), investment management, management, management and economics, finance and management, strategic marketing, retail management, logistics and supply chain management, international HRM, logistics and supply chain management, project management, strategic leadership, CPD; DBA, MBA, MSc, PhD, ExecMBA (Defence)

Cranfield Defence & Security www.cranfield.ac.uk/cds

cyber defence & information assurance, cyberspace operations, communication electronic warfare, defence acquisition management, defence simulation & modelling, scientific computation, explosive ordinance engineering, gun system design, military electronic systems/OR, information capacity development, international defence & security, military aerospace & airworthiness, program & project management, communication sensor electronic warfare, forensic computing, military vehicle technology, scientific computation, systems engineering for defence capacity; EngD, MSc, PGDip/Cert, PhD

UNIVERSITY FOR THE CREATIVE ARTS
www.ucreative.ac.uk (at Canterbury, Epsom, Farnham, Maidstone and Rochester)

architecture, fine art, graphic design: visual communications, illustration & animation, interior architecture & design, digital communication design, fashion, fashion journalism, fashion management & marketing, fashion promotion & imaging, graphic design, music journalism/promotion, acting & performance, advertising, computer games arts, digital film & screen arts, film production, glass, ceramics, metalwork, graphic communication, journalism/ & creative writing, media & communications/creative writing, photography, product design, sports journalism, textiles for fashion & interiors, interactive media production, media business management, tv production, computer animation arts, contemporary jewellery, creative arts for theatre & film, fashion accessories/atelier/buying retail management/design/ photography/media & promotion/textiles: print, photography, product design, silversmithing, goldsmithing & jewellery

Postgraduate; architecture, curatorial practice, fine art, urban design, creative industries management, design, innovation & brand management, fashion / management & marketing, fashion promotion & imaging, graphic design, creative arts education, animation, ceramics documentary practices, glass, illustration, interior design, journalism, jewellery, media communication, metalwork, photography, product design, textiles, crafts; BA(Hons), FD, Grad Dip, MA, MPhil, PGCert, PhD, MRes, FDA

UNIVERSITY OF CUMBRIA
www.cumbria.ac.uk

Faculty of Education, Arts & Business; www.cumbria.ac.uk/about us/faculties/ABS

Creative Arts: adventure media, contemporary fine art, digital/creative media, wildlife & media, art of games des, film & TV production, fine art, illustration, photography

Business School

accounting & finance, business administration, business entrepreneurship and computing innovations, business management and e-commerce/finance and accounting, computing/and IT, international business management, international marketing management, energy & sustainability, events leadership/education/social enterprise and management, leadership and management in health & social care, media leadership, sustainable leadership development; BSc(Hons), DipHE, PGDip, MA, MSc, MBA

Education

primary & early years (with QTS), non-QTS, PGCE primary & secondary, school direct, subject knowledge enhancement, academic practice, educational research, teaching and learning support, TESOL, academic practice, educational research, teaching and learning support; MSc, MBA, BA(Hons), MA, PGDip/Cert, PGCE, FdA, PhD, MPhil

Humanities

English/& creative writing, mass communications, theology, religious studies, journalism; BA(Hons), MA, Univ Certs

Law & Social Science

criminology & law/social science, law, youth & community work, applied psychology, applied forensic psychology, applied social science, interpersonal violence and abuse studies, law, legal and criminological psychology, international business law, psychological research methods; BA(Hons), BSc(Hons), LlM, MSc, PGCert

Performance

drama, event management, performing arts, performance, production, technical theatre, dance performance & drama performance/& music theatre performance; BA(Hons), FdA

Policing

policing, investigation & criminology, criminal justice, professional policing, strategic policing; DipHE, FdSc, BSc(Hons), MSc

Faculty of Health & Science; www.cumbria.ac.uk/about us/HealthScience

Forestry & Outdoor

adventure & environment, animal conservation science, conservation biology, outdoor & experiential learning, forestry, forest management, greening outdoor practice, marine freshwater & conservation, outdoor education/studies/leadership, trans-cultural European outdoor studies, woodland conservation; FDSc, BSc(Hons), MSc, PGDip

Health & Social Care

adv practice/cognitive behaviour therapy, applied public health, community special practice (district nursing/general practice nursing), paramedic practice, leadership & management in health & social care, early childhood studies, midwifery, mental health practice, non-medical prescribing (nursing/pharmacist), nursing (adult/child/learning disabilities/mental health), nursing practice, occupational health/nursing, physiotherapy, advanced practice occupational/clinical therapy, radiology, counselling & psychotherapy, evidence-based psychological approaches, management & leadership in health & social care, international health, specialist community public health nursing, diagnostic radiography, medical imaging, magnetic resonance, nuclear security management, ultrasound, physical activity & health development, practice development (developing paramedic practice/acute & critical care/aromatherapy/cardiac care/children & young people's mental health & wellbeing, diabetes management/palliative care/reflexology/respiratory care/stroke & rehabilitation/urological care/long term conditions), sexual health advice, sexual & reproductive health, social work, working with children & families/young people/older adults

Post Graduate; community specialist practice (learning disabilities nursing/general practice nursing/district nursing), counselling, diagnostic radiography, health & social care: dementia practice, management and leadership in health and social care, midwifery, non-medical prescribing for allied health professionals – independent prescribing for physiotherapists and podiatrists/radiographers/nurses/pharmacists, nursing adult/child/international/learning disability/mental health, nursing practice, occupational therapy, occupational therapy, paramedic science, physiotherapy, practice development (acute and critical care/ aromatherapy/children and young people's mental health and wellbeing/dementia care/ developing paramedic practice/diabetes management/emergency care/foundations of occupational health/long term conditions/mental health and wellbeing/ midwifery/occupational health/paediatric practice/palliative care/reflexology/respiratory care/ stroke and neurorehabilitation/stroke care/ wound care), radiation protection, sexual and reproductive health, social work, specialist community public health nursing (health visiting/occupational health nursing/school nursing/sexual health advising), working with children and families (child, young people and family studies/early childhood studies), working with individuals on the autism spectrum; BA, BSc(Hons), GradDip, MA, MSc, PgC/D, UC, UAD, DipHE, FdA, FdSc, MPhil, PhD, MBA, PGDip/Cert

Science & Engineering

applied sciences, forensic science, sustainable energy technology; animal conservation science, biology, forensic/& investigative science, marine & freshwater conservation, zoology; BSc, FdSc

Sport

physical activity/exercise & health, PE, sport & exercise science, sports coaching & development, sports rehabilitation/massage therapy, exercise & health, practice development: sport & exercise rehabilitation; BSc(Hons), BA(Hons), DipHE, MSc, PhD

DE MONTFORT UNIVERSITY
www.dmu.ac.uk

**Leicester Business School;
www.dmu.ac.uk/about-dmu/schools-and-departments/leicester-business-school;
also Department of Politics & Public Policy**
accounting & business management/economics/finance, advertising & marketing communications, business & globalisation/management/marketing, business entrepreneurship & innovation/economics/finance/HRM, business studies (economics/finance/strategy), economics, economics & finance/politics, finance, globalised accounting studies, HRM & international business, international relations & politics, international marketing & business, international relations, marketing, politics, public administration & management, housing, communities & regeneration
Postgrad; accounting & finance, advertising & PR management, business economics & finance/international relations/marketing/risk, diplomacy & world order, finance & investment, forensic accounting, global financial management, housing studies, international business & corporate responsibility/entrepreneurship/finance/HRM/management/international relations, management of human resources, marketing management, project management, risk management, strategic & digital marketing; MBAs, Exec MBA, business administration (global/housing); BA(Hons), BSc(Hons), DipHE, GDL/CPE, FdSc, MA, MPhil, MBA, MSc, PGDip/Cert, PhD

**Leicester De Montfort School of Law;
www.dmu.ac.uk/about-dmu/schools-and-departments/leicester-de-montfort-law-school**
law, law & criminal justice, HR & social justice, business law, international business/human rights law, law & business management, environment/employment/sports law & practice, medical law & ethics, food law, legal practice; LlB(Hons), LlM, LPC, DCCJ, MA, PGDip/Cert

**Leicester School of Architecture;
www.dmu.ac.uk/about-dmu/schools-and-departments/leicester-school-of-architecture**
architecture, architectural design/practice/technology, architecture & sustainability; BA, MArch, PGDip, MA, MSc

School of Arts; www.dmu.ac.uk/about-dmu/schools-and-departments/school-of-arts
arts, art & design, animation, arts & festival management, dance, drama studies, fine art, music, technology & innovation/performance, performing arts,

photography/ & video, cultural events management, performance practice; BA(Hons), MA, MSc

School of Design; www.dmu.ac.uk/about-dmu/schools-and-departments/school-of design

design crafts/products, furniture/interior/product design, furniture & product development, product & furniture design, design entrepreneurship/innovation/management; BA(Hons), MDes, MA

School of Fashion & Textiles; www.dmu.ac.uk/about-dmu/schools-and-departments/school-of fashion-and-textiles

contour fashion, fashion design/buying/textiles & accessories, footwear design, textile design, fashion management & marketing, fashion & textiles; BA(Hons), MA

School of Humanities; www.dmu.ac.uk/about-dmu/schools-and-departments/school-of-humanities

creative writing, English/language, history, humanities, inter religion relations, ELT, photography history & practice, management, law & humanities of sport, sports history & culture; BA(Hons), MA, PGDip

Leicester Media School; www.dmu.ac.uk/about-dmu/schools-and-departments/leicester-media-school

animation design, audio & recording technology, media production/technology, music technology & innovation/performance, creative sound technology, TV & film production technology, global media, film studies/with languages, game art design, graphic design, illustration, e-media, journalism, media & communication, photography, journalism, TV scriptwriting; BA(Hons), FdA, FdSc, MA, MSc

Institute of Creative Technologies; www.ioct.ac.uk

creative technologies; Masters, PhD

School of Computer Science & Informatics; www.dmu.ac.uk/about-dmu/schools-and-departments/school-of-computer-science-and informatics

business information systems, computer management for business, computer science/security/games programming, computing, cyber security, forensic computing for practitioners, information & communication technology, intelligent systems, mathematics, professional practice in forensics, software engineering; BSc(Hons), MSc, PGDip/Cert

School of Engineering & Sustainable Development; www.dmu.ac.uk/about-dmu/schools-and-departments/school-of engineering-and sustainable-development

mechanical engineering, mechatronics, electronic engineering, engineering management, climate change & sustainable development, energy & sustainable building design, industrial sustainability, physics, engineering & sustainable development; BSc(Hons), BEng(Hons), MSc

School of Allied Health Sciences; www.dmu.ac.uk/about-dmu/schools-and-departments/school-of-allied-health-sciences

advanced biomedical science, environmental protection/quality management, intercultural business communication, healthcare science (audiology), human communication, speech & language therapy, medical science; BSc(Hons), PGDip/Cert, MSc, FDSc, MA

School of Applied Social Sciences; www.dmu.ac.uk/about-dmu/schools-and-departments/school-of-applied-social-sciences

criminology & criminal justice/with psychology, education studies/ with languages, education with psychology, education practice, health psychology, policing studies, psychology/with criminology/education studies, psychology of health studies, psychological wellbeing, sociology, social work, work with communities & young people, work, health & communities, youth work & community development, working with young people & young people's services; BA(Hons), BSc(Hons), FD, MSc, PGDip/Cert

School of Nursing & Midwifery; www.dmu.ac.uk/about-dmu/schools-and-departments/school-of-nursing-and midwifery

palliative care, health and professional practice higher education/teacher qualification, non-medical prescribing, practice education, practice nursing, nursing (specialist practice), specialist community public health nursing, specialist community public health nursing; BSc/BSc(Hons), RSHDip, PGCert/Dip, MSc

School of Pharmacy; www.dmu.ac.uk/ about-dmu/schools-and-departments/ school-of-pharmacy

pharmacy, forensic science, pharmaceutical & cosmetic science, pharmaceutical biotechnology/quality,

independent prescribing, clinical pharmacy, prescribing quality by design for pharmaceutical industry; BSc(Hons), MPharm, MSc

---

UNIVERSITY OF DERBY
www.derby.ac.uk

College of Art & Design; www.derby.ac.uk/art

animation, art & design, dance, theatre arts/technical theatre/studies, fashion & textiles, fine art, art & design, graphic design, illustration, media production, music production, music technology & 0roduction, pop music, commercial photography, visual communication, film production, visual effect & post-production, film/ & photography, production design; BA(Hons), MDes, PhD, MPhil, Univ Cert/Dip,

College of Business; www.derby.ac.uk/ business

accounting and finance, accounting, business, accounting and finance, business studies, business management, business start-up, information technology management for business, international business/and finance, entertainment and leisure marketing, marketing and business intelligence/consumer psychology digital media, HRM, marketing, PR and advertising, marketing, banking and finance, economics for business Postgrad; logistics and supply chain management, accounting and finance, financial leadership, supply chain improvement, HRM, international business, international business and finance, business and reward management; BA(Hons), BSc(Hons), MSc, DBA, MBA, ProfDoc, MBus

College of Law, Humanities & Social Sciences; www.derby.ac.uk/lhss

Law & Criminology; www.derby.ac.uk/lhss/ law

law, intellectual property & information technology, international & comparative law, international politics of human rights & personal freedom, transnational criminal law, law with criminology/politics, legal practice, medical law, social & public law, corporate & financial law, cyber crime & e-investigation, criminal investigation; BA(Hons), BSc(Hons), MSc, LlB, LlM

International Policing, Law & Enforcement; www.derby.ac.uk/lhss/policing

police leadership, strategy and organisation; MSc

Humanities & Media; www.derby.ac.uk/ lhss/humanities

American studies, humanities, creative writing, English, film/& TV studies, history, professional writing, media studies/production, writing for performance, journalism; BA(Hons), MA, PGCert/Dip

Social & Political Science; www.derby.ac.uk/lhss/social-political-science

politics, international & global development, sociology; BA(Hons), BSc(Hons)

Computing & Mathematics; www.derby.ac.uk/computing

computer forensic investigation, advanced computer networks, computer games programming, computer science/networks, information technology/security, mathematics/& computing science, networks & security, mobile device software development, computer graphics production, mathematics/with education; BA(Hons), BSc(Hons), MA, MPhil/PhD, MSc, PGDip/Cert

College of Education; www.derby.ac.uk/ education

teacher status (QTS), education, early childhood studies, early childhood studies with early years teacher status, child and youth studies, education studies, children's and young people's services, special educational needs and disability; PGCE primary, primary/ secondary (school direct) with QTS, post 14 (education and training/with specialism – English: literacy, maths, or teaching learners with disabilities), education (career learning/community learning/early years/emotional education/ELTS/ ESOL/leadership and management/lifelong learning/ special educational needs and disabilities) early years teacher, education; BA(Hons), BEd, EdD, PGCE, MPhil, PhD, FdA

College of Health & Social Care; www.derby.ac.uk/health-and-social-care

applied social work, community specialist practice, creative expressive, therapies (dance, drama, music, art), dance and movement studies, diagnostic radiography, health and social care, international nursing, nursing (adult/mental health), occupational therapy, specialist community public health nursing systemic thinking and practice, working with young people and communities (youth work or community development) advanced occupational therapy community, advanced practice, art therapy, bone densitometry reporting, cognitive behavioural psychotherapy (adult or children and young people), compassion focused therapy, community specialist practice, dance movement psychotherapy, dramatherapy, doctor of health and social care practice, hand therapy, integrative counselling and psychotherapy, interprofessional practice education, leadership for healthcare improvement, management of long term conditions, medical ultrasound, mental health and wellbeing, mentoring in practice, occupational therapy, osteoporosis and falls management, non medical prescribing, DXA reporting for clinician, return to practice – nursing/radiography/occupational therapy), specialist community public health nursing, social work, systemic psychotherapy, systemic thinking and practice; BA(Hons), BSc(Hons), UniAdvDip, MSc, PGCert, MPhil, PhD, ProfDoc, DocHSC

College of Engineering & Technology; www.derby.ac.uk/engineering-technology

Engineering; architectural studies/technology and practice/design, civil engineering, civil and infrastructure engineering, construction, construction management and property development, electrical and electronic engineering, interior architecture and venue design, manufacturing and production engineering, mechanical engineering, mechanical and manufacturing engineering, motorcycle engineering, motorsport engineering, motorsport and motorcycle manufacturing engineering, property development, product design engineering, sound, light and live event technology, technology foundation programme Computing and Mathematics; analytics joint honours, computer forensic investigation, computer games modelling and animation/programming, computer networks and security, computer science, information technology, mathematics, mathematics and computer science, mathematics with education Postgrad; advanced computer networks, big data analytics, civil engineering and construction management, computational mathematics, control and instrumentation, cyber security, digital forensics and computer security, information technology, innovative engineering solutions, mechanical and manufacturing engineering, mobile app development, motorsport engineering, professional engineering, sustainable architecture and healthy building, technology; BSc(Hons), BA(Hons), MSc, FdSc/Eng, BEng(Hons), MPhil, PhD

College of Life & Natural Science; www.derby.ac.uk/science

biology, human biology, zoology, forensic science/with criminology/psychology, geography, geology, psychology, sport and exercise science/studies, sports massage and exercise therapies, sport psychology/coaching/development/management, outdoor Activities, environmental hazards Postgrad; behaviour change, conservation biology, biological sciences, forensic science, sport and exercise, applied petroleum geoscience, applied Acoustics, public health, health psychology; BSc(Hons), BA(Hons), FdSc, FdA, MPH, MSc, MPhil, PhD

UNIVERSITY CENTRE DONCASTER
www.don.ac.uk/university-centre-doncaster

illustration and concept art, fashion and textiles design, fine art and craft, graphic design, illustration and concept art, moving image production, early childhood development and learning in practice, supporting children with special educational needs and disability, early childhood studies, professional studies working with young people and the community, working with children and young people), applied social science, criminal justice, English, social psychology, business management, international football business management, live events production, contemporary performance practice, creative music technology, dance practice, PE and sports coaching, sports, fitness and exercise science, sports, exercise and health science, art, design and media, creative industries: practice, business and innovation, creative pattern cutting, early years, early childhood studies, education studies (primary / secondary),

literature and digital culture, leadership and management, business administration, advancing professional practice, teacher education and professional development, creative HRM, music technology; BA(Hons), BSc(Hons), MBA, MSc, PGDip/Cert, MA, PGCE, FdA, MSc, CertEd

UNIVERSITY OF DUNDEE
www.dundee.ac.uk

College of Art, Sciences and Engineering; www.dundee.ac.uk/case

School of Computing; www.computing.dundee.ac.uk

applied computing (games/human computing interaction, augmentative & alternate computing, business intelligence/computing, computing, computing with international business, computing/science/research, data science engineering, information technology & international business, user experience engineering, vision & imaging computing; BSc, MSc, PhD

Duncan of Jordanstone College of Art and Design; www.dundee.ac.uk/djcad

animation & VFX, art & humanities, art philosophy, art, society & publics, graphic design, interior/environmental/jewellery & metal/textiles design, digital interaction design, fine art, illustration, media arts & imaging, forensic/media/medical art, product design, textile design time-based art & digital film; BA, BSc(Hons), BDes, MSc, MFA, PhD, MPhil

School of Engineering, Physics and Mathematics; www.dundee.ac.uk/eps

civil engineering/design & materials, concrete engineering & environmental management, electronic & physics, geotechnical earthquake & offshore engineering, engineering, mathematics, mathematics & accountancy/financial economics/physics, applied/mathematics, mathematical biology, mechanical engineering, physics with renewable energy sciences/mathematics, renewable energy & environmental modelling, secondary education, structural engineering; BEng, BSc, MEng, MSc, MSci, PhD, PGDE, PGDip

Centre for Anatomy & Human Identification; www.dundee.ac.uk/cahil

anatomical sciences, advanced forensic anthropology, anatomy, anatomy & advanced forensic anthropology, anthropology for artists, forensic art & facial identification, forensic art, medical art; BSc, MBChB, BDS, MSc

College of Arts and Social Sciences; www.dundee.ac.uk/artsoc

School of Business; www.dundee.ac.uk/business

accountancy, business management, economic studies, finance, international business, postgraduate: accounting, management and strategy, accounting & finance, economics, finance, financial economics, international accounting/ business/business, accounting and finance, international business, marketing and HRM, international business and finance/ human resource management/management/marketing, management, management and accounting/ finance/ HR international business/marketing, professional accountancy; BSc, BAcc, BFin, MA, MRes, PGDip, PhD

Continuing Education; www.dundee.ac.uk/conted

arts & social sciences; MA

School of Education, Social Work and Community Education; www.dundee.ac.uk/eswce

childhood practice, community learning & development, education (primary), professional development (community engagement, leadership & management, tertiary education, volunteer management), healthcare/integrated services, volunteering, social work, education/leading learning & teaching/inclusion & learner support/nursery/early education/pupil care & support/adult literacies primary, policing studies, science (maths/sciences), educational psychology, international education, leadership & innovation, mathematical thinking, technical qualification FE, teaching in HE, secondary physics with science teaching/(FE)/HE); BA/BA(Hons), PGCert/Dip, MRes, DSW, PGDE, MSc, MA, PhD, MPhil, ProfDoc, DCLD, DEd, DEdPsych

Interdisciplinary Disability Research Institute (IDRIS)
Institute for Research and Innovation in Social Services (IRISS)

School of the Environment; www.dundee.ac.uk/socialsciences

Architecture: architecture, renewable energy & sustainable building, adv sustainability of built environment, adv sustainable urbanism, adv sustainability
Environmental Science: environmental science, geography
Geography: geography, catchment hydrology and management, social research methods/population and welfare, water hazards, risk & resilience
Town & Regional Planning: environmental sustainability, geography & planning, town regional planning, energy sustainability & international business; BSc, MA, BArch, MArch, PhD

School of Humanities; www.dundee.ac.uk/ humanities

American Studies
American studies (& jt degrees)
Centre for Archive and Information Studies; www. dundee.ac.uk/cias
archives & records management, records management & information rights/digital records, CPD
Gender, Culture & Society; www.dundee.ac.uk/ gender-culture-society
gender, society & culture
Languages; www.dundee.ac.uk/languagesstudies
French, German, Spanish, European languages & cultures, European studies, applied languages
English; www.dundee.ac.uk/English
English, English and film studies/modern languages (& jt degrees), philosophy & literature, women, comic & graphic novels, comics studies, theatre studies, writing practice, gender, culture & society, creative writing
European Studies
interdisciplinary courses, practical languages (French, German, Spanish), European studies
History; www.dundee.ac.uk/history
early America, European history, Greater Britain in the twentieth century, history, global empires, Scottish history, 20th century studies, Scottish historical studies

Philosophy; www.dundee.ac.uk/philosophy
philosophy, philosophy/& literature, continental/ recent analytic philosophy, women, culture & society, continental philosophy, art, philosophy, contemporary practice, jt degrees
Politics; www.dundee.ac.uk/politics
politics, international relations & politics, international security, international law/politics & security devolution & global governance
MA(Hons), MLitt, MSc, BSc, LlB, MPhil, PhD

School of Law; www.dundee.ac.uk/law

commercial & international commercial law, corporate & commercial law, competition & European private international law, international criminal justice & human rights, environmental law & sustainable development, international law, dual qualification degree, family law, law with language, Scots law, English law, international dispute resolution; LlB, LlM, PhD

Graduate School of Natural Resources Law, Policy and Management; www.dundee.ac.uk/postgradschool
mineral resource management, international oil & gas management, managing in energy industries; MBA, MSc

UNESCO Centre for Water Law, Policy and Science
water law; PGCert, LlM, PhD

Centre for Energy, Petroleum, & Mineral Law & Policy; www.dundee.ac.uk/cepmlp
energy law and policy, environmental law and policy, mineral law and policy, rural resources law and policy, oil and gas law and policy, petroleum taxation and finance, water law, mineral law and policy, natural resources law and policy, oil and gas law and policy, international oil & gas management, managing in the energy industries, international mineral resources; LlM, PhD, MBA, MSc

School of Psychology; www.dundee.ac.uk/ psychology

psychology, psychology of language, psychological research methods, developmental psychology, augmentative & alternative communication, psychology of mental health; BA(Hons), MA(Hons), PhD

College of Life Sciences; www.lifesci.dundee.ac.uk

biochemistry, biomedical/biological sciences, bioinformatics, drug discovery, cell signalling, cell & developmental biology, immunology, biology, molecular microbiology, neuroscience, pharmacology, physiological sciences, plant science; BSc(Hons), MRes, MSc, PhD

Schools of Research

Biological Chemistry & Drug Discovery (CLS); www. lifesci.dundee.ac.uk/bcdd

Div of Cell and Developmental Biology; www.lifesci. dundee.ac.uk/cdb

Div of Cell Signalling & Immunology; www.lifesci. dundee.ac.uk/csi

Drug Discovery Unit; www.drugdiscovery.ac.uk

Gene Regulation & Expression; www.lifescience. dundee.ac.uk/gre

Molecular Microbiology; www.lifesci.dundee.ac.uk/ mmb

Protein Phosphorylating & Ubiquitylation Unit; www. dundee.ac.uk/research

Div of Molecular Medicine; www.lifesci.dundee.ac.uk/ mm

Nucleic Acid Structure Research Group; www.dundee. ac.uk/research

Div of Plant Sciences; www.lifesci.dundee.ac.uk/pl

Scottish Institute of Cell signalling

College of Medicine, Dentistry and Nursing; www.dundee.ac.uk/cmdn

School of Medicine; www.medicine.dundee.ac.uk

premedical & medical courses, anatomy, applied orthopaedic technology, clinical research, forensic medicine, human genetics and experimental medicine, human reproduction, assisted conception and embryonic stem cells, international health, neuropharmacology & behaviour, cardiovascular & diabetes medicine, public health, motion analysis, cancer biology, oral cancer, health studies, global health and wellbeing, psychological therapy in primary care, quality diabetes care, quality improvement, simulation based education, sports and biomechanical medicine, stratified medicine and pharmacological innovation, orthopaedic and rehabilitation technology, othopaedic surgery, medical psychology, neuroscience, physiological sciences, physiology, sports biomedicine, immunology, oncology, trauma surgery, palliative care, psychiatry, cognitive behavioural psychotherapy, skin disease, cognitive behavioural psychotherapy, minimal access surgery, motion analysis, palliative care; MBChB, BMSc, MSc, MChOrth, MRes, MFM, PGDip/Cert, MD, MMSc, MSSc

School of Dentistry; www.dundee.ac.uk/ dentalschool

oral health science, orthodontics, prosthodontics, dental surgery, dental public health, cancer biology, oral cancer, forensic odontology; BMSc, BSc, MDPH, MRes, MDSc, MFDent

School of Nursing and Midwifery; www.dundee.ac.uk/medden

advanced practice, adult/child/mental health nursing, palliative care, midwifery, global health & well-being, health & social care, infection prevention & control, health studies, community health nursing, mental health, physiotherapeutics, quality improvement, clinical assessment governance, CPD, numerous Master modules, long term conditions, maternal, child & family help, health studies, maternal and infant health, health studies quality improvement; BN, BSc, MNurs, MPhil, MSc

School of Medicine Institutes

Division of Cardiovascular & Diabetes Medicine; Division of Imaging & Technology; Division of Neuroscience; Division of Population Health Sciences; Division of Molecular Medicine

Graduate School; www.graduate.cmdn.dundee.ac.uk

DURHAM UNIVERSITY
www.dur.ac.uk

Faculty of Arts and Humanities; www.dur.ac.uk/arts.humanities

Dept of Classics and Ancient History; www.dur.ac.uk/classics

ancient history & archaeology, ancient history, classics, classical past, ancient, medieval & modern history, ancient philosophy, Greece, Rome & the Near East

Dept of English Studies; www.dur.ac.uk/ english.studies

English literature studies & history/philosophy, medieval & Renaissance literary studies, studies in poetry, 20th-century literary studies, Victorian & romantic literary studies, educational studies, English literature & romantic studies, English literary studies

English Language Centre; www.dur.ac.uk/ englishlanguage

TESOL English for specific purposes/teaching young learners, English for academic purposes, English language teaching, applied linguistics for/in TESOL

Dept of History; www.dur.ac.uk/history

history, medieval history/& early modern/history, modern history, research methods (economic and social history), social & economic history

Dept of Music; www.dur.ac.uk/music

music, ethnomusicology, composition, musicology, British music, performance

School of Modern Languages and Cultures; www.dur.ac.uk/mlac

Arabic/English translation & interpreting, arts & social sciences, medieval & early modern studies, French, German, Hispanic studies, Italian, Russian, Chinese studies, modern languages & history, translation studies, culture & difference, visual arts & culture

Dept of Philosophy; www.dur.ac.uk/ philosophy

philosophy (& jt degrees), history & philosophy of science & medicine, metaphysics, ethics, aesthetics

Dept of Theology and Religion; www.dur.ac.uk/theology.religion

Christian theology (Anglican, Catholic studies), historical & systemic theology, Old Testament & related studies, theology, philosophy & theology, theology & religion, biblical studies, spirituality, theology & health, study of religion/film & religion, theology & ethics, theology & science, religion & society; BA(Hons), GDip, MA, MLitt, MMus, MTh, PhD

Faculty of Science; www.dur.ac.uk/ science.faculty

School of Biological and Biomedical Sciences; www.dur.ac.uk/ biological.sciences

biomedical sciences, biological sciences, biosciences, protein quality control in health & disease, cell biology, ecology, cellular & molecular biology & biochemistry

Dept of Chemistry; www.dur.ac.uk/ chemistry

chemistry (& jt degrees), numerous postgraduate research projects, natural science

Dept of Engineering and Computer Science; www.dur.ac.uk/ecs/computing.science

civil/electronic/mechanical engineering, communications engineering, computer science, general engineering, internet systems and e-business, new and renewable energy, software development for business, computer science & business/physics/mathematics, natural sciences

Dept of Earth Sciences; www.dur.ac.uk/ earth.sciences

earth sciences, climate & environmental change, geohazards, the solid earth, geoenergy, resources & waste, geology, natural sciences, geophysics, environmental/geosciences

Dept of Mathematical Sciences; www.dur.ac.uk/mathematical.sciences

mathematics, mathematical sciences, particles, strings & cosmology, jt degrees including statistics, physics

Dept of Physics; www.dur.ac.uk/physics

physics/& astronomy, particles, strings & cosmology, biophysical science

Dept of Psychology; www.dur.ac.uk/ psychology

developmental/cognitive neuroscience, developmental psychopathology, applied/psychology, research methods; BA(Hons), BEng, BSc(Hons), MA, MChem, MEng, MMath, MPhil, MPhys, MSc, MSci, PhD

Faculty of Social Science and Health; www.dur.ac.uk/science.health

School of Applied Social Sciences; www.dur.ac.uk/sass

criminology & criminal justice/sociology, anthropology & sociology studies, international social work & community development, social policy, social work, society & politics, social research methods (sociology/ social policy/criminology), managing community practice/youth work practice, community and youth work, sport, exercise & physical activity, CPD

Dept of Anthropology; www.dur.ac.uk/ anthropology

anthropology/& archaeology, evolutionary anthropology/medicine, health and human sciences, biological/medical anthropology, well-being, sustainability, culture & development anthropology, energy & society, sociocultural anthropology, research methods (anthropology)

Dept of Archaeology; www.dur.ac.uk/archaeology

archaeology/& ancient civilisations, archaeological science, conservation of archaeological & museum objects, international cultural heritage management, paleopathology, museum & artefact studies

Durham Business School; www.dur.ac.uk/dbs

economics, environmental and natural resource economics, experimental economics, public economics; finance, finance (accounting and finance/corporate and international finance/economics and finance/finance and investment/international banking and finance/international money, finance and investment, global finance; management, management (business ethics/entrepreneurship/finance/HRM/international business/supply chain logistics), Islamic finance/& management; global MBA, Durham EBS, corporate MBA EMBA

School of Education; www.dur.ac.uk/education

educational assessment, education studies, initial training, PGCE primary education with QTS, secondary education, intercultural education & internationalism, history of art, practice of education, technically enhanced education, research methods (education)

Dept of Geography; www.dur.ac.uk/geo

risk & environmental hazards, geography, contemporary human geography, research methods, natural science, risk, health & public policy, risk & security

School of Government and International Affairs; www.dur.ac.uk/sgia

Arab world studies, defence, development, diplomacy, conflict prevention & security/peace-building, global politics, international relations/studies, economics, philosophy/& politics, politics & international relations; BA(Hons), DBA, EdD, MA, MA(Ed), MBA, MAnth, MSc, MScW, PGCE, PGCert/Dip, PhD

Durham Law School; www.dur.ac.uk

European trade/international trade & commercial law, law, society & law, legal studies

School of Medicine, Pharmacy www.dur.ac.uk/school.health

clinical management, global health, health research methods, philosophy of science, interdisciplinary mental health, medical education, pharmacy, public policy and health, spirituality theology & health; BA(Hons), BA(Ed), BSc(Ed), BSc(Hons), Cert Leg Stud, LlB, LlM, MA, MBBS, MPhil, PGCert, PGCert/Dip, PGCE, PhD, MA, MPharm, MJur[a]Degrees validated by Durham University offered at:

CRANMER HALL, ST JOHN'S COLLEGE
www.cranmerhall.com

theology and ministry; BA, MA, diploma/certificate, Doc PhD

NEW COLLEGE DURHAM
www.newdur.ac.uk

applied business computing, applied sport & exercise science, business & management, community studies, children & young people, childhood studies, computing & networks, counselling, design, education/& training, health & wellbeing, graphics/web design, outdoor activity/leadership, podiatry, events/spa/tourism management, applied health & social care, public health & health progress, leadership in voluntary & community organisations, public & community service, management & administration in the public sector, supporting learning & teaching, retailing, social work, visual arts, web design; BA(Hons), BSc(Hons), FD, numerous non-graduate courses

ROYAL ACADEMY OF DANCE
www.rad.org.uk

ballet education, ballet/dance teaching studies, Benesh, dance education, movement notation; BA(Hons), Dip/CertHE, MTeach(Dance), licenciate, PGCE

USHAW COLLEGE
www.ushaw.ac.uk

theology & ministry; BA, Certs, Dipls, MA, PGCert/Dip

UNIVERSITY OF EAST ANGLIA
www.uea.ac.uk

Faculty of Arts and Humanities; www.uea.ac.uk/hum

American Studies; www.uea.ac.uk/am
American literature, American history, American & English literature, American studies/& film studies/creative writing

School of Art History & World Art Studies; www.uea.ac.uk/art-history
archaeology, history of art & literature, gallery & museum studies, history of art, cultural heritage & international development/museum studies, art history & literature, history & history of art, cultural heritage and international development, cultural heritage and museum studies, history of art, museum studies, the arts of Africa, Oceania and the Americas, world art studies, film studies/landscape & art history

School of Film, Television & Media Studies; www.uea.ac.uk/film-television-media
film & TV studies, film & English/American studies, media studies, film, TV & creative practice, film & history

School of History; www.uea.ac.uk/history
modern history, history, modern British history, history & politics/landscape/medieval/modern European history, early modern history

School of Literature, Drama & Creative Writing; www.uea.ac.uk/lit
biography & creative non-fiction, creative writing – poetry/prose/scriptwriting, drama, scriptwriting & performance, English & American literature, English literature & drama, literary translation, literature & history, medieval & early modern textual cultures, theatre directing, text & production, writing in the modern world

Politics, Philosophy, Language and Communication Studies; www.uea.ac.uk/ppl
Politics; literature and politics, international relations, international relations and European politics/modern history/modern languages/politics/media/development studies, philosophy and politics, regulation and competition, international public policy and public management, international security, politics, public policy and the environment, social and political theory, international development studies, management studies

Communication Studies; society, culture and media, broadcast journalism, modern language, intercultural communication with business management, modern language and film and TV: theory and practice, media and cultural politics, media, culture and society, translation and interpreting with modern languages, translation, media and modern language

Philosophy; philosophy, English literature and philosophy, philosophy and film studies/history, philosophy and literature

BA(Hons), MA, MPhil, PGDip, PhD, MRes

Faculty of Medicine & Health; www.uea.ac.uk/medicine-health-science

School of Rehabilitation Sciences; www.uea.ac.uk/rehabilitation-sciences

occupational therapy, physiotherapy, speech & language therapy, clinical education/research, human communication science, leadership/dementia care, leading innovation for clinical practitioners

Norwich Medical School; www.uea.ac.uk/medicine

medicine, surgery, clinical science/research/psychology/education, cognitive behavioural therapy, coloproctology, health economics/research, knee surgery, molecular medicine, onoplastic breast surgery, regional anaesthesia, health economics/research, CPD (numerous topics)

School of Health Sciences; www.uea.ac.uk/health-sciences

adult/ children's/learning disabilities/mental health nursing, midwifery, occupational therapy, operating department practice, paramedic science, physiotherapy, speech and language therapy, advanced practitioner: emergency care practitioner/midwife/neonatal nurse/nurse/occupational therapy/paramedic/pharmacist/physiotherapist, clinical education, clinical research, occupational therapy, physiotherapy, advanced musculoskeletal research and practice, leadership in dementia care, leading innovation for clinical practitioners

BA(Hons), BSc(Hons), ClinPsyD, DipHE, FD, MBBS, MCE, MD, MHeaRes, MPhil, MSc, PGDip/Cert, PhD, MRes, MA

Faculty of Science; www.uea.ac.uk/sci

School of Actuarial Science; www.uea.ac.uk/actuarial-science

actuarial science, business statistics

School of Biological Sciences; www.uea.ac.uk/biological-sciences

biochemistry, biological sciences, biomedicine, ecology, molecular biology & genetics, applied ecology & conservation, plant science, molecular medicine, plant genetics & plant improvement

School of Chemistry Science; www.uea.ac.uk/chemistry

chemistry, adv organic chemistry, biological and medicinal chemistry, chemical physics, chemical sciences, forensic & investigational chemistry

School of Computing Science; www.uea.ac.uk/computing

actuarial sciences, applied/advanced computing/science, business information systems, business statistics, computational biology, computer graphics/systems engineering/science, games development, information systems, knowledge discovery & data mining

School of Engineering; www.uea.ac.uk/engineering

energy engineering with environmental management

School of Environmental Sciences; www.uea.ac.uk/env

applied ecology, agriculture, environmental sciences, climate change, environmental assessment & management/chemistry/earth sciences, environmental geography & international development/climate change/geophysics, geography, meteorology & oceanography

School of Natural Science; www.uea.ac.uk/sci/natsci

natural science

School of Mathematics; www.uea.ac.uk/mathematics

mathematics, mathematics with business, energy engineering & environmental management

School of Pharmacy; www.uea.ac.uk/pha

pharmacy practice, pharmacy
BSc(Hons), GradDip, MPhil, MSc, MSci, PGDip, PhD, MMath, MChem, MNatSci

Faculty of Social Sciences; www.uea.ac.uk/ssf

School of Economics; www.uea.ac.uk/economics

economics/& accountancy, business economics, business/ finance & economics, economics of international finance & trade, economics of money, banking & capital markets, quantitative financial economics, media economics, environmental/experimental/industrial economics, international business finance & economics, philosophy, politics & economics, economics & international relations

School of Education and Lifelong Learning; www.uea.ac.uk/edu

advanced educational practice/practice, cognitive behavioural therapy, counselling/ focusing-orientated psychotherapy, education, learning & development/pedagogy & assessment, lifelong learning &

development; international perspective, mathematics education, PE, person-centred counselling studies, PGCE (primary/secondary), social science research methods

School of International Development; www.uea.ac.uk/international-development

geography and international development, international development/and the environment/with economics/overseas experience/social anthropology and politics, social anthropology and politics with overseas experience, media and international development/with overseas experience, agriculture and rural development, climate change and international development, conflict, governance and international development, development economics, education and development, environment/gender analysis and international development, globalisation business and sustainable development, impact evaluation for international development, international development, international social development, media and international development, water security and international development, social science research methods

Geography; www.uea.ac.uk/geography

geography, environmental geography & climate change/international development, geography & international development

Law School; www.uea.ac.uk/law

law, employment law, European legal systems, information technology & intellectual property law, international commercial & business law/competition law/trade law, law with American law/ French law & language, legal studies, media law, policy and practice

Norwich Business School; www.uea.ac.uk/nbs

accounting & finance/management, brand leadership, business information management, advanced/international business management, entrepreneurship, finance & management, HRM, international accounting & business management, investment & finance, management, marketing/& management, supply chain management, sustainable business

School of Social Work; www.uea.ac.uk/social work

social work, social science research methods

School of Psychology; www.uae.ac.uk/psychology

psychology, developmental psychology, cognitive psychology/neuroscience, social psychology, social science research

BA(Hons), BSc(Hons), CPE/Dip, DEd, GradDip, LlBHons, LLM, MA, MA/DipSW, MBA, MPhil, MRes, MSc, MScEd, PGCert, PGDip, PhD[a]Degrees validated by University of East Anglia offered by:

CITY COLLEGE NORWICH
www.ccn.ac.uk

applied social work, applied science & exercise, arts & wellbeing, business management (finance & accounting/HRM), culinary arts, dementia care, early/childhood studies/years, English & cultural studies/psychology, health studies, higher education in social practice, hospitality/tourism & leisure management, leisure & event management, HRM, leadership & management/in public services, mental health practice, psychology/& sociology, public services, retailing, social work, sport, health & exercise, travel & tourism management; BA(Hons), Cert/DipHE, FdA/Sc

---

EASTONOTLEY COLLEGE
www.eastonotleycollege.ac.uk

agriculture, agricultural engineering, countryside management, equine studies, motor vehicles engineering, animal studies, arboriculture, construction, fishery studies, floristry, horticulture, outdoor activities, veterinary nursing

THE UNIVERSITY OF EDINBURGH
www.ed.ac.uk

College of Humanities and Social Sciences; www.hss.ed.ac.uk

The Edinburgh College of Art; www.ed.ac.uk/schools-departments/edinburgh-college-art

School of Art: intermedia art, interdiscipline creative practice, painting, sculpture, photography, contemporary art practice/theory, cultural landscapes, material practice

School of Design: animation, fashion, film & TV, glass, graphic design, illustration, interior design, jewellery & silversmithing, performance costume, product design, textiles, film directing, interior architectural design, performance costume, film directing, glass, graphic design, interior architectural design, jewellery, textiles

Architecture & Landscape Architecture:

architectural history, architecture, landscape architecture; Postgraduate; advanced sustainable design, architectural & urban design, architectural conservation, architectural history and theory, architectural project management, architecture, art space nature, cultural landscapes, cultural studies, design and digital media, digital media design, landscape architecture, material practice, urban strategies & design, architecture by design, cultural studies, interdisciplinary creative practices, landscape architecture, reflective design practice

Reid School of Music: music, music technology, composition/for screen, composition & performance, digital composition & performance, musical instruments & research, acoustics & music technology, musicology

History of Art; history of art, art in the global middle ages, history of fine art, Renaissance & early modern studies, curating & criticism, Scottish art & visual culture, theory & display; BA, MA, MA(Hons), MSc, MArch, MLA, MPhil, PhD, MFA, Dip

The Business School; www.business-school.ed.ac.uk

accounting & finance, business & accounting/economics/finance/geography/law, business management, business with decision science/enterprise & innovation/HRM/Marketing/strategic economics, international business with foreign language, accounting & finance, banking & risk, carbon finance/management, economics, finance &

investment, HRM, international business & emerging markets, management, marketing/& business analysis; MA, MSc, PhD, MBA

School of Divinity; www.div.ed.ac.uk

divinity/classics, biblical studies, ethics, ministry, philosophy & theology, religious studies/& English literature, science & religion, theology/in history, world Christianity; MA(Hons), MTh, GradDip, MPhil, PhD

School of Economics; www.ed.ac.uk/schools-departments/economics

asset pricing, corporate finance, economics, international money & finance, economics analysis, econometrics/finance, economics, economics (large number of jt degrees), advanced topics in macroeconomics/microeconomics, economics of labour markets, adv time series econometrics, development economics development of economic thought & methodology, personnel economics, topics in economic history, economic policy, environment & natural resources, health economics, industrial organisation, international trade; MA(Hons), MSc, PhD

School of Health in Social Science; www.ed.ac.uk/schools-departments/health

advancing nursing practice/skills, nursing studies, nursing in clinical research, health nursing & science, nursing (adult branch), clinical psychology, counselling & psychotherapy, health, science & society, including social science in health, integrated service improvement, health & social care, clinical psychology, applied psychology for children and young people, psychology of mental health, children & young people's mental health and psychological practice, mental health and well-being of children, young people and families, cognitive behavioural therapy for children and young people, psychological interventions for children and young people, CPD courses, psychology of mental health; BNurs(Hons), MA, MSc, CPD, DClinPsych, PhD

School of History, Classics and Archaeology; www.shc.ed.ac.uk

Archaeology; archaeology, environmental archaeology, anthropology & social anthropology, ancient Mediterranean civilisations, history & archaeology, archaeological history & archaeology, archaeological

Europe, forensic archaeology, human/osteoarchaeology, Mediterranean archaeology

Classics; ancient history, classical studies, classics, Greek studies, Latin studies, ancient & modern history, ancient history & classical archaeology/ Greek/Latin, ancient Mediterranean civilisations, classical archaeology & Greek, history & classics

History; economic/ & social history, history, Scottish history, American history, social history, history jt degrees, law & history, social studies & history, contemporary history, gender history, intellectual history, medieval history, Islamic & Byzantine studies, modern British & Irish history, social & cultural history; MA(Hons), LlB, BSc, MPhil, PhD

School of Law; www.law.ed.ac.uk

Scottish legal system, family law, public law of the UK and Scotland, contract and unjustified enrichment, critical legal thinking, European law, other law or non-law courses, jurisprudence, delict, public law and individual rights, business entities, evidence and criminal law, property law, commercial law, succession and trust law, optional law or non-law courses, intellectual property law, commercial law, media law, human rights law, commercial law, comparative and European private law, competition law and innovation, corporate law, criminal law/criminology and criminal justice, European law, global crime, justice and security global environment and climate change law, human rights, innovation, technology and the law, intellectual property law, international banking law and finance, legal research, international economic law, international law, law, law and Chinese, history and philosophy of law, medical law and ethics; LlB, Graduate LlB, Dip, LlM/MSc, PhD

School of Literatures, Languages and Cultures; www.ed.ac.uk/schools-departments/literatures-languages-cultures

Asian Studies; Chinese, Chinese & history/linguistics/ history of art/economics/law, Japanese/& linguistics, Japanese society & culture, modern Chinese culture studies, Asian relations/religions/studies, East Asian religions, Sanskrit, Prakit, & Pali language & literature

Celtic and Scottish Studies; Celtic & Scottish studies Scottish ethnology, Gaelic & primary education, Scottish culture & heritage, Scottish culture, Celtic

English Literature; book history & culture, US literature, creative writing, play writing, creative writing with online learning, literature & society/

enlightenment, romantic & Victorian, literature & modernity, 1900 to the modern day

European Languages and Cultures; French, German, Italian, Russian, Scandinavian, medieval literatures & cultures, comparative & general literature

Film Studies and Theatre Studies; film studies, theatre & performance studies, film exhibition & curating, play writing

Islamic and Middle Eastern Studies; Persian studies/ civilisation, advanced Arabian, Middle East studies, comparative literature, European languages & cultures, English literature, European theatre, film studies, Islamic & Middle Eastern studies, Arabic world studies, international relations of Middle East with Arabic

Translation Studies; literature & transatlanticism, material cultures & study of the book, translation studies; MA(Hons), MSc, MPhil, PhD

Moray House School of Education; www.education.ed.ac.uk

academic practice, additional support for learning & community education, childhood practice, applied sport science, community education, dance science, developing education leadership & learning, digital education, education leadership & management/ Scottish qualification for headship, education, education, language-theory, practice & literacy, educational research, HE, international child protection management, inclusive & special education, language teaching, learning for sustainability, outdoor environment & sustainability education, performance psychology, physical activity for health, PE, primary education, sport policy, management & international development, social justice & community action, sport & recreation management, sport policy & international development, TESOL, strength & conditioning, sport coaching & performance, PGDE (primary/secondary/ Canadian); MA(Hons), BA(Hons), BSc(Hons), MSc, PGDip/Cert, MEd, EdD, MPhil, PhD

School of Philosophy, Psychology and Language Science; www.ppls.ed.ac.uk

ancient philosophy, philosophy, philosophy and English literature/English language/economics/ Greek/linguistics/mathematics/politics/psychology/ theology/modern languages, applied linguistics, cognition in science & society, psychological linguistics, cognitive science, cognition in science & society, developmental linguistics, evolution of language & cognition, English language, epistemology, ethics & mind, history & theory of psychology, human cognitive neuropsychology, learning/& English language, linguistics/jt degrees, mind, language & embodied cognition, psychology & philosophy/business studies/linguistics/sociology, psychology of reading/language, psychology/of individual differences, speech & language processing, visual cognition; MA(Hons), BSc(Hons), MSc/Dip, MA, MPhil, PhD

School of Social & Political Science; www.sps.ed.ac.uk

international relations/& law, international relations with quantitative methods; politics with quantitative methods; social anthropology, social anthropology & politics; social anthropology & social policy/development/social history/ south Asian studies; social anthropology, social anthropology & politics/social policy/development/social history/south Asian studies; social policy, social policy & law/politics/ economic history/sociology/social & political studies/economics; social work, social policy with quantitative methods, global & international sociology, sociology, sociology & psychology/politics/social & economic history/social anthropology/South Asian studies/quantitative methods, the internet and Society, genetics, nature and society, medical sociology armed force and society

Masters Programmes, African studies, childhood studies, comparative public policy, global crime, justice and security, global environment, politics and society, global health, health equalities, health systems and public policy, international and European politics, international development, international political theory, international relations, international relations of the Middle East, Middle East with Arabic, management of bioeconomy, innovation and governance, medical anthropology, nationalism studies, policy studies, science and technology society, social anthropology, social research, sociology and global change, social work, advanced professional studies (mental health officer award), human rights; BSc(Hons), MA, MA(Hons), MPhil/PhD, MSc, PGDip/Cert, MSW, LlM, Dip

College of Medicine and Veterinary Medicine; www.ed.ac.uk/schools-departments/medicine-vet-medicine

medicine, medical sciences, veterinary medicine, biomedical sciences, infectious diseases, neuroscience, pharmacology, physiology, reproductive biology, animal bioscience, public health, regenerative medicine: clinical & industrial delivery, reproductive sciences biosciences, applied animal behaviour & welfare, biomedical sciences, cardiovascular biology, dental implantology, human anatomy, integrative neuroscience, oral surgery/health science, orthodontics, paediatric dentistry, prosthodontics, regenerative medicine; clinical & industrial delivery/science, communication & public health, transfusion, transplantation & tissue banking

School of Clinical Sciences; www.ed.ac.uk/schools-departments/clinical-sciences

oral surgery, orthodontics, paediatric dentistry, prosthodontics, regenerative medicine: clinical and industrial delivery

School of Biomedical Sciences; www.ed.ac.uk/schools-departments/biomedical-sciences

biomedical sciences, biological sciences, medical sciences, science communication and public engagement, biodiversity, wildlife and ecosystem health, global health and infectious diseases, international animal health

School of Molecular Genetics & Population Health Sciences

The Royal (Dick) School of Veterinary Studies; www.ed.ac.uk/schools-departments/vet

animal biolscience one health, conservation medicine, international animal welfare, ethics & law, veterinary medicine & surgery, applied animal behaviour & animal welfare, equine science; BSc(Hons), MBChB, MSC, BVMS, DipCert, MPhil, PhD

College of Science and Engineering; www.scieng.ed.ac.uk

School of Biological Sciences; www.ed.ac.uk/schools-departments/biology

biochemistry, bioinformatics, biological sciences/& management, biotechnology, cell biology, developmental regeneration & stem cells, ecology, evolutionary biology, genetics, immunology, infectious diseases, medical biology, molecular biology, molecular genetics, plant science, zoology, biodiversity & taxonomy of plants, bioinformatics, drug discovery & translational biology, next generation drug direction, quantitative genetics & genome analysis, systems & synthetic biology, synthetic biology & biotechnology; BSc(Hons), MSc, MPhil, PhD

School of Chemistry; www.chem.ed.ac.uk

chemical physics, chemistry/with environmental & sustainable chemistry/materials chemistry, medicinal & biological chemistry, bioelectronics biosensors, sensor & imaging systems; BSc(Hons), MSc

School of Engineering; www.see.ed.ac.uk

Chemical Engineering with environmental engineering/management, materials & processes, energy systems

Civil and Environmental Engineering: civil engineering, structural engineering with architecture/management, structural & fire safety engineering

Electronics and Electrical Engineering: electrical engineering/& mechanical engineering/management/renewable energy, electronics & computer science/electronic engineering/electrical engineering (communications), electronics & software engineering

Mechanical Engineering: advanced materials applications, electrical & mechanical engineering, fluid and particle dynamics, manufacturing & process optimization, materials & processes, mechanical engineering with management/renewable energy

Institute for Energy Systems: environmental mitigation, energy delivery, renewable energy, restructuring and regulation, energy for sustainable environment

General Engineering

Engineering MSc Programmes

bioelectronics and biosensors, electronics, signal processing and communications, structural and fire safety engineering, sustainable energy systems, international master of science in fire safety engineering, structural engineering and mechanics, sensor and imaging systems; BEng(Hons), MEng(Hons), MSc, MPhil, PhD, EngD, PGDip

School for Informatics; www.inf.ed.ac.uk

informatics, artificial intelligence, cognitive science, computer science, software engineering, adv/ design informatics; BEng(Hons), MEng(Hons), BSc(Hons), MSc, MInf, PhD, MPhil

School of Geosciences; www.geos.ed.ac.uk

Ecological Sciences, Geography, Earth Science: geography, physical geography, geology, geophysics, archaeology, GIS, ecological & environmental science, environmental geoscience, carbon capture & storage/management, carbon capture and storage, carbon management, climate change management, earth observation, ecosystem services, environment, culture and society, environment and development, environmental sustainability, GIS, marine systems and policies, sustainable resource management; BSc(Hons), MSc, MEnvSci, PGCert, PhD

School of Mathematics; www.maths.ed.ac.uk

applied mathematics, mathematics & biology/business/management/music/physics, artificial intelligence/computer science & mathematics, economics & mathematics/statistics, philosophy & mathematics operational research, operational research(OR)/with risk/computational rationalisation, financial OR with statistics, financial modelling & optimisation, economics & statistics, computational/financial mathematics, financial mathematics & modelling; BSc(Hons), MA, MSc, PhD

School of Physics and Astronomy; www.ph.ed.ac.uk

astrophysics, physics, chemical physics, computational physics, mathematical physics, theoretical physics, physics and computer sci/mathematics/meteorology/music, high performance computing with data, science; BSc, MChemPhys, MPhil, MPhys, MSc, PGDip, PhD

EDINBURGH NAPIER UNIVERSITY
www.napier.ac.uk

The Business School; www.napier.ac.uk/ business-school

Accounting, Financial Services & Law; accounting, accounting and finance/financial management/corporate finance/economics/entrepreneurship/HRM/law/marketing management, banking & financial regulation, financial services, global investment banking, international banking & finance, international commercial law, international finance, law, law with accounting/ business management/entrepreneurship

Marketing, Tourism Languages; English as a foreign language, festival and event and hospitality management, festival and event management, festival and event management with entrepreneurship/HRM/language, hospitality & marketing management/service management/tourism management, hospitality management, hospitality management with entrepreneurship/HRM/ language, intercultural business communication, international business languages/ with entrepreneurship/HRM/management, international event & festival management, international marketing, international marketing with tourism and events, international tourism management, language with festival and event management/marketing management/tourism management, languages and intercultural communication, marketing, marketing management/ with consumer studies/entrepreneurship/language, marketing with digital media/ festival and event management/sales management, tourism and airline management, /hospitality management, marketing management, tourism management/with entrepreneurship/HRM/language, tourism marketing Management; business and enterprise, business management (banking, entrepreneurship, events, finance, HRM, leadership and innovation, marketing and sales, marketing, sales, strategy and governance, tourism and hospitality), business studies, business studies with entrepreneurship/finance/HRM/ marketing, economics with management, international/ HRM, HRM with financial management/ organisational psychology, international business management, international business studies/HRM; MBA; (banking, entrepreneurship, events, executive, finance, health management, tourism and hospitality, HRM, leadership and innovation, leadership practice, marketing and sales); BA, BA(Hons), MSc, MBA, MPhil, LlB, LlM, PGCert

Faculty of Engineering, Computing and Creative Industries; www.napier.ac.uk/ fecci

School of Computing; www.napier.ac.uk/ soc/Pages/Home.aspx
advanced networking, business information systems, computer network systems, computing/science/SWE, computing for educators, computing security systems, creative computing, digital media/global networks, interactive media design, games development/technology, information technology/systems development, adv security & cybercrime/digital forensics, adv/software engineering, project & programming management, sound design, web technologies/design & development, strategic ITC leadership; BEng/Hons, BSc/Hons, MPhil, MSc, PhD

Arts & Creative Industries; www.napier.ac.uk/sci/Pages/ SchoolOfArtsCreativeIndustries.aspx
adv film practice, acting for stage & screen/& education, advertising, communication, advertising & PR, creative advertising/writing, English/& acting/ film, environmental graphics, exhibition design, film, graphic design, interaction/interdisciplinary design, international journalism for media professionals, interior architecture, journalism, lighting design, music, music/(pop), photography, product design/ prototyping, magazine/publishing, motion graphics, publishing, screen project development, screenwriting, TV; BA, BA(Hons), BDes, BDes(Hons), BMus(Hons), MDes, MFA, MSc, PGCert/Dip, MA

Engineering & the Built Environment; www.napier.ac.uk/sebe/Pages/ default.aspx
architectural technology & building performance, adv materials engineering, adv structural engineering with management, automation & control, building surveying, civil engineering, civil & timber engineering/transportation, construction/& project/ management, electronic/computer/electrical engineering, energy & environmental engineering, engineering design, environmental sustainability, facilities management, maritime transportation project management, property development & valuation/ investment/construction management, quantity surveying, adv/structural engineering, real estate management & investment/surveying, safety & environmental management, renewable energy, timber industry management/engineering, transport management/planning and engineering; BSc, BSc(Hons), BEng, BEng(Hons), MEng, MSc, MSci, PGCert/Dip

Faculty of Health, Life & Social Science; www.napier.ac.uk/fhlss

Life, Sport & Social Sciences; www.napier.ac.uk/FHLSS/SLSSS/Pages/ Home.aspx
animal biology, applied criminology & forensic psychology, biomedical sciences, biological sciences, biotechnology for environmental sustainability, career guidance & development, criminology, drug design & biomedical science, psychology, sociology, social science, social research; conservation & management of protected areas, ecotourism, environmental biology, forensic biology, marine & freshwater biology, microbiology & biochemistry, psychology, pharmaceutical science, social sciences, careers

guidance, human performance, environmental sustainability & sociology, health & well being, medical biotechnology, psychology & sociology, veterinary psychology, sports & exercise science (coaching/sport performance, enhancement/conditioning/physiology/psychology/injury), wildlife biology & conservation, youth work; BSc(Hons), MSc, BA(Hons), PGCert/Dip, MPhil, MRes, PhD

School of Nursing, Midwifery and Social Care; www.napier.ac.uk/fhlss/NMSC/Pages/SchoolofNursing.aspx

nursing studies, nursing – child health/adult/mental health/learning disabilities, advanced practice (cancer care/child protection/neonatal nursing/diabetes nursing, midwifery, nursing & applied education/palliative care/management), clinical research, epilepsy care, health administration, international clinical research & technology; BMid, BN, DipHE, MSc, PGDip/Cert, MRes, MPhil, PhD

EDINBURGH COLLEGE OF ART
www.eca.ac.uk

Architecture & Landscape; architectural history, architecture, landscape architecture, architecture & urban design, architectural conservation, architectural history & theory, architectural project management, art, space & nature, cultural landscapes, cultural studies, design & digital media, material product, sound sign, urban strategy & design

School of Art; intermedia art, painting, photography, sculpture, animation, contemporary art practice/theory, cultural landscapes, material practice

History of Art; fine art, history of art, art in global images, theory & display, modern & contemporary art tradition, curating & criticism, Renaissance & early modern art, Scottish art & visual culture, 1750–2000

Design; animation, fashion, film & TV, glass, graphic design, illustration, interior design, jewellery & silversmithing, performance costume, product design, textiles, design informatics, film directing, interior architectural design, interior design, material practice music, music technology, digital composition & media/performance, acoustics, adv sustainable design, architectural & urban design

Reid School of Music; music, music technology, acoustics & music technology, composition, digital composition & performance, musical instrument design, musicology; BA(Hons), MA, MSc, MFA, MArch, MLA, MPhil, PhD, BMus, MMus

---

UNIVERSITY OF ESSEX
www.essex.ac.uk

Faculty of Humanities and Comparative Studies; www.essex.ac.uk/hcs

History; www.essex.ac.uk/depts/history.aspx

history (modern, social & cultural, American), film studies, joint honours in range of subjects, cultural & social, local & regional history, public history

Department of Literature, Film, and Theatre Studies; www.essex.ac.uk/depts/lifts.aspx

creative writing/& film /literature, drama/& literature/film studies/modern languages, English literature, English & United States literature, film studies, film & literature, literature & film studies/history of art/sociology/philosophy/history/modern language/

drama, literature & the environment, multimedia journalism, playwriting

Dept of Philosophy & Art History; www.essex.ac.uk/depts/spah

Art History; art history, art history & philosophy/history/modern language/literature/film studies, gallery & cultural criticism, curating contemporary art, gallery studies, art history for academic purposes, art history & theory

Philosophy; philosophy, philosophy, religion & ethics, philosophy & art history, philosophy & history/ mod languages/literature/law/human rights/politics/sociology, continental philosophy, critical social theory, philosophy & psychoanalysis, politics, philosophy & economics

Centre for Interdisciplinary Studies in the Humanities; www.essex.ac.uk/depts/centres-and-institutes/cish

Latin American Studies
Latin American studies with human rights/business management/modern languages/Spanish studies/sociology

European Studies
European studies/with politics or modern languages, government, law, philosophy & art history

American studies
American (US) studies with criminology/film, criminology & socio-legal research, organised crime, terrorism research & security

Liberal Arts
liberal arts with sociology/mathematics
BA(Hons), CertHE, Dip/MA, FdA, MA, MFA, MPhil, PGCert, PhD, LlB

Faculty of Social Sciences; www.essex.ac.uk/ss

Dept of Economics; www.essex.ac.uk/economics
accounting & financial economics, behavioural/business/financial economics, computational economics, economic analysis for public policy, financial markets & policy, financial & business economics, financial/econometrics, economics, economics with mathematics/history/mod languages, money & banking, numerous jt courses, financial/international/management economics

Dept of Government; www.essex.ac.uk/government
politics, international relations, political economics, elections, public opinions and parties, political theory and public policy, philosophy, politics and economics, economics and politics, politics with human rights, politics/international relations and modern languages, sociology and politics, modern history and international relations/politics, philosophy and politics, law and politics, politics, political science, multilevel governance in Europe, global and comparative politics, ideology and discourse analysis, international relations, political behaviour, political economy, political theory, public opinion and polling, international relations, political economy, politics, philosophy, politics and environmental issues, ethics, politics and public policy

Dept of Languages and Linguistics; www.essex.ac.uk/linguistics
modern languages, modern languages with film production and editing skills, language studies, French/German/Italian/Portuguese/Spanish and modern languages, modern languages and linguistics, modern languages and English language/TEFL/linguistics, large number of jt degrees with modern languages, Spanish, Portuguese and Brazilian studies, European studies with modern languages, applied linguistics, English language and linguistics/language acquisition/language disorders, linguistics, linguistic studies, psycholinguistics, sociolinguistics, sociolinguistics of the Arab world, TEFL, TESOL, translation, interpreting and subtitling, Chinese-English translation and interpreting, translation, interpreting and subtitling, translation and literature

Dept of Sociology; www.essex.ac.uk/sociology
anthropology, crime & the media, sociology & politics, criminology & media, criminological & socio-legal research, sociology & human rights/social anthropology, social psychology, media, culture & society, sociology, psychosocial studies, sociological research, survey methods for sociology; BA(Hons), BSc(Hons), Diploma, GradDip, MA, MPhil, MRes, MSc, PGDip, PhD, ProcDoc

Faculty of Law and Management; www.essex.ac.uk/lm

Essex Business School; www.essex.ac.uk/ebs
Centre for Global Accountability; Centre for Entrepreneurship Research; Essex Finance Centre; Essex Management Centre
finance/management with Mandarin, accounting with economics/finance/management, sociology and management, business management, business analytics, banking and finance/with mod language, finance, financial management, management and marketing, business management and modern languages, marketing, international business/marketing & entrepreneurship, business administration, accounting, accounting and management/finance/financial management, financial economics, computational finance, international accounting, international finance, finance and management, banking and finance, finance and investment, financial engineering and risk management, management, international management, management and organisational dynamics, marketing and brand management,

entrepreneurship and innovation, environment & resource management, global project management, organisation studies and international HRM, accounting and financial economics, computational finance and economics, advertising, marketing & the media, marketing and brand management, sociology and management, MBA topics; BA(Hons), BSc(Hons), BBA, MA, MSc, MBA

Human Rights Centre; www.essex.ac.uk/humanrightscentre

human rights & Latin American studies/law/philosophy/politics/sociology, human rights & cultural diversity/public law, human rights theory & practice, international human rights law, humanitarian law, economics, social & cultural rights, research methods

School of Law; www.essex.ac.uk/law

law/philosophy/politics/sociology/Latin American studies & human rights, economic social & cultural rights, EU commercial law, human rights & cultural diversity, international human rights & humanitarian law, international commercial & business law, international trade law, philosophy & law, theory & practice of human rights, human rights & public law; BA(Hons), BSc(Hons), DocProg, LlM, LLB, MPhil, MSc, PhD, MBA

Faculty of Science and Engineering; www.essex.ac.uk/se

Dept of Biological Sciences; www.essex.ac.uk/bs

biochemistry, biological sciences, biology, biomedical science, biotechnology, environmental & resource management, genetics, tropical marine biology, molecular medicine, sports & exercise science

School of Computer Science and Electronic Engineering; www.essex.ac.uk/csee

computer science, computer games, computer networks, information and communication technology, computer science, data science and analytics, computer systems engineering, computers with electronics, electronic engineering, telecommunication engineering, electronic engineering, computational finance, advanced computer science, advanced web engineering, artificial intelligence, big data and text analytics, cloud computing, computer engineering, embedded systems, intelligent systems and robotics, multimedia networking, computer networks and security, telecommunication and information systems, computational finance, financial computing, algorithmic trading

School of Health and Human Sciences; www.essex.ac.uk/hss

adult/mental health nursing, health sciences (care of the adult/mental health), public health, midwifery, clinical psychology, psychological wellbeing practitioner, oral health sciences (hygiene/therapy), speech & language/occupational therapy, physiotherapy, healthcare practice, CPD, social work, sports therapy

Department of Mathematical Sciences; www.essex.ac.uk/maths

actuarial science, mathematics & computing/economics/finance/accounting/humanities/statistics/humanities/management/computing, cryptography & network security computing & mathematics, data science/ & analytics, discrete mathematics & its applications, econometrics, financial decision-making with applications, management, mathematics & economics/physics/modern languages/humanities, operational research & computer science, statistics & data analysis/computer science/econometrics/operational research, mathematics for secondary teaching

Dept of Psychology; www.essex.ac.uk/psychology

advanced/psychology, cognitive neuropsychology/neuroscience, psychology with cognitive neuroscience, research methods in psychology, language & the brain; BA(Hons), BEng, BSc(Hons), GradDip, MA, MPhil, MRes, MSc, PGDip, PhD, ProfDoc

Degrees validated by the University of Essex offered at:

WRITTLE COLLEGE
www.writtle.ac.uk

agriculture, animal management & science, conservation & environment, conservation wild life/management, design, equine, floristry, horticulture, sport & exercise performance, veterinary physiology, applied equine science, livestock protection science, arable crop management, animal welfare & conservation,

conservation management under global change, energy resources management, horticultural crop production, post-harvesting technology, art & design, landscape architecture, & garden design, historic designed landscape; BA(Hons), BSc(Hons), CertMS, Certs, DipMS, FdAs, Higher Certs, MA, MBA, MSc, PGCert/Dip

UNIVERSITY OF EXETER
www.exeter.ac.uk

University of Exeter Business School; www.business-school.exeter.ac.uk

accounting & finance, business & accounting/management, management with marketing, business, business economics, economics, economics with econometrics/finance/politics

Postgrad: Accounting & Finance; accounting and finance/investment/management, financial analysis and fund management, financial mathematics, marketing and financial services, financial economics, money and banking

Economics: economics, economics and econometrics, economics and experimental economics, behavioural economics and finance, financial economics, money and banking

Management: international management, international tourism management, marketing, management, international supply chain management, IT management for business, HRM, MBA courses

BSc, BA(Hons), MBA, MPhil, MSc, MRes, PGDip/Cert, PhD

College of Engineering, Mathematics & Physical Sciences; www.emps.exeter.ac.uk/engineering

Computer Science: IT management for business, computer science/& mathematics, electronic engineering & computer science

Engineering: civil engineering, civil and environmental engineering, electronic engineering, electronic engineering and computer science, energy engineering, engineering and management, materials engineering, mechanical engineering (all above degrees available with international study or industrial experience), engineering

Postgrad: advanced materials engineering, advanced mechanical engineering, engineering management, international supply chain management, advanced civil & environmental engineering, water management, structural engineering

Geology: applied geology, engineering geology & geotechnics, mining geology, applied geotechnics

Mathematics: adv/mathematics, mathematical biology, mathematics with computer science/accounting/finance/management/economics/physics, financial management, natural science, financial mathematics, fluid dynamics, mathematics (climate science/mathematical biology/geophysical & astrophysical), mathematics with business & finance/computer science, engineering mathematics, computational mathematics

Medical Imaging: diagnostic radiography, medical imaging

Minerals & Mining Engineering: minerals/mining engineering, mining geology, surveying & land/environmental management, applied geotechnics, professional mining life cycle

Natural Sciences: natural sciences

Physics & Astronomy: physics/with astrophysics, biomedical physics, quantum systems, electromagnetic & acoustic materials, nanomaterials, natural science; BSc(Hons), BEng, MEng, MSc, MPhil, PhD, MPhys, MMath MPhys, MSci, PGCert/Dip, MGeol

College of Humanities; www.humanities.exeter.ac.uk

Archaeology: archaeology, archaeology and anthropology, archaeology with forensic science, ancient/history and archaeology, bioarchaeology, experimental archaeology

Classics & Ancient History: ancient history, classical studies, classics, ancient history and archaeology, art history and classical studies, classical studies and English/modern language/ philosophy/theology/French and Latin/history, classics & ancient history

Drama: drama, theatre practice, staging Shakespeare, drama & visual culture/English

English: English, English & history/geography/drama /film studies/modern language/art history/classical studies, English literary studies, American & Atlantic studies, enlightenment to romanticism, Renaissance literature, modern & contemporary, film studies, creative writing, criticism & theory

Film Studies: film studies/with English, modern languages, international film business

History: history & English/philosophy/visual culture/international relations/politics/art history, ancient history, early modern history, medieval studies, western esotericism, maritime/medical history, war & society, economic & social history

Liberal Arts: liberal arts

Theology & Religion: theology, classical studies, philosophy; BA, BSc, MPhil, PhD

College of Life & Environmental Sciences; www.lifesciences.exeter.ac.uk

Biosciences: animal behaviour, conservation biology and ecology, environmental sciences, evolutionary biology, human sciences, marine biology, zoology, biological sciences, biochemistry, biological and medicinal chemistry, applied ecology, conservation and biodiversity, conservation science and policy, evolutionary and behavioural ecology, food security & sustainable agriculture

Geography: geography, environmental science, European studies, climate change/& risk management, conservation science & policy, environment energy & resilience, feedback & resilience, critical human geography/science, sustainable development

Psychology: psychology, animal behaviour, applied psychology (clinical), social & organizational psychology, psychology with sports & exercise science, psychology research methods

Sport and Health Sciences: paediatric exercise & health, psychology with sport & exercise science, health & wellbeing, psychology research methods; BSc(Hons), MPhil, BA(Hons), DocCliniPsychology, MSc, PhD, PGCert/Dip, MRes, BClinSci, MSci

College of Social Science & International Studies; www.social sciences.exeter.ac.uk

Arabic & Islamic studies: Arabic & Islamic studies/Middle East studies, politics & international relations in the Middle East, Kurdish/East/Persian/Palestine/Gulf/Iranian studies, ethnopolitics, Middle East history

Graduate School of Education

special educational needs, education, TESOL, educational psychology, childhood & youth studies, English & education, sport science, professional studies, PGCE: primary; ages 5–11; English, mathematics, humanities, music, science; 7–11; art, modern languages, main secondary subjects, schools direct, teaching first training, intercultural teaching programme, art/music/science/modern foreign languages, early years, secondary sciences/design & technology/English with media/drama/modern foreign languages/geography/information, post compulsory education; EdD(generic/educational psychology/SNE/TESOL), educational research

School of Law

law, European (maitrise) law, international commercial/property law, international human rights law, intellectual property law, sociolegal research, legal practice, maritime law

Politics; politics/& international relations, politics, philosophy & economics, number of joint degrees with politics, history & politics, conflict, security & development, international relations/studies (& jt degrees), European politics, political thought, public administration, public administration, politics & international relations of the Middle East

Sociology, Philosophy & Archaeology: sociology/& anthropology/criminology, philosophy, archaeology & anthropology, sociology & anthropology/criminology, politics, philosophy & economics, philosophy & sociology of science, sociology & politics, philosophy, science & technology studies

Strategy & Security Institute; applied security studies; BA(Hons), MA, PhD, MPhil, MA, PhD, LlB, LlM, MRes, DEdPsych, EdD, MEd, MPubAdmin, MArabic

University of Exeter Medical School; www.exeter.ac.uk/medicine

clinical sciences, environmental & human health, medicine, surgery, medical sciences, applied health services research; BClinSci, BMBS, MSc, MS, MPhil, PhD, MD, PhD, MSc, PGDip/Cert, PGCE

Degrees validated by University of Exeter offered at:

UCP MARJON-UNIVERSITY COLLEGE PLYMOUTH ST MARK & ST JOHN
www.ucpmarjon.ac.uk

acting, applied sport science & coaching, armed forces executive MBA, armed forces sport, fitness and health science, business and management, business management (education studies/media production/outdoor adventure/sport), children and families, children and young people, children's physical education, church university certificates, coaching and fitness education, community and society, community development, disability research in professional practice, early childhood education, early childhood studies, early years/ initial teacher training status/teacher programme, education studies, English and creative writing, English language & linguistics, executive MBA, film, football coaching and development, health and social care, health and social welfare, health exercise and physical activity, journalism, learning support, music production, outdoor adventure education, outdoor studies, coaching and mentoring, PGCE primary, PGCE secondary education with modern foreign languages/PE (with QTS), PE (secondary ed) (with QTS), primary education (early years) (with QTS), primary education (with QTS), primary education, professional development – education, professional enquiry, professional studies (leadership & management/sport and health sciences/sport development/outdoor education/outdoor learning/adventure education/English literature, rehabilitation in sport and exercise, school direct, special educational needs, speech and language sciences/therapy, sport coaching and PE, sport development (coaching/PE/management), sport journalism, sports therapy, strength and conditioning, TESOL, youth and community work; BA(Hons), BA/BSc, BEd, FdA/Sc, MTL, BEd(Hons), MA, MEd, MSc, MBA, PGDip/Cert

FALMOUTH UNIVERSITY
www.falmouth.ac.uk

Falmouth School of Art
drawing, fine art, illustration, authorial practice

School of Architecture & Interior Design
architecture interior design, sustainable product design

School of Communication Design
creative advertising, graphic design

Fashion & Textiles Institute
fashion design/marketing/photography, performance sportswear design, textile design

Academy of Innovation & Research
creative education

School of Film & TV
animation & visual effects, film/ & TV

Academy of Music & Theatre Arts
creative events management, music theatre & entertainment management, acting, music, dance & choreography, creative music technology, music, pop

Institute of Photography
photography, press & editorial photography

School of Writing & Journalism
creative writing/& journalism, English, journalism & communication/creative writing, English & journalism/creative writing, sports journalism

Games Academy
computing for games, digital games
BA(Hons), Foundation Dip, MPhil, PhD, FdA, PGDip, MA, MFA

UNIVERSITY OF GLASGOW
www.gla.ac.uk

College of Arts; www.gla.ac.uk/colleges/arts

School of Critical Studies
English language/literature, Scottish literature, theology & religious studies, creative writing, medieval & Renaissance studies, modernities, literature, theory & culture, Victorian literature, value based practice (faith communities/health & social care/peacebuilding)

School of Culture & Creative Arts
electronics & music, film & TV studies, history of art/art world practice, music, theatre studies, Postgrad; art history: art: politics: transgression: 20th century avant-gardes/dress and textile histories/a history of collecting & collections/art in Germany/kunst in

Deutschland, art, law and business, art, style & design, arts of China, arts of Europe, composition, creative industries and cultural policy, creative practice: see popular music, curatorial practice (contemporary art), film & TV studies, film journalism, filmmaking and media arts, historically informed performance practice, media management, medieval & renaissance studies, modern & contemporary art, museum studies, music industries, popular music, musicology, playwriting & dramaturgy, sonic art, textile conservation, theatre history/practices/studies

School of Humanities

archaeology, Celtic civilisation/studies, classics, digital media & information studies, Gaelic, Greek, history, Latin, philosophy, Scottish history, American studies, ancient civilisations, archaeological studies, battlefield & conflict archaeology, Celtic & Viking archaeology, Celtic studies, classics, early modern history, history, history (history of medicine), gender history, information management & preservation (digital)/(archives & records management), landscape: integrated research & practice, material culture & artefact studies, medieval history, museum studies, philosophy, war studies

School of Modern Languages & Cultures

comparative literature, French, German, Hispanic studies, Italian, Portuguese, Russian, Spanish, comparative literature, cultures, societies & language, modern languages & cultures, translation studies, translation & professional practice, TESOL; BD(Min), BMus, DLitt, MA, MA(Hons), MLitt, MPhil, MTh, PhD, MFA, PGCert/Dip, MSc, MMus

College of Medical Veterinary & Life Sciences; www.gla.ac.uk/colleges/mvls

Institutes: Biodiversity, Animal Health & Comparative Medicine; Cancer Sciences, Cardiovascular & Medical Science, Health & Wellbeing, Infection, Immunity & Inflammation, Molecular, Cell & Systems Biology, Neuroscience & Psychology

Postgrad: Biomedical Science, biotechnology, infection biology, cancer sciences, bioinformatics, polyomics & systems biology

Medical & Clinical Sciences; clinical sciences, translational medical sciences, forensic toxicology, clinical trials & stratified medicine, human nutrition, medical physics, health professions education, medical genetics, oral & maxillofacial surgery, endodontics, fixed & removable prosthodontics

Animal & Plant Sciences; veterinary public health, animal welfare, science, ethics and law, quantitative methods in biodiversity, conservation & epidemiology, ecology and environmental biology, food security

Cardiovascular & Pharmacology; cardiovascular science; diabetes, clinical pharmacology, sport and exercise science & medicine, forensic toxicology

Health and Wellbeing; global mental health, health technology assessment, primary care, advanced practice in health care

Neuroscience & Psychology; brain sciences: from molecules to mind, applied neuropsychology

School of Medicine; www.gla.ac.uk/medicine

dentistry, medicine, nursing (community, adult, surgical, children, public health), advanced lymphoedema management, advanced practice in health care, child health, clinical nutrition, endodontics, fixed & removable prosthodontics, forensic toxicology, health-professions education/health professions education, healthcare chaplaincy, human nutrition, medical genetics, medical physics, translational medical sciences

School of Veterinary Medicine; www.gla.ac.uk/schools/vet

animal welfare science, ethics & law, quantitative methods in diversity, conservation & epidemiology, veterinary biosciences, animal reproduction, veterinary medicine & surgery, biomedical sciences, veterinary public health

BSc, BSc(Vet Sci), BVMS, MVPH, PhD, B(MedSci), MSc(MedSci/DentSci), MBChB, MD, MML, MMLE, MPC, MPH, PhD, BDS, BSc(Dent Sc), DDS, MSc, PGDip/Cert, MRes

College of Science & Engineering; www.gla.ac.uk/colleges/scienceengineering

School of Chemistry; www.gla.ac.uk/schools/chemistry

chemistry, chemical physics, medical chemistry

School of Engineering; www.gla.ac.uk/schools/engineering

aeronautical engineering, aerospace systems, biomedical engineering, civil engineering, civil engineering with architecture, electronic & software engineering, electronics & electrical engineering, electronics with music, mechanical design engineering, mechanical engineering, mechanical engineering with aeronautics, mechatronics, product design engineering

Postgrad; aeronautical engineering, aerospace engineering & management, aerospace systems, biomedical engineering, civil engineering/& management, computer systems engineering, electronics & electrical engineering/& management, mechanical engineering/ & management, mechatronics nanoscience and nanotechnology, product design engineering, structural engineering & mechanics, sustainable energy

School of Computing Science;
www.gla.ac.uk/schools/computing

computing science (numerous jt degrees incl physics/ mathematics), informatics, neuroinformatics, data science, electronic & software engineering/development, mobile/software engineering, software engineering, information/security/technology

School of Geographical & Earth Sciences;
www.gla.ac.uk/schools/ges

archaeology/geography, geography, business economics/geography, numerous jt degrees, central & east European studies/geographaquatic system science, coastal system management, freshwater system science, geoinformation technology and cartography, geomatics & management, geospatial and mapping sciences, human geography: spaces, politics & ecologies, marine system science

School of Mathematics & Statistics;
www.gla.ac.uk/schools/
mathematicsstatistics

mathematics, applied/pure mathematics, finance/ accounting & mathematics/statistics, biostatistics, adv/statistics, environmental/social statistics, financial modelling/finance, statistics

School of Physics & Astronomy;
www.gla.ac.uk/schools/physics

astronomy, physics, chemical/theoretical physics, astrophysics, physics: advanced materials/energy & the environment/global security/life sciences/nuclear technology, physics with mathematics/applied mathematics/computer science, sensor & imaging systems

School of Psychology; www.gla.ac.uk/
schools/psychology

psychology, brain imaging/sciences – from molecules to mind, psychological studies

BEng, BSc, EngD, MEng, MSc, PGDip, PhD, EngD, PGDip, MRes

College of Social Sciences;
www.gla.ac.uk/schools/social sciences

Adam Smith Business School;
www.gla.ac.uk/schools/business

Accountancy & Finance; accountancy, accountancy with finance/international accounting/languages/economics, international accounting & financial management, international finance & financial institutions/ corporate governance & accountability, international financial analysis, international corporate finance & banking, financial modelling

Business & Management; business & management with computing science/mathematics/statistics/law/ archaeology/Celtic civilisation/music/philosophy/ Russian/Scottish history/Scottish literature/Celtic studies/classics/comparative literature/digital media & information studies/English literature/French/Gaelic/ German/history of art/history/Latin/theology & religious studies/politics/psychology/public policy/business economics/classics/economic & social history/ economics/geography/sociology

Business Economics; business economics with law/ archaeology/business & management/economic & social history/geography/mathematics/philosophy/ politics/psychology/public policy, Scottish history/ sociology/central & east European studies

Economics; economics with accountancy/mathematics/statistics/law/comparative literature/English language/English literature/French/Greek/history/ Latin/music/philosophy/Russian/Scottish history/ Scottish literature/theatre studies/theology & religious studies/German/Spanish/archaeology/central & east European studies, economic & social history/ business & management/Celtic civilisation/geography/mathematics/politics/psychology/public policy/ sociology

Post Graduate; asset pricing & investment, banking & financial services, corporate governance & accountability, development studies, economic development, economics, banking & finance, environment & sustainable development, finance & economic development, finance & management, financial economics, financial forecasting & investment, financial modelling, financial risk management, international accounting & financial management, international banking & finance/business & entrepreneurship/ corporate finance & banking/development/finance/ finance & economic policy/financial analysis/management & design innovation/management & leadership/real estate & management/ strategic marketing/ trade & finance, investment banking & finance/ local economic development, management with enterprise & business growth/HR/international finance, business administration, quantitative finance; BA, BSc, MA, MAQ(SocSci), MAcc, MBA, MFin, MSc, PhD, MPA, MBA

School of Education; www.gla.ac.uk/schools/education

adv education for social change, adult & continuing education, addiction, childhood practice, children's literacy & literature, drugs & alcohol studies, education (primary, secondary), education studies, adv/community development, community learning/& development, music, education with teaching, inclusive education/policy & practice, drugs & alcohol studies, learning & teaching languages in primary school/HE, middle leadership & management in schools, primary PE, primary teaching qualification, professional development in education, professional practice with PGDE, psychological studies, religious & philosophical education, religious education, teaching adults, teaching, leadership & learning, technological education, TESOL, young people, social inclusion & change; BA(Hons), BTechEd, BEd, BTechS, EdD, MA, MA(Hons), MEd, MLitt, MSc, MusicBEd, PhD, IM, MEd, PGDE

School of Interdisciplinary Studies; www.gla.ac.uk/schools/interdisciplinary

environmental stewardship, health & social policy, tourism, heritage & development/sustainability, environment, culture & communication, primary education, environmental science, technology & society; BSc, MA, MLitt, PGCert/Dip, MSc, TQ

School of Law; www.gla.ac.uk/schools/law

law, law (no. of joint degrees including French, German, Portuguese, Spanish & Italian legal studies & language, corporate & financial law, intellectual property & digital economy, international company law & policy, international competition/commercial/property law, international law, international law & security/politics, professional legal practice, socio-legal studies; MRes, LlB, LlM, MRes, PGDip/Cert, PhD

School of Social & Political Science; www.ac.uk/schools/socialpolitical

Central & East European Studies, Economic & Social History, Politics, Social & Public Policy, Sociology; in combination with one of the following: Celtic civilisation/Celtic studies/classics, digital media & information/English literature/German/history of art/Italian/Latin/Scottish history/Scottish literature/comparative literature/Gaelic/philosophy/Portuguese/Russian/Spanish/business economics/economics/geography/history/mathematics politics/psychology/public policy/law/economic & social history & archaeology/Celtic studies/French/history/music/Scottish history/computing science/business & management/politics /public policy/Scottish history/politics & law/archaeology/English language/film & television studies/French/ Greek/history/music/philosophy/theatre studies/ theology & religious studies; MA, MA(SocSci), MSc, MRes, CPD, MLitt, EdD, PhD, PGCert/Dip

GLASGOW CALEDONIAN UNIVERSITY
www.gcu.ac.uk/ebe

School of Engineering & the Built Environment; www.caledonian.ac.uk/ebe

3D computer animation, 3D design for virtual environments, adv computer networking, advance networking engineering, applied instrumentation & control, audio technology with electronics/multimedia, audio systems engineering, building services engineering/surveying, climate justice, computer aided mechanical engineering, computer games (art & animation/design/software development/indie development), computer science, computing (information/web systs development), computer & electronics systems engineering, digital design (graphics), electrical & electronic engineering/energy engineering, engineering & the built environment, engineering, computing & the creative industries, construction management by blended engineering/economics, digital security/forensics, cyber security & networking, information technology/security, electrical power engineering, energy & environmental management/oil & gas, environmental civil engineering/management & planning, fire risk engineering, forensic investigation, graphic design for digital media, engineering, health & safety & environmental management, interior design, international project design/management (oil & gas), IT/ security/management for business, maintenance management, mechanical & power plant systems engineering, mechanical electronic systems engineering, mechanical engineering design/manufacture, networked security/systems engineering, web systems development, management/engineering oil & gas, occupational health & safety management, property management & valuation, quantity surveying, real estate management, software development for business, sustainable energy technology/management, telecommunication engineering, waste management; BA/BA(Hons), BEng/BEng(Hons), BSc/BSc(Hons), DipHE, MA/PGD, MSc/PGDip, PhD, FD, Dips

Glasgow School for Business & Society; www.caledonian.ac.uk/cbs

accountancy, business/& management, business resilience & crisis management, captive insurance marketing, citizenship & human rights, creative & cultural management, digital marketing, economics & finance/law/risk, fashion branding retailing/business, finance, investment & risk, global business law & regulation, global human rights law & regulation, Islamic finance, management, health history, HRM, investment, international banking, law with risk, international banking finance & risk management, international economics & finance, international business & hospitality management/marketing/tourism management, international contracting/HRM/brand management, international business & economics/finance/business/sports management/event management/fashion branding, international management/HRM/law/languages, international development/business management/fashion marketing/marketing/retail marketing/supply chain management, international retailing/operations & supply chain management, finance & risk, international multimedia communication/sports management/tourist management, law, learning contracts, leadership & management in public sector, management, marketing, media communication, multimedia journalism, marketing & enterprise, management, public sector finance, management, marketing, multimedia journalism, railway operations management, risk & law/management, social business & microfinance, social enterprise, social sciences, TV writing (fiction); BA(Hons), MRes, PhD, LlB, LlM, MSc, PGD/C, PhD, MBA

School of Health & Life Sciences; www.caledonian.ac.uk/hls

adv nursing practice, applied psychology, applied/biomedical science, biomolecular & biomedical science, clinical microbiology, clinical nutrition & health/physiology, diagnostic imaging studies, clinical ophthalmology & vision, counselling & psychology, diabetes care & management, digital health, education in /health & social care/adv professional practice, food bioscience, human nutrition & dietetics, human bioscience, life sciences, medical ultrasound, microbiology, musculoskeletal physiotherapy, nursing (adult/child/mental health/learning disabilities), nursing studies, occupational therapy, operating dept practice, optometry, orthoptics, ophthalmic dispensing, oral health science, pharmacology, podiatry, professional studies in nursing, psychology in forensic settings, physiotherapy, public health, radiography, radiotherapy & oncology, specialist community public health nursing, social work, theory of podiatric surgery, biomedical sciences, food bioscience, sociology, psychology, microbiology, pharmacology, psychology; BSc, BSc(Hons), DipHE, DPsych, MSc, OphthDisp, PGCert/Dip, PhD, MRes, BSc(Hons), BA(Hons), GradCert, MPhil, MSc, PGCert/Dip, PhD, ProfDoc, BMidwifery, BN

THE GLASGOW SCHOOL OF ART
www.gsa.ac.uk

architecture/studies, communication design, creative practices, design innovation & citizenship, digital culture, engineering with architecture, environmental/service design, fine art photography, interior/silversmithing & jewellery/fashion & textiles/product design engineering, fine art practice, graphics, graphic illustrative photography, interior design, international management & design/innovation, international heritage visualisation teaching & learning medical visualisation & human anatomy, painting & printmaking, product design engineering, sculpture & environmental art, serious games design, sound for the moving media; BA(Hons), BEng, BArch, DipArch, MA, MArch, MDes, MEng, MPhil, MRes, PhD, MFA, PGCert

UNIVERSITY OF GLOUCESTERSHIRE
www.glos.ac.uk

School of Accounting & Law; insight.glos.ac.uk/academicschools/dal/Pages/default.aspx

accounting & business/financial management, law

School of Art & Design; insight.glos.ac.uk/academicschools/dad/Pages/default.aspx

advertising, graphic design, fine art, illustration, photojournalism & documentary philosophy, photography/editorial & advertising, illustration, landscape architecture, visual communication

School of Business & Management; insight.glos.ac.uk/academicschools/dbm/Pages/default.aspx

accountancy & business management/financial management, business & marketing management, business management & strategy, business/information technology, economics, international business studies, marketing, advertising & branding, strategy, law, marketing management & branding/advertising, management studies, hospitality management, HRM/strategy, marketing, retail management, tourism management

School of Media; insight.glos.ac.uk/academicschools/dcmp/Pages/default.aspx

film/production/studies, sport/journalism, mass communication, media production, pop music, radio/TV production, music & media management

School of Computing & Technology; insight.glos.ac.uk/academicschools/dc/Pages/default.aspx

business information, computing, forensic computing, information technology, computer games design, multimedia web design, product design, dependable software, information security, information technology

School of Humanities; insight.glos.ac.uk/academicschools/dh/Pages/default.aspx

creative writing, English literature/language, history, religion, philosophy & ethics, theology & religious studies, creative & critical writing, philosophical & religious thought

School of Leisure; insight.glos.ac.uk/academicschools/delth/Pages/default.aspx

drama, events, events tourism/hotel and resort/ hotel resort and events/ hotel resort and tourism management, performing arts, sports management and development, strategic events/hospitality/sports/tourism management, tourism management, hospitality and tourism management, professional studies/in children's play

School of Natural & Social Sciences; insight.glos.ac.uk/academicschools/NSS/Pages/default.aspx

applied ecology, animal biology, biology, counselling, criminology, ecology & environmental science, geography, psychology/& criminology/sociology, psychotherapy, sociology, sustainable environment, applied social sciences, applied/business/criminal/forensic/occupational psychology

Sport & Exercise; insight.glos.ac.uk/academicschools/dse/Pages/default.aspx

sports (coaching/development/fitness), applied sport and exercise studies, sport and exercise sciences, sports and dance education, sports coaching and development/education, sports education and development/ science, sports fitness and physical activity, sports leadership/strength and conditioning/science/therapy, coaching science, physical activity, exercise and health practice, psychology of sport & exercise, sport and Christian outreach (sports chaplaincy), sport and exercise psychology, sports therapy

Institute of Education & Public Service; insight.glos.ac.uk/academicschools/education/Pages/default.aspx

children and young people's practice, early years, education and learning, health and social care practice, mental health practice, youth practice applied health studies, community care practice with vulnerable adults, community and district nursing specialist practice, early childhood studies with early years initial teacher training, early childhood studies, education studies, health, community and social care, non-medical prescribing, person-centred health care practice, social work/with adults, teacher training – primary, youth studies, youth work, QTS (primary and secondary), community and district nursing specialist practice leadership and management (social/care work, educational leadership, inclusive education, professional studies, non-medical prescribing, PGCE (primary/secondary), practice teacher, work with children, young people, families and their carers, youth work

BA/BA(Hons), BSc/BSc(Hons), DipSW, BEd, LlB, MA, MPhil, MRes, MSc, PGCert/Dip, MBA, CMS, DMS, FD, GradDip/Cert, CertHE

GLYNDWR UNIVERSITY
www.glyndwr.ac.uk

Institute for Arts, Science & Technology; www.glyndwr.ac.uk/en/ UniversityInstitutes/ ArtsScience&Technology

Creative Industries, www.glyndwr.ac.uk/en/UniversityInstitutes/ArtsScienceandTechnology/Cre

Applied Art; design: applied arts, art practice, design practice

Design Communication & Digital Art; design: animation, visual effects and game art/film and photography/graphic design and multimedia/illustration, graphic novels and children's publishing, digital art for creative media, creative media, communications & digital art

Fine Art; fine art, drawing, illustration

Creative Media Technology; music technology, sound technology, television production and technology, creative audio technology

Broadcasting & Journalism; broadcasting, journalism and media communications, print

Creative Writing; creative writing and history/English

English; English, English and creative writing/history

History; history, creative writing/English and history

Information Management; library and information practice/management

Theatre; theatre, TV & performance

BEng(Hons), FdEng, MSc, PhD, MPhil, MRes, MFA

Engineering and Applied Physics; www.glyndwr.ac.uk/en/UniversityInstitutes/ArtsScienceandTechnology/eng

Electrical and Electronic Engineering; electrical and electronic engineering

Renewable Energy Systems and Sustainability techniques; distributed generation

Aeronautical & Mechanical Engineering; aeronautical technology and mechanical engineering/

manufacture, aircraft maintenance, aircraft electronics & control, composites, engineering

Performance Car Technology; performance car technology, motorsport design and management, renewable energy and sustainable technologies

Industrial Engineering; industrial engineering

Mechanical Engineering; mechanical engineering, manufacture, manufacturing engineering

Digital and Radio Frequency Communication Systems; advanced electronic techniques, electrical and electronic systems, renewable energy systems and sustainability/distributed generation

BSc(Hons), MSc, MRes, FdEng, BEng, MEng, MPhil, PhD

Computing; www.glyndwr.ac.uk/en/UniversityInstitutes/ArtsScienceandTechnology/Cor

computer science, computer games development, computer network and security, computing philosophy, creative computing, immersive technology, informatics, intelligent computing, library and information management, library and information practice, telecommunications, computing, computer networks and security, computer games development, computer networking, learning and technology, creative audio technology, media technology; BSc(Hons), FdSc, MSc, MRes, PhD, MPhil, MComp

Biology & the Environment; www.glyndwr.ac.uk/en/UniversityInstitutes/ArtsScienceandTechnology/Biol

Built & Natural Environment: architectural design technology, building studies (construction/maintenance management), facilities management, housing studies, housing & sustainable communities, housing studies, supported housing, real estate, rural business, professional practice

Animal Studies & Equine Science: animal studies, equestrian psychology, equine science & welfare/management

Wildlife & Plant Biology
Science & Environment: formulation science, forensic science, geography, ecology & environment, photovoltaics, polymer & biopolymer science, chemistry with green nanotechnology
BSc(Hons), FdSc, MPhil, PhD

Management & Business;
www.glyndwr.ac.uk/en/
UniversityInstitutes/
ArtsScienceandTechnology

accounting and finance, business, business psychology, global business, management entrepreneurship, business management, hospitality, tourism & events management, HRM, executive/MBA, marketing & consumer psychology, project management, sports leadership & development/management, management; BA(Hons), FdA, PhD, MPhil, MA, MBA, MSc, ProfDoc, MBA

Sport & Exercise Sciences

sport & exercise sciences, sport leadership & development, sport coaching/management; BSc(Hons), MRes, MPhil, PhD

Institute for Health, Medical Science & Society; www.glyndwr.ac.uk/en/ UniversityInstitutes/ HealthMedicalScienceandSociety

Society

criminology & criminal justice, therapeutic childcare, health & social care, youth & community work/studies, social work, counselling children & young people, counselling skills, sociology
Childhood Studies; education and childhood studies, families and childhood studies, childhood studies: young children, special education needs, play/early childhood education, early childhood, care and education

Education

education, education (counselling and psychology/special educational needs, education studies, learning support: teaching and learning; special educational needs/post-compulsory education and training, professional education and training, person-centred and experiential counselling and psychotherapy, person-centred and experiential counselling and psychotherapy, education, dyslexia, professional development in HE, learning and technology, professional development (education), teaching of psychology

Health, Psychology & Social Care

health & social care (ageing & later life/management & leadership/mental health), health wellbeing & communities, person-centred and experiential counselling and psychotherapy, health care studies, health and social care, health and care studies, nursing post-registration
Community Practice; community specialist practice (community children's nursing/district nursing/general practice nursing), health studies, healthcare leadership and management, specialist community public health nursing (health visiting/school nursing), clinical/community practice
Occupational Health and Safety; environmental health management (environmental and public health/occupational health, safety and environmental management
Occupational Therapy; occupational therapy
Health and Medical Science; nursing and healthcare studies, advanced clinical practice, complementary medicine as complementary therapy for healthcare, health and social care, professional education, counselling studies with children and young people, public health, health sciences, specialist community public health nursing (schools visiting/health visiting), complementary therapy

Psychology

psychology, teaching of psychology
BA(Hons), BSc(Hons), FdSc, MSc, MPhil, DipHE, EdD, PGCert/Dip, GradDip

Science & Environment

polymer & bipolymer science, formulation science, photovoltaic cells, chemistry with green nanotechnology, forensic science, geography, ecology & environment; MRes, MPhil, PhD

Society & Community

Criminal Justice: criminology & criminal justice
Social Care: social work, therapeutic childcare, counselling & psychotherapy, counselling studies/with children & young people, health & social care
Social Science: public & social policy
Youth & Community: youth & community work/studies, education (youth & community work/counselling children & young people/counselling skills), sociology; Cert/DipHE, BA(Hons), FdA, MPhil, PhD, MA, ProfDoc

Social Sciences

social science; MRes, MPhil, PhD

Sport & Exercise Sciences;
www.glyndwr.ac.uk/en/
UniversityInstitutes/
HealthMedicalSciencesandSociety/
SportandExerciseSciences

sport & exercise sciences, sports coaching, sport leadership & development, sport management; BSc(Hons), MRes, MPhil, PhD

UNIVERSITY OF GREENWICH
www.gre.ac.uk

Faculty of Architecture, Computing & Humanities; www2.gre.ac.uk/about/faculty/ach

Dept of Architecture & Landscape

architecture & landscape architecture, garden design, landscape architecture, landscape management (land use), advanced landscape and urbanism, architectural design, architectural practice, architecture and construction, architecture, landscape architecture, landscape design

Dept of Built Environment

design and construction management, occupational safety, health and environment, property development and management, architecture and construction – research, construction management and economics, facilities management, occupational hygiene, project management – international, real estate/ development and investment, safety, health and environment, sustainable building engineering

Dept of Computing & Information Systems

business information system/technology, business computing, computer science, computer security and forensics, computer systems and networking, computing with digital media/games development, computing, software engineering, creative digital media, digital media technologies, games design and development, web technologies, business intelligence, computer science, computing and information systems, data warehousing and business intelligence, software engineering, enterprise systems and database administration, information security and audit, information systems management, management of business information technology, computer forensics and cyber security, computer forensics and the law, computer systems and network engineering, network and computer systems security

Dept of Creative Professions & Digital Arts

3D digital design and animation, graphic and digital design, digital film production, film and TV production, film studies, digital arts practice, media and communication, web design and content planning, film production, media and communication

Dept of Literature, Language & Theatre

drama/and English literature, professional dance and musical theatre, creative writing/and English literature, English language and literature, English literature/with creative writing, English language and ELT, international foundation programme with cultural studies, languages and international relations, English: literary London, language learning and Japanese language teaching, second language learning and teaching, humanities and social sciences – research

Dept of Law

criminology and criminal psychology, criminology, commercial law, law, law senior status, international criminology, international and commercial law, law – research

Dept of Mathematical Sciences

financial mathematics, mathematics and computing, mathematics with business, mathematics with economics, mathematics, statistics, applicable mathematics, computational finance, computing and mathematical sciences, computing and mathematical sciences

Dept of History, Politics & Social Sciences

history and English/ politics/ sociology, history, politics and international relations, sociology/and psychology, history, international maritime policy, maritime studies, international relations, humanities and social sciences – research, public policy and practice; BA(Hons), BSc(Hons), MSc, MA, PGdip/Cert, LlB, LlM, MPhil, PhD

Business School

accounting and finance, accounting and financial information systems, finance, business – research, finance and investment, financial management, international banking and finance, business management, business psychology, HRM, business – research, international HRM, business economics, business with law, economics with banking, economics with language, economics, international business with language, international business, business – research, business and financial economics, international business; advertising and marketing communications/ with language, events management, hospitality management, marketing, marketing with language, PR and communications, tourism management/ with language; business, events management, international tourism management, PR, strategic marketing communications, strategic marketing, business entrepreneurship and innovation, business logistics and transport management; business purchasing and supply chain management, business studies, business with finance, business with HRM/ language/law/ marketing, business, business – research, e-logistics and supply chain management, business administration, MBA project management for logistics, transport and logistics management; FD, BA(Hons) BSc(Hons), certs, MBA, DBA, MA, MSc, MPhil, PhD

Faculty of Education & Health; www2.gre.ac.uk/about/faculty/eduhe

Dept of Adult Nursing & Paramedic Science

assistant health and social care practitioner, health and social care: care, health and social care: early years care, acupuncture, nursing (pre-registration) – adult nursing, paramedic science, advanced practice in health and social care, nursing, specialist practitioner (district nursing)

Dept of Education & Community Studies

childhood and youth studies, early years teacher status/ (professional), early years, education studies, education, early years teacher status/ (professional), early years, education – research, education, youth and community

Dept of Family Care & Mental Health

mental health work, midwifery (pre-registration), nursing (pre-registration) – child nursing/learning disability/mental health nursing/sexual health, specialist community public health (health visiting and school nursing), health and social care – research, mental health nursing studies, safeguarding children

and young people, specialist community public health nursing (health visiting and school nursing)

Dept of Primary Education

primary education, primary education with QTS, primary education with mathematics specialism, school direct training programme (primary)

Psychology, Social Work & Counselling

counselling, health and social care, health and well-being, psychology with counselling, psychology, public health, social work; child and adolescent psychology, health and social care – research, psychology, social work, therapeutic counselling

Secondary, LLTE & PE & Sport

speech and language therapy, teaching in the lifelong learning sector, language and literacy education, teaching English (ESOL/literacy/and ESOL), teaching mathematics (numeracy), mathematics education, PE and sport, qualified teacher status (secondary school level), teaching literacy & ESOL in the lifelong learning sector, school direct training programme (secondary), secondary education computer science and information/ design and technology/mathematics/modern languages (French)/PE/, physics with mathematics, secondary education science with biology/chemistry/ physics, secondary musicians in education; FD, BScHons, BAHons, MA, MSc, PGCert/ Dip, PGCE, EdD, MPhil, PhD, CertHE, LlB

Faculty of Engineering & Science; www2.gre.ac.uk/about/faculty/engsci

Department of Civil Engineering

civil engineering

Department of Electrical, Electronic & Computer Engineering

computer engineering, computer network engineering, control and instrumentation engineering; electrical and electronic engineering technology, electrical and electronic engineering, electrical engineering, electronic engineering, engineering for intelligent systems, engineering technology, computer networking, computer systems and software engineering, electrical and electronic engineering, electrical power engineering, electronics and communications engineering, embedded systems, information and communications technology, wireless mobile communications, systems engineering

Department of Life & Sports Sciences

animal management, applied animal behavioural science and welfare, applied/ biomedical science, biological sciences, equine management, equine sports therapy and rehabilitation, horticulture, human nutrition, international agriculture, osteopathy, sports science with coaching/professional football coaching, sports science, applied plant science, strength and conditioning

Department of Mechanical, Manufacturing & Design Engineering

mechanical engineering, mechanical engineering technology, engineering research, manufacturing systems, mechanical and manufacturing engineering, professional engineering

Department of Pharmaceutical, Chemical & Environmental Sciences

chemistry, environmental science, forensic science/with criminology, geography, pharmaceutical sciences, biotechnology, environmental conservation, formulation science, GIS with remote sensing,

landscape ecology with GIS, pharmaceutical biotechnology, pharmaceutical sciences

Department of Technology Management & Enterprise

business administration, business technology management, design, innovation and entrepreneurship, engineering business management, engineering project management, information and communications technology, information technology management for business, project management, engineering management

Royal School of Military Engineering Foundation Degrees

building services engineering, construction management, electrical engineering, highway engineering and plant management; BEng(Hons), BSc(Hons), MEng, MSc, MPhil, PhD, MBiol, MOst, MChem, BA(Hons), FD

GRIMSBY INSTITUTE/UNIVERSITY CENTRE
www.grimsby.ac.uk

applied psychology, business management with accounting/marketing, events management, computing technology, commercial photography, counselling studies, creative music, creative & internet design, criminological studies with social science, children, young people and families, early childhood studies, digital film & TV production, education & training, English studies, fine arts practice, health & social care, hospital & healthcare (adult), industrial management in food manufacturing, integrated care, learning support, logistics & supply chain

management, marketing, mechanical engineering, mental health studies, operations management, make-up/design, man multi-platform journalism, performance, professional writing, public health & nutrition, applied psychology, refrigeration & air conditioning management, salon management, social care, special effect make-up for TV, strategic business environment, film & theatre, sports coaching, sport & recreation management, tourism/ & business management; BA(Hons), BSc(Hons), FdA, FdEd, FdSc, HEdDip, MA, MBA, MSc, PGCE

HARPER ADAMS UNIVERSITY
www.harper-adams.ac.uk

agriculture, agriculture with animal science/crop management/environmental management/mechanisation/marketing/farm business, welfare with animal behaviour/animal health/animal management/animal science/bioveterinary science, advanced veterinary nursing, veterinary nursing/and practice management, agricultural engineering, countryside/ & environmental management, off road vehicle design with marketing and management, agri-food marketing with business studies, food, nutrition and well-being, food & consumer studies, agri-business, agri-food

marketing with business studies, business management with marketing, rural enterprise and land management, rural property management, geography, agricultural law, agroecology, animal precision farming, animal management & welfare, applied mechatronic engineering, conservation and forest protection, crop precision farming, crop production, dairy business management, ecological applications, engineering precision farming, entomology, farm and agri-business management, food industry management, food & public health nutrition, food business innovation & entrepreneurship, food production & marketing, food studies, forestry management, fresh produce production, integrated pest management, international agri-business and food chain management, meat business management, negotiated studies, negotiated studies, plant nematology, plant pathology, poultry business management, precision farming, regional food production & global marketing, ruminant nutrition, rural estate and land management, rural sustainable energy, soil and water management, sustainable agriculture, veterinary nursing/pharmacy/physiotherapy/rehabilitation/ oncology nursing/therapy, weed science; BSc(Hons), FdSc, MBA, MSc, PGDip/Cert, MRes, PhD

Degrees validated by the Harper Adams University offered at:

ASKHAM BRYAN COLLEGE
www.askham-bryan.ac.uk

adventure, sport & public service, agriculture & land management, animal management & science, arboriculture, canine & feline training welfare, countryside management/collection & conservation, equine science, equine business & event management, equine sports management, sport surface management, arboriculture, applied/horticulture, landscaping & garden management, sport (outdoor & adventure education), veterinary health studies/nursing; BSc, BSc(Hons), Nat Dips, FD

HERIOT-WATT UNIVERSITY
www.hw.ac.uk

Energy, Geoscience, Infrastructure and Society

Architectural Engineering; architectural engineering/ with international studies, (interior) design
Civil and Structural Engineering; civil engineering / with international studies, structural engineering, structural engineering with architectural design/ international studies
Construction Management and Surveying; construction project management, quantity surveying
Urban Studies; urban planning and property development, geography, society and environment
Postgrad Taught Programmes;
Centre of Excellence in Sustainable Building Design; architectural engineering, architectural project management, building conservation (technology and management), carbon and energy management, construction project management, quantity surveying, sustainable urban management, urban and regional planning, urban strategies, design
Institute for Infrastructure & Environment; civil engineering, civil engineering and construction management, safety and risk management, safety, risk and reliability engineering, structural and foundation engineering, water and environmental management, water technology and desalination, ergonomics, engineering, psychology

Institute for Social Policy, Housing, Environment and Real Estate; real estate and planning, real estate investment and finance, real estate management and development; BSc(Hons, Ord), BEng, MEng, MRes, MSc, PGDip/Cert, PhD, Diploma

School of Mathematical and Computer Sciences; www.macs.hw.ac.uk
actuarial science/mathematics, computer science (artificial intelligence/games programming/software engineering), computer systems, financial mathematics/quantitative finance, financial risk management/engineering, information systems/interaction design/internet systems/management), mathematics, mathematics with computer science/finance/French/ German/physics/Spanish/statistics, mathematical statistics & actuarial science, statistics, quantitative financial risk management, software engineering, statistical modelling; BSc(Hons), MEng, MMath, MRes, MSc, PGDip/Cert, PhD

School of Engineering and Physical Sciences; www.eps.hw.ac.uk
Chemical Engineering: chemical engineering with energy engineering/pharmaceutical chemistry, industrial engineering (chemical)
Chemistry: chemistry with materials/ biochemistry/ computational chemistry/pharmaceutical chemistry,

dynamics and structure, materials chemistry, molecular chemistry, biological chemistry

Computing and Electronics: electrical power and energy, electrical power and energy, electrical and electronic engineering, industrial engineering (electrical and electronic), robotics, autonomous and interactive systems

Mechanical Engineering: mechanical engineering and energy, engineering/advanced energy, oil and gas technology, renewable energy and distributed generation, renewable energy engineering, smart grid demand management, sustainability engineering

Physics: chemical/engineering/engineering/mathematical physics, nanoscience, physics with energy science and technology, photonics & optoelectonic devices, image restoration for improving biological microscopy image resolution under diffraction limit, bio-image processing and analysis, bioprinting and biofabrication super-resolution biological imaging of stem cells, cancer cells and diabetic cells, spatial and temporal resolution, synthesis of novel chemical probes, image data signal processing, novel microscopic optical development, bio-processing, high resolution ultrasound imaging and signal processing, bioengineering

Engineering, engineering; BEng, BSc(Ord, Hons), EngD, MChem, MEng, MPhil, MPhys, PhD

School of Life Sciences; www.hw.ac.uk/sls

applied psychology (forensic science), engineering psychology with ergonomics, psychology/with human health/management, marine spatial, biological sciences (cell and molecular biology/human health/microbiology), bioprocesses, biotechnology, brewing and distilling, business psychology, food science/safety & health/nutrition, food & beverage science, food sciences, applied marine biology, climate change: managing the marine environment/ impacts & migration, environmental analysis & assessment, marine biodiversity & biotechnology, marine resource development & protection; BSc(Hons), MSc/Cert/Dip, PGDip, PhD

School of Management and Languages; www.hw.ac.uk/sml

accountancy & business law/finance, applied language studies, business/adminstration, business management with HRM/marketing/business law/ enterprise, business & finance, economics, economics & accountancy/business law/business management/ finance/marketing, finance/& business law, international business management, applied languages and translating (French/German, French/Spanish, German/Spanish, French/British sign language, German/British sign language), British sign language (interpreting, translating and applied language studies), languages (interpreting and translating) (French/Spanish/German/Spanish/French/British sign language), French/German/Spanish and applied language studies, international business management and languages, Chinese/French/German/Spanish as main language

Postgrad Programmes; Accountancy, Economics and Finance

Accounting; accounting, international accounting and finance/ environmental economics, strategy and international management accounting

Economics; economics, banking and finance, international finance and economic development

Finance; finance, finance and management, international banking and finance/economic development/ environmental economics

Business Management: investment management, international business management with finance/ HRM/logistics/ marketing/sustainability international fashion marketing, international marketing management, international marketing management with consumer psychology/digital marketing/sustainability, tourism management with business strategy, leadership and change, lean six sigma for operational excellence, managing business performance, operations management, strategic project management, European master in strategic project management, logistics and supply chain management with business performance/lean six sigma/marketing/shipping and port operations, logistics with green and sustainable supply chain management

Languages and Intercultural Studies: interpreting, interpreting and translating, Arabic-English interpreting and translating, Chinese-English interpreting and translating, translating, Arabic-English translating, Chinese-English translating, translating for business

Business Communication and Intercultural Studies: cultural resource management, international management and business communication; BA(Hons, Ord), GradDip, MA(Hons), MSc

Heriot-Watt Institute of Petroleum Engineering; www.pet.hw.ac.uk

marine resource management, marine renewable energy, petroleum engineering/geoscience, renewable energy development, reservoir evaluation & management; MPhil, MSc, PhD

School of Textiles and Design;
www.tex.hw.ac.uk

design for textiles (fashion, interior, art), fashion, fashion communication/marketing and retailing/menswear/technology/womenswear, interior design Postgrad Programmes; ethics in fashion (communication, consumerism and sustainability), fashion & textiles design/ innovation and new applications/ innovation and new applications/ management, strategic innovation management fashion and textiles; BA, BSc(Hons, Ord), MA, MSc, MPhil, PhD, Diploma

Edinburgh Business School;
www.ebsglobal.net

financial management, HRM, marketing, strategic planning; DBA, MBA, MSc

Degrees validated by Heriot-Watt University offered at:

EDINBURGH COLLEGE OF ART
www.eca.ac.uk

Architecture & Landscape Architecture; architectural history, architecture, architectural & urban design, architectural conservation, architectural history and theory, architectural project management, art space nature, cultural landscapes, cultural studies, design and digital media
School of Art; painting, photography, sculpture, contemporary art practice, material practice, interdisciplinary creative practices History of Art; fine art, history of art, art in the global middle ages, history of art, theory and display, modern and contemporary art, history, curating and criticism, renaissance and early modern studies

School of Design; animation, fashion, film & TV, graphic design, illustration, interior design, jewellery & silversmithing, performance costume, product design, textiles, design informatics, fashion, film directing, glass, material practice, performance costume
Reid School of Music; music, music technology, acoustics and music technology, composition, digital composition and performance, musical instrument research, musicology; BArch, MArch, MLA, MFA, BA(Comb), BSc(Hons, Ord), MA(Hons), MPhil, MSc, PhD, BMus(Hons), MMus

UNIVERSITY OF HERTFORDSHIRE
www.herts.ac.uk

Hertfordshire Business School;
www.herts.ac.uk/schools-of-study/
courses/business

accounting with finance/language, business administration/economics/analysis & consultancy, accounting & financial management, business, business with accounting/HRM, information systems/law/marketing, business administration, business & economics/event management/finance/HR/tourism, business study with language, economics, business economics/with language, business strategy with language, delivering organisational change, event management with marketing/tourism, finance with language/economics/HRM/language/information systems/investment management, information systems & marketing, global business, global economy & business institutions, HRM, information systems, IT for business, international business/management/tourist &

hospitality management/with language, international management/with tourism management, marketing for business, leadership & management in public services, management/studies, managing major projects, managing organisational change, marketing, marketing with fashion/language/advertising/digital communication, tourism management, professional studies, project management/practice, proprietary trading, sport management, strategic business information systems; BA/BSc, BA(Hons), BSc, DBA, DMan, MA, MBA, MPhil, MSc, PGCert/Dip, PhD, FD

School of Computer Science;
www.herts.ac.uk/courses/schools-of-
study/computer-science

advanced computer science, computer science (artificial intelligence/networks/software engineering), artificial intelligence/robotics, computer technologies (media systems/networks/software development), software development for business, computer networking principles, distribution systems & networks, elearning systems, information technology, software engineering; BSc(Hons), MEng, MPhil, MSc, PGCert/Dip, PhD, FD

School of Creative Arts; www.herts.ac.uk/courses/schools-of-study/creative-arts

three-dimensional design, 3D computer animation and modelling, contemporary design crafts (ceramics and glass/jewellery/interior architecture and design, model design (character and creative effects/model effects/special effects), applied arts, contemporary textiles digital media arts, interactive media, product design, interior & spatial design, model design, musical management/technology, songwriting & music production, visual effects for film & TV, music composition for film & media, music & sound technology, photography, screen cultures; BA(Hons), MA, PGCert/Dip, MSc, MPhil, PhD, FdA, DipHE

School of Education; www.herts.ac.uk/courses/schools-of-study/education

early years/leadership, early childhood education, education studies/with learning & teaching/special education & disabilities, working with young people, education studies, PGCE (primary, education: secondary: biology, chemistry, physics), practice based teaching, primary education, teaching & learning, CPD, primary/secondary education; BA(Hons), BEd, EdD, FdA, MA, MPhil, PGCert/Dip, PGCE, PhD, MSc, MLT

School of Engineering & Technology; www.herts.ac.uk/courses/schools-of-study/engineering-and-technology

aerospace engineering/systems/management/space technology with pilot studies/with space technology, aerospace systems engineering, with pilot studies, aerospace technology with pilot studies/management, automotive engineering/with motorsport technology/management, biomedical engineering, broadband & telecommunication networks, broadcast media technology, computer & network technology, construction management, data communication & electronics, adv digital systems, digital systems, embedded intelligent systems, mechanical engineering/& mechatronics, motorsport technology, digital systems & computer engineering, electronics/electrical engineering, adv digital systems, manufacturing management, mobile & smart systems, operations &

supply chain management, radio & mobile communication systems; BSc(Hons), BEng, MEng, MSc, PGDip/Cert, MPhil, PhD

School of Health and Social Work; www.herts.ac.uk/courses/schools-of-study/health-and-social-work

contemporary healthcare/nursing, adv physiotherapy (neuromuscularskeletal), cognitive behavioural therapy, diagnostic imaging/radiography, dietetics/adv practice, interventions, medical imaging & radiation sciences/diagnostic imaging/image interpretation/oncology/radiation science/ultrasound, mental health recovery & social inclusion, midwifery/& women's health/with RM, nursing (children, adults, mental health, learning disability), nutrition, radiotherapy & oncology, applied/paramedic science, physiotherapy, special community nursing, social intervention, social work, specialist community public health nursing, clinical research; BSc(Hons), DHRes, FDSc, MPhil, MSc, PGCert/Dip, PhD

School of Humanities; www.herts.ac.uk/courses/schools-of-study/humanities

English language & communications or English literature or philosophy, or history, combined with one of the following subjects: acting & screen performance, American studies, creative writing, teaching, ELT, film, French, German, Italian, Spanish, Japanese, history, journalism & creative writing, media cultures, computing, mass communication, modern literary cultures, new media publishing, philosophy, journalism & media/communication, creative writing & media, film & TV aesthetics, global film & TV; BA(Hons), MA, MPhil, PGCert/Dip, PhD

School of Law; www.herts.ac.uk/courses/schools-of-study/law

law, commercial law, international law, legal practice, maritime law, commercial & workplace mediation, government & politics; BSc(Hons), Diploma, LIB(Hons), LlM, MPhil, PGDip, PhD, GradCert

School of Life & Medical Sciences: www.herts.ac.uk/courses/schools-of-study/life-and-medical-sciences

animal/equine management, adv clinical pharmaceutics, biochemistry, biological/biomedical/science, biotechnology, business psychology, cardiology & stroke, contemporary therapeutic counselling, counselling, dermatological skills & treatment, medical healthcare simulation, health & medical education, psychiatric/mental health practice, public health, nutrition, therapeutic counselling, environmental management for agriculture/business, human/physical geography, molecular biology, pharmaceutical/& health science/analysis, pharmacology, pharmacovigilance, advancing/pharmacy practice, mental health & practice, molecular biology, optometry, pharmacy, pharmaceutical practice, research in clinical psychology, psychology clinical/business/health/occupational/personal/organisational, physiology, public health, sports studies/therapy, sport & exercise science, sustainable agriculture & food security, sustainable planning & environmental management/& transport, water & environmental management; BSc/BSc(Hons), MSc, PGCert/Dip, FdSc, CertHE, MHMEd

School of Physics, Astronomy and Mathematics; www.herts.ac.uk/courses/schools-of-study/physics-astronomy-and-mathematics

astrophysics, financial mathematics, mathematics, physics; BSc(Hons), MPhil, MSc, PhD, MPhys

Degrees validated by the University of Hertfordshire offered at:

HERTFORDSHIRE REGIONAL COLLEGE
www.hrc.ac.uk

3D dimensional design, art & design, business with HRM/accounting/information systems/marketing computing technologies, fine art practice, graphic design, visual merchandising; FD

NORTH HERTFORDSHIRE COLLEGE
www.nhc.ac.uk

accounting/information systems/ computing technology, business/with HRM, creative enterprises-fashion & textile, early years, marketing, sports studies, business with HRM/accounting/information systems/marketing; FD, extended degrees

---

OAKLANDS COLLEGE
www.oaklands.ac.uk

animal/equine management, business/with management/information,, construction management, early years, engineering & technology, fine arts practice, sports studies; FD, extended degrees

---

WEST HERTS COLLEGE
www.westherts.ac.uk

accounting with HRM/information systems/law/marketing, engineering, fashion & textiles, graphic design, illustration, business/ & management, media & photography, sports studies, teaching; FD, Dip teaching

---

THE UNIVERSITY OF HUDDERSFIELD
www.hud.ac.uk

School of Applied Sciences;
www.hud.ac.uk/sas

Chemical & Biological Sciences: analytical chemistry/bioscience, chemistry with chemical engineering/forensic science, biochemistry, chemical engineering/science, biology (molecular & cellular), food nutrition & health, forensic & analytical science, forensic anthropology/entomology, forensic science (body fluids/DNA/toxicology), molecular biochemistry/biology/genetics, pharmaceutical & analytical science, food science, pharmaceutical chemistry, nutrition & public health, accelerator applications;

BA(Hons), BSc(Hons), MA, MChem, MPharm, MSc, MSci, PhD

School of Art, Design and Architecture; www.hud.ac.uk/ada

animation, architecture, adv architectural design, adv project management in construction, professional practice in management of architecture, sustainable architecture construction/& project management, contemporary arts & illustration, costume/with textiles, design integrate & building information modelling, digital media, fashion communication & promotion/design with marketing & production/textiles, fashion and textiles buying management, fashion textile practices, fine art, graphic design/& animation, illustration, photography, product design, spatial design, surface design for fashion & interiors/textile design/surface design/textile crafts & design, surveying, urban design; BA(Hons), BSc(Hons), CertHE, DipHE, FdA, FdSc, MA, MArch, MSc

University of Huddersfield Business School; www.hud.ac.uk/uhbs

accountancy and finance/financial services, finance and economics, accounting, banking/and finance, international finance with law

management, organisational behaviour, HRM, strategic leadership, operations, project management, cross-cultural studies, change management, and e-commerce

transport & logistics management, air transport & logistics management, supply chain management with logistics, logistics & supply, supply chain management, global logistics and supply chain management, economics, international business, financial services, information management, entrepreneurship, environmental management and journalism, enterprise development, marketing PR, advertising and marketing communications, sports promotion and marketing, economics, international business, marketing, risk, disaster and environmental management, management law, law and practice, legal practice, commercial law, international law; BA(Hons), FdA, DPubAdmin, GradDipLaw, LlB(Hons), LlM, MBA, MSc, PGCE, PGDip, PGDip/Cert, GradDip, CPE

School of Computing and Engineering; www.hud.ac.uk/ce

adv computer science, automotive & motorsport engineering, creative music technology, electronics & communication engineering, electronic engineering & computer systems, motorsport engineering, computing science/& informatics, electrical engineering, construction & project management, embedded systems engineering, energy engineering, engineering, engineering control systems & instrumentation, information systems management, mechanical engineering/design, music & sound for image, music technology & audio systems, pop music production, software development/engineering, engineering & technology management, turbocharging engineering, web technologies/design; BEng(Hons), MEng, MSc, PhD, UniFdCert

School of Education; www.hud.ac.uk/sepd

early childhood education with early years teaching status, early years, education human resource, development and training, religion and education, teacher training (lifelong learning) primary education (early years and key stage 1), TESOL, education and professional development, educational management and administration, learning support, teacher training (lifelong learning), early childhood studies, early years initial teacher training, education, education and youth work studies, guidance professional studies, international education, leadership in education and public services, learning and development management, teacher training (lifelong learning) primary education (early years and key stage), PGCE with QTS, teacher training primary education (general) PGCE with QTS/ primary/secondary school direct PGCE/ secondary business education/design technology/mathematics PGCE with QTS, teacher training secondary music/science with biology/chemistry physics PGCE with QTS, teacher training, secondary ICT and computer science, PGCE with QTS, ESOL, technology enhanced learning, action research for education, education, education and youth work studies, guidance professional studies, higher education/practice, leadership in education and public services, learning and development management, teacher training (lifelong learning), teaching in lifelong learning, technology enhanced learning; BA(Hons), CertEd, FdA, MA, PGradDip/Cert, PGCE, EdD

Human and Health Sciences; www.hud.ac.uk/hhs

Health Sciences: health professions, midwifery, nursing, occupational therapy, operating dept practice, physiotherapy, podiatry, community nursing practice (district nursing), health studies (advanced diabetes care/advanced practice in acute and critical care/advancing midwifery practice/health professional education: teaching/healthy lifestyles/long-term conditions, health studies, podiatry, public health nursing practice: health visiting/school nursing, theory of podiatric surgery

Social Sciences: behavioural sciences, counselling studies, criminology, health and social care, international politics, investigative psychology, politics/& criminology/ sociology, psychology & investigation, psychology/with counselling/ criminology, social research and evaluation, social work, sociology and criminology, sociology, social research and evaluation DipHE, MA, MSc, PGDip/Cert, PhD, ProfDoc

Music, Humanities and Media; www.hud.ac.uk/mhm

drama/and English language/& literature/modern language/creative writing/applied linguistics,

drama, dance & performance, English language & English literature with a modern language/creative writing, English and history/politics, history with a modern language, broadcast journalism, film studies & drama/English literature/ history, journalism, media and popular culture, music journalism, sports journalism, music and sound for image, music, music technology – creative music technology/& popular music, music technology/performance, labour history, health and social history, religious dissent and conflict, performance, commercial music, including sound design and film; BA(Hons), FdA, MA, PdF, PhDs, MMus, PGDip, MEnt, EntD

UNIVERSITY OF HULL
www.hull.ac.uk

Faculty of Arts and Social Sciences; www.hull.ac.uk/fass

Drama, Music & Screen

drama & theatre, theatre practice, music/& theatre/ practice, jazz/& pop music, performance, composition, creative writing/English/history/philosophy & film studies, web design & development/experience, creative music technology, digital design/media studies, digital arts, applied digital media, film studies & drama, game & entertainment design, digital design, media & screen studies

English

English & American literature & culture, English language & literature, English language research, creative writing/ with American studies/English/ philosophy/religion, English literature, modern & contemporary literature, literary & visual cultures studies, English in jt degrees

History

history (20th century/social/economic/archaeological), history with maritime history/history of art, archaeological & medieval history, historical research, history & religion, Chinese & history/ American studies/English language & literature

School of Law

law, international law, senior status, law with business/criminology/foundation English/French/ German/Spanish, law & legislative studies/history/ politics, philosophy, international business law, restorative justice

Languages, Linguistics & Culture

Chinese/French/German/Italian Spanish studies, Chinese with American studies/English/film studies/ history/politics & international studies/husiness/management/marketing, translation studies, TESOL, American studies with creative writing/history/English/film studies, modern language studies, combined language degrees

Politics, Philosophy & International Studies

politics, British politics & legislative studies, politics & international relations/history/war & security studies, philosophy, politics & economics, war & security studies, civilization, terrorism & dissent, EU governance, globalisation & governance, global political economy, global communication & international politics, international politics/political economy, international law & politics, strategy & international security

Social Sciences

anthropology & sociology/criminology/philosophy/ religion, criminology & sociology/law/forensic science/ sociology & anthropology & gender studies, sociology, social work, community & youthwork studies, media studies, applied social research, restorative justice, theology, women & gender studies, social & community studies/behavioural studies, BA(Hons), BMus, BSc(Hons), LlB, LLM, MA, MEd, MMus, MPhil, MR/MRes, PGDip/Cert, PhD

The Hull University Business School; www.hull.ac.uk/hubs

accounting, business, business economics, economics with mathematics, financial management, management, marketing, supply chain management, business management, international business, accounting and finance

MSc degrees; advertising and marketing, business management, economics and business, energy markets, finance and investment, financial management, financial mathematics, HRM, international business, logistics and supply chain management, management consulting, marketing management, money, banking and finance, strategic brand management, MBA degrees

BA(Hons), BSc(Hons), MBA, MPhil, MRes, MSc, PhD, MBA, BSc(Econ), MSc(Econ)

Faculty of Health and Social Care; www.hull.ac.uk/fhsc

nursing (adult/mental health/children's/learning disability nursing, operating department practice, practice teacher, educator in practice, return to practice, midwifery, the associate practitioner/health and social care, practice skills for health and social care, operating department practice, clinical psychology, cognitive behavioural therapy, practice skills for health and social care, working with children and young people in a learning context, working with children, young people and families, health and social care of adults, the theory and practice of counselling; Adv Diploma, BSc(Hons), FD, MPhil, MRes, PhD, Univ Cert, PGDip/Cert, DClinPsy

The Hull York Medical School; www.hyms.ac.uk

anatomical science, biomedical science, cancer, cardiovascular medicine, child health, clinical sciences, clinical techniques & skills, cognitive behavioural therapy, dermatology, evidence-based decision making, gastrointestinal medicine, health professions education, human anatomy & evolution/science, immunology, medicine, medical education/science, medical & human science, mental health, metabolic & renal medicine, pathology, person-centred care, population health & medicine, public health, reproduction, respiration, sport, health & exercise science, surgery, interacted degrees; BSc(Hons), MBBS, MPhil, MA, MRes, MSc/Dip/Cert, PGCert/Dip, PhD

Faculty of Education; www2.hull.ac.uk/ifl

learning support, childhood studies, integrative counselling, education and learning, learning and teaching – primary education with QTS, early childhood education and care, early childhood studies, higher education, education and society, education/& technology, education studies (social inclusion & special needs/early childhood/early years teaching, inclusive education, social inclusion and special needs, education and early learning, children's inter-professional studies, inclusive teaching training, teaching English (literacy/mathematics) in the lifelong learning sector, ESOL, teaching maths (numeracy) in the lifelong learning sector, educational studies, initial teacher training, PGCE primary: early years (3–7 years) 5–11, PGCE secondary (numerous subjects), primary teaching, sustained professional development, early childhood studies, inclusive education, leadership and learning, schools direct, teaching and learning; BA, EdD, FD, GradCert, MA, MEd, MPhil, MSc, PGCE, PhD, PGCert(HE), CertEd, MTL, FD

Postgraduate Medical Institute; www2.hull.ac.uk/pgmi

post-graduate medical education; PGCME, MD, MPhil, PhD

Faculty of Science & Engineering; www.hull.ac.uk/science

Biological, Biomedical & Environmental Sciences: aquatic zoology, biology, biomolecular science, chemical science, chemistry with analytical chemistry/forensic science/toxicology/molecular medicine/nanotechnology, human biology, marine and freshwater biology, zoology, translational oncology

Chemistry: biological chemistry, chemistry, analytical chemistry with toxicology, forensic science/& criminology/toxicology, pharmaceutical science, molecular medicine, nanotechnology, toxicology, registration, evaluation & authorisation of chemicals

Computer Science: computer science/engineering, games development/programming, computer software/systems development, information systems, computer graphics/games programming, NET distribution systems/development, computer systems engineering

Engineering: automatic control & logistics technology, chemical engineering, computer aided engineering, electrical/& electronic engineering, mechanical engineering, medical engineering, product innovation, embedded systems, wireless systems engineering, plant & process/process engineering management, logistics/technology, petroleum, oil & gas chemical engineering management/technology

Geography, Environment & Earth Sciences: human/physical geography, geology/with physical geography, renewable energy, geography & history/business/management, archaeology & human geography/environments

Physics & Mathematics: physics/with astrophysics/mathematics, nanotechnology, philosophy, mathematics, financial mathematics

Sports Science, Health & Exercise Science: applied exercise for health, applied sport science for performance, sports coaching & performance science, sport & exercise nutrition, sports rehabilitation

Psychology: psychology, clinical applications of psychology, health psychology, psychology & health, clinical psychology; BA, BEng, BSc, BSc/MEng, MPhil, MPhys, MPhysGeog, MRes, MSc, PhD, FdEng, MPharmSci

Degrees validated by the University of Hull offered at:

BISHOP BURTON COLLEGE
www.bishopburton.ac.uk

agriculture resource management, applied animal behaviour & welfare/management, applied bioscience, art, countryside management (gamekeeping/fisheries management) event management, environmental conservation, equine business management/studies/science/therapy & rehabilitation/sports performance/sports coaching, fashion & clothing design, multidisciplinary design, floristry design, garden design & horticulture, horticulture (gardens & green space management), policing & criminology/forensic investigation, sports coaching, tourism & hospitality management; BA(Hons), BSc(Hons), FDA/Sc, MSc, PGCE

DONCASTER COLLEGE
www.don.ac.uk

illustration and concept art, fashion and textiles design, fine art and crafts, graphic design, illustration and concept art, moving image production, early childhood studies, education studies (primary/secondary), early childhood development and learning in practice, early years, supporting children with special educational needs and disability, early childhood studies, professional studies working with young people and the community, education, working with children and young people, advancing professional practice, applied social science, criminal justice, social psychology, English, business management, international football business management, live events production, contemporary performance practice, creative music technology, dance practice physical education and sports coaching, sports, fitness and exercise science, integrated technology, sports, exercise and health science, creative industries: practice, business and innovation, creative pattern cutting, literature and digital culture, business administration, HRM, creative music technology, relationship therapy; BA(Hons), BSc, BSc(Hons), FD, HND, MA, MSc, PGCE, PGCert/Dip, MBA

IMPERIAL COLLEGE, LONDON
www3.imperial.ac.uk

Faculty of Engineering;
www3.engineering.imperial.ac.uk
Aeronautics: adv composites, adv aeronautical engineering, adv computational methods for aeronautics/flow management and fluid-structure interaction, composites: the science, technology and engineering application of advanced composites

Bioengineering: bioengineering, biomedical engineering, biomedical device design & entrepreneurship, medical design

Chemical Engineering: chemical engineering/with nuclear engineering, adv chemical engineering with biotechnology/process systems engineering/structured product engineering, process automation, instrumentation and control

Civil & Environmental Engineering: civil/structural engineering, civil & environmental engineering, earthquake engineering, engineering geology, general structural engineering, geotechnics, concrete structures/and business management sustainable development, environmental engineering and business management/ sustainable development, hydrology and business management/sustainable development/ water resources management, soil mechanics/and business management/engineering seismology/environmental geotechnics/sustainable development, structural steel design/and business management/ sustainable development, transport/ and business management/sustainable development

Computing: adv/computing, computational mathematics, computing science, games vision & interactivity, software engineering, mathematics & computer science – pure mathematics & computational logic/computational statistics, mathematical logic, secure software systems, visual information programs, robotics & image-guided intervention, computing (artificial intelligence/ (computational management science/machine learning/secure software systems/software engineering)

Earth Science & Engineering: geology, geophysics, environmental/petroleum geoscience/geophysics, metals & energy finance, petroleum engineering/ geophysics, remote sensing

Electrical & Electronic Engineering: electronic & electrical engineering, analogue & digital integrated circuit design, information engineering, communications & signal processing, control systems, future power networks

Materials: adv/material science & engineering/management, aerospace materials, biomaterials & tissue engineering, biomedical engineering & biomaterials, materials & nuclear engineering, advanced materials, composites, nuclear engineering

Mechanical Engineering: adv/mechanical engineering, nuclear engineering, innovation design engineering, global engineering design; BEng, MA, MEng, MSc, MSci, PhD, MRes

Faculty of Medicine; www1.medicine.imperial.ac.uk

medicine, allergy, biomedical research/science, cancer biology, cardiorespiratory nursing, clinical research design & management, epidemiology, experimental neuroscience, human molecular genetics, human nutrition, immunology, infection management for pharmacists, medical robotics & image-guided intervention, medical ultrasound, molecular biology & pathology of viruses, molecular medicine, neuroscience, paediatrics & child health, preventative cardiology, public health, quality & safety in healthcare, reproductive biology, surgery, surgery education, translational medicine

BSc, CAS, MB BS, MEd, MPH, MRes, MSc, MSci, PhD

Imperial College Business School; www3.imperial.ac.uk/business-school

accounting, actuarial finance, adv corporate finance, brand management, data science & management, economics & strategy for business, finance, global business, innovation management, innovation, investment & wealth management/entrepreneurship & management, international health management, management, managerial economics, marketing/ management, materials & energy finance, mergers & acquisition, people & organisational behaviour, private equity finance, project management, risk management and financial engineering, social media, strategic marketing, business analytics, finance and accounting, international health management; BSc, MBA, MSc, PhD

Faculty of Natural Sciences; www3.imperial.ac.uk/naturalsciences

Chemistry: chemical biology/health & design, bioimaging sciences, chemistry and management/medicinal chemistry/molecular physics/French, German, Spanish for science, green chemistry, nanomaterials, plant chemical biology, drug discovery & development, theory & simulation of materials, catalysis: chemistry and engineering, green chemistry, energy and the environment, nanomaterials, plant chemical biology

Life Sciences: biology, theoretical systems biology, bioinformatics & theoretical systems biology, biomedical science, biosystematics, biotechnology, biology, ecology & environmental biology, microbiology, plant science & biodiversity, taxonomy & biomedicine, zoology, biodiversity informatics and genomics, chemical biology of crop sustainability and protection, conservation science, ecology, molecular &

cellular biosciences, molecular plant and microbial sciences quantitative biology, structural molecular biology, systems and synthetic biology, applied biosciences and biotechnology, computational methods in ecology and evolution, ecological applications, ecology, evolution and conservation/ research, ecosystem and environmental change, taxonomy and biodiversity, tropical forest ecology

Mathematics: applied/pure mathematics, computational statistics/logistics, mathematical sciences/ & finance, mathematical physics, statistical financial management, statistics, numerical analysis

Physics: physics, optics and photonics, controlled quantum dynamics, nanophysics, photonics, physics with shock physics, physics with music/education, plastic electronics materials, plasmonics & metamaterials, quantum fields and fundamental forces, theoretical physics, theory and simulation of materials; BSc, MRes, MSci, PhD

Materials: aerospace materials, biomaterials and tissue engineering, materials science and engineering, materials with management/nuclear engineering, advanced materials science and engineering, nuclear engineering

Dyson School of Design Engineering; design engineering

KEELE UNIVERSITY
www.keele.ac.uk

Faculty of Health; www.keele.ac.uk/facs/health

School of Medicine; www.keele.ac.uk/depts/schoolofmedicine
biomedical science/engineering, cell and tissue engineering, clinical audit, end of life care, health professionals education, healthcare leadership & management, biomedical blood science, biomedical science/engineering, foundation medical practice: medical education, medical ethics & law/palliative care, medical humanities, medical science (anatomical sciences/clinical audit, end of care in non-specialist settings/leadership & management continuing professional development, individual health, primary care, parasitology, natural sciences with neuroscience/psychology/biochemistry/biomedical science, anatomy, vector biology, foundation medical practice/ethics, geriatric medicine, leadership & management, medical science/practice, medicine, obstetrics & gynaecology, stroke treatment, surgery, medical science (obstetrics & gynaecology/stroke/surgery)

School of Pharmacy; www.keele.ac.uk/schools/pharm
adv professional practice (pharmacy), clinical (hospital) pharmacy, pharmacist, public health/community pharmacy, independent prescribing, medicines, research evaluation, prescribing studies, pharmaceutical science, technology & business, research and evaluation, community pharmacy, pharmacy, independent medicines use review, pharmaceutical drug development and business management, professional Masters

School of Nursing and Midwifery; www.keele.ac.uk/depts/ns
acute care, adult/children's nursing/mental health/ learning disabilities, adv professional practice, applied clinical anatomy, clinical practice, critical care, end of life care, independent practice development, midwifery, operating department practice, pain science & management, physiotherapy (neurology/rheumatology/cardiorespiratory nursing), advancing professional practice (AHPS, nursing and midwifery), neurological rehabilitation, neuromusculoskeletal healthcare, specialist community nursing – district nursing, specialist community public health nursing – health visiting/specialist school nursing

School of Health and Rehabilitation; www.keele.ac.uk/depts/pt
applied clinical anatomy, health science/social care, individual health, neurological rehabilitation, neuromusculoskeletal healthcare, osteopathy, pain science management, physiotherapy, rehabilitation science; MBChB, BSc, MSc, MSci, MPharm, PGCert/Dip, MMedSci, MPhil, PhD, MD

Faculty of Humanities and Social Sciences; www.keele.ac.uk/facs/humass

Keele Management School; www.keele.ac.uk/schools/ems
accounting/& finance/financial management, business management/economics/administration,

economics, industrial relations & employment law, European industrial relations & HR, finance & IT/management/risk management, HRM, international business & law, leadership & management, management & IT, marketing; MA, MBA, MSc, PGCert, PGDip, UnivCert

School of Humanities; www.keele.ac.uk/schools/hums

American studies, English, English and American literatures, humanities, media communication/global media & culture, history, philosophy, Russian music & music technology

Keele Law School; www.keele.ac.uk/depts/law

child care law & practice, gender, human rights, globalization & justice, medical ethics & law/palliative care, law, law with politics/criminology, law & society, safeguarding adults, law policy & practice, international business & law

School of Politics, International Relations and Philosophy; www.keele.ac.uk/spire

diplomatic studies, environmental politics, environment, European politics & culture, global security, international relations, parties & elections, philosophy, politics

School of Public Policy and Professional Practice; www.keele.ac.uk/schools/pppp

PGCE (international) education, international: adv professional development, developing educational practice, educational/studies/international, PGCE (primary, secondary, subject knowledge enhancement, pre-teaching training), initial teacher training (primary/secondary), teacher education, teaching & learning, social work, education, health executive/systems/policy, gerontology, health executive, health services management, HE teaching & learning, community health, gerontology, professional leadership & management, schools direct (primary/secondary/partner schools); GradDip Law, EdD, LlB, LLM, MA, MBA, MRes, MSc, PGCE, PGDip/Cert, PhD

Faculty of Natural Sciences; www.keele.ac.uk/facs/sci/

School of Computing and Mathematics; www.scm.keele.ac.uk

actuarial science, adv/computer science, creative computing, finance/ management and IT, information systems, mathematics (pure, applied, statistics), project management, web & internet technologies, analytics for business and research, project management

School of Life Sciences; www. keele.ac.uk/depts/bi

biomedical blood science, molecular parasitology and vector biology, neuroscience, scientific research training

School of Physical and Geographical Sciences; www.keele.ac.uk/schools/dps

chemistry, chemical sciences, medicinal chemistry, analytical, materials & surface chemistry, spectroscopy, bioinorganic chemistry, chemical ecology, forensic science, green chemistry and clean energy, organic chemistry, photochemistry, applied environmental science, environment and sustainability, environmental sustainability & green technology, geography, geology, geoscience, human/physical geography, forensic science, astrophysics, physics, applied geography, geoscience research, geology and earth sciences, physical geography & environmental science, human geography, environment & sustainability, mathematics

School of Psychology; www.keele.ac.uk/depts/ps

psychology, child development, clinical psychology research, counselling psychology, psychology/health & wellbeing; BA, BSc, DClinPsy, DSc, MGeoscience, MRes, MSc, PGCert, PGDip, PhD

UNIVERSITY OF KENT
www.kent.ac.uk

Faculty of Humanities; www.kent.ac.uk/ humanities

Kent School of Architecture; www.kent.ac.uk/architecture

architecture, architectural visualisation, architecture & urban design/sustainable development, architectural conservation

School of Arts; www.kent.ac.uk/arts

art history/ and classical & archaeological studies/ English and American literature/ film/modern European language, classical and archaeological studies and film, drama and English and American literature/theatre, European arts (history and philosophy of art), film and drama/ religious studies/ practice, history and philosophy of art and drama/English and American literature, film, media arts, philosophy, Postgrad: arts criticism, contemporary performance practice, curating, drama and theatre, drama: practice, European theatre and dramaturgy, film, film with practice, film: practice by research, history & philosophy of art, photographic studies, physical acting, Shakespeare, stand up comedy, theatre directing

School of English; www.kent.ac.uk/english

English/American literature/creative writing, postcolonial studies/literature, creative writing, critical theory, Dickens & Victorian culture, 18th century studies, jt degrees, contemporary literature

School of European Culture & Languages; www.kent.ac.uk/secl

ancient history, archaeology, classical & archaeological studies/history, European studies (Humanities), heritage management, Hellenic & Hellenic near east, drama, linguistics, applied linguistics for TESOL, history, medical humanities, modern French/German/Hispanic/Italian studies & comparative literature, Italian theory, world literature, modern European literature, philosophy, medical humanities, religion, Roman history & architecture

School of History; www.kent.ac.uk/history

American studies, history, European history, history of science, modern history, medieval & modern studies, war studies, war, media & society, science, communication & society, science technology &

society; BA(Hons), BSc(Hons), MA, MArch, MDram, MPhil, PhD

Faculty of Science; www.kent.ac.uk/stms

Dept of Bioscience; www.kent.ac.uk/bio

biology, biomedical sciences, biochemistry, biotechnology & bioengineering, drug design, infectious diseases, reproductive medicine/science & ethics, cancer biology, science, community & society

School of Computing; www.cs.kent.ac.uk

adv/computer science – artificial intelligence/consultancy/networks, computing/ & entrepreneurship, computational intelligence, computer animation, computing security, IT consultancy, adv software development, networks & security

School of Engineering and Digital Arts; www.eda.kent.ac.uk

advanced/electronic/computer systems engineering, architectural visualisation, bioengineering, broadband & mobile communications networks, computer animation, digital visual effects/arts, electronic & communications engineering/computer systems, embedded systems & instrumentation, engineering with finance, information security/biometrics, mobile applications design, multimedia technology & design, wireless communication & signal processing

School of Mathematics, Statistics & Actuarial Science; www.kent.ac.uk/lsmsas

applied/actuarial science, financial mathematics, mathematics & statistics, financial & risk, investment, mathematics/accounting/finance, risk, mathematics & secondary education, mathematics & its applications, statistics with finance

Medway School of Pharmacy; www.msp.kent.ac.uk

medicines management, pharmacy/& physiology, general pharmacy practice, independent supplementary prescribing, applied drug discovery, applied bioscience technology, pharmacology & physiology

School of Physical Sciences; www.kent.ac.uk/physical-sciences

astrophysics, astronomy, space science & astrophysics, forensic science/ & forensic chemistry, chemistry, physics, applied optics, astronomy & planetary science, forensic imaging/science, functional materials; BA(Hons), BEng, BSc(Hons), DClinPsych, MD, MRes, MPhil, MSc, MSurg, PCert, PDip, PhD

School of Sport & Exercise Science; www.kent.ac.uk/sportscience

sport & exercise science/management, sports therapy/science/management, sports therapy, sport for exercise & health science, optimal performance; BSc(Hons), MSc, ProfDoc, MPhil, PhD

Faculty of Social Sciences; www.kent.ac.uk/socsci

School of Anthropology and Conservation; www.kent.ac.uk/sac

anthropology (social/biological/medical), anthropology & conservation, anthropology of ethnicity nationalism & identity, conservation & management, environmental anthropology/studies, liberal arts, social/visual anthropology, social anthropology & computing, conservation & international wildlife trade/ tourism, conservation biology, conservation project management, ethnobotany, evolution & human behaviour; BA(Hons), BSc(Hons), MA, MSc, PhD

Kent Business School; www.kent.ac.uk/kbs

accounting & finance/management, business administration, business & management, business, business analytics, international business/management, logistics & supply chain management, human resource management, management science, marketing; BA(Hons), BBA, BSc(Hons), MBA, MEBA, MPhil, MSc

School of Economics; www.kent.ac.uk/economics

agricultural economics & policies, applied economics & international development, econometrics, economics, finance, financial economics, economic development, international finance & economic development, economics & computing/Spanish; BSc(Hons), MPhil, PhD, MSc

Kent Law School; www.kent.ac.uk/law

international/criminal justice, English law, European legal studies, numerous joint degrees, English & French/German/Spanish/Italian law, European law, international environmental/commercial law, international criminal justice, international law & international relations, English & American law, medical law & ethics, senior status, law & psychology/accounting & finance, law & business, medical law & ethics, law & languages; BA(Hons), LlB, LlM, MPhil, PhD, GradDip

Centre for Journalism; www.kent.ac.uk/journalism

journalism, international multimedia journalism, journalism & the news industry; BA(Hons), MA

School of Politics and International Relations; www.kent.ac.uk/politics

comparative politics, international conflict analysis/relations, European & global governance, international relations & international law, international security & politics of terror, peace & conflict studies, political theory & practice of terror, security & terrorism; BA(Hons), MA, MPhil, PhD, PGDip

Dept of Psychology; www.kent.ac.uk/psychology

applied psychology, cognitive psychology, clinical/developmental psychology, forensic psychology, group processes & intergroup relations, organisational psychology, psychology, psychology & social anthropology/sociology/law, social/& applied psychology, research methods; BSc(Hons), MPhil, MSc, PhD

School of Social Policy, Sociology and Social Research; www.kent.ac.uk/sspssr

autism studies, criminal justice and criminology, criminology/& cultural studies/social policy/sociology, cultural studies and comparative literature/film/history & philosophy of art/social anthropology, health and social care, intellectual and developmental disabilities, management in primary care, social policy and politics/sociology, social sciences, social work, sociology and economics/politics/social anthropology/Italian, statistical social research

Postgrad; advanced child protection, advanced social work – practice and research, analysis and intervention in intellectual and developmental disabilities, applied behaviour analysis, applied health research, civil society, NGO and non-profit studies, environmental social science, international social policy, methods of social research, philanthropic studies, political sociology, applied psychology, community care, cultural and global criminology, medicine and health sciences, mental health, migration studies, personal social services, sociology, urban studies; BA(Hons), BSc(Hons), GradDip/Cert Diplomas, MA, MPhil, MSc, PhD

KINGSTON UNIVERSITY
www.kingston.ac.uk

Faculty of Art, Design and Architecture; www.kingston.ac.uk/faculties/#design

UG; art & design: history and practice, fashion, filmmaking, fine art and art history, fine art, graphic design, historic building conservation, illustration animation, interior design, photography, product and furniture design

PG; architecture, art market appraisal (professional practice), art & space, communication design & the creative economy/ illustration, creative practice, curating contemporary design, design: product and space/ & the creative economy, experimental film, fashion, fashion: knit, fashion & the creative economy, film (experimental), fine art, historic building conservation, landscape architecture, landscape and urbanism, museums and galleries/ & the creative economy, photography, professional practice architecture, sustainable building design and performance, sustainable design, urban design and planning; BA(Hons), FdA, FdSc, MA, MSc, PGCert/Dip, FDip, BSc(Hons), MFA, MArch, MLA

Faculty of Arts and Social Sciences; www.fass.kingston.ac.uk

UG; Economics, History & Politics; applied economics, business economics, economics, financial economics, history, human rights, politics/ and international relations, politics, humanities

Humanities; creative writing, English language and communication, English literature, French, journalism, Spanish, screen studies

Performance & Screen Studies; dance, drama, film studies, music, creative music technologies, TV and new broadcasting media, media and communication, psychology, criminology and sociology

Criminology, Psychology & Sociology; criminology, psychology, sociology
economics, history and politics

PG; Economics; applied econometrics, development and international economics, economic policy, financial economics, international politics and economics, philosophy/ and political economy

History: Politics; human rights, international conflict, international relations, terrorism and political violence, humanities

Creative Writing: creative writing, creative writing and publishing, English literature, applied linguistics for language teaching

Journalism; journalism, magazine journalism

Philosophy; aesthetics and art theory, contemporary European philosophy, modern European philosophy, philosophy and contemporary critical theory, philosophy

Publishing; Performance & Screen Studies; film making, film studies, media and communication

Music: composing for film and TV, music education, music, music performance, production of popular music

Criminology and Sociology; criminological psychology, criminology

Psychology: behavioural decision science, child psychology, clinical applications of psychology, psychology

The Media/Performing Arts and the Creative Economy; creative writing and the creative economy, film making/journalism/publishing/the creative economy, music and the creative economy

BA(Hons), BMus, MA, PGCert/Dip, LlM, EdD, MMus, MSc, MFA

Faculty of Law & Business; www.business.kingston.ac.uk

Kingston Business School

accounting/banking & finance, business IT, finance & business, management, business information technology & operational management, logistics & supply chain management, marketing & communications, advertising/commercial design/writing & creative industries, fashion/film making/museums & galleries/music/publishing managing in the creative economy, international business management/with enterprise/marketing/professional management, leadership & management in health, international/HRM, business psychology, internal communications, corporate communications, marketing communication & development, marketing & brand management, strategic marketing, general law, corporate & financial law, employment/medical law, environmental law & sustainability, international commercial law, legal studies, strategic project management, leadership, HRM, professional practice

Kingston School of Law

international law, law, law with business, law with criminology, real estate management, corporate and financial law, dispute resolution, employment law,

environmental law and sustainability, general law, international commercial law, law with law of international trade, legal studies, employment law and mediation, real estate, employment law and mediation
BA(Hons), BSc(Hons), DBA, FdA, GradDip Law, LlM, MA, MBA, MSc, PhD

Faculty of Science, Engineering & Computing; www.kingston.ac.uk/#sec

Engineering Undergraduate Courses;
Aerospace and Aircraft; aerospace engineering, astronautics & space technology, aerospace engineering, aerospace engineering (maintenance, repair and overhaul), aircraft engineering, aviation studies for commercial pilot training
Automotive and Mechanical; automotive engineering, mechanical engineering, motorsport engineering/motorsport engineering (motorcycle)
Chemistry and Pharmaceutical Sciences; biochemistry, biomedical science, chemistry, forensic science, medical biochemistry, pharmaceutical and chemical sciences, pharmaceutical science, pharmacology
Civil and Construction; building surveying, civil engineering, construction management, quantity surveying consultancy
Computing, Information Systems and Games Development, Software; computer graphics technology, computer science, computer science (games programming/network communications), computing and mathematics, computing with business, cyber security & computer forensics with business, games technology, information systems /internet business, software engineering, software engineering
Geography, Geology, Earth Sciences & Environment; environmental hazards and disaster management, geography, human/physical geography, sustainable development, geology, environmental management/with business, environmental science, geography with business
Life Sciences; biochemistry, biological sciences, biological sciences with business, biological sciences (environmental biology/human biology/medical biology), biomedical science, exercise, nutrition and health, forensic biology, forensic science/with: criminology, medical biochemistry, nutrition, pharmacology, pharmacology with: business, sport analysis and coaching, sport science/with business
Technology; computer graphics technology, creative technology, media technology
Related Courses; applied architectural stonework & conservation, historic building conservation

Postgraduate Courses; advanced industrial & manufacturing systems, advanced product design engineering, aerospace engineering, analytical chemistry/with management studies, automotive engineering (commercial vehicle technology/hybrid and electric vehicles), biomedical science with management studies/ (haematology/medical microbiology), building surveying, cancer biology, computer animation, embedded systems, embedded systems/with management studies/computer vision), engineering projects & systems management, environmental & earth resource management, forensic analysis, game development (design/(programming), GIS & science, hazards & disaster management, information systems, information systems (e-commerce/health information management), IT & strategic innovation, management in construction/with law/civil engineering), mechanical engineering, mechatronic systems, network & information security/with management studies, networking & data communications/ with management studies, pharmaceutical analysis/ with management studies, pharmaceutical science/with management studies, pharmaceutical technology, pharmacy practice (overseas pharmacists assessment programme) professional engineering, quantity surveying, renewable energy engineering, software engineering/ with management studies, software engineering (web)/ with management studies, structural design & construction management/ with sustainability, sustainability & environmental change, sustainable environmental development with management studies, user experience design;
BSc(Hons), BEng, FdSc, FdEng, MComp, MPh, MPharmSci, MPhil, MSc, PhD, PGCert/Dip, MEng

Faculty of Health, Social Care Sciences & Education; www.healthcare.kingston.ac.uk

UG; breast imaging, child centred interprofessional practice, early years, early years: education & leadership in practice/leadership and management/teaching and learning, healthcare practice, midwifery/registered midwife, nursing/registered nurse, paramedic science, physiotherapy, primary teaching leading to QTS, radiography (diagnostic/therapeutic), social work, special educational needs & inclusive practice, working with children & young people, advanced social work 1
PG; applied exercise for health, child centred interprofessional practice, clinical leadership, clinical practice, education, professional studies in education, ELT, healthcare practice, midwifery/registered

midwife for registered nurses/midwifery/registered midwife, nursing/registered nurse, physiotherapy, practice education, primary teaching leading to QTS, professional development in social work, professional education & training, radiography: breast evaluation/medical imaging, medical imaging (mammography)/oncology practice), rehabilitation, secondary teaching leading to QTS, social work; BSc(Hons), DipHE, FdSc, EdD, MREs, MPhil, MSc, MA, MSW, PGCert/Dip, PhD, PGDip, FdA, FdSc, PGCE, GradCert

LANCASTER UNIVERSITY
www.lancs.ac.uk

Faculty of Arts and Social Sciences: www.lancs.ac.uk/fass/faculty

European Languages and Cultures; www.lancs.ac.uk/fass/eurolang

dance/English language & French studies/German studies/Spanish studies, French studies/German studies/Spanish studies – large number of jt degrees, management studies and European languages, modern languages, modern languages and cultures, languages & culture

Sociology; www.lancs.ac.uk/fass/sociology

media & cultural studies, sociology, social work, gender & women's studies

Educational Research; www.lancs.ac.uk/fass/edres

educational research, education & social justice, HE research, evaluation & enhancement, e-research & technology enhanced learning

English and Creative Writing; www.lancs.ac.uk/fass/english

English literature/language & creative writing/literature & practice, English literature & history/linguistics/religious studies/French/German/Spanish/film studies, creative writing & fine art/theatre/film/dance, English, English literary studies, film studies, creative writing/art, contemporary literature, from decadence to modernism, 1890–1945, American literature from 1900, Shakespeare, contemporary literature, advanced creative writing, creative non-fiction, short fiction, poetry and experiment, narrative and new media, world literature

History; www.lancs.ac.uk/fass/history

history, medieval & Renaissance studies, medieval & early modern/modern/heritage history, heritage & public history, number of research modules

Lancaster Institute for the Contemporary Arts; www.lancs.ac.uk/fass/licr

dance, design interactions, film, film, media and cultural studies, fine art, marketing and design, theatre, contemporary arts consultancy, design management, international innovation (design), research (art, design, film studies, theatre and performance)

School of Law; www.lancs.ac.uk/fass/law

law, bioethics, medical law, European legal studies, international business & corporate law, international human rights/law, law & criminology, criminology & society, human rights & the environment, diplomacy & international law, terrorism law, international law & international relations/politics

Linguistics & English Language; www.ling.lancs.ac.uk

English language, linguistics & Chinese/philosophy, English language & creative writing/Chinese/French/German/Spanish/the media/linguistics, applied/linguistics, English language & literary studies, language teaching, language & linguistics, teaching English (TESOL/TEFL), language testing

Politics, Philosophy & Religion; www.lancs.ac.uk/fass/ppr

international relations, politics, politics and international relations, peace studies and international relations, politics, philosophy, politics and economics, conflict, development and security, conflict resolution and peace studies, diplomacy and foreign policy, diplomacy and international law/international relations/religion, international law and international relations

religion and conflict, Quakerism in the modern world, diplomacy and religion, philosophy and religion, religious studies, religious studies, diplomacy and religion, philosophy and religion, religious studies, politics, philosophy and religion, religion and conflict, bioethics and medical law philosophy, ethics, philosophy, religion, philosophy with Chinese/politics/religious studies, philosophy, politics and economics

history, philosophy and politics, numerous joint degrees in philosophy

School of Health and Medicine; www.lancs.ac.uk/shm/faculties

Biomedical & Life Sciences; www.lancs.ac.uk/shm/bls

biochemistry/with biomedicine or genetics, biomedical sciences, applied bioscience & business management, biological sciences, biomedical & life sciences, premedical studies, biology/with psychology

Lancaster Medical School; www.lancs.ac.uk/shm/med

medicine & surgery, medical statistics, biomedical science, biomedicine, biomedical and life sciences, clinical psychology, health research, environmental and biochemical toxicology, quantitative methods for science, social science and medicine, medical leadership, medical education, epidemiology, cellular responses to DNA damage, clinical research, premedical studies, science & technology in clinical practice, reproductive immunology, toxicology, parasitology, quantitative methods in health research; BSc(Hons), CertHE, DClinPsych, MBChB, MBiomed, MD, MHospice leadership, MPhil, MRes, MSc, PGDip/Cert, PhD

Lancaster University Management School; www.lums.lancs.ac.uk

UG; accounting and economics/management studies, accounting, auditing and finance; accounting, finance and computer science/mathematics, advertising and marketing, business analytics and consultancy, business economics, business studies, economics, economics & geography/international relations/mathematics/politics, entrepreneurship (with management), European management (French/German/Italian/Spanish), European-Latin American management (Mexico), finance (industry), finance and economics/management studies (industry), finance and management studies (industry), management, management mathematics, management studies and European languages, management and entrepreneurship, management and IT, management and organisation (HRM), management and organisation, management, politics and international relations, marketing, marketing management, marketing and design, marketing with psychology, organisation

studies and psychology/sociology, philosophy, politics and economics

Post Graduate Programmes; accounting & financial management, advanced financial analysis, advanced marketing management, e-business & innovation, economics, entrepreneurship, innovation & practice, finance, financial analysis, human resources & consulting, human resource & knowledge management, information technology, management & organisational change, international business & strategy, international innovation, logistics & supply chain management, management, management science & marketing analytics, marketing, money, banking & finance, operational research & management science, politics, philosophy & management, project management, executive MBA, MBA, practising management, international executive management, leadership practice & responsibility, philosophy & management, project management, quantitative finance; MRes, BA(Hons), BSc(Hons), BBA, MEcon(Hons), MRes, PGDip, MBA, LlM, MPhil, PhD, MA

Faculty of Science and Technology; www.lancs.ac.uk/shm/sci-tech/faculties

Chemistry; www.chemistry.lancs.ac.uk

chemistry, environmental chemistry, chemistry & spectroscopy, chemical theory & computation, chemical synthesis

Computing & Communication; www.lancs.ac.uk/sci-tech/departments/computing_and_communication

business information & information systems, computer science/& mathematics, computer systems & electronics, communications/computer/systems, cyber security, data science, high wire, software engineering, IT for creative industries, international innovation (computer science/telecommunications), computer systems engineering

Engineering; www.engineering.lancs.ac.uk

chemical engineering, communication systems & electronics, engineering, engineering project management, electronic/electrical engineering, international innovation (electronics), mechatronics, mechanical engineering/with project management, nuclear science & engineering, sustainable engineering, computer systems engineering, aerospace safety engineering, smart systems engineering

Lancaster Environment Centre; www.lec.lancs.ac.uk

biological/biomedical sciences, biology, ecology & conservation, environmental/biology/chemistry/ science, environment, earth/& environmental science, economics/& geography, contamination, risk assessment and remediation, data science for the environment, ecology, ecology and conservation, energy and the environment, environment and development/law, environment, culture and society, environmental management and consultancy, environmental science, environmental science and technology, environmental and biochemical toxicology, food challenges for the 21st century, geography, human rights and the environment, international innovation / (environmental science), plant sciences, resource and environmental management, sustainable agriculture and food security: sustainable water management, volcanology and geological hazards

Mathematics and Statistics; www.maths.lancs.ac.uk

mathematics, computer science and mathematics, financial mathematics, mathematics & philosophy/ statistics/psychology/theoretical physics/economics, quantitative methods for science/social science/

medicine, statistics & operational research, accountancy, finance & mathematics, management mathematics, statistics, data science, quantitative finance

Natural Sciences; www.naturalsci.lancs.ac.uk

combined science, combined technology, natural sciences

Physics; www.lancs.ac.uk/depts/physics

astrophysics, cosmology, nanoscience, physics, space science, theoretical physics/with mathematics, particle physics

Psychology; www.psych.lancs.ac.uk

development psychology/disorders, language, organisational studies & psychology, linguistics & psychology/French/German/Spanish, psychology, psychology of advertising, social psychology, psychological research methods, language, speech & hearing

Biological sciences

biological sciences

BEng(Hons), BSc(Hons), MChem, MEng(Hons), MPhil, MPhys(Hons), MRes, MSc, MSci(Hons), PGDip, PhD

Degrees validated by Lancaster University offered at:

BLACKPOOL AND THE FYLDE COLLEGE
www.blackpool.ac.uk

automotive engineering and technology (automotive/ motorsport), business and financial management, criminology and criminal justice, digital production and film making, early childhood studies, English: communication at work, English: language, literature and writing, environmental science waste, resources and technology), events management, family support and wellbeing, fashion and costume for performance, fine art and professional practice, graphic design and visual communication, health and social care (adults/ children), history and heritage/heritage management, hospitality and licensed retail management, hospitality management, human biosciences, interactive media development, international resort tourism management, management in the workplace, marine biology and coastal zone management, mechanical and production engineering, mechanical engineering, mechatronics, media writing with production, musical theatre, network engineering security and systems administration, photography, professional certificate in education, professional practice health and social care (children and families/combined health/learning disability/ mental health), professional practice in early years, project management, public services and the community, software engineering and game development, sports coaching and exercise instruction, sports studies and development, teaching and learning support, tourism enterprise management, working with young people; FD, BEng(Hons), BA(Hons), BSc(Hons), PGCE

EDGE HILL UNIVERSITY
www.edgehill.ac.uk

Faculty of Education; www.edgehill.ac.uk/education

design and technology education/English education/ mathematics education/modern foreign languages education/religious education with QTS, secondary science (biology/chemistry) education with QTS, secondary science (physics) education, child development & children's learning/& development, early years education, early years leadership, early years learning with QTS, management and enterprise, international early years education, teaching, learning & mentoring practice, working with children & young people, early years education/primary education with QTS, PGCE, early years/primary English education/mathematics specialist/primary modern languages education/primary science education with QTS, early years initial teacher training, early years teacher status, early years practice, professional development, teaching in the lifelong learning sector; simulation and clinical learning, specialist dyslexia training, specialist primary mathematics practice, teaching and learning in clinical practice, clinical education, education, management of international HE, qualitative educational research, specialist primary mathematics practice, post-compulsory education and training, simulation and clinical learning, specialist primary mathematics practice, teaching, learning & mentoring, spld (dyslexia) with ambda/ ats, teaching and learning in clinical practice, working with children & young people in diverse settings; BA(Hons), BSc(Hons), CertHE, FD, PGCE, MA, MTL, PGCert

Faculty of Health & Social Care; www.edgehill.ac.uk/health

children's nursing/learning disabilities & social work, childhood and youth studies, adv fertility practice, childhood nursing/learning disabilities & social work, family & community studies, health & social care, integrated children's & young people practice, nursing studies (adult, learning disabilities, mental health, children's), midwifery, operating department practice, paramedic practice, children's health & wellbeing, health & social wellbeing, leadership & management in children's services, learning disability nursing/children nursing & social work, mental health law & ethics, teaching & learning in clinical practice, simulation & clinical learning, nutrition & health, complementary therapies, counselling &

psychotherapy, playwork intervention, psychosocial analysis of offending behaviour, support for families & communities, social work, applied clinical nutrition, clinical and health research, clinical education, cognitive behavioural psychotherapy, dental implantology, evidence based practice, international midwifery/nursing studies, leadership development, learning disabilities studies, person-centred play therapy, practice education, professional clinical practice, public health and wellbeing/nutrition, surgical care practice, workplace medical learning; BSc(Hons), Dip/CertHE, FdA/Sc, MA, MRes, MCh, MPhil, MSc, MPhil, PhD, PGCert

Faculty of Arts and Science

Biology; www.edgehill.ac.uk/biology
biology, human biology, genetics, ecology, conservation management; BSc(Hons), MSc

Business School; www.edgehill.ac.uk/ business
accountancy, accounting, finance & management, studying business, business and economics/management/accounting and finance/HRM/leisure and tourism/marketing, business innovation and enterprise, international business, business and management (enterprise), business service sector management, marketing & business administration, critical management research, leadership & management development, business administration (finance/HRM/IT/ marketing), marketing & digital communication, marketing with advertising/PR; BSc(Hons), MA, MSc, MRes, MBA, FD

Dept of English and History; www.edgehill.ac.uk/history
English language/literature, history, pop/culture, humanities

Computing; www.edgehill.ac.uk/ computing
computing (application development/games programming/information systems/networking, security and forensics), IT management for business, web design & development, advanced software application development, computer security & networks, computing, cyber security, information security and IT management, IT (mobile computing), web design & development; BSc(Hons), MSc, MRes, FdSc

Law & Criminology; www.edgehill.ac.uk/law

law, law with criminology/politics, criminology/& criminal justice/law/psychology/sociology, international business & commercial/justice & human rights law, policing

Media; www.edgehill.ac.uk/media

advertising, animation, digital SFX animation, film studies/with film production, film & TV production, media, TV/music and sound, motion graphics, music/production, pop music, PR, critical screen practice, film and media, media management; BA(Hons), MA, MRest

Dept of Geography; www.edgehill.ac.uk/geography

environmental science, geography, geology, human/physical geography

Performing Arts; www.edgehill.ac.uk/performingarts

drama/ & dance, visual theatre, making performance, dance movement psychotherapy, visual/musical theatre, theatre design, performance arts, creative & cultural education

Dept of Psychology; www.edgehill.ac.uk/psychology

psychology, educational psychology, sport & exercise psychology

Dept of Social Science; www.edgehill.ac.uk/social science

childhood & youth studies, early childhood studies, sociology

Dept of Sport & Physical Activity; www.edgehill.ac.uk/sport

coach education, PE and school sport, sport and exercise psychology, sport and exercise science, sports development and management, sports therapy, football rehabilitation, sport and exercise, sports development, sports studies; BA(Hons), BSc(Hons), FDA, FDSc, LlB(Hons), MA, MSc, PhD, MBA, MRes, PGDip

UNIVERSITY OF LEEDS
www.leeds.ac.uk

Faculty of Arts; www.leeds.ac.uk/arts

School of English; www.leeds.ac.uk/english

American literature & culture, critical & cultural research, English language/literature, modern & contemporary/Renaissance literature, post-colonial literary & cultural studies, romantic literature & culture, theatre & global development, English literature & linguistics/theatre studies, English & film studies, Victorian literature, jt degrees

School of History; www.leeds.ac.uk/history

history, international history & politics, modern history, race & resistance, social & cultural history, jt hons courses

School of Philosophy, Religion & History of Science; www.leeds.ac.uk/religion_philosophy_and_history_of_science

philosophy, philosophy, ethics and religion, philosophy, politics and economics, hilosophy, psychology and scientific thought, religion, politics and society, theology and religious studies, religion and public life, religious studies and global development, religious studies and global development, theology and religious studies, history & philosophy of science, philosophy of science, history of science, technology & medicine

Institute for Colonial and Post-colonial Studies; www.leeds.ac.uk/icps

post-colonial literary & cultural studies, race & resistance, world cinema, modern languages & cultures

School of Modern Languages and Cultures; www.leeds.ac.uk/smlc

Arabic & Middle Eastern/Islamic studies, Asia-Pacific studies, Chinese, Japanese, South/East Asian studies, Thai studies, French, German, Italian, linguistics & phonetics, Russian & Slavonic studies, Spanish, Portuguese and Latin, applied translation studies, diplo applied translation studies, audiovisual translation studies, conference interpreting and translation studies, diplo conference interpreting, professional language and intercultural studies, Arabic/English translation, linguistics, linguistics and English language teaching, middle eastern and Islamic studies, Chinese studies, Chinese business/and the Asia pacific, East Asian regional development, Japanese business/studies, world cinemas, numerous jt honours; BA(Hons), MA, MPhil, PGDip, PhD

Faculty of Biological Studies; www.fbs.leeds.ac.uk

biochemistry, biology, biological science, bioscience, biotechnology, biodiversity & conservation, infection, immunology & human disease, plant science & biotechnology, ecology & environmental biology, biodiversity & conservation, genetics, human physiology, medical biochemistry/microbiology/sciences, microbiology, neuroscience, pharmacology, virology, sport & exercise sciences, sport science & physiology, zoology; BSc(Hons), MRes, MSc, PhD, MBiol

Faculty of Business; www.fbs.leeds.ac.uk

Leeds University Business School; www.leeds.ac.uk/lbs

UG; accounting and finance, business analytics, business economics, economics, economics and finance, economics and management, HRM, international business, international business and economics/finance/marketing, management, management and the human resource, management with marketing, Arabic and management, Asia Pacific studies and economics/management, Chinese and economics/management, economics, economics (numerous jt degrees), management, management (numerous jt degrees)

Post Grad; accounting and finance, actuarial finance, advertising and design, advertising and marketing, banking and international finance, business analytics and decision sciences, business psychology, coproducing health, corporate communications and PR, economics, economics and finance, engineering, technology and business management, enterprise, executive MBA, finance and investment, financial mathematics, financial risk management, full time MBA, global innovation management, global supply chain management, HRM, information systems & information management, international business, international marketing management, management, organizational behaviour, organizational psychology, strategic management in the global environment; BSc(Hons), BA(Hons), ExecMBA, MA, MBA, MPhil, MSc, PhD

Faculty of Education, Social Sciences & Law; www.essl.leeds.ac.uk

School of Education; www.education.leeds.ac.uk

childhood studies, technology, education and learning, international educational management, education and professional enquiry, special educational needs, provision for children with developmental disorders, deaf education, English as an additional language and education, TESOL studies, TESOL and ICT, TESOL for young learners, TESOL teacher education, educational research methods, clinical education, children & inclusive education, language education, learning, leadership & policy, mathematics/science education, teaching; PGCE schools direct primary, secondary (provision for children with learning difficulties), developmental disorders, teaching, teacher education & learning, teaching English (TESOL) & ICY/studies/teacher education, teaching English for academic professional purposes; BA(Hons), MA, MSc, PGCert, MEd, PGCE, PhD

School of Law; www.law.leeds.ac.uk

law, criminal justice & criminology/criminal law, law & French law, European & international business law/corporate law/trade/banking & finance law, intellectual property law, international law, international banking & finance/business/corporate law, international & European human rights law, law & finance, security & justice, senior status; LlB, LlM, MSc, MA, PhD

School of Politics and International Studies; www.leeds.ac.uk/polis

economics & politics, international development/relations, economics & politics, politics & parliamentary studies, disablement/& global development, theatre & religious studies/global development, international development & politics of the Middle East, conflict, development & security, security, terrorism & insurgency, public administration; BA, MA, MPhil, PhD

School of Sociology and Social Policy; www.sociology.leeds.ac.uk

sociology, social policy, social policy and crime, interdisciplinary social policy and sociology/social and public policy, social policy with enterprise, politics and sociology, politics and social policy, geography and sociology, sociology and international relations, social research

Postgrad; work, care and migration, international social transformation, social and political thought, global racism studies, disability studies, disability and global development/special education/social policy, gender studies, gender, sexuality and the body; BA(Hons), MA, MPhil, PGCert, PhD

Faculty of Engineering;
www.engineering.leeds.ac.uk

School of Civil Engineering;
www.engineering.leeds.ac.uk/civil

architectural engineering, civil & environmental engineering/structural engineering, civil engineering with project management, international construction management & engineering, engineering project management, water, sanitation & health engineering, structural engineering, environmental engineering & project management

School of Computing;
www.engineering.leeds.ac.uk/comp

applied computer science, computer science, computer science with artificial intelligence/distributed systems/ mathematics, electronics and computer engineering; Postgrad; advanced computer science, advanced computer science (cloud computing/data analytics/intelligent systems), mathematics and computer science, mobile computing and communications networks

School of Electronic and Electrical Engineering;
www.engineering.leeds.ac.uk/elec

electronic engineering, electronic and electrical engineering/communications engineering, electronics and computer engineering/renewable energy systems, mechatronics and robotics, music, multimedia and electronics; Postgrad; communications & signal processing, digital communications networks, electrical engineering and renewable energy systems, electronic and electrical engineering, embedded systems engineering, engineering, technology and business management, mechatronics and robotics, mobile computing and communications networks

Mechanical Engineering;
www.engineering.leeds.ac.uk/mech

aeronautical/& aerospace engineering, automotive engineering, adv/mechanical engineering, mechatronics & robotics, medical engineering, oilfield corrosion engineering, product design, tribology of surfaces & interfaces

School of Chemical & Process Engineering;
www.engineering.leeds.ac.uk/chemical

aviation technology with/management/pilot studies, chemical & energy/materials/minerals/nuclear engineering, chemical engineering, energy & environment, fire & explosion engineering, food processing engineering, materials science & engineering, sustainable energy science, petroleum engineering; BEng, MEng, MSc, MSc(Eng), MPhil, PhD

Faculty of the Environment;
www.leeds.ac.uk/foe

School of Earth & Environment;
www.see.leeds.ac.uk

geological sciences, geophysical sciences, environmental science, meteorology and climate science, environment and business, sustainability and environmental management; Postgrad; exploration geophysics, structural geology with geophysics, engineering geology petroleum exploration, climate change and environmental policy, environment and development, sustainability and business, sustainability and consultancy, climate and atmospheric science

School of Geography;
www.geog.leeds.ac.ukw

geography, geography/with transport studies/mathematics/management/economics, geography–geology, GIS, river basin dynamics & management with GIS

Institute for Transport Studies;
www.its.leeds.ac.uk

economics with transport studies, geography with transport planning, planning & the environment/engineering, transport economics, sustainability (transport)

Earth & Biosphere Institute;
www.earth.leeds.ac.uk/ebi

global change & the biosphere; BA(Hons), BSc(Hons), MA, MGeol, MGeophys, MRes, MSc, PGCert/Dip, PhD, MEnv, MGeol

Faculty of Mathematics and Physical Science; www.maps.leeds.ac.uk

School of Chemistry;
www.chemi.leeds.ac.uk

chemistry, chemical process research & development, analytical medicinal chemistry, polymers, colorants & fine chemicals, chemical biology & drug design, natural sciences, chemistry & mathematics

School of Food Science and Nutrition; www.food.leeds.ac.uk

food biotechnology, food quality & innovation, nutrition, food science/& nutrition, food studies

School of Physics and Astronomy; www.physics.leeds.ac.uk

physics/with astrophysics, theoretical physics, physics with business management

School of Mathematics; www.amsta.ac.uk

actuarial/financial mathematics, actuarial finance, statistics; BSc(Hons), MChem, MMath, MNatSci, MPhil, MPhys, MSc, PhD, GradDip

Faculty of Medicine & Health; www.leeds.ac.uk/medhealth

Leeds Dental Institute; www.leeds.ac.uk/dental

dental hygiene & dental therapy, clinical dentistry, restorative/implant dentistry, dental nursing/surgery/technology, dental public health, paediatric dentistry, oral science

School of Healthcare; www.healthcare.leeds.ac.uk

adult/child/adult nursing, adv practice, healthcare sciences (audiology/cardiological physiology), midwifery, diography, social work, leadership management in health & social care, child health, education in primary care, health management, planning and policy, hospital management, health research, psychotherapy and counselling, pharmacy practice, medical imaging, prescribing and patient assessment, social work, systemic family therapy, stroke care, systemic practice

Leeds School of Medicine; www.leeds.ac.uk/medicine

clinical embryology/science, applied health, medical humanities/primary care, clinical sciences (medical imaging/molecular medicine/international health, medicine and surgery, clinical embryology/and assisted reproduction technology, epidemiology and biostatistics, medical imaging, health economics, health informatics, health management/planning and policy, international health, public health/ (international), child health, education in primary care, family therapy, health research, molecular medicine, diagnostic imaging, psychiatry, psychoanalytic observational studies, stroke care

School of Psychology; www.psych.leeds.ac.uk

adv/psychology, psychological approach to health, psychology (industrial/international)
BHSc, BSc(Hons), CPD, DClinPsych, GradDip, MA, MBChB, MD, MMedSci, MPH, MPsycObs, MSc, PGDip/Cert, PhD

Faculty of Performance, Visual Arts and Communication; www.leeds.ac.uk/pvac

School of Media & Communication; www.media.leeds.ac.uk

broadcast journalism, communication & media, film, photography & media, journalism, new media, media industries, PR & society

School of Design; www.design.leeds.ac.uk

adv/textile design, adv/textiles, advertising & design, art & design, design, fashion design/marketing, fashion, enterprise & society, graphic and communication design, medical textiles, textile innovation & branding

School of Fine Art, History of Art and Cultural Studies; www.leeds.ac.uk/fine_art

cultural and media studies, fine art, fine art with contemporary cultural theory/ history of art/museum and gallery studies, history of art, history of art with cultural studies/museum studies; Postgraduate; arts management and heritage studies, critical and cultural theory, art gallery and museum studies, fine art, history of art

School of Music; www.leeds.ac.uk/music

app psychology of music, critical & applied musicology, critical & experimental composition, music, music (industry/performance), music & management, computer music, musicology, performance, music & management/enterprise

School of Performance & Cultural Industries; www.pci.leeds.ac.uk

culture, creativity & entrepreneurship, dance, managing performance, performance design/culture & context, theatre & performance, writing for performance and publication, app theatre intervention
BA(Hons), GradDip, MFA, BMus, BSc(Hons), MA, MMus, MSc, PhD

Degrees validated by University of Leeds offered at:

COLLEGE OF THE RESURRECTION
www.mirfieldcollege.org.uk

theological studies, ministry & theology, liturgy;
BA(Hons), DipHE, MA, MPhil, PGDip, PhD

LEEDS COLLEGE OF ART
www.leeds-art.ac.uk

creative advertising, creative practice, digital film, games & animation, fashion, fine art, graphic design, illustration, photography, printed textiles & surface pattern design, visual communication; BA(Hons), FD, MA

LEEDS COLLEGE OF MUSIC
www.lcm.ac.uk

music (classical/pop/production/business), composition, creative practice, jazz, musicology, performance /& composition; BA(Hons), FD, MA, PGDip, MMus

LEEDS TRINITY UNIVERSITY
www.leedstrinity.ac.uk

English; www.leedstrinity.ac.uk/departments/English
English & film studies/journalism/media/writing, creative writing, Victorian studies; BA(Hons), BSc(Hons), MA, MSc, PhD

History; www.leedstrinity.ac.uk/departments/history
history/& English, Victorian studies; BA(Hons), MA

Children, Young People & Families; www.leedstrinity.ac.uk/cyp
supporting children & families in social context/ education/learning & additional needs, education studies, child and family welfare studies, professional practice: early childhood studies/education, supporting young people, children and families; BA(Hons), FD, MA, PGCert, PGCE

Business, Management & Marketing: www.leedstrinity.ac.uk/departments/business
accounting/& business, business, business & management/marketing, business management, international business, financial management, finance & accountancy, management, marketing & media; BA(Hons), MA/PGDip, MBA

Primary education; www.leedstrinity.ac.uk/departments/primary
primary education, early years, later years (QTS)/ primary education/PE & sport; BA(Hons), PGCE

Secondary Education; www.leedstrinity.ac.uk/departments/secondary
education, secondary education, PE & sport, PGCE primary, secondary (10 subjects), teacher training (SCiTT), schools direct; BSc(Hons), PGCE, MA

Sport Health & Nutrition; www.leedstrinity.ac.uk/departments/shln
health and wellbeing, secondary education, physical education and sport, primary/secondary physical education and sports development, primary/secondary physical education and sports coaching, sport and exercise sciences (sports nutrition/sports psychology/strength and conditioning), sport, health, exercise and nutrition, nutrition, food and health supporting learning: sport, physical education and health; BSc(Hons), BA(Hons), MSc

Journalism; www.leedstrinity.ac.uk/ departments/cfj

journalism, broadcast/magazine/sport/radio/print journalism, creative & professional writing, English & journalism; BA(Hons), BA, PGDip

Media, Film & Culture; www.leedstrinity.ac.uk/departments/ media

media & marketing, film & TV studies, film studies, media, TV production; BA(Hons)

Theology & Religious Studies; www.leedstrinity.ac.uk/departments/ theology

philosophy, ethics & religion, theology, religious studies, Catholic religious studies; BA(Hons), MA, Cert

Victorian studies; www.leedstrinity.ac.uk/ departments/victorian.studies

Victorian Studies; MPhil, PhD

Psychology; www.leedstrinity.ac.uk/ departments/psychology

psychology, forensic/sport/psychology, psychology & child development; BSc(Hons), PhD

NORTHERN SCHOOL OF CONTEMPORARY DANCE
www.nscd.ac.uk

contemporary dance; BPA(Hons), PgDip, MA, FD

YORK ST JOHN UNIVERSITY
www.yorksj.ac.uk

Faculty of Arts; www.yorksj.ac.uk/arts/ faculty.of.arts

applied theatre, music composition, computer science/aided design, contemporary literature, American studies, creative writing, film production, English literature, film studies, fine arts, graphics/ interiors design, history, human geography, mass communication, media, product design, theatre & performance; FD, BA(Hons), PGCert/Dip, MA

Faculty of Education & Theology; www.yorksj.ac.uk/education-theology

PGCE, primary/secondary education, education studies, early childhood studies, academic practice, religious studies, improving professional practice, initial teacher education, contemporary religion, evangelism, supporting learning, theology & ministry/religious studies, chaplaincy studies, military chaplaincy, religion, philosophy & ethics, religion & education/public life, Christian theology, Catholic studies, theology & ministry, primary education with QTS, teacher education, children, school leadership, schools direct, children, sociology, children, young people & families, youth & community work; MFL, BA(Hons), GradDip, PGDip, PGCE, PhD

Faculty of Health & Life Sciences; www.yorksj.ac.uk/health-and-life-sciences

applied cognitive psychology, biomedical sciences, counselling/supervision, coaching & /psychotherapy studies, occupational therapy, physiotherapy, psychology, community & clinical social psychology, psychology/of child & adolescent development, applied sport & exercise science, nutrition & exercise for health, PE/& sport coaching/youth sport, sports development & coaching, sports science & injury rehabilitation, strength & conditioning; BA(Hons), MA, MSc, PGDip/Cert, PhD

York St John Business School; www.yorksj.ac.uk/business

accounting & finance, business management/& HRM/languages/finance, business administration with finance/design management/media management, business information technology, coaching & mentoring, applied linguistics TESOL, English language & linguistics, design & creativity, languages, British sign language & English language/literature, French/German/Spanish/Japanese and English literature/language, strategic/HRM, marketing management/ web technology, global marketing, languages, leadership & management, leading innovation & change, international business, international tourism management/& hospitality management, tourism

management/& marketing, MBA (finance/design/marketing); BA(Hons), FD, MA, PGDip/Cert, MBA

LEEDS BECKETT UNIVERSITY
www.leedsbeckett.ac.uk

Faculty of Arts, Environment & Technology; www.leedsbeckett.ac.uk/aet

The Leeds School of Art, Architecture & Design; www.leedsbeckett.ac.uk/aet/#art-architecture-design

architecture, architectural professional practice, art & design, artist teacher in art & design, design practice, fashion, fine art, interior architecture & design, urban design, graphic art & design, professional studies, landscape architecture & design, urban design

School of Built Environment & Engineering; www.leedsbeckett.ac.uk/aet/#built-environment-engineering

adv engineering management, building/engineering studies/services engineering, civil engineering/& construction, construction/commercial/management, strategic/project management, facilities management, architectural technology, building/quantity surveying, environmental engineering & construction, health & neighbourhood planning, housing/strategy, housing, regeneration & urban management, planning law & practice, strategic project management, project management/construction, town & regional planning, UK planning law & dispute practice, sustainable urban planning

School of Computing, Creative technology & Engineering; www.leedsbeckett.ac.uk/aet/#computing-creative-technology

advanced engineering management, business information systems/intelligence, computer forensics/& security, computer science computing, computer sustainable engineering, creative media/technology, digital forensics & security, electrical & electronic engineering, food engineering, information management/systems, managing software development, web applications development, software development/engineering, mobile device applications, information & technology/management, broadcast media technologies, computer animation technology, computer animation/& special effects & visual effects, creative technology, 3D visualisation & interactive environments, networking systems engineering

School of Film, Music & Performing Arts; www.leedsbeckett.ac.uk/aet/#film-music-performingarts

music performance/production/technology, dance, audio engineering, performance, music for moving image, sound & music for interactive games, sound design

Northern Film School

animation, film making, film & TV

School of Cultural Studies & Humanities; www.leedsbeckett.ac.uk/as/cs

English/& history, English literature, history, media, communication & cultures, English contemporary literature, social history; BA(Hons), BSc(Hons), DipHE, FdAA, GradCert, MPhil, MRes, MSc, PGDip

Faculty of Business and Law; www.leedsbeckett.ac.uk/fbl

Leeds Business School; www.leedsbeckett.ac.uk/fbl/leeds_business_school

accounting/& finance, business, business studies/administration/economics, business & management/HRM/management studies, action by facilitation, corporate governance/communications, economics for business/& finance, executive leadership, financial economics, applied finance, HRM, international HRM, international business/communications/business law/trade & finance, journalism, leadership & change, management, marketing, marketing & advertising management, PR & communication/journalism/strategic communication, retail marketing management, supply chain management & logistics, MBA(Executive/Graduate)

Leeds Law School; www.leedsbeckett.ac.uk/lbs/law

law, legal practice, commercial, international business law; BA(Hons), HND, LlB(Hons), LlM, MA, MSc, PGDip/Cert, MBA, DBA

Faculty of Health & Social Sciences; *www.leedsbeckett.ac.uk/hss*

adv practice, adv social work practice, adv diabetics education, adv biotechnical research, acoustics, art psychology/practice, biomedical sciences (human biology/microbiology/molecular biology/physiology/pharmacology/research,), chaplaincy in health & social care, community specialist practitioner – community children's nursing/district nursing/health visiting/schools nursing/occupational health nursing, community & youth studies, counselling & therapeutical studies/psychotherapy, criminology/& psychology/sociology, dietetics, eating disorders, environmental health, health & safety regulation, health & community care, interdisciplinary psychology, interpersonal & counselling skills, international nursing (adult health/mental health), nutrition/in practice, mental health studies/practice, microbiological technology, nutritional health, occupational therapy, osteopathy, playwork, play-based therapy, physiotherapy, psychology/& society, psychological therapies, psychotherapy, public health – environmental health/nutrition, safety health & environmental management, social work, sociology, speech & language/exercise therapies, sports & exercise therapy, support work, therapeutic counselling/play skills, toxicological sciences, youth work & community development, young people, communities & security, CPD; BA(Hons), BSc(Hons), CertHE, HNC, MA, MSc, PGDip/Cert, Prof Dip, DipHE, FdAA, GradCert, MPhil, MRes, PGDip, MBioms

Carnegie Faculty; *www.leedsbeckett.ac.uk/carnegie*

childhood and early years, higher and further education, childhood studies, education studies, internationalisation inclusion training in intellectual disability for educators in Europe, partnerships with schools playwork researchers, childhood outdoor & adventurous activities, psychology, strength & coordination, PE, leisure, sport & culture, PE with outdoor education, sport & exercise science, sport & business management/development/management/coaching/studies, sport physical activity & health, sport & exercise medication, psychology of sport & exercise, international/event management, sport event management, sport & exercise/biomedicine/nutrition/physiology/health/psychology/science/therapy, sport, law & society, conference & exhibition management, entertainment management, managing cultural & major events, event sponsorship and fundraising; BA(Hons), BSc(Hons), FdSc, PGCE, PGCert/Dip, MA, PhD, Prof DocEd

UNIVERSITY OF LEICESTER
www.le.ac.uk

College of Arts, Humanities and Law; *www2.le.ac.uk/colleges/artshumlaw*

School of Archaeology & Ancient History; www.le.ac.uk/ar

ancient history, archaeology, classical Mediterranean, history, historical archaeology, archaeology of the Roman world

School of English; www.le.ac.uk/ee

English studies, English, English & American studies/history/French/Spanish, English language & modern literature & creative writing/linguistics, Victorian studies

Dept of History of Art and Film; www.le.ac.uk/ha

the country house in art, history & culture, film studies and visual arts/English/media studies, history of art/& English, film & film cultures

School of History; www.le.ac.uk/hi

contemporary history, English local history & family history, history, history and politics/international relations/ancient history/archaeology/English/American studies, urban history/conservation, European urbanisation

School of Law; www.le.ac.uk/law

law, international/human rights/commercial law, public international law, general law, law with French law, law & criminology/politics/languages

School of Modern Languages; www.le.ac.uk/ml

European studies, French/German/Italian/ & English, modern language studies, modern languages with management/EFL/film studies, translation & interpreting/, international communication & culture, translation studies,

Museum Studies; www.le.ac.uk /ms

art museum/& gallery studies, heritage & interpretation, learning & visitor studies in museums & galleries; BA(Hons), BSc(Hons), LlB, LlM, MSC, MA/GradDip, MPhil, PhD

College of Science and Engineering; www2.le.ac.uk/colleges/science

Dept of Chemistry; www.le.ac.uk/ch

chemistry, cancer chemistry, chemistry with forensic science, pharmaceutical chemistry, chemical research (biological/green/physical chemistry), forensic science & criminal justice

Dept of Computer Science; www.cs.le.ac.uk

advanced computational methods/distributed systems/software engineering, agile software engineering technologies, computer science, computing, computing with management, software engineering for financial services, web applications & services, cloud computing

Dept of Engineering; www2.le.ac.uk/departments/engineering

advanced control & dynamics, advanced engineering, advanced materials engineering, aerospace engineering, communications & electronic engineering, control & signal processing, adv/electrical & electronic engineering, embedded systems & control engineering, general engineering, information & communication engineering, adv/mechanical engineering, software & electronic engineering

Dept of Geography; www.le.ac.uk/geography

environmental informatics, geography, geology, GIS with industry, global environmental change, human/physical geography, sustainable management of natural resources

Dept of Geology; www2.le.ac.uk/departments/geology

applied & environmental geology, crustal processes, geology, geography, rock physics & boreholes, palaeobiology, palaeoenvironments, palaeoclimates

Dept of Mathematics; www2.le.ac.uk/departments/mathematics

mathematics, actuarial science, data analysis for business intelligence, financial mathematics/& computation, mathematical modelling in biology, mathematics with management/economics/actuarial science

Dept of Physics and Astronomy; www2.le.ac.uk/departments/physics

astronomy, physics, physics with nanotechnology/astrophysics/space science & technology/planetary science, space exploration systems; BA(Hons), BSc(Hons), BEng/MEng, MA, MChem, MComp, MGeol, MMath, MPhil, MPhys, MSc, MSci, PGDip, PhD

College of Medicine, Biological Sciences and Psychology; www2.le.ac.uk/colleges/medbiopsych

bioinformatics, cancer cell and molecular biology, molecular pathology and therapeutics of cancer, molecular genetics, chronic disease and inflammation, infection and immunity, cell physiology and pharmacology, forensic psychology, psychological research methods, applied health research, diabetes, integrated provision for children and families

School of Biological Sciences; www2.le.ac.uk/departments/biologicalscience

bioinformatics, biological sciences (biochemistry/genetics/microbiology/physiology with pharmacology/zoology), medical genetics, biochemistry/microbiology/physiology, molecular genetics, cell physiology & pharmacology

Dept of Medical & Social Care Education Medicine; www2.le.ac.uk/departments/msce

medicine, operating department practice, physiotherapy, social work

medicine, cancer cell studies & molecular medicine/biology, bioinformatics, cardiovascular sciences, clinical science, health sciences, infection & immunisation, medical statistics, medical & social care education, molecular pathology/toxicology, mountain medicine, occupational psychology, operating department practice, pain management, physiotherapy, primary care research, social science applied to health, child & adolescent mental health, integrated provision for children & families, social work

School of Psychology; www2.le.ac.uk/departments/psychology

psychology/with sociology/cognitive neuroscience/media, clinical/forensic psychology, applied forensic psychology, forensic legal psychology, occupational psychology, psychology of work; DocClinPsych, BSc, MBChB, MBioSci, MD, MSc, PostgradDip/Cert, PhD

College of the Social Sciences
www.le.ac.uk/colleges/socsci

Dept of Criminology; www2.le.ac.uk/departments/criminology

applied/clinical/criminology, terrorism, security & policing, criminology

Dept of Economics; www2.le.ac.uk/departments/economics

banking & finance, business/financial economics, economics, business analysis & finance, financial risk management

School of Education; www2.le.ac.uk/departments/education

action research, educational studies, education, educational leadership, learning & teaching, understanding and managing children/mental health problems and children with social, learning/emotional and behavioural difficulties, specialist assessment and teaching of pupils with specific learning difficulties, promoting language development in the early years, issues in mathematics/science/English education, mentoring and coaching, developing leadership in education, teaching mathematics, teaching English for academic purposes, education and sustainable development, PGCE primary/secondary education, teachfirst, TESOL & applied linguistics

Institute of Lifelong Learning; www2.le.ac.uk/departments/lifelong-learning

advice work, counselling, creative writing, drug and alcohol counselling and treatment, global ecology, humanities and arts, leadership and business management, managing voluntary and community organisations, psychology, psychodynamic counselling and psychotherapy, risk, crisis and disaster management, psychodynamic counselling and psychotherapy

School of Management; www2.le.ac.uk/departments/management

accounting, finance, management studies, marketing, finance, economics, politics, business administration, global financial markets, HRM & training, management & economics/politics

Dept of Media & Communication; www.le.ac.uk/mc

communications & globalization, media & PR/advertising, film & media, new media & society, media & communication/society, media, culture & society, journalism studies

Dept of Politics and International Relations; www2.le.ac.uk/departments/politics

diplomatic studies, politics & international relations/history, politics & sociology/history/management studies/economics, human rights & global ethics, international security, politics of the EU, law with politics, international relations & world order, intelligence & security, political conflict & violence

Dept of Sociology; www2.le.ac.uk/departments/sociology

politics & sociology, psychology with sociology, media, culture & society, migration studies, sociology, contemporary sociology, social research; BA(Hons), DocSocSci, EdD, FD, MA, MBA, MPhil, MSc, PGCE, PGDip/Cert, PhD, CertHE

Degrees validated by the University of Leicester offered at:

NEWMAN UNIVERSITY
www.newman.ac.uk

accountancy & finance, applied social sciences, computing financial education, early childhood education & culture, EYETT, drama/art/economics & education, English & drama/creative writing/history/theology, studies in primary education, education, business management, business & media production, education/counselling studies with children, history & English/theology/education/sociology, public health history, Victorian studies, mathematics, psychology & counselling studies, young people & families, counselling, primary education (QTS)/early years, PGCE secondary computer science & IT (QTS), education & counselling studies, counselling studies & working with children, young people & families, integrative counselling, early childhood education, PGCE primary education with QTS, school direct, integrative counselling/psychotherapy, sports coaching science/tournament golf, sport & exercise studies/psychology, sports coaching & science/tournament golf, PE & sports science, sport & exercise psychology, working with children, young people & families/& education studies, teaching & learning support assistant, studies in primary education, theology & education studies/history/English/education studies, philosophy, religion & education, contemporary Christian theology, PGCE primary, secondary education (several subjects, QTS), chaplaincy with young people, English & drama/creative writing/education/film studies/theology, English literature, philosophy, religion & English, history & education/theology/public

history, Victorian studies, sports management, management studies with IT, business accounting, psychology/education & counselling studies, clinical/applications of/psychology, integrative psychotherapy (children, adolescents, adults), psychology & counselling studies, criminology, social science, mathematics/chemistry, youth & community studies; BA/BSc(Hons), FD, MA, MPhil, PGCE, PhD, MBA

UNIVERSITY OF LINCOLN
www.lincoln.ac.uk

College of Arts; www.lincoln.ac.uk/college of arts

animation, architecture, sustainable architectural design, art, architecture/& design, art & design research, art, architecture & design, conservation of historic objects/studies, conservation & restoration, conservation studies, contemporary curatorial practice, creative advertising, design, design/exhibition & museums, development & regeneration, fashion studies, fine art, graphic design, illustration, interactive design, interior design/architecture/enterprise, international design enterprise, product design, planning/& urban design, sustainable architectural design, 21st-century literature, audio production, choreography, community radio, creative writing, dance, digital imaging/arts, digital media, drama/& English, film & TV, English, English studies, history, historical studies, medieval studies, journalism, war & international human rights, sports/science & environment, journalism (investigative/arts/digital/sports), journalism, war & human rights/PR, media & cultural studies, media production, media, film & TV production, music, photography, PR: settlement; BA(Hons), BArch, GradDip, MA, MArch, MPhil, PhD, MRes

College of Social Science; www.lincoln.ac.uk/home/collegeof socialscience

Centre for Educational Research & Development
educational research & development, PGCE secondary, social research

Lincoln Business School
accountancy & finance, accounting, advertising & marketing, business & finance/management/ marketing, business studies, economics, finance, business administration/studies, business management/military, international business management/tourism management, social research, engineering management/military, event management, HRM, HRD, logistics management/military, marketing

School of Health & Social Care
adv professional practice in social work, nursing, nursing (mental health), health & social care, professional practice, interprofessional practice (mental health professional), non-medical/independent prescribing, social research, social work

Lincoln Law School
law, law & criminology, international business law, international law, social research

School of Psychology
psychology, psychology with clinical forensic psychology, developmental psychology, social research

School of Social & Political Science
politics, sociology, politics & social policy, criminology, criminology & international relations/politics/social policy, global justice, social research, social science

School of Sport & Exercise Science
physical activity & health development, sports & exercise science, sports development & coaching, sport & PE, sports coaching/development, strength & conditioning in sport
BA(Hons), BSc(Hons), CertHE, DClinPsy, MA, MClinRes, MPhil, PGCert, PhD, LlB(Hons), LlM, MBA, MPhil, MRes, MSc, EdD

College of Science; www.lincoln.ac.uk/science

Lincoln School of Chemistry
chemistry, forensic chemistry/science, research in analytical/biological/environmental chemistry, conservation science

Lincoln School of Engineering
engineering, electrical engineering (control systems/electronics/power & energy)

Lincoln School of Computer Science
computer information systems, computer science, games computing, intelligent systems, social computing

School of Life Science
animal behaviour & welfare/science, clinical animal behaviour, biochemistry, biology, biomedical science, bioveterinary science, biotechnology, evolution & ecology, life sciences

School of Mathematics & Physics
mathematics, physics, mathematics & physics, pure/applied mathematics, computational physics

Lincoln School of Pharmacy; www.lincoln.ac.uk/home/lsp
pharmacy, pharmaceutical science

National Centre for Food Manufacturing
food manufacture (operations management/quality assessment & technology management), food manufacture & technology

Centre for Educational Research & Development
educational research, social research, PGCE secondary; BA(Hons), BSc(Hons), BEng(Hons), MEng(Hons), FdSc, MA, MComp, MPhil, MRes, MSc, PhD, EdD, PhD, MPharm

Degrees validated by the University of Lincoln offered at:

EAST RIDING COLLEGE
www.eastridingcollege.ac.uk

access to higher education, applied digital media, early childhood policy & practice, education & professional development, computing, applied digital media, contemporary media design, inservice PGCE, lifelong learning, learning support, sport coaching & exercise/health science; BA(Hons), FdA, FdEd, FdSc, PGCE

HULL COLLEGE
www.hull-college.ac.uk

Faculty of Arts

Hull School of Art & Design; www.hull-college.ac.uk/hull-school-of-art-and-design
technical and theatre production, acting with theatre practice, animation, architecture, broadcast media, creative practice, dance, design (interior, product, designer maker), fashion, film-making & creative media, production, fine art, games design, graphic design, illustration, journalism & digital media, music production/theatre, photography, textiles, web design, visual culture: theory and practice; BA(Hons), FdA, MA, MArch

Faculty of Business & Science
leadership and management, teacher education, business and management, professional portfolio, travel & tourism, hospitality management, leadership and management in health & social care settings, criminology, sport, young children's learning and development, health, exercise and lifestyle and health and social care, engineering, sustainable construction, computing and logistics, green skills, renewable energy, digital; FdA, FdSc, BSc(Hons), BA(Hons), PGCE

NORTH LINDSEY COLLEGE
www.northlindsey.ac.uk

business studies, business & HRM, biochemistry, bioscience, leadership & management, applied studies, early childhood, computing information systems, learning support, integrated engineering (electrical/mechanical), English, history, social science, sport development & coaching, PGCE, sport & exercise science (personal training/coaching); BA(Hons), Dips, FdA/Sc/Ed/Eng, Grad Cert Ed, PGCE

UNIVERSITY OF LIVERPOOL
www.liv.ac.uk

Faculty of Health & Life Sciences; www.liv.ac.uk/health_and_life_sciences
Dentistry; www.liverpool.ac.uk/dentistry
dental hygiene/therapy/surgery, orthodontics, endodontics
Health Sciences; www.liverpool.ac.uk/health-sciences/
adv practice in healthcare, diagnostic radiography, health & veterinary studies, nursing, occupational therapy, orthoptics, physiotherapy, radiotherapy, CPD
Medicine; www.liverpool.ac.uk/medicine
medicine, surgery, medical science, public health
Psychology; www.liverpool.ac.uk/psychology
psychology, investigative & forensic psychology, mental health psychology, organisational & business psychology, research methods
Life Sciences; www.liverpool.ac.uk/life-sciences
anatomy & human biology, biological/& medical sciences, microbiology, molecular biology & biotechnology, pharmacology, physiology, tropical disease biology, zoology, advanced biological science (numerous subjects)
Veterinary Science; www.liverpool.ac.uk/veterinary-science
veterinary science, veterinary science, veterinary reproduction studies/physiology/professional studies/business management, veterinary practice, bovine reproduction

Institute of Ageing & Chronic Disease; www.liv.ac.uk/ageing-and-chronic-diseases
anatomy & human biology, clinical sciences, musculoskeletal ageing

Institute of Infection & Global Health; www.liv.ac.uk/infection-and-global-health
infection biology, microbiology & immunology, epidemiology & population health, critical care, dental microbiology, epidemiology/ & population health, food security, gastrointestinal diseases, global health, immunology, infectious diseases, infection & global health (medical/veterinary), infection & immunity, medical microbiology, medical parasitology, neurological science, one health medical/veterinary), respiratory diseases, veterinary epidemiology/ immunology/ microbiology/ parasitology/pathology/ virology), virology

Institute of Integrative Biology; www.liv.ac.uk/integrative-biology
advanced biological sciences, biochemistry, evolution, ecology & behaviour, functional & comparative genomes

Institute of Psychology, Health & Society; www.liv.ac.uk/psychology-health-and-society
medicine and surgery, psychology, dental surgery, clinical psychology, health services research, medical education, mental health psychology, organisational and business psychology, psychiatry, psychology, primary care, public health, reading in practice

Institute of Translational Medicine; www.liv.ac.uk/translational-medicine
physiology, pharmacology, anatomy & human biology, biomedical science & translational medicine, biostatistics, cancer biology, cancer medicine, cellular and molecular physiology, child health, gastroenterology, haematology and leukaemia, medical imaging, ocular oncology, orthopaedic biology, pancreatology, pathology, pharmacology, radiotherapy, surgery and oncology, women's health

BSc(Hons), BN, BVSc, BDS, MBChB, FD, PGCert/Dip, MRes, MSc, MPhil, PhD, MD, MChOrth, MCommH, D/MClinPsychol, MDS, MPH, MRCPsych, MTCH&CP, MTropMed, MTropPaed

Faculty of Humanities & Social Sciences; www.liv.ac.uk/ humanities_and_social_sciences/hss

School of the Arts; www.liv.ac.uk/arts

Architecture; www.liv.ac.uk/lsa/index.htm
architecture, digital integrated design, sustainable architectural design, design studies

Communications & Media; www.liv.ac.uk/ communication-and-media/index.htm
communications & media, politics & mass media

English; www.liv.ac.uk/english/index.htm
applied linguistics, English, directed studies/modern & contemporary literature/Renaissance & 18th century literature, Victorian literature, reading in practice, TESOL

Music; www.liv.ac.uk/music/index.htm
music, pop music, music industry

Philosophy; www.liv.ac.uk/philosophy/index.htm
philosophy, philosophy & mathematics/law, art aesthetics & cultural institutions

Combined Honours
combined honours, science programme, two/three subject, first/second year

School of History, Language & Culture

History; www.liv.ac.uk/history/index.htm
history, 18th century worlds, 20th century history, international slavery studies, archives & records management, cultural history, medieval & Renaissance studies

Irish Studies; www.liv.ac.uk/irish/index.htm
Irish studies, understanding conflict

Politics; www.liv.ac.uk/politics/index.htm
politics, international politics & policy, politics & international business, international relations & security,

Archaeology, Classics & Egyptology; www.liv.ac.uk/ sace/index.htm
archaeology, classics/ & ancient history, classical studies, archaeology/of ancient civilisations, evolutionary anthropology, Egyptian archaeology, Egyptology, ancient history & archaeology

Modern Language & Cultures; www.liv.ac.uk/soclas/ index.htm
French, German, Basque, Catalan, Portuguese, Italian, Spanish, Latin American studies, Chinese, modern languages, film studies; BA(Hons), MA, MArch, MPhil, PhD, MAML, LAML

School of Law & Social Justice; www.liv.ac.uk/law-and-social-justice/ index.htm

Liverpool Law School; www.liv.ac.uk/law/index.htm
law, law & business & accounting/finance/business studies/criminology/philosophy/French/German/Italian/Spanish, international human rights/business law, European law, law, medicine & healthcare

Dept of Sociology, Social Policy & Criminology; www. liv.ac.uk/sociology-social-policy-and-criminology
sociology, sociology, criminology & security/psychology/politics, law with criminology, sociology & history/philosophy, social policy/criminology, research methodology (sociology & social policy), criminological research, social research

School of Management; www.liv.ac.uk/ management

University of Liverpool Management School: accounting & finance, business administration (football industries) big data management, business economics/management, economics, finance, finance & investment management, international business, marketing, finance & management, managing business enterprise projects, football industries, global leadership, law with accounting/business, operations & supply chain management, programme & project management, management entrepreneurship/ finance, management, managing international development, thoroughbred horseracing industry; BA(Hons), MA, MMus, MPhil, MBA, PhD, MRes, PGDip/Cert

Faculty of Science & Engineering; www.liv.ac.uk/science_and_engineering

School of Engineering; www.liv.ac.uk/ engineering

adv/aerospace engineering/pilot studies, adv engineering management, adv anufacturing systems & technology, biomedical engineering, civil engineering, civil & structural/environmental engineering, adv/mechanical engineering/with business, industrial design, mechanical engineering, mechanical & materials engineering, nuclear power engineering, product design & management, simulation in aerospace engineering, sustainable structural engineering

Electrical Engineering & Electronics; www.liv.ac.uk/eee

avionic systems, computer science & electronic engineering, electrical & electronic engineering, engineering, foundation engineering, mechatronics & robotic systems, microelectronic systems & telecommunications, energy & power systems, telecommunications & wireless systems

Dept of Computer Science; www.csc.liv.ac.uk systems/engineering

computer science, electronic commerce computing, computer information systems, internet computing, software development, artificial intelligence, e-finance, mathematics and computer science, computer science and electronic engineering, combined honours, advanced computer science/with internet economics, big data and high performance computing

School of Environmental Sciences; www.liv.ac.uk/environmental-sciences

earth sciences, geology (North America), geology and geophysics, geology and physical geography, geology, geophysics (geology/physics), geology & geophysics, ocean sciences, geography and oceanography, marine biology with oceanography, sea level: from coast to global ocean, ecology and environment, marine biology, marine biology with oceanography, conservation & resource management, marine planning & management environment, geography, geology & physical geography, oceans, climate and physical geography, contemporary human geography (research methods), environment and climate change, environmental science, geographic data science, population and health, geography and planning, environment and planning, urban regeneration and planning, town and regional planning, environmental assessment and management, marine planning and management, town and regional planning, urban regeneration and management, urban design and property development, environmental sciences, conservation and resource management

School of Physical Sciences

Chemistry; www.liv.ac.uk/chemistry/index.htm

chemistry, medicinal chemistry with pharmacology, adv chemical science (organic with catalysis/chemical synthesis/biomolecular chemistry/nanoscale with materials interfacial chemistry), chemistry with nanotechnology

Mathematical Sciences; www.liv.ac.uk/mathematical-sciences/

mathematics, actuarial mathematics, pure/applied mathematics, mathematical sciences, financial mathematics, mathematical/theoretical physics, statistics & probability, mathematics with economics/computer science/education/physics/European languages/ statistics

Physics; www.liv.ac.uk/physics

physics, astronomy, astrophysics, mathematical/theoretical physics, nuclear science/& technology, physics with medical applications/astronomy/nuclear science, physics for new technology, medical physics & clinical engineering, radiometrics: instrumentation & modelling; BSc(Hons), MChem, BEng, MEng, DEng, MPhil, MMath, MPhys, MESci, MRes, MSc, PhD, MSc(Eng), MMarBiol, MEcol

---

Degrees validated at the University of Liverpool offered by:

LIVERPOOL HOPE UNIVERSITY
www.hope.ac.uk

Faculty of Arts & Humanities; www.hope.ac.uk/artsand humanities

Business School; accounting, business management, law, marketing, business & management, HRM/D, Int MBA, marketing management

Drama, Dance & Performance Studies; creative & performance arts, dance, contemporary pop theatre, drama & theatre studies

English; English language/literature, popular literatures

Fine & Applied Art; art & design history, design, fine art, art history & curating, creative practice, museum & heritage studies

History & Politics; history, international relations/& politics, peace studies

Law; law

Media & Communications; media & communications, creative writing, creative practice, film & media

Music; music, creative practice, pop music & music

Social Work, Care & Justice; children & youth, social policy/work, health & wellbeing, youth & community

Social Science; criminology, sociology

Theology, Philosophy & Religion; biblical studies, Christian theology, philosophy & ethics/religion, theology, world religions, biblical & pastoral theology, Jewish studies, theology & religious education BA(Hons), BSc(Hons), MA, PGCert, BMin, MMin, FdA, MSc, BDes, LlB

Faculty of Education; www.hope.ac.uk/education

education studies, development psychology & disability studies/early childhood studies, early childhood studies, special educational needs & disability studies, school direct, PGCE/primary secondary education/disability studies (with QTS), teacher education, childhood & youth studies, education (children & young people, disability studies, early childhood, leadership & management, music education, RE, SEN, subject specialisms, teaching & learning), education & computer science/English language/English literature/geography/mathematics/music; BA(Hons), MA, EdD, PGCE

Faculty of Science; www.hope.ac.uk/science

Mathematics & Computer Science: computing, computer science, information technology, mathematical informatics, mathematics, electronic engineering

Geography & Environmental Science: environmental science/management, tourism, geography

Health Sciences: biology, applied exercise physiology, biological sciences, skills acquisition and human movement, human biology, exercise and ageing, nutrition, sports nutrition, sport and exercise science, international sports management, sport and physical education, bioinformatics and systems biology, sport psychology

Psychology: psychology, sports psychology, cognitive neuroscience & neuroimaging

Social Work, Care & Justice: social work, criminology, criminal justice, social policy; BA(Hons), BSc(Hons), MA, MBA, MPhil, MSc, PhD

LIVERPOOL JOHN MOORES UNIVERSITY
www.ljmu.ac.uk

Faculty of Arts, Professional & Social Studies: www.ljmu.ac.uk/APS

Liverpool Business School; www.ljmu.ac.uk/lbs

accounting & finance, business administration (MBA) studies/management, business & PR, digital/financial/marketing, finance, entrepreneurship, HRM, management, marketing, resource management

School of Law; www.ljmu.ac.uk/LAW

law, law & criminal justice, European law, forensic psychology, global crime, justice & security, international business, corporate & finance law, legal practice; BA(Hons), BSc(Hons), DBA, MBA, LlB, LlM, MA, MBA, MPhil, MRes, MSc, PGDip/Cert, PhD

Liverpool School of Art & Design; www.ljmu.ac.uk/LSA

architecture, art & design, fashion/innovation & realisation, graphic design & illustration, fine art, history of art, exhibition studies, urban design

Liverpool Screen School; www.ljmu.ac.uk/LSS

creative writing, English, drama, media production, international news journalism, journalism, writing, screenwriting, film studies

School of Humanities & Social Science; www.ljmu.ac.uk/HSS

critical social science, criminology & psychology/sociology, English, media & cultural studies, modern/history, mass communications, media/& cultural studies, communication, literature & cultural history, policing studies, cities, culture & creativity, sociology; BA, BA(Hons), BDes, DipArch, DipHE, MA, MPhil, MRes, PG, PGCE, PhD

Faculty of Education, Community and Leisure: www.ljmu.ac.uk/ECL

Centre for Public Health

public health, international public health, public health (addictions), public health: policy and practice, epidemiology, public health intelligence, research methods, health improvement, health protection, violence, alcohol and tobacco control, work based learning, understanding addictions, addictions: interventions and policies, epidemiology, public health intelligence, research methods, health Improvement, health protection, violence, alcohol and tobacco control, work based learning, understanding addictions, addictions: interventions and policies

School of Education, Leisure & Allied Health

early childhood studies, education studies and early years/special inclusive needs/mathematics, education and European studies, dance practices, events management, tourism and leisure management, food and nutrition, food design and technology, inclusive sports development, outdoor education, PE, primary education studies, sport and nutrition for health, sport business/ coaching/ development, international approaches to early childhood and Montessori education, education and society, international events management, international tourism management, sport coaching, learning, development and support

School of Teacher Education & Professional Learning

education (PGDE) with qualified teacher status: PGDE in primary education with QTS, primary foundation stage/key stage 1 (3–7 years), primary with mathematics/specialism (5–11 years), religious education, advanced educational practice (dyslexia/ leadership and management/teaching and learning science/special educational needs coordination), school direct – initial teacher training

School of Nursing & Allied Healthcare

nursing with registered nurse status (adult/child/ mental health, midwifery with registered midwife status, health and social care for individuals, families and communities, health and social care development, special community practitioner children's nursing/district nursing/health visiting/school nursing) paramedic practice, advanced healthcare practice, counselling and psychotherapeutic practice, social work, improving access to psychological therapies in primary care, continuous professional development; BA(Hons), BSc(Hons), EdD, FD, MA, MPhil, MRes, PGCert, PGDip, PhD

Faculty of Science; www.ljmu.ac.uk/ faculties/scs

School of Sport & Exercise Science; www.ljmu.ac.uk/sps

sport & exercise science/physiology, clinical biomechanics/exercise psychology, science & football, app/ sports psychology, clinical exercise physiology, sport nutrition

School of Pharmacy & Biomolecular Sciences; www.ljmu.ac.uk/PBS

biomedical sciences, biochemistry, industrial biotechnology, forensic science, applied chemical & pharmaceutical science, clinical/pharmacy, drug discovery & development, virology, pharmaceutical manufacture & quality control

School of Natural Sciences & Psychology; www.ljmu.ac.uk/NSP

animal behaviour, applied psychology, bioarchaeology, criminology & psychology, forensic psychology & criminal justice, forensic anthropology, human/ forensic/applied psychology, health psychology, geography, zoology, biology, wildlife conservation & UAV technology, forensic psychology & criminal justice, natural sciences, primate behaviour & conservation; BSc(Hons), MPhil, MPhys, MRes, MSc, PGCE, PhD

Astrophysics Research Institute www.ljmu.ac.uk/astro

physics, astronomy, observational/ astrophysics; BSc(Hons), PhD

Faculty of Technology & the Environment; www.ljmu.ac.uk/faculties/ TAE

School of Computing & Mathematical Sciences; www.ljmu.ac.uk/cmp

adv/computer studies/forensics, multimedia computing, computer games technology, computer network security, software engineering, wireless & mobile computing, cyber security, mathematics

School of Engineering & Technology & Maritime Operations; www.ljmu.ac.uk/ ENG

audio and music production, control and automation engineering, electrical and electronic engineering, electrical power engineering, electronic engineering, electronics and software engineering, extended engineering and technology, management, transport and logistics, marine operations, maritime business and management, maritime studies, mechanical and manufacturing engineering/marine engineering, mechanical engineering/ with management, nautical science, product design engineering

Postgraduate Courses; electrical power and control engineering, international transport, trade and logistics, manufacturing engineering, marine and offshore engineering, maritime management, maritime operations management, mechanical engineering, microelectronic systems design, port management, telecommunications engineering

School of the Built Environment; www.ljmu.ac.uk/BLT

architectural technology, building services engineering/ project management, building surveying, civil and environmental engineering, civil engineering, civil engineering and architecture/construction management, construction management, quantity surveying, real estate management/ and business
Postgrad; applied facilities management, architectural engineering, civil engineering, commercial building surveying, commercial property management, construction project management, project management, quantity surveying and commercial

management, smart technologies for infrastructure and buildings, water, energy and the environment; BA(Hons), BSc(Hons), FdSc, MPhil, MSc, PGCert, PGCE, PGDip, PhD

Faculty of Health & Applied Social Services; www.ljmu.ac.uk/HEA

adv healthcare practice, child nursing, environmental health, health and social care/for families, individuals & communities/practice, health sciences, midwifery, nursing (adult/child/mental health/paramedic practice), neonatal/diabetes care, public health, social work, specialist community practitioner (district nursing/public health nursing, school visiting/health visiting), counselling, psychotherapy, adv paediatric nursing; BA(Hons), BSc, DNurs, DMidw, DPH, DipHE, FD, FdA MPhil, MRes, MSc, PGDip/Cert

UNIVERSITY OF THE ARTS LONDON
www.arts.ac.uk

Camberwell College of Art & Design; www.camberwell.arts.ac.uk

3D design, art & design, conservation, drawing, graphic design, visual arts (bookmaker arts/design maker/illustration/fine arts digital/printmaking), illustration, painting, photography, sculpture; BA(Hons), Dip, FdA, MA, MPhil, PGDip, PhD, MFA

Central Saint Martins College of Art & Design; www.csm.arts.ac.uk

acting, applied imagination in creative industries, architecture: spaces and objects/cities & innovation, art: exhibition studies, art theory & philosophy, art & design/science, art, exhibition studies/moving image/ theory & philosophy, ceramic design, character animation, culture, communication design, criticism & curation, art & design (ceramics/furniture/jewellery), directing, dramatic writing, fashion design/ knitwear/marketing/menswear/womenswear/fashion production/journalism/promotion/communication/ print, fashion & theory, fashion, communication: fashion history & theory/communication & promotion, fashion journalism, fine art, graphic design, industrial design, innovation management, jewellery design, journalism design, screen acting/directing/ writing, material futures, narrative environments, performance design & practice, photography,

product design, textile design; BA(Hons), FdA, FD, GradDip, MA, MPhil, PGCert/Dip, PhD

Chelsea College of Art & Design; www.chelsea.arts.ac.uk

art & design, curating & collections, fine art, graphic design communication, interior & spatial design, textile design; BA(Hons), FdA, Foundation Dip, GradDip, MA, MPhil, PGCert/Dip, PhD, MRes

London College of Communication; www.lcc.arts.ac.uk

advertising, animation, applied branding & identity, arts & lifestyle journalism, book arts, design for art direction, design management & cultures, design for visual communication, graphic communication for interactive & moving image, contemporary graphic media, documentary film, film practice, film & TV, games design, graphic design, graphic brands & moving image/identity, graphic & media design, graphic branding, information & interface design, illustration & visual media, interactive design culture, international journalism (online) journalism (print/online/TV/magazine/sports), live events & TV, photojournalism & documentary, marketing, media & cultural studies, media communication/critical practice, photography, photojournalism & documentary photography, photographic portfolio development, printmaking, product design, PR, publishing, production for live events & TV, magazine publishing, screenwriting, service design innovation, sound arts/& design, spatial design, TV; BA(Hons), FdA, ABCDip, MA, MDes, MRes, MSc, PGDip

London College of Fashion;
www.fashion.arts.ac.uk

international preparation for fashion, 3D effects for performance and fashion, bespoke tailoring, Cordwainers fashion bags and accessories: product design and innovation/footwear: product design and innovation, costume for performance, creative direction for fashion, fashion:(business/buying and merchandising/contour design/design and development/design technology: menswear/womenswear/illustration/jewellery/journalism/management/marketing/media/pattern cutting/photography/PR and communication/sportswear/styling and production, textiles: embroidery/ knitwear/print fashion: retail management), retail branding and visual merchandising, marketing and promotion, hair and make-up, design and technology, design and marketing, buying and merchandising, visual merchandising and branding, beauty and spa management, hair and make-up for film and TV/ fashion: styling and photography

Postgraduate; international fashion production management, cosmetic science, international fashion management, executive MBA (fashion), fashion; management, fashion design management, fashion enterprise creation, fashion entrepreneurship and innovation, fashion retail management, strategic fashion marketing, fashion: buying and merchandising, costume design for performance, fashion cultures, fashion curation, fashion futures, psychology for fashion professionals, applied psychology in fashion, footwear, fashion design technology womenswear, pattern and garment technology, footwear: production and manufacture, fashion media styling, fashion journalism, fashion media production, fashion photography; BA(Hons), BSc(Hons), diplomas, FD, MA, PGDip/Cert, MDes

Wimbledon College of Art;
www.wimbledon.arts.ac.uk

art & design, digital theatre, drawing, fine art (painting/sculpture/print & time-based media), interactive media, painting, print & time-based media, theatre & screen (costume design/interpretation/set design for screen/ technical arts & special effects, theatre design); BA(Hons), FdA, MA

LONDON CONTEMPORARY DANCE SCHOOL
www.theplace.org.uk

advanced dance training, choreography, contemporary dance, dance training & education, improvisation, performance studies; BA, PGDip, MA

LONDON METROPOLITAN UNIVERSITY
www.londonmet.ac.uk

Faculty of Social Sciences & Humanities;
www.londonmet.ac.uk/faculties/
faculty-of-social-sciences-and-
humanities

community development and leadership, creative writing/and English literature, criminology and law/policing/ psychology/ sociology/ youth studies, dance, digital media design, digital media, diplomacy and international relations/law, early childhood studies, education and social policy, education studies/and English literature, English literature,

fashion marketing and journalism, film and TV studies, health and social care/social policy, international relations and law/politics, international relations, peace and conflict, international relations, journalism, film and TV studies – journalism and digital media, journalism, media and communications, media, communications and journalism, Montessori early childhood practice, police studies, procedure and investigation, politics, public health and health promotion/social care, public service management, social science, social sciences and humanities, sociology and social policy – social work, sociology, theatre and performance practice, youth studies, youth work

Postgraduate; child abuse, conference interpreting, counter-terrorism studies, creative writing, crime, violence and prevention, criminology, early childhood studies, education, filmmaking, health and social care, management and policy, intelligence and security studies, international human rights and social justice, international relations, international security studies, interpreting, journalism, learning and teaching in HE, public administration, media and communications, PGCE (early years, primary (5–11), school direct early years, school direct secondary citizenship/English with media/mathematics/modern languages/music/PE/science with biology/physics/biology/chemistry/physics), policing, security and community safety, public health, screenwriting, security studies, social policy and evaluation, social policy, social work, specialised translation, supporting older children and young people with dyslexia /SplDs, teaching Arabic, TESOL and applied linguistics, translation/and technology, violence against women, women and child abuse; BA(Hons), BSc(Hons), EdD, MPA, MA, MPhil, MRes, MSc, PGCert/Dip, PhD, FdA, PGCE, ProfDoc

Sir John Cass Faculty of Art, Architecture and Design; www.thecass.com

architectural history, digital architecture & manufacture, theory & interpretation, animation, architecture/ & digital design systems, interior architecture, architecture & interior design, architecture, art & design, art design media, energy & sustainability, spatial planning & urban design, art, media & design, curating the contemporary, fashion, fashion & textiles, film & animation/media & music, drawing, film & broadcast production, fine art, furniture & product design, graphic design, illustration, interior design/& decoration, jewellery & silversmithing, music technology (audio systems/music production/sound for media), musical instruments, painting, photography, product design, textile design; BA(Hons), PGCert, FdA, MA, MPhil, MSc, PhD, ProfDip

Faculty of Life Sciences & Computing; www.londonmet.ac.uk/depts/flsc

Electronics, Networking & Communications Engineering

computer networking/systems engineering, computing, electronic & computer/communications engineering, telecommunications & network engineering, computer networking & security, network management & security, telecommunication & network engineering

Applied Computing

business computing systems, business IT, computer forensics & IT security, computer networking & IT security, computing & business IT, IT, software engineering, computing technology & mathematics

Mathematics

mathematics & computer science/statistical modelling, mathematical sciences, mathematics

Computer Science & Creative Technologies

computer science, computer games programming, games modelling, animation & effects, computing, computing, technology & mathematics, software engineering; BSc(Hons), FdSc, MEng, MRes, MSc, PhD

School of Human Sciences; www.londonmet.ac.uk/depts/fls/hhs

biochemistry, bioethics, biological sciences, applied/ biology, biotechnology, appl/biomedical science, blood science, chemistry, diet, food & nutrition, dietetics & nutrition, food science, football & community sport, forensic science, health, herbal medicinal science, human nutrition (public health/sport), medical bioscience, medical genetics, molecular & pharmaceutical science, obesity & weight management, personal training and fitness consultancy, pharmaceutical science, pharmacology, sports dance therapy, sports psychology & coaching, sport science & PE, sport nutrition, sports rehabilitation & therapy, sports science & therapy

School of Psychology; www.londonmet.ac.uk/depts/flsdops

applied/psychology, addiction & mental health, child & family mental health, psychology & sociology, psychology of counselling/health/psychology, business/consumer/criminal/forensic, occupational/organisational psychology; BSc(Hons), DipHE, FdSc, GradDip/Cert, MOst, MOstMed, MSc, Prof Doc, PGDip/Cert

Faculty of Business & Law; www.londonmet.ac.uk/faculties/ faculty-of-business-and-law

accounting & finance, airline, airport & aviation management, advertising, marketing communications & PR, banking & finance/compliance, brand management, business management & marketing/ law/administration, business, innovation & creative enterprise, business economics, economics/& finance, events management, fashion marketing & business management, fashion retail management, finance, finance (accounting), international financial strategy, intelligence & security studies, international banking, financial & company law, international business, international family & child law, financial service law, regulation & compliance, HRM, marketing management, international business management, international common law/family law, international law, international trade, transport & maritime law, international marketing communications, legal practice, law/with international relations, management & strategic leadership, maritime law, marketing & communications, music industry management/& enterprise, music business & live entertainment, sports/business/management, tourism & travel management, transport & logistics management, executive & professional courses; DPS, FdSc, GradConv, MA, MBA, DBA, MSc, PGDip, ProfDoc, LlB, LlM, PGDip

THE LONDON SCHOOL OF OSTEOPATHY
www.lso.ac.uk

osteopathy; MOst

LONDON SOUTH BANK UNIVERSITY
www.lsbu.ac.uk

Faculty of Arts and Human Sciences; www.lsbu.ac.uk/#ahs

Arts, Media; www.lsbu.ac.uk/ahs/ departments/artsmedia
critical arts management, creative media industries (journalism/cultural management), digital film & video/photography/new media, film & media/photography, film/cultural & media studies, society & digital media; BA(Hons), MA, MPhil, PhD

Culture, Writing & Performance; www.lsbu.ac.uk/ahs/departments/cwp
arts & festivals management, critical/arts management, English/with creative writing, film & English studies, film practice/studies, cultural management, game cultures, independent film practice, film/& media studies, media writing, multimedia journalism, English/writing, new media, theatre practice; BA(Hons), MA, PhD, MPhil

Education; www.lsbu.ac.uk/departments/ education
PCGE: early years, graduate teacher training/PGCE with QTS (primary/secondary maths/school direct), careers education/development/guidance with OCG, education/studies, education-autism, learning and teaching, in HE, education for sustainability, postcompulsory education, practice education community practice teacher, sustainability equality & diversity; BA(Hons), Cert, FdA, MA, MPhil, PhD, PGDip/Cert, EdDoc, PGCHE

Law; www.lsbu.ac.uk/departments/law
law, business/criminal/medical/family law, common law, crime & litigation, entertainment & media law, human rights, international human rights and development/criminal law, law, legal studies, criminality social research methods, law with criminology/ psychology/sociology, civil litigation & dispute resolution; GradDip, LlB(Hons), LLM, CPE

Psychology; www.lsbu.ac.uk/departments/ psychology
addiction psychology & counselling, investigative forensic science, psychology, criminology, clinical psychology, child development, forensic sports psychology, mental health clinical psychology, advanced cognitive psychotherapy, practice; BSc(Hons), GradDip, MSc, PhD

Social Sciences; www.lsbu.ac.uk/ahs/ departments/socialsciences
criminology with law/psychology, development studies, education for sustainability, gender & sexuality, refugee studies, social policy, social research methods, sociology/with criminology, social science, social work; BA(Hons), BSc(Hons), MSc, PhD, PGDip/Cert

Urban, Environmental & Leisure Studies; www.lsbu.ac.uk/ahs/departments/uels

built environment studies, development & urbanism, development studies, housing studies, international tourism & hospitality/travel management, planning policy and practice, town planning, sustainable communities, urban and environmental planning/ regeneration and community development, urban planning design/regeneration, tourism, leisure & hospitality management; BA(Hons), FdA, HNC, MA, MSc, PGCert/Dip, MPhil, PhD

Faculty of Business; www.bus.lsbu.ac.uk

accounting/& entrepreneurship, finance, business administration/management/project management/ studies/enterprise/intelligence, finance, corporate governance, digital business, economics, international finance/banking/investment/business with finance/accounting, management in civil society, financial management, business information technology/intelligence, high performance/human centred computing, international investment & finance/banking/accounting/intelligent systems/management, IT management for business, internet & database systems, multimedia computing, small business development, strategic information IT, digital marketing, public administration, HRM/D, HR practice, international business, international health services & hospital management, international human resources/HRM/management/marketing, management & marketing, marketing/communications management, Chinese business practice, charity finance/& accounting, public administration & management, fundraising & marketing; MA, D/MBA, PGDip/Cert, MSc, BTEC, HND, DMS, CM, BSc(Hons), BA(Hons), MPA, CM

Faculty of Engineering, Science & Built Environment, www.lsbu.ac.uk/esbe

Dept of Applied Sciences; www.lsbu.ac.uk/ esbe/departments/appsci

applied biology, applied science, baking technology, chemical & process engineering, biochemistry, culinary art, engineering, food & nutrition, food safety & control, food science, forensic science/with criminology, human biology, human nutrition, microbiology, petroleum engineering, sport & exercise science, sport coaching & analysis; BA(Hons), BEng(Hons), BSc(Hons), FdSc, MSc/PgCert/PgDip

Dept of Engineering & Design; www.lsbu.ac.uk/esbe/departments/engdes

biomedical engineering & instrumentation, civil engineering, computer-aided design/engineering, computer systems & networks, computer systems management, design & manufacturing management, electrical & electronic engineering, engineering product design, enterprise, mechanical engineering/ design, mechatronics/engineering/embedded & distributed systems, power distribution, product design, sports product design, telecommunications & computer networks engineering, quality engineering management, structural engineering, systems for environmental services, sound design, transport engineering & policy; BEng(Hons), BSc(Hons), FdEng, MRes, MSc, PGDip

Dept of the Built Environment; www1.lsbu.ac.uk/esbe/departments/ builtenv

architecture, architectural technology/engineering, built environment, commercial management (quantity surveying), construction/management/project management, construction economics, housing studies, planning buildings for health, property development & planning management, property management (building surveying), surveying (building or quantity building surveying, real estate, urban & environmental design; BA(Hons), FdSc, HNC, PGDip/Cert, MSc

Dept of Urban Engineering; www1.lsbu.ac.uk/esbe/departments/ urbeng

architectural engineering, building services engineering, civil engineering, environmental & architectural acoustics, structural engineering, transport engineering & planning, sustainable energy systems, urban planning design/regeneration, town planning, planning, policy & practice; BEng(Hons), BSc(Hons), FdEng, HNC, HND, MSc, PGDip/Cert

Faculty of Health & Social Care: www.lsbu.ac.uk/faculties/hsc

health & social care (hospital care/maternity support/ mental health care/primary care/rehabilitation therapy), health visiting (specialist community practice nursing), nursing (advanced practice/children's/learning disabilities/mental health/neonatal practice/occupational health), midwifery, professional nursing practice (adult), children's adv nursing practice, radiography (diagnostic/therapeutic/reporting), clinical technology, diagnostic imaging, operating dept practice, occupational therapy, perioperative practice, social work, primary & social care, neuromusculoskeletal management, non medical prescribing, breast imaging, ultrasound, child health studies, acute & psychiatric intensive care, forensic/mental health practice, health visiting, international health services & hospital management, mental health/& primary care, occupational health nursing, public health & health promotion, schools nursing, continuous professional development, therapeutic radiography, traditional Chinese medicine (acupuncture), workplace health management; FdSc, BSc, BSc(Hons), DipHE(-Hons), MSc, PGDip/Cert, PhD, University AdvDip, ProfDoc, MCMAc

UNIVERSITY OF EAST LONDON
www.uel.ac.uk

School of Arts and Digital Industries;
www.uel.ac.uk/ad

acting, advertising, animation, computer games design/development, creative & professional writing, cultural studies, dance, digital media design, drama, applied theatre & performance, English literature, film-making, fine art, graphic design, fashion, film, heritage studies, history, international fashion management, illustration, sports/journalism, magazines, media & communication, music technology/performance & production, photography, print design, theatre directing, writing imaginative practice; BA(Hons), BSc/BA, FdA, GradCert, MA, MPhil, MSc, PGC, PhD, ProfDoc

School of Combined Honours;
www.uel.ac.uk/combined

range of subjects for which combined honours courses are conducted

School of Architecture, Computing and Engineering; www.uel.ac.uk/ace

architecture, architectural design technology, interior design, product design, architecture: computing and design/design/interpretation and theories/sustainability and design/urban design, landscape architecture
civil engineering, civil engineering and surveying/construction management, engineering, business information systems, civil engineering, structural engineering, surveying & mapping science
computing for business, computing, computer science; postgraduate; business information technology, data science, information security/and computer forensics, software engineering, electrical & electronic engineering, product design, construction management, mechanical engineering; BA/BEng(Hons), BA/BSc, BSc(Hons), MPhil, MSc, PhD, ProfDoc

Royal Docks Business School;
www.uel.ac.uk/business

School of Business & Law

accounting & finance, business management (finance/HR/marketing) investment/risk management, economics, entrepreneurship, event management, finance & risk, hospitality & international tourist management, HRM, international business/& leadership/HR/marketing management, international accounting/banking & finance, international tourism management, Islamic finance, luxury brand management, music industry management, marketing, sports management; BA(Hons), DBA, HND, LlB, MA, MBA, MPhil, MSc, PGDip, PhD

Cass School of Education & Communities;
www.uel.ac.uk/education

early years, early childhood education and care, early childhood with health promotion/psychology/special education, early childhood studies, early years ITT, education with psychology, education studies, special education/& additional learning needs, autism spectrum & education, social work, child care and education, creative leadership in education, education, English language teaching, post-qualifying professional practice, social work, special educational needs/coordination, teaching in HE, youth and community work, secondary teacher training, school direct, subject knowledge enhancement, post compulsory teacher training, teacher training, primary (core), primary with early years (3–7)/, English/English as an additional language, English/humanities and RE/ICT and computing/ early years (3–7)/modern languages/music, PGCE secondary education (numerous subjects), PGCE (primary education), mathematics with education & QTS, Madrassah teaching/teacher, early years/primary teacher training, post compulsory teacher training, youth & community work, social work/with adults/children

& families, post qualifying professional practising/ teacher, mentoring & supporting behaviour, CPD; BA(Hons), EdD, FdA, MA, PGCE, PGDip, ProfDoc, UnivCert

School of Health, Sport and Bioscience; www.uel.ac.uk/hsb

biotechnology, contemporary nursing practice, health promotion/and health services management, health science, human biology, medical physiology, podiatry, public health/and health promotion/ health services management, adv practice for health professions, applied/health science, biochemistry, bioinformatics/promotion, bioscience, biomedical science, biotechnology/management, health informatics, health service management, toxicology, pharmacology, phyto/pharmaceutical science, sport and exercise science, sport, PE and development, sports coaching, sports therapy, physiotherapy, podiatric medicine, sports science/psychology, strength & conditioning, toxicology; BA(Hons), BSc(Hons), FdSc, MPhil, MSc, PGCert, PhD, ProfDoc, MRes

School of Law & Social Science; www.uel.ac.uk/lss

anthropology, anthropology with North American studies/psychosocial studies/sociology, anthropology & human rights & justice; criminology & criminal justice/psychology/psychosocial studies/sociology; art/systemic psychotherapy, child & adolescent primary mental health care & work, child protection & complex child care, child, adolescent & family mental well-being, conflict, displacement & human security, human rights, consultation & the organisation: psychoanalytical approaches, counselling in educational settings, consultation & the organisation (psychoanalytical approaches), emotional features in learning & teaching, infant mental health, international development, international development & anthropology/NGO management/international politics/public health/health, international politics, Islamic & Middle Eastern studies; law, law general, law with anthropology/criminology/international

politics/sociology, international business law, international law with criminal justice/financial markets/ international relations/world economy, international relations; narrative research, NGO & development management, psychodynamic approach to working with adolescents/people with learning disabilities/ personality disorders, psychosocial studies/with professional practice/art/criminology, psychoanalytic/ observation studies, psychoanalytic psychotherapy with children, parents & young people, systemic psychotherapy, psychosocial approaches to working with adolescents/with people with learning disabilities, psychosocial perspectives on working with people with personality disorders, refugee studies/ with community development, therapeutic communication with children, sociology/(professional development), sociology with anthropology/criminology/ international politics, sociology with law, systematic psychotherapy, terrorism studies, transport, sustainability & society, working with groups, working with people with eating disorders; BA(Hons), BSc(Hons), LlB, LlM, MSc, PostGDip, DChPsych, MSystPsych, MPsych, DConsOrg, ClinPsyD, ProfDoc, DEdChPsy

School of Psychology; www.uel.ac.uk/ psychology

child psychology, clinical and community psychology, forensic psychology, psychology, psychology with psychopharmacology, psychology with sociology, psychology, applied positive psychology and coaching psychology, business psychology, clinical and community psychology, criminal and investigative psychology, international humanitarian psychosocial consultation, occupational and organisational psychology, clinical psychology, counselling/ psychology, counselling and psychotherapy, counselling psychology, integrative counselling and coaching, career coaching, applied positive psychology and coaching psychology, integrative counselling and coaching; BA(Hons), BSc(Hons), ClinPSyD, FdA, GradDip/Cert, MA, MSc, ProfDoc, DAppEdChPsych, MPsych, UnivCert

UNIVERSITY OF WEST LONDON
www.uwl.ac.uk

London College of Music; www.uwl.ac.uk/ academic-schools/music

dance, music, performance/management, music technology with music performance, music performance/

& recording, music with foundation, musical theatre, performance/& music management/technology, record production, applied sound engineering

Masters level study: adv music technology, composition (concert music/electronic music/ film and television), musical theatre, music industry management and artist development, popular music performance; BA(Hons), BMus(Hons), BSc, DipHE, FdA, FdMus, MA, MMus, PGCert, PGDip

Ealing School of Art, Design, & Media; www.uwl.ac.uk/academic-schools/art_design_media

advertising, fashion & textiles, film production, graphic design (visual communication & illustration), motion graphics, photography, broadcast journalism, broadcasting, luxury design innovation & brand management, visual effects, Postgrad; advertising, branding & communication, art direction for film and TV, film production, luxury design, innovation & brand management, creative writing, PR; BA(Hons), FdA, MA, DipHE, MPhil

School of Psychology, Social Care & Human Sciences; www.uwl.ac.uk/academic-schools/psychology

psychology, psychology with counselling theory/substance use and misuse studies/criminology/applied forensic investigation, global health psychology, health psychology, substance use and misuse studies, social work, clinical hypnotherapy, nutritional therapy/therapeutics, forensic science, psychology with applied forensic investigation; BSc(Hons), BA(Hons), CertHE, DipHE, FdSc, MA, MPhil, MSc, PGCert, PhD

School of Nursing, Midwifery & Healthcare; www.uwl.ac.uk/academic-schools/nursing-midwifery

advancing practice (midwifery/leadership), midwifery, health & social care, healthcare promotion & public health, professional practice, improvement science, workforce planning, learning disability/adult/child/mental health nursing, midwifery/& women's health, operating department practice, psychosocial interventions for psychology, strategic workplace planning, BSc, DipHE, FdSc, MA, MM, MPhil, PGDip, PhD

The Claude Littner Business School; www.uwl.ac.uk/academic-schools/business

accounting & finance, business studies with finance/internship/HRM/marketing, credit management, computing & information systems, finance & accounting/risk management, HRM, management, managing human resources, international business management/business & commercial law/marketing, management (health & social care), management studies (health & social care); DMS, FdA, GradCert, GradDip, MA, MBA, MPhil, MSc, PGDip, PhD

Ealing Law School; www.uwl.ac.uk/academic_schools/law

law, criminology/with law/psychology, criminal policing & forensics, investment & arbitration law, international/business & commercial/banking & finance/investment law, finance law, legal practice; GradDip, LLB, LLM, PhD

London School of Hospitality & Tourism; www.uwl.ac.uk/academic-schools/hospitality-tourism

airline & airport management, events management/with tourism, food & professional cookery, hospitality/operations management, hospitality management & food studies/operations management, international culinary arts/hotel management, international tourism & aviation management, luxury hospitality management tourism, travel & tourism/management; BA, DipHE, FdA, GradCert, MA, MPhil, PGDip, PhD

School of Computing & Technology; www.uwl.ac.uk/academic-schools/computing

applied sound engineering, applied project management, computer science, computing/ & information systems, creative computing, cyber security, information management/systems, information technology for business/management, electronic/electrical engineering, engineering, mobile computing, software engineering, architectural design/technology, building surveying, sustainability & built environment, civil engineering, civil & environmental engineering, construction/project management/architectural technology, structural engineering, sustainability & the built environment; BSc, FdSc, HND, MSc, MPhil, PhD

UNIVERSITY OF LONDON; BIRKBECK
www.bbk.ac.uk

School of Arts; www.bbk.ac.uk/arts

English & Humanities: arts & humanities, screen writing, English, contemporary/medieval/ literature & culture, creative writing/producing, culture & critical studies, humanities & cultural studies, medical humanities, text & performance, theatre & drama studies, medieval literature & culture, modern & contemporary literature, Renaissance studies, Romantic studies, theatre studies & English, theatre directing/& drama studies, Shakespeare & contemporary performance, Victorian studies

European Culture & Languages: French/German/ Iberian and Latin American Studies, Japanese, modern languages, linguistics and languages, language and management and language, language and history, language and film/media, comparative literature, cultures and thought, language teaching, politics with language, Spanish, Portuguese and Latin American cultural Studies, TESOL, world cinema

History of Art: history of architecture & landscape studies, history of art, understanding visual art, world art & artefacts, arts & humanities/media management, history of art & design/philosophy, museum cultures

Film, Media & Cultural Studies: arts management, digital media management, film and media studies, journalism, media practice, screenwriting, understanding visual arts, culture and language (French/ German/ Japanese/Portuguese/Spanish), linguistics and Japanese, journalism

BA, CertHE, MA, MPhil, PhD, PGDip/Cert

School of Business, Economics and Informatics; www.bbk.ac.uk/business

Economics, Mathematics and Statistics; economics, mathematics and statistics; economics and finance, mathematical finance, mathematics and statistics, applied statistics, economics, financial economics, financial risk management, mathematics, econometrics, finance, statistics, economic and social policy/business, financial economics/with accounting, mathematics and accounting/economics/management/statistics

Management: international business, accounting & management, applied accountancy & business, business, business innovation/& e-business, corporate governance, management, HRM, international

business & marketing, creative industries, management, management for personal assistants, marketing, sports marketing, professional studies, funeral management

Computer Science & Information Systems: information technology, web design/ technology, web systems, computer science, information technology, cloud & data technology, adv computing technologies, computing for financial services, computing services, data analytics, information & web technologies, information systems & management, intelligent technologies, learning technologies

Organisational Psychology: business psychology, career management/ & coaching, HRD & consultancy, HRM, management consultancy & organisational change, occupational psychology, organisational behaviour/psychology; BSc(Econ), BSc, CertHE, MPhil, PhD, MSc, MRes

School of Law; www.bbk.ac.uk/law

law, criminology & criminal justice, constitutional & political law, law & theory, law (general), human rights, international economic law/justice & development, criminology & criminal justice, human rights law; LlB, MPhil, PhD, LlM, BSc

School of Science; www.bbk.ac.uk

Biological Sciences: biomedicine, life sciences for subjects allied to medicine, analytical bioscience, bio-business, bioinformatics with systems biology, health and disease, microbiology, principles of protein structure, protein crystallography, structural biology, structural molecular biology, techniques in structural molecular biology

Earth & Planetary Sciences: geology, earth sciences, environmental geology, planetary science with astronomy, geochemistry

Psychological Sciences: psychology, psychology for education professionals, cognition & computation, cognitive neuroscience & neuropsychology, developmental science, educational neuroscience, psychological research methods, functional neuroimaging; MRes, PGDip/Cert, BSc, MPhil, PhD, FD, CertHE

School of Social Sciences, History and Philosophy; www.bbk.ac.uk/sshp

Applied Linguistics & Communication: intercultural communication/for business & professions, education/lifelong learning, higher education, linguistics & language (Italian, German, Japanese, Portuguese, Spanish), linguistics studies, applied linguistics, intercultural, language teaching

Geography, Environmental & Development Studies: community leadership, development studies, social anthropology, social policy and the care sector, sociology, community development and public policy, development studies with environment, environmental management, environmental science, social science(s), social anthropology, children, youth and international development, climate change management, countryside and protected area management, development studies/and social anthropology, environment and sustainability, environmental management (countryside management/protected area management), GIS, social and cultural geography, community, youth and voluntary sector, international childhood studies

History, Classics & Archaeology: history, archaeology, archaeological practice, classical archaeology, classical studies, contemporary history & politics, early modern history, European history, gender, sexuality & sociology/culture, psychoanalysis, history & culture/international relations, history in Britain, history of ideas, medical history

Philosophy: philosophy, politics, philosophy, history

Politics: global politics & international relations, politics, history & philosophy, European politics & policy, global governance & emerging powers, global politics, international security & global governance, Middle East in global politics, nationalism & ethnicity, politics, population, migration & education, public politics & management, social & political theory, social research

Psychosocial Studies: psychosocial studies, social science, culture, diaspora, ethnicity, psychoanalysis, history & culture, psychoanalytical studies, education, power & social change, psychodynamics of human development; BA, BSc, MA, MRes, MPhil, PhD, MPhilSt, CertHE, FDSc

UNIVERSITY OF LONDON; COURTAULD INSTITUTE OF ART
www.courtauld.ac.uk

conservation of easel paintings, curating the art museum, history of art, Buddhist art, conservation of wall painting, curating the art museum; BA(Hons), GradDip, MA, PGDip, MPhil, PhD

UNIVERSITY OF LONDON; GOLDSMITHS
www.goldsmiths.ac.uk

Dept of Anthropology; www.gold.ac.uk/anthropology
anthropology, anthropology & media/sociology/history, cultural politics, applied anthropology & community development, Latin American studies, development & rights, history, sociology & political science, social/visual anthropology, applied anthropology & community development/community & youth work, development & rights, visual practice, politics, philosophy & economics; BA(Hons), MPhil, PhD, MRes

Dept of Art; www.gold.ac.uk/art
fine art/& history of art, art writing, creative/curating, digital arts computing; BA(Hons), MFA, MPhil, PhD

Centre for English Language & Academic Writing; www.gold.ac.uk/eap
art, English language, humanities & social science, media, communication, counselling & therapy, creative & cultural industries, design, music; GradDip, IntCert

Centre for Cultural Studies; www.gold.ac.uk/cultural-studies
cultural studies/industry, critical theory & practice, interactive media: post-colonial culture & global policy; MA, MPhil, PhD

Dept of Computing; www.gold.ac.uk/computing
computing, business computing, computer science, computational arts, computer games & entertainment/art & design, computational arts, computing & information science, creative computing, creative &

cultural entrepreneurship, data science, digital journalism/sociology/arts/music computing, games programming, journalism; BMus, BA/BSc(Hons), MFA, MPhil, MSc, PhD, MA

Dept of Design; www.gold.ac.uk/design

design, design education, PGCE design & technology, design – critical practice/ & environment/& innovation, creative & cultural entrepreneurship, design futures/& metadesign, fashion, innovation in practice; BA(Hons), BSc(Hons), BEng/MEng, MPhil, MRes, PhD, GradDip/Cert, PGCE

Dept of Educational Studies; www.gold.ac.uk/educational-studies

artist teachers & contemporary practice, children's literature, education, culture & society, education: writer/teacher, education teacher training (PGCE) – primary/secondary (standard/flexible), school direct, education: culture, language and identity, education: school-based explorations, writer/teacher, management of learning and teaching in HE, multilingualism, linguistics and education, art practice and learning; BA(Hons), DPS, MA, MPhil, PhD, PGCE

English Studies, Comparative Literature & English Language; www.gold.ac.uk/ecl

English & American literature, English & comparative literature/drama/history/creative writing/media, children's literature, English & comparative literary studies, creative and life writing, multilingualism, linguistics and education, sociocultural linguistics, writer/teacher; BA(Hons), MA, MPhil, MRes, PhD

Dept of History; www.gold.ac.uk/history

history, history & anthropology/history of ideas/politics, English & history; BA(Hons), MA, MPhil, MRes, PhD

Institute for Creative and Cultural Entrepreneurship; www.gold.ac.uk/icce

arts management, creative & cultural entrepreneurship, cultural policy/& tourism/relations & diplomacy, museum & gallery entrepreneurship, arts administration & cultural policy, fashion; MA, MPhil, PhD

Institute of Management Studies; www.gold.ac.uk/institute-management-studies

business computing, consumer behaviour, global leadership, management of innovation, management & entrepreneurship, occupational psychology, psychology with management, economics; MSc, BSc

Dept of Media and Communications; www.gold.ac.uk/media-communications

anthropology & media, media & communications/sociology/English, brands communications & culture, creative & cultural entrepreneurship, digital media/journalism, filmmaking, gender & culture, journalism, promotional media/PR, global media & transnational communications, photography: the image & the electronics arts, radio, filmmaking (screen documentary), script writing, TV journalism, political communications; BA(Hons), MA, MPhil, PhD, MRes

Dept of Music; www.gold.ac.uk/music

arts administration & cultural policy, composition, contemporary music studies, pop music, creative practice, creative & cultural entrepreneurship, ethnomusicology, historical musicology, music, music computing/performance & related studies, studio composition; BMus(Hons), BMus/BSc(Hons), MA, MMus, MPhil, PGCert, PhD, GradDip

Dept of Politics; www.gold.ac.uk/politics

economics, politics & public policy, international studies, international studies & Chinese, politics, politics & international relations, politics, philosophy & economics, history & politics, sociology & politics, art & politics, international relations; BA(Hons), DPS, MA, MPhil, MRes, PhD

Dept of Theatre & Performance; www.gold.ac.uk/theatre-performance

drama, drama and theatre arts/English, applied theatre: drama in educational community and social contexts, arts administration and cultural policy, creative and cultural entrepreneurship, musical theatre, performance making, performance & culture, writing for performance, world theatre; BA(Hons), MA, PGCE

Dept of Psychology; www.gold.ac.uk/psychology

cognitive (& clinical) neuroscience, music, mind & brain, clinical psychology/& health services, psychology, psychology with clinical psychology/cognitive neuroscience/management, science of psychology, genetics & education/social relations, forensic psychology; FD, BSc(Hons), MPhil, MSc, PhD

Dept of Sociology; www.gold.ac.uk/sociology

sociology, anthropology/media & sociology, politics, philosophy & economics, sociology/& politics/criminology/Chinese, cities & society, brands, communication & culture, critical & creative analysis, gender, media & culture, human rights, culture & social justice, photography & urban cultures, social research, visual sociology, digital sociology; BA(Hons), MA, MSc, MPhil, PhD

Dept of Visual Cultures; www.gold.ac.uk/visual-cultures
contemporary art theory, fine art/ & history of art, research architecture, contemporary art theory, research architecture, curatorial/knowledge, visual culture; BA(Hons), MA, MPhil, PGDip, PhD

UNIVERSITY OF LONDON; HEYTHROP COLLEGE
www.heythrop.ac.uk

Abrahamic religions, biblical studies, canon law, Christian spirituality/theology, Christianity & inter-religious relations, contemporary ethics, divinity, pastoral/mission/theology, philosophy/& religion, philosophy in education, philosophy of religion & ethics in religion, philosophical studies, psychology of religion, study of religions, theology; BA, Certs, BD, GradDip, MA, MRes, MPhil, PhD

UNIVERSITY OF LONDON; INSTITUTE IN PARIS
www.ulip.lon.ac.uk

French studies/with history, Paris studies – history & culture, international relations; BA, MA, MPhil, PhD, LlM

UNIVERSITY OF LONDON; INSTITUTE OF EDUCATION
www.ioe.ac.uk

Teacher Training: primary PGCE, secondary PGCE: numerous secondary subjects, post-compulsory education
UG; school direct, early years initial teacher training, school centred initial teacher training, education, working with children: education and well-being, education studies, psychology with education, social sciences/ with quantitative methods, education studies, professional practice in the lifelong learning sector, education,
PG; adult literacy, language and numeracy, advanced educational practice, applied educational leadership and management, applied linguistics, art and design in education, child development, citizenship, history or religious education (humanities), clinical education, comparative education, curriculum, pedagogy and assessment, development education and global learning, developmental and educational psychology, digital media, culture and education, early years education, education (psychology), education and international development/ technology, education, gender and international development/ health promotion and international development, educational assessment/neuroscience/planning, economics and international development, effective learning and teaching, English education, evaluation, inspection and educational improvement, geography education, higher and professional education, history of education, leadership, lifelong learning, literacy learning and literacy difficulties, special educational needs, mathematics education, museums and galleries in education, music education, philosophy of education, policy studies in education, primary education (policy and practice), professional education and training, psychology of education, quantitative research methods, reading recovery and literacy leadership, research for public policy and practice, science education, social justice and education, social pedagogy: working with children and families, social policy and social research, sociology of childhood and children's rights sociology of education, special and inclusive education, specific learning difficulties (dyslexia), speech, language and communication needs in schools: advanced practice,

teaching, teaching and learning in higher and professional education, TESOL; BEd, Certs, DedPsy, EdD, GradDip, MA, MBA, MPhil, MRes, MSc, MTg, PGCE, PhD, MTL, BA/BSc, FD, MTeach

UNIVERSITY OF LONDON; KING'S COLLEGE LONDON
www.kcl.ac.uk

The School of Arts & Humanities: www.kcl.ac.uk/humanities

ancient history, classical and modern Greek studies, classical archaeology, classical studies/ & comparative literature/French/English, classics (Greek & Latin), comparative literature/ with film studies, digital culture, English, English with film studies, European politics, film studies, French & German/ history/management/philosophy/Spanish, French, French with English/film studies, German & history/music/philosophy, German & Portuguese/management/Spanish/English, film studies, Greek with English, history, liberal arts, mathematics & philosophy, music, philosophy, philosophy & Spanish, physics & philosophy, Portuguese & Brazilian studies/French/English, religion, philosophy & ethics, religion, politics & society, Spanish & Latin American studies/Portuguese/management/English/ film studies, theology, war studies & history/philosophy Postgrad; advanced musical studies, ancient history, arts & cultural management, biblical studies, Christianity & the arts, classical art & archaeology, classical studies, classics, comparative literature, contemporary literature, culture & theory, critical methodologies, cultural & creative industries, digital asset & media management, digital culture & society. digital curation, digital humanities, early modern English literature: text & transmission, early modern history, eighteenth-century studies, English: 1850–present, European history, European public policy, European studies, film studies, French literature & culture, German & comparative literature, history, history of philosophy, international political economy, Jewish studies, language & cognition, late antique & Byzantine studies, medical humanities, medieval English/history/studies, modern history, music, nineteenth-century studies, philosophy, philosophy of medicine/psychology, religion in contemporary society, science, technology & medicine in history, Shakespeare studies, Spanish, Portuguese & Latin American studies, systematic theology, theatre & performance studies, theology & religious studies, world history & cultures

BA(Hons), MA, BMus, MMus, MRes, MSc, GradDip, MPhil, PhD

Faculty of Life Science & Medicine; www.kcl.ac.uk/lsm

This Faculty comprises the institutions listed below. Each provides education and research in their appropriate specialist area, offering degrees at undergraduate, postgraduate and research level

School of Bioscience Education, GKT School of Medical Education, Analytical & Environmental Sciences Division, Asthma, Allergy & Lung Biology, Bioscience Education, Cancer Studies, Cardiovascular, Centre for Global Health, Centre of Human & Aerospace Physiological Sciences, Cicely Saunders Institute of Palliative Care and Rehabilitation, Diabetes & Nutritional Sciences, Genetics & Molecular Medicine, Imaging Sciences & Biomedical Engineering, Immunology, Infection & Inflammatory, Life Science & Medicine, Pharmaceutical Science, Health & Social Care Research, Medical Education, Randall Division of Cell & Molecular Biophysics, Transplantation Immunology & Mucosal Biology, Women's Health, Department of Anatomy, Department of Biochemistry, Department of Genetics, Centre of Immunology, Department of Neuroscience, Department of Nutrition & Dietetics, Department of Pharmacology & Therapeutics, Department of Pharmacy & Forensic Science, Department of Physiology, Department of Physiotherapy, Institute of Psychiatry, Psychology, Physiotherapy; GradCert/Dip, MRes, MSc, PGDip, MPhil, PhD, MD

Dental Institute; www.kcl.ac.uk/dentistry

dentistry, developmental & human biology, digital culture, conscious sedation for dentistry, dental public health, endodontology, maxillofacial & craniofacial technology, orthodontics, paediatric dentistry, periodontology, prosthodontics, regenerative dentistry, special care dentistry; BDS, MClinDent, MOrth, MSc, PGDip, BA

Institute of Psychiatry; www.iop.kcl.ac.uk

psychology, neuroscience & neuropsychology/clinical applications, cognitive behavioural therapies for children & adolescents/psychosis, health psychology, mindfulness; BSc, BA, DClinPsy, GradCert, MSc, PGDip, MPhil, PhD, MD

School of Law; www.kcl.ac.uk/law

law, English & French/German/American/Hong Kong/Australian law, politics, philosophy & law, medical ethics & law, economics for competition law, EU competition/competition law, European/EU law, global ethics & human values, intellectual property & information law, international business/financial law, law with American/European/transnational legal studies, medical ethics/mental health & law, UK/US/EU copyright law; LlB, LLM, MA, MPhil, MSc, PhD

School of Medicine; www.kcl.ac.uk/schools/medicine

medicine, nutrition, adv neuromusculoskeletal physiotherapy, dietetics, physiology, cardiovascular res, immunology, translational cancer medicine, clinical pharmacology, drug development, clinical/medical/radiochemical imaging, medical engineering/physics, radiopharmaceutics, medical/vascular ultrasound, nuclear medicine, nutrition, pain, science & practice, palliative care, primary health care, public health, adv physiotherapy/paediatrics, clinical dermatology, clinical imaging, rheumatology, translational medicine, ultrasound in emergency treatment; MBBS, MPH, MSc, DDip/Cert, MD, MPhil, PhD

Florence Nightingale School of Nursing & Midwifery; www.kcl.ac.uk/nursing

midwifery studies with registration, nursing practice, nursing studies with registration (adult nursing, children's nursing, mental health nursing), nutrition & dietetics, advanced practice (district midwife with registration, nursing/leadership/midwifery/specialist community public health nursing/health visiting/school nursing, clinical nursing/research, education for healthcare professionals, health studies, neuroscience; BSc(Hons), DipHE, DHC, DPhil, MRes, MSc, PGCert/Dip

School of Natural & Mathematical Sciences; www.kcl.ac.uk/nms

Chemistry; chemistry, chemistry with bioscience, analytical science for industry, biopharmaceuticals, medical imaging sciences, pharmaceutical analysis & quality control, pharmaceutical technology, education (chemistry), radiopharmaceutics & pet radiochemistry, science education

Informatics; computer science, computer science with intelligent systems/management robotics, electronic & information engineering, electronic engineering, electronic engineering with management, mathematics & computer science, robotics & intelligent systems, adv computing, adv software engineering, computing & internet systems, computing & security, computing, IT, law & management, electronic engineering with management, engineering with management, intelligent systems, mobile & personal communications, mobile internet research, robotics, telecommunications & internet technology, telecommunications research, web intelligence

Mathematics; mathematics & philosophy/physics/computer science/management & science, financial theoretical physics, complex modelling systems, mathematics

Physics; physics & mathematics/philosophy/medical applications/theoretical physics, robotics & intelligent systems; BEng, BSc, MSc, MPhil, MSci, GradDip, PhD

School of Social Science and Public Policy; www.kcl.ac.uk/sspp

Management: business management, accounting, accountability & financial management, HRM & organizational analysis, international management/marketing, public service policy & management, risk analysis

Education & Professional Studies: English language & linguistics, education, PGCE, Latin with classics, biology, chemistry, English, IT and computer, science, computer science, mathematics, modern foreign languages, physics/ with mathematics, religious education, schools direct, applied linguistics and ELT, international/ child studies, education in arts & cultural setting, education programmes, language & cultural diversity, TESOL

Political Economy: politics of international economy, international politics/studies/conflict studies, public policy, political economy

War Studies: international relations, war studies & history, conflict, security & development, history of war, intelligence & international security, international conflict studies, international peace & security, non-proliferation & international security, science & security, South Asia & global security, terrorism, security & society, war studies, air power in the modern world, international relations & contemporary war, war in the modern world

Defence Studies: defence studies, international security & strategy, war studies, history of warfare, international conflict studies, international peace & security, terrorism, security & society, war studies & history/philosophy, South Asia & global security, conflict security & development, intelligence & international security, non-proliferation & international security

Geography: aquatic resource management, climate change: environment, science and policy/history, culture, society, disasters, adaptation and development, environment and development, environment, politics and globalisation, environmental monitoring, modelling and management, geopolitics, territory

and security, 19th-century studies, risk analysis, sustainable cities, tourism, environment and development, water: science and governance

Social Science, Health & Medicine: ageing & society, bioethics & society, gerontology, global health & social justice, health & society/promotion, medicine, science & society, ageing & public policy, research methods; BA, MA, MSc, MRes, GradDip, PGDip/Cert, FD, DThMin, DrPS, MPhil, PhD, EdD

UNIVERSITY OF LONDON; LONDON SCHOOL OF ECONOMICS & POLITICAL SCIENCE
www.lse.ac.uk

Departments at LSE:

Accounting, Anthropology, Economics, Finance, Geography & Environment, Government, International History, International Relations, Law, Management, Mathematics, Media and Communications, Philosophy, Logic and Scientific Method, Social Policy, Sociology, Statistics

UG

applied statistics and actuarial science, business mathematics and statistics, statistics with finance, actuarial science, economic history, economic history with economics, economics and economic history, economics, econometrics and mathematical economics, economics with economic history, environmental policy with economics, environment and development finance, finance, history, international relations/and history, international relations, language studies, law, mathematics & economics, philosophy, politics and economics (philosophy and economics, philosophy, logic and scientific method, social policy, social policy and economics, social policy and sociology, social policy with government, sociology, societal psychology: theory and applications

PG

accounting & finance, anthropology & development, applicable mathematics, behavioural science, China in comparative perspective, city design & social science, comparative politics, conflict studies, criminal justice policy, culture & society, development management/studies, econometrics & mathematical economics, economic history, economics, economics & management, economy, economics, risk & society, empires, colonisation & globalisation, environment & development, environmental economics & climate change, environmental policy & regulation,

European policy, European studies/ideas, ideologies & identities, finance & private equity, financial mathematics, gender, gender development & globalisation/media & culture/policy & inequalities, global health/history/politics, health, communication & development, history of international relations, human geography & international studies, human resources, & organisations, human resource management, human rights, inequalities & social science, international development & humanitarian emergencies, international health policy, international management, international management & public policy, international political economy, international relations/theory, law & accounting, law, anthropology & sociology, local economic development, management & strategy, management science, media & communication (data & society/media & communications governance), media, communication & development, organisational & social psychology, philosophy & public policy, philosophy of science/social science, political economy of Europe/late development, political science & political economy, political sociology/theory, politics & communication, population & development, public management & governance, public policy & administration, quantitative economic history, real estate economics & finance, regional & urban planning, regulation, religion in the contemporary world, risk & finance/stochastics, social anthropology, social & cultural psychology, society & public communication, social policy (European & comparative social policy, social policy & planning/development, social research methods, sociology (contemporary social thought/research), statistics, financial statistics, theory & history of international relations, urbanisation & development;

Numerous doctoral and other research qualifications are awarded

BA(Hons), BSc(Hons), Dips, EMBA, LlM, ELLM, MBA, MPA, MPhil, MRes, MSc, MA, PhD

UNIVERSITY OF LONDON; LONDON SCHOOL OF JEWISH STUDIES
www.lsjs.ac.uk

Jewish education, Jewish studies, school direct; MA

UNIVERSITY OF LONDON; QUEEN MARY
www.qmul.ac.uk

Humanities & Social Sciences

School of Business & Management; www.busman.qmul.ac.uk

Undergraduate; business management, marketing and management, accounting and management Postgrad; public administration, marketing, management, management and organisational innovation, international HRM and employment relations, international financial management, international business, international business and politics, business and management, accounting and management, accounting and finance; BSc, MSc, MPA, MRes, PhD

School of Economics & Finance; www.econ.qmul.ac.uk

accounting & finance, banking/ & finance, economics/ & finance/politics/finance & management/statistics & mathematics, economics, statistics & mathematics, finance & econometrics, finance, investment & finance, law & economics/finance, mathematical finance, wealth management; BSc, MPhil, MSc(Econ), PhD

School of English and Drama: www.sed.qmul.ac.uk

Dept of Drama
drama, drama & English/French/German/Hispanic studies/Russian/film studies, theatre & performance

Dept of English
English/& drama/film studies/history/modern language/French/German/English literature/Hispanic studies/Russian, English literature & linguistics, English literature, early modern studies, 1300–1700, 18th century literature and romanticism, Victorian literature, writing in the modern age, contemporary writing, post colonial & global writing; BA(Hons), MA, MRes, PhD

School of Languages, Linguistics & Film; www.sllf.qmul.ac.uk

honours combinations of French, German, Hispanic studies, Russian, Catalan languages, Portuguese, with English language/literature, business management, film studies, linguistics, politics, history, drama, Anglo-German cultural relations, comparative literature with language/film/linguistics, applied linguistics for English literature, documentary practice, linguistics, language teaching, Anglo-German relations; BA(Hons), MA, PhD

Dept of Geography; www.geog.qmul.ac.uk

geography, cities & cultures, community organizing, environmental geography/science/with business management, human geography, environmental science: integrated management of freshwater environment, global development futures, London studies; BA(Hons), BSc(Econ), BSc(Hons), MA, MSc, PhD

Dept of History; www.history.qmul.ac.uk

modern & contemporary/medieval/history, history & politics/film studies/English/German/French/comparative literature, European Jewish history, global imperial history, medieval & Renaissance/American/ cultural history, Middle Eastern studies, global & imperial history, history of political thought & intellectual history; BA(Hons), MA, PhD

School of Law; www.law.qmul.ac.uk

law, English & European law, law & ; politics, banking and finance law, commercial and corporate law, comparative and international dispute resolution, competition law, computer and communications law, criminal justice, energy and natural resources law, environmental law, European law, human rights law, immigration law, insurance law, intellectual property law, international business law, international dispute resolution (arbitration/mediation), international economic law, international finance law, international shipping law, law and economics/finance, law by research, laws, legal theory, management of intellectual property, media law, medical law, public international law, trade marks law and practice; Dips, LlB, LlM, MPhil, MSc, PGDip/Cert, PhD

Dept of Philosophy; www.philosophy.qmul.ac.uk

philosophy; MPhil, PhD

School of Politics & International Relations; www.politics.qmul.ac.uk

international relations, British politics, theory & practice, international/public policy, European public policy, politics/& economics/law/history/business management/French/German/Russian/Hispanic studies, international business & politics, numerous postgrad modules available; BA(Hons), MA, MPhil, MRes, PhD

School of Medicine & Dentistry; www.smd.qmul.ac.uk

Barts and The London School of Medicine and Dentistry; www.smd-edu.qmul.ac.uk/medicine

medicine, surgery, dentistry, aesthetic medicine, biomedical science (medical microbiology), burn care, clinical dermatology, clinical drug development, clinical microbiology, critical care, diabetes, endocrinology and diabetes, forensic medical sciences, gastroenterology, global health, law and governance, global public health and policy, healthcare research methods, health systems and global policy, inflammation: cellular and vascular aspects, international primary health care, mental health and law, mental health: psychological therapies/transcultural mental healthcare, migration, culture & global health, molecular pathology and genomics, neuroscience and translational medicine, pharmaceutical & innovative therapies, reconstructive microsurgery, regenerative medicine: science and application, sport and exercise medicine, surgical skills and sciences, trauma sciences/(military and austere), dental clinical sciences, dental materials, dental public health, dental technology, endodontic practice, experimental oral pathology (oral sciences), oral biology, oral medicine, orthodontics, paediatric dentistry, periodontology, prosthodontics

Research Institutions

Barts Cancer Institute
Bizard Institute of Cell and Molecular Science
Institute of Dentistry
Institute of Health Science and Education
William Harvey Research Institute
Wolfson Institute of Preventative Medicine
BDS, BMedSci, FD, MBBS, BDental Science, MBBS, MClinDent, MD, MRes, MPhil, BSc, MSc, NVQ, PGDip, PhD, MPrth, PG Cert/Dip, MRes

Department of Science & Engineering

School of Biological and Chemical Sciences; www.sbcs.qmul.ac.uk

aquatic biology, biochemistry, bioinformatics, biology, biomedical sciences, chemistry, chemical research, ecology & evolutionary genomics, ecological & environmental biology, freshwater & marine ecology, immunology, medical/genetics, neuroscience, pharmaceutical chemistry, pharmacological & innovative therapies, plant & fungal taxonomy; diversity & conservation, psychology, zoology; BSc(Hons), FD, MPhil, MSci, PhD

School of Electronic Engineering & Computer Science; www.eecs.qmul.ac.uk

computer systems engineering, electrical and electronic engineering, electronic engineering, information and communications technologies, information technology management for business, multimedia and arts technology, computer science, computer science and mathematics/multimedia/business management/and accounting, computer systems engineering, electronic engineering & telecommunications, electronics with music and audio systems, big data science, computer vision, computing and information systems, digital signal processing, electronic engineering by research, media and arts technology by research, software engineering, sound and music computing, telecommunications & wireless systems/management, software engineering; BEng, BSc(Eng), MEng, MSc, PhD, MSci

School of Engineering and Materials Science; www.sems.qmul.ac.uk

aerospace engineering, biomedical engineering & clinical materials, computer-aided engineering, design, innovation & creative engineering, materials & design, materials science & engineering, dental materials, biomaterials, adv/mechanical engineering, materials research, medical materials/electronics & physics/science, polymer science & nanotechnology, sustainable energy systems/engineering/materials; BEng, BSc, MEng, MPhil, MRes, PhD

School of Mathematical Sciences; www.maths.qmul.ac.uk

mathematics, actuarial science, computer science & mathematics, economics, statistics & mathematics, pure mathematics, statistics, financial economics, finance & accounting, mathematical finance, maths with business management, networks science, mathematical/financial computing; BSc(Hons), MPhil, MSc, MSci, PGDip/Cert, PhD

School of Physics & Astronomy; www.ph.qmul.ac.uk

astrophysics, astronomy, physics, theoretical physics, particle physics; BSc(Hons), MSc, MSci, PGDip, PhD

UNIVERSITY OF LONDON; ROYAL HOLLOWAY
www.rhul.ac.uk

Faculty of Arts; www.rhul.ac.uk/ departments/arts

Dept for Classics; www.rhul.ac.uk/classics

ancient history/with philosophy, classical studies, classics, classical studies & drama/Italian, English & classical studies/Latin, French & classical studies/ Greek/Latin, Greek, German & classical studies/ Greek, ancient & medieval history, classical art & archaeology, classical studies & comparative literature & culture/philosophy/French, classics, reception, rhetoric, history, Helenic studies; BA(Hons), MA, MRes, MPhil, PhD

Dept of Drama & Theatre; www.rhul.ac.uk/ drama

applied & participative theatre, drama/ & creative-writing/philosophy/music/dance/English/classics/ theatre studies/modern language, contemporary performance practices, playwriting; BA(Hons), MPhil, PhD

Dept of English; www.rhul.ac.uk/english

English, English & philosophy/classics/modern languages/film studies/drama/creative writing/history/ Latin/music, creative writing, English literature, modern & contemporary literature, medieval studies, poetic practice, Shakespeare, Victorian literature, art, culture, comparative literature; BA, MA, PhD

Dept of Media Arts; www.rhul.ac.uk/ media-arts

documentary by practice, international broadcasting, production, film studies, screenwriting/producing for TV & film, film, TV & digital processes, international TV industries; BA(Hons), MA, MPhil, PhD

Dept of Modern Languages, Literature & Culture; www.rhul.ac.uk/mllc

French, German, Italian, Spanish, Hispanic studies, contemporary literature & culture, film, visual arts, visual cultures & international film, liberal arts, linguistics, multilingual studies; BA, BSc, MA, MA by Research, PhD

Dept of Music; www.rhul.ac.uk/Music

music, composition, music & drama/economics/modern foreign language/history/mathematics/philosophy/political studies/physics, advanced musical studies; BA(Hons), BMus, MMus, MPhil, PhD

Faculty of History & Social Sciences; www.rhul.ac.uk/departments/hss

Dept of Law, Criminology & Sociology; www.rhul.ac.uk/criminologyandsociology

law, criminology & sociology/psychology, consumption, culture & marketing, forensic psychology; BSc, MA, PhD

Dept of Economics; www.rhul.ac.uk/ economics

economics, economics & management/mathematics, economics, policy & international relations, accounting, finance & economics, financial & business economics, policy economics, finance, computational finance, economics with French/German/Spanish/ Italian/music/political studies; BSc, MSc, PhD

Dept of European Studies; www.rhul.ac.uk/ EuropeanStudies

European studies (French/Spanish/Italian/German), European research, social science; BA

Dept of Social Work; www.rhul.ac.uk/ socialwork

social work, work with children & families; BA(Hons), MA, MSc

Dept of History; www.rhul.ac.uk/history

history, public history, late antique & Byzantine studies, crusader studies, ancient & medieval history,

Holocaust studies, medieval studies, modern history & politics, history & international relations/music/ English/philosophy/ French/German/Spanish; BA, MA, PhD

School of Management; www.rhul.ac.uk/ management

accounting & finance, management & organisations, business & management, entrepreneurship, business information systems, consumption, culture & marketing, marketing, international accounting/business/ HRM, management, project management, sustainability & management; BSc, MA, MBA

Dept of Politics & International Relations; www.rhul.ac.uk/politicandir

politics and international relations/philosophy, geography/economic policy & international relations, history & international relations, politics, philosophy and economics (PPE), politics and international relations, politics with philosophy/economics/ French/music/Spanish with political studies, multilingual studies with international relations, European studies (French/German/Italian/Spanish, contemporary political theory, elections, public opinion and parties, international public policy, international relations, media, power & public affairs, politics, transnational security studies; BA(Hons), BSc(Hons), MA, MBA, MSc, MPhil, PhD, PGCert, Grad Dip, PGDip

Faculty of Science; www.rhul.ac.uk/ departments/science

School of Biological Sciences; www.rhul.ac.uk/biological-sciences

biochemistry, biology, ecology & evolution & behaviour/the environment, molecular biology, biomedical sciences, medical biochemistry, plant molecular sciences, psychology, zoology; BA(Hons), BSc(Hons), MSc, PhD

Dept of Computer Science; www.cs.rhul.ac.uk

computer science/& management, computing & business, artificial intelligence, computational finance, big data, digital media, information security, software engineering; BSc(Hons), MPhil, MSc, PhD

Dept of Earth Sciences; www.rhul.ac.uk/ earthscience

environmental geology/geoscience, geoscience, geology, petroleum geology, environmental geology, physical geography & geology, petroleum geoscience, geopolitics & security; BSc, MSC, MSci, PhD

Dept of Geography; www.rhul.ac.uk/ geography

geography, human/physical geography, physical geography & geology, politics & international relations, creative writing, place, environment, writing, geopolitics & security; BA, BSc, MA, MSc, PhD

Dept of Mathematics; www.ma.rhul.ac.uk

mathematics, maths of cryptology & communication, economics with statistics, finance & mathematics, mathematics for applications, mathematics with physics/philosophy/management/foreign language/ music/statistics, information security, joint degrees; BSc(Hons), MSc, MSci, PhD

Dept of Physics; www.rhul.ac.uk/physics

physics/with mathematics/philosophy/music, astrophysics, experimental physics, particle physics, theoretical physics, Masters by research; BSc(Hons), MPhil, MPhys, MSc, PhD

Dept of Psychology; www.rhul.ac.uk/ psychology

psychology, applied/social psychology, cognitive behavioural theory, criminology & psychology, psychological development & developmental disorders, clinical psychology & mental health, clinical & cognitive neuroscience; BSc(Hons), DClinPsych, MSc, PhD

UNIVERSITY OF LONDON; ROYAL VETERINARY COLLEGE
www.rvc.ac.uk

applied biological/veterinary research, bioveterinary sciences, biological science (animal behaviour & welfare & ethics), comparative pathology, intensive/ livestock health & production, veterinary nursing/ medicine, wild animal health/biology, veterinary/ education/epidemiology & public health, risk analysis in food security, science education, sustainable agriculture in health & food safety, one health (infectious diseases); BSc(Hons), BVetMed, FdSc, MPhil, PhD, MVMed, MRes, MSc, PGDip/Cert

UNIVERSITY OF LONDON; SCHOOL OF ORIENTAL AND AFRICAN STUDIES
www.soas.ac.uk

Faculty of Languages & Cultures;
www.soas.ac.uk/languagecultures

Undergraduate Degrees; African language and culture, African studies, ancient Near Eastern studies, Arabic/and Islamic studies, Chinese (modern and classical), Chinese studies, English, Hebrew and Israeli studies, international management and South East Asian Studies, Islamic studies, Japanese/studies, Korean, linguistics, Middle Eastern studies, Persian, South Asian studies, South Asian studies (Bengali/Hindi/Nepali/Sanskri/Urdu pathways), South East Asian studies, Turkish

Numerous Undergraduate (Combined) Degrees

Postgraduate Degrees; postcolonial studies, cinema, nation and the transcultural, global cinemas and the transcultural, Japanese post-war film genres and the avant-garde, Japanese transnational cinema, theory and practice of translation (Asian and African languages), intensive language (Arabic/Japanese/Korean), advanced Chinese studies, African literature, ancient Near Eastern languages, anthropological research methods and Nepali, applied linguistics and language pedagogy, Arabic literature, Chinese literature/studies, Islamic societies and cultures, Islamic studies, Israeli studies, Japanese literature/studies, Korean literature/studies, language documentation and description, languages and cultures of South Asia, linguistics, Near and Middle Eastern studies, Pacific Asian studies, sinology, South Asian area studies, South East Asian Studies, Taiwan studies, theory and practice of translation (Asian and African languages), Turkish studies, Iranian studies

Research Degrees; African studies, Chinese and Inner Asian Studies, interdisciplinary programmes (comparative literature, cultural studies and postcolonial studies), Japanese and Korean studies, linguistics, Near and Middle Eastern studies, South Asian studies, South East Asian studies

Diplomas & Certificates; Sanskrit, ancient Near Eastern studies, Arabic studies, modern Hebrew, Persian, South Asian studies, Turkish studies

Faculty of Law & Social Sciences;
www.soas.ac.uk/lawsocialsciences

Undergraduate Degrees; international management and South East Asian studies, international relations, politics, development economics, economics, international management

Taught Masters Degrees; law, banking law, environmental law, international economic law, law and gender, law in the Middle East and North Africa, South Asian law, gender studies and law, gender and sexuality, politics (with language), African politics, Asian politics, comparative political thought, development economics, development studies (special reference to Central Asia/economics with reference to Africa/environment and development/South Asia/the middle east), environment, politics and development, finance and development, globalisation and development, labour, social movements and development, Middle East politics, migration mobility and development, political economy of development, politics of China, research for international development, violence, conflict & development, global diplomacy

Research Degrees: economics, Certificate in political studies

Faculty of Arts & the Humanities;
www.soas.ac.uk/artshumanities

Undergraduate Degrees; development studies, international management and South East Asian studies, international relations, politics, development economics, economics, international management (China/Japan and Korea/Middle East and North Africa), management, senior status (law), economics, law

Masters Degrees; Chinese law, dispute and conflict resolution, environmental law, human rights, conflict and justice, international economic law, international law, international and comparative commercial law, Islamic law, law and gender, law, the Middle East and North Africa/culture and society/development and governance, gender studies/and law, gender and sexuality, legal studies, Chinese law, dispute and conflict resolution environmental law and sustainable development, human rights law, law, development and globalisation, politics with (language), finance and management, African politics, Asian politics, comparative political thought, development economics/studies, development studies (Central Asia), economics with reference to Africa/environment and development/South Asia/Asia Pacific region/Middle East, environment, politics and development, finance and development/financial law, global economic governance and policy, globalisation and development, international management (China/Japan/Middle East and North Africa) international politics, labour, social movements and development, Middle East politics, migration mobility and development, political economy of development, politics of China, politics of conflict, rights & justice, public financial management, public policy and management, research for international development, state,

society and development, violence, conflict & development, global diplomacy

Research Degrees; music, anthropology & sociology, art & archaeology, history, media studies, study of religions

Diplomas; postgraduate Asian art course, diploma or certificate

Certificates; certificate in the study of religions
BA(Hons), LlB, LlM, MMus, MRes, MPhil, MSc, PGDip, PhD, Certs, Dips

UNIVERSITY OF LONDON; THE SCHOOL OF PHARMACY
www.pharmacy.ac.uk

pharmacy, clinical pharmacy, international practice and policy, pharmaceutics, pharmaceutical formulation and entrepreneurship, drug delivery, drug discovery and development/pharmacy management,

medicinal natural products and phytochemistry, experimental pharmacology and therapeutics, drug sciences; Certs, MPharm, MSc, PGDip, PhD, MRes

UNIVERSITY OF LONDON; UNIVERSITY COLLEGE LONDON (UCL)
www.ucl.ac.uk

UCL School of Life and Medical Science (including UCL Medical School); www.ucl.ac.uk/slms

Faculty of Brain Sciences; www.ucl.ac.uk/brain-sciences

UG: linguistics, psychology, psychology for medics, psychology & language science

PG: Audiology and Hearing Research; advanced audiology, audiological science, audiological science with clinical practice, medical otology and audiology (audiovestibular medicine/medical ENT practice)

Ophthalmology and Vision Research; clinical ophthalmic practice, clinical ophthalmology, ophthalmology with clinical practice

Psychiatry and Mental Health Sciences; clinical/mental health sciences

Neurology and Neuroscience; clinical neurology, clinical neurology, clinical neuroscience, neurology for clinical trainees

Speech and Language Therapy; speech and language sciences

Clinical Psychology; cognitive behavioural therapy for children and young people, low intensity cognitive behavioural interventions

Faculty of Life Sciences; www.ucl.ac.uk/life-sciences

UG; Biosciences: biochemistry, biological sciences (including genetics, human genetics, biodiversity and conservation and zoology), biomedical science, biotechnology, human sciences/human evolutionary sciences, immunology, molecular biology, neuroscience, genetics/human genetics, pharmacology, physiology, anatomy, cell and developmental biology

Institute of Child Health

advanced physiotherapy (cardiovascular and paediatric) or physiotherapy studies (cardiovascular and paediatric), cell and gene therapy, child and adolescent mental health, paediatrics and child health (advanced paediatrics, community child health, gastroenterology and global child health) paediatric neuropsychology (applied and clinical), biomedicine, paediatrics and child health

Faculty of Medical Sciences; www.ucl.ac.uk/medical-sciences

UG; applied medical sciences, clinical science, orthopaedic science, surgical science, immunology, infection & cell pathology, medicine

UCL Medical School; medicine surgery, clinical & professional development

Division of Medicine; applied medical sciences, advanced biomedical imaging, clinical and public health nutrition, eating disorders and clinical nutrition, clinical drug development, drug design

UCL Cancer Institute

cancer

UCL Eastman Dental Institute

advanced aesthetic dentistry, conservative dentistry, dental sedation and pain management, endodontic practice, endodontics, endodontology, implant dentistry, oral medicine, oral surgery, oral and maxillofacial surgery, orthodontics, paediatric dentistry, periodontology, prosthodontics, restorative dental practice, special care dentistry

Division of Infection & Immunology; immunology, infection & cell pathology, immunology & infection, healthcare associated infection control, infection and immunity, mycology

Division of Surgery & Interventional Science; burns, plastic & reconstructive surgery, evidence-based healthcare, musculoskeletal science, nanotechnology & regenerative medicine, performing arts medicine, perioperative medicine, sports medicine, exercise & health, surgical & interventional sciences, trauma & orthopaedics, rehabilitation and assistive technologies, physical therapy in musculoskeletal healthcare and rehabilitation, orthopaedics, orthopaedic science, surgical sciences, introduction to systematic reviews, perioperative fluid therapy

Wolfson Institute for Biomedical Research

drug discovery

Faculty of Population Health Sciences; www.ucl.ac.uk/populationhealth-sciences

child health, paediatrics & child health, international health, women's health & communicable disease, prenatal genetics, fetal medicine, reproductive science & women's health, haemoglobinopathology, epidemiology & healthcare, health informatics, dietetics & public health, health & society, social epidemiology, health physiology, sexually transmitted disease, & HIV, cardiovascular science, cancer, cardiorespiratory sciences, general & adolescent paediatrics, genes, development & disease, infection & immunity, neurosciences & mental health, nutritional & surgical sciences, population health sciences; BSc(Hons), DipCDSc, IbSc, MBBS, MClinDent, MD(Res), MPhil, MRes, MSc, MSci, PGCert/Dip, PhD, MOrth, MRD

The Bartlett, Faculty of the Built Environment

Built Environment: www.bartlett.ucl.ac.uk

School of Architecture: adv architectural research, architectural/& interdisciplinary studies/digital theory, architectural design, urban design, architectural history, architecture, historic urban environments, adaptive architecture & computation, spatial design, architecture & cities

School of Construction & Project Management: project management for construction, construction economics & management, project enterprise & management, strategic management of projects, infrastructure investment and finance

Development Planning: building and urban design in development, development administration & planning, environment and sustainable development, social development practice, urban development planning, urban economic development

Advanced Spatial Analysis: smart cities & urban analytics, smart cities, advanced spatial analysis & visualisation

School of Graduate Studies: adaptive architecture & computation, advanced architectural studies, environmental design & engineering, facility & environment management, heritage science, light & lighting, sustainable heritage, built environment, spatial design architecture & cities, environmental design & engineering, urban design & city planning

School of Planning: urban planning, design & management, urban studies, planning and real estate, inter-disciplinary urban design, dip spatial planning, international planning, international real estate & planning, urban regeneration, sustainable urbanism, planning, design & development, mega infrastructure planning appraisal, housing development, transport and city planning

Energy Institute: energy demand studies, economics & policy of energy & the environment

Sustainable Resources: economics & policy of energy & the environment, sustainable use of resources & the environment

Sustainable Heritage; sustainable heritage

BSc(Hons), Diplomas, EngD, MA, MArch, MPhil, MSc, PhD, PGDip, MRes

Faculty of Engineering Sciences; www.ucl.ac.uk/engineering

Civil, Environmental & Geomatic Engineering; www.cege.ucl.ac.uk

civil engineering, earthquake engineering with disaster management, environmental systems engineering, geomatics for building information analytics, GIS, hydrographic surveying, transport, transport health & policy, spatio-temporal analytics & big data mining, engineering for international design, geoinformatics for building information modelling, surveying, integrated design management

Biochemical Engineering; www.ucl.ac.uk/biochemeng

biochemical engineering, bioprocessing of new medicines, synthetic biology

Chemical Engineering; www.ucl.ac.uk/chemeng

chemical engineering/with biochemical engineering, chemical process engineering

Computer Science; www.cs.ucl.ac.uk

computer science, mathematical computation, business analytics, computational finance, computational statistics and machine learning computer graphics, vision and imaging, financial systems engineering, financial risk management, information security, machine learning, networked computer systems, software systems engineering, web science and big data analytics, ICT innovation, computer science, financial computing

Electronic and Electrical Engineering; www.ee.ucl.ac.uk

electronics engineering with communications engineering/computer science/nanotechnology, electrical & electronic engineering, internet engineering, nanotechnology, integrated photonic & electronic systems, space science & engineering, satellite communications development, telecommunications/engineering/with business, wireless & optical communications

Management Science and Innovation; www.ucl.ac.uk/msi

information management for business, technological entrepreneurship: theory & practice, entrepreneurial finance, management, technology entrepreneurship

Mechanical Engineering; www.ucl.ac.uk/mecheng

engineering (mechanical) with business/finance, marine engineering, mechanical engineering, naval architecture, power systems engineering, biomaterials & tissue engineering, engineering with innovation & enterprise

Medical Physics & Bioengineering; www.ucl.ac.uk/medphys

biomedical; engineering, medical imaging/computing, physics & engineering in medicine, medical physics, radiation physics; MEng, BSc, Certs, MEng, MPhil, MRes, MSc, PGDip, PhD

Faculty of Mathematical and Physical Sciences: www.ucl.ac.uk/maps-faculty

Chemistry; www.ucl.ac.uk/chemistry

chemistry, chemical physics, drug discovery, chemical research, materials for energy & the environment, medicinal chemistry, molecular modelling/& materials science

Earth Sciences; www.ucl.ac.uk/es

earth science, environmental geoscience, geology, geophysical hazards, geophysics, geosciences, natural hazards, natural sciences, risk & disaster reduction

Mathematics; www.ucl.ac.uk/mathematics

mathematics with economics/modern languages/management studies/physics/statistics, mathematical modelling, financial mathematics

Physics and Astronomy; www.phys.ucl.ac.uk

astronomy, astrophysics, physics, theoretical physics, high energy physics, planetary science, nanotechnology

Science and Technology Studies; www.ucl.ac.uk/sts

science, technology & society, natural sciences, history & philosophy of science, philosophy, medicine & society

Space and Climate Physics; www.mssl.ucl.ac.uk

space science & engineering, technology management, systems engineering management

Statistical Science; www.ucl.ac.uk/stats

statistics, economics & finance/languages, statistics, mathematics & statistical science, statistics/& management for business, medical statistics; BSc, BSc(Econ), EngD, MRes, MSc, MSci, PhD

Faculty of Arts & Humanities; www.ucl.ac.uk/ah

English; English, English and a modern language, English; issues in modern culture, English linguistics, medieval and Renaissance studies, early modern studies

European Social & Political Studies, Dutch, French, German, Italian, Russian, Spanish, Scandinavian studies, Spanish & Latin American studies, East European language & culture, Hebrew & Jewish studies, anthropology, economics, geography, planning, political science, philosophy, international relations, history, law

Greek & English; Latin: classics: languages & literature, ancient world studies, reception of classical world

Hebrew & Jewish studies: Jewish history, language & culture, history (central & E Europe) & Jewish studies, ancient languages

Information Studies: library & archive information studies, archive & information studies/records management, digital humanities, publishing, information science

Philosophy: philosophy, philosophy and economics/Greek/history of art, philosophy, politics and economics of health

European Languages, Culture & Society: French, Dutch, German, Italian, Spanish, Portuguese & Latin American studies, comparative literature, translation studies, language, history & culture, Scandinavian studies

Slade School of Art

fine art, sculpture, history & theory of art, critical studies; BA(Hons), BFA, MA, MPhil, MRes, PhD, MFA

Faculty of Law; www.ucl.ac.uk/laws

law, law & adv studies/another legal system (Australia, Singapore), French/German/Hispanic law, competition/comparative/corporate law, criminal justice, family & social welfare, dispute resolution, environmental law & policy, family law, human rights/intellectual property law, international banking & finance/commercial law, international law, jurisprudence & legal theory, legal history, litigation & dispute resolution, maritime law, public law, law with another legal subject, law & economics, EU law; LlB and Baccalaureus Legum, LlBHons, LlM, MPhil, PhD

Faculty of Historical and Social Sciences; www.ucl.ac.uk/shs

Anthropology; www.ucl.ac.uk/anthropology

anthropology, anthropology, environment & development, ethnographic & documentary film, social & cultural anthropology, materials, evolution & anthropological design, human evolution & behaviour, medical anthropology, materials & visual culture; BA(Hons), BSc(Hons), MA, MPhil, MRes, MSc, PhD

Archaeology; www.ucl.ac.uk/archaeology

archaeology & anthropology, archaeology of eastern Mediterranean/& Middle East, artefact studies, ancient history & Egyptology, bioarchaeology & forensic archaeological science, classical archaeology & classical civilization, comparative art & archaeology, conservation for archaeology & museums, culture, materials & design, archaeology & heritage of Asia, cultural heritage studies, Egyptian archaeology, environmental archaeology, forensic archaeological science, GIS, managing archaeological sites, Mediterranean archaeology, museum studies, palaeoanthropology & palaeolithic archaeology, principles of conservation, public archaeology, skeletal & dental bioarchaeology, technology & analysis of archaeological materials, urban archaeology; BA(Hons), BSc(Hons), MA, MPhil, MSc, PhD

Economics; www.ucl.ac.uk/economics

economics, econometrics, economics & business with European social & political studies, economics & geography/statistics/philosophy/mathematics, microeconomics, macroeconomics, statistics & economics & finance/languages, economic policy; BSc(Hons), MSc, PhD

Geography; www.geog.ucl.ac.uk

geography, economics and geography, environmental geography, aquatic science, climate change, conservation, environmental mapping/modelling, environment, science and society, GIS geospatial analysis, global migration, globalisation, remote sensing, urban studies; BA(Hons), BSc(Hons), MSc, PhD

History; www.ucl.ac.uk/history

history, history with a European language, ancient history/and Egyptology, ancient world, ancient history, Chinese health and humanity, Dutch golden age, European history, history of political thought and intellectual history, late antique and Byzantine studies, transnational studies; BA(Hons), MA, MPhil, PhD

History of Art; www.ucl.ac.uk/art-history

history of art/with material studies, human & non human and nonhuman in medieval art, the values of design in the Italian renaissance, theories of authorship in early modern Italian art, early modern horror (16th/17th centuries), cannibalism and the early modern image, the senses and the rise of capital, tracing the body: technologies of representation in 18th and 19th century France, vision, tourism, imperialism: art and travel in the British empire, 1760–1870, art and technology in nineteenth-century France, politics of the image Germany 1890–1945, photographic cultures: photography's publics & the production of politics, American media: publicity and the logics of surveillance, race/place-exotic/erotic, inhabiting art: communes, colonies, squatting, contemporary art and globalization, art as theory: the writing of art; BA(Hons), MA, MPhil, PhD

Political Science; www.ucl.ac.uk/spp

political science & international relations, European social & political studies, human rights, security studies, democracy & comparative politics, international/European public policy, global government & ethics, public policy, legal & political theory, philosophy, politics & economics, global/public administration & management; MA, MPhil, MSc, PhD, MPA

School of Slavonic and Eastern European Studies; www.ssees.ucl.ac.uk

languages/literature & culture, politics & society, economics & business, history, politics & economics; BA(Hons), MA, MPhil, MRes, PhD

UNIVERSITY OF LOUGHBOROUGH
www.lboro.ac.uk

Faculty of Engineering; www.lboro.ac.uk/eng

Aeronautical and Automotive Engineering; www.lboro.ac.uk/departments/tt/

aeronautical engineering, automotive engineering/systems engineering

Chemical Engineering; www.lboro.ac.uk/departments/cg

advanced/chemical engineering/IT & management, advanced process engineering, chemical engineering with management

Civil and Building Engineering; www.lboro.ac.uk/departments/cv

air transport management, architectural engineering & design management, civil engineering, commercial management & quantity surveying, construction engineering management/project management, construction business management, energy demand studies, low energy building services engineering, low carbon building design & modelling, transport, building, infrastructure in emergencies, water & waste engineering/environmental management

Electronic, Electrical & Systems Engineering; www.lboro.ac.uk/departments/el

digital communication systems, electronic & electrical engineering, mobile communications, networked communications, renewable energy systems technology, systems engineering

Mechanical and Manufacturing; www.lboro.ac.uk/departments/mm

adv engineering, adv manufacturing engineering & management, engineering design & manufacture, innovative manufacturing engineering, mechanical engineering, product design engineering, sports technology, sustainable engineering; BEng, BSc(Hons), MDes, MRes, MSc, PhD, Cert, Dip

Faculty of Science; www.lboro.ac.uk/sci

Faculty of Chemistry; www.lboro.ac.uk/departments/cm

chemistry, analytical & pharmaceutical science, analytical chemistry, chemistry/& analytical science/sport science, environmental studies, pharmaceutical science & medicinal chemistry, medicinal & pharmaceutical chemistry; BSc(Hons), MChem, MSc, PhD

Dept of Computer Science; www.lboro.ac.uk/departments/co

adv/computer science, computer science/& mathematics/AI/management, IT management for business, information management, computing & management, internet computing & network security, web development; BSc(Hons), MSc, PhD, PGDip/Cert

Dept of Materials; www.lboro.ac.uk/departments/materials

automotive materials, design with engineering materials, materials engineering/science & technology, polymer science & technology, biomaterials; BEng/MEng, BSc(Hons), Dip Industrial Studies, MSc, PGDip/Cert, PhD

School of Mathematical Sciences; www.lboro.ac.uk/departments/maths

industrial mathematical modelling, mathematical finance, mathematics, financial mathematics, mathematics & accounting & financial management/sports science/economics/management/mathematics education/statistics; BSc(Hons), MSc, PhD

Dept of Physics; www.lboro.ac.uk/departments/ph

adv physics, astrophysics & cosmology, engineering physics, physics, physics & maths/management/sports science/cosmology, quantum & mathematical physics, physics of materials; BSc(Hons), MSc, PhD

Faculty of Social Sciences and Humanities; www.lboro.ac.uk/ssh

School of the Arts; www.lboro.ac.uk/departments/sota

fine art, graphic communication & illustration, textiles, innovation & design, 2D/3D visualisation, art & design (studio practice), arts & the public sphere, studio ceramics, methodologies & practice; BA(Hons), MA, MSc, MPhil, PhD

School of Business & Economics; www.lboro.ac.uk/departments/sbe

Business: accounting & financial management, banking, finance & accounting/management, business analytics/psychology, entrepreneurship & innovation management, finance & management/investment, management in creative organisations, information management & business studies/computing, international business/crisis management/management, management sciences, marketing, retailing marketing & management, work psychology
Economics: economics, economics with management, business economics & accounting/geography/politics/finance, international economics, banking & finance
Executive Education: management & leadership, automotive management, occupational health & safety management, healthcare management; BSc(Hons), MA, MSc, MRes, MPhil, PhD, Cert, Dip, MBA

Loughborough Design School; www.lboro/departments/lds

design/ergonomics, ergonomics (human factors in design/in health & community care), ergonomics & human factors, product/industrial design & technology, design & innovation for sustainability, human factors in transport/for inclusive design, interaction design; BA, MA, MSc, MDes, PGCE with QTS

Dept of English & Drama; www.lboro.ac.uk/departments/ea

creative writing, drama, English, history, English & sports science/history/American studies/business studies/publishing, politics with English; BA(Hons), MA, PhD

Dept of Politics, History & International Relations; www.lboro.ac.uk/departments/phis

history & geography/English/international relations/politics, politics & international relations, international financial & political relations; BSc(Hons), MPhil, MSc, PhD

Dept of Geography; www.lboro.ac.uk/departments/gy

geography, geography & management/economics/sports management/sports science, globalization & society/sport science, human geography research, international financial & political relations, environmental monitoring for management; BSc, MPhil, MSc, PhD

School of Sport, Exercise and Health Sciences; www.lboro.ac.uk/departments/ssehs

human biology, psychology, sport and exercise science, exercise physiology, human biology, musculoskeletal medicine, musculoskeletal sport science and health, PE with QTS, psychology of sport and exercise, sociology of sport, sport and exercise nutrition, sport coaching, sport management, sports biomechanics, sports science with management, English/geography/mathematics and sports science, sports science and physics, geography and sport management; BSc(Hons), MPhil, MSc, PhD

Dept of Social Sciences; www.lboro.ac.uk/departments/socialsciences

communications and media studies, conversation analysis, discursive psychology, criminology & social policy, digital media & society, global media & cultural industries, global political communication, media & cultural analysis, media, culture & society, social psychology/with criminology, sociology; BSc(Hons), MPhil, MSc, PhD

Teacher Education Unit; www.lboro.ac.uk/departments/teu
initial teacher training (mathematics/PE); MSc, PGCE, QTS

UNIVERSITY OF MANCHESTER
www.manchester.ac.uk

Faculty of Engineering and Physical Sciences: www.eps.manchester.ac.uk

School of Chemical Engineering and Analytical Science; www.ceas.manchester.ac.uk
adv/chemical engineering, adv process integration & design, chemical engineering/energy & the environment/year abroad; BEng, MEng, MSc, PhD

School of Chemistry; www.chemistry.manchester.ac.uk
chemistry/medicinal chemistry/industrial experience, polymer & materials science & engineering; BSc(Hons), EngD, MChem, MEnt, MPhil, MSc, PhD

School of Computer Science; www.cs.manchester.ac.uk
artificial intelligence, computer science, computer systems engineering, computer science with business and management/ mathematics, computer science (human computer interaction), software engineering/ with industrial experience/mathematics, advanced computer science, advanced web technologies, artificial intelligence, computer systems engineering, computer security, data and knowledge management, digital biology, multi-core computing, semantic technologies, advanced computer science and IT management, information management, computer science foundation; BSc(Hons), MEng, MEnt, MPhil, MSc, PhD

School of Earth, Atmospheric & Environmental Sciences; www.seaes.manchester.ac.uk
earth sciences, environmental sciences, policy & management, geochemistry, geography, geology, environmental & resource geology, geology with planetary science, petroleum engineering, geoscience, pollution & environmental control; BSc(Hons), MEarthSci, MEng, MSc, PhD

School of Electrical and Electronic Engineering; www.eee.manchester.ac.uk
communication engineering, advanced control & systems engineering, digital signal processing, electrical & electronic engineering/industrial experience, electrical power systems engineering, mechatronic engineering, power electronics, machines & drives, renewable & clean technology; BEng(Hons), Dip, BSc(Hons), EngD, MEng(Hons), MPhil, MSc, PhD

School of Materials; www.materials.manchester.ac.uk
materials science and engineering, materials science and engineering with biomaterials/polymers/ metallurgy corrosion/textile technology, textiles, textile science and technology, fashion management/marketing/buying and merchandising; Postgrad, advanced engineering materials, biomaterials, corrosion control engineering, international fashion marketing/retailing, polymer materials science and engineering, textile technology (technical textiles); BSc, MEng, MPhil, PhD

School of Mathematics; www.maths.manchester.ac.uk
actuarial science and mathematics, mathematics, mathematics and philosophy/ statistics/modern language/business & management/finance/financial mathematics, computer science and mathematics/ with industrial experience, mathematics and physics, mathematical finance, pure mathematics & mathematical logic, statistics; Postgrad; actuarial science, applied mathematics, mathematical finance, pure mathematics & mathematical logic, statistics; BSc, MMath, MPhil, MSc, PhD

School of Mechanical, Aerospace and Civil Engineering; www.mace.manchester.ac.uk
adv manufacturing technology & systems management, aerospace engineering with industrial experience/ management, civil engineering /(enterprise)/ with industrial experience, civil and structural engineering, mechanical engineering with industrial experience/management, management of projects,

advanced manufacturing technology and systems management, reliability engineering and asset management, mechanical engineering design, thermal power and fluid engineering, renewable energy and clean technology; BEng, EngD, MEng, MEnt, MPhil, MSc, PhD

School of Physics & Astronomy; www.physics.manchester.ac.uk

physics, physics & astrophysics/mathematics/theoretical physics/philosophy, astronomy and astrophysics, nonlinear dynamics, nuclear physics, nuclear science and technology, particle physics, soft matter and liquid crystals, theoretical physics, astronomy and astrophysics, biological physics, condensed matter physics, nonlinear dynamics, photon physics, soft matter and liquid crystals, applications of graphine and related nanomatter; BSc, EngD, MMath & Phys, MPhys, MSc, PhD

Faculty of Humanities; www.humanities.manchester.ac.uk

School of Arts, Languages and Cultures; www.arts.manchester.ac.uk

American Studies; American studies, English literature/history and American studies

Archaeology; ancient history and archaeology, archaeology, archaeology and anthropology/archaeology and art history

Art History & Visual Studies; archaeology and art history, history of art and a modern language, art gallery & museum studies, art history, arts management, policy & practice

Chinese Studies; Chinese and Japanese, Chinese and linguistics, Chinese studies, English language/French/German/Italian/Russian and Chinese, modern language and business and management (Chinese), Portuguese/Russian/Spanish and Chinese, Spanish and Chinese history, conference interpreting, intercultural communication, languages & cultures, translation & interpreting studies

Classics and Ancient History; ancient history, classical studies, Latin & English literature/Italian/linguistics/Spanish/French, classics and ancient history

Drama; drama, drama & English literature/screen studies/music, applied theatre (theatre & performance), arts management, policy & practice, screen studies, theatre & performance

English Literature and Creative Writing; English literature, English literature and a modern language/American studies/linguistics, English literature with creative writing, English studies, English studies

(literature and Culture 1200–1700/modernism and after/postcolonial literatures/contemporary literature and culture, gender, creative writing, medieval studies, screenwriting

French Studies; English language & French, English literature/European studies and a modern language (French), French & modern language (various), French studies, history & French, history of art and a modern language (French), modern language & business & management (French), Middle Eastern language and a modern European language, conference interpreting, intercultural communication, languages & linguistics, languages & cultures, translation & interpreting studies

German Studies; English language & German, English literature/European studies and a modern language (German), French & German, German & Chinese/Italian/Japanese/ linguistics/Portuguese/Russian/Spanish, German studies, history & German, history of art and a modern language (German), modern language & business & management (German), German, Arabic, Hebrew, Turkish or Persian (Middle Eastern language and a modern European language), conference interpreting, intercultural communication, languages & linguistics, languages & cultures, translation & interpreting studies

History; history and American studies, history and Arabic/modern language/ sociology, modern history with economics/politics, cultural history, early modern history, modern British history, modern European history, social and economic history, war, conflict and culture, world history, history of science, technology and medicine, medieval studies

Italian Studies; English language & Italian, English literature/European studies and a modern language (Italian), French/German/history & Italian, history of art and a modern language (Italian), Italian & Chinese/linguistics/Portuguese/Russian/Spanish/ Japanese, Italian studies, modern language & business & management (Italian), intercultural communication, languages & cultures, languages & linguistics, translation & interpreting studies

Japanese Studies; Chinese/English language/French/German/Italian & Japanese, Japanese studies, linguistics/Portuguese/Russian/Spanish and Japanese, modern language and business and management (Japanese)

Linguistics & English Language; Chinese/English literature/French/German/Italian and linguistics, linguistics, linguistics and Arabic, Japanese/Portuguese/Russian/screen studies/social anthropology/sociology/Spanish; English language, English language and Arabic/Chinese/French/German/Japanese/Portuguese/Russian/screen studies/Spanish, intercultural communication, linguistics

Middle Eastern Studies; Arabic studies, English language/history/linguistics and Arabic, Arabic and a modern European language, modern language and business and management (Arabic); Middle Eastern studies, conference interpreting, languages and cultures, translation and interpreting studies

Music; music, composition, electroacoustic music composition, musicology

Religions & Theology; comparative religion & social anthropology, religions & theology, theological studies in philosophy & ethics, medieval studies, religions & theology

Russian & East European Studies; English language and Russian/modern language (Russian), European studies and a modern language (Russian), French/German/Italian/history and Russian, history of art and a modern language (Russian), linguistics and Russian, Russian and Chinese/Japanese/ Portuguese/Spanish, Russian studies, modern language and business and management (Russian); intercultural communication, languages and cultures, translation and interpreting studies

Spanish, Portuguese & Latin American Studies; English language & Portuguese/Spanish, English literature and a modern language (Portuguese/Spanish), European studies and a modern language (Portuguese/Spanish), French & Portuguese/Spanish, German & Portuguese/Spanish, history & Spanish, history of art and a modern language (Portuguese/Spanish), history/Italian & Portuguese, Italian & Spanish, linguistics & Portuguese/Spanish, modern language & business & management (Portuguese Chinese/Russian), Russian & Spanish, Spanish & Chinese/Portuguese, Spanish, Portuguese & Latin American studies, intercultural communication, languages & cultures, languages & linguistics, translation & interpreting studies

Translation & Intercultural Studies; conference interpreting, intercultural communication, translation & interpreting studies; BA(Hons), MA, MMus, MSc, PML, PhD

School of Education; www.education.manchester.ac.uk

digital technologies, communication and education, education (international), educational leadership, psychology of education, TESOL, PGCE primary, secondary (numerous subjects), PGCE primary school direct 5–11, PGCE secondary school direct (numerous subjects), English language & education, management & leisure

School of Environment, Education & Development; www.seed.manchester.ac.uk
Planning and Environmental Management
planning, urban and regional planning, urban studies, environmental impact assessment & management, urban regeneration and development, global urban development and planning, urban design and international planning, real estate development, real estate asset management

Manchester Institute of Education
English language for education, management and leisure, digital technologies, communication and education, education (international), educational leadership, psychology of education, TESOL

Teacher Training; PGCE courses; primary, secondary (range of secondary education subjects); PGCE School direct courses; primary school direct 5–11, secondary school direct (range of secondary education subjects)

Manchester School of Architecture
architecture, architecture & urbanism

Geography
geography, geography & geology/international studies/planning, environmental governance, environmental monitoring, modelling & reconstruction, GIS, international development

Institute for Development, Policy & Management
development economics and policy, development finance, global health, global urban development and planning, human resource development (international development), HRM and development (international development), ICTs for development, international development, international development: development management/environment, climate change and development/globalisation, trade and industry/politics, governance and development policy/poverty, inequality and development/poverty, conflict and reconstruction/public policy and management, management and implementation of development projects, management and information systems: change and development, organisational change and development

BA(Hons), DCons, DEd, EdD, MA, MEd, MPhil, MSc, PGCE, PGCert/Dip, PhD, UGCert/Dip, BArch, MArch, MGeog, MPlan, IMPRE

School of Law; www.law.manchester.ac.uk
criminology, law with criminology, criminology and quantitative methods, philosophy/politics, social anthropology and criminology, law, law with

criminology/politics; corporate governance, health-care ethics and law, healthcare ethics, intellectual property law, international business and commercial law, international financial law, international trade transactions, public international law, security and international law, transnational dispute resolution; BA, LlB, LlM, MA, MPhil, MSc, MRes, PGDip/Cert, PhD, BASS, MDiplo

Manchester Business School; www.mbs.manchester.ac.uk

accounting, information technology management for business, information technology management for business (strategy and economics), information technology management for business (marketing), international business, finance and economics, international management/with American business studies, management, experience, management (accounting and finance), HRM, management (innovation, sustainability and entrepreneurship), management (international business economics), management (international studies), management (marketing)

The above courses provide the opportunity for professional or industrial experience; management with compliance, management with trusts and estates

Masters Courses: accounting and finance, finance, finance and business economics, quantitative finance: financial engineering/risk management, business analytics: operational research and risk analysis, innovation management and entrepreneurship, international business and management, business analysis and strategic management, management, corporate communications and reputation management, marketing, operations, project and supply chain management, HRM and industrial relations, international HRM and comparative industrial relations, organisational psychology, business psychology; Master of Enterprise, full-time/global part-time/global executive MBA; BA, BSc, MBA, MBus, MDA, MEnt, MPA, MRes, MSc, PhD, DBA, PGCert

School of Social Sciences; www.socialsciences.manchester.ac.uk

economics and social studies, social sciences, accounting and finance, business studies, business studies and economics/politics/sociology, development studies, economics, economics and philosophy/finance/economics and politics/sociology, finance, criminology and quantitative methods, philosophy and criminology/politics/quantitative methods, politics and criminology/social anthropology/sociology/ quantitative methods, social

anthropology and criminology/philosophy/sociology quantitative methods, sociology and criminology/philosophy/quantitative methods, economics, philosophy, politics and international relations, politics, philosophy and economics, sociology, social anthropology; Postgrad; econometrics, economics (economics of health/environmental economics), economics and econometrics, economics, financial economics, philosophy, politics, human rights, political science, law and political science, international politics, international political economy, international relations, political economy, theoretical political economy, finance, business & employment, political economy of development, society, space and environment, political science, democracy and elections, European politics & policy, governance and public policy, political theory, ethics and political philosophy, politics, research, social anthropology, anthropological research, social anthropology – cities and migration/culture, ethnography and development/Latin American studies/visual and sensory media, visual anthropology, social statistics, social research methods and statistics, sociology, sociological research; BAEcon, BSc, MA, MRes, MSc, PGDip, PhD, BASS, BEconSc

Faculty of Life Sciences: www.ls.manchester.ac.uk

anatomical sciences, biochemistry, biology with science & society, biological sciences, biology, biology with science & society, biomedical sciences, biotechnology/& enterprise, cell biology, cognitive neuroscience and psychology, developmental biology, genetics, biology, life sciences, medical biochemistry, microbiology, molecular biology, neuroscience, optometry, pharmacology, physiology, plant sciences, zoology; BSc, MNeuroSci, MRes, MSc, PhD

Faculty of Medical & Human Sciences; www.mhs.manchester.ac.uk

School of Dentistry; www.dentistry.manchester.ac.uk

dental implantology, dental public health, dentistry, endodontics, fixed & removable prosthodontics, oral & maxillofacial surgery, orthodontics, periodontology, restorative & aesthetic dentistry; BDS, BSc, MDen, MDPH, MSc, MSc(Clin), PGDip/Cert, PhD

School of Medicine; www.medicine.manchester.ac.uk

medicine, surgery, audiology, adv professional practice & leadership, advanced audiology studies, advanced practice in forensic mental health, cardiovascular health & disease, clinical biochemistry, clinical and health psychology/health services pharmacy, clinical pharmacy, clinical research, clinical rheumatology, community pharmacy public health services, deaf education, dental implantology, dental public health, digital biology, endodontics, fixed and removable prosthodontics, forensic psychology and mental health, genetic counselling, genetic medicine, health data science, health care ethics and law, health and social care, health psychology, investigative ophthalmology and vision sciences, medical education, medical imaging, medical microbiology, medical mycology, medical virology, modelling and simulation in pharmacokinetics and pharmacodynamics, occupational hygiene, occupational medicine, orthodontics, periodontology, primary mental health care, psychosocial interventions for psychosis, public health and primary care, reproduction & pregnancy, restorative and aesthetic dentistry, skin ageing and aesthetic medicine, social work, tissue engineering for regenerative medicine, translational medicine; ChB, MB, MD/ChM, MPH, MPhil, MRes, MSc, PGCert, PGDip, PhD, BSc(Hons), APIMH, Ad Dip, CPD Dip

School of Nursing and Midwifery & Social Work; www.nursing.manchester.ac.uk

advanced nursing/midwifery studies, clinical research, health & social care, midwifery, adult/child/mental health nursing, psychosocial interventions for psychosis, dementia care, primary mental health care, social work; BMidwif, BNurs, MA, MClinRes, MPhil, MRes, MSc, PGCert, PGD, PGDip, PhD

School of Pharmacy & Pharmaceutical Sciences; www.pharmacy.manchester.ac.uk

clinical & health services pharmacy, clinical pharmacy, community pharmaceutical public health service, independent prescribing, pharmaceutical industrial advanced training, pharmacological technology and qualitative assessment, pharmacy, modelling & simulation in pharmacokinetics/dynamics; MPharm, MPhil, MSc, PGCert/Dip, PhD

School of Psychological Sciences; www.psych-sci.manchester.ac.uk

approve mental health professional practice, cognitive neuroscience & psychology, psychology, healthcare science (audiology), speech & language therapy, advanced audiology studies, advanced practice in forensic mental health, audiology, clinical and health psychology, deaf education, forensic psychology & mental health, forensic psychology and mental health, neuroimaging for clinical and cognitive neurosciences, psychology; BSc, MPhil, MRes, MSc, PGDip, PhD, ClinPsyD

MANCHESTER METROPOLITAN UNIVERSITY
www.mmu.ac.uk

Manchester School of Art; www.artdes.mmu.ac.uk

acting, animation, architecture/& urbanism, art history, collaborative practice, contemporary art history/curating, contemporary visual culture, design (ceramics/furniture/glass/jewellery/lab), design cultures, drawing, embroidery, fashion (knitwear/menswear/womenswear/fashion graphics/art direction), film & media studies, filmmaking, fine art/& history of art, graphic design & art direction, illustration/& animation, interactive arts, interior design, graphic art & design, interior/3D design, landscape architecture/design, media arts, photography, product design, textiles for fashion, textiles in practice, theatre design; BA(Hons), BArch, BL and Arch, MA, MEnterprise, MPhil, PGDip/Cert, PhD, MFA, MSc

Faculty of Health, Psychology & Social Care; www.hpsc.mmu.ac.uk

Health Professions; Nursing; Social Work & Social Change

adult nursing, contemporary health practice, counselling, emergency medicine, forensic psychology, health & social care, professional practice development, psychology/& criminology, social work, social care, specialist public community public health nursing (health visiting or school nursing), speech pathology, advanced physiotherapy, cardio-respiratory physiotherapy/advanced physiotherapy, manual therapy/musculoskeletal physiotherapy/neurological therapy/advanced physiotherapy, physiotherapy, psychology/biology/criminology/education studies/forensic psychology/forensic science/philosophy/

psychology/psychology/sociology, psychology with counselling and psychotherapy, speech pathology & therapy/& language therapy, community health; BA(Hons), BSc(Hons), BA/BSc, MA, FdA, DipHE, PGCert/Dip, PhD, MPhil

Faculty of Humanities, Languages & Social Sciences; www2.hlss.mmu.ac.uk

English; English, English and American literature/creative writing/film/Arabic/Chinese/Japanese/Urdu, English; French/history/linguistics/philosophy/politics/social history/Spanish/German

Italian/TESOL/sociology, education studies, creative writing, English studies

history, politics & philosophy, history, American history, ancient history, ancient and medieval history, medieval and early modern history, modern history, war and society; philosophy, environment, technology & philosophy, ethics, religion & philosophy, politics, international politics, public services, international relations, European philosophy, European philosophy (aesthetics), international relations and global communications, public administration

Language, Linguistics & TESOL: Arabic, French, German, Italian, Japanese; linguistics, Spanish, TESOL, Urdu, applied linguistics, TEFL

Journalism, Information & Communication; information and communications, multimedia journalism, web development, digital media and communications, apprenticeship technology solutions, information management, library and information management, multimedia journalism, international fashion journalism

Sociology; criminology, criminology and sociology, criminology and sociology/with quantitative methods, criminology with quantitative methods, sociology, sociology with quantitative methods, criminology/psychology, education studies/sociology, English/sociology, philosophy/sociology, applied quantitative methods, sociology and global change, probation officer qualifications, British studies for foreign teachers, community engagement training; BA(Hons), BSc(Hons), PGDip/Cert, MA, MPhil, PhD, LlB, LlM, MSc

Faculty of Science & Engineering; www.sci-eng.ac.uk

School of Healthcare Science

biomedical science, dental technology, physiology (physical activity & health), healthcare science (physiological sensing/life sciences), human biology,

cellular pathology, clinical biochemistry, haematological transfusion science, medical microbiology; BSc(Hons), MSc

School of Computing, Mathematics & Digital Technology; www.scmdt.mmu.ac.uk

adv/computer science, computer & network security, computing, computer forensics & security, computer games technology, computer science, engineering with management, games design & development, information systems, media technology, multimedia & web computing, software engineering, web technologies, mathematics, financial mathematics, economics/mathematics, computing, mathematics & digital science; FdSc, BSc(Hons), MSc, PGDip/Cert, PhD, BA/BSc(Hons)

School of Engineering; www.soe.mmu.ac.uk

automotive engineering, applied/physics, computer & network technology, electrical & electronic engineering, engineering with management, design engineering, industrial communications & automation, mechanical engineering, product/design & technology, computer networks, apprenticeship technology solutions; BSc(Hons), BEng(Hons), MSc, PGDip/Cert, MPhil, PhD

School of Science & the Environment; www.ssty.mmu.ac.uk

Biology & Conservation Ecology

animal behaviour, biology/& chemistry/psychology, biological recording, bird conservation, conservation biology/genetics, ecology & conservation, environmental management & business, forensic biology, wildlife biology, GIS, microbiology & molecular biology, countryside/environmental management, sustainable aviation; BSc(Hons), MSc, PGDip/Cert, MPhil, PhD

Chemistry & Environmental Science

chemistry, chemical/& pharmaceutical science, biology & chemistry, environmental science, forensic science & applied criminology/medicinal & biochemical/pharmaceutical chemistry/psychology, medicinal & biological chemistry, forensic biochemistry; MChem, BSc(Hons)

Geography & Environmental Management

geography, environmental management & business/sustainability, human/physical geography, GIS studies, sustainable aviation; BSc(Hons), PGCert/Dip, MSc, MPhil, PhD, MGeog

Faculty of Business & Law;
www.business.mmu.ac.uk

Accounting and Finance; banking and finance, economics and finance, finance/& business, professional accounting, economic and financial analysis, financial planning and business management, taxation and fiscal policy, sustainable performance management

Business Management & Leadership; business, business administration, business administration with information technology, business/economics, business management with law, HRM/with CPD, international business/marketing, business management, international business management, business technology and analytics, finance and business, financial planning and business management, international business management, international HRM, leadership, leadership in health and social care, logistics and supply chain management, management, management and leadership, business administration (MBA), place management, project management, strategic business management

Digital Business and Communications; business technology and analytics, digital communications management, PR and digital communications, digital marketing

Economics; economics, business/economics, economics & international business/politics/ mathematics/ banking, applied economics, economic & financial analysis, taxation/fiscal policy

Marketing, Advertising and Public Relations; business/marketing, digital media/marketing, advertising and brand management, marketing management, PR/and marketing/ digital communications/media management, marketing (communications/creative advertising), place management

Sports Management; sports management, sports marketing management

Human Resources; human resources, HRM

Retail; retailing, logistics and supply chain management

Business Technology; business technology

BA(Hons), BSc(Hons), MA, MSc, MBA, DBA, PhD, FD, PGCert/Dip

Manchester Law School;
www.law.mmu.ac.uk

law, legal practice, legal management; LlB(Hons), LlM, MPhil, PhD, Grad Dip, PGCert, GDl

Faculty of Education;
www.ioe.mmu.ac.uk

Initial Teacher Training; primary education with QTS, PGCE, primary education, PGCE secondary education – numerous subject specialisms, early years teacher initial teacher training leading to early years teacher status (EYTS), Schools Direct, early years and childhood studies, education studies, inclusive education and disability studies, youth and community work, religion, education and community, early years teacher status, supporting teaching & learning, education, inclusive education and special educational needs, research, education, autistic spectrum conditions, childhood studies and practice in the early years, education leadership & management, inclusive education and special educational needs, language education, science, technology, engineering and maths, specific learning difficulties, teaching and learning, special educational needs coordination, mentoring & coaching, specific learning difficulties FE/HE; BA(Hons), BA/BSc, Certs, EdD, FD, MA, MPhil, MSc, PGDip/Cert, PhD

Hollings Faculty;
www.hollings.mmu.ac.uk

Department Apparel

fashion buying & merchandising, fashion design & technology (womenswear/sportswear/menswear), int fashion/practice/promotion; BA(Hons)

Department of Food, Nutrition & Hospitality

events management, events, hospitality and tourism, food business entrepreneurship, hospitality business management, nutritional sciences, tourism management, food innovation, food safety, responsible food, nutrition and health, occupational safety, health and environment; BA(Hons), BSc(Hons), FdA, FdSc, MA, MPhil, PhD, BTech

MMU Cheshire;
www.cheshire.mmu.ac.uk

Dept of Business & Management Studies;
www.cheshire.mmu.ac.uk/bms

business, business management with logistics/financial management/marketing, events management (creative industries), global business management, marketing/management, sports development, strategic leadership & change, sustainable management; BA/BSc, BA(Hons), FD, MBA, MSc, MPhil, PhD

Dept of Contemporary Arts; www.cheshire.mmu.ac.uk/dcu

contemporary arts, contemporary theatre & performance, creative music production, creative writing, dance, drama, music, popular music, communal practice; BA(Hons), MA, MPhil, PhD

Dept of Exercise & Sports Science; www.cheshire.mmu.ac.uk/exspsci

coaching and sport development, coaching studies, exercise & sport (biomechanics/coaching/physiology/psychology/sport development), science, PE & sports pedagogy, sport development, sport & exercise science; BA, BSc, FD, MA, MSc

MIDDLESEX UNIVERSITY
www.mdx.ac.uk

School of Arts and Design; www.mdx.ac.uk/aboutus/Schools/art-and-design

animation, architecture/art & design, 3D animation & games, illustration, jewellery, photography, fine art, games design, graphic design, design futures/crafts, fashion/ design, fashion communication & styling, fashion textiles, interior architecture/design, interiors, interior design, fashion, printmaking, spatial cultures; BA(Hons), MA, FdA, MSc, PhD

Middlesex University Business School; www.mdx.ac.uk/aboutus/Schools/business-school

Economics and International Development; Accounting and Finance; International Management and Innovation; Leadership, Work and Organisation
Accounting & Finance; business accounting, banking and finance, business management (finance), financial services/management, accounting and finance, Postgrad; banking and finance, accounting, finance/ accounting practice, investment & finance,
Business and Management; international business, business management (marketing/finance/Spanish/innovation/Mandarin/human resources/innovation/supply chain management/ project management), int business & trade, int international business admin, business and management (HR), music business and arts management Postgrad; banking and finance, media management, marine surveying
Economics; economics, business economics, Postgrad; behavioural economics in action, global supply chain management
Human Resource Management; business, business management (HR), int/HRM HRM, Postgrad; HRM/development, globalisation and work
Marketing; marketing, business management (marketing), advertising, PR and media, Postgrad; marketing communications/management, e-marketing and social media

Tourism and Hospitality Management; international tourism management, international tourism management (Mandarin), international hospitality and tourism management, international tourism management (Spanish), Postgrad; arts management
MBAs; innovation management and entrepreneurship, shipping and logistics, oil and gas, strategic management and leadership; BA(Hons), BSc(Hons), MA, MSc, PhD, MBA, MProf, PGCert/Dip

School of Health and Education; www.mdx.ac.uk/aboutus/Schools/health-and-education

Education; early childhood studies/ with early years teacher status, early years initial teacher training, learning and teaching, education studies; Postgrad; leading inclusive education, higher education, education (drama), pre-teaching and training
Integrative Medicine; professional practice in acupuncture/ayurvedic herbal medicine, herbal medicine/Chinese herbal medicine
Healthcare Science; medical physiology (cardiovascular science), honours healthcare science (medical engineering/rehabilitation engineering/cardiac physiology/neurophysiology)
Mental Health; professional practice in mental health nursing, care leadership and management, nursing (mental health), Postgrad; mental health and substance use (dual diagnosis), mental health studies, promoting mental health in adolescents and young people, leading and developing public and community services, child, adolescent and family mental health work, dementia care and practice, child and family mental health work, professional practice (health, social care, public and community sectors)
Midwifery; midwifery, Postgrad; midwifery studies, neonatal care
Nursing; professional practice in practice nursing/mental health nursing, care leadership and management, European nursing (adult), nursing (adult/

child), veterinary nursing, Postgrad; nursing studies, leading and developing public and community services, mental health studies nursing, professional practice (health, social care, public and community sectors)

Social Work; care leadership and management, social work; Postgrad; comparative drug and alcohol studies, advanced professional practice in social work (adults), promoting mental health in adolescents and young people, leading and developing public and community services, evidence based parenting; supervision theory, child, adolescent and family mental health work, advanced professional practice in social work (practice education), evidence based parenting: supervision & leadership, advanced professional practice in social work (children and families), child and family mental health work, social work, professional practice (health, social care, public and community sectors), Veterinary Nursing; veterinary nursing

CertHE, DipHE, BSc, MSc, PGDip, PGCE

School of Law; www.mdx.ac.uk/aboutus/Schools/law

law, law with international relations/human rights/criminology, European law and politics, commercial law, law and social sciences, international politics, economics and law, international politics and law, Postgrad; employment law, international business law, legal research, minorities, rights and the law; BA(Hons), Grad Dip, LlB, LlM, PGDip/Cert, D/MProf, FdA, MPhil, PhD

School of Media and Performing Arts; www.mdx.ac.uk/aboutus/Schools/performing-arts

Film, Media & English; arts management, audiovisual literary translation, business & legal translation, media & culture studies, performing arts, advertising and PR & media, creative writing/technology, dance studies/performance, English literature and language, film, journalism/publishing/English language & media, media technology, novel writing, theatre arts, professional practice in dance technology & pedagogy, pop music, music business and arts; BA(Hons), MA, MSc, PhD

School of Science and Technology; www.mdx.ac.uk/aboutus/Schools/science-and-technology

Computer & Communications Engineering; Computer Science, Design Engineering & Mathematics; Natural Sciences

biomedical & biological science, biology (environmental biology/biotechnology/molecular biology), clinical biochemistry, business information systems/technology/management, computer & network security/management, computer communications/& networks/forensics/company networks & IT, computer forensics/science/systems engineering, electronic security & digital forensics, engineering & computing mobile systems & communication, design engineering/& electronics/embedded/robotic systems/manufacturing management, engineering, game design, computer science & information technology, visual analytics, mechatronics, product design & engineering, environment, environmental policy/culture, environmental health/science, sustainable environmental management/development, mathematics, natural sciences, complementary health (herbal medicine, acupuncture, traditional Chinese medicine), applied public health, environmental health, occupational safety & health management, risk management, building information modelling management, design engineering manufacturing management, engineering management, mobile telecommunications, project management, telecommunications engineering; BSc(Hons), BEng, MEng, MA, MSc, PGCert/Dip, MPhil, PhD

Psychology

psychology with education/sociology marketing, psychology, psychology with neuroscience/HRM/counselling skills/criminology, applied clinical health psychology, psychoanalysis, applied psychology, forensic psychology, criminology with forensic psychology, health psychology; BA(Hons), BSc(Hons), MA, MSc, DocProf, MPhil, PhD

Sport and Exercise Science and Rehabilitation

sport and community development, sport and exercise science /performance analysis, sport and exercise rehabilitation, sport and exercise science (strength and conditioning/teaching and coaching sport), sport and exercise nutrition, strength and conditioning, sport performance analysis, sport and exercise science (physiology), sport, exercise and physical activity for special populations, sport and exercise science (psychology/biomechanics), sport rehabilitation, sport physiotherapy and exercise; BSc(Hons), MSc, PhD, DocProf

UNIVERSITY OF NEWCASTLE UPON TYNE
www.ncl.ac.uk

Faculty of Humanities and Social Sciences; www.ncl.ac.uk/hass

School of Architectural Planning and Landscape; www.ncl.ac.uk/apl

architecture, architecture & practice/and management/urban planning, architectural design research/ planning & leadership, digital architecture, experimental architecture, future landscape imaginaries, geography & planning, architectural planning/landscape, planning for sustainable & climate change, landscape architectural studies, planning & environmental research/sustainability & climate change, international spatial planning, regional development & spatial planning, sustainable building & environment, town planning, urban design/planning; BA, BArch, Cert, Dip, MA, MPhil, MSc, PGCert, PhD, MPlan, MRes

School of Arts and Cultures; www.ncl.ac.uk/sacs

Music; www.ncl.ac.uk/sacs/music

folk & traditional music, analysis, musicology, music, musical history, popular & contemporary music, composition, performance, ethnomusicology, mixed media; BA, BMus, Diploma, MA, MLitt, MMus, MPhil, PhD

Fine Art; www.ncl.ac.uk/sacs/fineart

fine art; BA(Hons), MFA, MPhil, PhD

Media & Cultural Studies; www.ncl.ac.uk/sacs/ digitalmedia

media, communication & culture, media & journalism/PR/culture, international multimedia journalism, digital film production; Dip, BA(Hons), MA, MRes, PhD

Museum, Gallery and Heritage Studies; www.ncl.ac. uk/sacs/icchs

art museum & gallery studies, art as enterprise, heritage studies, heritage, heritage & tourism management, museum studies; MA, MPhil, MPrac, PGCert, PGDip, PhD

Business School; www.ncl.ac.uk/nubs

accounting and finance, business accounting and finance, business management, international business management, marketing/ & management, economics, economics and finance/business management, accounting/mathematics/politics and economics

Postgrad; banking & finance, finance, financial accounting & business, international economics & finance/financial analysis, quantitative finance & risk management, strategic planning & investment, adv international business management, e-business, e-business (e-marketing/information systems), international/HRM, arts business creativity, innovation, creativity & entrepreneurship, adv international business management & marketing, international marketing, operations, logistics & supply chain management, operations management, logistics & accounting; MBAs (full-time, global)

School of Education, Communication and Language Sciences; www.ncl.ac.uk/ecls

speech and language sciences, education: PGCE/ secondary, coaching and mentoring, innovative pedagogy and curriculum, education: international perspectives, international development and education, education research, education and communication, education and applied linguistics, applied linguistics research, applied linguistics and TESOL/ education, evidence based practice, language pathology, speech and language sciences, speech and language therapy, clinical linguistics and evidence based practice (research) and applied linguistics and TESOL/ education (including counselling/international business management/international marketing/international relations/media, applied educational psychology

BA(Hons), BSc(Hons), DAppEdPsych, EdD, MA, MEd, MSc, PGCE, PhD, QTS

School of English Literature, Language, Linguistics; www.ncl.ac.uk/elll

English language/literature, English lit: 1500–1900, linguistics/with Chinese/Japanese/French/German/ Spanish, creative writing, classical studies & English, film theory & practice, language practice acquisition, modern & contemporary studies; BA(Hons), MA, MLitt, MPhil, PGCert, PhD

Geography, Politics and Sociology; www.ncl.ac.uk/gps

geography, physical/human geography, local & regional development, regional development & spatial planning, government/& European Union studies, international political economy, international studies, international politics (global justice & ethics/

205

critical geopolitics/globalization, politics/& economics/sociology/history), sociology, social research, world politics & popular culture; BA(Hons), BSc(Hons), MA, MSc, PhD

Global Urban Research Unit; www.ncl.ac.uk/guru
cities and international development, power, place & materiality, planning & environmental dynamics, cities, security & vulnerability; MPhil, PhD

Institute of Health and Society; www.ncl.ac.uk/ihs/
public health & health services research, epidemiology, global public health, epidemiology & health service research, social sciences & health research; MSc, PGDip/Cert, MRes, MD, PhD

School of History, Classics & Archaeology Studies; www.ncl.ac.uk/historical
ancient history/& archaeology/politics, archaeology, British history, classical studies/& English, classics/& ancient history, English literature & History, European history, Greek & Roman/Byzantine archaeology, heritage, history & archaeology, history, politics/& history, history of medicine, Roman frontier studies; BA(Hons), MA, MLitt, MPhil, PhD

Newcastle Law School; www.ncl.ac.uk/nuls
environmental regulation & sustainable development, criminology, European legal studies, international legal studies, international business law, law (complete range of legal areas taught at UG level); LlB, LlM, MPhil, PhD

Centre for Learning and Teaching; www.ncl.ac.uk/cflat
innovative pedagogy & curriculum, coaching and mentoring for teacher development, teaching and learning in HE, educational research in practice, educational leadership, educational leadership and management, information, communication and entertainment technology, international development and education, pedagogy and learning, inclusive education, educational leadership and management, information, communication and entertainment technology, international development and education, pedagogy and learning, education & communication, applied educational psychology, PGCE primary & secondary education, educational research; EdD, MA, MEd, PGCE, DEdPsy, DAppEdPsy, IPhD

Newcastle Centre for the Literary arts/ www.ncl.ac.uk/ncla
creative writing; MA, PhD, PGCert

School of Modern Languages; www.ncl.ac.uk/sml
modern languages, translation and interpreting, modern languages (French, German, French and German, French and Spanish, German and Spanish or French, German and Spanish) Portuguese, Dutch, Catalan or Quechua, Chinese studies, Japanese studies, translating/& interpreting, Latin American interdisciplinary studies, film: theory and practice, modern languages and business studies, modern languages and linguistics, Spanish, Portuguese and Latin American studies; BA(Hons), MA, MLitt, PhD

Policy, Ethics and Life Sciences Research Centre; www.ncl.ac.uk/peals
reproduction & genetic medicine, families, kinship & childhood, embodiment & identity; PhD

Centre for Research in Linguistics and Language Science; www.ncl.ac.uk/linguistics
linguistics, European or Asian language, English language/& literature, applied linguistics and TESOL, clinical linguistics research, evidence based practice in communication disorders, language pathology, linguistics (with English language/language acquisition/European languages), applied linguistics research; BA(Hons), MA, MEd, MSc, PhD

Centre for Urban and Regional Development Studies; www.ncl.ac.uk/curds
cities, security and vulnerability, cities and international development, planning and environmental dynamics, power, place and materiality; MA, PhD

Faculty of Medical Sciences: www.ncl.ac.uk/aboutpeoplestudies academic/biosciences
biochemistry, biomedical genetics/science, medical microbiology, biotechnology, medical science, pharmacology, psychological science, clinical education/psychology, sociology, medical science

Newcastle Biomedicine; www.ncl.ac.uk/biomedicine
Biomedical and Biomolecular Science; biomedical sciences, biochemistry, biomedical genetics, exercise biomedicine, pharmacology, physiological sciences, medical science

Medicine; medicine, surgery
Psychology; psychology, biology/mathematics/nutrition and psychology

Biomedicine; clinical and health sciences, clinical research/clinical research (ageing)/leadership), clinical leadership, clinical education, clinical psychology, cognitive behavioural therapy, genomic medicine, health services research, low intensity psychological therapies, medical sciences, clinical sciences (physiological sciences with specialisms in: cardiac, vascular, respiratory and sleep science, gastrointestinal physiology and urodynamic science), clinical sciences (medical physics with specialisms in: radiotherapy physics, radiation safety, imaging with ionising radiation, imaging with non-ionising radiation), oncology and palliative care, cancer studies, praxis cognitive behavioural therapy studies, psychology (clinical and health psychology/ clinical and forensic psychology), public health, public health and health services research, social science and health research, clinical and health sciences, transplantation BA, BSc(Hons), DClinPsychol, MB, MClinEd, MClinRes, MD, MRes, MSc, MSci, PGCert/Dip, PhD, MBBS

School of Dental Sciences; www.ncl.ac.uk/dental

clinical implants surgery, conscious sedation in dentistry, dental surgery, dentistry & dental science, orthodontics, restorative dentistry, dental hygiene & therapy; BDS, DDS, MSc, PGDip/Cert, PhD, MPhil

Faculty of Science, Agriculture & Engineering; www.ncl.ac.uk/aboutpeoplestudies/academic/sage

School of Agriculture, Food and Rural Development; www.ncl.ac.uk/afrd

agri-business management, animal science agriculture, agriculture with agronomy, agriculture with animal production science, agriculture with management, countryside management, environmental science, rural studies, food & human nutrition, food marketing & nutrition,
Postgrad; food and rural development research, environmental resource assessment, biodiversity conservation and ecosystem management, organic farming and food production systems, agricultural and environmental science; BSc(Hons), MPhil, MSc, PhD

School of Biology; www.ncl.ac.uk/biology

biology, cellular & molecular biology, ecology & environmental biology, ecological consultancy, industrial & commercial biotechnology, wildlife management; BSc(Hons), MSc, MRes, PhD

School of Chemical Engineering and Advanced Materials; www.ncl.ac.uk/ceam

applied/process control, bioprocessing engineering, chemical engineering, clean technology, industry, materials, design & engineering, process automation/control, sustainable/chemical engineering, renewable energy flexible training/enterprise and management; BEng(Hons), MEng(Hons), MSc, PGDip

School of Chemistry; www.ncl.ac.uk/chemistry

chemistry, drug chemistry, medicinal & synthetic product, chemistry with medicinal chemistry, structural chemistry & spectroscopy, synthetic & medicinal chemistry; BSc(Hons), MChem(Hons), MPhil, MSc, PhD

Civil Engineering and Geosciences; www.ncl.ac.uk/ceg

civil engineering, civil and structural engineering, civil and surveying engineering, earth science, surveying and mapping science, GIS, physical geography, civil and surveying engineering Postgrad; environmental engineering, environmental consultancy, environmental/and petroleum geochemistry, structural engineering, geotechnical engineering, engineering geology, transport planning and its/engineering/business management/environment, hydrogeology and water management, flood risk management, hydroinformatics, hydrology and climate change, hydroinformatics and water management, renewable energy, enterprise and management; BEng, PostgradCert/Dip, BSc(Hons), MEng, MPhil, MSc, PhD

Computing Science; www.cs.ncl.ac.uk

computer game engineering, cloud computing, computer security and resilience, computer science – bioinformatics, computational systems biology, adv/computing science, mobile & distributed systems, games engineering, biocomputing, security & resilience, human-computer interaction, software engineering, e-business & information systems, neuroinformatics, synthetic biology; BSc(Hons), MPhil, MSc, MComp, PhD

Electrical, Electronic and Computer Engineering; www.ncl.ac.uk/eece

automation and control, communications & signal processing, digital electronics, electrical & electronics engineering, electronics & computer engineering, electrical power, electronic communications, computer engineering, power distribution, wireless embedded systems, electrical power, microelectronics, power distribution, wireless embedded systems; BEng, EngD, MEng, MPhil, PhD

Newcastle Institute for Research on Sustainability; www.ncl.ac.uk/sustainability
research projects; MPhil, MRes, PhD

Digital Institute; www.ncl.ac.uk/digitalinstitute
research projects; PhD

Newcastle Centre for Railway Research; www.ncl.ac.uk/newrail
rail freight & logistics, organisation, management & economics of train movement; MSc, PhD

School of Marine Science and Technology; www.ncl.ac.uk/marine
marine biology and oceanography, marine zoology, engineering and science in the marine environment integrated, marine engineering, marine transport & management, naval architecture, offshore and environmental technology, offshore engineering, pipeline engineering, renewable energy enterprise and management, small craft technology, subsea engineering and management, technology in the marine environment, marine technology; BSc(Hons), MEng, MRes, MSc, PGDip/Cert, PhD

Mathematics and Statistics; www.ncl.ac.uk/maths
mathematics, financial mathematics/with management, mathematics & statistics/accounting/economics/psychology/management, mathematical sciences, pure mathematics, applied mathematics, statistics; BSc(Hons), MMath, MMathStat, MPhil, PhD

School of Mechanical & Systems Engineering; www.ncl.ac.uk/mech
mechanical engineering, mechanical design and manufacturing engineering, mechanical and low carbon transport engineering, mechanical engineering with mechatronics/bioengineering, biomedical engineering, design and manufacturing engineering, low carbon transport engineering, mechatronics, microsystems engineering, rail freight and logistics, biomedical engineering, MEMS, design, manufacture and materials, fluid dynamics and thermal systems; BEng, MEng, MSc, PhD

Centre for Rural Economy; www.ncl.ac.uk/cre
food & rural development; MPhil, MSc, PhD, MRes

Sir Joseph Swan Institute for Energy Research; www.ncl.ac.uk/energy
renewable energy, enterprise & management; MRes, MSc, PhD

UNIVERSITY OF NORTHAMPTON
www.northampton.ac.uk

School of Science & Technology: www.northampton.ac.uk/science-technology

Division of Computing; www.northampton.ac.uk/about-us/academic-schools/school-of-science-and-technology/subject-areas/computing
business computing (systems/web design), computer games development, computing, computing (computer networks engineering/computer systems engineering/graphics and visualisation/internet technology and security/mobile computing/software engineering), computing (internet technology and security/computer networks engineering/software engineering/immersive technologies/ environmental informatics, IT service management, web technology & security; BA/BSc, BSc(Hons), MSc, PhD

Division of Engineering; www.northampton.ac.uk/about-us/academic-schools/school-of-science-and-technology/subject-areas/engineering
civil engineering, construction management, electro-mechanical engineering, electrical and electronic engineering, engineering, lift/& escalator engineering/technology, mechanical/production engineering, non-destructive testing; BSc(Hons), BTEC, FdSc, BEng(Hons), MEng, MSc, ProfCert

**Environmental Sciences;
www.northampton.ac.uk/about-us/
academic-schools/school-of-science-and-
technology/subject-areas/environmental-
and-geographical-sciences**

arboriculture, country & wildlife management, environmental management, environmental science (climate change/landscape ecology/waste), geography
(human/physical), international development &
human geography, international environmental management, wildlife conservation, horticulture & garden design, applied equine studies, equine behaviour
and welfare, equine management/therapies, agriculture, horticulture & garden design, land, BSC
management; BA/BSc, BSc(Hons), FdSc, HND,
MBA, MSc, UnivCerts

**Leather Technologies;
www.northampton.ac.uk/about-us/
academic-schools/school-of-science-and-
technology/subject-areas/leather-
technology**

leather technology/development (professional),
leather technology (leather science/environment/mar-
keting & business); BSc(Hons), BTEC NC, Cert/Dip,
MSc, PhD/MPhil, Univ Dip

**Wastes Management;
www.northampton.ac.uk/about-us/
academic-schools/school-of-science-and-
technology/subject-areas/wastes-
management**

adv/wastes management, waste management pollution technology, wildlife management, resource
management; BSc(Hons), MSc, FdSc

*The School of The Arts;
www.northampton.ac.uk/about-us/
academic-schools/school-of-the-arts*

**Division of Design;
www2.northampton.ac.uk/arts/home/
Design**

architectural technology, design, graphic design,
interior design, product design, design (textiles/foot-
wear/graphic communication/photographic commu-
nication/product & spatial innovation/illustration/
fashion & textiles), web design games art; BA(Hons),
BSc(Hons), MA

**Division of Fine Art (Art);
www2.northampton.ac.uk/arts/home/Fine
Art**

drawing, fine art, illustration, painting & drawing,
photographic practice,, fine art, photography, art &
design, music studies, pop music, English & culture/
contemporary; BA(Hons), FDA, MA

**Division of Media;
www2.northampton.ac.uk/arts/home/
Media**

advertising, creative writing, film & screen studies,
media production, media production & moving
image, events management, broadcasting/multime-
dia journalism, digital film production, digital marketing; BA(Hons), MA

**Division of Performance Studies;
www2.northampton.ac.uk/arts/home/
performance**

acting, dance, drama, theatre practice, performing
arts, pop music, music practice & production;
BA(Hons), MA, PhD, BA/BSc

**Division of Fashion;
www2.northampton.ac.uk/arts/home/
Division-of-Fashion**

fashion, footware & accessories, interior design,
printed textile fashion, surface design & printed
textiles, international fashion marketing, textiles for
fashion; BA(Hons), MA

*School of Education;
www.northampton.ac.uk/about-us/
academic-schools/school-of-education*

early years education, early childhood studies,
education (primary), early years (primary/early
years/secondary/PGCE), education, education studies, childhood & youth, developmental & educational psychology, early young people teacher status
(–5), education management & leadership, ELT,
graduate teacher programme (GTP), initial teacher
training, learning & teaching, practice education,
special education needs & inclusion, post-compulsory education & training, primary mathematics,
OCR Level 5 and Level 7, specific learning difficul-
ties/dyslexia, PGCE (primary/early years/secondary),
Schools Direct; PGCE; QTS, GTI, BA(Hons), GTP,
PGCE, BSc(Hons), BA/BSc, FD, CertHE, FD, PhD

School of Health;
www.northampton.ac.uk/about-us/academic-schools/school-of-health

dental nursing, autonomous healthcare practice, cancer care, community practice, applied/cancer studies, counselling, health studies, health & social care (community care), mental health non-medical prescribing, midwifery, international nursing studies, nursing (adult/children's/learning disabilities/mental health), learning disability nursing, adv occupational therapy, palliative & supportive care, paramedic science, adv podiatry, professional practice, public health; BSc(Hons), MPhil, PGCert, PhD, FD

Northampton Business School;
www.northampton.ac.uk/about-us/academic-schools/northampton-business-school

accounting/& finance, banking & financial planning, business/& management, business computing/entrepreneurship/studies, corporate governance & leadership, economics/& business/management, enterprise development, events management/& business entrepreneurship, fashion marketing, international marketing strategy, finance, financial services management, HRM, income generation & tendering, international accounting/banking & finance/business/business communications/development/logistics & trade financing/leadership/marketing studies, business administration systems, international development & human geography/economics, international marketing strategy(logistics/marketing/events management/business entrepreneurship), international tourism management/development, leadership & management, management, management (HR/international/marketing/tourism/finance), marketing management, sports marketing/enterprise, travel & tourism management, web design; BA(Hons), BA/Bsc(Hons), CMS, DBA, DMS, FdA, HND, MA, MBA, MSc, PGDip (marketing), MBL, ProfDip

School of Social Sciences;
www.northampton.ac.uk/about-us/academic-schools/school-of-social-sciences

History; www.northampton.ac.uk/about-us/academic-schools/school-of-social-sciences/subject-areas/history
history, social & cultural history, history & English/educational studies

Law; www.northampton.ac.uk/about-us/academic-schools/school-of-social-sciences/subject-areas/law
criminal legal practice, international business law/criminal law & security/commercial law, law, appl criminal justice, offender management, police & criminal justice, law & criminology, public service interpreting law

Psychology; www.northampton.ac.uk/about-us/academic-schools/school-of-social-sciences/subject-areas/psychology
child & adolescent health, counselling children & young people, development & educational/sport & exercise psychology, counselling, psychology, psychology & law/marketing/drama/English/educational studies, transpersonal psychology & consciousness

Social Science/Sociology; www.northampton.ac.uk/about-us/academic-schools/school-of-social-sciences/subject-areas/sociology
international relations, sociology, police & criminal justice service, probation & policing, urban affairs, community practice, social work, sociology, youth & community work, social psychology, social care & educational studies

Politics; www.northampton.ac.uk/about-us/academic-schools/school-of-social-sciences/subject-areas/politics
media studies, philosophy, politics, media, philosophy, politics, international relations, politics, international relations

Criminology; www.northampton.ac.uk/about-us/academic-schools/school-of-social-sciences/subject-areas/criminology
criminology

Human Geography; www.northampton.ac.uk/about-us/academic-schools/school-of-social-sciences/subject-areas/human-geography
geography (human/physical)

Police and criminal justice; www.northampton.ac.uk/about-us/academic-schools/school-of-social-sciences/subject-areas/police-and-criminal-justice
police & criminal justice studies, offender management

Urban Affairs; www.northampton.ac.uk/ about-us/academic-schools/school-of- social-sciences/subject-areas/urban- affairs

sustainable communities

FdA, BA(Hons), BSc(Hons), BA/BSc, MA, LlB, LlM, PhD

Youth and Community Work

youth and community work; MA

UNIVERSITY OF NORTHUMBRIA AT NEWCASTLE
www.northumbria.ac.uk

Faculty of Business & Law

Newcastle Business School; www.northumbria.ac.uk/sd/academic/bs

accounting/& finance, business studies, business leadership & corporate management, business with economics/financial management/HRM/international management/logistics & supply chain management/ hospitality & tourism management, business with financial entrepreneurship/management/law/finance/ marketing/marketing management, entrepreneurial business management, finance & investment man-agement, global finance management, international management with logistics & supply chain manage-ment/marketing management/public administration/ business management, business & law (MBA), HRM/ & development, global financial management/busi-ness management, global/logistics & supply chain management, travel & tourism management, inter-national HRM, investment management, interna-tional business management with French/Spanish, international business administration/hospitality & tourism management/HRM/management/banking & finance/business, leadership & corporate, marketing management/studies, public administration, tourism & hospitality management, strategic marketing; BA, DBA, MA, MBA, MSc, PhD

Northumbria School of Law; northumbria.ac.uk/sd/academic/law

advanced legal practice, law, bar practice/profes-sional training, business/commercial/employment law, business with legal management, data protection law, & information governance, employment law in practice, information rights law and practice, inter-national commercial/trade/environmental law/HRM, law with business/international business, legal prac-tice, medical law, professional practice in mental

Sport

sport strength & conditioning, sport therapy/studies, performance & coaching, sport development & PE, sport marketing management, sport & exercise science, sports studies & education studies/business/ marketing/multimedia/psychology; BA(Hons), BSc(Hons), MSc

health, mental health law, ; GradCert, LlM, LlB, LPC, PGCert, MLaw, MSc, MBA

Faculty of Arts, Design & Social Sciences: www.northumbria.ac.uk/sd/academic/ sass

Dept of Arts; www.northumbria.ac.uk/sd/ academic/sass/about/arts

arts, arts & media management, music management & promotion, conservation of fine art, cultural/events management, performance, events & conference management, fine art/& education, music manage-ment, museum & heritage management, preventive conservation, theatre & performance; MA, MRes, BA(Hons), FD

Dept of Humanities; www.northumbria.ac.uk/sd/academic/ sass/about/humanities

American studies, applied linguistics, TESOL, crea-tive writing/in the classroom, English literature/& creative writing/history, history/& politics, journalism & English literature, history/& politics, linguistics, English language & literature/studies; BA(Hons), MA, PGCert, MRes, PhD, PGCert

Dept of Media & Communication Design; www.northumbria.ac.uk/sd/academic/ sass/about/media

animation, film & TV studies, graphic design, interactive media design, mass communication with management/PR/business/advertising, media, media & journalism, media production, journalism/& Eng-lish literature; BA(Hons), MA

Dept of Social Sciences & Languages; www.northumbria.ac.uk/sd/academic/sass/about/socscience

criminology & sociology/criminal justice, modern foreign languages (French, Spanish), English for academic purposes, international development/with philanthropy/policy analysis, public administration, social sciences, politics, sociology; BA(Hons), BSc, MSc, MPA, MRes, MA, PhD, MPA

Northumbria Design

3D design, design for industry, design/management, fashion management & entrepreneurship/communication/marketing/graphic design, design for interactive design futures, interactive media design, interior design, motion graphics & animation, multidisciplinary design innovation, performance production design; BA(Hons), BSc(Hons), MA, MSc, MRes, MPA, PhD, PGCert/Dip

Faculty of Engineering & Environment: www.northumbria.ac.uk/sd/academic/ee

Architecture & the Built Environment

architectural technology/engineering/studies, architecture, building design management/project management/services engineering, building design management & building information modelling, building surveying, built environment, quantity surveying, construction project management, civil engineering, project management/for construction, environmental management/health, disaster management & development, future cities, housing policy/with professional practice/& management, interior architecture, housing policy & management, international/real estate management, planning & real estate/development, quantity surveying/construction/for housing, project management, real estate, renewable & sustainable energy technology, surveying (minerals), sustainable development in the built environment; BA(Hons), BSc(Hons), MArch, BEng(Hons)

Computer Science & Business Technology

computer animation & VFX, computer games programming, computer design & production, computer & network technology/IT/science, information governance & e-disclosures, mathematics & computer science, web design & development/computing, computer & digital forensics; BSc, BEng, MEng

Mechanical & Construction Engineering

electrical & electronic engineering, electrical power engineering, engineering management, mechanical design/engineering, mechanical & automotive technology, microelectronic & communications engineering, pipeline integrity management, product design technology, professional engineering, renewable sustainable energy technologies; BSc, BEng, MEng

Mathematics & Information Science

mathematics/with business management, business information management/systems, information technology management/for business, information & library management/records management; BSc(Hons)

Physics & Electrical Engineering

physics, astrophysics, electronic design engineering, electric power engineering, microelectronic & communication engineering, electrical & electronic engineering

Geography

geography, physical geography, geography & the environment, disaster management & sustainable development, environmental health, safety, health & environmental management; BSc(Hons), BA(Hons), FdSc, MA, MSc, PGDip/Cert, PhD, ProfDip

Faculty of Health & Life Sciences

School of Health, Community & Education Studies; www.northumbria.ac.uk/sd/academic/shes

Health: clinical practice (adv critical care practice), clinical exercise physiotherapy, emergency care practice, health science, health in contemporary society, midwifery studies, healthcare/nursing leadership, nursing studies/registered nurse/child/mental health/adult/learning disabilities, occupational therapy, operating dept practice, physiotherapy, public health; AdvDipHE, BSc, MSc, PGDip, MClinPract, MNurs

Education: academic practice, childhood studies & early years, creative writing in the classroom, autism, early primary education, education with teaching & learning, guidance, counselling & early years, PGCE early years & primary/secondary, early years education/& disability studies, education studies/leadership, professional practice, post-compulsory education & training (literacy/numeracy), education with curriculum development/learning disabilities, adult learners with learning difficulties/disablement, leadership & management in integrated children's services, psychoanalytical observational studies, systematic teacher training, teaching lifelong learning (English literacy/(CPD)/mathematics/numeracy), teaching dyslexic children, secondary education (art, craft & design/PE), special education needs & inclusion, schools direct, TESOL; BA(Hons), MSc, MA, MTL, Cert/DipHE, PGDipCert

Social Work: social work/with children, young people & their families/in mental health services; BSc(Hons), PGDip/Cert, ProfDoc, PhD, Prof Doc

School of Life Sciences; www.northumbria.ac.uk/sd/academic/lifesciences

Biology, Food & Nutrition Science

applied biology, applied sciences, biology with forensic biology, biotechnology, food science/ & nutrition, human nutrition, nutritional science, microbiology; BSc(Hons), MSc

Chemical & Forensic Science

applied sciences, biomedical sciences, human biosciences, forensic science, drug design with pharmacological analysis, pharmaceutical chemistry, medical science; BSc(Hons), MC

Biomedical Sciences; www.northumbria.ac.uk/sd/academic/lifesciences/ad/biomed/bmsug txt]applied science, biomedical sciences, human biosciences, medical science; BSc(Hons)

Psychology

psychology with criminology/sport science, psychology, health psychology, occupational psychology, organisational psychology, psychology of health & wellbeing, psychology of sport & exercise behaviour; BSc(Hons), MSc, MRes

Sport & Exercise Science

applied sport science with coaching/exercise science, psychology & sport science, sport exercise & nutrition, clinical exercise psychology, psychology of sport & exercise behaviour, sport & exercise physiology, strength & conditioning; BSc(Hons), MSc, MRes

Sport Development

sport, sport coaching, sport development/management/with coaching, international sport management, professional practice in sport coaching, sport marketing; BA(Hons), BSc(Hons), MSc

UNIVERSITY OF NOTTINGHAM
www.nottingham.ac.uk

Faculty of Arts; www.nottingham.ac.uk/arts

School of American and Canadian Studies; www.nottingham.ac.uk/american

American & Canadian literature/history & culture/studies, American studies with English/history/Latin American studies/studies, American studies with film & TV studies, American studies (history/literature/visual culture), American studies with Canadian Literature/Canadian studies/European study, English and American studies; BA(Hons), MA, MRes, PhD

Dept of Archaeology; www.nottingham.ac.uk/archaeology/index.aspx

archaeology, archaeology, historical archaeology, archaeology and history of art/geography/classical civilisation/ history, natural sciences, Viking studies, archaeology, archaeological science, Mediterranean archaeology; BA(Hons), BSc(Hons), MA, MPhil

Art History; www.nottingham.ac.uk/art-history

history of art, history of art & English/archaeology/history, art history, visual culture; BA(Hons), MA

Dept of Classics; www.nottingham.ac.uk/classics

classical civilisation with art history/archaeology/English/philosophy, ancient history, classical literature, classics, English/& Latin, visual culture of classical antiquity, history; BA(Hons), MPhil/PhD

Dept of Culture, Film & Media; www.nottingham.ac.uk/cfm

cultural industries & entrepreneurship, international media & communications studies, critical theory & politics/cultural studies, modern languages & critical theory, film & TV studies, French/German/Portuguese, numerous jt degrees; BA(Hons), MA, MPhil

School of English; www.nottingham.ac.uk/english

English, English language & literature, applied linguistics/English language, creative writing, communication & entrepreneurship, creative English studies/language teaching, English literature, literary linguistics, Viking & Anglo Saxon studies, American studies/history of art/French/German/history/philosophy and English; BA(Hons), MA, MPhil, MSc, PGDip, PhD

Dept of French & Francophone Studies; www.nottingham.ac.uk/french

French studies, modern languages, French and contemporary Chinese studies, French/beginners French and English/ history/ international media communications studies/ politics/ philosophy, modern European studies/economics, modern language studies, modern languages with business/ translation, law with French and French law, management studies with French, comparative literature, translation studies, modern languages and critical theory; BA(Hons), MA, MPhil, PhD

Dept of German Studies; www.nottingham.ac.uk/german

English and German, German and contemporary Chinese studies/philosophy/politics, German, modern languages, modern language studies, modern European studies, modern languages/with business, economics with German, law with German and German law, management with German, modern and contemporary German studies, modern languages and critical theory, comparative literature studies, literatures in translation; BA(Hons), MA, MPhil, PhD

School of History; www.nottingham.ac.uk/history

history, ancient history, archaeology, British history, church history, gender history, women's studies & global gender history, environmental/international history, contemporary Chinese studies, art history, politics, local & regional history, medieval studies, modern history, Viking studies, warrior societies; BA(Hons), MA, MPhil, PhD

School of Humanities; www.nottingham.ac.uk/humanities

archaeology, art history, classics, music, culture, languages & area studies, philosophy/& theology, theology & religious studies, systemic & philosophical theology, church history; BA(Hons), BSc(Hons), MA, MSci, MSc, MPhil, PhD

School of Culture, Languages & Area Studies; www.nottingham.ac.uk/clas

American & Canadian studies, culture, film & media, comparative literature, combined studies with languages, Chinese (English) translation & interpreting, French & Francophone studies, German studies, Russian & Slavonic studies, Spanish, Portuguese & Latin American & Canadian studies, translation studies & interpreting; BA(Hons), MA, MPhil, PhD

Music; www.nottingham.ac.uk/music

music, early music, music on stage & screen, music theory & analysis, musicology, history & culture, music & philosophy; BA(Hons), MPhil, PhD

Dept of Philosophy; www.nottingham.ac.uk/philosophy

philosophy/& theology, philosophy & music/classical civilisation/English studies/French/German/economics/physics/psychology, religion, philosophy & ethics, philosophy, politics & economics, politics; BA(Hons), MA, MPhil, PhD

Russian & Slavonic Studies; www.nottingham.ac.uk/slavonic

modern languages, modern languages/with business/ studies, modern European studies, Russian studies, history and east European cultural studies, Russian and contemporary Chinese studies, economics with Russian, Russian, Serbian/Croatian, Slovene, Russian and east European studies, literatures in English translation, translation studies, comparative literature, modern languages and critical theory; BA(Hons), MA, MPhil

Spanish, Portuguese and Latin American Studies; www.nottingham.ac.uk/splas

modern languages, economics/English/history and Hispanic studies, modern languages with translation, Hispanic studies, law with Spanish and Spanish law, management with Spanish, modern European studies, modern languages/with business, Spanish and contemporary Chinese studies, Spanish and international media and communications studies, modern languages and critical theory, comparative literature, translation studies; BA(Hons), MA, MPhil, PhD

Faculty of Science; www.nottingham.ac.uk/science

School of Biosciences; www.nottingham.ac.uk/biosciences

agriculture, agricultural and crop science/environmental science, livestock science, animal science, biotechnology, environmental science/biology, food science, microbiology, nutrition/and dietetics/food science, advanced dietetic practice, advanced genomic and proteomic sciences, agrifood, animal nutrition, plant science, applied bioinformatics, applied biomolecular technology, applied biopharmaceutical biotechnology and entrepreneurship, behaviour change, brewing science/and practice, brewing and packaging, brewing/principles and practice, clinical nutrition, crop biotechnology and entrepreneurship, crop improvement, dietetics, food production management, food production management, food science and engineering, global food security, industrial physical biochemistry, nutritional sciences, plant genetic manipulation, sensory science, sustainable bioenergy/and industrial biotechnology, techniques in cell and development biology; BSc(Hons), Cert, Grad Dip, MRes, MSc, MNutrition, MPhil, PhD

School of Chemistry; www.nottingham.ac.uk/chemistry

chemistry, biochemistry, medical/& biological chemistry, chemistry, nanoscience, molecular physics, biochemistry & biological chemistry, natural sciences, green & sustainable chemistry; BSc(Hons), MChem, MPhil, MSc, MSci, PhD

School of Computer Science; www.nottingham.ac.uk/computerscience

computer science, computer science and artificial intelligence, software engineering, data science, information technology, human-computer interaction; BSc(Hons), MPhil, MSc

School of Mathematical Sciences; www.maths.nottingham.ac.uk/

mathematics, financial mathematics, data science, mathematics and economics/management studies, physics and astronomy, mathematical physics, natural sciences, financial and computational mathematics, gravity, particles and fields, mathematical medicine and biology, pure mathematics, scientific computation/with industrial mathematics/mathematical medicine and biology, statistics/and applied probability; BSc(Hons), MSc, MMath, PhD

School of Pharmacy; www.nottingham.ac.uk/pharmacy

medicinal & biological chemistry, pharmacy, drug discovery & pharmacological science; MPharm, MRes, MSc, MSci, PhD

School of Physics & Astronomy; www.nottingham.ac.uk/physics

astronomy, mathematical physics, medical physics, nanoscience, physics, physics & philosophy/astronomy/medical physics/nanoscience/theoretical astrophysics/physics/European language, chemistry & molecular physics, condensed matter theory, particle theory, ultracold atoms, magnetic resonance; BSc(Hons), MSc, MSci, PhD, MRes, MPhil

School of Psychology; www.nottingham.ac.uk/psychology

psychology/& cognitive neuroscience, brain imaging, psychology/& philosophy, psychology research-methods; BSc(Hons), MSc, PhD, DAppPsych, DEdPsych

Faculty of Engineering; www.nottingham.ac.uk/engineering

Dept of Architecture & Built Environment; www.nottingham.ac.uk/abe

architectural environment engineering, architecture, architecture & environmental design, design, energy conversion & management, environmental design, renewable energy & architecture, sustainable built environment/energy & entrepreneurship, sustainable tall buildings/building technology, theory & design, sustainable urban design, sustainable energy entrepreneurship, digital architecture & tectonics; BA(Hons), BArch(Hons), BEng(Hons), Dip Arch, MEng, MPhil, PhD

Dept of Chemical and Environmental Engineering; www.nottingham.ac.uk/scheme

chemical engineering/with environmental engineering, efficient fossil energy techniques; BEng(Hons), MEng(Hons), MPhil, MRes, MSc, PhD

Dept of Electrical & Electronic Engineering; www.nottingham.ac.uk/eee

electronic engineering, electronic and computer engineering, electrical engineering and renewable energy systems, electrical engineering, electronic engineering, electronic and computer engineering/communications engineering, electronic and communications engineering, electrical and electronic engineering/with management/mathematics, electrical transportation systems and infrastructure, modern telecommunications, electrical and electronic engineering and entrepreneurship, electrical engineering for sustainable and renewable energy, electronic communications and computer engineering, photonic and optical engineering, power electronics, sustainable transportation and electrical power systems, sustainable energy engineering, biophotonics, electromagnetics design, bioengineering imaging and sensing, electronic communications and computer engineering, photonic and optical engineering, power electronics and drives; BEng, MEng, MPhil, MRes, MSc, PGDip, PhD

Dept of Civil Engineering; www.nottingham.ac.uk/civil

civil engineering, civil & environmental engineering, civil engineering, civil engineering (engineering surveying/highways and transportation/structural engineering), risk and reliability methods, environmental management and earth observation, engineering surveying with GIS, positioning and navigation technologies; BEng(Hons), MEng(Hons), MPhil, MSc, PhD

Dept of Mechanical, Materials and Manufacturing Engineering; www.nottingham.ac.uk/schoolm3

advanced materials, aerospace technologies, applied ergonomics & the human factor, biomedical materials science, bioengineering, biomaterials & biomechanics/imaging & sensing/the digital body, human factors & ergonomics, manufacturing engineering & management, mechanical engineering, product design & manufacture, usability & human-computer interaction; BEng, MEng, MSc, PGCert, PhD

Faculty of Medicine & Health Science; www.nottingham.ac.uk/mhs/index.aspx

School of Life Sciences; www.nottingham.ac.uk/life-sciences

biochemistry, biology, genetics, neuroscience and zoology (biochemistry and molecular medicine, human genetics and tropical sciences), medicine, pharmacy, biochemistry & biological chemistry, biochemistry & genetics, clinical science, drug discovery and pharmaceutical sciences, immunology and allergy, integrated physiology in health and disease, microbiology and immunology, molecular genetics and diagnostics, molecular medical microbiology, sports and exercise science; BSc, MSc, MSci, PhD, MRes, MPharm, BMMS

School of Medicine; www.nottingham.ac.uk/scs

epidemiology and public health, public health, public health (international health), child health, obstetrics & gynaecology, assisted reproduction technology, cancer and stem cells, cancer immunology and biotechnology, oncology, stem cell technology, psychiatry and applied psychology, clinical psychology, forensic and criminological psychology, forensic psychology, management psychology, mental health research, occupational psychology, work and organisational psychology, workplace health and wellbeing, medical education, habilitation and ageing, health psychology, rehabilitation psychology, rheumatology, orthopaedics and dermatology, sports and exercise medicine, clinical neuroscience, translational neuroimaging; FRCS(Orth), MMedSci, DM, MSc, PhD, BM, BS, MPH, DForensPsych

Faculty of Social Sciences, Law & Education; www.nottingham.ac.uk/social-sciences/index.aspx

School of Contemporary Chinese Studies; www.nottingham.ac.uk/chinese

accounting & finance for contemporary Chinese, business & economy of contemporary China, globalisation & /contemporary Chinese studies, international relations & contemporary Chinese studies; BA, MSc, MSci, PhD

Economics; www.nottingham.ac.uk/economics

economics, economics and econometrics/international economics, economics with Chinese studies/French/German/Hispanic studies/Russian, economics and philosophy, mathematics and economics, politics and economics, philosophy, politics and economics, applied economics, economic development and policy analysis, applied economics and financial economics, economics, economics and development economics, economics and financial economics, behavioural economics; BA(Hons), BSc(Hons), MPhil, PGDip, PhD

School of Education; www.nottingham.ac.uk/education

adv counselling practice, counselling/children & young people / & psychotherapy, creativity, arts, literacy & learning, creative professional practice in arts & education, education, initial teacher training, school direct/school central ITT, (PGCE) – secondary (English, geography, history/international, humanistic counselling, international advice & support, mathematics, modern languages, science), PGCE (primary), mentoring & coaching/beginner teachers, educational leadership & management, special needs, trauma studies, learning technology & education, person-centred experiential counselling & psychotherapy, teaching English for academic purposes, special needs, TESOL, TCOL; BA(Hons), MA, MPhil, MRes, PGCE, PGCert/Dip, PhD, SCITT, EdD

School of Geography; www.nottingham.ac.uk/geography

geography/with Chinese/business, environmental management, GIS, geospatial intelligence, environmental geoscience, human geography, physical geography, landscape & culture, contaminated land management; BA(Hons), BS(Hons), MArts, PhD, MRes

School of Law; www.nottingham.ac.uk/law

law, law with French & French law/German and German law/Spanish & Spanish law, senior status law, American/Australian/European/Chinese/New Zealand law, environmental law, human rights law, international law/& development, international commercial law, criminal justice, international criminal law, European law, international law, international law/and development, law & environmental science, maritime law, public international law, procurement law, security & terrorism, senior status, sociolegal & criminal research; BA(Hons), LlB, LlM, MA, MSc, PhD

Nottingham University Business School; www.nottingham.ac.uk/business

accountancy, finance, accounting and management, international management, industrial economics/with insurance, management, management with French/German/Spanish/Chinese studies, accounting and finance, banking and finance/risk/managerial economics, business and management, corporate social responsibility, corporate strategy & governance, entrepreneurship, innovation and management, finance and investment, HRM and organisation, industrial engineering/information systems and operations management, international business, logistics and supply chain management, management, management, science and operations management, marketing, operations management, risk management supply chain and operations management, sustainability, applied biopharmaceutical biotechnology and entrepreneurship, communication/crop biotechnology/cultural industries/electrical and electronic engineering and entrepreneurship
MBAs; finance, entrepreneurship, corporate social responsibility, executive
BA(Hons), MBA, MA, MSc

Politics & International Relations; www.nottingham.ac.uk/politics

Asian & international studies, diplomacy, international relations/ & global issues, international security & terrorism, politics/& economics/contemporary history/history/American studies/German/French, social and global justice, war & contemporary conflict, European politics, politics, philosophy & economics; BA(Hons), MA, MPhil, MRes, PhD

School of Sociology and Social Policy; www.nottingham.ac.uk/sociology

criminology, global citizenship, identities & human rights, science & technology public administration/policy, social & cultural studies, international/social policy, social work, sociology/& social policy, criminology & social policy; BA(Hons), MA, MPA, MPhil, MSWS, PhD, PGCert, MPA

NOTTINGHAM TRENT UNIVERSITY
www.ntu.ac.uk

School of Animal, Rural and Environmental Sciences; www.ntu.ac.uk/ares

animal science, environmental conservation and countryside management, horticulture/garden design, sport horse management and coaching, wildlife conservation, food science and technology, animal biology, zoo biology, environmental conservation/science, equine sports science, equestrian psychology and sports science, geography (physical), geography, wildlife conservation, international horticulture, veterinary nursing science, food science and technology, horticulture
Postgrad: biodiversity conservation, endangered species recovery and conservation, equine performance, health and welfare, global food security and development, applied anthrozoology, animal health and welfare, food industry management; BSc(Hons), MSc/MRes/PGCert/PGDip, FdSc

School of Architecture, Design and Built Environment; www.ntu.ac.uk/adbe

adv property design engineering, architecture, architectural technology & design, built environment studies, civil engineering design & construction, commercial management, construction/management, interior architecture & design, international real estate investment & finance, civil engineering, furniture & product design, building/quantity surveying, planning & development, real estate, construction management, medical product design, planning/& design, urban design & residential development, product design (business/finance), project management (construction), property finance & investment, innovation & management, quantity surveying & construction, smart design, structural engineering/with management/materials, smart design; BSc(Hons), MA, MSc, MArch, PGDip/Cert, PhD

School of Art & Design; www.ntu.ac.uk/art

fashion design, fashion knitwear design and knitted textiles, fashion communication and promotion, fashion management, fashion marketing and branding, international fashion business, textile design innovation, fashion and textile design, creative pattern cutting, international fashion management, fashion marketing, fashion communications, luxury fashion brand management, art & design media practice, graphic design, photography, media creatives, costume design and king, decorative arts, design for film and television, fine art, theatre design, branding and identity, illustration, graphic design theory and practice, film practice, puppetry and digital animation, fine art; BA(Hons), GradDip, MA, MPhil, PhD, FdA, MFA

School of Arts & Humanities; www.ntu.ac.uk/hum

English, broadcast/magazine/newspaper/documentary/print journalism, creative writing, global studies, European studies, film & TV, Chinese (Mandarin), TESOL, ELT, history, Holocaust & genocide studies, international relations, museum & heritage management, English literature, human security & environmental change, international development, linguistics, media journalism with communication, media globalisation, media, philosophy, French, Spanish, German, Italian, Latin American studies; BA(Hons), MA, PGDip/Cert, MPhil, PhD

Nottingham Business School; www.ntu.ac.uk/nbs

business management, management and leadership, business, management, economics, economics with business/international finance & banking/trade & development, accounting and finance, international business/with French/Spanish, management and HRM/international business/finance/marketing/global supply chain management/entrepreneurship, management & HR/marketing, global management & marketing, entrepreneurship/marketing, marketing, digital marketing, branding & marketing, business administration, management and leadership, public services management, HE administration, management & leadership; BA(Hons), DBA, MBA, MSc, BIntBan, MBA, BSc(Hons)

School of Education; www.ntu.ac.uk/edu

primary education (PGCE), PGCE secondary science/design and technology, secondary science education, Schools Direct training, post compulsory education & training, school centred initial teacher training, mathematics and secondary education, childhood studies, education studies, early years and digital learning, special and inclusive education and digital learning, early years and psychology/special and inclusive education, education studies and early years/psychology/special and inclusive education, psychology/special and inclusive education, secondary design and technology education, science, engineering and mathematics education, computing in education, education studies, education, early years initial teaching training, primary and secondary teaching, primary, secondary and post-compulsory teaching; BA(Hons), BSc(Hons), MA, MSc, FdA, PGDE, PGCE, PGCert, ProfCert, ProfDoc

Nottingham Law School; www.ntu.ac.uk/nls

law, business law, corporate & insolvency law, human rights & justice, employment law, health law & ethics, European/& insolvency law, international law, intellectual property law, international/trade & commercial law, law & criminality/psychology, oil, gas & mining law, senior status, sports law, legal practice; GDL, GradDip, LlB, LlM, LPC, PhD

School of Science & Technology; www.ntu.ac.uk/sat

Biological Sciences, biomedical science, biochemistry, microbiology, pharmacology, applied biosciences, bioinformatics, biotechnology, environmental management, molecular cell biology, pharmacology, neuropharmacology, molecular microbiology

Chemistry, pharmaceutical and medicinal chemistry, advanced materials engineering, analytical chemistry, pharmaceutical analysis, pharmaceutical and medicinal science

Computer Science, computer science (games technology), software engineering, computer systems engineering, computer systems (networks), computer systems (forensic and security), computing, digital media technology, information systems, information and communication, technology, computer science, computer systems engineering, computing systems, computer games systems, internet and security, cloud and enterprise computing, interactive media engineering, engineering (cybernetics and communications/electronics), engineering management, data analytics for business, computer science, electronic systems

Forensic Science, forensic science (physical), forensic biology

Mathematics, financial mathematics, computer science and mathematics, sport science and mathematics

Physics, physics with nuclear technology/forensic applications/astrophysics, medical and materials imaging

Sport science and management, sport and exercise science, coaching and sport science, exercise, nutrition and health, sport and leisure management, exercise physiology, performance nutrition, performance analysis, biomechanics, sport and exercise psychology; FdSc, MChem, MRes, MSc, MSci, PhD, MComp(Hons), MMath

School of Social Sciences; www.ntu.ac.uk/soc

applied child psychology, adv professional practice in careers guidance, criminology, children's services, counselling & psychotherapy, forensic mental health/psychology, health & social care, international relations, psychology/ with criminology/sociology, psychological research methods, psychology, well-being & mental health, politics, professional practice, public health, social work, sociology/& politics, youth justice/work/studies; BA(Hons), MA, MRes, MSc, PGDip/Cert, PhD, ProfDoc

Degrees validated by Nottingham Trent University offered at:

SOUTHAMPTON SOLENT UNIVERSITY
www.solent.ac.uk

www.solent.ac.uk/courses

Art, Design & Fashion

Fashion

fashion, fashion buying & merchandising, fashion graphics, fashion marketing with management, fashion photography, fashion promotion & communication, fashion styling, fashion with PR, make-up & hair design, writing fashion & culture, fashion retail/management/journalism, fashion merchandising management

Photography

photography, fashion photography, photojournalism

Visual Arts & Design

animation, computer & video games, computer generated images, fine art, graphic design/web & mobile devices, illustration, interior design/decoration, product design, special effects, visual art, fashion, web design & management, digital graphics for web; BA(Hons), BSc(Hons), FdA, MA

Built Environment

architectural technology, construction management, interior design/decoration, civil engineering, quantity surveying; BA(Hons), BSc(Hons)

Business, Management and Law

accounting & finance, international business economics, business & economics, international/business management, business (professional development), business administration, international management, business, business & management/marketing, law, politics & international relations, professional practice, business administration, criminology & criminal justice, management, project management, promotional media, retail management, business management, HRM, personnel & development, law, international trade regulation, business information technology, information technology management, information technology for business, international trade research, advertising, events management, fashion buying & merchandising, fashion promotion & communication, fashion with PR, marketing/with advertising/management, music promotion & culture, PR & communication, sound media, advertising & PR, media communication & culture, creative advertising, PR; BA(Hons), BSc(Hons), LlB, LlM, FdA, MBA, PGD, MSc

Computing, Games and Networking; computing & video games, computer games, software development, computer generation imagery, computer networks & web design, computer systems & networks, digital analysis, network security management, web design & management/development, computing, software engineering, business information technology, information technology management, information technology for business; BA(Hons), BSc(Hons)

Engineering and Yacht Design; electronic engineering, engineering design & manufacture, mechanical engineering, production design, manufacturing & mechanical engineering, applied acoustics, yacht &

power craft design, yacht design, & production, BEng(Hons), BA(Hons), BSc(Hons), MSc

Geography and Tourism; geography with environmental studies/marine studies, events management, international/tourism management, adventure & outdoor activities; BA(Hons), BSc(Hons)

Maritime; maritime, business, shipping & port management, marine engineering & management, marine electrical & electronic engineering, marine engineering, international marine business – international shipping & logistics, shipping operations, management; BEng(Hons), BSc(Hons), FdEng, MSc

Media and Media Technology; broadcasting systems, computer generated imagery, digital media, film, film & TV studies, film production, live sound, technology, music systems, outside broadcasting (production operations), screenwriting, sound engineering, sound for film, TV special effects/production, TV & video production, TV postproduction/studio production, marketing with advertising management, music management/promotion, media culture & production, media production/writing, audio engineering/technology, digital music, live sound technology, media technology, music studio technology, outside broadcast/production operations, social media, sound engineering, sound for film, TV & games, TV production technology; BSc(Hons), BA(Hons)

Music and Performance; live & studio performance, live sound technology, pop music journalism/production, sound for film, TV & games, music management & promotion; BSc(Hons), BA(Hons)

Health and Social Sciences; criminal investigation with psychology, criminology/psychology, psychology (criminal behaviour/counselling), fitness/management & personal training, health, exercise & physical activity, psychology (counselling/criminal behaviour/education/health), criminology & counselling, social work, criminology & criminal justice; BA(Hons), BSc(Hons), MSc

Sport and Fitness; applied sport science, athletic performance, fitness & physical training, fitness management & sport training, health, exercise & physical activity, sports coaching & development, adventure & extreme sport management, football studies/& business, sport & PE, sport studies, sport & development, athlete performance & peak performance; BA(Hons), BSc(Hons), MA, MSc

Writing and Communication; English & education/creative writing/film/magazine journalism/PR/screenwriting, media writing, fashion journalism, journalism, magazine journalism, multimedia journalism, photojournalism, pop music/sports journalism, advertising/& PR, event management, fashion buying & merchandising, fashion promotion & communication, fashion with PR, PR & communications, marketing with advertising management, media communication & culture, promotional media, music/production/promotion/management, publishing, social media; BA(Hons), MA

THE OPEN UNIVERSITY
www.open.ac.uk

Faculties of the University and Qualifications conferred

Faculty of Arts; www.open.ac.uk/Arts
BA(Hons), MA, PGDip, PhD

Faculty of Health & Social Care; www.open.ac.uk/health-and-social-care
BA/BSc(Hons), FD, MA, CertHE, Dip/CertHE

Open University Business School; www.open.ac.uk/business-school
BA/BSc, Diplomas, Dip/CertHE, FD, MA, MSc, PGDip/Cert, MBA

Faculty of Education & Language Sciences; www.open.ac/uk/education -and-language-studies
Ba(Hons), BSc(Hons), Diplomas, Cert/DipHE, Certificated, PGCE, PGDE, QTS, MEd, DEd

Open University Law School; www.open.ac.uk/law
LlB(Hons), PGDip, LlM

Faculty of Mathematics, Computing & Technology; www.open.ac.uk/mathematics-computing-and-technology
BSc(Hons), BA/BSc(Hons), BEng(Hons), MEng, FD, Dip/CertHE, DipHE, MSc

Faculty of Science; www.open.ac.uk/science

BSc(Hons), DipHE, FD, MSc

Faculty of Social Sciences; www.open.ac.uk/social-sciences

BSc(Hons), BA(Hons), FD, DipHE, Dip/CertHE, MA, PGDip

Institute of Educational Technology; www.open.ac.uk/iet

MAODE, EdD, PhD

Courses Offered

Arts & Humanities

criminology and law, humanities, philosophy and psychological studies, politics, philosophy and economics, youth justice studies, psychology/ and law, classical studies, English language and literature, English literature/and creative writing, history, design and innovation, computing & IT, language studies

Business & Management

business management, business management (sport and football), computing & IT and a second subject, healthcare practice, combined professional studies, management, accounting

Computing & IT

computing and IT, computing and IT practice, computing & IT and a second subject

Design

design and innovation

Education, Childhood & Youth

childhood and youth studies, youth work, early years, youth justice studies, sport, fitness and coaching, mathematics and its learning, working with young people, primary teaching and learning, working with young people, childhood practice, primary teaching and learning, sport and fitness, professional practice, supporting teaching and learning in primary schools, sport, fitness and management, mathematics education, working together for children, effective practice (youth justice)
BA(Hons), BSc(Hons), Diplomas, Cert/DipHE, Certificates, PGCE, PGDE, QTS, MA, MEd, DEd

Environment & Development

international studies, environmental management and technology, environmental science, natural sciences, design and innovation, environmental studies

Engineering

engineering, environmental management and technology, engineering

Health & Social Care

health and social care, health sciences, healthcare and health science, nursing practice, adult nursing, psychology with counselling, childhood and youth studies, social work, youth work, youth justice studies, mental health nursing, healthcare practice, counselling, working with young people, childhood practice, social care, adult health and social care, children and families, health and social care, promoting public health, end-of-life care, working together for children, effective practice (youth justice)

Health & Wellbeing

sport, fitness and coaching, healthcare and health science, health sciences, mental health nursing, sport and fitness, healthcare practice, sport, fitness and management, health sciences, end-of-life care, promoting public health

Languages

humanities, language studies, English language and literature, English literature, English literature and creative writing, classical studies

Law

criminology and law, psychology and law, laws, youth justice studies

Mathematics & Statistics

mathematics and statistics, computing & IT and a second subject, economics and mathematical sciences, mathematics, mathematics and physics, mathematics and its Learning, mathematics education

Medical Sciences

health sciences, paramedic science

Nursing & Healthcare Practice

nursing practice, health and social care, health sciences, children and families, healthcare with health science, healthcare practice, promoting public health

Psychology & Counselling

combined social sciences, philosophy and psychological studies, computing & IT and a second subject, criminology and psychological studies, psychology, psychology and law, psychology with counselling, forensic psychology, social psychology, childhood and youth studies, counselling, healthcare practice, children and families

Science

health sciences, natural sciences, mathematics and physics, environmental science, environmental studies, environmental management and technology, environment, paramedic science, physics, astronomy and planetary science

Social Sciences

combined social sciences, politics, philosophy and economics, economics and mathematical sciences, environmental studies, philosophy and psychological studies, social policy and criminology, computing &

IT and a second subject, criminology and psychological studies, forensic psychology, psychology, psychology and law, psychology with counselling, criminology and law, international studies, youth justice studies, social psychology, childhood and youth studies, counselling, combined social sciences, environmental management and technology, social policy and criminology, criminology and law, healthcare practice, children and families

Technology

environmental management and technology

UNIVERSITY OF OXFORD
www.ox.ac.uk

Division of Humanities; www.ox.ac.uk/ divisions/humanities

Rothermere American Institute; www.rai.ox.ac.uk

American studies/history/politics/literature; MSt

Faculty of Classics; www.classics.ox.ac.uk

classics, classics and English/ modern languages/ oriental studies, classical archaeology and ancient history, ancient and modern history, Greek and/or Roman history, Greek and/or Latin languages and literature, ancient history, classical languages and literature, classical archaeology, late antique & Byzantine; BA(Hons), MPhil, MSt, DPhil

Ruskin School of Drawing and Fine Art; www.ruskin-sc.ox.ac.uk

art history & theory, contemporary art, drawing, fine art, theoretical & practice-led research, history of art & visual culture; BFA, MLitt, DPhil

Faculty of English, Language & Literature; www.english.ox.ac.uk

English language and literature (650–1550; 1550–1700; 1600–1830; 1800–1914; 1900–present day), English & modern languages/classics/history, literature in English, English language, English & American studies, English studies/medieval studies, history & English, Shakespeare, women's studies: film aesthetics, studio world literatures in English; BA(Hons), DPhil, MLitt, MPhil, MSt

History of Art Department; www.hoa.ox.ac.uk

history of art, authenticity and replication in art and visual culture, French painting, 1880–1912, gothic: artistic originality and the transmission of style in

medieval art, image and thought, media and modernity: art and mass culture, 1880–2000, portraiture as genre, the apparatus of art history, theories of vision: the eye and the gaze, women, art and culture in early modern Europe
BA(Hons), DPhil, MLitt, MSt

Faculty of History; www.history.ox.ac.uk

ancient & modern history, British history, British and European history, from 1500 to the present, economic and social history, global and imperial history, history of art and visual culture, history of science, medicine and technology, late Antique and Byzantine studies, medieval history, modern South Asian Studies, US history; BA(Hons), DPhil, MPhil, MSc, MSt, MLetters

Faculty of Linguistics, Philology and Phonetics; www.ling-phil.ox.ac.uk

comparative philology & comparative philosophy, historical philology, structure of language, Indo-European languages, linguistics theory, philology & phonetics, psychology, philosophy, & linguistics, modern languages & linguistics; BA, MPhil, PhD, MSt

Faculty of Medieval & Modern Languages; www.mod-langs.ox.ac.uk

Celtic, comparative literature, medieval literature, cultural studies, Czech, Catalan, Galician, French, German, Slavonic languages, enlightenment, women's studies, film aesthetics, medieval studies, linguistic theory, history & modern languages, modern Greek, Italian, language history, linguistics/ medieval & modern languages, European & mid Eastern languages, general linguistics, Italian, Polish, Portuguese, Russian, Spanish, Slavonic languages, modern Greek, Yiddish; BA(Hons), DPhil, MPhil, MSt

Faculty of Music; www.music.ox.ac.uk

chamber music, choral studies/conducting performance, composition & analysis, dance music, musicology, ethnomusicology, historical musicology, jazz, musical history/theory, the motet in the 14/15th centuries, orchestration, music analysis & criticism, performance & interpretation, psychology of music, theory & analysis, source studies, technology of composition, south Western music theory; BMus, DPhil, MA(Hons), MPhil, MSt, MLitt

Faculty of Oriental Studies; www.orinst.ox.ac.uk

Arabic, Persian, Turkish, Sanskrit, Buddhist studies, Aramaic with Syriac, Armenian, Coptic, Hindi and Urdu, Korean, Old Iranian, Pali, and Prakrit, Chinese studies, Armenian, Pali, Hindi & Urdu, classic & oriental studies, eastern Christianity, Egyptology & ancient Near East, European & Middle East languages, Asia & Near Asian studies, Hebrew & Jewish studies, Islamic world, Japanese studies, Korean studies, theology & oriental studies; BA(Hons), DPhil, MPhil, MSt

Faculty of Philosophy; www.philosophy.ox.ac.uk

early modern philosophy, knowledge and reality, ethics: philosophy of mind, philosophy of science and social science, philosophy of religion, the philosophy of logic and language, aesthetics, medieval philosophy: Aquinas/Duns Scotus and Ockham, the philosophy of Kant, post-Kantian philosophy, theory of politics, Plato, Republic, Aristotle, Frege, Russell and Wittgenstein, formal logic, philosophy of physics, philosophy of mathematics, philosophy of science, philosophy of cognitive science, the philosophy and economics of the environment, philosophical logic, Plato, Latin philosophy, jurisprudence; BA(Hons), BPhil, MPhil, PhD

Faculty of Theology; www.theology.ox.ac.uk

theology & religion/oriental studies, philosophy & theology, Old Testament, New Testament, biblical interpretation, Christian ethics, philosophical theology, science & religion, modern/Reformation/scholastic/patristic theology, ecclesiastical history, the study of religions, issues in theology, Judaism and Christianity in the Graeco-Roman world; BA(Hons), BTh, MTh, MSt, MLitt, MPhil, DPhil, PGDip/Cert

Division of Mathematical, Physical and Life Sciences: www.ox.ac.uk/divisions/mpls

Dept of Chemistry; www.chem.ox.ac.uk

chemical biology, inorganic chemistry, mathematical techniques, medical chemistry, molecular biochemistry/& chemical biology, organic chemistry/reactions/synthesis, organometallic chemistry, physical & theoretical chemistry, quantum mechanics, reaction mechanisms, solid state chemistry, spectroscopy, theoretical chemistry, thermodynamics; DPhil, MChem, MSc

Dept of Computer Science; www.cs.ox.ac.uk

computer science, mathematics & computer science, modelling & scientific computing, mathematics & foundations of computer science & philosophy, software engineering, software & systems security; BA(Hons), MSc, DPhil, PhD

Dept of Engineering Science; www.eng.ox.ac.uk

automotive engineering, aerothermal engineering, micromechanics and materials modelling, mechanical performance and integrity, advanced structures, biotechnics, hydraulics, sustainable energy, environmental engineering, bioprocesses, process systems, chemical engineering, production engineering, optoelectronics, microelectronics, communications, power electronics, machine vision and robotics, machine learning, multivariable control, nonlinear and predictive control, medical imaging and informatics, cellular engineering and therapy, dynamic systems, chaos, optimization and mathematical models, autonomous intelligent machines and systems CDT, gas turbines aerodynamics CDT; DPhil, MEng, MSc, EngD

Life Science Interface; Doctoral Training Centre; www.lsi.ox.ac.uk

biological systems, biological experimental techniques, biological physics, organic chemistry, molecular genetics & cell biology, mathematical biology, medicinal chemistry, programming, bioinformatics, statistical data systems, structural biology; DPhil

Division of Materials; www.materials.ox.ac.uk

materials science, materials structures & mechanical properties of metals, electrical/mechanical properties, nanoelectronics, materials economics, non-metallic materials, composites, polymers, packaging/

superconducting/semiconducting materials, structural & nuclear materials, device materials, nanomaterials, process & manufacturing, characterisation, computational nuclear modelling; DPhil, MEng, MSc, MS, MEm

Mathematical Institute; www.maths.ox.ac.uk

mathematics, mathematics and statistics/philosophy/computer science/theoretical physics, partial differential equations: analysis and applications, industrially focused mathematical modelling, mathematical modelling and scientific computing, mathematics and foundations of computer science, mathematical finance, mathematical and computation finance, computation and applied statistics; BA(Hons), DPhil, MCF, MFoCS, MS, MSc, MMath

Dept of Physics; www.physics.ox.ac.uk

physics, atmospheric oceanic & planetary physics, astrophysics, biological physics, condensed matter physics, cosmology, general relativity, quantum theory, sub-atomic physics, particle physics, physics, atomic & laser/theoretical/molecular physics, physics & philosophy; BA(Hons), DPhil, MPhys, MPhysPhil

Dept of Plant Science; www.plants.ox.ac.uk/plants

biochemistry & systems biology, biological science, cell biology/physiology, cell & development biology, comparative developmental genetics, ecology, evolution & systematics, plant science; DPhil, MRes, MSc

Dept of Statistics; www.stats.ox.ac.uk

applied statistics, mathematics & statistics, applied probability & research in statistics; BA(Hons), DPhil, MMath, MSc, PGDip

Dept of Zoology; www.zoo.ox.ac.uk

animal behaviour/welfare, ageing biology, biological science, disease, ecology, evolution, food science, molecular biology & bioinformatics, indigenous biology, ornithology, integrative bioscience, wildlife conservation; DPhil, MRes, MSc

Biological Science; www.biologyy.ox.ac.uk

organisms, cells & genes, ecology, qualitative methods, evolution, adaptation to the environment, cell & developmental biology, animal behaviour, disease, plants

Division of Medical Sciences; www.ox.ac.uk/divisions/medical_science

Dept of Biochemistry; www.bioch.ox.ac.uk

molecular cell biology, biological chemistry and biophysical chemistry, organic chemistry and maths & statistics, macromolecular structure and function, bioenergetics and metabolism, genetics and molecular biology, cell biology, molecular immunology, plant molecular biology, neuropharmacology, membrane transport, glycobiology, human disease, bionanotechnology, systems biology and signalling to the nucleus, biochemistry, medical sciences, chromosome & developmental biology, structural biology, infection, immunity and translational medicine; DPhil, MBiochem, MSc, PhD

Nuffield Dept of Clinical Medicine; www.ndm.ox.ac.uk

cancer biology, genetics & genomics, immunology & infectious diseases, protein science & structural biology, physiology, cellular & molecular biology, tropical medicine & global health; PhD, MSc

Dept of Clinical Neurosciences; www.ndcn.ox.ac.uk

medicine, biomedical sciences, experimental psychology, psychology, biochemistry, clinical neurology, functional MRI of the brain, anaesthesia, ophthalmology; DPhil, MSc

Dept of Experimental Psychology; www.psy.ox.ac.uk

clinical/experimental psychology, psychology, philosophy & linguistics, neuroscience, psychological research; BA(Hons), DPhil, MSc

Radcliffe Department of Medicine

Division of Cardiovascular Medicine, Oxford Centre for Diabetes, Endocrinology and Metabolism, MRC Weatherall Institute of Molecular Medicine, Nuffield Division of Clinical Laboratory Sciences, The Oxford Acute Vascular Imaging Centre, Centre for the Advancement of Sustainable Medical Innovation Investigative Medicine Division

Nuffield Dept of Obstetrics & Gynaecology; www.obs-gyn.ox.ac.uk

obstetrics & gynaecology, clinical embryology; MSc, DPhil

Dept of Oncology; www.oncology.ox.ac.uk

oncology, radiation biology, experimental therapeutics, clinical pharmacy, medical oncology, radiation oncology & radiobiology; DPhil, MRes, MSc

Department of Orthopaedics, Rheumatology and Musculoskeletal Sciences; www.ndorms.ox.ac.uk

orthopaedics, rheumatology, musculoskeletal sciences, translational medicine & medical technology, immunology; MSc, DPhil

Dept of Paediatrics; www.paediatrics.ox.ac.uk

paediatric infection and immunity, paediatric infectious diseases, international child health, paediatric endocrinology and diabetes, paediatric haematology, neonatology, paediatric gastroenterology and nutrition, HIV infection and immune control, molecular infectious diseases, developmental immunology, paediatric neuroimaging and pain, vaccinology; PhD, MSc

Sir William Dunn School of Pathology; www.path.ox.ac.uk

bacteriology and virology, cell biology, immunology, microbiology and molecular biology; DPhil

Dept of Pharmacology; www.pharm.ox.ac.uk

pharmacology, experimental therapeutics, research in pharmacology, practical drug therapy, medical chemistry for cancer; MSc, DPhil

Dept of Physiology, Anatomy and Genetics; www.dpag.ox.ac.uk

ion channels & transporters, functional genomics & genetics, neuroscience, cardiovascular science; MPhil, MSc, DPhil

Nuffield Department of Population Health; www.ndph.ox.ac.uk

global health science, population technology, population health, ethics & law, medical sociology, population pathology, integrated population health, global health, preventive medicine; DPhil, MSc

Nuffield Dept of Primary Health Sciences; www.phc.ox.ac.uk

patient and the doctor, communication skills telehealth and self-management of long-term conditions, evidence-based health care, behavioural medicine, cancer research, evidence-based medicine, health service economics and organisation, chronic kidney disease, clinical trials, tobacco addiction, diabetes and long-term conditions, health experiences research, heart failure research, hypertension, infectious diseases research; DPhil, MSc

Dept of Psychiatry; www.psychiatry.ox.ac.uk

experimental psychology, psychology & philosophy, psychology & linguistics, philosophy & linguistics, mood disorders, behavioural & cognitive neurosciences, schizophrenia & psychiatry, human development, clinical trials, translational neurosciences, experimental medicine, criminality & aggression, self harm mental health, epidemiology, society & mental health, neuropsychological treatment, psychiatry & medicine, emotion & motivation, clinical neuroscience, psychopharmacology; MSc, DPhil, MRCPsych

Nuffield Dept of Surgical Science; www.surgery.ox.ac.uk

endovascular neurosurgery, integrated Immunology, surgical science, ageing and degenerative diseases, cancer, cardiac/cardiovascular sciences, cell biology and genes, clinical trials and epidemiology, diabetes, evidence-based medicine, immunology, musculoskeletal science, neurosciences, oncology, stem cells, translational medicine and medical technology; DPhil, MCh, MS, MSc

Division of Social Sciences; www.socsci.ox.ac.uk

School of Anthropology and Museum Ethnography; www.anthro.ox.ac.uk

social anthropology, social anthropology of selected regions, topics in material anthropology, themes in anthropology, medical anthropology, cognitive & evolutionary anthropology, material & museum anthropology, migration studies, refugee & forced migration studies, material anthropology & museum ethnography; BA, BSc, DPhil, MPhil, MSc

Pitt Rivers Museum; www.prm.ox.ac.uk

material anthropology, museum ethnography, sound & music; DPhil, MPhil, MSc

School of Archaeology; www.arch.ox.ac.uk

archaeology & anthropology, bioarchaeology, Eurasian prehistory, classical archaeology & ancient history, historical & classical chronology, materials & technology, chronology, Eurasian prehistory, Palaeolithic archaeological science; BA(Hons), DPhil, MLitt, MSc, MSt

SAID Business School; www.sbs.ox.ac.uk

law and finance, major programme management, MBA economics and management, management studies, executive MBA, financial economics, strategic management, financial strategy, global business, organisational leadership, strategy and innovation, cyber risk for managers, finance, high performance leadership, performing leaders, private equity, real estate, women's transforming leadership; BA, Dip, MBA, Exec MBA, MSc

Dept of Economics; www.economics.ox.ac.uk

economics, macroeconomics, microeconomics, quantitative economics, British economic history since 1870, command & transitional economies, comparative demographic systems, econometrics, economics of developing countries, economics of industry, finance, game theory, international economics, labour economics & industrial relations, mathematical methods, microeconomic theory, money & banking, philosophy & economics of the environment, public economics, economics, economics for development, financial economics; BA(Hons), DPhil, MEng, MSc

Dept of Education; www.education.ox.ac.uk

applied linguistics, education (comparative & international education/higher education/learning & technology/research), learning and teaching/in HE, PGCE (numerous secondary subjects, Schools Direct), teaching English in university setting; DPhil, MSc, PGCE, PGDip

School of Geography & the Environment; www.geog.ox.ac.uk

geographical research, space, place and society, earth system dynamics, African societies, biogeography, biodiversity and conservation, climate change and variability, climate change impacts and adaptation, complexity, cultural spaces: geographies of affective experience, desert landscapes and dynamics, European integration, forensic geography, geographies of finance, geographies of nature, geopolitics in the margins, heritage science and conservation, post-Soviet Russia in transition, transport and mobilities, geography and the environment, biodiversity, conservation and management, environmental change and management, nature, society and environmental governance, water science, policy and management; BA(Hons), DPhil, MSc

School of Interdisciplinary Area Studies; www.area-studies.ox.ac.uk

African studies, modern Japanese studies, contemporary Chinese studies, Russian & East European studies, Latin American studies, Middle Eastern studies, public policy in Latin America, contemporary India; MSc, MPhil, DPhil

Dept of International Development; www.qeh.ox.ac.uk

development studies, economics for development, international development, refugee & forced migration studies, global governance, diplomacy; Cert/Dip, DPhil, MPhil, MSc

Oxford Internet Institute; www.oii.ox.ac.uk

social science of the internet, information, communication & the social sciences; DPhil, MSc

Faculty of Law; www.law.ox.ac.uk

law, law with law studies in Europe, legal studies, law and finance, criminology and criminal justice, administrative law, commercial law, English and French law, comparative law, competition law, constitutional law, environmental law, EU law, law and finance, human rights law, intellectual property law, jurisprudence, labour law, medical law and ethics, law of property, public international law, regulation, corporate law, law of obligations, socio-legal studies; BA(Hons), BCL, Dip, DPhil, MJur, MLitt, MPhil, MSc, MSt, PGDip

Oxford Martin School; www.oxfordmartin.ox.ac.uk

research in health & medicine, energy & environment, technology & society, ethics & governance

Oxford-Man Institute of Quantitative Finance; www.oxford-man.ox.ac.uk

consumer and socially responsible finance, data analysis and patterns in data, decision making under uncertainty and asset allocation, efficient markets, risk premia and market anomalies, electronic trading, numerical methods and high performance computing in finance, pensions, investments and hedge fund industry, stability of financial systems

Dept of Politics & International Relations; www.politics.ox.ac.uk

history and politics, international relations, philosophy, political theory, philosophy, politics and economics, politics (comparative government/European politics and society/political theory), PPE; BA(Hons), DPhil, MLitt, MPhil, MSc

Dept of Social Policy & Intervention; www.spi.ox.ac.uk

comparative social policy, evidence-based social intervention and policy evaluation, social policy or social intervention, social policy, social intervention

BA, MPhil, MSc

Dept of Sociology; www.sociology.ox.ac.uk
sociology, history & politics, human sciences, philosophy, politics & economics, sociology and demography; BA(Hons), DPhil, MPhil, MSc

OXFORD BROOKES UNIVERSITY
www.brookes.ac.uk

Faculty of Business; www.brookes.ac.uk/about/faculties/business

Business School; www.business.brookes.ac.uk
accounting and finance, automotive management, business and business and automotive management, business and enterprise/management/marketing management/social enterprise, business management, business management, international, business, enterprise and entrepreneurship/management and communications, economics, economics, finance and international business/politics and international relations, events management, finance, accounting, finance, international business, and economics, HRM, international business management, international business, finance, and economics, international relations, economics and politics, management, business and marketing, management, international business/marketing, marketing (and business) management, marketing management
Postgrad; accounting, accounting and finance, business management, e-business, coaching and mentoring/ practice, economics, economics, financial, financial economics, hospitality, events and tourism management, international hotel and tourism management, international/HRM, HRM, international hospitality, events and tourism management, international hotel and tourism management, international management, international management and international relations, international trade and logistics, strategic management and leadership, management, strategic management and leadership, marketing, mentoring and coaching/ practice, strategic management and leadership, tourism and hotel management; BA(Hons), BSc(Hons), Certs, DCM, DBA, Dips, FdA, MA, MBA, MRes, MSc, PhD

Oxford International Centre for Publishing; www.publishing.brookes.ac.uk
publishing media, publishing, publishing studies, book history and publishing culture, digital publishing, journals publishing; Cert, BA(Hons), European Master's in Publishing, MA

Oxford School of Hospitality; www.hospitality.brookes.ac.uk
international hospitality management, events & tourism management, international hotel & tourism management, food; BSc(Hons), MSc

Faculty of Human & Life Sciences; www.hls.brookes.ac.uk

Dept of Biological & Medical Sciences; www.bms.brookes.ac.uk
animal behaviour & welfare/biology & conservation, applied animal management, biological sciences, biology, biomedical science, conservation ecology evolution & development, environmental management/science, human biology, infection, prevention & control, biosciences, medical genetics & genomics, medical science, equine science/& management/thoroughbred management, life sciences; BA(Hons)/BSc(Hons), MSc, PGDip, PhD, BMedSci

Dept of Clinical Health Care; www.chc.brookes.ac.uk
adult & mental health nursing, adult nursing, adv practice (clinical), cancer studies, children's/ & mental health nursing, health and social care, nursing studies, leadership in clinical practice, non-medical prescribing, operating department practice, palliative care, paramedic emergency care; BSc(Hons), FdSc, FdA, MA, MSc, PgDip/Cert, MPhil, PhD

Dept of Psychology; www.psychology.brookes.ac.uk
psychology, developmental psychology; BSc(Hons), BA(Hons), MPhil, PhD, MSc, PGDip/Cert

Dept of Social Work & Public Health; www.swph.brookes.ac.uk
community children's nursing/in the home, district nursing, midwifery, public health, specialist community public health nursing, social work; BSc(Hons), BA(Hons), PGDip/Cert, Cert HE, MA, MSc, MPhil

Dept of Sport & Health Science; www.shs.brookes.ac.uk

management in health & social care, nutrition, physiotherapy, higher professional education, sport & exercise science, sports coaching & PE, sports science, applied human nutrition, applied sports & exercise nutrition, contemporary occupational therapy, rehabilitation; BSc(Hons), BA(Hons), Cert/DipHE, MSc, PGDip/Cert, MOst, MSc, MPhil, PhD

Faculty of Humanities & Social Sciences; www.brookes.ac.uk/about faculties/hss

School of Education; www.education.brookes.ac.uk

early/childhood studies, early years, education/studies, adv educational practice, CPD, education & lifelong learning, English language & communication, education (leadership & management/TESOL), PGCE primary/secondary/post-compulsory education, primary teacher education, school direct, special educational needs support for learning, challenging behaviour, children's literature, primary mathematics, teaching English as an additional language, early childhood, working with children with literacy difficulties; BA(Hons), BSc(Hons), CertEd, FdA, MA, MPhil, PGCE, PGDip, PhD, QTS, DEd

Dept of English & Modern Languages: www.english-language.brookes.ac.uk

English, English literature, creative writing, drama, European business, culture & language, French, Spanish, Japanese studies, app langs; BA(Hons), MA

Dept of History, Philosophy & Religion; www.history.brookes.ac.uk

history, history of medicine, history of art, philosophy, religion & theology, communication, media & culture, ministry; BA(Hons), MA, FdA

School of Law; www.law.brookes.ac.uk

law, international/economic/human rights/trade & commercial law, international law & international relations, public international law, legal practice; BA/BSc, LlB, PGDip, GradDip, LlM

Dept of Social Sciences; www.social-sciences.brookes.ac.uk

anthropology, geography, international relations/& politics, primate conservation, international studies, international relations, sociology, policing; BA/BSc, MA, MSc, GradDip, FdA

Faculty of Technology, Design & Environment; www.brookes.ac.uk/tde

School of Architecture; www.architecture.brookes.ac.uk

architecture, interior architecture, built environment, development & emergency practice, humanitarian action & conflict, shelter after disaster, international architectural regeneration & development, applied design in architecture, sustainable building: performance & design; BA(Hons), MArch, MArchD, PhD, FdA

School of Arts; www.arts.brookes.ac.uk

fine art, composition & sonic art, art & design, contemporary arts/& music, creative arts & design practice, music, fine art, graphic design, illustration narrative & sequential, composition & sonic arts, contemporary arts/& music, social sculpture, film studies/popular cinema, publishing/media/& language, book history & popular culture, digital international publishing; BA(Hons), BA/BSc, MA, MPhil, PhD, FdA

Dept of Planning; www.planning.brookes.ac.uk

built environment, environmental assessment & management, spatial planning, historic conservation, city & regional planning, planning/& property development, tourism environment & development, urban design/planning development & transitional regions & regional regeneration; BA(Hons), MPlan, MSc, PhD, MPhil, PGDip/Cert, FBE

Dept of Real Estate & Construction; www.rec.brookes.ac.uk

built environment, construction project management, investment finance, quantity surveying & commercial management, real estate/management, spatial planning, project management in the built environment; BSc(Hons), MSc, PhD

Dept of Computing & Communication Technologies; www.cct.brookes.ac.uk

computer science, computing for robotic systems, computing & informatics, information technology management for business/systems & management, mobile computing, computer vision, mobile wireless & communications, network computing, software engineering, multimedia production, software for business, sound mobile & high-speed telecommunications networks, wireless communication systems, digital media production; BSc(Hons), MSc, PhD

Dept of Mechanical Engineering & Mathematical Science; www.mems.brookes.ac.uk
mathematics, mathematical sciences, data visualisation & modelling, mechanical engineering, motorsport engineering/technology, automotive engineering, racing engine design, electronic engineering; BSc(Hons), BA(Hons), B/MEng, MSc, MRes, MPhil, PhD

UNIVERSITY OF PLYMOUTH
www.plymouth.ac.uk

Faculty of Arts; www.plymouth.ac.uk/faculties/arts

School of Architecture, Design and Environment; www1.plymouth.ac.uk/schools/ade
architecture, architectural technology & the environment, architectural engineering, design thinking, 3D design, building surveying & the environment, high performance buildings, sustainable construction/cost management/project management, construction management & the environment; BA(Hons), MA, MRes, MArch, MSc

School of Art & Media; www.plymouth.ac.uk/schools/artmedia
digital art & technology, graphic communication with typography, film & video, fine art, illustration, media arts, contemporary art/film practice, film & video, photography/& the book/land; BA(Hons), MA, MArch, GradDip, MRes, PhD, MSc, BSc

School of Humanities & Performing Arts; www.plymouth.ac.uk/schools/hpa
art history, choreography, computer music, dance/theatre performance, literature, history, heritage & archaeology, English & creative writing/history/French/Spanish/culture/publishing, events management, fine art & art history, history with international relations/politics/Spanish, modern/music, music & sound production, primary music, theatre & performance, the speaking dance; BA(Hons), MA, PGDip/Cert, MRes, PhD

Faculty of Health & Human Science; www.plymouth.ac.uk/faculties/hhc

School of Nursing & Midwifery; www.plymouth.ac.uk/schools/school-of-nursing-and midwifery
adult/child/health/mental health nursing, adv practice in healthcare, developmental nursing, contemporary healthcare (advancing practice/child/health genetics/midwifery); BSc(Hons), MSc, PGDip

School of Health Professions; www.plymouth.ac.uk/schools/hp
dietetics, mental health, adv/occupational therapy, adv professional practice (dietetic/neurological rehabilitation/occupational therapy/paediatric dietetics/physiotherapy), optometry, paramedic practitioner physiotherapy, podiatry, social work; BSc(Hons), DipHE, MSc, PGCert, PGDip

School of Psychology; www.plymouth.ac.uk/school_of_psychology
psychology, psychological studies, adv psychology, clinical psychology, psychology with human biology/sociology/criminology & criminal justice/international relations, research methods; BSc(Hons), MSc, PGDip

School of Education; www.plymouth.ac.uk/schools/education
children's workforce, early childhood studies, early childhood studies, education, teaching in the lifelong learning sector, education studies, primary (numerous primary subjects/digital literacy/early childhood studies/special educational needs), education studies, inclusive education, international study of early childhood, learning for sustainability, PGCE (education and training/teaching in the lifelong learning sector/primary early years), PGCE secondary (numerous secondary subjects), professional leadership, teaching and learning, special educational needs coordination; BEd, CertEd, MA, MSc, Masters in Teaching & Learning, PGCE, Dip, PGCert, ProfDoc, FdA

Faculty of Business;
www.plymouth.ac.uk/faculties/business

Plymouth Business School;
www.plymouth.ac.uk/schools/plymouth-business-school

accounting and finance, business, business administration, business economics, business enterprise, business management/ with business English, business studies, economics, economics with international relations/law/politics, financial economics, international business with economics/French/Spanish, international finance, international management, international supply chain and shipping management, international supply chain management, international trade and operations, management, management, government and law, management practice, maritime business and logistics, maritime business and maritime law, marketing, shipping and logistics; BA(Hons), BSc(Hons)

Plymouth Graduate School of Management; www.plymouth.ac.uk/schools/pgsm

accounting and finance, brand and design management, business administration, business and management, digital and social media marketing, entrepreneurship/ and international development, finance/ and investment, HRM, international business, international finance, international logistics/procurement and supply chain management, international shipping, management, marketing management, operations and supply chain management, public administration; MBA, DPA, DPubAdmin, PGDip, MPhil, ResM, PhD, MSc, MA

Plymouth Law School;
www.plymouth.ac.uk/schools/law

law, law and business, law with criminology and criminal justice studies, marine environmental law and sustainability, criminology and criminal justice studies, criminology and criminal justice studies with international relations/politics/ psychology/ sociology, police and criminal justice studies, criminology; BA(Hons), BSc(Hons), LlB, LlM, MSc, PGDip

School of Tourism & Hospitality;
www.plymouth.ac.uk/schools/th

business and tourism, cruise management, events management, hospitality management, hospitality, tourism and events management, tourism management, tourism and hospitality management, tourism management, international hospitality management, tourism and hospitality management; BSc(Hons), BA(Hons), MSc, PGDip

School of Government;
www.plymouth.ac.uk/schools/school-of-government

international relations, international relations with French /law/ politics/Spanish/psychology, politics with criminology and criminal justice studies, French/politics/history, international relations with law/Spanish/public management and business, public services, public management, social research methods, international relations: global security & development; BSc(Hons), MSc, DPA

Faculty of Science & the Environment;
www.plymouth.ac.uk/faculties/science

School of Biological Sciences;
www.plymouth.ac.uk/schools/school-of-biological-science

animal behaviour & welfare, animal conservation science, biological sciences, biosciences, conservation biology, environmental biology, sustainable aquaculture systems, zoo conservation biology; BSc(Hons), PGDip, MSc

School of Computing & Mathematics;
www.plymouth.ac.uk/schools/compmath

computer science, computer & information security, computer systems & networks, computing & games development, data modelling & analytics, electrical & electronic engineering, mathematics/with statistics/education/finance/high performance computing, network systems engineering, robotics, robotic technology/engineering, signal processing; BSc, MSc, MRes

School of Geography, Earth & Environmental Sciences;
www.plymouth.ac.uk/schools/sogees

chemistry, applied/geology, environmental science/conservation, extended science, geography/& international relations/ocean science, physical geography, planning, sustainable environmental management; BA(Hons), BSc(Hons), MGeol, MSc, MRes, PGCert

School of Marine Science & Engineering;
www.plymouth.ac.uk/schools/mse

civil and coastal engineering, civil engineering, hydrography for professionals, marine and composites technology, marine biology, marine biology and coastal ecology/oceanography, marine technology, mechanical design and manufacture, mechanical engineering, mechanical engineering with composites, navigation and maritime science, ocean exploration and surveying, ocean science, ocean science and marine conservation, oceanography and coastal processes; Postgrad; advanced hydrography for professionals, applied marine science, civil engineering, coastal engineering, hydrography, marine biology, marine renewable energy; BSc(Hons), MEng, MRes, MSc, BEng, FdSc, PGDip

School of Psychology; www.plymouth.ac.uk/ school_of_psychology

psychology, psychological studies, adv psychology, psychology with human biology/sociology/criminology & criminal justice studies/international relations, clinical psychology, psychology research methods; BSc(Hons), MSc, PGDip

Plymouth University Peninsular School of Medicine and Dentistry; www.plymouth.ac.uk/peninsular

Plymouth University Peninsular School of Dentistry

Plymouth University Peninsular School of Medicine

The School of Biomedical & Healthcare Sciences

medicine, surgery, clinical education, healthcare management, leadership and innovation, physician, remote and global healthcare, remote healthcare, simulation and patient safety, dental surgery, restorative dentistry, biomedical science, health and fitness, healthcare science (life sciences/physiological sciences), human biosciences, nutrition, exercise and health; MBBS, BDS, MD, MS, MPhil, PhD, PGDip/Cert, MSc, MClinEd

Degrees validated by the University of Plymouth offered at:

SOUTH DEVON COLLEGE
www.southdevon.ac.uk

animal science, child development & education, coaching, healthcare practice, biosciences, business, civil and coastal engineering, computing, criminology and psychology, engineering technologies, extended science, fashion with textiles, film and photography, game and interactive design, higher apprenticeships, professional practice in construction, operations management, history with English, illustration arts, law, marine science, psychology with sociology, sport and exercise science, sustainable construction and the built environment, three dimensional design, tourism, hospitality and events management, yacht operations; FdSc, FdA, BSc(Hons), CertHE

TRURO & PENWITH COLLEGE
www.trurocollege.ac.uk

action photography, applied media, applied social science, archaeology, art & design, biomedical science, bioscience, business, childhood education, children & young people's workforce, commercial music performance & production, applied/computer technology, computer games design & production, community studies (development & youth work), counselling studies, early childhood education, education/and training, education in lifelong learning sector, English studies, environmental & public health/nutrition, exercise, health & fitness/nutrition, health & social care, geography & sociology/environment, history & heritage, human behaviour studies, illustration (digital), interior design practice, law, managing business resources, media advertising, photography & moving image, post-compulsory education & training, music performance, outdoor education, photography & digital imaging, public services, PGCE, silversmithing & jewellery, sports coaching & performance/rehabilitation, web technology; BA(Hons), BSc(Hons), FdA, FdSc, PCET, PGCE, UnivCert/Dip

UNIVERSITY OF PORTSMOUTH
www.port.ac.uk

*Portsmouth Business School;
www.port.ac.uk/departments/faculties/
portsmouthbusinessschool*

Accounting & Finance, Economics, Human Resource & Marketing Management, Law, Strategy & Business Systems

accountancy and financial management, accounting and business, accounting with finance, business and HRM/management/systems management, business economics, business enterprise development, business with business communication, digital marketing, economics, economics and management, economics, finance and banking, finance with business communication, financial management for business, hospitality management, hospitality management with tourism, HRM with psychology, international business, law, law with business/business/communication/criminology/international relations, leadership, business and management, marketing, marketing with business communication/psychology

Postgraduate; accounting and finance, business administration (DBA), business and management, business economics, finance and banking, coaching and development, corporate finance, corporate governance and law, digital marketing, finance, forensic accounting, HRD, HRM, innovation management and entrepreneurship, international finance and banking, international HRM, law, leadership and management, marketing, MBA(executive), project management, risk, crisis and resilience management, sales management, strategic quality management, strategic quality management, business and management; BA(Hons), BSc(Hons), MSc, BSc(Econ)(Hons), PGDip/Cert, MPhil, PhD, LlB, LlM, MBA, DBA

Faculty of Creative and Cultural Industries; www.port.ac.uk/departments/faculties/facultyofcreativeartsandindustries

Portsmouth School of Architecture; www.port.ac.uk/departments/academic/architecture/

architecture, interior architecture & design, professional practice, sustainable architecture, urban design, historic building conservation; BA(Hons), MA, MArch, MSc

School of Art & Design; www.port.ac.uk/school-of art-and-design

design for digital media, fashion & textile design, fine art, graphic design, illustration, photography; BA(Hons), MA

School of Creative Media & Performing Arts; www.port.ac.uk/departments/academic/creative-media-and-performing-arts

creative & media writing, drama/& performance, English/film studies & creative writing/film studies, entertainment technology, media studies/& entertainment technology, music theatre; BA(Hons), MA, MRes

School of Creative Technologies; www.port.ac.uk/departments/academic/ct

animation/with business communication, computer animation/with business communication, computer games/enterprise/technology/with business communication, digital media, entertainment technology, music and sound technology, music computing, TV and broadcasting/with business communication/film production/TV and film production with business communication, creative professional practice; BA(Hons), BSc(Hons), FdSc, MSc

Faculty of Humanities and Social Sciences; www.port.ac.uk/departments/faculties/facultyofhumanities

Institute of Criminal Justice Studies; www.port.ac.uk/departments/academic/icjs

counter fraud and criminal justice studies, crime and criminology/criminal justice/forensic studies, criminology with psychology, law with criminology, policing and investigation, risk and security management

Postgrad counter fraud and counter corruption studies, crime science, investigation and intelligence, crime science, instigation and intelligence, criminology and criminal justice/criminal psychology, international criminal justice, policing, policy and leadership, criminal justice, security risk, management, security management; BSc(Hons), FdA, LlB, MScDCrim Studs, DCrimJ, ProfDoc

School of Education and Continuing Studies; www.port.ac.uk/departments/academic/school-of-education-and-continuing- studies

childhood & youth studies/with psychology, early childhood studies/with psychology, early years care & education/initial teacher training, education & training studies, education leadership & management, humanities & social science, PGCE in numerous subject courses/post-compulsory education/schools direct/teacher training, learning support, learning & teaching; BA(Hons), CertEd, FdA, MA, MSc, PGCE, PGCert, EYPS

School of Languages & Area Studies; www.port.ac.uk/school-of-languages-and-area-studies

American studies & history, applied languages, combined modern languages, communication & English studies/language, English language, European studies/ & international relations, French/German studies, humanities & social science, international development studies/& languages, international relations & language, international trade & business communication, logistics & business communications, languages & business studies/European studies/law, logistics, Spanish studies, Spanish & Latin American studies, international transport & business, applied linguistics & TESOL, translation studies; BA(Hons), MA

School of Social, Historical and Literary Studies; www.port.ac.uk/departments/academic/school-of-social-historical-and-literary-studies

English & history/media studies/languages & literature, English with psychology, government, history/& politics, history of war, culture & society, international relations & history/politics/European studies, journalism/with English literature/language/media studies, media studies, politics, psychology, sociology/& criminology/psychology, literature, history, history of war, culture & identity/society, humanities & social science, public administration; BA(Hons), BSc(Hons), FdA, MPA, MSc

Faculty of Science; www.port.ac.uk/departments/faculties/facultyofscience

School of Biological Sciences; www.port.ac.uk/departments/academic/biology

applied aquatic biology, biology, biochemistry, marine biology, science; BSc(Hons), MSc, MPhil, PhD, MRes

School of Earth and Environmental Sciences; www.port.ac.uk/departments/academic/isees

engineering geology/ & geotechnics, environmental geology & contamination, crisis & disaster management, environmental science, geological hazards, geological & environmental hazards, geology, marine environmental science, palaeontology, applied physics, physics, astronomy & cosmology, science; BSc(Hons), MEng(Hons), MSc, MRes, MPhys

Department of Geography; www.port.ac.uk/departments/academic/geography

geography, coastal & marine resources management, geography & GIS, human geography, physical geography, science; BA(Hons), BSc(Hons), MSc, MRes

The Dental Academy; www.port.ac.uk/departments/academic/dentalacademy

dental hygiene/therapy/nursing; BSc(Hons), CertHE, FdSc

School of Health Sciences and Social Work; www.port.ac.uk/departments/academic/shssw

acute clinical healthcare, health & social care, human physiology/communications science, speech, language & communication science, operating dept practice, paramedic science, social work, radiography (diagnostic/therapeutic), science; DipHE, FdSc, GradDip, BSc(Hons), MSc, ProfDoc

Pharmacy & Biomedical sciences; www.port.ac.uk/departments/academic/pharmacy

applied/biomedical science, healthcare sciences, pharmacy/practice, pharmacology, biomedicine, science; FdSc, BSc(Hons), MSc, MRes, MPharm(Hons)

Psychology; www.port.ac.uk/departments/academic/psychology/

psychology, forensic/psychology, applied psychology of intellectual disabilities, psychology & law, child forensic studies, science; BSc(Hons), MSc, PGCert, MPhil, PhD, MRes

Sport & Exercise Science; www.port.ac.uk/ departments/academic/sportscience

sport & exercise science/psychology, exercise & fitness management, sports management with business communication, sports development/business management/performance, sport science & management, clinical exercise science, science; BSc(Hons), MSc, MRes

Faculty of Technology; www.port.ac.uk/ departments/faculties/ facultyoftechnology

Civil Engineering & Surveying; www.port.ac.uk/departments/academic/ sces

civil engineering, construction engineering management, property development, civil engineering with environmental/geotechnical/structural engineering, construction project management, building/quantity surveying, technology; BSc(Hons), BEng(Hons), MEng, MSc, MRes

Computing; www.port.ac.uk/departments/ academic/comp

business information systems, computer science, computing, computing & information systems/security, security & information technology, forensic computing, computing security, information systems, technology, software engineering, web technologies, forensic/IT; BSc(Hons), MSc, MRes

Mathematics; www.port.ac.uk/ departments/academic/maths

mathematics, mathematics for finance & management/with statistics, logistics & transportation/supply chain management, technology; BSc(Hons), MSc, PgCert/Dip, MPhil, PhD, MRes

Engineering; www.port.ac.uk/ departments/academic/eng

computer-aided product design, computer engineering/networks, computer network planning & management, communication systems engineering, electronic engineering, electronic systems engineering, engineering & technology, mechanical & manufacturing engineering, mechanical engineering, petroleum engineering, product design & modern materials/innovation, adv manufacturing technology, communication network planning/administration & management, electronic & telecommunication engineering, electrical and power systems management, technology/management, petroleum & gas engineering; BSc(Hons), BEng(Hons), MEng, MSc, MRes

Learning at Work; www.port.ac.uk/ departments/academic/learning atwork

occupational health & safety management, partnership, technology; PGCert, MA/MSc

QUEEN MARGARET UNIVERSITY COLLEGE
www.qmu.ac.uk

School of Arts, Social Sciences & Management; www.qmucassam

international hospitality and tourism management, events management, business management, film /PR and media, media, marketing, drama and performance, theatre and film studies, costume design and construction, acting for stage and screen, psychology/ and sociology, MBA, MBA with hospitality, international management & leadership/with Hospitality, public sector governance, PR, arts, festival and cultural management, social justice

School of Health Sciences; www.qmu.ac.uk

dietetics, nutrition, applied pharmacology and human biology, dietetics, public health nutrition, nursing, occupation therapy, arts/music/therapy, clinical research, collaborative working, education health, podiatry, diabetes, physiotherapy, radiography, diagnostic radiography, therapeutic radiography, mammography, radiotherapy and oncology, diagnostic radiography, radiotherapy, podiatric medicine, theory of podiatric surgery, pharmacology, global health, sexual & reproductive health, social justice development & health, social development & health, international health, for podiatrists, speech & language therapy, hearing and audiology
BA/BA(Hons), BSc/BSc(Hons), MA, MBA, PGDip-Cert, MSc, PhD, ProfDoc, HECert/Dip

UNIVERSITY OF READING
www.reading.ac.uk

Faculty of Arts & Humanities;
www.reading.ac.uk/fah

School of Arts & Communication Design; www.reading.ac.uk/sacd

art, film, film & theatre, graphic communication, fine art, history of art, theatre, art and theatre/history of art/philosophy/psychology, film, theatre & TV, Samuel Beckett, book design, creative enterprise (communication design/art/film), typeface design, typography & graphic communication; BA(Hons), MA, MA(Res), MFA, MPhil, PhD

School of Humanities; www.reading.ac.uk/humanities

Classics: ancient history, classics, classical studies, ancient history and archaeology, archaeology and classical studies, ancient history and history, classical and medieval studies/English/history of art, museum and classical studies, classics and ancient history, the classical tradition, the city of Rome, ancient maritime trade and navigation

History: history, archaeology/ancient history and history, history and economics/English/French/German/international relations/Italian/philosophy, history and politics

Philosophy: philosophy, ethics value and philosophy, PPE philosophy politics and economics, philosophy and classical studies/English literature/international relations/politics, art and philosophy, history of art/psychology/history and philosophy, ethics and political theory

BA(Hons), MA, MPhil, PhD

School of Literature & Languages

Dept of Modern Languages & European Studies; www.reading.ac.uk/modern-languages-and-european-studies/mles-home.aspx

European Studies: European studies, European studies with a major European language

French Studies: French studies, European studies with French, French and German/Italian/Spanish/economics/English language/English literature/history/international relations/management, international management and business administration with French

German Studies: German studies, European studies with German, German and French/ Italian/Spanish/economics/English language/English literature/

history/international relations/management, international management and business administration with German

Italian Studies: Italian studies, European studies with Italian, Italian and German/Spanish/economics/English language/English literature/history/international relations/management, international management and business administration with Italian

Spanish Studies: European studies with Spanish, Spanish and French/Italian/German/English language/English literature/history/management

Postgrad: Franco-British history, Modern Italian history, French studies, German studies, Italian Studies; BA(Hons), MA, MA(Res), PhD

Dept of English Language & Applied Linguistics; www.reading.ac.uk/english-language-and-applied-linguistics/elel/home.aspx

English language/literature, applied linguistics, English language teaching; BA(Hons), MA, MA(Res), PhD

Dept of English Literature; www.reading.ac.uk/english-literature

English literature, English literature and Italian/politics/German/French/Spanish, English with French/English and European literature and culture, English literature and international relations/classical studies/French history and English literature, philosophy and English literature/ and film & theatre/art, applied English language and English literature, English, children's literature, early modern literature and drama, Victorian literature and culture; BA(Hons), MA, MA(Res), PhD

Faculty of Social Sciences;
www.reading.ac.uk/internal/fss

Institute of Education; www.reading.ac.uk/education

education, theatre arts, education and deaf studies, children's development and learning, postgraduate initial teacher education and training (secondary ITPGCE), language and literacy in education, equity, inclusion and improvement, early years teacher status, postgraduate professional development, special educational needs coordinators, early years, creative arts, English language teaching, English education, inclusive education, global futures, leadership and management, information and communication technology, mathematics teaching, primary education, music education; BA(Hons), FdA, PGCE, PhD, EdD

School of Law; www.reading.ac.uk/law

law, advanced legal studies, legal studies in Europe, international law, human rights, international commercial law, law and economics, international banking law/corporate finance/financial regulation, oil and gas law, intellectual property law and management; DPhil, LlB, LLM, MARes, MRes, MSc, PhD

School of Politics & International Relations; www.reading.ac.uk/spirs

politics and international relations/economics, war, peace and international relations, English literature and international relations/politics, economics/French/Italian/philosophy/history and international relations, history/economics and politics, philosophy, politics and economics; Postgrad; international relations, diplomacy, international security studies, strategic studies, military history and strategic studies, public policy, politics and international relations; BA(Hons), MA, MPhil, MRes, PhD

The School of Economics; www.reading.ac.uk/economics

economics, economics and finance/econometrics, business economics, accounting/politics/international relations/history/French/German/Italian/ geography/ mathematics & economics, European studies/with optional language, philosophy, politics; Postgrad; public policy, business economics, business economics in emerging developing markets, economics of international business and finance, emerging and developing economies, international economic development and business, banking and finance in emerging and developing economies, banking and the financial systems in the global economy, economics of climate change, law; BA(Hons), BSc(Hons), MSc, PhD

Henley Business School; www.henley.ac.uk

accounting and business/economics/finance/management, business and management, entrepreneurship, entrepreneurship and management, international business and management, international management and business administration with French/German/Spanish, international business and finance, management with information technology, finance and investment banking/psychology/management, real estate, investment and finance in property, rural property management, real estate with urban planning & development; Postgrad; accounting and financial management/international management, entrepreneurship and financing/management, international business, international business and finance, international HRM, marketing and international management, international management, health and social care management, leadership, applied management, international securities, investment and banking, capital markets, regulation and compliance, corporate finance, financial engineering, financial risk management, international shipping and finance, investment banking and Islamic finance, investment management, behavioural finance, business information management, information management & systems, business technology consulting, informatics, management information systems, informatics, spatial planning and development, spatial planning and research, international housing development and management, international planning and sustainable urban management, rural land and business management, real estate, real estate finance, corporate real estate, real estate investment and finance, conservation of the historic environment; MBA, DBA, BA(Hons), BSc(Hons), MA, MSc, PhD

Faculty of Life Sciences; www.reading.ac.uk/internal/lifesci

School of Agriculture, Policy & Development; www.reading.ac.uk/apd

agriculture, agricultural business management/development economics, agricultural economics, agriculture & development, applied development studies, animal science, climate change & development, consumer behaviour & marketing, development finance/policy, environment & development, environmental & countryside management, food marketing/& business economics, food economics & marketing, food security & development, research agricultural & food economics, international development, rural land business management; BA(Hons), BSc(Hons), MPhil, PhD

School of Biological Sciences; www.reading.ac.uk/biologicalsciences

biochemistry, biological sciences, biomedical sciences, ecology & wildlife conservation, microbiology, molecular medicine, plant diversity, species identification & survey skills, wildlife management & conservation, zoology; BSc(Hons), MPhil, MSc, PhD

School of Chemistry; www.reading.ac.uk/chemistry

chemistry, chemistry with forensic analytics, chemistry for life and the environment, materials chemistry, molecular chemistry, chemical research; BSc(Hons), MSc, MChem, PhD, Dip

School of Chemistry, Food & Pharmacy; www.reading.ac.uk/fcfp

chemistry, food science/technology, forensic analysis, medical chemistry, nutrition & food science, pharmacy, quality assurance; BSc(Hons), MPharm, MSc, PhD, MChem

School of Psychology & Clinical Language Sciences; www.reading.ac.uk/pcls

psychology, psychology and philosophy/art/neuroscience/ mathematics/finance, psychology, childhood and ageing, psychological theory and practice, speech and language therapy, language sciences and psychology, research methods in psychology, cognitive neuroscience, development and psychopathology, clinical aspects of psychology, language sciences, evidence-based psychological treatment; PGDip/Cert, BSc(Hons), MSc, PhD, MSci

Faculty of Science; www.reading.ac.uk/internal/facsci

School of Systems Engineering; www.reading.ac.uk/sse

artificial intelligence, adv computer science/and informatics/communication, cybernetics, digital signal processing electronic engineering, IT, robotics, systems engineering; BEng, BSc(Hons), FdSc, MEng, MPhil, MRes, MSc, PhD

School of Construction Management and Engineering; www.reading.ac.uk/CME

building/quantity surveying, construction management & surveying, construction in emerging economies, construction cost management, design & management of sustainable built environment, project management, renewable energy, technology & sustainability; BSc(Hons), MPhil, MSc, PGDip, PhD

School of Mathematical & Physical Sciences; www.smps.reading.ac.uk/

mathematics, statistics, meteorology, mathematics with finance and investment banking, computational mathematics, mathematics and economics/meteorology/meteorology/ psychology/statistics, data assimilation and inverse methods in geoscience, financial engineering; BSc(Hons), MMath, MPhil, MSc, PhD

School of Human & Environmental Science; www.reading.ac.uk/shes

archaeology, ancient history and archaeology/classical studies/history/museum studies, environmental science, geography and economics, human/and physical geography, environmental science, Postgrad; archaeology, archaeology of medieval Europe, archaeology of the Middle East, environmental archaeology, environmental management, environmental pollution; BSc(Hons), MSc, MA, MPhil, PhD

ROBERT GORDON UNIVERSITY
www.rgu.ac.uk

Faculty of Health and Social Care

School of Applied Social Studies; www.rgu.ac.uk/social

applied social sciences, corporate responsibility & energy, social care/work, sociology; BA(Hons), GradCert, MSW, MSc, PGDip, PhD

School of Health Sciences; www.rgu.ac.uk/health

Health Professions; Health & Exercise Professions; Laboratory, Biomedical & Sport Sciences
applied biomedical science, adv nursing/district nursing, bioscience, biomedicine, biochemistry, clinical biomechanics/pharmacological practice, health practice/promotion & public health, forensic & analytical science, clinical practice, diagnostic radiography, mental health nursing, nutrition, occupational therapy, pharmacy, physiotherapy, applied sport & exercise science, sports nutrition & dietetics, sport biomedicine, laboratory, biochemical & sport sciences, instrumental analytical science (proteomics & metabolomics/drug analysis & toxicology/sport biomedicine/oilfield chemicals), public health; BSc(Hons), CertHE, MPhil, MSc, PhD, MNursing, BNursing, BMidW, MPhysiotherapy, PGCert, MRes, MPharm

School of Nursing & Midwifery; www.rgu.ac.uk/nursing

acute/adult/children & young people/mental health, occupational health practice, adv clinical practice, adv district nursing, midwifery, public health nursing; BNurs, DipHE, MPhil, MSc, PhD, MNurs, MRes, BMidW

School of Pharmacy & Life Sciences; www.rgu.ac.uk/pharmacy-life

biomedical science, bioscience with biomedical sciences, forensic and analytical science, pharmacy, nutrition, nutrition and dietetics, clinical pharmacy practice, environmental science, instrumental analytical science environmental analysis/drug analysis and toxicology/oilfield chemicals/DNA analysis, proteomics and metabolomics, clinical pharmacy service development; MPharm, MSc, PGDip, PhD, DocProfPract

Aberdeen Business School; www.rgu.ac.uk/abs

Accounting & Finance: accounting, finance, strategic accounting, financial management, oil & gas accounting/finance
Management: business management; international business management, management, management studies, management with HRM, project management, corporate governance, business administration, energy management, health safety and risk management, HRM, international business, oil and gas management, public administration, purchasing and supply chain management, quality management
Law: law, law & management, online law, construction law & arbitration, employment law & practice, international commercial law/trade, oil & gas law, legal practice, mediation
Communication, Marketing & Media: fashion management, international hospitality management, journalism, management with marketing, media, PR, digital marketing, fashion management, corporate communication and public affairs, international marketing management, international tourism/and hospitality management, journalism, events management

Information Management: information management, information and library studies, information and library studies, digital curation, organisational learning
BA/BA(Hons), DBA, DInfSc, LlB, LlM, MBA, MPA, MPhil, MSc, PGDip/Cert, PhD, MSc, DInfSci, Grad Cert

Faculty of Design & Technology

School of Computing, Science & Digital Media; www.rgu.ac.uk/computing

business information technology, computer science, computer graphics & animation, computer network management & design, information & network security, data science, digital media: design, production & development, computing software technology with network management, information engineering, application/software development, software engineering, IT for oil & gas industry; BSc(Hons), MSc, PGCert/Dip, PhD

School of Engineering; www.rgu.ac.uk/eng

electrical & electronic engineering, mechanical engineering, offshore engineering, oil & gas/drilling & well/petroleum production engineering, energy & sustainability, offshore renewables, renewable engineering, subsea engineering, petroleum engineering; BSc(Hons), BEng, MEng, MPhil, MSc, PhD

Gray's School of Art, Design & Craft; www.rgu.ac.uk/grays

art & design, commercial photography, contemporary art practice, fashion design, fashion & textile design, painting, 3D design; BA/BA(Hons), BDes/BDes(Hons), MDes, MRes, PGDip/MA

The Scott Sunderland School of Architecture and Built Environment; www.rgu.ac.uk/sss

architectural studies/technology, architecture, architectural/construction technology, construction/project management, design management, quantity/building surveying, commercial practice for the energy sectors, visualisation in architecture and the built environment; GradDip, MArch, MSc, PhD, BSc(Hons)

ROEHAMPTON UNIVERSITY
www.roehampton.ac.uk

Dept of Dance; www.roehampton.ac.uk/dance

dance studies, ballet studies, dance anthropology/choreography/studies, SE Asia dance studies, choreography/& performance, community dancing, global dancing/identities & institutions; BA, MA, PGDip/Cert, MRes, MFA

Dept of Drama, Theatre & Performance; www.roehampton.ac.uk/drama-theatre-and-performance

drama, drama studies, theatre & performance studies, performance & creative research; BA(Hons), MPhil, MRes, MA, PhD

Dept of English & Creative Writing; www.roehampton.ac.uk/English-and-creative-writing

creative/ & professional writing, modern literature & culture, English literature, children's literature; BA, MA, MPhil, PhD

Dept of Humanities; www.roehampton.ac.uk/humanities

classical civilization, classical research, history, philosophy, Christian ministry, historical research, practical theology, studies in contemporary Catholicism, theology & religious studies/leadership, religion & gender, ministerial theology; BA, MTh, PGDip, MPhil, PhD

Department of Education; www.roehampton.ac.uk/education

dyslexia – identification, assessment, provision, enhancing inclusive education, education, education leadership & management, early childhood studies, education policy, PGCE (primary education/secondary education/schools direct (primary/secondary), psychology for educational professionals, social research methods, special & inclusive education needs & inclusion, sounds of intent, sports coaching/practice; BA(Hons), BA/BSc, EdD, FdA, Froebel Cert and Grad Cert, MA, MPhil, PGCE Primary/Secondary, PhD

Dept of Life Sciences: www.roehampton.ac.uk/life-sciences

anthropology/of health, social anthropology, biological sciences, biomedical sciences, biomechanics, health sciences, nutrition & health, clinical neuroscience/nutrition, life sciences, nutrition & health, obesity: risks & prevention, primate biology, behaviour & conservation, stress & health, social anthropology, sport psychology, psychology of sport & exercise physiology/science/psychology, zoology; BA, BSc, MSc, MPhil, PGDip, PhD

Dept of Media, Culture & Language; www.roehampton.ac.uk/media-culture-and-language

English language and linguistics, film, French/and Spanish, mass communications, media, culture and identity, photography, Spanish, translation; Postgrad; accessibility and filmmaking, applied linguistics and TESOL, audiovisual translation, film and screen cultures, media communication and culture, specialised translation; BSc, BA, MA, MRes, MPhil, PGDip, PhD

Dept of Psychology; www.roehampton.ac.uk/psychology

psychology, psychology and counselling, therapeutic psychology; Postgrad; art psychotherapy, attachment studies, counselling psychology, dance movement psychotherapy, dramatherapy, integrative counselling and psychotherapy, music therapy, play therapy; BSc, PsychD, MA, MPhil, PhD, ProfDoc, MSc

Dept of Social Sciences; www.roehampton.ac.uk/social-sciences

criminology, law/ & criminology, human rights/international relations/policy & practice, sociology; BA/BSc, MA, PGDip/Cert, PhD

Roehampton Business School; www.roehampton/business

accounting, business management, business management and accounting/digital media/ economics/entrepreneurship/retail marketing, HRM, international business, marketing, marketing and multimedia; Postgrad; accounting and finance, international management, international management with accounting/finance/HRM /marketing, marketing, MBA, project management, information systems management, strategic HRM, strategic supply chain management; MBA, PGDip/Cert, BA/BSc, BSc(Hons), MSc, MPhil, PhD

THE ROYAL ACADEMY OF DANCE
www.rad.org.uk

ballet education, dance education, professional dancers' teaching diploma; BA(Hons), CertHE, Dip

ROYAL ACADEMY OF DRAMATIC ART
www.rada.org

acting, technical theatre & stage management, theatre lab/directing, text & performance, production & design; BA(Hons), MA, FD

ROYAL AGRICULTURAL UNIVERSITY
www.rau.ac.uk

agriculture & applied farm management, food production & supply management, business management, international food and agribusiness, equine management, real estate and land management, international rural development, sustainable agriculture and food security, food safety and quality management, real estate and land management, equine, agriculture & farm management, archaeology and historic landscape conservation, British wildlife conservation, business and rural enterprise management, environmental conservation & heritage management; FdSc, BSc(Hons), BSc(Hons), GradDip, MSc, MA, MBA

Degrees validated by the Royal Agricultural University offered at:

ASKHAM BRYAN COLLEGE
www.askham-bryan.ac.uk

adventure, sport & public service, agriculture & land management, animal management & science, arboriculture, canine & feline training welfare, countryside management/collection & conservation, equine science, equine business & event management, equine sports management, sport surface management, arboriculture, applied/horticulture, landscaping & garden management, sport (outdoor & adventure education), veterinary health studies/nursing; BSc, BSc(Hons), Nat Dips, FD

ROYAL BALLET SCHOOL
www.royalballetschool.org.uk

classical ballet training, performing dancing/arts, professional dance; BTEC, NatDip

ROYAL COLLEGE OF ART
www.rca.ac.uk

School of Architecture; www.rca.ac.uk/ Default.aspx?ContentID=160131

architecture, interior design, architecture research

School of Communication; www.rca.ac.uk/ Default.aspx?ContentID=160132

animation, information experience design, visual communication, communication research

School of Design; www.rca.ac.uk/ Default.aspx?ContentID=501976

design interactions/products, global innovation design /engineering, service design, vehicle design, design research

School of Fine Art; www.rca.ac.uk/ Default.aspx?ContentID=160134

painting, photography, printmaking, sculpture, moving image, fine art/research

School of Humanities; www.rca.ac.uk/ Default.aspx?ContentID=160135

critical writing in art & design, curating contemporary art, critical and historical studies, history of design, humanities research

School of Material; www.rca.ac.uk/ Default.aspx?ContentID=160133

ceramics & glass, fashion menswear/womenswear/ footwear/accessories & millinery, goldsmithing, metalwork & jewellery, silversmithing, textiles, materials design; MA, MPhil, PGCert, PhD

ROYAL COLLEGE OF MUSIC
www.rcm.ac.uk

advanced vocal performance, composition, composition for screen, conducting, contemporary culture, ensemble performance, opera, performance, historical/orchestral performance, music/in context, performance science, physics & musical performance, vocal studies; DipRCM, BMus, BSc, PGDip, MMus, DMus, GradDip, MPerf, MSc, ArtDip

THE ROYAL COLLEGE OF ORGANISTS
www.rco.org.uk

teaching, choral directing; CertRCO, ARCO, FRCO, LTRCO, DipCHD

ROYAL CONSERVATOIRE OF SCOTLAND
www.rcs.ac.uk

Music

keyboard, education, vocal studies, opera, piano for dance, strings, woodwind, brass, repetiteurship, timpani & percussion, Scottish music, composition, creative & contextual studies, conducting, jazz, Scots music/pipe music; BA(Hons), BMus(Hons), MA, MMus, MOpera, MPhil, PGDip, PhD

Drama

acting, classical & contemporary text (acting/directing), contemporary performance practice, performance in British sign language/English digital film & TV, modern ballet, technical & production arts & design, musical theatre/directing/performance

Dance

modern ballet

Production

production arts & design, production technology & management

Screen

digital film & TV

Learning & Teaching

learning support & administration, higher art education, learning & teaching in art education/higher arts education/Gaelic arts/performance; BA(Hons), BMus(Hons), MA, MMus, MOpera, MPhil, PGDip, PhD

ROYAL NORTHERN COLLEGE OF MUSIC
www.rncm.ac.uk

composition, conducting & repetiteurship studies, chamber music, keyboard studies, strings, jazz, vocal studies, wind, brass & percussion, music, musicology, music psychology, musical performance, orchestral studies, performance arts leadership, popular music practice/performance, solo performance, specialist instrument techniques; BA(Hons), MusB, MMus, MPhil, PhD, GradDip, MPerf

---

UNIVERSITY OF ST ANDREWS
www.st-andrews.ac.uk

Faculty of Arts

School of Art History; www-ah.st-andrews.ac.uk

art history (with numerous joint degrees), ancient history, gallery studies; GradCert, GradDip, MA, MLitt, MPhil, PhD

School of Classics; www.st-andrews.ac.uk/classics

ancient history, classics, classical studies, Greek, Latin; MA, MLitt, MPhil, PGDip, PhD

School of Economics & Finance; www.st-andrews.ac.uk/economics

analytical finance, finance, applied economics, economics, international strategy & economics, financial economics, money, banking & finance, microeconomics, macroeconomics, sustainable development; BSc, MA, MSc, MPhil, PhD, MA/BSc

School of English; www.st-andrews.ac.uk/english

creative writing, English, medieval & Renaissance English, 18th century, Romantic & Victorian studies, early modern & 18th century studies, English/Scottish/Irish/American literature, modern & contemporary literature, Shakespeare & Renaissance literary culture, women, writing & culture; GradDip, MA, MLitt, MPhil, PhD

School of History; www.st-andrews.ac.uk/history

book history, central & Eastern European studies, environmental history, history, Iranian studies, medieval history/& archaeology, Middle East studies/history, early/modern history, intellectual history, medieval history, Scottish historical studies/history, transnational history, Reformation studies; GradDip, MA, DLitt, MPhil, PhD

School of International Relations; www.st-andrews.ac.uk/intrel

international relations (numerous jt hons degrees), international security studies, international political theory, Middle East & Central Asian security studies, peace & conflict, terrorism studies; MA, MLitt, MPhil, MRes, PhD

School of Management; www.st-andrews.ac.uk/management

sociology of finance, international marketing, HRM, scenario thinking non-governmental organisations, contexts, contributions and challenges, corporate social responsibility, accounting and reporting, consuming culture, social history of advertising, entrepreneurship and small business development, change complexity and innovation, international business, international banking, strategies for global business management, social theory and work organisation, sustainable development and management, creative industries, management of change, corporate finance and control, finance and management, international business, management, management and information technology, managing in the creative industries, marketing; BSc, DipRes, MA, MLitt, MSc, MRes, PhD

School of Modern Languages; www.st-andrews.ac.uk/modlangs

Arabic, comparative literature, cultural identity studies, French/German/Italian studies, Russian, Central & Eastern European studies, Persian, Spanish, Spanish & Latin American studies, medieval studies, Middle Eastern literatures & cultures; DLang, MA, MLitt, MPhil, PGDip, PhD

School of Philosophical, Anthropological & Film Studies; www.st-andrews.ac.uk/philosophy

Philosophy; philosophy and ancient history/Arabic/art history/biblical studies/classical studies/classics/economics/English/French/German/ Greek/international relations/Italian/Latin/management/mathematics/mediaeval history/ modern history/ psychology/Russian/Scottish history/social anthropology/Spanish/statistics/ theological studies, logic and philosophy of science and computational science, internet computing, mathematics, physics, statistic; Postgrad: epistemology, mind and language, history of philosophy, logic and metaphysics, moral, political and legal philosophy

Social Anthropology; social anthropology and Arabic/art history/classical studies/economics/ English/French/geography/international relations/Italian/mediaeval history, middle east studies, modern history, philosophy, psychology, Russian, Scottish history/Spanish/theological studies, social anthropology with geography, economics with social anthropology; Postgrad; social anthropology and American Indian studies, social anthropology with Pacific studies, anthropology, art and perception

Film Studies; film analysis, film history, world cinema, and film theory, theory and practice of research in film

Music; understanding music, making music, reading opera, advanced performance, concert performance, Scottish music, electronic music

BSc, MA, MLitt, MPhil, MRes, PhD, PGDip

Faculty of Divinity

School of Divinity; www.st-andrews.ac.uk/divinity

bible & the contemporary world, biblical studies, divinity, Hebrew, New Testament, Old Testament, theological studies/interpretation of scripture, biblical language & literature, scripture & theology, systematic & historical theology, theology, theological studies, imagination & the arts, numerous jt honours degrees; BD, MA, MLitt, MPhil, MTheol, PGDip, PhD

Faculty of Medicine

Bute Medical School; www.medicine.st-andrews.ac.uk

health psychology, medicine, surgery, community health, molecular medicine; BSc, MD, MPhil, MSc, PhD, MRes

Faculty of Science

School of Biology; www.biology.st-andrews.ac.uk

behavioural biology, biochemistry, biology, biology and economics/geography/ geology/ logic and philosophy of science/ mathematics or statistics/ psychology, cell biology, ecology & conservation, evolutionary biology, marine biology, molecular biology, psychology with biology, zoology; Postgrad; marine mammal science, ecosystem-based management of marine systems, sustainable aquaculture; BSc, MPhil, MRes, PhD, PG Dip/Cert, MSc

School of Chemistry; www.st-andrews.ac.uk/chemistry

biomolecular/chemical sciences, biological chemistry, chemical science, inorganic/physical/organic chemistry, materials chemistry, medicinal chemistry, chemistry & physics, chemical science; BSc, MChem, MSci, PGDip, PhD, PG Dip/MSc

School of Computer Science; www.cs.st-andrews.ac.uk

advanced/computer science, AI, human-computer interaction, internet computer science, information technology, computing/management & IT, networks & distributed systems, software engineering, dependable software systems, jt degrees; BSc, MPhil, MSc, PhD, MSci(Hons)

School of Geography & Geosciences; www.st-andrews.ac.uk/gg

geology, environmental earth sciences, geography, sustainable development, sustainable energy; BSc, MA, MLitt, MPhil, MRes, MSc, PGCert, PGDip, PhD, MGeol

School of Mathematics & Statistics; www.maths.mcs.st-andrews.ac.uk

applied mathematics, applied statistics & data mining, mathematics, pure mathematics, statistics; BSc, GradDip, MA, MLitt, MMath, MPhil, MSc, PhD

School of Physics & Astronomy; www.st-andrews.ac.uk/physics

astrophysics, physics, theoretical physics & mathematics, photonics & optoelectronic devices, physics & mathematics/computer science/logic & philosophy of science/chemistry, physics & astronomy; BSc, EngDoc, MPhys, MSc, PhD, MSci

School of Psychology & Neuroscience; www.psy.st-andrews.ac.uk

behavioural & neural sciences, evolutionary & comparative psychology, adults with learning disabilities, neuroscience, perception, psychology, health psychology, adult support, protection & safeguarding; BSc, MA, MPhil, MRes, MSc, PhD

UNIVERSITY OF SALFORD
www.salford.ac.uk

College of Arts & Social Sciences: www.famss.salford.ac.uk

School of Arts & Media; www.salford.ac.uk/arts-media

Art and Design; fashion: design, image making and styling, graphic design, interior design, photography, visual arts, communication design/contemporary fine art/creative education/product innovation, fashion innovation: communication/design/digital/entrepreneurship

English; English drama, English and drama/creative writing, English language, English literature/with English language, Anthony Burgess and his contemporaries, experimental practice, literature in the academic and cultural world, writing workshop, creative writing: innovation and experiment, literature, culture and modernity

Journalism; journalism (broadcast/multimedia/journalism (news), journalism and English, international and online journalism, news/broadcast/sport

Media; animation, computer and video games, English/and film studies, media technology, professional broadcast techniques, TV and radio, media, media production (animation/children's TV production/ post-production for TV/TV drama production), wildlife documentary production

Music; music: creative music technology/musical art/ popular music and recording

Performance; dance, performance, comedy writing/ media & performance, digital performance, theatre & performance practice, TV & radio scriptwriting

Politics & Security; contemporary history and politics, contemporary military and international history, international relations and politics, politics, international politics and media/security, intelligence and security studies, terrorism and security

English and Creative Writing; creative writing: innovation and experiment, literature, culture and modernity

TESOL & Linguistics/applied linguistics; BA(Hons), BSc(Hons), PGDip, MA, PGDip/Cert, PhD, MRes

School of Humanities, Languages & Social Sciences; www.salford.ac.uk/humanities

criminology/& sociology, law with criminology, psychology & criminology, sociology, intelligence & security services, English language/& linguistics/ English literature, modern language studies (Arabic/ French/German/Spanish/French /Italian), translation & interpreting studies, modern language studies (combinations of Arabic/EFL/Chinese/French/German/Italian/Hispanic studies), TESOL/linguistics & applied linguistics, translating for international business; BA(Hons), MA, PGDip/Cert, LlB

College of Business & Law; www.salford.ac.uk/cbl

Salford Business School; www.salford.ac.uk/business-school

accounting and finance, business and economics/ financial management/management/tourism management, business information technology, business management with law/sport, corporate law, enterprise, leadership and management, HRM, international business, international events management, marketing, law, law (media and digital industries), law with criminology, management

Postgrad; accounting and finance, digital marketing, financial services management, global management, HRM & development, information systems management, international banking and finance, international business, international business law, international business with law, international commercial law, international corporate finance, international events management, international management, Islamic banking and finance, management, marketing, procurement, logistics and supply chain management, project management, social business and sustainable marketing, Salford MBA; BA(Hons), BSc(Hons), CertHE, DipHE, FD, GradCert/Dip, LlM, MA, MSc, MBA, MPhil, ProfDip, ProfPGDip, PhD

Salford Law School; www.salford.ac.uk/law

construction law & practice, environmental/health case law, international business law & regulation, international social justice, law/& criminality/finance/ Spanish, law, law (media & digital industries), corporate law, law with criminology/management; LlB, LlM, MA, MSc, PGCert/Dip

College of Health & Social Care; www.fhsc.salford.ac.uk

School of Health Sciences; www.salford.ac.uk/health-sciences

diagnostic radiography, exercise, physical activity and health, occupational therapy, physiotherapy, podiatry, prosthetics and orthotics, psychology, psychology and counselling, psychology and criminology, sport rehabilitation
Postgrad; advanced medical imaging, advanced occupational therapy, advanced physiotherapy, applied psychology (therapies), cancer survivorship, clinical gait analysis, geriatric medicine, lower limb health, disease and rehabilitation, media psychology, nuclear medicine imaging, occupational and vocational rehabilitation, public health, service transformation and integration in health and social care, sports injury rehabilitation, strength and conditioning, trauma and orthopaedics (lower limb/spinal/ upper limb), ultrasound imaging; BSc(Hons), MSc, PGDip/PGCert, MPhil, PhD

School of Nursing, Midwifery & Social Work; www.salford.ac.uk/nmsw

counselling and psychotherapy: professional practice, criminology/and sociology, enhancing professional health care practice, integrated practice in learning disabilities nursing and social work, midwifery, nursing (adult/children and young people's/ mental health), social policy, social work, sociology
Postgrad; advanced counselling & psychotherapy studies, advanced practice (health and social care), applied social work practice, cognitive behavioural therapy/psychotherapy, counselling and psychotherapy studies, dementia: care and the enabling environment, diabetes care, leadership and management for healthcare practice, leading education for health and social care reform, leading education in practice: midwifery, military veterans' health and wellbeing, nursing/ (adult, mental health or children & young people), nursing: research, practice, education, international, palliative and end of life care, social policy, social work, the criminal justice process; BSc(Hons), MA, ProfDoc, MSc, PGDip/PGCert

College of Science & Technology; www.fsee.salford.ac.uk

School of the Built Environment; www.sobe.salford.ac.uk

architecture, architectural design & technology, BIM & integrated design, building/quantity surveying, construction, construction project management, construction law & practice/management, project management in construction, real estate & property management; BSc(Hons), DBEnv, DConstMangt, DRealEst, MSc, MPhil, PGDip/Cert, PhD, ProfDoc

School of Computing, Science & Engineering; www.cse.salford.ac.uk

audio acoustics, adv computer science, adv control systems, aeronautical engineering, aircraft engineering/technology with pilot studies, aerospace engineering, audio production, civil/& architectural engineering, computer networks/science, databases & web-based systems, data communication networks, audio production, gas engineering & management, industrial & commercial combustion engineering, information security, mathematics, mechanical engineering, multimedia & internet technology, petroleum & mechanical engineering/gas engineering, physics with acoustics, professional sound & video technology, pure & applied/physics, robotics & embedded systems/automation, software engineering, structural engineering, transport engineering & planning, digital media, video, audio & social technologies, web development; BEng, BSc(Hons), HND, MEng, MEnt(Tech), MPhys, MSc, PGDip, PG(Tech)

School of Environmental & Life Sciences; www.els.salford.ac.uk

biochemistry, biology, biomedical science, environmental health, environmental management, environmental studies, geography, human biology and infectious diseases, human geography, medicinal chemistry, pharmaceutical science, wildlife and practical conservation, wildlife conservation with zoo biology

Postgrad; analytical bioscience and drug design, biomedical science, biotechnology, environmental and public health, environmental assessment and management, environmental modelling, GIS, molecular parasitology and vector biology, occupational safety, health and wellbeing, safety, health and environment, wildlife documentary production; BSc(Hons), BA(Hons), MSc, MA, FD, PGDip

Degrees validated by University of Salford offered at:

RIVERSIDE COLLEGE, HALTON
www.riversidecollege.ac.uk

sport coaching and sport development, computing and systems development, counselling; Dip, FD, FdSc, BSc(Hons)

UNIVERSITY OF SHEFFIELD
www.sheffield.ac.uk

Faculty of Arts & Humanities; www.sheffield.ac.uk/faculty/arts-and-humanities

Dept of Archaeology; www.sheffield.ac.uk/archaeology

archaeology, classical and historical archaeology, prehistoric archaeology, archaeology and history/Slavonic studies/Hispanic studies/French/German, archaeology, religion, theology and theology; Postgrad; Aegean archaeology, archaeology of the classical Mediterranean, medieval archaeology, landscape archaeology, material culture studies, archaeological materials, osteoarchaeology, environmental archaeology and palaeoeconomy, human osteology and funerary archaeology, palaeoanthropology, experimental archaeology; BA(Hons), BSc(Hons), MA, MPhil, MSc, PhD, MSt

Dept of Religion, Theology & the Bible; www.sheffield.ac.uk/theology

religion, theology & the bible, philosophy/French/German & religion, biblical literature and English, archaeology, religion theology & the bible, religion, theology, the bible & linguistics & religion, religion, theology and the bible with other arts and humanities subjects

Postgrad; theology, ministry and theology, ministry and biblical studies, theological studies, liturgy; BA(Hons), MA, PGDip/Cert

Dept of French; www.sheffield.ac.uk/french

French studies, French & archaeology/business management/economics/English/German/Hispanic studies/history/linguistics/music/philosophy/politics/religion/Russian, modern languages, French & Dutch, Czech, Japanese & Luxembourg, Chinese studies, Polish; BA(Hons), MA, MPhil, PhD

School of English Literature, Language and Linguistics; www.sheffield.ac.uk/english

18th/19th-century studies, applied linguistics with TESOL, creative writing, English language studies, English literature, English language & linguistics, language acquisition, language & literature/linguistics, English & theatre studies, English studies, theatre & performance studies; BA(Hons), MA, MPhil, PhD

Dept of Germanic Studies; www.sheffield.ac.uk/german

German studies, German & archaeology/business management/economics/English/French/Hispanic studies/history/linguistics/music/philosophy/politics/religion/Russian/Luxembourg studies, modern languages, 19th century German literary studies, 20th century German literary writing, modern German thought, post-war German politics, modern German political culture, Dutch literature since 1945, linguistics of Dutch, linguistics of German; comparative Germanic linguistics; BA(Hons), MPhil, PhD

Dept of Hispanic Studies; www.sheffield.ac.uk/hispanic

Hispanic studies & archaeology/business management/economics/English/French/history/linguistics/music/philosophy/politics/religion/Russian, applied Hispanic studies, Catalan studies, Japanese, Polish, Chinese studies, Czech, Latin American studies, modern language studies; BA(Hons), MA, MPhil, PhD

Dept of History; www.sheffield.ac.uk/history

history, American history, early/modern history, historical research, international/medieval history, numerous dual honours degrees; BA(Hons), MA, MPhil, PhD

School of Languages & Cultures; www.sheffield.ac.uk/slc

Catalan, Czech, Dutch, French, Germanic studies, Hispanic studies, feminine & gender studies, cultural history, intercultural communication, modern languages, multilingual information & international development, Polish, Russian, Russian and Slavonic studies, Spanish, Luxembourgish, Japanese, screen translation, translation studies, numerous jt degrees; BA(Hons), MA, MPhil, PhD

Department of Music; www.sheffield.ac.uk/music

music, music management/performance, ethnomusicology, musicology & composition, traditional music of the British Isles, sonic arts, world music, numerous jt degrees, music and psychology in education, psychology of music; BA(Hons), BMus(Hons), DPhil, MA, MMus, PhD

Dept of Philosophy; www.sheffield.ac.uk/philosophy

philosophy, metaphysics, epistemology, logic, philosophy of language & the mind, ethics, politics & value, political theory, cognitive studies, numerous joint degrees; BA(Hons), MA, MPhil, PhD, PGDip

Russian & Slavonic Studies; www.sheffield.ac.uk/russian

Russian studies, Polish studies, Czech studies, translation studies, screen translation, intercultural communication, multilingual information management, European gender studies, numerous jt degree courses; BA(Hons), MA, MPhil, PhD

Faculty of Engineering; www.sheffield.ac.uk/faculties/engineering

Dept of Aerospace Engineering; www.sheffield.ac.uk/aerospace

aerospace materials, aerospace engineering/with private pilot instruction, aerostructures & aerodynamics, adv manufacturing technologies, avionics, adv control systems & systems engineering, mechatronics & robotic engineering; BEng, MEng, MPhil, MSc, PhD, PGDip, MSc(Res), MSc, MSc(Eng)

Dept of Automatic Control & Systems Engineering; www.sheffield.ac.uk/acse

control systems engineering, computer systems engineering, computational intelligence & robotics, mechatronic & robotic engineering, systems & control engineering, engineering management; BEng, MEng, MPhil, MSc, PhD

Dept of Bioengineering; www.sheffield.ac.uk/bioengineering

bioengineering, biomedical engineering, biomanufacture, biomaterials with tissue engineering, biomaterials & regenerative medicine, dental materials science, medical devices & systems; BEng, MEng, MSC

Dept of Chemical & Biological Engineering; www.sheffield.ac.uk/cbe

biological and bioprocessing engineering, biochemical engineering, chemical engineering, chemical engineering with energy/chemistry/biotechnology/nuclear technology/modern language, environmental & energy engineering, process safety & loss prevention; BEng, MEng, MPhil, MSc, MSc(Eng), PhD

Dept of Civil & Structural Engineering; www.sheffield.ac.uk/civil

civil engineering, civil and structural engineering, structural engineering and architecture, architectural engineering design, civil engineering with a modern language, architectural engineering design, earthquake and civil engineering dynamics, steel construction, structural engineering, structural and concrete engineering, water engineering; BEng, MEng, MPhil, MSc, PGDip/Cert, PhD

Dept of Computer Science; www.sheffield.ac.uk/dcs

computer science, computer science and mathematics, artificial intelligence and computer science, software engineering, information technology management for business, software development for business, physics with computer science, advanced software engineering, advanced computer science, advanced computer science (computer graphics and virtual reality/enterprise computing/verification and testing), computer science with speech and language processing, software systems and internet technology, data communications, information systems; BEng, BSc, MComp, MEng, MPhil, MSc, MSc(Eng), PhD

Dept of Electronic & Electrical Engineering; www.sheffield.ac.uk/eee

electrical engineering, electronic engineering, electrical and electronic engineering, electronic and communications engineering, digital electronics, microelectronics, electronic & electrical engineering with a modern language, advanced electrical machines, power electronics and drives, data communications, electronic and electrical engineering, semiconductor photonics and electronics, wireless communication systems; BEng, MEng, MPhil, MSc, PhD

Dept of Materials Science & Engineering; www.sheffield.ac.uk/materials

adv/aerospace materials, adv aerospace/materials/nuclear materials manufacturing, adv metallurgy, adv solid state chemistry & its applications, materials science & engineering (biomaterials/industrial management/modern language), ceramic science & engineering, polymers & polymer composites science & technology, nuclear science & technology/engineering & science, biomaterials & regenerative medicine, material science & nanomaterials; BEng, EngD, MEng, MPhil, MSc, MRes, PhD, MMet

Dept of Mechanical Engineering; www.sheffield.ac.uk/mecheng

advanced/mechanical engineering, advanced manufacturing technologies, aerodynamics & aerostructures, automotive engineering, mechatronics & robotic engineering, mechanical engineering with Spanish/French/Italian/German/industrial management, nuclear technology; BEng, MEng, MPhil, MSc, MSc(Res), PhD

Faculty of Medicine, Dentistry & Health; www.sheffield.ac.uk/faculties/medicine-dentistry-health

The Medical School; www.sheffield.ac.uk/medicine

human metabolism/nutrition, infection & immunity, medicine, medical education, molecular/& genetic medicine, musculoskeletal ageing, reproductive &

developmental medicine, translational neuroscience, translational oncology, orthoptics, surgery, vision & strabismus; BMedSci, MBChB, MD, PhD, PGCert/Dip

School of Clinical Dentistry; www.sheffield.ac.uk/dentalschool

clinical dentistry, dental hygiene and therapy, dental implantology, dental materials science, dental public health, dental surgery, dentistry, endodontics, diagnostic oral pathology, orthodontics, paediatric dentistry, periodontics, prosthodontics, dental public health, dental technology; BDS, ClinDent, Diploma, MSc, MClinD, MDPH, MMedSci, MPhil, PhD

Health & Related Research; www.sheffield.ac.uk/scharr

adv emergency care, clinical research, health services, public health (management & leadership), health economics & decision making, European public health (health service research/management & leadership), international health technical management/management & leadership; MSc, PGDip/Cert, MPH, MEuro PubHealth

Dept of Human Communication Sciences; www.sheffield.ac.uk/hcs

acquired communication disorders, cleft & speech, cleft palate studies, clinical communication studies, language & communication impairment in children, language & literacy, speech difficulties, speech & language sciences; AdvCert, BMedSci(Hons), BSc(Hons), MMedSci, MPhil, MSc, PGCert/Dip, PhD

Dept of Human Metabolism; www.sheffield.ac.uk/humanmetabolism

molecular medicine, translational neuroscience, human nutrition, vision & strabismus; B/MMedSci, MSc, MRCPsych, PGCert, PhD, MD

Dept of Infection & Immunity; www.sheffield.ac.uk/infectionandimmunity

molecular medicine, translational neuroscience; BMedSci, MSc, MRCPsych

Dept of Neuroscience; www.sheffield.ac.uk/neuroscience

translational neuroscience; BMedSci, MSc, MRCPsych

School of Nursing & Midwifery; www.sheffield.ac.uk/snm

acute care, cancer care, adult nursing studies, advanced practice, adv neonatal nurse practitioner, dementia care, health & social care studies/human sciences, high dependency & critical care, infection control, long term conditions, maternity care, midwifery, neonatal intensive care, nursing studies, nurse practitioner, occupational health nursing, palliative care, public health, primary/critical/cancer/neonatal intensive care; BMedSci, MMedSci, MMid, MPhil, PGCert, PhD

Dept of Oncology; www.sheffield.ac.uk/oncology

clinical oncology, cancer studies, supportive care, surgical oncology, urology, inflammation & tumour targeting, translational medicine; MSc, MSD, PhD

The Faculty of Science;
www.sheffield.ac.uk/faculties/science

Dept of Animal & Plant Sciences; www.sheffield.ac.uk/aps

animal behaviour, biology, conservation & biodiversity, ecology, plant sciences, ecology & environment, evolution & behaviour, plant-environment interaction/science, ecology & conservation biology/environment, plant & microbial biology, molecular science, plant-environment interchange, plant & microbial biology, population & community ecology, zoology; MBiolSci, PhD, MPhil, MEnvSci

Dept of Biomedical Science; www.sheffield.ac.uk/bms

biomedical science, integrative physiology and pharmacology, molecular and cellular basis of human disease, stem cell and regenerative medicine; BSc(Hons), MSc, PhD

Dept of Chemistry; www.sheffield.ac.uk/chemistry

chemistry, polymers for advanced technologies, science communication, biological chemistry, chemical physics, chemistry with biological & medicinal chemistry; BSc, MChem, MPhil, MPhys, PhD

Dept of Molecular Biology & Biotechnology; www.sheffield.ac.uk/mbb

biochemistry, biochemistry & genetics/microbiology, molecular cell biology, biology, biological chemistry, genetics, human & molecular biosciences, medical genetics/biochemistry, microbiology/molecular cell biology, biochemistry, microbiology, molecular biology, biology, medical microbiology; BSc(Hons), MBiolSci, PhD

Dept of Physics & Astronomy; www.sheffield.ac.uk/physics

astronomy & astrophysics, physics with astrophysics/computer science/philosophy, chemical physics, medical physics, nanoscale science and technology, physics, theoretical physics; BSc(Hons), MPhys, MSc, PhD

Dept of Psychology; www.sheffield.ac.uk/psychology

cognitive studies, cognitive & computational neuroscience, cognitive neuroscience & human neuroimaging, science communication, psychology, psychological research studies; BA(Hons), BSc(Hons), DClinPsych, MA, MPhil, MSc, PhD

School of Mathematics & Statistics; www.sheffield.ac.uk/maths

mathematics, statistics, financial maths, statistics with medical applications, maths with language; BSc, MSc, PhD, MMath, MComp

Faculty of Social Science;
www.sheffield.ac.uk/faculty/social-science

School of Architecture; www.sheffield.ac.uk/architecture

architecture, architectural design, architecture regeneration, designing learning environments, structural engineering & architecture, digital design & international built environment, sustainable architectural studies, urban design; BA(Hons), MArch, MPhil, MSc, PhD, MEng

School of East Asian Studies; www.sheffield.ac.uk/seas

Chinese studies, East Asian studies, adv/Japanese studies, modern/Korean studies, jt honours degrees; BA(Hons), MA, PhD

Dept of Economics; www.sheffield.ac.uk/economics

economics, accounting & financial management & economics, business finance & economics, economics & mathematics/politics/philosophy/finance/business management, financial economics, economics & health economics, international finance and economics, money, banking & finance, French/German/Hispanic studies/Russian & economics; Adv Cert, BA(Hons), BSc(Hons), MSc, PhD

Sheffield School of Law; www.sheffield.ac.uk/law

law, biotechnological law and ethics, corporate & commercial law, law (European & international), law with French/German/Spanish/criminology, social policy & criminology, European health law & policy, French/German/Spanish, law, international law, international criminology, international commercial law & practice, global policy & law, international/& European law, politics & governance, legal practice; LlB, LlM, MAPhil, PhD, GradDip

Sheffield Management School; www.sheffield.ac.uk/management

accounting and financial management, business management, international business management, business management with Japanese studies/Chinese studies/French/German/Hispanic studies/Korean studies/Russian, accounting and financial management and economics/mathematics, business management & economics/mathematics, business management and economics/mathematics/social policy/sociology; Postgrad; creative and cultural industries management, entrepreneurship and management, finance and accounting, global marketing management, HRM, information systems management, international management, international management and marketing, leadership and management, logistics and supply chain management, management, management (international business), marketing, management practice, occupational psychology, work psychology; MSc, MPhil, PhD, Sheffield MBA, ExecMBA

Dept of Politics; www.sheffield.ac.uk/politics

politics, European law/& governance & politics, European & global affairs, international relations/political economy, global politics and law/security/justice, globalisation & development, governance & public policy, international relations & politics, international politics & security studies/public policy, political theory, politics/& history/sociology/economics/philosophy/French/German/Russian/Hispanic studies; BA, MA, MPhil, PhD

Dept of Sociological Studies; www.sheffield.ac.uk/socstudies

business management & social policy/sociology, dementia studies, sociology/& English language/history/politics/criminology, integrated practice with children & families, social policy/politics & sociology, social research, sociology; BA(Hons), MA, MPhil, PhD

Dept of Town & Regional Planning; www.sheffield.ac.uk/trp

architecture/& town & regional planning, cities & global development, commercial real estate, geography & planning, international development & planning, real estate planning/& development, town & regional planning, urban studies/design & planning & planning, planning research, applied GIS, TR; BA(Hons), MA, MPlan, PhD

The School of Education; www.sheffield.ac.uk/education

applied professional studies in education, children, schools & families, education, culture & childhood, education, policy & practice, education: early childhood education/early childhood/language & education, educational child psychology, globalising education, higher education, language, learning & teaching, literacy & learning, policy & practice, PGDE (English, geography, history, mathematics, modern languages & science), school direct, psychology & education, educational research; EdD, MA, MEd, MPhil, PhD, PCHE, DEdPsy

Dept of Geography; www.sheffield.ac.uk/geography

geography, applied GIS, environmental change & international development, food security & food justice, geography & planning, international development, polar & alpine change; BA(Hons), BSc(Hons), MEnvSci, PhD, MPH

School of Information; www.sheffield.ac.uk/is

data science, electronic & digital library management, health informatics, information management, information systems/management, librarianship, library & information service management, multilingual information management; MA, MChem, MSc, MSc(Res), PhD/MPhil

Dept of Journalism Studies; www.sheffield.ac.uk/journalism

global/magazine journalism, journalism studies, international political communication, broadcast journalism, print journalism, science communication; BA, MPhil, PhD

Dept of Landscape; www.sheffield.ac.uk/landscape

landscape architecture, landscape management, architecture & landscape, landscape studies, landscape research; BA(Hons), BSc(Hons), MA, PGDip, PhD, MLA, BA/BSc

SHEFFIELD HALLAM UNIVERSITY
www.shu.ac.uk

Faculty of Arts, Computing, Engineering & Science; www.shu.ac.uk/art/faculties.aces

Art & Design; www.shu.ac.uk/prospectus/subject/art-design/

art & design, creative art practice, fashion design/management & communication, fine art, graphic design, illustration, interior design, design (packaging/graphics/product/interiors), product design: jewellery & metalwork/furniture, product design, PGCE secondary design technology/illustration; BA(Hons), MA, MArt, MDes

Media, PR & Journalism; www.shu.ac.uk/prospectus/subject/media-pr-journalism

journalism, digital media production, international broadcast journalism, PR, media, sports journalism, cultural communication & computer, cultural policy & management, photography, PR/ & media, games design; BA(Hons), MA, MPhil, PhD, PGCert/Dip

Computing; www.shu.ac.uk/prospectus/subject/computing

animation/& digital effects, advanced computer networks, big data analytics, business information systems, business & ICT, computing, computer & network engineering/information security, computer science, computer security with forensics, computer & network engineering, computing management/networks, database professionals, data science, digital media production, enterprise systems professional/innovation & management, forensic & security technologies, games/software design/development, IT with business technologies/digital media/networks, IT professional, IT with business studies, information systems/security, networking professional, software engineering, software development, web & cloud computing, web systems design, PGCE (secondary computing); BEng, BSc(Hons), FdSc, GradDip, MComp, MSc, MPhil, PhD

Engineering; www.shu.ac.uk/prospectus/subject/engineering

advanced engineering/management, aeronautical/aerospace/electronic engineering, advanced design/aeronautical materials engineering/engineering metals, automation & control engineering/control & robotics, automotive engineering, computer & network engineering, electrical & electronic engineering, engineering & mathematics, engineering (mechanical) food/manufacturing engineering, forensic engineering, industrial management, integrated engineering (manufacturing/materials/electrical), logistics & supply chain management, materials engineering, adv/mechanical engineering, mechanical & automotive engineering, product design, railway engineering, sports technology/engineering, telecommunication & electronic engineering, PGCE (engineering/design & technology); BSc(Hons), BEng, FdSc, MBA, MSc, PhD

Mathematics; www.shu.ac.uk/mathematics

mathematics education with QTS, data science, mathematics education, mathematics, PGCE secondary mathematics, subject knowledge/mathematics, engineering with mathematics; BSc(Hons), MSc, PhD, CertHE, MA/PGDip

Media Arts; www.shu.ac.uk/prospectus/subject/media-arts

animation/& digital effects, digital media production, fashion & media, media, games design/software development, international documentary production, fine art, journalism, film & media production, photography, PR/ & media, filmmaking; BA(Hons), MA, MComp, MArt, MSc

Faculty of Development & Society; www.shu.ac.uk/faculties/ds/nbe

Natural & Built Environment

architectural technology, architecture, building/quantity surveying, built environment, business property management, construction/project management/engineering, built environment, environmental science/management, human/geography, GIS, planning & geography, urban regeneration planning, planning & geography, real estate, project management in the built environment, transport planning; BSc(Hons), MPhil, MSc, PGDip/Cert, PhD, MBA

Criminology & Community Justice; www.shu.ac.uk/prospectus/subject/law

law, law & criminology, applied human rights, forensic criminology/science/law/psychology/accounting, international commercial law; BEng, BSc(Hons), FdSc, MA/PGDip/PGCert, MSc

Education; www.shu.ac.uk/prospectus/subject/education-studies

Asperger's syndrome, autism spectrum, early/childhood studies, early years/education with QTS/teaching, design & technology, education, educational studies with psychology & counselling, education & learning support, English & educational studies, knowledge enhancement in mathematics, languages & TESOL (French/Spanish/German), learning & teaching in HE/in primary education with QTS, mathematics/science with education & QTS, mentoring & coaching in educational leadership/FE, mentoring for learning & teaching/educational leadership, mathematics with education & QTS, PE & school sport, post-16 education & training, teaching & learning in the primary sector/with QTS/early years/ HE, special needs coordination, education studies, primary ed with QTS, design & technology/science with education & QTS, PGCE (early years education, learning & skills, mathematics education, primary, secondary – broad range of taught subjects – secondary citizenship), youth work

Teacher Education: post-16 education & training, teach first, school direct, special educational needs, teaching English for academic purposes; BA(Hons), CertE, EdD, FdA, MA, MPhil, MSc, PGCert/Dip, PhD, PGCE

Environment; www.shu.ac.uk/prospectus/subject/environment

environmental management/science; BSc(Hons), MPlan, MSc/PGDip/PGCert

English; www.shu.ac.uk/prospectus/subject/english

creative writing, writing, English & history, English/ language/literature, TESOL, English language teaching, ESOL, secondary English, English by research; BA(Hons), PGCE, MA, PGDip, MPhil, PhD

History; www.shu.ac.uk/prospectus/subject/history

history, English & history, criminology, politics, local & global history, imperialism & culture, history by research; PGCE, BA(Hons), MA, PGDip, MPhil, PhD

Stage & Screen; www.shu.ac.uk/prospectus/subject/stage-screen

animation & visual effects, film studies, film and media/production, international documentary production, performance & professional practice/for stage & screen, film studies & screenwriting; BA(Hons), FdA, MA, MArt, MA/PGDip/PGCert

Geography; www.shu.ac.uk/prospectus/subject/geography

geography/and planning, GIS, human geography; BA(Hons), BSc(Hons), MSc, PGDip/Cert, PGCE

Law; www.shu.ac.uk/prospectus/subject/law

law applied human rights, forensic accounting/ criminology/psychology/science, law with criminology, maîtrise en droit Francais; LlB, LLM, MSc, PGCert/Dip

Planning, Regeneration & Housing; www.shu.ac.uk/planning

geography & planning, GIS, human geography, built environment, business property management, urban planning, urban regeneration; BA(Hons), BSc(Hons), MPlanning and Transport, MSc/PGDip, DipHE, MBA

Psychology; www.shu.ac.uk/psychology

psychology, applied cognitive neuroscience, cognitive analytic therapy, criminology & psychology, developmental/forensic/industrial/organizational psychology, clinical cognitive neuroscience, education with psychology & counselling, health psychology, psychology & sociology, sexual & relationship psychotherapy, sport & exercise psychology; BSc(Hons), MRes/PGDip/PGCert, MSc, ExecMBA

Sociology & Politics; www.shu.ac.uk/prospectus/subject/sociology-politics/

applied social science, applied human rights, business, cultural studies, criminology/& sociology, education, human geography, politics, psychology/& sociology, public health, social sciences, sociology, planning and policy; BA(Hons), GradDip, MA, MPhil/PhD, MRes/PGDip/PGCert

Faculty of Health & Wellbeing; www.shu.ac.uk/faculties/hwb

Sport and Active Lifestyles; www.shu.ac.uk/prospectus/subject/sport-active-lifestyles

adv sport coaching practice, PE & school sport, professional studies, sports & development/with coaching, sport journalism/technology/engineering/ studies/coaching, physical activity, sport & health, secondary physical education, sports journalism/ studies, app/sport & exercise science, sport & exercise psychology, international/sport business management; BA(Hons), BSc(Hons), MA, MSc, PGDip/Cert, ProfDoc, PGCE

Biosciences & Chemistry; www.shu.ac.uk/bio

analytical chemistry, biochemistry, biology, biomedical/laboratory sciences, biosciences, biotechnology, chemistry, forensic science, human biology, molecular & cell biology, pharmaceutical analysis, pharmacology and biotechnology, professional studies, secondary science; BSc(Hons), MSc/PGDip/PGCert, ProfDocBiomedSc, PGCE

Diagnostic Radiography; www.shu.ac.uk/prospectus/subject/diagnostic-radiography

advanced diagnostic imaging practice, advancing professional practice, diagnostic radiography, medical ultrasound, radiological studies, healthcare education, health & social care leadership & management, professional studies; DocProf Studies (Health and Social Care), BA(Hons), BSc(Hons), MSc/PGDip/PGCert

Nursing & Midwifery; www.shu.ac.uk/faculties/lwb/departments/nursing-midwifery

advancing professional practice (paediatrics), applied nursing (learning disabilities) and generic social work, approved mental health professional nursing, community specialist practice, nursing (adult/child/mental health, public health/primary & community care), specialist community public health nursing/health visiting & nursing, health and social care leadership & management, healthcare education, maternal health care, midwifery, medical ultrasound, supportive and palliative care, primary care nursing/district nursing, professional practice (nursing/midwifery), prostate cancer care, health visiting and school nursing, social work, sports studies/practice, professional studies; AdvDip, AdvProfDev, BA(Hons), BSc(Hons), DocProfStud, FD, MSc/PGDip/PGCert

Centre for Medical & Dental Education; www.shu.ac.uk/faculties/hwb/medical

MSc, PGCert/Dip

Occupational Therapy; www.shu.ac.uk/occupational

applying/occupational therapy, advancing (paediatric) practice, vocational rehabilitation, healthcare education, health and social care leadership & management, vocational rehabilitation, professional studies; BSc(Hons), DocProf, MSc/PGDip/PGCert

Operating Department Practice; www.shu.ac.uk/odp

operating dept practice, advancing professional practice, health & social care leadership/management, healthcare education, professional studies; DipHE, DocProfStud, MSc/PGDip/Cert

Paramedic Studies; www.shu.ac.uk/paramedic

paramedic practice, advancing professional practice, health and social care leadership & management, healthcare education, professional studies; DipHE, MSc, PGDip/Cert, ProfDoc

Physiotherapy; www.shu.ac.uk/physio

advancing/applying physiotherapy practice, physiotherapy (practice based), applied sport & exercise science, adv professional practice (paediatrics), radiological studies, health and social care leadership/& management, healthcare education, vocational rehabilitation, medical ultrasound therapy, manual therapy, professional studies; BA(Hons), BSc(Hons), MSc, PGCert, PGDip, ProfDoc

Radiotherapy and Oncology; www.shu.ac.uk/radiotherapy

adv practice radiotherapy & oncology, adv professional practice, healthcare education, prostrate cancer care, radiotherapy planning, radiotherapy & oncology in practice, supportive and palliative care, health and social care leadership/& management, radiological studies, professional studies; BA(Hons), BSc(Hons), DipHE, MSc/PGDip/PGCert, ProfDoc

Social Work; www.shu.ac.uk/socialwork

applied nursing (learning disabilities) & generic social work, social work, specialist mental health practice/practitioner, working with children, young people & families, youth & community work, youth work, health and social care leadership & management, professional studies; BA(Hons), GradDip, MSc, PGDip, MSW, PGCert, DocSocWork, FD

Sheffield Business School; www.shu.ac.uk/sbs;

Accounting, Banking & Finance; www.shu.ac.uk/prospectus/subject/accounting-banking-finance/

accounting & finance, banking & finance, business & finance/financial management, business economics, international finance & banking/economics/investment, finance & investment, business accounting, financial management, forensic accounting, risk management; BA(Hons), MA, MSc, PGDip/Cert

Business & Management; www.shu.ac.uk/prospectus/subject/business-management

business, business and management/marketing/HRM/finance/financial management/ICT, built environment, business admin/economics/studies/management, business & enterprise management/English, business information systems, business property management, charity research management, coaching & mentoring, facilities management, financial management, food marketing management, global supply chain management, HRM/D, HR leadership, international business/studies/with languages, international business management, IT with business studies, strategic marketing, HRM/HR development, leadership & management, logistics & supply chain management, managing global business, organisational development & consultancy, industrial management, international business management/HRM/marketing/business studies, languages with business/tourism, marketing, marketing communication & advertising, professional business practice(sales & sales leadership), quality management, sales leadership, secondary business education, total quality management & organisational excellence, sports business management, strategic operations management, Exec MBAs (psychology/facility management/built environment); BSc(Hons), DBA, FD, GradDip, Exec MBA, PGCE, MBA, MPhil, MSc, PGCert, PGDip, PhD, MRes

Languages; www.shu.ac.uk/prospectus/subject/languages/

business & English, English language teaching, languages with TESOL/international business/tourism/marketing, international business studies & languages (French/German/Spanish), teaching English for academic purposes; GradDip/Cert, MPhil, PGCert, PhD

Tourism, Hospitality & Events Management; www.shu.ac.uk/prospectus/subject/tourism-hospitality-events

international/events management with arts & entertainment/tourism/experiental marketing, cultural policy & management, events management, events & leisure management, international events and conference management, international hospitality/tourism management/hotel management, international events management/with tourism, international tourism & hospitality business management, tourism management, tourism & hospitality business management, hospitality business management/with conference & events/culinary arts, secondary design & technology (food technology); BSc(Hons), FdSc, HND, MA, MPhil, MSc, PGCert, PGDip, PhD

UNIVERSITY OF SOUTH WALES
www.southwales.ac.uk

Faculty of Creative Industries;
www.southwales.ac.uk

School of Drama & Music; www.southwales.ac.uk/drama-music
Dance & Performance;
dance, performance & media, scriptwriting, theatre & drama, performing arts, live event technology; Postgrad; drama
Music & Sound
creative sound & music, music business, contemporary music performance, creative and therapeutic arts, pop, creative industries (popular music technology), music technology, sound engineering, Postgrad; music therapy, songwriting and production, music engineering and production

School of Media; www.southwales.ac.uk/school/media
Journalism & Media
film studies, journalism, media production, media, culture and journalism, performance and media, photojournalism, scriptwriting, Postgrad; drama
Film
film, creative industries (film and video), documentary film and TV, film studies, Postgrad; film producing
Animation, Games & Visual Effects
animation (2D and stop motion), computer animation, computer games design, computer games enterprise, game art, visual effects and motion graphics, Postgrad; animation, computer animation, games enterprise, visual effects

School of Art & Design; www.southwales.ac.uk/art-design

Art

creative & therapeutic art, art practice, art & design, film & TV set design, art psychotherapy, arts practice/fine art/art health & wellbeing

Design

illustration, advertising design, computer games design, fashion design, fashion promotion, graphic communication, interior design, TV and film set design, fashion marketing and retail design, Postgrad; computer animation, graphic communication, visual effects

Photography

photography, creative industries (photography, fine art, photojournalism, documentary photography; Postgrad; documentary photography

Fashion

fashion design/promotion/marketing/retail design, photography for fashion & advertising; BA(Hons), FdA, MFA, MA, MPhil, DDes, Dip Found, BMus(Hons), MSc, PhD

Faculty of Computing, Engineering & Science; www.southwales.ac.uk/computing-maths

Computing & Mathematics

Computing

computer science, computer systems engineering, computer forensics, computer games development, computer security, computing, computing mathematics, information communication technology, information technology management for business, software engineering, computer systems engineering; Postgrad; computer forensics, computer science, computer systems security, computing and information systems, cyber security, mobile computing

Mathematics

mathematics, computing mathematics, financial mathematics

Engineering; www.southwales.ac.uk/school-engineering

Aerospace Engineering

aeronautical engineering, aircraft maintenance engineering

Civil Engineering

civil engineering, fire safety engineering, Postgrad; civil engineering and environmental management, civil and structural engineering, dispute resolution, lean and six-sigma management

Electrical & Electronic Engineering

computer systems engineering, electrical and electronic engineering, information technology, renewable energy systems, Postgrad; electronics and information technology, embedded systems design, mobile and satellite communications, optoelectronics

Mechanical Engineering

automotive engineering, mechanical engineering, energy systems engineering, professional engineering

Renewable & Sustainable Energy

renewable energy systems, sustainable energy systems

Lighting & Live Event Technology

live event technology, lighting design & technology

Property, Construction & Surveying

project management (surveying) quantity surveying & commercial management, Postgrad; asset management & development, building information modelling & sustainability, dispute resolution, safety, health & environmental management

BSc(Hons), BA(Hons), BEng(Hons), MEng, MSc, UnivHCert, MComp(Hons), MMus

Faculty of Business & Society; www.southwales.ac.uk/faculty-business-society

Business School; www.southwales.ac.uk/bus-school

business management, business, business studies, business and accounting/finance/HRM/management/marketing/supply chain management, event management, HRM, international business, logistics and supply chain management, marketing, retail management, finance and investment, business studies, retail management; Postgrad; procurement and supply, business administration, engineering management, fashion marketing, HRM, international business and enterprise, international logistics and supply chain management, leadership and management, management, marketing, project management, PR, strategic digital marketing, strategic procurement management, (MBA) HRM/public service management, entrepreneurship practice, mentoring for entrepreneurial practice

School of Humanities & Social Sciences; www.southwales.ac.uk/hass

History

history, history with English, history by research

English & Creative Writing

English, English & history, English by research, writing, English & creative writing

Religious Studies

religious studies, Buddhist studies

Public Services & Emergency Services

public services, global/governance, community development & cross-section collaboration, health & public services management

Criminology

criminology & criminal justice/& youth justice, forensic science & criminology, criminology & law/psychology/sociology, criminology & social justice, criminal justice

Sociology

sociology with criminology/education/psychology

Combined studies

combined studies

Welsh

Welsh in the workplace with education/English/law

Youth & Community

childhood studies, working for/with children & young people, youth & community work/youth justice

School of Law, Accounting & Finance; www.southwales.ac.uk

Accounting & Finance

accounting and finance, forensic accounting, finance and investment, financial planning, investment and risk, Postgrad; accounting and finance/financial management, finance/and investment, forensic audit and accounting, Islamic banking and finance, management and development of international financial systems, trading and risk

Law

law, legal practice, law and business, criminology and criminal justice and law, paralegal studies, law with criminology and criminal justice, law with Welsh in the workplace, Postgrad; intellectual property law, international commercial law, law, legal practice, dispute resolution

BA(Hons), BA/BSc, BSc(Hons), DocPublServ, FCert, FdA, GradDip Law, LlB(Hons), LlM/PhD, MA/PDip/Cert, MSc, CertHE, PGDip, MBA, DBA

Faculty of Life Science & Education

School of Psychology, Early Years & Therapeutic Studies/pet; fbs.glam.ac.uk/psychology

Psychology

applied psychology, criminology and criminal justice with psychology, psychology, psychology with behaviour analysis/cognitive behavioural therapy/counselling/criminology/developmental disorders/education, sociology with psychology, sport psychology

Postgrad; behaviour analysis and therapy, business psychology, clinical and abnormal psychology, developmental disorders, health psychology, play therapy, play and therapeutic play, psychology by research, systemic/psychotherapy, behaviour analysis supervised practice, consultative supervision

Psychotherapy & Counselling

creative and therapeutic arts; Postgrad; systemic counselling, art psychotherapy, consultative supervision, counselling children and young people, integrative counselling and psychotherapy, music therapy, cognitive behavioural psychotherapy, systemic counselling/psychotherapy

School of Education; www.southwales.ac.uk/school-education

Welsh in the workplace with education, early years education and practice, history with education, childhood development, childhood studies, psychology/sociology with education, childhood development, early years education and practice; Postgrad; child and adolescent mental health, childhood studies, developing professional practice in higher education, early years, education, education for sustainable development and global citizenship, ICT & education, leadership & management (education/post compulsory education and training/FE/PCET), professional practice in higher education, religious education, special educational needs (SEN / autistic spectrum), teaching English (TEAL/ TESOL/TEYL) developmental disorders, developing professional practice in higher education, specific learning difficulties, PGCE: post compulsory education and training, SEN attention deficit hyperactivity disorder/developmental co-ordination disorder (dyspraxia)

Health, Sport & Professional Practice

Sport

sports development, clinical physiology, football/rugby coaching and performance, sport psychology/coaching, sports coaching and performance, sports studies, sports and exercise science, strength and conditioning, community football/rugby coaching and development, Postgrad; performance coaching, sport, health and exercise science, sports coaching/and performance, sports physiotherapy (sports and exercise rehabilitation), sports and exercise medicine, youth sports coaching

Chiropractic
chiropractic
Social Work & Social Care Management
social work, health & social care, sociology
Policing & Security
police sciences, Postgrad;community and partnerships, international policing

Care Science; www.southwales.ac.uk/care
Nursing & Health Science
community health & wellbeing, professional practice (nursing), specialist community public health nursing (health visiting/occupational health nursing/ school health nursing, nursing (adult/child/learning disabilities/mental health), health care nursing support worker education, dementia studies, community health and wellbeing; Postgrad; acute and critical care, community health studies (community children's nursing/district nursing/learning disabilities nursing, practice nursing, professional practice (health care studies/violence reduction), occupational health (nursing/technician), professional practice, health; Postgrad; advanced clinical practitioner,

clinical practice for nurses and midwives, community health studies (children's community nursing/community learning disabilities nursing, district nursing/practice nursing), diabetes, diagnostic clinical ultrasound (abdomen and small parts/superficial structures/clinical echocardiography/gynaecology/musculoskeletal/obstetrics and related gynaecology/vascular ultrasound), disaster healthcare, education for health and social care professionals, endocrinology, professional practice, professional practice (learning disability/ mental health/research/vulnerable person), public health, specialist community public health nursing (health visiting/ school health nursing), clinical endodontics, nursing studies, sports and exercise medicine, acute and critical care, education for health and social care professionals, palliative care, SEN specific learning difficulties, return to practice

Midwifery
midwifery, professional practice (midwifery); BA(Hons), BSc(Hons), BN, FoundCerts, CertHE, MSc, BMid, PGCert/Dip, FD

UNIVERSITY OF SOUTHAMPTON
www.soton.ac.uk

Faculty of Business and Law;
www.southampton.ac.uk/faculties/
faculty_business_law.html

School of Law; www.soton.ac.uk/law
law, law & psychology, commercial & corporate law, crime analysis, European law/legal studies, general law, insurance law, IT & commerce, international law/business law/legal studies, maritime law; LlB, LlM, MPhil, PhD

Southampton Business School; www.sbs.ac.uk/business-school
accounting and finance business history, business innovation, business management, business philosophy, business entrepreneurship, international marketing, management, management sciences/and accounting, management with entrepreneurship, marketing, music and management sciences, management sciences and German, accounting and management, business analytics, corporate risk & security management, digital marketing, finance, global enterprise and entrepreneurship, HRM, business administration, international banking & financial studies/marketing, financial studies, international

financial markets, international management, knowledge and information systems management, leadership and management in health and social care, management science & finance, marketing analytics, marketing management, organisational change management, project management, risk and finance, risk management, strategy and innovation, supply chain management and logistics; BSc(Hons), MSc, PhD, MBA, DBA, PGCert, MPhil

Winchester School of Art; www.soton.ac.uk/wsa
advertising design/management, communication/fashion/textiles design, design/fashion management, contemporary curation, fashion & textile design, fashion design (knitwear for fashion/textiles/woven textiles/printed textiles), games design & art, graphic arts/design, illustration, luxury brand management, photography, fine art, fashion marketing/management/& branding, global media management, motion graphics, printmaking, textile design; BA(Hons), MA, MPhil, PhD

Faculty of Engineering & the Environment; www.southampton.ac.uk/engineering

Acoustical Engineering

acoustical engineering, acoustics & music, engineering

Aeronautics and Astronautics

aeronautics & astronautics, aeronautics & astronautics (aerodynamics/air vehicle systems design/computational engineering design/engineering management/materials and structures/spacecraft engineering

Mechanical Engineering

mechanical engineering (acoustical engineering/advanced materials/aerospace/automotive/biomedical engineering), computational engineering and design, engineering management, mechatronics, naval engineering, sustainable energy systems

Computer Science and Software Engineering

electrical and electronic engineering (EEE), electrical engineering, electromechanical engineering, electronic engineering, information technology in organisations, web science

Environmental Science

environmental management with business, environmental monitoring and modelling, environmental sciences

Audiology

healthcare science (audiology)

Civil & Environmental Engineering

civil engineering/& architecture, civil & environmental engineering

Ship Science

ship science, ship science/advanced materials/engineering management/naval architecture/naval engineering/yacht & small craft, offshore engineering
Postgrad
Audiology; audiology, clinical and health research, clinical practice
Engineering; aerodynamics and computation, biomedical engineering, civil engineering, coastal and marine engineering and management, computational engineering design, energy and sustainability, energy and sustainability, engineering in the coastal environment, engineering materials, marine technology, maritime engineering science (advanced materials/marine engineering/maritime computational fluid dynamics/naval architecture/offshore engineering/maritime engineering science /yacht and small craft), mechatronics, propulsion and engine systems engineering, race car aerodynamics, sound and vibration studies, space systems engineering, surface engineering and coatings, sustainable energy technologies, transportation planning and engineering
Environmental Science; biodiversity and conservation, environmental monitoring and assessment, environmental pollution control, integrated environmental studies, water resources management, unmanned aircraft systems design; BEng, MEng, BSc(Hons), MEnvSci(Hons), DClinPract, MRes, MSc, MPhil, PhD, EngD

Faculty of Health Sciences; www.soton.ac.uk/healthsciences

midwifery, nursing (adult and child/adult and mental health/adult/child/mental health), clinical practice, healthcare science (cardiovascular and, respiratory and sleep science), healthcare: management, policy and research, occupational therapy, physiotherapy, podiatry, public health practice: specialist community public health nursing, advanced clinical practice (advanced nurse practitioner)
Postgrad; advanced clinical practice (children and young people/critical care/(district nursing/children's community nursing/midwifery/neonatal/standard), advanced rehabilitation technologies, clinical and health research, clinical leadership in cancer, palliative and end of life care, health and rehabilitation, health sciences (standard, mental health and neonatal), nursing – adult, child, mental health, leadership and management in health and social care, midwifery, physiotherapy, specialist community public health nursing
BSc(Hons), BN(Hons), BMid(Hons) MSc, PGDip, MPhil, PhD, MRes, DocClinPract, PGDip

Faculty of Humanities; www.soton.ac.uk/about/faculties/faculty_humanities

Archaeology; www.southampton.ac.uk/archaeology/

archaeology, archaeology and anthropology/geography/history; Postgrad; archaeological computing (GISW and survey), archaeological computing (virtual pasts), business and heritage management, ceramic and lithic analysis for archaeologists, maritime archaeology, osteoarchaeology, palaeolithic archaeology and human origins, Rome and the Mediterranean, social archaeology

English; www.southampton.ac.uk/english

English, English & jt degrees, English literary 18th-century studies, 20th/21st century literature, medieval & Renaissance culture, creative writing

Film; www.southampton.ac.uk/film

film, film studies, film & cultural management, film (jt degrees)

History; www.southampton.ac.uk/history

history, modern history, jt hons incl archaeology, English, foreign language, philosophy, Jewish history & culture, 18th century studies, medieval & Renaissance culture

Modern Languages; www.southampton.ac.uk/ml/

modern languages – contemporary European studies, English language studies/French/German/linguistics studies/Spanish, Portuguese and Latin American studies, applied linguistics for language teaching, applied linguistics (research methodology), English language teaching, language acquisition research, transnational studies, ELT/TESOL studies

Music; www.southampton.ac.uk/music

acoustics/English/French/German/philosophy/mathematics and music, music and management sciences; Postgrad; 18th-century studies, medieval and Renaissance culture, music (performance, composition, musicology)

Philosophy; www.southampton.ac.uk/philosophy

philosophy: jt hons degrees incl sociology, politics, mathematics, foreign language, philosophy, politics, economics, aesthetics; BA(Hons), MA, MRes, MPhil, PhD, CertHE, MMus, MA/MSc

Faculty of Medicine; www.southampton.ac.uk/faculties/faculty_medicine.html

Medicine; www.southampton.ac.uk/medicine

allergy, public health, diabetes best practice, genomic medicine, biomedical sciences/cell biology & immunology of cancer, immunity & infection, medicine, surgery, stem cell science, public health/nutrition, health sciences; BM, MSc, BMedSci, PGDip/Cert, PhD, DM

Faculty of Natural and Environmental Sciences; www.soton.ac.uk/about/faculties/faculty_natural_environmental-sciences

Biological Sciences; www.soton.ac.uk/biosc

biochemistry, adv biological science, wildlife conservation, biochemistry/biomedical science, pharmacology, biology/and marine biology, neuroscience, zoology, biomedical sciences, chemistry and biochemistry, ecology; BSc(Hons), Cert/DipHE, MPhil, PhD, BNatSci, MBiSCi, MEcol, MSci

Chemistry; www.soton.ac.uk/chemistry

chemistry, chemistry and biochemistry/maths/medicinal sciences, ocean chemistry, chemistry by research, instrumental analytical chemistry; BSc(Hons), MPhil, PhD, MSci, MChem

National Oceanography Centre, Southampton; www.noc.soton.ac.uk

marine biology, oceanography, geology, geophysics; BSc, MSc, MSci

School of Ocean and Earth Science; www.soton.ac.uk/soes

marine biology with oceanography, ocean chemistry, oceanography, oceanography with French/physical geography, geology with physical geography; Postgrad; ocean science, geology and geophysics, vertebrate palaeontology, engineering in the coastal environment, marine environment and resources; BSc(Hons), MSci, BNatSci, MRes, MPhil, PhD

Faculty of Physical and Applied Sciences; www.soton.ac.uk/about/faculties/faculty_physical-applied_sciences

Electronics and Computer Science; www.ecs.soton.ac.uk

computer science and software engineering, electrical and electronic engineering, electrical engineering, electromechanical engineering, electronic engineering, information technology in organisations, web science; Postgrad; embedded computing systems, artificial intelligence, biodevices, computer science, cyber security, data science, embedded systems, energy and sustainability with electrical power engineering, microelectromechanical systems (MEMS), microelectronics systems design, nanoelectronics and nanotechnology, software engineering, system on chip, systems, control and signal processing, web science, web technology, wireless communications, optical fibre technologies, photonic technologies; BEng, MEng, MSc, MComp, PhD

Optoelectronics Research Centre; www.orc.soton.ac.uk

optical fibre technologies, photonic technologies; MSc, PhD

Physics & Astronomy; www.phy.soton.ac.uk

astronomy, theoretical high energy physics, space environment physics, quantum, light & matter, particle physics, physics/with astronomy/nanotechnology/space science/photonics/mathematics; BSc(Hons), European Masters, MPhy, PhD

Faculty of Social and Human Sciences; www.soton.ac.uk/about/faculties/ facultysocial_human-sciences

School of Education; www.southampton.ac.uk/education

education, education & training (primary), educational studies with psychology/training, education (management & leadership/practice & innovation/specific learning difficulties (dyslexia)/mathematics & science), PGCE (primary, numerous secondary subjects/FE learning & skills), school direct, PCET, PGCE sciences, SKE computer sciences subject knowledge enhancement/mathematics subject knowledge enhancement/physics subject knowledge enhancement; BSc(Hons), BA(Hons), MSc, MA(Ed), CertEd, MPhil, PhD, EdD

Geography & Environment; www.soton.ac.uk/geography

geography, geography with geology/oceanography, geology/oceanography with physical geography, (social sciences) population and geography; Postgrad; applied GIS and remote sensing, GIS, sustainability, sustainability (consultancy/sustainability/population/research
BSc(Hons), BA(Hons), MA, MSc, MPhil, PhD

School of Mathematics; www.soton.ac.uk/maths

actuarial science, mathematical studies, mathematical physics, mathematics with actuarial science/astronomy/biology/computer science/finance/music/OR/physics/statistics/French/German, OR/& finance/statistics/economics, mathematics, statistics with applications in medicine; BSc(Hons), MMath, MSc, PGDip, PhD

School of Psychology; www.southampton.ac.uk/psychology

psychology/& education/criminology/law, anxiety & depression, foundations of clinical psychology, psychology, research methods, CBT/theory, health psychology; BSc(Hons), MSc, MPhil, PhD, PGDip

School of Social Sciences; www.southampton.ac.uk/socsci

accounting and economics, criminology, criminology and psychology, economics, economics and actuarial science/finance/management sciences/philosophy/international relations, modern history and politics, mathematics, operational research, statistics and economics, philosophy and politics/sociology, politics, politics and economics/French/German/international relations, politics and Spanish (or Portuguese) and Latin American studies, population and geography, social policy and criminology, sociology, sociology and criminology/social policy/anthropology
Postgrad; economics, politics & international relations, social statistics & demography, sociology & social policy; BSc(Hons), BA(Hons), MEcon, MSc, MPhil, PGDip, PhD

Southampton Statistical Sciences Research Institute; www.southampton.ac.uk/s3ri

demography, actuarial science, statistics, statistics with applications in medicine, official statistics, public health, public health – nutrition/management/intelligence/global health, social statistics (research methods/social statistics); MSc, PGDip/Cert, PhD

STAFFORDSHIRE UNIVERSITY
www.staffs.ac.uk

Faculty of Business, Education & Law; www.staffs.ac.uk/academic_depts/fbel

Staffordshire University Business School; www.staffs.ac.uk/business

Accounting & Finance: accounting & business/ finance, business administration (finance), international accounting & financial management, Islamic finance & accounting

Business, Management & Enterprise: business, business and HRM/marketing management, business management/ and enterprise, international business management, business administration (finance/international), economics for business analysis, economics of globalisation and European integration, leadership & management

Economics: economics for business analysis, economics of globalisation & European integration, business & economics

Human Resource Management: HRM, business & HRM, leadership & management, strategic HRM, personnel practice, professional development

Marketing: marketing management, business & marketing management, digital marketing, professional marketing, digital strategy

Tourism & Events: tourism management, events management

Professional Courses; MBA (finance/international)

BA, BSc, MA, MBA, MPhil, MSc, PGCert/Dip, PhD, PGCE, FD

School of Education; www.staffs.ac.uk/depts_education

early childhood studies with early years teaching status (EYTS), education, teaching learners with cognitive difficulties in the lifelong learning sector, PGCE; post compulsory education and training, international education, early years teacher status (EYTS), qualified teacher status (QTS), primary; PGCE (art and design/computer science/design and technology/economics and business/mathematics/ social sciences), qualified teacher learning and status (QLTS); Postgrad; early childhood, education, higher and professional education

BA(Hons), MA, MPhil, PhD, EdD, FD, PGCert/Dip

School of Law; www.staffs.ac.uk/academic_depts/law

law, business law, criminology, family law, healthcare & ethics, international sports law, international trade & commerce, legal practice; LlB, LlM, MPhil, PhD, GradDip, CPE, LPC

Faculty of Arts & Creative Technologies; www.staffs.ac.uk/academic_depts/fact

School of Art & Design; www.staffs.ac.uk/academic_depts/artanddesign

3D design: ceramics/contemporary jewellery and fashion accessories/crafts, advertising and brand management, animation, art cartoon and comic arts, art/design foundation year, design for outdoor living, fine art, graphic design, heritage interior design, illustration, interior design, photography, photojournalism, product design, retail design, stop motion animation and puppet making, surface pattern design, textile surfaces, transport design, VFX: visual effects and concept design, computer games design, computer games design and programming, games art, computer gameplay design and production; Postgrad; 3D computer games design, arts and creative technologies, ceramic design, creative futures: 3D design/advertising and brand management/animation/applied theatre/contemporary art practice/design/graphic design/heritage and culture/ illustration/photography/product design/surface pattern design/textile design/VFX, design management, writing; BA(Hons), BSc(Hons), BEng, FD, MA, MSc, PGDip/Cert

School of Film, Sound and Vision; www.staffs.ac.uk/academic_depts/fsv

acting and screen performance/theatre arts, advertising, film and music video production, experimental film production, film, TV and radio studies, media (film) production, radio production

Film; digital film and post production technology, film production technology, film and television production technology

FX; CQI and digital effects, digital film and 3D animation technology, games concept design

Music; creative music technology, music technology/ with management, sound design

Postgrad; arts and creative technologies, digital feature film production, film by negotiated learning (raindance), music technology, theatre practice by negotiated learning; BA(Hons), BSc(Hons), MA, MSc, PGDip/Cert

School of Journalism, Humanities & Social Sciences; www.staffs.ac.uk/academic_depts/jhss

Journalism; broadcast journalism, English and journalism, games journalism and PR, journalism, PR, music journalism and broadcasting, professional sports writing and broadcasting, sports journalism, sports PR and journalism

Humanities and Social Sciences; creative writing, crime, terrorism and deviance, English literature, English and creative writing, history (modern/and international), sociology, sociology, crime and deviance

Postgrad; arts and creative technologies, broadcast journalism, journalism, sports broadcast journalism, continental philosophy, development policy and practice, international history, international policy and diplomacy, international relations, social and cultural theory, sociology, terrorism, crime and global security, transnational organised crime; BA(Hons), MA, MSc, BA, FdA, MFA, MPhil, MSc, PhD

Faculty of Computing, Engineering & Science; www.staffs.ac.uk/academic_depts/fecs

School of Computing; www.staffs.ac.uk/academic_depts/computing

applied computing, information systems, computer systems for business, professional/computing, mobile applications device development, computing science, computer games programming, cybersecurity, computer networks & security, forensic computing, software engineering, network computing, web development/design

School of Engineering; www.staffs.ac.uk/academic_depts/engineering

automotive engineering/technology/sport, motorsport engineering, motorsport technology, aeronautical technology, electronic engineering, electrical engineering, engineering, telecommunications engineering, mathematics & statistics, PGCE in mathematics, mechanical engineering, mechatronics, product design engineering, mechanical/manufacturing technology, advanced technology, professional education

School of Sciences; www.staffs.ac.uk/academic_depts/sciences

animal biology & conservation, biology, biomedical science, forensic biology, human biology, ecology & conservation, healthcare science management, forensic/investigative science, policing & criminal investigation, crime scene investigation, fire investigation, firearm examination, geography, environment & sustainability, geography & mountain leadership, governance & sustainable development, invertebrate biology & conservation, sustainability & environmental management; BA, BEng, BSc, FdSc, MEng, MSc, MPhil, MRes, PGCE, PGCert, PGDip, PhD

Faculty of Health Sciences; www.staffs.ac.uk/academic_depts/health

School of Nursing & Midwifery; www.staffs.ac.uk/academic_depts/nursingandmidwifery

adult/children's/mental health nursing, integrated care practice, midwifery, mental health, Postgrad; advanced clinical practice, advanced forensic practice (custody health/sexual assault/sexual assault and custody health professional), health care practice (ageing/contraception and sexual health/mental health/nursing), specialist community public health nursing (health visiting or school nursing), specialist practice – district nursing, health studies, health and welfare studies; DAHP, DM, DN, MPhil, MRes, MSc, PGDip/Cert, PhD, DipHE, FD

School of Psychology, Sport & Exercise; www.staffs.ac.uk/academic-depts/pse

psychology, forensic psychology, sport development & coaching, PE & youth coaching, counselling/therapy & practice, psychotherapeutic counselling, psychology & child development/counselling/criminology, applied sport & exercise psychology/science, sport studies/therapy, sport & exercise psychology, sports coaching with PE, clinical biomechanics, clinical psychology, cognitive behavioural therapy, health psychology, mechanics of diabetes foot, sport strength & conditioning, gait analysis

School of Social Work, Allied & Public Health; www.staffs.ac.uk/academic-depts/swaph

paramedic science, health and social care, paramedic science, operating department practice, social welfare law, policy and advice practice, social work, anaesthetic care

Postgrad; negotiated learning – health, social work practice, negotiated learning – health, osteopathy, ageing, mental health and dementia, medical education, physical activity and public health, public health

(health informatics), social welfare law, policy and advice practice, public health
BSc, MA, MPhil, MSc, PGCert, PGDip, PhD, MOst, Adv Univ Dip, FD

UNIVERSITY OF STIRLING
www.external.stir.ac.uk

School of Applied Social Science; www.stir.ac.uk/social-science
criminology, criminology and sociology, social work, sociology and social policy; Postgrad; adult services, support and protection, advanced practice skills (child welfare and protection), applied social research/(criminology/social statistics and social research), applied studies (child welfare and protection), applied studies (management and leadership in social services), child, welfare and protection, counselling & psychotherapy, criminological research, dementia studies, educational research, housing studies, management in social services, social enterprise, social work studies; BA, GradCert, MSc, PGCert, PGDip, PhD

School of Arts & Humanities; www.stir.ac.uk/schools/arts-and-humanities

Communications, Media & Culture; History & Politics, Law & Philosophy, Literature & Language
digital media, education (primary), professional education (primary) with specialism in modern languages/the environment/early years, European film and media, film and media, French, global cinema and culture, heritage and conservation, history, journalism studies, law, modern languages, politics, politics (international politics), politics, philosophy and economics: PPE, religion, Scottish history
Postgrad; Atlantic studies, corporate social responsibility, creative writing, diplomatic studies, diplomacy, English language and linguistics, environment, heritage and policy, environmental policy and governance, film studies: theory and practice, gender studies (applied), historical research, humanities, international conflict and cooperation, international energy law and policy, media and communications management, media management, media research, modern Scottish writing, business, international trade and diplomatic studies,

diplomacy and security studies, philosophy, public policy, publishing studies, Renaissance studies, Spanish & Latin American studies, strategic communication & public relations, strategic public relations/& communication management, the Gothic imagination, translation studies, translation studies with TESOL; MPP, DDip, BA, LLB, LLM, MSc, MLitt, MRes, MPhil, PhD

School of Education; www.ioe.stir.ac.uk
education (primary/secondary), professional education with specialism in modern languages/environment/early years, tertiary education (TQFE/TQAE), EFL, educational leadership, professional learning & leadership, enquiry, teaching qualifications in adult education/FE, TESOL teaching qualification in adult education/FE, tertiary education, educational research; BA, BSc, EdD, MEd, MPhil, MRes, MSc, PGCert/Dip, PhD, UnivCert

School of Natural Sciences; www.stir/schools/natural-sciences

Institute of Aquaculture; www.aqua.stir.ac.uk
aquaculture, aquaculture: sustainable aquaculture, aquaculture: sustainable aquaculture, aquatic food security, aquatic pathobiology, aquatic veterinary studies, marine biotechnology, marine biology, sustainable aquaculture; BSc, MPhil, MSc, PGCert, PGDip, PhD

School of Biological & Environmental Sciences; www.sbes.stir.ac.uk
applied biological science, biology, cell biology, conservation biology & management, conservation & sustainability, ecology, environmental geography/management/science/outdoor education, environmental management (conservation/energy); BSc, MPhil, MRes, MSc, PGCert, PGDip, PhD

Dept of Computing Science & Mathematics; www.cs.stir.ac.uk

advanced/computing, big data, business computing, computing science, computing for financial markets/business, IT, mathematics/& its applications, information technology, software engineering; BSc, MSc, PhD, MBA

Dept of Psychology; www.psychology.stir.ac.uk

psychology, health psychology, psychological research methods, autism/child development/evolution & behaviour/measuring perception/psychology of faces, evolutionary psychology, psychology applied to health, psychological therapy in primary care; BA, BSc, MSc, PGDip, PhD

School of Nursing & Midwifery & Health; www.nm.stir.ac.uk

advanced/professional practice/care practice, health & wellbeing of the older person, health profession & paramedical practice/studies/research/visiting, midwifery, nursing (adult, mental health), welfare & benefits advice; BM, BN, BSc, DAHP, DM, DN, MPhil, MRes, MSc, PGDip, PhD, DipHE, DClin, Grad Cert

School of Sport; www.sports.stir.ac.uk

health & exercise sciences, performance coaching, psychology of sport, sport & exercise science, sport coaching/management/nutrition, sports studies; BA, BSc, MPhil, MSc, PGDip, PhD

Stirling Management School; www.stir.ac.uk/management

accountancy/& finance, banking & finance, international accounting & finance, investment analysis, business administration, business studies, finance, business & management, HRM, international business, international management studies/European languages & society management/& intercultural studies, international accounting & finance/HRM, management, marketing, retailing, retail marketing, behavioural science for management, economics, energy management; BA, BSc, MBA, MSc, PhD, BAcc, MPhil, PGDip, MBA, MRes, MBM

Institute for People-Centred Healthcare Management
PhD

Institute for Retail Studies
retail studies; PhD

Institute for Social Marketing
PhD

Institute for Socio-Management
PhD

STOCKPORT COLLEGE
www.stockport.ac.uk

childcare: early years practice/working with children and young people, childhood studies, computing: enterprise computing, design: graphic arts and design/illustration/motion design/interior design with sustainability, forensic science, health and social care, contemporary photography, television production; various HND/Cs in engineering; BA, FdA, FdSc

UNIVERSITY OF STRATHCLYDE
www.strath.ac.uk

Strathclyde Business School; www.strath.ac.uk/business

accounting, business/administration/enterprise, business analysis & technology, economics, finance, hospitality & tourism management, HRM, management, marketing, business law, international business & modern languages

Postgrad: applied economics, business analysis & consulting, economics & finance, finance, HRM, hospitality & tourism leadership, international accounting & finance/banking management/HRM/marketing, investment & finance, marketing, equality in pay & reward, finance & management, global energy management/sustainable cities, hospitality & management, leadership studies, operational research, qualitative finance, supply chain management, tourism marketing management; BA, MSc, MBA, DBA, MPhil, PhD, MRes, PGCert/Dip, MBM

Faculty of Engineering;
www.strath.ac.uk/engineering

Dept of Architecture; www.strath.ac.uk/architecture

architecture, architectural studies, adv architectural design/international, urban design, architectural design for conservation of built heritage, sustainable engineering: architecture & ecology; BSc, MArch, MRes, MSc, PGCert, PGDip

Biomedical Engineering;
www.strath.ac.uk/biomedeng

medical devices, biomedical engineering, medical technology, prosthetics & orthotics, rehabilitation studies; EngD, MPhil, MRes, MSc, PGCert, PGDip, PhD, BEng, MEng

Dept of Chemical & Process Engineering;
www.strath.ac.uk/chemeng

adv chemical & processing engineering, chemical engineering, chemical processing, chemical/process & technology management; BEng, MEng, MSc, PGCert, PGDip, PhD

Dept of Civil & Environmental Engineering;
www.strath.ac.uk/civeng

civil & environmental engineering, civil engineering, environmental engineering/health, entrepreneurship, hydrogeology, sustainability & environmental studies, geo environmental engineering, integrated pollution prevention & control; BEng, BSc, MEng, MPhil, MRes, MSc, PhD

Dept of Design, Manufacture & Engineering Management; www.strath.ac.uk/dmen

adv engineering technology & systems, adv electrical power, computer-aided engineering design, digital creativity, global innovation management, lean six sigma for process, mechatronics & automation, operations management in engineering, product design engineering/design & innovation, production engineering design, production engineering & management, sports engineering, supply chain management, management, sustainable engineering/product development; BEng, BSc, MEng, MSc, PGCert, PGDip

Dept of Electronic & Electrical Engineering;
www.strath.ac.uk/eee

electronic & electrical engineering, electronic & electrical engineering with business studies, electrical energy systems, electronic & digital systems, electrical & mechanical engineering, computer & electronic systems; Postgrad; wind energy systems, communications, control & digital signal processing, signal processing, electronic & electrical engineering, electrical power engineering with business, advanced electrical power engineering
BEng, MEng, MSc, PGCert, PGDip

Dept of Mechanical & Aerospace Engineering; www.strath.ac.uk/mecheng

aero-mechanical engineering, mechanical engineering, mechanical engineering with aeronautics/financial management/materials engineering; Postgrad; sustainable engineering: renewable energy systems and the environment, advanced mechanical engineering, advanced mechanical engineering with aerospace/energy systems/materials/power plant technologies; BEng, MEng, MPhil, PGCert, PGDip, PhD

Dept of Naval Architectural & Marine Engineering; www.strath.ac.uk/na-me

naval architecture and marine engineering/ocean engineering/small craft engineering, Postgrad; marine engineering, offshore floating systems, sustainable engineering: offshore renewable energy, subsea engineering, ship & offshore structures, ship & offshore technology, marine technology
BEng, MEng, MPhil, MSc, PGCert, PGDip, PhD

Faculty of Humanities & Social Sciences;
www.strath.ac.uk/humanities

Undergraduate; Arts & Social Studies: English studies, French, history, Italian, journalism & creative writing, psychology, politics, Spanish
Education: childhood practice, education & social services, primary education, teaching with chemistry/mathematics/physics
Law: law, law with a modern language
Social Work: social work
Speech and Language: speech & language pathology
Sports Science: BA(Hons), BSc(Hons), BEd, LlB
Postgrad: Social Work & Social Policy; advanced residential childcare, child and youth care studies by distance learning, social services management
Education: PDGE primary, PDGE secondary, adult guidance, applied education and social research, autism, early childhood studies, educational support, Gaelic immersion for teachers, management & leadership in education, education, philosophy with children, supporting bi-lingual learners in mainstream classroom, supporting teacher learning

Government & Public Policy: public policy, international public policy, European public policy, political research, international politics and organisations
Humanities: historical studies, health history, investigative journalism, digital journalism, literature, culture & place, north Atlantic world c900 – c1800, creative writing
Law: advocacy, construction law, climate change law and policy, criminal justice & penal change, professional legal practice, human rights, internet law & policy, international economic law, international law & sustainable development, mediation & conflict resolution, employment and labour law
Psychological Sciences & Health: educational psychology, counselling, counselling skills, research methods in psychology, clinical health psychology MSc, PGDip/Cert, PGCE, PGDE, BEd, MEd, MLitt, LlM, DEdPsy, PGCert/Dip, MCounselling, MPhil, EdD, MRes

Faculty of Science; www.strath.ac.uk/science

Dept of Pure & Applied Chemistry; www.chem.strath.ac.uk

chemistry, chemistry with analytical chemistry, chemistry with drug discovery, forensic chemistry, forensic and analytical chemistry, applied chemistry and chemical engineering, chemistry with teaching, forensic science, medicinal chemistry; BSc, MChem, MSc, PGDip, PhD

Dept of Computer & Information Sciences; www.strath.ac.uk/cis

enterprise/business information systems, computer & electronic systems, adv/computer science, adv/software engineering, mobile computing, information & library studies, information management, mathematics with computer science; BEng, BSc, MEng, MPhil, MRes, MSc, PGCert, PGDip

Dept of Mathematics & Statistics; www.mathstat.strath.ac.uk

mathematics, mathematics, statistics & accounting/economics/finance, mathematics & physics, mathematics with teaching, mathematics & computer science, quantitative finance, research topics; BSc, MSc, PhD, MMath

Dept of Physics; www.strath.ac.uk/physics

applied/advanced physics, nanoscience, optical technologies, photonics & device fabrication, mathematics with physics, physics with teaching; BSc, MPhys, MSc, PhD

Strathclyde Institute of Pharmacy & Biomedical Sciences; www.strath.ac.uk/sipbs

advanced pharmaceutical manufacturing, biomedical sciences, clinical pharmacy, industrial biotechnology, pharmaceutical analysis, pharmaceutical quality and good manufacturing practice, biomedical sciences, biochemistry; BSc, MPharm, MPhil, MSc, PGCert, PGDip, PhD, MRes

UNIVERSITY CAMPUS SUFFOLK
www.ucs.ac.uk

Faculty of Arts, Business and Applied Social Science; www.ucs.ac.uk/Faculties-and-Centres/Faculty-of-Arts, -Business-and-Applied-Social-Science/Faculty-of-Arts, -Business-and-Applied-Social-Science.aspx

Department of Arts and Humanities

computer games design, dance, English, film, fine art, graphic design/graphic illustration, history, interior architecture and design, photography, arts practice, digital film practice, screenwriting & film studies

Department of Children, Young People and Education

early years practice, early childhood studies, early learning, special educational needs and disability

studies, childhood and youth studies, learning and teaching

Department of Psychology, Sociology and Social Work

criminology, criminology and youth studies, psychology and criminology, psychology and sociology, psychology and youth studies, social care practice, sociology and youth studies, social work

Suffolk Business School

accounting and financial management, business & management, HRM, event management, event management and tourism management/business management, management for the heritage sector, business administration (MBA), HRM, professional practice in heritage management, enterprise, leadership &

tourism; FdA, BA(Hons), MA, PGDip/Cert, FdSc, MSc, MBA

Faculty of Health and Science; *www.ucs.ac.uk/faculty-of-health-and-science*

Department of Health Studies

health care practice (acute care/end of life/long term care/mental health/dementia care), public health, operating department practice, diagnostic radiography, midwifery, public health, radiotherapy and oncology, specialist community public health nursing (school nurse or health visiting), clinical effectiveness,

healthcare education, leadership and service innovation, paramedical science

Department of Nursing Studies

adult nursing, children's health nursing, mental health nursing, acute health care practice, nurse practitioner, advanced health care practice

Department of Science and Technology

bioscience, communication technology: network engineering/software engineering, computer games design/programming, nutrition and human health, sport and exercise science; Postgrad; regenerative medicine; BSc(Hons), MSc, DipHE, MA, FdSc, PGDip/Cert

---

UNIVERSITY OF SUNDERLAND
www.sunderland.ac.uk

Faculty of Applied Sciences; *www.sunderland.ac.uk/faculties/apsc*

Dept of Computing, Engineering & Technology; www.sunderland.ac.uk/faculties/apsc/ourdepartments/cet

mechanical engineering, engineering management, power engineering, engineering management, automotive engineering, manufacturing engineering, computer systems engineering, engineering, network systems, electronic and electrical engineering, computer forensics, telecommunications engineering, project management, network computing, health information management, games software development, computing, information technology management, applied business computing, computer science, network systems; BA, BEng, BSc, FdSc, MSc

Dept of Pharmacy, Health & Well-being; www.sunderland.ac.uk/faculties/apsc/ourdepartments/phw

nursing, medicines management, physiological sciences, biopharmaceutical science, pharmacy, clinical pharmacy, pharmaceutical science, drug discovery and development, independent prescribing for pharmacists, biomedical science, biopharmaceutical science, pharmaceutical and biopharmaceutical formulations, healthcare science: physiological/life sciences, biomedical science, overseas nursing programme, sport and exercise sciences, sports coaching, project management, environment, health and safety, exercise, health and fitness, healthcare science:

physiological/life sciences, environmental management and assessment, sports coaching
BA, BSc, FdA, MPharm, MSc, PGCE, Univ Dip, PGDip, Adv Dip

Dept of Psychology; www.sunderland.ac.uk/faculties/apsc/ourfaculty/ourdepartments/psychology

counselling, psychology, psychology with counselling, psychological research; BA, FdA, MA, MSc

Dept of Sport & Exercise Sciences; www.sunderland.ac.uk/faculties/apsc/ourdepartments/sport/

sport & exercise sciences, sports coaching/development, exercise/sport health & fitness, sport, exercise & fitness; BA, BSc, FdA, MSc

Faculty of Arts, Design & Media; *www.sunderland.ac.uk/faculties/adm/*

Dept of Arts & Design; www.sunderland.ac.uk/faculties/adm/ourfaculty/ourdepartments/departmentofartsdesign

animation, broadcast and digital media, dance, drama music, fashion, film, media and cultural studies, fine art, art and design, glass, ceramics, graphics advertising and media, illustration, PR, photography, fine art, curating, journalism and PR, sports journalism, magazine journalism photography, design studies, animation and design, media production (film and TV), radio, media & cultural studies; BA, BSc, FdA, MA

Faculty of Business & Law; *www.sunderland.ac.uk/faculties/bl*

Sunderland Business School; www.sunderland.ac.uk/faculties/bl/departments/business

accounting & finance, accountancy & financial management, applied management/investment, banking & finance, business/financial management, business & management/enterprise management/HRM/marketing, marketing management, international tourism & hospitality management, HRM, innovation & enterprise, investigative management, events/travel management, international management, leadership & change management, marketing/management, sports management, MBA (HRM/hospitality management/innovation & enterprise/supply chain management/transformation/global business/general management/marketing); BA(Hons), FD, CertHE, MBM, MBA, MA, MSc, PGDip

Dept of Law; www.sunderland.ac.uk/faculties/bl/departments/law

law, criminal law & procedure, human rights, business law; LlB, LlM, LPC, BA(Hons)

Dept of Tourism, Hospitality & Events; laww.sunderland.ac.uk/faculties/bl/departments/tourism/

international hospitality & tourism management, tourism management, events management, travel & tourism, tourism & events/hospitality (jt degrees); BA(Hons), BA/BSc, FD, BSc(Hons)

Faculty of Education & Society

Dept of Education; www.sunderland.ac.uk/faculties/es/ourfaculty/ourdepartments/departmentofeducation

childhood studies, community and youth work studies, history, English education with QTS, education and care, education and training, education studies – combined subjects, social sciences, criminology, health and social care, social work, English and creative writing, combined subjects, education and curriculum studies secondary, English education, mathematics education ostgrad; post compulsory education, education, PGCE; business/design and technology/English/geography/computer science education/mathematics/primary education/science with biology/science with chemistry/science with physics education, School Direct, international education, special educational needs co-ordination, social work, teaching and learning in HE, TESOL, education overseas; BA, BSc, MA, PGCE, FD, PGDip/Cert, MSc

Dept of Culture; www.sunderland.ac.uk/faculties/es/ourfaculty/ourdepartments/departmentofculture

English, creative writing, history, modern foreign languages, politics, TESOL BA, BSc, MA, PGCE

Dept of Social Sciences; www.sunderland.ac.uk/faculties/es/ourfaculty/ourdepartments/departmentofsocialsciences

childhood studies, community & youth studies, community engagement, criminology, education & care, health & social care, practice development, social work, sociology, supporting career learning & development, working with young people, social sciences; BA, FdA, MA, BA(Hons), BEng(Hons), BSc(Hons), EdEng, FdSc, LLM, MBA, MSc, PGCE, PGCert

Degrees validated by University of Sunderland offered at:

SUNDERLAND COLLEGE
www.sunderlandcollege.ac.uk

applied music practice, art and design, business & management, counselling, health & social care, practice dance, drama, exercise health & fitness, health & safety management, leadership & management, sports coaching/development, travel & tourism; FdA, FdSc, HNC/D

UNIVERSITY OF SURREY
www.surrey.ac.uk

Faculty of Arts & Human Sciences; www.surrey.ac.uk/fahs/

School of Arts; www.surrey.ac.uk/schoolofarts

Dance; dance; Postgrad; dance cultures, creative practices and direction

Media, Digital Arts & Film; digital media arts, film, film and video production engineering, media, culture and society; Postgrad;film, digital arts

Music; creative music technology, actor musician, music and sound recording;Postgrad; sound recording/psychoacoustic engineering, musical theatre, practice of voice and singing, creative practices and leadership, music

Theatre; theatre and performance, theatre, acting, actor musician, musical theatre, professional production skills; Postgrad; theatre, acting, musical theatre, contemporary theatre making, creative practices and direction

Sound Recording; music and sound recording; Postgrad; sound recording/psychoacoustic engineering; BA(Hons), BSc(Hons), BMus, MA, PhD, MPhil, MMus, PGDip

School of English & Languages; www.surrey.ac.uk/englishandlanguages

Communication, Languages & Translation Studies; applied languages (French and Spanish/German and French/Spanish), business management and French business management and German/Spanish, English literature and French/German/Spanish, liberal arts and sciences, Postgrad; business interpreting in Chinese and English, business translation with interpreting, communication and international marketing, intercultural communication with international business, interpreting, TESOL, translation studies, translation studies with intercultural communication

English Literature & Creative Writing; creative writing, English literature, English literature and French/German/Spanish, English literature with creative writing, liberal arts and sciences; Postgrad; creative writing, English literature, higher education, English (literature, creative writing or linguistics), intercultural communication

Liberal Arts & Sciences; liberal arts and sciences; BA(Hons), BSc(Hons), MA, PhD

School of Politics; www.surrey.ac.uk/politics

politics, international politics, politics & sociology/economics, politics with policy studies, international relations, European politics & policy; BA(Hons), BSc(Hons), MSc, MPhil, PhD

School of Psychology; www.surrey.ac.uk/psychology

psychology, environmental/health/social psychology, occupational & organisational psychology, supervision & consultation: psychotherapeutic & organisational approaches, liberal arts & science; BSc(Hons), MSc, PsychD, PhD, PGCert/Dip

School of Sociology; www.surrey.ac.uk/sociology

sociology/& criminology, law with criminology, media, culture and society, social research methods, media studies, politics wiih sociology; BA(Hons), BSc(Hons), MA, MSc, PsychD, PGDip, LlB

Dept of Economics; www.econ.surrey.ac.uk

economics, energy economics & policy, business economics/ & finance, international economics, finance & development, economics & finance/politics/mathematics, economics for public policy, health economics, international economics, finance and development; BSc, MSc, PhD

Faculty of Engineering & Physical Sciences; www.surrey.ac.uk/feps

Dept of Computing; www.surrey.ac.uk/computing

computer science, computing & information technology, information systems, information security; BSc, MSc, PhD

Dept of Electronic Engineering; www.ee.surrey.ac.uk

electronic engineering, electrical and electronic engineering, electronic engineering with audio-visual systems/communications/nanotechnology/ space systems, communications networks and software, computer vision – electronic engineering, medical imaging, microwave engineering and wireless subsystems design, mobile and satellite communications: mobile communications systems, multimedia signal processing and communications, nanotechnology & nanoelectronic devices, satellite communications engineering, signal processing and machine intelligence, space engineering; BSc, MMath, MSc, PhD

Dept of Mathematics; www.surrey.ac.uk/maths

mathematics, financial mathematics, mathematics with statistics, mathematics music, biosystems, dynamical systems & partial differential equations, strings & geometry, and fluid mechanics & meteorology, MSc, MMath, MSc, PhD

Dept of Physics; www.surrey.ac.uk/physics

physics, medical imaging, medical physics, physics with astronomy, nuclear astrophysics/satellite technology/mathematics, radiation & environmental protection; BSc, MSc, MPhys

Division of Chemistry; www.surrey.ac.uk/chemistry

chemistry/with forensic investigation, medicinal chemistry, drug discovery; BSc, MSc, MChem, MRes, PhD

Division of Civil, Chemical & Environmental Engineering; www.surrey.ac.uk/cce

Dept of Civil & Environmental Engineering

civil engineering, bridge engineering, structural engineering, water & environmental engineering, infrastructure engineering & management, advanced geotechnical engineering

Dept of Chemical & Process Engineering

chemical engineering, chemical & biosystems engineering, petroleum refining, information/& processing systems engineering, process & environmental systems engineering, renewable energy, process systems engineering;

Centre for Environmental Strategy

environmental strategy, sustainable development, sustainable tourism; BEng, MEng, MSc, PGCert, PGDip, PhD

Division of Mechanical, Medical & Aerospace Engineering; www.surrey.ac.uk/mma

advanced materials, aerospace/mechanical engineering, biomedical/medical engineering; BEng, MEng, MSc, PGCert, PGDip, PhD, MPhil

School of Health & Social Care; www.surrey.ac.uk/healthandsocialcare

Department of Biochemistry & Physiology; Department of Microbial & Cellular Sciences; Department of Nutrition & Metabolism; School of Health & Social Care

adult/child/mental health nursing, midwifery, operating department practice, paramedic practice, delivering quality healthcare, education for professional practice, health care management, nursing studies (adult/mental health), primary and community care (community children's nursing/district nursing/general practice nursing), public health practice (health visiting/school nursing), health sciences, education for professional practice, delivering quality healthcare, public health practice/health visiting), biochemistry, biological sciences, biomedical science, child nursing, food science and microbiology, microbiology, nutrition, nutrition/dietetics, nutrition and food science, sports and exercise sciences, veterinary biosciences, veterinary medicine, applied toxicology, genetic toxicology and environmental mutagenesis, health and clinical sciences, human nutrition, medical microbiology, nutritional medicine, pharmaceutical medicine/with clinical pharmacology, systems biology, toxicology, veterinary microbiology, public clinical pharmacology, genetic toxicology, veterinary microbiology; BSc(Hons), MSc, DipHE, PGCert/Dip, PhD, DClinPract, BVi, DipHE

Faculty of Business, Economics & Law; www.surrey.ac.uk/fbel

Surrey Business School; www.surrey.ac.uk/sbs

accounting & finance, banking & finance, business/& retail management, business analytics/management, business management (entrepreneurship/HRM/marketing), entrepreneurship, HRM, international business management, international financial/marketing/management, investment management, operations & logistics management, international retail management, management, marketing management, sustainable enterprise management, extractive industries, the environment & sustainability; BSc, DBA, MBA, MSc, PhD

School of Law; www.surrey.ac.uk/law

law, international/international commercial law, law & international studies/criminology, senior status; LLB, LLM, MA, PhD, MRes

School of Hospitality & Tourism Management; www.surrey.ac.uk/shtm

air transport management, international hospitality/& tourism management, international event/hotel management, strategic hotel management, tourism development/management/marketing, sustainable tourism; BSc(Hons), MSc, PhD, MBA

Department of Health Care Management and Policy; www.surrey.ac.uk/hcmp
health care management; MSc, PhD

Degrees validated by the University of Surrey offered at:

FARNBOROUGH COLLEGE OF TECHNOLOGY
www.farn-ct.ac.uk

accounting, aeronautical engineering, business management/& computing, combined/media production, computing with networking education (early childhood studies/early years practice/learning, early years education and practice, early years care and education, early years (children & education), electronic engineering, English literature & criminology/sociology, graphic design, health care practice, hospitality management, HR management, lifelong learning, mechanical engineering, modern history & contemporary/sociology/English literature, management (hospitality), photography, psychology & marketing/criminology/criminology/English literature, salon & spa management, sports science/human performance, sports coaching, personal training & fitness, software engineering; BA(Hons), BSc(Hons), FdA, FdSc, FdEng, PGEd

NESCOT (NORTH EAST SURREY COLLEGE OF TECHNOLOGY)
www.nescot.ac.uk

applied biomedical science, applied biological and healthcare science, computing, business accounting & technology management, osteopathic medicine, perfusion science, sports therapy, education and training, education, education & training, education studies

Additional Nongraduate Courses;acoustics, biomedical science, business management, health & social care, computing/& IT, early years, educational support, music technology, orthopaedic medicine, osteopathic medicine, photography, photo-imaging, perfusion science, psychodynamic counselling, sports therapy, teacher training, teaching & learning in lifelong learning sector, travel & tourism management; BA(Hons), BSc(Hons), DipHE, FdA, FdSc, MSc, PGDip, Masters, MOst, BOst

ST MARYS UNIVERSITY
www.smuc.ac.uk

applied physics, business law/management, bioethics & medical law, creative writing/first novel, drama, drama and applied/physical theatre/theatre arts, education and social science, education, culture & society, English, geography, history, Irish studies, law, management studies, media arts, human/nutrition, philosophy, physical and sport education, primary education/with QTS, psychology, education pedagogy & professional practice in PE, values & practice/international students, PGCE (primary/secondary), sociology, sport rehabilitation, science sport science, sports coaching science, strength and conditioning, theology and religious studies, tourism/management, applied linguistics & ELT, Gothic: culture, subculture, counterculture, education: leading innovation & change, Irish studies, physical theatre, film & screen media, sports journalism, theatre directing, psychology and counselling, charity management, international business practice, international tourism development, managing for sustainability, applied sport and exercise physiology, applied sports nutrition/psychology, sports coaching/health & fitness, public history, sport rehabilitation, strength and conditioning, health, fitness & physical activity, healthcare chaplaincy, pastoral ministry, youth ministry, theology, Catholic school leadership, religion, politics and conflict resolution; BA, BSc, FdA, LlB, LLM, MA, MPhil, MSc, PGCE, PGCert, PGDip, PhD

UNIVERSITY OF SUSSEX
www.sussex.ac.uk

Brighton & Sussex Medical School; www.bsms.sussex.ac.uk

medicine, surgery, mobile medical education, anaesthesia and perioperative medicine, cardiology, dementia studies, global health, leadership and commissioning, medical education, medical research, psychiatry, public health; MoMEd, MA, MSc, MRes, MD, MPhil, PGCert, PGDip, PhD

School of Business, Management & Economics; www.sussex.ac.uk/aboutus/schoolsdepartments/bmec

Dept of Business & Management; www.sussex.ac.uk/bams

accounting and finance, business and management studies, finance, international business, marketing and management, law with business

Postgrad; banking and finance, financial risk and investment analysis, global supply chain and logistics management, HRM, international accounting and corporate governance, international management, international marketing, management, management and entrepreneurship/finance; Masters in business administration MBA; BA, BSc, MSc, PGDip, LlB, MPhil, DPhil

Dept of Economics; www.sussex.ac.uk/economics

economics, economics & international development/international relations/management studies/politics/finance/business, business & management studies, development economics, finance & business, mathematics with economics, PPE, international economics, international finance; BA, BSc, GradDip, MSc, MPhil, MMath, DPhil

Dept of Science & Technology Policy Research (SPRU); www.sussex.ac.uk/spru

science & technology policy, energy policy for sustainability, innovation for sustainable international development, technology & innovation management, managing innovation & projects; DPhil, MPhil, MSc

School of Education & Social Work; www.sussex.ac.uk/aboutus/schoolsdepartments/esw

Dept of Education; www.sussex.ac.uk/education

childhood & youth: theory & practice, early years, education, education, pedagogy & practice, education studies, working with children & young people, initial teacher education, international education & development, overseas teacher education, PGCE: primary, 11–18/7–14 maths/modern foreign languages/secondary (numerous subjects)/international, school direct, subject knowledge enhancement; BA, MA, PGCE, PGCert/Dip, EdD, MPhil, PhD, MSc, QTS

Dept of Social Work & Social Care; www.sussex.ac.uk/socialwork

childhood & youth studies, leadership & management in integrated children's services/& supervision in children's services, supervision of children's services, effective practice in children's services, practice education, social work, social work & social care, social research methods; BA, DPhil, MA, MPhil, MSc, PGCert, DSW

School of Engineering & Informatics; www.sussex.ac.uk/ei

Engineering & Design: advanced mechanical engineering, automotive/mechanical engineering, electrical/& electronic engineering, computer engineering, digital communications & business management, engineering, product design, computer science & AI, computing for/with digital media, evolutionary & adaptive systems, games & multimedia environments, intelligent systems, Postgrad; advanced computer science, computing with digital media, evolutionary & adaptive systems, human-computer interaction, information technology with business and management, intelligent systems, management of information technology, web development

BA, BSc, BEng, MEng, DPhil, MA, MComp, MPhil, MSc, PGCert

School of English; www.sussex.ac.uk/aboutus/schoolsdepartments/english

drama: theatre and performance, drama studies and English/film studies/a language; American studies and English, English, English and art history/film

studies/history/media studies, English language and literature, philosophy and English, English language and linguistics/literature
Postgrad; English language and literature, applied linguistics, creative and critical writing, English: literature, culture and theory, literature and philosophy, modern and contemporary literature, culture and thought, sexual dissidence; BA, DPhil, MA, MPhil

School of Global Studies; www.sussex.ac.uk/aboutus/ schoolsdepartments/global

Dept of Anthropology; www.sussex.ac.uk/ anthropology

anthropology, anthropology & cultural studies/history/a language, anthropology & international development/geography/international relations, anthropology of development/social transformation, social anthropology of global economy; BA, DPhil, MA, MSc

Dept of Geography; www.sussex.ac.uk/ geography

geography, geography & international relations/ development/anthropology/a language, climate change & policy/development, migration studies; BA, BSc, DPhil, MA, MPhil, MSc

International Development; www.sussex.ac.uk/development

international relations & development, sociology & international development, international development & anthropology/economics/geography/French/ Italian/Spanish, anthropology & international development, environment, development & policy; BA, MA, MPhil, DPhil

Dept of International Relations; www.sussex.ac.uk/ir

conflict, security & development, geopolitics & grand strategy, global political economy/governance, international security, international relations & anthropology/law/modern languages/politics/sociology/ geography/development/economics; BA, LlB, DPhil, MA

School of History, Art History & Philosophy; www.sussex.ac.uk/aboutus/ schoolsdepartments/hahp

Dept of American Studies; www.sussex.ac.uk/americanstudies

American studies, American studies with history/ English/film studies/politics/law; BA, MA, MPhil, DPhil, LlB

Dept of Art History; www.sussex.ac.uk/ arthistory

art history, art history & museum curating/with photography/film studies/English; BA, MA, MPhil, DPhil

Dept of History; www.sussex.ac.uk/history

contemporary history, history/& American studies/ English/philosophy/sociology/anthropology/film studies, intellectual history/politics, intellectual history; BA, MPhil, DPhil, MA

Dept of Philosophy; www.sussex.ac.uk/ philosophy

philosophy, philosophy and English/sociology, philosophy, politics and economics, history/politics and philosophy; Postgrad; literature and philosophy, philosophy, social and political thought; BA, MA, MPhil, DPhil

School of Law, Politics & Sociology; www.sussex.ac.uk/aboutus/ schoolsdepartments/lps

Dept of Politics; www.sussex.ac.uk/politics

history and politics, politics, politics and economics/ law with politics, philosophy, politics and economics; Postgrad; corruption and governance, European governance and policy, international politics; BA, DPhil, MPhil

Sussex Law School; www.sussex.ac.uk/law

law, criminal law & criminal justice, international criminal law/trade law/financial law/commercial law, law & business/American studies/international relations/politics/criminology/a language/climate change/media, information technology & intellectual property law; CPE, DPhil, GradDip, LLB, LLM, MPhil, MSc

Dept of Sociology; www.sussex.ac.uk/ sociology

sociology, criminology/& sociology, sociology/with cultural studies/politics/media studies/international relations/philosophy/Italian/Spanish, international development, gender studies, social sciences; BA, DPhil, MA, MPhil, MSc

School of Mathematical & Physical Sciences; *www.sussex.ac.uk/aboutus/ schoolsdepartments/mps*

Dept of Mathematics; www.sussex.ac.uk/ maths

mathematics, computational mathematics, corporate & financial risk management, financial mathematics, mathematics with finance, economics/physics; BSc, DPhil, MMath, MPhil, MSc, PGDip

Dept of Physics & Astronomy; www.sussex.ac.uk/physics

astronomy, astrophysics, cosmology, physics, astrophysics, theoretical/particle physics, frontiers of quantum technology, mathematics with physics; BSc, DPhil, MPhil, MPhys

School of Life Sciences; *www.sussex.ac.uk/aboutus/ schoolsdepartments/lifesci*

Biochemistry & Biomedicine; www.sussex.ac.uk/lifesci/biochemistry

biochemistry, biomedical science, genetic manipulation & molecular cell biology, biosciences

Evolution, Behaviour & Environment; www.sussex.ac.uk/lifesci/ebe

biology, bioscience, ecology, conservation & environment, genetics, zoology, evolution, behaviour & environment

Genome Danger & Stability; www.sussex.ac.uk/gdsc

various research topics

Neuroscience; www.sussex.ac.uk/lifesci/ neuroscience

neuroscience, biosciences, medical neurosciences, neuroscience with cognition science/psychology; BSc, DPhil, MPhil, MChem, MSc

School of Media, Film & Music; *www.sussex.ac.uk/aboutus/ schoolsdepartments/mfm*

Dept of Media & Film; www.sussex.ac.uk/ mediaandfilm/

English and film studies, film studies, journalism, media practice, media and communications/cultural studies, American studies and film studies, anthropology and cultural studies, art history/drama studies and film studies, English and media studies, history and film studies, sociology and cultural studies/media studies; Postgrad; digital documentary, digital media, film studies, filmmaking, gender and media, international journalism, journalism, journalism and documentary practice/media studies, media practice for development and social change, media and cultural studies; BA(Hons), MA, PhD, MPhil

Dept of Music; www.sussex.ac.uk/music

music, music technology, music & sonic media; BA, BSc, DPhil, MA, MPhil, PhD, PGDip

School of Psychology; *www.sussex.ac.uk/aboutus/ schoolsdepartments/psychology*

psychology, psychology with cognitive science/neuroscience; Postgrad; applied social psychology, cognitive neuroscience, experimental psychology, foundations of clinical psychology and mental health, low-intensity psychological interventions for children and young people, psychological methods, psychological therapy experimental psychology, clinical psychology & mental health, low intensity interventions for children & young people, psychological methods/therapy; BSc, MRes, MSc, PGDip

SWANSEA UNIVERSITY
www.swansea.ac.uk

College of Arts & Humanities; *www.swansea.ac.uk/artandhumanities*

American studies, ancient and medieval history, classics, ancient history and Egyptology, Welsh, English – Chinese translation and interpreting, English language, TESOL and English language, English literature/with creative writing, French, German, history, Italian, media and communication, medieval studies, modern languages, translation and interpreting, politics and international relations, Spanish, war and society

Postgrad; ancient Egyptian culture, ancient history and classical culture, ancient narrative literature, Chinese-English translation and language teaching, classics, PR, creative writing, development and human rights, digital media, early modern history, English literature, journalism, media and globalisation, gender and culture, history, international journalism, international relations, international security and development, medieval studies, modern history, politics, public policy, TEFL, translation and interpreting, professional translation, war and society, Welsh writing in English, translation technology; BA, MA, MPhil, MSc, MScEcon, PhD, GradDip

College of Business & Economics & the Law; www.swansea.ac.uk/business

School of Management; www.swansea.ac.uk/som

accounting & finance, business management (marketing/entrepreneurship/operations & supply management/business analytics/HRM)/finance/media/ebusiness/management consultancy)/operations & supply management, economics, economics & business/finance, finance/& business analytics, international banking and finance/management financial management, financial forecasting & investment, investment management, management; BA, BSc, MBA, MPhil, MSc, MScEcon, PhD

School of Law; www.swansea.ac.uk/law

law, law & American studies/criminology/economics/French/German/law & history/Italian/politics/Spanish/media/Welsh, international maritime/trade/commercial/commercial and maritime/oil & gas law, intellectual property & commercial practice, law, crime & criminal justice, continuing professional legal studies; LlB, LlM, GDL, MPhil, PhD

College of Engineering; www.swansea.ac.uk/engineering

aerospace engineering, chemical engineering, desalination and water re-use, fuel technology, membrane technology, civil engineering, computational mechanics, computer modelling and finite elements in engineering mechanics, computer modelling in engineering, research in civil engineering, electronic and electrical engineering, communication systems, power engineering and sustainable energy, nanoscience to nanotechnology, research in electronic

and electrical engineering, environmental engineering, materials science and engineering, sports materials, materials engineering, steel technology, research in materials engineering, steel process and product development, mechanical engineering, research in mechanical engineering, medical engineering, research in tissue engineering and regenerative medicine; nanotechnology, sports science, sports materials; BEng, EngD, MEng, MPhil, MRes, MS

College of Human & Health Sciences; www.swansea.ac.uk/HumanandhealthSciences

adult/child/mental health nursing, health and social care, healthcare science (audiology/cardiac physiology/nuclear medicine/radiotherapy physics/respiratory and sleep sciences), health & social care, critical care practice, enhanced neonatal care, child public health, geography & social policy, primary care development, maternal care, midwifery, osteopathy, paramedic science, psychology, social work, social policy, criminology & social policy/psychology, childhood studies, developmental and therapeutic play, education for health professions, advanced practice in health care/infection control, adv critical care, approved mental health professional, chronic conditions management, community and primary health care practice, health care law & ethics, infection prevention and control, non-medical prescription, public health & health promotion/partnerships in care, social work, health care management, abnormal and clinical psychology, cognitive neuroscience, long term & chronic conditions management, research methods in psychology, social research methods; BA, BSc, BMid, BN, DipHE, HND, LLB, MA, MPhil, MSc, MScEcon, PGCert/Dip, PhD, DipHE, MOst, BScEcon

College of Medicine; www.swansea.ac.uk/medicine

medicine, surgery, genetics, biochemistry, medical genetics, medical biochemistry, rural & remote health, applied analytical science, applied liquid chromatography and mass spectrometry, autism and related conditions, clinical sciences (medical physics), health data science, health informatics, leadership for the health professions, life science and healthcare enterprise, medical radiation physics, nanomedicine, trauma surgery, trauma surgery (military), education for the health professions (human and health sciences), health informatics, life science and health care enterprise, medicine and life sciences, medical and health care studies, chemistry, education for the health professions; BSc, MBBCh, MD, MPhil, MSc, PhD, MRes, DProf, PGCert

College of Science; www.swansea.ac.uk/science

Dept of Biosciences; www.swansea.ac.uk/biosci

biology, biological sciences, biosciences, marine biology, zoology, environmental biology, conservation & resource management, high performance & scientific computing

Dept of Computer Science; www.swansea.ac.uk/compsci

computer science, software engineering, computing & software engineering, adv software technology

Dept of Geography; www.swansea.ac.uk/geography

geography, human geography, physical geography, physical earth science, geography & geoinformatics/European studies, environmental dynamics & climate change, geographical information & climate change, high performance & scientific computing, earth observation, environmental dynamics, glaciology, global environmental modelling, global migration, media geographies, social theory and space, urban studies

Dept of Physics; www.swansea.ac.uk/physics

physics, theoretical physics, physics & nanotechnology, particle physics & cosmology, antimatter physics, cold atoms and quantum optics, laser physics, lattice gauge theory, nanotechnology, quantum fields & strings, theoretical particle physics, high performance & scientific computing

Dept of Mathematics; www.swansea.ac.uk/maths

mathematics, pure/applied mathematics, mathematics for finance, mathematics & physics/geoinformatics/computing for finance, high performance & science computing, stochastic processes, theory & application; BSc, MEng, MMath, MPhil, MPhys, MRes, MSc, PhD, FSc

UNIVERSITY OF TEESSIDE
www.tees.ac.uk

School of Arts & Media; www.tees.ac.uk/schools/sam

Art: digital arts & design, fine art
Design: comics, graphic novels and sequential design, contemporary fashion, design for the creative industries, fashion enterprise, graphic design, interior architecture, interior design, textile design, digital arts and design, future design
English: English studies, creative writing
History: history, cultural history, European history, local & regional history
Media & Journalism: broadcast media production, journalism, journalism, journalism (magazine/sport), journalism and news practice, media studies, multimedia journalism/PR, TV & film production, mass communication
Performing Arts & Music: music technology, performing arts, dance, performance and events production, performance for live and recorded media; BA(Hons), BSc(Hons), FdA, MA, MPhil, MSc, PhD

School of Computing; www.tees.ac.uk/schools/scm

computer/character/animation/games, computer animation & visual effects, computer character animation, computing, computing (networks), games AI/development/systems, digital story telling, games & animation, creative digital media, concept art form, computer science, computer games design/programming/art, computer & digital forensics, computing networking, web & multimedia, web design, computer & digital forensics, computing security & networks, data science, information visualisation, IT project management, mobile application development, software engineering, technical illustration, user experience design; BA, BSc, DProf, FdSc, MA, MPhil, MProf, MSc, PGDip, PhD

School of Health & Social Care; www.tees.ac.uk/schools/soh

adult social care, social care, dental hygiene and dental therapy, dental nurse practice, diagnostic radiography, midwifery, nursing studies (adult/learning disabilities/mental health), occupational therapy, operating department practice, paramedic practice, physiotherapy, social work, nursing in the home/ district nursing, specialist community public health nursing (health visiting/occupational health/school nursing), food and nutrition

Postgrad; advanced clinical practice, advanced clinical practice (cardiac care/management of long-term health conditions/manipulative therapy/neurological rehabilitation), advanced practice in integrated care, advanced social work studies, advancing human factors in health and social care, advancing practice, advancing quality improvement in health and social care/ safety and governance in health and social care, applied behavioural analysis, autism practice, clinical psychology, clinical research, clinical research and evidence-based medicine, cognitive behaviour therapy, cognitive behaviour therapy, diagnostic radiography, evidence-based medicine, evidence-based medicine, evidence-based medicine (anaesthesia, perioperative medicine and pain), evidence-based practice, forensic radiography, health and social care, health and social care sciences (generic pathway/ integrated and palliative end-of-life care perspectives/public health), innovation and transformational change, leadership in health and social care, manipulative therapy, medical ultrasound, midwifery studies, neurological rehabilitation, nursing (advanced cardiac care/advanced nurse practitioner/specialist field), nursing in the home/district nursing, occupational therapy, orthopaedics, physiotherapy, prehospital care, primary mental health care, public health, service improvement, social work, specialist community public health nursing (health visiting), specialist community public health nursing (occupational health nursing/school nursing), surgical care practitioner (cardiothoracic surgery/surgical care surgery/orthopaedic surgery), surgical gastroenterology and minimally invasive surgery, the management of long-term health conditions, transformational leadership in health and social care, research degrees

BA, BSc, Cert/DipHE, FdSc, MCh, MA, MPhil, MSc, PGCert/Dip, MRes, DClinPsy, Doc Health & Social Care

Science & Engineering; www.tees.ac.uk/ schools/sse

aeronautical engineering, aerospace engineering, chemical engineering, civil engineering, civil engineering with disaster management/with industry, electrical and electronic engineering, electrical and electronic engineering with industry, engineering, instrumentation and control engineering, instrumentation and control engineering, mechanical engineering, petroleum and gas engineering, food science and engineering

Postgrad; civil and structural engineering, electrical power and energy systems, instrumentation and control engineering (oil and gas), mechanical engineering, oil and gas management, petroleum engineering, project management, research degrees, energy and environmental management

BEng, BSc, FdEng, MPhil, MRes, MSc, PGDip, PhD

School of Social Sciences, Business & Law; www.tees.ac.uk/schools/sssbl

accounting and finance, applied accounting and business finance, business management, business with law, business and computing, marketing, public services, tourism and aviation, tourism and events management, travel and tourism, business finance and accounting, international business management, marketing, tourism management, civil engineering with disaster management, law with business management, psychology with business management, criminology, criminology and sociology, criminology with law/psychology/youth studies, crime and investigation, crime scene science, childhood and youth studies, early childhood studies, education and training, education studies, education, research degrees, crime and investigation, law, law with business management, policing, crime scene science, forensic science, criminal investigation, business law, criminal law, international law, medical law), research degree, psychology, psychology and counselling, psychology and criminology, psychology with business management, counselling psychology, forensic psychology, health psychology, research degrees, clinical psychology, social research methods, fitness instruction and exercise therapies, outdoor leadership, physical activity, exercise and health, sport and exercise (applied exercise science/applied sport science/coaching science/personal training/ sport studies), sport and fitness, sports coaching and exercise, sports development, sports therapy, sports therapy and rehabilitation, applied sports rehabilitation, movement science and multimodal rehabilitation, sport and exercise, sports therapy, strength and conditioning, research degrees; BA, BSc, DProf, FdA, FdSc, FdSocSc, GradCert, CertEd, LLB, LLM, MA, MPhil, MProf, MSc, PhD, DBA PGDip

Degrees validated by the University of Teesside offered at:

ASKHAM BRYAN COLLEGE
www.askham-bryan.ac.uk

adventure, sport & public service, agriculture & land management, animal management & science, arboriculture, canine & feline training welfare, countryside management/collection & conservation, equine science, equine business & event management, equine sports management, sport surface management, arboriculture, applied/horticulture, landscaping & garden management, sport (outdoor & adventure education), veterinary health studies/nursing; BSc, BSc(Hons), Nat Dips, FD

TRINITY COLLEGE LONDON
www.trinitycollege.co.uk

dance, drama & speech, music, performing & teaching, theory & composition, English language, teaching English; PGDip, Music Diplomas, Teaching Diplomas

UNIVERSITY OF ULSTER
www.ulster.ac.uk

Faculty of Arts, Design & the Built Environment; www.adbe.ulster.ac.uk

Belfast School of Architecture; www.adbe.ulster.ac.uk/schools/archdesign
architectural technology and management, architecture, interior design, product and furniture design; BSc(Hons), BDes(Hons), MArch

Belfast School of Art; www.adbe.ulster.ac.uk/artdesign
animation, art & design, contemporary applied arts, graphic design and illustration, fine art, interaction design, multidisciplinary design, photography, textile art, design and fashion; BDes(Hons), BA(Hons), MFA

School of the Built Environment; www.adbe.ulster.ac.uk/schools/built_environment
building engineering and materials, building surveying, civil engineering, construction engineering and management, construction building & project management, energy and building services engineering, environmental health, housing management, planning and property development, property investment, appraisal and development, quantity surveying and commercial management, transport planning, transportation, environmental health management and practice, fire safety engineering, housing studies, infrastructure engineering, hydrogen safety engineering, renewable energy and energy management, built environment; BEng, BSc, MEng, MPhil, MSc, PGCert, PGDip, PhD

Faculty of Arts; www.arts.ulster.ac.uk
Creative Technologies; cinematic arts, design, drama, music, English, history, Irish, applied languages; Chinese, French, German, Spanish
Interactive Media Arts; journalism, media & production, media studies, applied languages and translation (French/German/Spanish), arts, Celtic studies, Chinese, creative technologies, cultural heritage and museum studies, dance, dance with drama/Irish/music, design for creative practice, documentary practice, drama, drama with advertising/computing/dance/Irish/marketing/music/ psychology, English, English: jt degrees in number of subjects, film studies, film studies: jt degrees in number of subjects, French, French: jt degrees in number of subjects, German, German: jt degrees in number of subjects, history, history; jt degrees in number of subjects, humanities, interactive media arts, Irish, Irish: jt degrees in number of subjects, Irish history, Irish history & politics/society, Irish language/and literature, Irish literature in English, journalism, journalism: jt degrees in number of subjects, media management and policy, media studies, media studies and production, media studies: jt degrees in number of

subjects, modern Irish, modern languages – French/German/Spanish, museum practice and management, music, music with dance/drama/Irish/psychology, photo imaging minor, professional translation, Spanish, Spanish: jt degrees in number of subjects; BA(Hons), MA, MPhil, PGDip, PhD, MRes, BMus, MMus, MDes, CertHE

Faculty of Computing & Engineering; www.compeng.ulster.ac.uk

School of Computing & Information Engineering; www.compeng.ulster.ac.uk/cie

computing, computing (games development/internet systems), computing with accounting/business/education/geography/psychology, professional software development; BSc, MSc, PGDip, PhD

School of Computing & Intelligent Systems; www.scis.ulster.ac.uk

computer science, computer science (software systems development), computer games development, electronics & computer systems, computer engineering, information and communication technologies, information technologies, computer games, modelling and animation, creative computing (design/games), computational intelligence
BEng, BSc, MSc, PGDip, PhD

School of Computing & Mathematics; www.infj.ulst.ac.uk/cm/

computational technology, computing science, mathematics/with computing, health informatics, computational intelligence, computing systems, interactive multimedia design, computing science, software engineering, professional software development; BSc, MSc, PGCert, PGDip, PhD

School of Engineering; www.seng.ulster.ac.uk/eme

biomedical engineering, clean technology, electronic engineering, engineering management, mechanical/mechatronics engineering, sports technology, technology/design, adv composites & polymers, manufacturing management, nanotechnology; BSc, BEng, MEng, MSc, PGDip, PhD

Faculty of Life & Health Sciences; www.science.ulster.ac.uk

School of Biomedical Sciences; www.biomed.science.ulster.ac.uk

biology, applied biosciences, biomedical and healthcare sciences, biomedical and bio-industrial sciences, biomedical sciences, biomedical science (pathology), dietetics, food and nutrition, human nutrition, optometry, stratified medicine, Postgrad; medical professional practice, biomedical science, cataract and refractive surgery, clinical visual science, diabetes, dietetics, food and nutrition, food regulatory affairs, human nutrition, medical and healthcare biotechnology, nutraceuticals, functional foods and supplements, sports and exercise nutrition, stem cell biology, stratified medicine, systems biology, veterinary public health; BSc, DMedSc, GradCert, MPharm, MSc, PGCert, PGDip

School of Environmental Sciences; www.science.ulster.ac.uk/envsci

marine science, environmental science, geography, environmental science with business, computing, education, international development or psychology, coastal zone management, marine spatial planning, environmental management, environmental management with/and geographic information system, environmental toxicology and pollution monitoring, GIS; AB, BSc, DEnvSci, MPhil, MRes, MSc, PGCert, PGDip, PhD

School of Health Sciences; www.science.ulster.ac.uk/health

health science, health physiology, occupational therapy, physiotherapy, podiatry, diagnostic radiography & imaging, radiology & oncology, speech & language therapy, lower limb preservation in diabetes, advancing practice in an AHP specialism, respiratory health, stroke care, sensory integration, clinical physiology, medicines management; BSc, MClinRes, MSc, PGCert/Dip

School of Nursing; www.science.ulster.ac.uk/nursing

nursing (adult/mental health), specialist nursing practice, specialist community public health nursing, specialist nursing practice, health & wellbeing, health studies, health & social care (learning disability) Postgrad; non-medical prescribing, specialist nursing practice, health studies, health and wellbeing, health promotion and public health nursing, education for nurses and midwives; BSc, CertHE, MSc, PGCert, PGDip, MPhil, PhD

School of Psychology; www.science.ulster.ac.uk/psychology

applied behaviour analysis, applied psychology (mental health), careers guidance, health psychology, psychology, social psychology; BSc, MSc, PGDip

School of Sports; www.science.ulster.ac.uk/sports

physical activity, exercise and health, sports coaching, sport & exercise sciences, sports studies (sport: theory and practice), Postgrad; physical activity and public health, sport and exercise nutrition, sports development and coaching, sport and exercise psychology, sport and exercise medicine/science; BSc, FdSc, MPhil, MSc, DPhil, PGDip, PhD

Faculty of Social Sciences; www.socsci.ulster.ac.uk

School of Communication; www.socsci.ulster.ac.uk/comms

communication, advertising & marketing/PR, communication management and PR, therapeutic communication and counselling studies, counselling – professional development, communication, advertising and marketing, communication and PR (advertising/political lobbying/healthcare), counselling and therapeutic communication, digital media communication, communication management in healthcare, professional development in counselling, therapeutic communication and counselling studies, language and linguistics (with an optional specialism in counselling studies), counselling and therapeutic communication, language and linguistics, English language and linguistics, communication and PR(advertising/political lobbying/healthcare), communication management and PR communication and PR (advertising/political lobbying/healthcare); BSc, MPhil, MSc, PGCert, PGDip, PhD

School of Education; www.socsci.ulster.ac.uk/education

PGCE (post-primary, primary, in numerous school subjects, FE), Certificate in Teaching, contemporary society, educational leadership & management, education with numerous jt degree subjects, ICT, international development, teaching & learning, library & information management, middle leadership, working with children and youth, conflict transformation and peace building, further education teaching skills, inclusive & special education, information and communication technology, leadership & management, TESOL; MEd, PGCE, PGCert, PGDip, BA(Hons), BSc(Hons), MSc

School of Law; www.socsci.ulster.ac.uk/law

law, law & criminology/politics/accountancy/HRM/marketing/Irish/sociology/politics, legal practice, gender, conflict & human rights, commercial law, human rights law & transitional justice, clinical legal education; LLB, LLM

School of Criminology, Politics & Social Policy; www.socsci.ulster.ac.uk/policy

criminology and criminal justice, criminology, law with criminology, politics with criminology, social policy with criminology, sociology with criminology, health and social care policy, politics, politics with criminology, law with politics, sociology with politics, public administration, social policy, social policy with criminology/sociology, social research skills with specialisms; BSc, MPA, PGCert, PGDip, LlB, MPhil, PhD

School of Sociology & Applied Social Studies; www.socsci.ulster.ac.uk/sociology

community development/youth work, restorative practices, profession development/in social work, sociology with social work/criminology/HRM/drama/politics/psychology, law with sociology; BSc, MSc, PGCert, PGDip, LlB

Graduate School of Professional Legal Education; www.socsci.ulster.ac.uk/gsple

legal practice; PGDip

Ulster Business School; www.business.ulster.ac.uk

accounting & law/advertising/HRM/managerial finance/marketing, advertising/management, adv accounting, advertising and HRM, advertising with accounting/computing/drama/Irish psychology, business administration, business management/economics, business studies/ with specialisms, business economics with accountancy/ marketing, business with specialisms, business & accounting/advertising/computing/drama/education/environmental science/HRM/international development/Irish/marketing/media studies/psychology/retail studies/Spanish/economics/supply chain excellence, business development & innovation, consumer studies, business improvement, business information systems, business studies & business with numerous jt degree subjects, developing managerial performance, economics, finance and investment analysis, HRM, HRM & marketing, international business/event management, international hospitality management, international travel and tourism/tourism management, management, international travel and tourism studies with languages, leisure and events management, management and leadership development, management practice, marketing, middle management, advanced accounting, applied management, MBA, business development and innovation, business improvement, business studies, creative technologies, event management, executive leadership, financial services, innovation management in the public service, international business, international hotel and tourism management, international tourism development, management & corporate governance, middle management, marketing, strategic management;BSc, BSc(Hons), MBS, CertHE, AdvDip, MBA, MSc, PGDip

UNIVERSITY OF WALES TRINITY SAINT DAVID
www.uwtsd.ac.uk

Faculty of Applied Design & Engineering; www.uwtsd.ac.uk/fade

School of Applied Computing; http:/ www.uwtsd.ac.uk/undergraduate/applied-computing

wireless communications systems, computer networks technology, computer systems and electronics, electrical and electronic engineering, applied computing, business computing, business information technology, cloud computing, computer games development, computer graphics and visualisation, computer networks, computing and information systems, GES and environmental conservation, mobile computing and application development, robotics and intelligent systems, software engineering, web development, information technology management for business, applied computing, computer networks, ecommerce; BEng, BSc, MSc

School of Automotive Engineering; www.uwtsd.ac.uk/automotive-engineering

advanced engine design/with manufacturing, automotive engineering/with manufacturing, motorcycle engineering/with manufacturing, motorsport engineering/ with manufacturing, powertrain engineering/ with manufacturing; BEng, BSc, MEng

School of Architecture, Built & Natural Environment; www.uwtsd.ac.uk/built-natural-environment

architectural conservation, architectural technology/ & glass, building surveying, civil engineering/and environmental management, environmental conservation, environmental sciences, habitat management, marine and coastal geography, project & construction management, property management, quantity surveying/& commercial management, renewable energy and the built environment, sustainable construction, waste resource management and logistics, sustainable construction, environmental conservation & management, property and facilities management; BSc, MSc

School of Engineering, Logistics & Manufacturing; www.uwtsd.ac.uk/logistics-manufacturing-engineering

Logistics and Transport (Including Motorsport Management); food logistics, humanitarian logistics, logistics services, logistics, military logistics, motorsport logistics, engineering project management Mechanical and Manufacturing Engineering; composites engineering, energy and environmental engineering, extreme sports engineering, humanitarian engineering, mechanical and manufacturing engineering, mechanical engineering, engineering project management, lean and agile manufacturing, logistics, non-destructive testing and evaluation; BSc, BEng, MA, MSc

Faculty of Art & Design; www.uwtsd.ac.uk/art-design

School of Design & Applied Arts www.uwtsd.ac.uk/applied-arts

product design, product design & technology/innovation, automotive design, transport design, industrial design, transportation design, glass, glass in the public arts, architectural glass arts, surface pattern design (contemporary applied arts practice/textiles for fashion/textiles for interiors), surface pattern design (fashion object), textiles (contemporary dialogues)
BA(Hons), MA, MDes, MPhil, PhD

The School of Film & Digital Media

3D computer animation, creative computer games design, digital arts/film & TV production, sonic art, music technology, 3D computer animation, multi-media, creative sound production, film and visual culture, new media production; BA, MA, BSc, MPhil, PhD

School of Fine Art & Photography

art & design, fine art (combined media/painting & drawing/3D & sculptural practice), photography in the arts, photojournalism, fine art/photography (contemporary dialogues), art practice (environmental art/community/health and wellbeing), applied arts, design, fine art; FD, BA(Hons), MArt, MA, MPhil, PhD

School of Visual Communication; www.uwtsd.ac.uk/visual-communication

graphic design, illustration, advertising and brand design, visual communication (contemporary dialogues); BA(Hons), MPhil, PhD

Art & Design Research

textiles, fine art/visual communication/photography (contemporary dialogues), industrial design, product design and innovation, transportation design, 3D computer animation, multimedia, creative sound production, applied arts, design, fine art; MA, PhD, MSc

Faculty of Humanities & Performing Arts; www.uwtsd.ac.uk/faculty-of-humanities-performingarts

School of Archaeology, History and Anthropology

Archaeology; archaeology, archaeology professional practice, environmental archaeology, nautical archaeology, archaeology of Egypt and the near east, ancient history and archaeology, archaeology and anthropology, archaeology and classical studies/history/medieval studies/heritage studies, nautical archaeology and heritage studies, archaeology with forensic studies/education studies/ancient Egyptian culture/heritage management/ digital humanities; jt degrees with education studies and other subjects

Ancient Civilisations; cultural astronomy and astrology, engaged anthropology, landscape management and environmental archaeology, local history, heritage practice, medieval studies, landscape and environmental archaeology, cultural astronomy and astrology, heritage practice, medieval studies

History and Medieval Studies; history, medieval studies, ancient and medieval history, modern historical studies, conflict and war, history and heritage studies/ancient history/anthropology/

archaeology/English/medieval studies/philosophy/theology, medieval studies and heritage studies/ Chinese civilisation/Chinese studies/anthropology/ archaeology/ classical studies/English/modern historical studies/philosophy, history with heritage management/digital humanities, medieval studies with heritage management, jt degrees with education studies and other subjects

Postgraduate Courses; cultural astronomy and astrology, engaged anthropology, landscape management and environmental archaeology, local history, heritage practice, medieval studies

School of Classics

Classical Studies; classical studies, classical civilisation, classics, classical studies and archaeology/ English/medieval studies/philosophy/theology/religious studies/heritage studies/education studies/ Greek/Latin/ancient Egyptian culture/heritage management/digital humanities/creative writing; jt degrees with education

Ancient history; ancient history, ancient history and archaeology, ancient civilisations, ancient and medieval history, classical civilisation, ancient history and anthropology/history/heritage studies, ancient history with Latin/ancient Egyptian culture/heritage management/digital humanities/education studies, ancient history, education studies & anthropology/ classical studies/ history/archaeology/ religious studies, ancient history, classical studies

Postgrad; ancient history, classical studies, classics, ancient religions

School of Cultural Studies

Chinese Studies; number of jt degree courses in Chinese studies, Mandarin, Chinese civilisation

Creative Writing; creative writing and English/philosophy/publishing/heritage studies/digital humanities/heritage management/education studies/classical studies

English & English with TEFL; English, joint degrees, jt degrees with education studies

Postgraduate Degrees; applied philosophy, creative writing, creative and script writing, English with TEFL, European philosophy, medieval and early modern literature, modern literature, ethics, literary studies, medieval literature

School of Theology, Religious Studies and Islamic Studies

study of religions, theology, Islamic studies, religious studies, Islamic studies and religious sttudies, theology, philosophy, numerous jt degrees offered with religious studies, education studies

The School of Performing Arts

acting, dance, theatre design and production, Welsh medium courses

Postgrad; ancient religions, biblical interpretation, Islamic studies, study of religions, Christian theology, church history, bible & theology, religious studies/ experience; BA, MA, FD, MRes, GradDip, MEd, CertHE, MPhil, PhD

Faculty of Business & Management; www.uwtsd.ac.uk/business-management

Swansea Business School

accounting, business and finance, business management, e-business, marketing management, business information technology, business computing, entrepreneurship, HRM, international business, management and leadership, marketing management, sustainable management, law and business, skills in the workplace, business and finance law and business, public services, management skills for the workplace, financial management Postgrad; financial management, marketing, digital marketing, HRM, MBAs in: international tourism, sports Management, public services management, e-MBA, Professional programmes in human resource management, human resource practice, learning and development; BA, MA, MBA, MSc, DBA, MPhil, PhD BSc

School of Sport, Health & Outdoor Education

health & exercise and sport studies, health, nutrition and lifestyle, outdoor education, outdoor fitness, personal training (health & exercise), physical education, sport therapy, public services, law & public services, health and social care, health management, children and young people, sports management Postgrad; outdoor education, physical education; BA, BSc, MA, FDA

The School of Tourism and Hospitality

events management, international travel and tourism management, leisure management, tourism management, Postgrad: international tourism management, sports management, events management, international tourism, sports management; BA, MBA, MA

Wales Institute for Work-Based learning

professional practice; BA(Hons), FdA, CertHE, DProfPract, MA, PGCert/Dip

Faculty of Performance; www.uwtsd.ac.uk/performance

School of Performing Arts

acting, dance, theatre design and production

Centre for Contemporary Performance

technical theatre, applied drama, performing arts (contemporary practice)

Welsh Academy of Voice

advanced vocal studies, advanced pianoforte studies; BA, BSc, MA, FdA

Faculty of Education & Community; www.uwtsd.ac.uk/education-andcommunitity

School of Early Childhood

early childhood, early literacy

School of Social Justice and Inclusion

advocacy, inclusive studies for teaching assistants, social inclusion, social inclusion (inclusive education/ additional needs/communities, families and individuals/ health and social care/ youth and community work), primary education studies, youth work, equality and diversity in society, playwork, young people's health and wellbeing, additional learning needs, learning support, supporting learning and teaching, counselling skills, education studies, counselling skill and interdisciplinary studies, counselling studies and psychology, psychotherapeutic practice: emotion-focused therapy, humanities with education studies

School of Welsh and Bilingual Studies

Celtic studies, bilingualism & multilingualism, Welsh learners, applied bilingualism (Welsh with English)

School of Psychology

psychology, counselling studies and psychology, applied social and health psychology, adolescent psychology, applied psychology, anthropology/religious studies/religion/ethics/philosophy with applied psychology; CertHE, BA, BSc, MA, PGDip, FdA

South West Wales Centre of Teacher Education

PGCE primary/secondary with QTS, PGCE secondary: art & design/computing and ICT business studies, maths 11–18, maths 11–16 with ICT, biology, design and technology, geography, physics, science 11–16, English, history, modern foreign languages, religious education, Welsh, chemistry, all with QTS

UNIVERSITY OF WARWICK
www.warwick.ac.uk

Faculty of Arts; www2.warwick.ac.uk/ fac/arts

Dept of Classics & Ancient History; www2.warwick.ac.uk/fac/arts/classics

ancient history & classical archaeology, ancient visual & material culture, visual & material culture in ancient Rome/Greece, classical civilization/with philosophy, classics (Latin/ancient Greek), English & Latin literature, Italian & classics, Italian literature; BA, MA, MPhil, PhD

Dept of English & Comparative Literary Studies; www2.warwick.ac.uk/fac/arts/english

English literature, creative writing, English & theatre studies, pan-romanticisms, world literatures, writing, translation & transcultural studies; BA, MA, MPhil, PhD, Diploma

School of Comparative American Studies; www2.warwick.ac.uk/fac/arts/cas

History, Literature and Cultures of the Americas, comparative American studies; BA, MA

Dept of Film & TV Studies; www2.warwick.ac.uk/fac/arts/film

film & literature/TV studies, research in film & TV, film studies, French/German/Italian & film studies, history & film; BA, MA, MPhil, PhD

Dept of French Studies; www2.warwick.ac.uk/fac/arts/french

English & French, French studies with history of art/German/Italian studies/film studies/ stage & theatre German/history/international studies/Italian/politics/film/sociology, film, research in French and Francophone studies, translation, writing and cultural difference, pan-romanticisms, French studies by research culture & thought, French & francophone studies, translation, writing & cultural differences, theatre studies, jt honours (German with modern languages); BA, MA, MPhil, PGDip, PhD

Dept of German Studies; www2.warwick.ac.uk/fac/arts/german

German cultural studies, German studies, German with business studies/French/international studies/ Italian/Spanish/history, pan-romanticism, translation, writing & cultural differences; BA, MA, MPhil, PGDip, PhD

Dept of Hispanic Studies; www2.warwick.ac.uk/fac/arts/Hispanic

Hispanic studies, Hispanic studies with Arabic, Chinese, French, German, Italian, Japanese, Portuguese, Russian, film studies, theatre studies or politics and international studies

Dept of History; www2.warwick.ac.uk/fac/arts/history

history, 18th-century studies, comparative American history, global history, history, literature and cultures of the Americas, history and philosophy/politics/sociology/French/German/Italian/film, history of medicine, religious/cultural & social history 1500–1700; BA, MA, MPhil, PhD

Dept of History of Art; www2.warwick.ac.uk/fac/arts/arthistory

history of art, art history with Italian/French, Venice & its legacies; British art; BA, MA, MPhil, PGDip, PhD

Dept of Italian; www2.warwick.ac.uk/fac/arts/italian

English & Italian literature, Italian & classics/European studies, history of art, Italian & film studies/international studies/theatre studies, Italian with French/German translation, modern languages, reseach in Italian, translation, writing & cultural differences; BA, MA, MPhil, PGDip, PhD

School of Theatre; www2.warwick.ac.uk/fac/arts/theatre

theatre consultancy, international performance research, creative & media enterprise, global media & communication, theatre & performance studies, French/German/English/Italian & theatre studies; BA, MA, MPhil, PhD

Faculty of Medicine; www2.warwick.ac.uk/fac/med

Warwick Medical School

medicine & surgery, advanced clinical practice for health care professionals, child health, diabetes, diabetes (paediatrics), digital healthcare, dentistry, endodontics, health sciences/research, health sciences (musculoskeletal care/plastic surgery/retinal screening – diabetes), health services management, implant dentistry/with supervised oral surgery clinical training, interdisciplinary biomedical research, leadership for healthcare, medical education/leadership, orthodontics/with supervised dental clinical training, pre-hospital critical care, public health, reproductive health, research methods in health sciences, restorative dentistry with supervised dental clinical training/ aesthetic dentistry, trauma and orthopaedic surgery, biomedical cell biology, health science, mental health & wellbeing, metabolic & vascular health, microbiology; MBChB, MD, MMedSci, MPhil, MSc, MA, MS, PhD, PGCert, MPH

Faculty of Science; www2.warwick.ac.uk/fac/sci

Dept of Life Sciences; www2.warwick.ac.uk/fac/sci/lifesci

biochemistry, biomedical science, biological sciences, biotechnology, bioprocessing & business management, environmental bioscience in changing climate, food security, integrative medical microbiology & virology, medical bioscience & business management, sustainable crop production, agronomy for the 21st century; BSc, MD, MPhil, MSc, PhD

Dept of Chemistry; www2.warwick.ac.uk/ fac/sci/chemistry

chemistry, analytical science, biomedical chemistry, chemical biology, chemistry/with medical chemistry, molecular/physical chemistry, chemistry with scientific writing, diamond science & technology, polymer chemistry, polymer science, analytical and polymer science, methods & instrumental techniques, molecular analytical science, scientific communications and research, analytical & polymer science; BSc, MChem, MSc, PhD, ChM

Dept of Computer Science; www2.warwick.ac.uk/fac/sci/dcs

computer & management sciences/business studies, cognitive systems, computer science/& applications, computing systems engineering, data science/analytics, discrete mathematics; BSc, MEng, MPhil, MSc, PhD

School of Engineering; www2.warwick.ac.uk/fac/sci/eng

general engineering, engineering with sustainability/ business management, automotive engineering, automotive engineering with business management/ robotics/sustainability, civil engineering with business/ business management/ engineering with sustainability, computer systems engineering, electronic engineering with business management, electronic engineering with communications, engineering business, engineering and business studies, engineering with business management, electronic engineering with business management, manufacturing and mechanical engineering with business/management, mechanical engineering with business management, engineering and business studies, engineering business management, manufacturing and mechanical engineering/ with business management/robotics/ sustainability, mechanical engineering, mechanical engineering with business management/fluid dynamics, sustainability

Postgrad; advanced mechanical engineering, biomedical engineering, communications and information engineering, energy and power engineering, sustainable energy technologies, tunnelling and underground space; BEng, BSc, EngD, MPhil, MSc, PhD

Dept of Mathematics/Warwick Mathematics Institute; www2.warwick.ac.uk/fac/sci/maths

discrete mathematics, mathematics, mathematics & business/physics/statistics/MORSE studies/economics/philosophy, mathematics in real world systems; Postgrad; advanced study in mathematical sciences, mathematics, interdisciplinary mathematics, financial mathematics; BSc, MMath, MSc, PhD

Dept of Physics; www2.warwick.ac.uk/fac/ sci/physics

mathematics & physics, physics/& business studies, Master project options; BSc, MPhys, MSc, PhD, MMathPhys

Dept of Psychology; www2.warwick.ac.uk/ fac/sci/psych

psychology, behavioural & economic science, clinical psychology, psychology, psychological research; BSc, MPhil, MSc, PhD, Doc ClinPsych

Dept of Statistics; www2.warwick.ac.uk/ fac/sci/statistics

statistics & mathematics/economics, operational research, data science, MORSE, financial statistics; MMathStat, MPhil, MSc, PGDip, PhD

Warwick Systems Biology Centre; www2.warwick.ac.uk/fac/sci/biology systems

Faculty of Social Sciences; www2.warwick.ac.uk/fac/soc

Centre for Applied Linguistics; www2.warwick.ac.uk/fac/soc/al

English language teaching, intercultural communication/for business & the professions, language, culture & communication; BEd, BA(Hons), EdD, MA, MPhil, PGCert, PGDip, PhD

Dept of Economics; www2.warwick.ac.uk/fac/soc/economics

economics, economics & industrial organisation/politics & international studies, finance & economics, mathematics & economics, MORSE, politics, philosophy & economics; Postgrad; economics, economics and international financial economics, economic development and growth, behavioural and economic science; BA, BSc, BSc/Ec, MEcMSc, PGDip, PhD, MRes

Warwick Institute for Employment Research; www2.warwick.ac.uk/fac/soc/ier

Research; PhD

Dept of Philosophy; www2.warwick.ac.uk/fac/soc/philosophy

continental philosophy, philosophy, philosophy & literature/maths/psychology/classical civilisation, philosophy of mind, philosophy, politics & economics; BA, BSc, MA, MPhil, PGDip, PhD

Dept of Politics & International Studies; www2.warwick.ac.uk/fac/soc/pais

politics, politics and international studies/ sociology, politics, international studies and quantitative methods/modern languages
Postgrad; political & legal theory, research in PAIS, PAIS: big data & quantitative methods, US foreign policy, international development, public policy, international politics & Europe/Asia, international security, international political economy, international relations; BA, MA, MPhil, PhD

Dept of Sociology; www2.warwick.ac.uk/fac/soc/sociology

sociology, sociology & quantitative methods, sociology with specialisms in social policy/research methods/cultural studies/gender, history & sociology, sociology & law, public policy; Postgrad; sociology, social research, social and political thought, gender and international development, science, media, and public policy; BA, MA, MPhil, PGDip, PhD

School of Health & Social Studies; www2.warwick.ac.uk/fac/soc/shss

applied social studies, health studies, health & social studies, specialist social work; MA, MPhil, PGDip, PhD

Warwick Business School; www2.wbs.warwick.ac.uk/fac/soc/

accounting & finance, international business, international management, management, information systems management & innovation, Postgrad; accounting & finance, behavioural finance, business (consulting/ finance & accounting/ leadership/ marketing), business analytics, finance, finance & economics, financial mathematics, HRM & employment relations, information systems management & innovation, international business, management, marketing, MBA, Exec MBA, Global Energy MBA; BA, BSc, MA, MBA, MPA, MPhil, MSc, PGDip, PhD

Centre for Education Studies; www2.warwick.ac.uk/fac/soc/ces

education studies, educational innovation, drama education and ELT, drama and theatre education, innovation in education, educational leadership and management, religions and education, innovation in education, international education and development, subject pedagogy development, innovation in education; BA, MA, PGCert & awards

Warwick School of Law; www2.warwick.ac.uk/fac/soc/law

law, European law with French law or German law, law and business studies/humanities/social sciences; Postgrad; advanced legal studies, international corporate governance and financial regulation, international development law and human rights, international economic law; BA, LLB, LLM, MPhil, PhD, PGCert, PGDip

UNIVERSITY OF WEST OF SCOTLAND
www.uws.ac.uk

School of Business & Enterprise; www.uws.ac.uk/schools/business-school

accounting, applied enterprise, business/& English language, events management, HRM international finance & accounting, law & business, marketing, tourism management, Postgrad; accounting, creative branding, digital marketing, finance and accounting, financial accounting, HRM, international events management, international financial management, international HRM, international management, international marketing management, logistics and supply chain management, management accounting; BA, BSc, MSc, MBA, EMBA, PGDip/Cert

School of Media, Culture and Society; www.uws.ac.uk/schools/school-of-media-culture-and-society

broadcast production, commercial music, commercial sound production, contemporary screen acting, criminal justice, digital art, filmmaking and screenwriting, journalism, musical theatre, performance, politics, psychology, social policy, social science, social work, sociology, sports journalism, technical theatre; Postgrad; alcohol and drug, applied social science, broadcast journalism, careers guidance and development, creative media practice, filmmaking, music: innovation & entrepreneurship, psychology, screenwriting, songwriting and performance; BA, BA(Hons), BAcc, ExecMBA, MA, MSc, PGDip, PhD

School of Science & Sport; www.uws.ac.uk/schools-of-science

adv/applied biomedical science, biotechnology, applied bioscience & zoology/forensic science, chemistry, environmental health, forensic science, occupational safety & health, exercise & health science, sport & exercise science, sports coaching/development, biotechnology, drug design & discovery, personal fitness & practice, project management, psychology, quality management, waste & clean technologies; BSc/BSc(Hons), CertHE, GradDip/Cert, MSc, PhD

School of Engineering & Computing; www.uws.ac.uk/schools/school-of-engineering

aircraft engineering, business technology, chemical engineering, civil engineering, computer animation, computer games development/technology, computer networking, computer-aided design, computing, computing science, engineering management, information technology, mechanical engineering, mechatronics, music technology, physics, physics with nuclear technology, product design & development, web and mobile development; Postgrad; advanced computer systems development, computer-aided engineering, engineering management, enterprise software systems, information technology, mobile web development, smart networks; BEng(Hons), PGDip/Cert, MSc, BA(Hons), BSc(Hons), CertHE

School of Health, Nursing & Midwifery; www.uws.ac.uk/schools/school-of-health-nursing-and-midwifery

adult nursing, integrated health and social care, integrated health and social care with administration, mental health nursing, midwifery

Postgrad; acute mental health care, adult nursing, advancing practice, child protection, cognitive behavioural therapy, health studies, health studies (family health/maternal and child health), healthcare associated infection improvement, later life studies, maternal and child health in advanced neonatal paediatric practice, mental health nursing, mental health practice, midwifery, neonatal nursing, personality disorder, professional health studies, public health nursing, sexual and reproductive health, specialist community public health nursing (health visiting/occupational health), specialist practitioner (district nurse), vulnerability, working with older people; BSc(Hons), MSc, PGCert/Dip, DipHE

School of Education; www.uws.ac.uk/schools/school-of-education

childhood practice, childhood studies, community education, education, ESL; Postgrad; artist teacher, coaching and mentoring, enhanced educational practice, inclusive education, leadership for learning, mental health and education, teaching and learning in HE, education (primary), education (secondary), TESOL, artist teacher, enhanced educational practice, coaching & mentoring; BA, BEd MEd, PGCert/Dip

THE UNIVERSITY OF WESTMINSTER
www.wmin.ac.uk

Faculty of Architecture & the Built Environment; www.westminster.ac.uk/about-us/faculties/architecture

architectural technology, architecture, designing cities: planning and architecture, interior architecture, architecture and environmental design, urban design, property and planning, international planning and sustainable development, urban and regional planning, housing practice, building engineering, building surveying, construction management, property and planning, quantity surveying and commercial management, real estate, architectural technology building information management, construction commercial management, construction project management, facilities and property management, property finance, real estate development tourism and events management, tourism management, tourism planning and management, tourism with business events and conference management, tourism management, events and conference management, air transport planning and management, logistics and supply chain management, transport planning and management

BA, BSc, MA, MPhil, MSc, PGCert, PGDip, PhD, MArch

Faculty of Science & Technology; www.westminster/about-us/faculties/science-and-technology

Biomedical Sciences & Biosciences; biomedical sciences, human and medical science, pharmacology & physiology, applied biomedical science, healthcare science diagnostics, applied biomedical science, biomedical sciences (haematology/cancer biology/cellular pathology/clinical biochemistry/immunology/medical microbiology), biomedical sciences, medical molecular, biology (bioinformatics), medical molecular biology life sciences, applied biotechnology, pharmacology

Business Information Systems; business information systems, business intelligence and analytics, database systems

Complementary Medicine; Chinese medicine/acupuncture, herbal medicine

Computer and Network Engineering; computer network security, computer networks and communications, computer systems engineering

Computer Science and Software Engineering;computer networks, computer science, software engineering, cyber security and forensics

Electronic Engineering; electronic engineering, embedded systems, microelectronic system design, mobile, wireless and broadband communications

Multimedia and Games Computing; research in electronics computer games development, multimedia computing

Nutrition; human nutrition (nutrition & exercise science), human nutrition, international public health nutrition, public health nutrition, sport and exercise nutrition

Psychology; cognitive neuroscience, psychology, business psychology, cognitive rehabilitation, health psychology

BSc, FdSc, MA, MPhil, MSc, PGCert, PhD, BEng, MEng

Faculty of Media, Arts & Design; www.westminster.ac.uk/about-us/faculties/media

animation, applied sound for interactive media, audio production, commercial music performance, communication/policy, contemporary media practice, design for communication, digital media & communication, diversity & the media, fashion/buying/business management, management/design/merchandise management, film, TV, film & TV; theory, culture & identity/directing/production/theory, global media, graphic communication design, illustration & visual communication, international media, business journalism media development/management/business, music business management, clinical photography, photographic arts/studies, documentary photography & photojournalism, medical journalism, media campaigning & social change, multimedia journalism (broadcasting/PR & online), PR/& advertising, radio production, social media, mixed media & fine art, TV production, social media, culture & society; BA, BMus, BSc, FdA, GradDip, MA, PGDip

Faculty of Social Sciences & Humanities; www.westminster.ac.uk/about-us/faculties/humanities

Criminology; criminology, sociology and criminology

English; Arabic/Chinese and English language/English literature, English language/English literature and creative writing/English literature/French/linguistics/Spanish, English literature, linguistics and creative writing; Postgrad; creative writing: writing the city, cultural and critical studies, English language and creative writing/linguistics/literature, English literature: modern and contemporary fictions, TESOL, TESOL & creative writing

History; English literature and history, history and politics, history

Languages; Arabic and English language/English literature/linguistics, Chinese & English language/literature, Chinese and linguistics, English language and French/Spanish, English literature and French/Spanish, French and linguistics/Spanish, international relations and Arabic/Chinese/French/ Spanish, linguistics and Spanish, translation studies (French, Spanish), bilingual translation, international liaison and communication, specialised translation, translating cultures, translation and interpreting

Linguistics; Arabic and linguistics, Chinese and linguistics, English language and linguistics, English literature and linguistics, French and linguistics, linguistics and creative writing, linguistics and Spanish, TESOL,

Politics & International Relations; development studies and international relations, history and politics, international relations and Arabic/Chinese/French/ Spanish, international relations, politics and international relations, politics, international relations and democratic politics, international relations and security, international relations; BA, MA, MPhil, PhD, MRes

Westminster Law School

European legal studies, law, law with French law, solicitors exempting, conflict prevention, dispute resolution, corporate finance law, entertainment law, international and commercial dispute resolution law, international banking law, international commercial law, international law; LlB, LlM, MLaw, GradDip

Westminster Business School; www.westminster.ac.uk/schools/business

Accounting, Finance & Economics; accounting with management, international business economics, business management (accounting/economics/finance & financial services), finance with management, finance & accounting, finance, banking & insurance, global finance, international economic policy & analysis, investment & risk finance

Business & Management; business – international, business management (accounting/economics/entrepreneurship/finance & financial services/HRM/international business/law/marketing), purchasing & supply chain management, international business (with Arabic/Chinese/French/German/Spanish), international marketing, marketing communication/management, business communication for digital economy, international business & management, international development management/HRM, management, business management (MBA), project management

Human Management Resource; HRM, international HRM

Marketing: business management – marketing, international marketing, marketing communications/management; BA, MA, MBA, MPhil, MSc, PGCert, PhD

THE UNIVERSITY OF WINCHESTER
www.winchester.ac.uk

Faculty of Arts; www.winchester.ac.uk/aboutus/universitystructure

American studies, American studies & politics/history, creative writing, creative & professional writing, English literature, English language studies, English with American literature; Postgrad; creative and critical writing

writing for children, broadcast television and media production, digital media design/ development, film production/studies, mass communication, media and audio communication/ communication, media, communication and advertising/journalism/social media, Postgrad; digital media practice

choreography and dance, comedy performance and production, drama, musical theatre, performing arts, street arts: performance and production, theatre for children and young people, theatre production (arts and stage management), vocal and choral studies Postgrad; cultural and arts management; Doc Creative Arts, BA, FdA, MA, PGCert/Dip, PhD

Faculty of Humanities and Social Sciences; www.winchester.ac.uk/aboutus/universitystructure/hss

Dept of Archaeology; www.winchester.ac.uk/academicdepartments/archaeology/Pages/Archaeology.aspx

archaeology, archaeological practice, ancient, classical & medieval studies, cultural heritage & resource management

Dept of Applied Social Studies; www.winchester.ac.uk/academicdepartments/applied-social-studies

applied/criminology, fashion: media & marketing, forensic science, sociology, geography

Dept of Theology, Religion & Philosophy; www.winchester.ac.uk/academicdepartments/theology/Pages/Theology-religionandphilosopy

history, civilisations & beliefs, religious studies, theology & religious studies, death, religion & culture, orthodox studies, religion, ethics & society, reconciliation & peacekeeping, philosophy/theology & ethics, funereal celebrancy

Dept of History; www.winchester.ac.uk/academicdepartments/history/Pages/history.aspx

history, historical studies, history & the medieval world/modern world, global history & politics, ancient, classical/ & medieval studies, politics & global studies

Dept of Psychology; www.winchester.ac.uk/academicdepartments/psychology/Pages/Welcome.aspx

psychological science/disorders, psychology & child development/cognition, psychology, psychological research methods, forensic psychology, social psychology

BA, BSc, MA, MPhil, MRes, MSc, PGCert, PGDip, PhD, MTh

Faculty of Education, Health and Social Care

Dept of Education & Liberal Arts; www.winchester.ac.uk/academicdepartments/edstudiesandliberalarts

education studies, education studies (early childhood), modern liberal arts; BA, MA

Dept of Teacher Development; winchester.ac.uk/academicdepartments/teacherdevelopment

primary education with recommendation for QTS, PGCE primary/secondary religious education, early years IT, education, school leadership; BEd, MEd, EdD

Dept of Interprofessional Studies; www.winchester.ac.uk/academicdepartments/Interprofessionalstudies

academic departments childhood, youth and community studies, primary practice, social work, nursing studies, childhood studies, early years initial teacher training, medical education, health and social care; BA(Hons), BSc(Hons), MA, FdA, Dip

Faculty of Business Law & Sport; www.winchester.ac.uk/academicdepartments/Winchester%20Business%20School/Pages/WinchesterBusinessSchool.aspx

Winchester Business School; www.winchester.ac.uk/academic-departments/winchester-business-school

accounting & finance, business management/with enterprise & innovation, business administration, events management, fashion, media & marketing, international fashion marketing, management, managing contemporary issues with environment & development, marketing, sustainable business; BA, FdA, MBA, MSc, PGCert, PGDip, FD

Dept of Law; www.winchester.ac.uk/academicdepartments/law

law, intellectual & information rights law, medical law & ethics; BA/LLB, LLB, LlM, GradDip

**Dept of Sports Studies;
www.winchester.ac.uk/
academicdepartments/SportsStudies/
Pages/Sportsstudies.aspx**
sports coaching, sports management/studies, sport &
society, applied sport & exercise science, sport &
exercise psychology; BA, BSc, FdA, MA, PGDip

UNIVERSITY OF WOLVERHAMPTON
www.wlv.ac.uk

Faculty of Arts; www.wlv.ac.uk/about-us/our-schools-and-institutions/faculty of arts

Wolverhampton School of Art
visual communication, visual communication (graphic design/illustration), photography, applied arts,
fashion and textiles, fine art, interior design, art and
design, applied arts, product design, visual
communications

School of Humanities
English; English & deaf studies/education studies/
film studies/history/philosophy
Creative and Professional Writing; creative and
professional writing and English/film studies/media
and communication studies/philosophy
English Language; English language and creative and
professional writing/ linguistics/media and communication studies/media and cultural studies
Linguistics; linguistics and English language/deaf
studies, linguistics and TESOL
Philosophy; philosophy and English/film studies/
law/politics religious studies/war studies
Religious studies; religious studies and education
studies/philosophy/sociology/
Cultural Heritage; cultural heritage
Postgrad; English, transmedia screenwriting, human
science, popular culture
School of Media; Animation, Games & Film Production; animation, computer games design, video and
film production, art and design, commercial video
production
Broadcasting, Film & Media Studies; broadcasting
and journalism, film studies, media and communication studies, media and cultural studies, film studies
and philosophy, film, media and cultural studies,
English and film studies, creative and professional
writing and film studies, media and cultural studies
and English language, media and cultural studies

and sociology, film, media and communication
studies, broadcast journalism
Postgrad; film studies, contemporary media, PR &
corporate communication

School of Performing Arts
dance; drama, dance science, drama; music; music
technology, musical theatre, music technology and
popular music, popular music, sound production,
music, audio technology, musical theatre; BA(Hons),
BSc(Hons), MA, MSc, BA(Muis), FdA

Faculty of Education, Health and Wellbeing

Institute of Education
Teaching; primary teaching, secondary teaching,
school direct, post-compulsory education, modern
foreign languages, early years primary (3–7 years),
primary education (5–11 years, PGCE; primary/
general primary with mathematics/school direct
tuition, education studies/and English, childhood
studies, family and community studies, childhood
and family studies and education studies, childhood
and family studies and social policy/sociology,
special needs, childhood and family studies, special
needs and inclusion studies/ and education studies,
childhood studies with early years teacher status
(EYTS), early years services, supporting children in
primary education, education, academic practice in
higher education, post-compulsory education, childhood, family and community studies, special needs
and inclusion studies, education studies, mentoring;
BA(Hons), BEd(Hons), BAPCE, CertED, PGCert,
DEd, PGCE, FdA

Institute of Health Professions
nursing (adult/child/mental health/community
health/learning disabilities), midwifery, health and
social care practice (offender health), nursing studies
(palliative and end of life care), specialist community

291

public health nursing (health visiting/school nursing/ district nursing/general), clinical nursing, school nursing, practice nursing, non-medical prescribing, health and wellbeing (learning, education and progression, sexual health), emergency practitioner (top-up) health and social care practice, health studies, health and social care (restraint reduction), nursing studies, paramedic science, developing palliative and end of life care practice, lymphoedema care, advanced practice for allied health professionals (diabetology/musculoskeletal disorders), commissioning for health and social care, emergency planning resilience and response, education for health, social care and allied professionals, health and social care/wellbeing, healthcare leadership, medical education, mental health, midwifery, nursing, specialist clinical nursing, service improvement, advanced clinical practice, physician associate studies, assistant practitioner (foot health assistant/ perioperative), advanced clinical practice, emergency practitioner, nursing studies/acute care/cardiac care/care of the older person/emergency care/critical care/neonatal-intensive care/orthopaedic care/renal care/stroke care/learning disabilities/mental health and psychological interventions; BNurs(Hons), BSc(Hons), MSc, PGCert/Dip, DipHE, FD

Institute of Psychology

psychology, psychology (counselling psychology/ criminal behaviour), counselling psychology, occupational psychology, applied child psychology; BSc(Hons), PGCert, MSc, PhD, ProfDoc

Institute of Public Health, Social Work & Care

public health & wellbeing
health & social care, health studies, public health
Social Care; social care, social care & criminology & criminal justice/deaf studies/health studies/sociology/ social policy
Social work; social work; FD, BSc(Hons), MA/MSc, MPhil, MPH

Faculty of Science & Engineering; www.wlv.ac.uk/about-us/our-schools-and-institutions

School of Architecture & Built Environment

architectural design technology, architecture, interior architecture and property development, building/ quantity surveying, civil engineering, civil and environmental engineering, construction/project management, commercial/management and quantity surveying, environmental health, advanced technology management, computer aided design for construction, building information modelling, civil engineering/management, construction law and dispute resolution, climate change management, environmental management/pollution control/technology, waste and resource management, construction and the built environment, environment and geography, environmental health, advanced technology management, computer aided design for construction, building information modelling, climate change management; BSc(Hons), BEng(Hons), MSc, PGCert

School of Biology, Chemistry & Forensic Science

Biology; animal behaviour and wildlife conservation, biochemistry, biological sciences, biotechnology, genetics and molecular biology, microbiology, molecular bioscience
Chemistry; chemistry, chemistry with secondary education (QTS)
Forensic Science; forensic science, forensic science and criminology
Postgrad; molecular biology with bioinformatics, computational bioinformatics, forensic genetics and human identification, forensic mark comparison, fire scene investigation, medical biotechnology, applied microbiology and biotechnology; BSc(Hons), MSc, MSci

School of Biomedical Science & Physiology

biomedical science, healthcare science (biomedical science/physiology), human biology, medical science, biomedical science (cellular pathology/clinical biochemistry/haematology)/medical microbiology); BSc(Hons), MSc, MD, DMedSci

School of Engineering

aerospace engineering, automotive engineering, chemical engineering, electronic and telecommunications engineering, mechanical engineering, mechatronics engineering, motorsport engineering, technology; Postgrad; advanced technology management, manufacturing engineering, polymer engineering design, rapid product development and advanced manufacturing; BEng(Hons), MEng, BSc(Hons), PGCert

School of Mathematics & Computer Science

mathematics, mathematical sciences, industrial mathematics, business information systems, computer science, computer science (games development/ software engineering), computer systems engineering, computing. information technology/

management/security, computing, digital media design, computer games development, computing software development, games & digital media, Postgrad; mathematics, cybersecurity and digital forensics, information technology management, strategic information technology management, information technology, computer science, information technology, mobile and wireless systems engineering, web and mobile application development; BSc(Hons), MSc, PGCert

School of Pharmacy

pharmaceutical science, pharmacology, pharmacy, pharmaceutical science (drug discovery & design/science), independent prescribing, pharmaceutical analysis/pharmaceutical manufacture/pharmaceutical quality assurance/pharmaceutical sciences); BSc(Hons), MPharm, MSc

Faculty of Social Sciences; www.wlv.ac.uk/about-us/our-schools-and-institutions

The Wolverhampton Business School

accounting & finance, business administration, international/business management, business & finance/HRM/marketing management/accounting/banking & finance/hospitality management, coaching & mentoring, employability & enterprise, event & venue management, HRM, HRD & organisational change, innovation & entrepreneurship, leadership, management, marketing & enterprise management/HRM, marketing management, healthcare leadership, medical education, leadership, sport management, tourism management economics and politics/social policy/sociology/business, marketing and events management business management, event and venue management, international hospitality management, tourism management, accounting and finance, HRM, international business management, marketing management, business and accounting/finance/HRM, marketing management, business, Postgrad; coaching and mentoring, finance and accounting, healthcare leadership, HRD and organisational change, HRM, innovation and entrepreneurship, international banking and finance, international business management, management, marketing, event and venue management, international hospitality management/managing PR for events and venues

Postgrad Certs, Dips; management studies, healthcare leadership, HRD and organisational change, HRM, leadership, marketing, medical education, event and venue management, international hospitality management; MBA, BA(Hons), BSc(Hons), FdA, MA, PGCert/Dip, MSc

Wolverhampton Law School; law, accounting and law, business and law

law and philosophy, law, social science and communication studies, social policy and law, Postgrad; international corporate and financial law, law, professional practice, common professional examination, legal practice; BA(Hons), LlB(Hons), PGDip/Cert, LPC, LlM

School of Sociology, History & Political Studies

history, politics, war studies, sociology, social policy and criminology, uniformed services, interpreting and deaf studies; Postgrad; conflict studies, military history, history of the first world war; BA(Hons) MA, FD, BSc(Hons)

UNIVERSITY COLLEGE WORCESTER
www.worc.ac.uk

Institute of Education; www.worc.ac.uk/departments/institute-of-education

early childhood/years, education (early years), education studies, educaton & training, primary initial teacher education, PGCE primary school direct training and school direct salaried; secondary assessment/education and training diploma in teaching English (literacy and ESOL), subject knowledge enhancement, education studies, learning support, teaching: school direct secondary primary initial teacher education PGCE secondary early childhood professional practice, early years teacher teaching, improving practice in education, enhancing learning & teaching strategies, improving practice in education, early childhood, teaching primary modern foreign languages PGCE primary subject knowledge enhancement, education timetable, educational management and leadership, special and inclusive education, higher education, mentoring and coaching for leadership in education; QTS, BA, CertHE, FdA, MA, MSc, PGCE, PGCert, PGDip

Institute of Health & Society; www.worc.ac.uk/departments/institute-of health-and-society

advancing practice, physiotherapy, occupational therapy, child & adolescent mental health, psychology, forensic psychology, counselling psychology business/occupational psychology, counselling, applied psychology, applied psychology, nursing, midwifery, paramedic science, physician associate, public health, professional development, professional development for health sciences; BSc(Hons), BANurs, DipHE, FdA, FdSc, GradDip, MA, MSc, PGCert, PGDip/Cert, DHSc

Institute of Humanities & Creative Arts; www.worc.ac.uk/departments/institute-of-humanities-and-creative-arts

animation, digital film production, creative & professional writing, computing, creative digital media, digital film production, fine art practice, game art design, graphic design/ & multimedia, illustration and screenwriting, journalism/ and media & cultural studies. fine art, history, archaeology & heritage studies, creative & professional writing, English literary studies, geography, politics: people & power and sociology, English language studies, English literary studies, screenwriting, sociology, education studies/ history/human geography/media & cultural studies/politics: people and power and sociology, psychology and sociology, sociology and sports studies; BA, MA, MSc, FdA

Institute of Science & the Environment; www.worc.ac.uk/departments/institute-of-science-and-the-environment

animal biology, archaeology and heritage studies, biology, arboriculture, archaeology & heritage studies, biochemistry, biology, ecology, environmental science, forensic and applied biology, geography, horticulture, human biology, human geography, human nutrition, mathematics, physical geography, plant science; Postgrad; archaeological landscapes, sustainable development advocacy, research in biology/river science/ ecology and environmental management, evaluation for a sustainable future; BSc, FdSc, MSc, PGCert/Dip

Institute of Sport & Exercise Science; www.worc.ac.uk/departments/652.htm

cricket coaching & management, sports coaching science with disability sport, European basketball coaching science, applied sport science, cricket coaching & management, dance and community practice, football business management and coaching, outdoor adventure leadership & management, physical education (PE), PE and dance/ outdoor education, sport business management, sports coaching science/ with disability sport, sport development & coaching, sports studies, sports therapy, research in socio-cultural studies of sport and exercise, sports coaching, sports management; BSc, MSc, MPhil, PhD, MRes

Worcester Business School; www.worc.ac.uk/departments/655.html

accounting, business, computing, computer games design & development; Postgrad; HRM, management, finance, leadership & management/(heritage), international management, marketing, MBA; business administration; executive leadership & management, management, international business management, marketing, advertising & PR, many joint degrees with combinations of the above subjects; BA(Hons), BSc(Hons), DBA, GradCert, MBA, MSc, MA, PGCert/Dip, MRes

UNIVERSITY OF YORK
www.york.ac.uk

Dept of Archaeology; www.york.ac.uk/ depts/arch

archaeology, archaeology and heritage, historical archaeology, bioarchaeology;Postgrad; archaeological information systems, bioarchaeology, digital heritage, early prehistory, human anatomy and evolution, zooarchaeology, the archaeology of buildings, conservation studies, cultural heritage management, field archaeology, historical archaeology, medieval archaeology, landscape archaeology, mesolithic studies; BA, BSc, MA, MPhil, MSc, PhD

Dept of Biology; www.york.ac.uk/depts/ biol

biology, biochemistry, biomedical sciences, bioscience technology, biotechnology & microbiology, computational biology & bioinformatics, ecology & environmental management, post-genomic biology, genetics, molecular cell biology; BSc, MPhil, MRes, MSc, PhD, MBiol

Dept of Chemistry; www.york.ac.uk/depts/chemistry

chemistry, chemistry/management & industry/resources & the environment, green chemistry & sustainable industrial technology; BSc, MChem, MPhil, MSc, PhD

Dept of Computer Science; www.cs.york.ac.uk/depts

adv computer science, computer science/with AI/embedded systems, engineering/philosophy/mathematics, automaton, robotics engineering, computing, cyber security, human-centred interactive technologies, information technology, safety critical systems, social media & interactive technology, software engineering; BEng, BSc, MEng, MMath, MPhil, MSc, PGCert, PGDip

Dept of Economics & Related Studies; www.york.ac.uk/depts/econ

economics, economics and finance/econometrics, economics, econometrics and finance, economics and mathematics/history, mathematics and finance, economics and philosophy/politics, philosophy, politics and economics; Postgrad; development economics and emerging markets, econometrics and economics, economics and public policy, economics, economics and finance, finance, finance and econometrics, financial engineering, health economics, project analysis, finance and investment; BA, BSc, MSc, PGCert, PGDip, PhD

Dept of Education; www.york.ac.uk/depts/educ

applied linguistics for English/language teaching, English in education, psychology in education, educational studies, language & literature in education, teaching English (young learners/TESOL), PGCE (English, history, maths, economics, geography, foreign languages, sciences, teaching & learning, teacher training), global & international citizenship, science education & learning, sociology & education; BA, MA, MPhil, PhD

Dept of Electronics; www.york.ac.uk/depts/elec

avionics, audio & music technology, autonomous robotic engineering, communications engineering, digital systems engineering/signal processing, digital media systems, electronic engineering, electronics & communication, engineering management, internet & wireless technology, music technology/systems, electrical engineering with nanotechnology/business management; BEng, MEng, MSc, MPhil, PhD

Dept of English & Related Literature; www.york.ac.uk/depts/engl

English, English & history/history of art/linguistics/philosophy/politics, culture & thought after 1945, English literary studies, film & literature, medieval literatures & languages, literature of the Romantic period, 1775–1832, medical history and humanities, modern and contemporary literature and culture, poetry and poetics, Renaissance literature, 1500–1700, Victorian literature and culture; BA, MA, MPhil, PhD

Dept of Environment; www.york.ac.uk/depts/eeem

environmental economics & environmental management, environmental geography/science, environmental economics & ecology, environmental science & management, environment, corporate social responsibility & environmental management, human geography & environment, marine environmental management BSc, MPhil, MSc, MEnv, PGDip, PhD

Centre for Health Economics; www.york.ac.uk/he

economic evaluation of health technologies, health policy, mental health policy, health econometrics & data; MSc, PhD

Dept of Health Sciences; www.york.ac.uk/depts/healthsciences

applied health research, health sciences, health & social care, /practice/associate practitioner public health, midwifery practice, nursing studies (adult/child/learning disability/mental health), organisational development, public health; BA, BSc, DipHE, MPhil, MSc, PGCert, PGDip, PhD, MPH, FD, MNursing, Dip

Dept of History; www.york.ac.uk/depts/hist

history, history with politics/history of art/philosophy/economics/French/English, early modern history, heritage, history and the parish church, medieval history, modern history, public history, contemporary history and international politics, culture and thought after 1945, 18th century studies, medical history and humanities, medieval studies,

Renaissance and early modern studies, women's studies; BA, GradCert, MA, MPhil, PhD, PGDip;

Dept of History of Art; www.york.ac.uk/depts/histart

history of art, stained glass conservation & heritage management, English history/history of Art, history of art (architectural history and theory/British art/medieval art and medievalisms/sculpture studies; BA, MA, MPhil, PhD

Hull York Medical School; www.hyms.ac.uk

undergraduate qualifying medical courses, biomedical sciences, human sciences, medical sciences, public health, health professional education; MBBS, MSc, PGCert, MD, PhD, MPhil, PGCME, BSc

Centre for Applied Human Rights; www.york.ac.uk/cahr

applied/defending human rights, international human rights law & practice; LlM, MA, PhD, PGCert

Dept of Language & Linguistic Science; www.york.ac.uk/depts/lang

linguistics, English language & linguistics, combinations of French/German/Spanish/English, linguistics & French/German/Spanish/mathematics/philosophy, philosophy & French/German, comparative syntax and semantics, linguistics, phonetics and phonology, phonological development, psycholinguistics, sociolinguistics, linguistics by research, forensic speech science; BA, MA, MPhil, MSc, PhD

York Law School; www.york.ac.uk/law

law, international corporate & commercial law, international human rights & practice, theory & practice of clinical legal education, senior status, legal & political theory; LLB, LLM, MPhil, PhD

Dept of Mathematics; www.york.ac.uk/depts/maths

mathematics, mathematics with computer science/economics/physics/statistics/finance/philosophy, financial engineering, adv mathematical biology, statistics & computational finance, mathematical finance; BA, BSc, MMath, MPhil, MRes, MSc, PGCert, PGDip, PhD

Centre for Modern Studies; www.york.ac.uk/modern-studies

culture & thought after 1945; MA

Dept of Music; www.york.ac.uk/depts/music

music, numerous undergraduate modules, community music, music production, music & sound recording, music education; BA, MA, MPhil, PhD, PGDip/Cert

Dept of Philosophy; www.york.ac.uk/depts/phil

philosophy, philosophy with computer science/economics/physics/English/mathematics/history/sociology, PPE; BA, BSc, GradDip, MA, MPhil, PGCert, PGDip, PhD

Dept of Physics; www.york.ac.uk/depts/physics

physics, physics with astrophysics/mathematics/philosophy, theoretical physics, fusion energy; BA, BSc, MMath, MPhil, MPhys, MSc, PhD, GradDip

Dept of Politics; www.york.ac.uk/depts/poli

politics with international relations/English/history/economics/philosophy/politics, political research, conflict, governance & development, international political economy/relations, political philosophy, public administration & public policy/international development, PPE, political & legal theory, tolerance, postwar recovery studies, international humanitarian studies, political research; BA, MA, MSc, PGDip, PhD

Dept of Psychology; www.york.ac.uk/depts/psych

developmental/cognitive neuroscience, applied/forensic psychology, development disorders & clinical psychology, psychology; BSc, MPhil, MRes, MSc, PhD

Dept of Social Policy & Social Work; www.york.ac.uk/depts/spsw

applied social science (children & young people/crime & criminal justice), applied social science & social policy, comparative applied social & pubic policy, criminology, delivery & change/strategy for public services, global social justice/crime & justice international development, policy management & government, public administration, public policy & management, public management in the information age, social policy, social work, sociology & political science, comparative & international social policy; BA, MA, MPhil, MRes, PGCert, PhD, MPA

Dept of Sociology; www.york.ac.uk/depts/soci

sociology, sociology with criminology/ social psychology, sociology/education, philosophy/sociology, social and political sciences/ with philosophy; Postgrad; criminology/ and social research, culture, society and globalization, social media and social research, social media and management, social media and interactive technologies; BA, MA, MPhil, MSc, PhD

Dept of Theatre, Film & Television; www.york.ac.uk/depts/tft

contemporary cinema & TV, digital film & TV production, interactive media, interactive TV & society, post-production with visual effects/sound design, theatre, film & TV production, theatre writing, directing & performance; BA, MA, MPhil, MSc, PhD

York Management School; www.york.ac.uk/depts/management

business and management, management, business and management, management accounting, business and finance management, marketing, actuarial science, Postgrad; international business and strategic management, management accounting and financial management, HRM; BA, BSc, MA, MPhil, MRes, MSc, PhD

YORKSHIRE COAST COLLEGE
www.yorkshirecoastcollege.ac.uk

www.yorkshirecoastcollege.ac.uk/ highereducation/index.php

historical & performance costume for stage & screen, education (teaching in lifelong learning sector), children, young people and families, social care, early childhood studies, sport and recreation management, tourism management, events management; BA, FdA, FdEd, GradCert

Part 5

Qualifications Awarded by Professional and Trade Associations

THE FUNCTIONS OF PROFESSIONAL ASSOCIATIONS

Qualifications

Some associations qualify individuals to act in a certain professional capacity. They also try to safeguard high standards of professional conduct. Few associations have complete control over the profession with which they are concerned. Some professions are regulated by the law, and their associations act as the central registration authority. Entry to others is directly controlled by associations that alone award the requisite qualifications. If a profession is required to be registered by the law and is controlled by the representative council, a practitioner found guilty by his or her council of misconduct may be suspended from practice or completely debarred by the removal of his or her name from the register of qualified practitioners. In other professions the consequence of misdemeanour may not be so serious, because the profession does not exercise the same degree of control.

The professions registered by statute, and therefore subject to restrictions on entry and loss of either privileges or the right to practise on erasure, are listed in Table 5.1. Certain other professions are closed.

Table 5.1 Professions registered by statute

Profession	Statutory committee controlling professional conduct
Architects	Architects Registration Board
Dentists	General Dental Council
Doctors	General Medical Council
Professions supplementary to medicine: arts therapists, biomedical scientists, chiropodists/podiatrists, clinical scientists, dieticians, hearing aid dispensers, occupational therapists, operating department practitioners, orthoptists, paramedics, physiotherapists, practitioner psychologists, prosthetists/orthotists, radiographers, speech and language therapists and social workers	Health and Care Professions Council (HCPC)
Nurses and midwives	Nursing and Midwifery Council
Opticians and optometrists	General Optical Council
Osteopaths	General Osteopathic Council
Patent attorneys	Chartered Institute of Patent Attorneys
Pharmacists, pharmacy technicians	General Pharmaceutical Council
Teachers	The National College for Teaching and Leadership

Study

Some associations give their members an opportunity to keep abreast of a particular discipline or to undertake further study in it. Such associations are especially numerous in medicine, science and applied science. Many qualifying associations also provide an information and study service for their members. Some of the more famous learned societies confer added status upon distinguished practitioners by electing them to membership or honorary membership.

Protection of Members' Interests

Some associations exist mainly to look after the interests of individual practitioners and the group. A small number are directly concerned with negotiations over salary and working conditions.

MEMBERSHIP OF PROFESSIONAL ASSOCIATIONS

Qualifying associations

The principal function of qualifying associations is to examine and qualify people who wish to become practitioners in the field with which they are concerned. As already indicated, some regulate professional conduct and many offer opportunities for further study. Membership is divided into grades, usually classified as corporate and non-corporate. Non-corporate members are those not yet admitted to full membership, mainly students; they are divided from corporate membership by barriers of age and levels of responsibility and experience. The principal requirement for admission to membership is the knowledge and ability to pass the association's exams; candidates may be exempted from the association's exams if they have acceptable alternative qualifications.

Non-corporate or affiliated members

Non-corporate members are those who are as yet unqualified or only partly qualified. They are accorded limited rights and privileges, but may not vote at meetings of the corporate body. Most associations have a student membership grade. Students are those who are preparing for the exams that qualify them for admission to corporate membership. Some associations have licentiate and graduate membership grades, which are senior to the student grade. Graduates are those who have passed the qualifying exams but lack other requirements, such as age and experience, for admission to corporate membership.

Corporate or full members

Corporate members are the fully qualified constituent members of incorporated associations. They are accorded full rights and privileges and may vote at meetings of the corporate body. Corporate membership is often divided into two grades: a senior grade of members or fellows and a general grade of associate members or associates.

Honorary members

Some associations have a special class of honorary members or fellows for distinguished members or individuals who have made an outstanding contribution to the profession in question.

Examinations and requirements

Professionals normally become corporate members by exam or exemption, with or without additional requirements. Many final professional exams are of degree standard, and a number of professional qualifications are accepted by employers as evidence of competence at operational level. Ongoing professional development is encouraged by most associations to ensure members' skills and knowledge are up to date and relevant.

The transition from the general grade of membership to the senior can be automatic in some associations (for instance, on reaching a prescribed age), but in others the higher grade is reached only after the submission of evidence of research or progress in the profession.

Qualifying exams are usually conducted in two or more stages. The first stage leads to an Intermediate or Part I qualification, the second leads to a Final or Part II or Part III qualification, which is about the standard of a degree.

Gaining professional qualifications

Prospective students can study by any of the following means:

- correspondence courses (distance learning and/or online support);

- personal attendance at the schools maintained by some associations (eg the Architectural Association School of Architecture);

- further and higher education institutions.

ACCOUNTANCY
Membership of Professional Institutions and Associations

ASSOCIATION OF ACCOUNTING TECHNICIANS

140 Aldersgate Street
London EC1A 4HY
Tel: +44 (0)20 3735 2434
Fax: 020 7397 3009
E-mail: aat@aat.org.uk
Website: www.aat.org.uk

AAT is the UK's leading qualification and membership body for accounting professionals. We have over 125,000 members including students, people working in accountancy and self-employed business owners, in more than 90 countries worldwide. Established in 1980 to ensure consistent training and regulation for accounting staff, our qualifications provide a progression route to CIMA, CIPFA, ICAS, ICAEW and ACCA.

MEMBERSHIP
Student Member
Affiliate Member
Full Member (MAAT)
Fellow Member (FMAAT)

QUALIFICATION/EXAMINATIONS
AAT Accounting Qualifications
Entry Award in Accounting (AAT Access)
Entry Certificate in Accounting
Introductory Certificate in Accounting
Introductory Diploma in Accounting and Business

(16–19-year-olds)
Intermediate Diploma in Accounting
Advanced Diploma in Accounting
Advanced Certificate in Taxation and Ethics
AAT Bookkeeping
Introductory Award in Bookkeeping
Intermediate Certificate in Bookkeeping
Advanced Certificate in Bookkeeping and Ethics
AAT Computerised Accounting
Introductory Award in Computerised Accounting
Intermediate Award in Computerised Accounting
Advanced Certificate in Computerised Accounting and Ethics
AAT Small Business Courses
Introductory Award in Accounting Skills to Run Your Business
AAT Essentials (One day courses)

DESIGNATORY LETTERS
MAAT and FMAAT

ASSOCIATION OF CHARITY INDEPENDENT EXAMINERS

The Gatehouse
White Cross
South Road
Lancaster
Lancashire LA1 4XQ
Tel: 01524 34892
Fax: 01524 34892
E-mail: info@acie.org.uk
Website: www.acie.org.uk

ACIE provides support, training, conferences, resources and qualifications for independent examiners of charity accounts throughout the UK (*subscriptions apply*). Further information at the website: www.acie.org.uk

Registered charity in E&W 1139609 & SC039066. Registered company limited by guarantee 7461134; registered in England at 4–6 Grimshaw St, Burnley BB11 2AZ.

MEMBERSHIP
Affiliate
Full Member (with category of Associate or Fellow)

QUALIFICATION/EXAMINATIONS
Associate (limited re: size and type of charity by one of five authorisation bands – see website): ACIE
Fellow (all UK charities eligible for IE): FCIE

DESIGNATORY LETTERS
ACIE, FCIE

CHARTERED INSTITUTE OF INTERNAL AUDITORS

13 Abbeville Mews
88 Clapham Park Road
London SW4 7BX
Tel: 020 7498 0101
Fax: 020 7978 2492
E-mail: membership@iia.org.uk
Website: www.iia.org.uk

The Chartered Institute of Internal Auditors (IIA) is the only professional body in the UK and Ireland focused exclusively on internal auditing and we are passionate about supporting, promoting and training the professionals who work in it. Every year we help internal auditors at every stage of their career with training, qualifications and technical resources.

MEMBERSHIP
Student Member
Affiliate Member
Voting Member (PIIA, CMIIA)

Head of Internal Audit Service Member
Fellow (FIIA, CFIIA)

QUALIFICATION/EXAMINATIONS
IIA Certificate in Internal Audit and Business Risk (IA Cert)
IIA Diploma (PIIA)
IIA Advanced Diploma (CMIIA)
IT Auditing Certificate

DESIGNATORY LETTERS
IA Cert, PIIA, CMIIA, FIIA, CFIIA

CIMA – THE CHARTERED INSTITUTE OF MANAGEMENT ACCOUNTANTS

26 Chapter Street
London SW1P 4NP
Tel: 020 8849 2251
E-mail: cima.contact@cimaglobal.com
Website: www.cimaglobal.com

CIMA is the employers' choice when recruiting financially qualified business leaders.

The Chartered Institute of Management Accountants, founded in 1919, is the world's leading and largest professional body of Management Accountants, with 183,000 members and students operating at the heart of business in 168 countries. CIMA works closely with employers and sponsors leading-edge research, constantly updating its qualification, professional experience requirements and continuing professional development to ensure it remains the most relevant international accountancy qualification for business.

MEMBERSHIP
Member
Associate (ACMA)
Fellow (FCMA)

QUALIFICATION/EXAMINATIONS
Certificate in Business Accounting
CIMA Professional
Certificate in Islamic Finance
Diploma in Islamic Finance

DESIGNATORY LETTERS
ACMA, FCMA

ICAEW (THE INSTITUTE OF CHARTERED ACCOUNTANTS IN ENGLAND AND WALES)

Metropolitan House
321 Avebury Boulevard
Milton Keynes MK9 2FZ
Tel: 01908 248 250
E-mail: careers@icaew.com
Website: icaew.com/careers

ICAEW is a world leading professional membership organisation that promotes, develops and supports over 140,000 chartered accountants worldwide. We provide qualifications and professional development, share our knowledge, insight and technical expertise, and protect the quality and integrity of the accountancy and finance profession.

MEMBERSHIP
ACA (Associate of the Institute of Chartered Accountants in England and Wales) FCA (Fellow Chartered Accountant)

QUALIFICATION/EXAMINATIONS
The ICAEW chartered accountancy qualification, the ACA, is one of the most advanced learning and professional development programmes available. It has integrated components which give an in-depth understanding across accountancy, finance and business. Combined they help build the technical knowledge, professional skills and practical experience needed to become an ICAEW Chartered Accountant. There is more than one way to start the ACA, find out more at icaew.com/careers

The ICAEW Certificate in Finance, Accounting and Business (ICAEW CFAB) provides fundamental knowledge and skills in finance, accounting and business. ICAEW CFAB consists of the same six exam modules as the first level of the ACA qualification. It can be studied as a stand-alone qualification or as an entry route to the ACA. There are no entry requirements and it is achievable in as little as 12 months through online learning, self-study or classroom tuition. Find out more at icaew.com/cfab

DESIGNATORY LETTERS
ACA, FCA

ICAS (INSTITUTE OF CHARTERED ACCOUNTANTS OF SCOTLAND)

CA House
21 Haymarket Yards
Edinburgh EH12 5BH
Tel: 0131 347 0100
E-mail: caeducation@icas.org.uk
Website: icas.org.uk

ICAS is a professional body for around 19,000 world class business professionals who work in the UK and in more than 100 countries around the world. Our members have all achieved the internationally recognised and respected CA qualification. We are an educator, examiner, regulator, and thought leader. ICAS is the first professional body for accountants and was created by Royal Charter in 1854.

MEMBERSHIP

To qualify as a CA, trainees must enter and complete a training contract with an ICAS authorised employer for a prescribed period, normally three years. They must achieve relevant work experience requirements and key competencies, study for and pass three stages of examinations and complete a course and assignment in Business Ethics. For further information please see the ICAS website.

QUALIFICATION/EXAMINATIONS

The CA qualification syllabus contains ten subjects leading to three stages of exams.

Test of Competence (TC) contains five subjects: Financial Accounting, Principles of Auditing and Reporting, Finance, Business Management, Business Law.

Test of Professional Skills (TPS): Taxation, Advanced Finance, Financial Reporting, Assurance and Business Systems.

Test of Professional Expertise (TPE) contains a multidisciplinary case study designed to apply theoretical knowledge and practical skills to a real-life situation.

In addition to including ethics within the three levels, Business Ethics forms a standalone subject and assessment.

DESIGNATORY LETTERS
CA

INSTITUTE OF FINANCIAL ACCOUNTANTS

Burford House
44 London Road
Sevenoaks
Kent TN13 1AS
Tel: 01732 458080
Fax: 01732 455848
E-mail: mail@ifa.org.uk
Website: www.ifa.org.uk

The IFA was established in 1916 and is the oldest body of non-Chartered Accountants in the world. We represent members and students in more than 80 countries, providing qualifications for those wishing to work in financial management and accountancy, and CPD for qualified Financial Accountants, particularly in SMEs.

MEMBERSHIP

Financial Accounting Executive
Associate (AFA)

Fellow (FFA)

QUALIFICATION/EXAMINATIONS

IFE Level 4 Award for SME Tax Advisers (QCF)
IFA Level 4 Award for SME Financial Accounting (International Standards) (QCF)
IFA Level 4 Diploma for SME Financial Accountants (QCF)
IFA Level 5 Diploma for SME Financial Managers (QCF)

IFA Level 5 Diploma for SME Finance and Business Managers (QCF)

The Diploma in IFRS for Accounting Professionals and the Diploma in IFRS for Business

DESIGNATORY LETTERS
QCF

INTERNATIONAL ASSOCIATION OF BOOK-KEEPERS

Suite 5
20 Churchill Square
Kings Hill
West Malling
Kent ME19 4YU
Tel: 0844 3303527
Fax: 0844 3303514
E-mail: mail@iab.org.uk
Website: www.iab.org.uk

The IAB specializes in providing high-quality, accredited and regulated financial and business qualifications. We continue to be the leading international membership body for professional book-keepers. Established in 1973, we now have many thousands of students and members worldwide.

MEMBERSHIP
Associate (AIAB)
Member (MIAB)
Fellow (FIAB)

QUALIFICATION/EXAMINATIONS
Award in Bookkeeping (Level 1)
Award in Manual Bookkeeping (Level 1)
Award in Computerized Bookkeeping (Level 1)
Certificate in Bookkeeping (Level 2)
Award in Manual Bookkeeping (Level 2)
Award in Computerized Bookkeeping (Level 2)
Certificate in Bookkeeping (Level 1)
Certificate in Bookkeeping (Level 3)
Diploma in Bookkeeping (Level 3)
Certificate in Manual Bookkeeping (Level 3)
Award in Computerized Bookkeeping (Level 3)
Diploma in Accounting to International Standards (Level 4)
Certificate in Payroll (Level 1)
Certificate in Payroll (Level 2)
Award in Computerized Payroll (Level 2)
Diploma in Payroll (Level 2)
Diploma in Payroll (Level 3)
Award in Computerized Payroll (Level 1)
Award in Computerized Payroll for Business (Level 1)
Certificate in Computerized Payroll for Business (Level 2)
Certificate in Computerized Payroll for Business (Level 3)
Award in Computerized Payroll (Level 3)
Award in Computerized Accounting for Business (Level 1)
Certificate in Computerized Accounting for Business (Level 2)
Certificate in Computerized Accounting for Business (Level 3)
Diploma in Accounting and Advanced Bookkeeping (Level 3)
Diploma in Small Business Financial Management (Level 3)
Diploma in Cost and Management Accounting (Level 3)
Diploma in Financial Information for Managers (Level 4)
Diploma in Personal and Business Tax (Level 4)

DESIGNATORY LETTERS
NCF, QCF

THE ASSOCIATION OF CHARTERED CERTIFIED ACCOUNTANTS

London WC2A 3EE
Tel: 020 7059 5000
Fax: 020 7059 5050
E-mail: info@accaglobal.com
Website: www.accaglobal.com

ACCA is the largest and fastest-growing international accountancy body, with over 424,000 students and 147,000 members in 170 countries. The ACCA Qualification is an established route to professional status, and we offer continued support to our members throughout their careers.

MEMBERSHIP
Associate (ACCA)
Fellow (FCCA)

QUALIFICATION/EXAMINATIONS
Foundations in Accountancy

Certificate in International Finance Reporting
Certificate in International Finance Reporting Standard for SMEs
Diploma in International Finance Reporting
The ACCA Qualification
MBA (awarded by Oxford Brookes University; accredited by the Association of MBAs)

DESIGNATORY LETTERS
ACCA, FCCA

THE ASSOCIATION OF CORPORATE TREASURERS

51 Moorgate
London EC2R 6BH
Tel: 020 7847 2540
Fax: 020 7374 2598
E-mail: enquiries@treasurers.org
Website: www.treasurers.org

The ACT is the professional chartered body for treasury and sets the benchmark for international treasury excellence. The ACT leads the profession through its globally recognised treasury qualifications by defining standards and championing continuing professional development.

MEMBERSHIP
eAffiliate Member
Student Member
Affiliate Member
Associate Member
Member

Fellow
Corporate Member

QUALIFICATION/EXAMINATIONS
Certificate in Treasury Fundamentals
Certificate in Treasury
Certificate in International Cash Management
Diploma in Treasury Management
MCT Advanced Diploma

DESIGNATORY LETTERS
CertTF, CertT, CertICM, AMCT, MCT

THE ASSOCIATION OF INTERNATIONAL ACCOUNTANTS

Staithes 3
The Watermark
Metro Riverside
Newcastle upon Tyne
Tyne & Wear NE11 9SN
Tel: 0191 493 0277
Fax: 0191 493 0278
E-mail: aia@aiaworldwide.com
Website: www.aiaworldwide.com

AIA was founded in 1928 as a global accountancy body and has recognition as a Recognised Qualifying Body for statutory auditors, supervisory status for its members in the Money Laundering Regulations 2007 and an Awarding Body in the UK. AIA is a Prescribed Body in the ROI and is recognised in over 30 countries worldwide.

MEMBERSHIP
Student Member
Graduate Member
Academic Member
Associate (AAIA)
Fellow (FAIA)
Honorary Member
Retired Member

QUALIFICATION/EXAMINATIONS
Professional Accountancy Qualification
Recognised Professional Qualification (Statutory Audit)
QCF Level 5 Certificate in Accountancy
QCF Level 6 Diploma in Accountancy
QCF Level 7 Diploma in Professional Accountancy
Auditing Diploma
IFRS Diploma
Management Accounting & Costing Diploma
IFRS for SMEs Certificate

DESIGNATORY LETTERS
AAIA, FAIA

THE CHARTERED INSTITUTE OF PUBLIC FINANCE AND ACCOUNTANCY (CIPFA)

77 Mansell Street
London E1 8AN
Tel: 020 7543 5600
Fax: 020 7543 5700
E-mail: students@cipfa.org.uk
Website: www.cipfa.org.uk

The Chartered Institute of Public Finance and Accountancy (CIPFA) is *the* professional body for people in public finance. Our 14,000 members work throughout the public services and as the only UK professional accountancy body to specialise in public services, CIPFA's qualifications are the foundation for a career in public finance.

MEMBERSHIP
Affiliate
Associate
Full Member

QUALIFICATION/EXAMINATIONS
CIPFA Professional Qualification
Professional Qualification in Public & Corporate Accounting
Integrated Qualification for Auditors
Certificate in International Public Sector Financial Reporting
Certificate in International Public Sector Accounting Standards
Certificate in Financial Reporting for Academies

DESIGNATORY LETTERS
CPFA

THE INSTITUTE OF CERTIFIED BOOKKEEPERS

London Underwriting Centre
3 Minster Court
Mincing Lane
City of London EC3R 7DD
Tel: 0845 060 2345
Fax: 01635 298960
E-mail: info@bookkeepers.org.uk
Website: www.bookkeepers.org.uk

The ICB is the largest bookkeeping institute in the world. Our aims are to promote bookkeeping as a profession, to improve training in the principles of bookkeeping, and to establish qualifications and the award of grades of membership that recognize academic attainment, work experience and professional competence, and thereby enable qualified bookkeepers to gain recognition as an integral part of the financial world.

MEMBERSHIP
Registered Student
Affiliate
Associate Member (AICB)
Member (MICB)
Fellow (FICB)

QUALIFICATION/EXAMINATIONS
Level 1: Certificate in Basic Bookkeeping

Level 2: (Intermediate): Certificate in Computerized Bookkeeping
Level 2: (Intermediate): Certificate in Manual Bookkeeping
Level 3: (Advanced): Diploma in Computerized Bookkeeping
Level 3: (Advanced): Diploma in Manual Bookkeeping
Level 3: (Advanced): Diploma in Payroll Management
Level 3: (Advanced): Diploma in Self-Assessment Tax Returns
Level 4: (Advanced): Diploma in Financial Management (Drafting Financial Statements, Management Accounting, Personal Taxation and Business Taxation)

DESIGNATORY LETTERS
AICB, MICB, FICB

ACOUSTICS
Membership of Professional Institutions and Associations

INSTITUTE OF ACOUSTICS

St Peter's House
45–49 Victoria Street
St Albans
Hertfordshire AL1 3WZ
Tel: 01727 848195
Fax: 01727 850553
E-mail: ioa@ioa.org.uk
Website: www.ioa.org.uk

The IOA is the UK's professional body for those working in acoustics, noise and vibration, and has more than 3,000 members in research, educational, environmental, government and industrial organizations. It offers professionally recognized courses

and is licensed by the Engineering Research Council to offer registration at Chartered and Incorporated Engineer levels.

MEMBERSHIP
Student

Affiliate
Technician Member (TechIOA)
Associate Member (AMIOA)
Member (MIOA)
Fellow (FIOA)
Honorary Fellow (HonFIOA)
Incorporated Engineer (IEng)
Chartered Engineer (CEng)
Sponsor

QUALIFICATION/EXAMINATIONS
Certificate of Competence in Environmental Noise
Measurement

Certificate of Competence in Workplace Noise Risk
Assessment
Certificate Course in the Management of Occupational Exposure to Hand–Arm Vibration
Certificate Course in Building Acoustics
Measurements
Diploma in Acoustics and Noise Control

DESIGNATORY LETTERS
TechIOA, AMIOA, MIOA, FIOA, HonFIOA, IEng,
CEng

ADVERTISING AND PUBLIC RELATIONS
Membership of Professional Institutions and Associations

CHARTERED INSTITUTE OF PUBLIC RELATIONS

52–53 Russell Square
London WC1B 4HP
Tel: 020 7631 6900
Fax: 020 7631 6944
E-mail: info@cipr.co.uk
Website: www.cipr.co.uk

The CIPR, founded in 1948, is the professional body for PR practitioners and has more than 9,000 members, to whom it offers information, advice, support and training. Our aim is to raise standards within the profession through the promotion of best practice and our members abide by our strict code of professional conduct.

MEMBERSHIP
Student
Affiliate
Associate (ACIPR)

Member (MCIPR)
Fellow (FCIPR)
Global Affiliate

QUALIFICATION/EXAMINATIONS
Foundation Award in Public Relations
Advanced Certificate
Diploma

DESIGNATORY LETTERS
ACIPR, MCIPR, FCIPR

INSTITUTE OF PRACTITIONERS IN ADVERTISING

44 Belgrave Square
London SW1X 8QS
Tel: 020 7235 7020
Fax: 020 7245 9904
E-mail: web@ipa.co.uk
Website: www.ipa.co.uk

The IPA is the UK's leading professional body for advertising, media and marketing communications agencies. We promote the services of our member agencies, which have access to a range of services and benefits, including a Legal Department, Information Centre and training courses provided by our Professional Development Department.

MEMBERSHIP
Personal Member (MIPA)
Fellow/Honorary Fellow (FIPA)
Member Agency

QUALIFICATION/EXAMINATIONS
Foundation Certificate

Advanced Certificate
LegRgs Certificate
Commercial Certificate
Search Certificate
Excellence Diploma
Eff Test

DESIGNATORY LETTERS
MIPA, FIPA

INSTITUTE OF PROMOTIONAL MARKETING

70 Margaret Street
London W1W 8SS
Tel: 020 7291 7730
E-mail: contact@theipm.org.uk
Website: www.theipm.org.uk

The Institute of Promotional Marketing represents promoters, agencies and service partners engaged in promotional marketing in the UK by protecting, promoting and progressing effective sales promotion across all media channels through its education, legal advice, awards, and other products and services.

MEMBERSHIP
Corporate Member

QUALIFICATION/EXAMINATIONS
IPM Certificate
IPM Incentive & Motivation Diploma
IPM Diploma
Legal Code Certification (LCC)

DESIGNATORY LETTERS
MISP

LONDON SCHOOL OF PUBLIC RELATIONS

118A Kensington Church Street
London W8 4BH
Tel: 020 7221 3399
Fax: 020 7243 1730
E-mail: info@lspr-education.com
Website: www.lspr-education.com

Established in 1992, the London School of Public Relations (LSPR) provides up-to-date training courses for those wishing to enter public relations as a career or for those already in PR or an information/communications job who require up-to-date practical training awarded with a professional development qualification.

LSPR provides the following courses:
DIPLOMA:
- PR & Reputation Management
  ADVANCED CERTIFICATES:
- Branding and Brand Management

- Corporate Social Responsibility
- Issues and Crisis Management
- Leadership and Personal Branding
  CERTIFICATES:
- Writing for Business
- Feature Writing
- Social Media

Our Diploma, *PR & Reputation Management*, is awarded to delegates upon successful completion of a 10-day full-time intensive course or an 8-week part-time evening course (twice weekly, 6.30pm–8.30pm).

The Advanced Certificate courses run for 5 days, Monday–Friday. The Certificated courses are offered as day and evening courses.

LSPR also runs training programmes in Leadership, CSR, Reputation Management, Stakeholder Analysis, Crisis and Issues Management, Branding, Corporate Identity, Media Relations and Feature and Press Release Writing. Courses are also offered in-house for clients.

LSPR training programmes are approved and recognised by the Institute of Training and Occupational Learning (ITOL). LSPR operates globally with franchises, in association with international PR bodies and agencies.

MEMBERSHIP
Institute of Training and Occupational Learning

QUALIFICATION/EXAMINATIONS
* Diploma: Examination, Assessment and a Final project
* Advanced Certificates: Critical Thinking Exercises
* Certificates: Projects and exercises

AGRICULTURE AND HORTICULTURE
Membership of Professional Institutions and Associations

INSTITUTE OF HORTICULTURE

Capel Manor College
Bullsmoor Lane
Enfield
Middlesex EN1 4RQ
Tel: 01992 707025
E-mail: ioh@horticulture.org.uk
Website: www.horticulture.org.uk

The IoH represents all those professionally engaged in horticulture in the UK and the Republic of Ireland. Our main aim is to promote the profession and its importance in food and ornamental plant production, improving the environment, providing employment and as the leisure pursuit of gardening. We are also developing CPD and mentoring schemes for our members and liaise with government and other bodies on matters of interest or concern.

MEMBERSHIP
Student Member, Affiliate, e-Affiliate, Associate (AI Hort), Member (MI Hort), Fellow (FI Hort), Group Membership

DESIGNATORY LETTERS
AI Hort, MI Hort, FI Hort

ROYAL HORTICULTURAL SOCIETY

RHS Garden Wisley
Woking
Surrey GU23 6QB
Tel: 01483 226500
E-mail: qualifications@rhs.org.uk
Website: www.rhs.org.uk

The Royal Horticultural Society is a recognized awarding body offering a range of qualifications in horticultural knowledge and skills. Part-time courses leading to RHS qualifications are offered by approved centres throughout the UK and Ireland, and by distance-learning providers. The RHS School of Horticulture provides courses in practical horticultural skills.

RHS Level 1 Introductory Award in Practical Horticulture

RHS Level 1 Award in Practical Horticulture

RHS Level 2 Certificate in the Principles of Plant Growth, Propagation and Development

RHS Level 2 Certificate in the Principles of Garden Planning, Establishment and Maintenance

RHS Level 2 Certificate in the Principles of Horticulture

RHS Level 2 Certificate in Practical Horticulture

RHS Level 2 Diploma in the Principles and Practices of Horticulture

RHS Level 3 Certificate in the Principles of Plant Growth, Health and Applied Propagation

RHS Level 3 Certificate in the Principles of Garden Planning, Construction and Planting

RHS Level 3 Certificate in Practical Horticulture

RHS Level 3 Diploma in the Principles and Practices of Horticulture

Master of Horticulture (RHS)

Wisley Diploma in Practical Horticulture

THE ROYAL BOTANIC GARDEN EDINBURGH

20A Inverleith Row
Edinburgh EH3 5LR
Tel: 0131 552 7171
Fax: 01312 482901
E-mail: education@rbge.org.uk
Website: www.rbge.org.uk

The RBGE was founded in the 17th century as a physic garden, growing medicinal plants. Now it extends over four gardens boasting a rich living collection of plants, and is a world-renowned centre for plant science and education.

Certificate in Botanic Illustration

Certificate in Herbology

Certificate in the Principles of Horticulture (RHS Level 2)

Certificate in Practical Field Botany

Certificate in Practical Horticulture

Diploma in Botanical Illustration

Diploma in Garden Design

Diploma in Garden History

Diploma in Herbology

HND/BSc in Horticulture with Plantsmanship

MSc in The Biodiversity and Taxonomy of Plants

AMBULANCE SERVICE
Membership of Professional Institutions and Associations

AMBULANCE SERVICE INSTITUTE

Suite 183
Maddison House
226 High Street
Croydon CR9 1DF
E-mail: enquiries@asi-international.com
Website: www.asi-international.com

The ASI is a non-union, non-political, independent institute whose membership is dedicated to raising the standards and quality of ambulance provision and thereby improving the professionalism and quality of care available to patients. Membership is open to non-NHS personnel as well as to employees of NHS Ambulance Services.

MEMBERSHIP
Student
Member (MASI)
Licentiate (LASI)
Associate (AASI)
Graduate (GASI)
Fellow (FASI)

QUALIFICATION/EXAMINATIONS
The Institute offers professional examinations and qualifications in the areas of Pre-Hospital Care, Control and Communications, and Management, for those who desire a career in the ambulance service.

DESIGNATORY LETTERS
MASI, LASI, AASI, GASI, FASI

ARBITRATION

Membership of Professional Institutions and Associations

THE CHARTERED INSTITUTE OF ARBITRATORS

12 Bloomsbury Square
London WC1A 2LP
Tel: 020 7421 7444
Fax: 020 7404 4023
E-mail: info@ciarb.org
Website: www.ciarb.org

The CIArb is a not-for-profit, UK-registered charity with 12,000 members worldwide that exists to promote and facilitate the settlement of private disputes by arbitration and alternative dispute resolution. We provide training for arbitrators, mediators and adjudicators and act as an international centre for practitioners, policy-makers, academics and those in business concerned with the cost-effective and early settlement of disputes.

MEMBERSHIP
Associate (ACIArb)

Member (MCIArb)
Fellow (FCIArb)

QUALIFICATION/EXAMINATIONS
Introductory Certificate
Advanced Certificate
Diploma

DESIGNATORY LETTERS
ACIArb, MCIArb, FCIArb

ARCHAEOLOGY
Membership of Professional Institutions and Associations

CHARTERED INSTITUTE FOR ARCHAEOLOGISTS

Miller Building
University of Reading
Reading
Berkshire RG6 6AB
Tel: 0118 378 6446
E-mail: admin@archaeologists.net
Website: www.archaeologists.net

CIfA is a professional organisation for all archae-ologists and others involved in protecting and understanding the historic environment, with more than 3,000 members. We advance the practice of archaeology and allied disciplines by promoting professional standards and ethics for conserving, managing, understanding and enjoying our heritage.

MEMBERSHIP
Student
Affiliate
Practitioner (PCIfA)
Associate (ACIfA)
Member (MCIfA)
Registered Organisation

ARCHITECTURE
Membership of Professional Institutions and Associations

ARCHITECTS REGISTRATION BOARD

8 Weymouth Street
London W1W 5BU
Tel: 020 7580 5861
Fax: 020 7436 5269
E-mail: info@arb.org.uk
Website: www.arb.org.uk

The ARB is the regulatory body for architects in the UK. Only individuals registered with the Board can use the title 'architect'. Applicants must have passed the recognized exams at a school of architecture in the UK (or have an equivalent non-UK professional qualification) and have at least 2 years' practical experience working under the supervision of an architect.

CHARTERED INSTITUTE OF ARCHITECTURAL TECHNOLOGISTS (CIAT)

397 City Road
London EC1V 1NH
Tel: 020 7278 2206
Fax: 020 7837 3194
E-mail: info@ciat.org.uk
Website: www.ciat.org.uk

CIAT represents professionals working and studying in the field of Architectural Technology. We are internationally recognised as the qualifying body for

Chartered Architectural Technologists (MCIAT) and Architectural Technicians (TCIAT).

MEMBERSHIP
Student Member
Profile Candidate
Associate (ACIAT)

Architectural Technician (TCIAT)
Chartered Architectural Technologist (MCIAT)
Honorary Member (HonMCIAT)

DESIGNATORY LETTERS
ACIAT, TCIAT, MCIAT

ROYAL INSTITUTE OF BRITISH ARCHITECTS

66 Portland Place
London W1B 1AD
Tel: 020 7580 5533
E-mail: info@riba.org
Website: www.architecture.com

The Royal Institute of British Architects is the UK body for architecture and the architectural profession. We provide support for our 40,500 members worldwide in the form of training, technical services, publications and events, and set standards for the education of architects, both in the UK and overseas. We also work with government to improve the design quality of public buildings, new homes and new communities.

MEMBERSHIP
Student Member
Affiliate Member
Associate Member
Chartered Member
Chartered Practice

ART AND DESIGN
Membership of Professional Institutions and Associations

BRITISH ASSOCIATION OF ART THERAPISTS

Claremont
24–27 White Lion Street
London N1 9PD
Tel: 020 7686 4216
E-mail: info@baat.org
Website: www.baat.org

The BAAT is the professional organization for art therapists in the UK and has its own Code of Ethics of Professional Practice. We maintain a comprehensive directory of qualified art therapists and work to promote art therapy in the UK through 20 regional groups. We also have a European section and an international section.

MEMBERSHIP
Trainee Member

Associate Member
Full Member
Honorary Member
Fellow
Corporate Member

QUALIFICATION/EXAMINATIONS
The BAAT organizes a programme of CPD courses for Art Therapists. For details see the website.

BRITISH ASSOCIATION OF PAINTINGS CONSERVATOR-RESTORERS

PO Box 258
Norwich NR13 4WY
Tel: 01603 516237
Fax: 01603 510985
E-mail: office@bapcr.org.uk
Website: www.bapcr.org.uk

The BAPCR (founded in 1943 as the Association of British Picture Restorers) is the professional association for conservator-restorers of paintings and has more than 400 members worldwide. Our aims are to advance the profession by providing means for CPD to our members and thereby a service to the public.

MEMBERSHIP
Associate (Student)
Associate
Fellow

D&AD (BRITISH DESIGN & ART DIRECTION)

Britannia House
68–80 Hanbury Street
London E1 5JL
Tel: 020 7840 1111
Fax: 020 7840 0840
E-mail: info@dandad.co.uk
Website: www.dandad.org

Founded in 1962, D&AD is a professional association and educational charity with a membership of more than 2,000, working on behalf of the design and advertising communities. Our mission is to set creative standards, educate and inspire the next creative generation, and promote the importance of good design and advertising to business as a whole.

MEMBERSHIP
Awarded
Professional
Education Network

SOCIETY OF DESIGNER CRAFTSMEN (SDC)

24 Rivington Street
London EC2A 3DU
Tel: 020 7739 3663
E-mail: info@societyofdesignercraftsmen.org.uk
Website: www.societyofdesignercraftsmen.org.uk

The Society, which was founded in 1887 as the Arts and Crafts Exhibition Society, is the largest and oldest multi-craft society in the UK. Our aim is to emphasize designer-making where innovation, originality and quality are important; we provide promotional services and exhibiting opportunities to members.

MEMBERSHIP
Associate
Licentiate (LSDC)
Member (MSDC)
Fellow (FSDC)

QUALIFICATION/EXAMINATIONS
Membership is by direct application by an individual craftsman and assessment is on quality of craftsmanship and design.

New graduates can be assessed at New Designers or College degree show following graduation.

Application forms and criteria are on our website.

DESIGNATORY LETTERS
LSDC, MSDC, FSDC

THE CHARTERED SOCIETY OF DESIGNERS

1 Cedar Court
Royal Oak Yard
Bermondsey Street
London SE1 3GA
Tel: 020 7357 8088
Fax: 020 7407 9878
E-mail: info@csd.org.uk
Website: www.csd.org.uk

The CSD, which was founded in 1930, is the professional body for designers and has more than 3,000 members. We promote sound principles of design in all areas in which design considerations apply, further design practice and encourage the study of design techniques for the benefit of the community.

MEMBERSHIP
Student Member
Associate (Assoc. CSD)
Member (MCSD)
Fellow (FCSD)

DESIGNATORY LETTERS
MCSD, FCSD

THE INDEX OF PROFESSIONAL MASTER DESIGNERS

Kensington House
33 Imperial Square
Cheltenham Spa
Gloucestershire GL50 1QZ
Tel: 08701 161823
Fax: 08702 626146
E-mail: masterdesigners@kensington-house.com

The Index was formed to provide a register of designers practising in all areas of design. Our objectives are to enable designers to achieve recognition and attain qualifications and also to accredit schools and training organizations offering suitable courses.

MEMBERSHIP
Student

Professional Designer (IPMD (DIP))
Master Designer (IPMD (MAS))

QUALIFICATION/EXAMINATIONS
Certificate of Excellence – Interior Design Students

DESIGNATORY LETTERS
IPMD (DIP), IPMD (MAS)

ASTRONOMY AND SPACE SCIENCE
Membership of Professional Institutions and Associations

THE BRITISH INTERPLANETARY SOCIETY

27/29 South Lambeth Road
London SW8 1SZ
Tel: 020 7735 3160
Fax: 020 7587 5118
E-mail: info@bis-space.com
Website: www.bis-space.com

The BIS was formed in 1933 and has been at the forefront of actively promoting new ideas on space exploration at technical, educational and popular levels for 80 years. We serve the interests of those professionally involved with space, promote fundamental space research, technology and applications, encourage technical and scientific space studies, and undertake educational activities on space topics.

MEMBERSHIP
Member
Fellow (FBIS)

DESIGNATORY LETTERS
FBIS

AVIATION
Membership of Professional Institutions and Associations

THE GUILD OF AIR PILOTS AND AIR NAVIGATORS

Cobham House
9 Warwick Court
London WC1R 5DJ
Tel: 020 7404 4032
Fax: 020 7404 4035
E-mail: gapan@gapan.org
Website: www.gapan.org

The Guild, an active Livery Company of the City of London, represents pilot and navigator interests within all areas of aviation. Most of our members are, or have been, professional licence holders, or hold a private licence. Our aims include promoting the highest standards of air safety, liaising with all authorities connected with licensing, training and legislation, providing advice and facilitating exchange of information.

MEMBERSHIP
Associate
Freeman
Upper Freeman

QUALIFICATION/EXAMINATIONS
Master Air Pilot Certificate
Master Air Navigator Certificate
Master Rearcrew Certificate

THE GUILD OF AIR TRAFFIC CONTROL OFFICERS

Membership Services
4 St Mary's Road
Bingham
Nottingham
Nottinghamshire NG13 8DW
Tel: 01949 876405
Fax: 01949 876405
E-mail: caf@gatco.org
Website: www.gatco.org

Founded in 1954, GATCO is an independent professional organization that exists to promote honourable practice and the highest standards in all aspects of aviation. It is dedicated to the safety of all who seek their livelihood or pleasure in the air.

MEMBERSHIP
Student Member
Associate Non-Operational Member
Associate Operational Member
Full Member
Corporate Member
Membership category changes will be implemented and become effective 1st June 2016 after ratification at the 2015 AGM. This only affects the Full Member and Associate Member categories.

QUALIFICATION/EXAMINATIONS
Qualifying criteria apply to all membership categories. Further information should be sought from GATCO Ltd, Membership Services.

AWARDS
Membership of Professional Institutions and Associations

CONFEDERATION OF PROFESSIONAL AWARDING BODIES (COPAB)

40 Archdale Road
East Dulwich
London SE22 9HJ
Tel: 0208 693 0555
Fax: 0208 693 0555
E-mail: secretary@copab.net; profblankson@snnp.org.uk
Website: www.copab.net

DESIGNATORY LETTERS
MCOPAB

BANKING

Membership of Professional Institutions and Associations

IFS UNIVERSITY COLLEGE

8th Floor
Peninsular House
36 Monument Street
London EC3R 8LJ
Tel: 0207 4447111
Fax: 0207 4447115
E-mail: customerservices@ifslearning.ac.uk
Website: www.ifslearning.ac.uk

ifs University College is the university college for financial education. London-based, it is a registered charity that exists to ensure a flow of talented individuals into the financial services industry and related sectors. Its qualifications enable individuals to reach their full professional potential, drawing on 130 years of experience in the industry.

MEMBERSHIP
Member
Student Member

Associate
Fellow
Chartered Associate
Chartered Fellow

QUALIFICATION/EXAMINATIONS
Offering a wide range of qualifications for those employed or aspiring to a career in the financial services industry, and for consumers. For details see www.ifslearning.ac.uk

THE CHARTERED INSTITUTE OF BANKERS IN SCOTLAND

Drumsheugh House
38B Drumsheugh Gardens
Edinburgh EH3 7SW
Tel: 0131 473 7777
Fax: 0131 473 7788
E-mail: info@charteredbanker.com
Website: www.charteredbanker.com

The Chartered Institute of Bankers in Scotland provides world-class professional qualifications for both the UK and international markets. Our vision for the financial services industry is one of professionalism. We are the only organisation in the world entitled to award the designation 'Chartered Banker' to its members.

MEMBERSHIP
Student
Affiliate
Associate (ACIBS)

Member (MCIBS)
Fellow (FCIBS)

QUALIFICATION/EXAMINATIONS
Certificate
Diploma
Advanced Diploma
Chartered Banker

DESIGNATORY LETTERS
ACIBS, MCIBS, FCIBS

BEAUTY THERAPY AND BEAUTY CULTURE
Membership of Professional Institutions and Associations

BRITISH ASSOCIATION OF BEAUTY THERAPY AND COSMETOLOGY LTD

BABTAC Limited
Ambrose House, Meteor Court
Barnett Way
Barnwood
Gloucester GL4 3GG
Tel: 0845 250 7277
Fax: 01452 611599
E-mail: info@babtac.com
Website: www.babtac.com

BABTAC was formed in 1977 and is a non-profit-making organization for beauticians and therapists in the UK. Members work to a rigorous code of ethics and good practice, both in terms of the treatments and therapies they offer and the way they conduct their relationships with their clients. CIBTAC, an international, educational awarding body that works closely with BABTAC, offers over 30 internationally recognized diplomas in beauty and complementary therapies to accredited colleges and students in the UK and abroad.

MEMBERSHIP
Student Member
Associate Member
Full Therapist Member
Full Hairdresser Member
Salon and Spa Member
International Member

QUALIFICATION/EXAMINATIONS
BABTAC offers a programme of short courses. For details see the BABTAC website. For CIBTAC diplomas see www.cibtac.com/courses_home.htm

BRITISH INSTITUTE AND ASSOCIATION OF ELECTROLYSIS LTD

40 Parkfield Road
Ickenham
Middlesex UB10 BLW
Tel: 08445 441373
E-mail: sec@electrolysis.co.uk
Website: www.electrolysis.co.uk

The BIAE is a non-profit-making organisation that demands a high standard of skill and ethical conduct from its members, who are spread throughout the UK and overseas. Candidate Electrolysists must complete the rigorous assessments, both theoretical and practical, of the BIAE Examining Board before being accepted onto the Register.

MEMBERSHIP
Member

QUALIFICATION/EXAMINATIONS
Certificate in Remedial Electrolysis (CRE)

FEDERATION OF HOLISTIC THERAPISTS

18 Shakespeare Business Centre
Hathaway Close
Eastleigh
Hampshire SO50 4SR
Tel: 023 8062 4350
Fax: 023 8062 4396
E-mail: info@fht.org.uk
Website: www.fht.org.uk

The FHT is the leading and largest professional beauty, sports and complementary therapist association in the UK, which has been representing the interests of holistic therapists since 1962. The FHT leads the industry by offering its members a Code of Conduct and Professional Practice, public liability insurance, access to regulation, a robust CPD programme with auditing, class-leading journal, local therapist network, and comprehensive business and public affairs updates.

MEMBERSHIP
Student
Affiliate
Associate
Member
Fellow
International

QUALIFICATION/EXAMINATIONS
Please see the FHT's website.

DESIGNATORY LETTERS
MFHT, FFHT, AFHT, AfFHT

ITEC

2nd Floor, Chiswick Gate
598–608 Chiswick High Road
London W4 5RT
Tel: 020 8994 4141
Fax: 020 8994 7880
E-mail: info@itecworld.co.uk
Website: www.itecworld.co.uk

ITEC is a leading international specialist examination board, providing high quality qualifications specialising in: Beauty & Spa Therapy, Hairdressing, Complementary Therapies, Sports & Fitness and Customer Service.

QUALIFICATION/EXAMINATIONS
Beauty & Spa Therapies
Hairdressing
Complementary Therapies
Sports & Fitness
Customer Service

BIOLOGICAL SCIENCES
Membership of Professional Institutions and Associations

INSTITUTE OF BIOMEDICAL SCIENCE

12 Coldbath Square
London EC1R 5HL
Tel: 020 7713 0214
Fax: 020 7837 9658
E-mail: mail@ibms.org
Website: www.ibms.org

The IBMS is the professional body for biomedical scientists in the UK. We aim to promote and develop the role of biomedical science within healthcare to deliver the best possible service for patient care and safety.

MEMBERSHIP
eStudent
Associate
Licentiate (LIBMS)
Member (MIBMS)
Fellow (FIBMS)
Company Member

QUALIFICATION/EXAMINATIONS
Certificate of Achievement Part I and II
Certificate of Competence (also required for registration with the Health and Care Professions Council (HCPC))
Specialist Diploma in:
Cellular Pathology, Clinical Biochemistry, Clinical Immunology, Cytopathology, Haematology &
Transfusion Science, Histocompatibility & Immunogenetics (developed in conjunction with BSHI), Medical Microbiology, Transfusion Science, Virology.
Diploma of Biomedical Science
Diploma of Specialist Practice
Higher Specialist Diploma in:
Cellular Pathology, Clinical Chemistry, Cytopathology, Haematology, Immunology, Histocompatibility & Immunogenetics (developed in conjunction with BSHI), Medical Microbiology, Transfusion Science, Virology.
Diploma of Higher Specialist Practice
Complementary qualifications/examinations related to areas of scientific expertise (available to Members and/or Fellows)
Certificates and Diplomas of Expert Practice
Advanced Specialist Diplomas

DESIGNATORY LETTERS
LIBMS, MIBMS, FIBMS

SOCIETY OF BIOLOGY

Charles Darwin House
12 Roger Street
London WC1N 2JU
Tel: 020 7685 2550
E-mail: info@societyofbiology.org
Website: www.societyofbiology.org

The Society of Biology aims to be a single unified voice for biology: advising government and influencing policy; advancing education and professional development; supporting members; and engaging and encouraging public interest in the life sciences.

MEMBERSHIP
Associate Member (AMSB)
Member (MSB)
Fellow (FSB)

Chartered Biologist (CBiol)
Affiliate
Sudent
BioNet

DESIGNATORY LETTERS
AMSB, MSB, FSB, CBiol

BREWING
Membership of Professional Institutions and Associations

INSTITUTE OF BREWING & DISTILLING

33 Clarges Street
Mayfair
London W1J 7EE
Tel: 020 7499 8144
Fax: 020 7499 1156
E-mail: enquiries@ibd.org.uk
Website: www.ibd.org.uk

The IBD is a members' organization dedicated to the education and training needs of brewers and distillers and those in related industries. We do this by offering a range of internationally recognized qualifications and the training to support them, through either direct instruction or distance learning.

MEMBERSHIP
Member
Honorary Member
Senior Member
Fellow (FIBD)
Honorary Fellow
Corporate Member
Student Member
Member in Retirement
Certificate Member

QUALIFICATION/EXAMINATIONS
Certificate in the Fundamentals of Brewing and Packaging of Beer (FBPB) (City & Guilds Level 2)

Certificate in the Fundamentals of Distilling (FD) (City & Guilds Level 2)
General Certificate in Brewing (GCB) (City & Guilds Level 3)
General Certificate in Distilling (GCD) (City & Guilds Level 3)
General Certificate in Packaging (GCP) (City & Guilds Level 3)
Diploma in Packaging (Dipl.Pack) (City & Guilds Level 4)
General Certificate in Spirits Packaging
General Certificate in Malting
Diploma in Brewing (Dipl.Brew) (City & Guilds Level 4)
Diploma in Distilling (Dipl.Distil) (City & Guilds Level 4)
Master Brewer (MBrew)

DESIGNATORY LETTERS
Dipl.Brew, Dipl.Distil, Dipl.Pack, MBrew, FIBD, Hon FIBD

BUILDING
Membership of Professional Institutions and Associations

INSTITUTE OF ASPHALT TECHNOLOGY

PO Box 15690
BATHGATE EH48 9BT
Tel: 01506 238397
E-mail: info@instituteofasphalt.org
Website: www.instituteofasphalt.org

The IAT is the UK's professional body for persons working in asphalt technology and those interested in aspects of the manufacture, placing, technology and uses of materials containing asphalt or bitumen.

A fully audited CPD system for members has been available since 1994 and is now also offered in computerized format for ease of data entry and auditing, via members' own PCs.

MEMBERSHIP
Student
Technician (Tech.IAT)
Affiliate (AIAT)
Associate Member (AMIAT)
Member (MIAT)

Fellow (FIAT)
Honorary Fellow (Hon FIAT)

DESIGNATORY LETTERS
Tech.IAT, AIAT, AMIAT, MIAT, FIAT, Hon.FIAT

THE CHARTERED INSTITUTE OF BUILDING

Englemere
Kings Ride
Ascot
Berkshire SL5 7TB
Tel: 01344 630700
Fax: 01344 630777
E-mail: reception@ciob.org.uk
Website: www.ciob.org

The CIOB is the international voice of the construction industry. CIOB members are largely Construction Managers engaged in managing the development, conservation and improvement of the built environment, with a common commitment to achieving and maintaining the highest possible standards.

MEMBERSHIP
Student Member
Associate (ACIOB)
Incorporated (ICIOB)
Member (MCIOB)
Fellow (FCIOB)
Chartered Environmentalist (CENV)
Student in Employment
Educationalist
Concessionary

QUALIFICATION/EXAMINATIONS
The CIOB has routes to membership to suit a range of professionals from those with degrees or vocational qualifications to those with experience but no formal qualifications. All our members have a strong commitment to improve and develop themselves in a challenging and exciting career.
Chartered Member status is recognized internationally as the mark of a skilled professional in the construction industry. CIOB members are from a wide range of professions in the construction industry.

To find out more about our membership qualifications and joining the CIOB just visit our website www.ciob.org

The CIOB Awarding Body offers a suite of qualifications to enable site operatives to progress into management roles.
Level 3 Diploma in Site Supervisory Studies
Level 4 Certificate in Site Management
Level 4 Diploma in Site Management
The CIOB qualifications develop the skills and confidence to manage and coordinate all types of construction projects. The site management qualifications are nationally recognized and allow the learner to progress to higher education and National Vocational Qualifications (NVQs).

For more information on the Site Management Qualifications visit the website at www.ciob.org.uk/education/courseinfo/sitemanagement

DESIGNATORY LETTERS
ACIOB, ICIOB, MCIOB, FCIOB, CENV

THE INSTITUTE OF CARPENTERS

32 High Street
Wendover
Buckinghamshire HP22 6EA
Tel: 0844 879 7696
Fax: 01296 620981
E-mail: info@instituteofcarpenters.com
Website: www.instituteofcarpenters.com

The IOC was founded in 1890 to oversee training for carpenters and joiners and maintain high professional standards at a time when many feared that traditional skills were being lost. Today, while remaining committed to our original aims, we embrace many other wood craftsmen, such as shopfitters, furniture and cabinetmakers, boat builders (woodworking skills), structural post & beam carpenters (heavy structural timber framers), wheelwrights, wood carvers and wood turners, and offer professional status to those holding recognized qualifications.

MEMBERSHIP
Student
Mature Student
Affiliate

Licentiate (LIOC)
Member (MIOC)
Fellow (FIOC)
College Member
Corporate Member
Corporate Associate

QUALIFICATION/EXAMINATIONS
Foundation Examination
Intermediate Examination
Advanced Craft Examination
Fellowship Examination
Setting-Out Course

DESIGNATORY LETTERS
LIOC, MIOC, FIOC

THE INSTITUTE OF CLERKS OF WORKS AND CONSTRUCTION INSPECTORATE OF GREAT BRITAIN INC

28 Commerce Road
Lynch Wood
Peterborough PE2 6LR
Tel: 01733 405160
Fax: 01733 405161
E-mail: info@icwci.org
Website: www.icwci.org

The ICWCI is the professional body that supports quality construction through inspection. As a membership organization, we provide a support network of meeting centres, technical advice, publications and events to help keep our members up to date with the ever-changing construction industry.

MEMBERSHIP
Student

Licentiate (LICWCI)
Member (MICWCI)
Fellow (FICWCI)
Life Member
Honorary Member

DESIGNATORY LETTERS
LICWCI, MICWCI, FICWCI

BUSINESS STUDIES
Membership of Professional Institutions and Associations

ASSOCIATION OF BUSINESS RECOVERY PROFESSIONALS (R3)

8th Floor
120 Aldersgate Street
London EC1A 4JQ
Tel: 020 7566 4200
Fax: 020 7566 4224
E-mail: association@r3.org.uk
Website: www.r3.org.uk

The Association of Business Recovery Professionals (known by its brand name 'R3') is the leading professional association for insolvency, business recovery and turnaround specialists in the UK. A not-for-profit organization, it promotes best practice for professionals working with financially troubled individuals and businesses, and provides a forum for debate on key issues facing the profession.

MEMBERSHIP
New Professional (Student) Member
New Professional (Networking) Member
Associate Member (AABRP)
Full Member (MABRP)
Fellow (FABRP)

QUALIFICATION/EXAMINATIONS
R3 provides comprehensive Continuing Professional Education in the field of Insolvency and Restructuring. For details of courses see R3's website.

DESIGNATORY LETTERS
AABRP, MABRP, FABRP

INSTITUTE OF ASSESSORS AND INTERNAL VERIFIERS

PO Box 1138
Warrington WA4 9GS
Tel: 01925 485 786
E-mail: office@iavltd.co.uk
Website: www.iavltd.co.uk

The IAV is the professional organization representing assessors and internal verifiers in the UK in vocational training and assessment.

MEMBERSHIP
Affiliate Member
Associate Member
Licentiate Member

THE ACADEMY OF EXECUTIVES & ADMINISTRATORS

PO Box 93
Moreton-in-Marsh GL56 9WG
Tel: 01386 277973
E-mail: info@academyofexecutivesandadministrators.org.uk
Website: www.academyofexecutivesandadministrators.org.uk

The Academy of Executives & Administrators was founded in 2002 to give professional status and recognition to the knowledge and skills of executives and administrators. We encourage excellence and flexibility in the changing environment of executive and administrative roles, and support lifelong learning to help members fulfil their career ambitions.

MEMBERSHIP
Student Member (StudAEA)
Associate Member (AMAEA)
Member (MAEA)
Fellow (FAEA)
Companion (CAEA)

QUALIFICATION/EXAMINATIONS
Associate Diploma for Business Economists
Associate Diploma for Financial Managers
Associate Diploma for Assistant Accountants
Associate Diploma for Assistant Corporate Accountants
Associate Diploma for Trainers
Certified Administration Practitioner
Certified Executive Practitioner
Certified Budget and Planning Practitioner

THE ACADEMY OF MULTI-SKILLS

Head Office
Suite 3, Third Floor, 148 Cambridge Heath Road
London E1 5QJ
Tel: (0)709 201 2910
E-mail: registrar@academyofmultiskills.co.uk
Website: www.academyofmultiskills.co.uk

The Academy of Multi-Skills was founded in 1995 to give professional recognition to multi-skilled personnel, skilled trades, crafts and professions. The Academy encourages a positive and energetic attitude to the challenges of careers that require diversity, creativity and intellect, and recognizes the valuable contribution that these skills provide to society.

MEMBERSHIP
Technician (TAMS) GBP 70
Associate (AAMS) GBP 80
Fellow (FAMS) GBP 90
Doctoral Fellow (DFAMS) GBP 100

QUALIFICATION/EXAMINATIONS
Members may choose to enhance their qualifications via our diploma, HND, post-graduate and doctoral diploma courses.

We have arrangements with other prestigious organisations which our members may choose to join to obtain further qualifications.

Discounts are available to our members from organisations ranging from books to overseas conferences.

DESIGNATORY LETTERS
TAMS, AAMS, FAMS, DFAMS

THE FACULTY OF SECRETARIES AND ADMINISTRATORS WITH THE ASSOCIATION OF CORPORATE SECRETARIES

Brightstowe
Catteshall Lane
GODALMING
Surrey GU7 1LJ
Tel: 01483 437323 dedica
Fax: 0871 288 6935 on req
E-mail: admin@facultyofsecretaries.org.uk
Website: www.facultyofsecretaries.org.uk

The Faculty and Association is a professional body for company and corporate secretaries whose prime qualified designation is that of Certified Public or Corporate Secretary. Since 1930 the Faculty has been a leader in promoting good but liberal governance through qualified corporate secretaries.

The Faculty kitemark is now a key marker for organisation in Public, Private, Community and

Voluntary Sector showing induction training in Corporate Secretaryship combined with a study of the organisation to embed the concept of reasonableness and care for others in organisations operation and decision taking.

MEMBERSHIP
Membership Fellows (FFCS)
Associates (AFCS)
Member (MACS)
Ordinary Member
Student Member
Licentiate (LFCS)
Corporate

QUALIFICATION/EXAMINATIONS
Part 1 The Generic Business Assessment to ONC/D Level

Part 2 Professional Papers in Company Secretarial Practice, Company Law and Management, Secretarial and Administrative Practice, Commercial Law
Part 3 Professional Meetings Law and Procedure, Company Taxation, Accountancy and Finance, Company Law
Assessment of Senior Personnel for direct entry now involves a viva voce interview and rated questions on company secretaryship as well as exemptions based on an agreed list of qualifications and a declaration of working with the general ethos of the faculty.
The Society of Teachers in Business Education monitors this interview process.

DESIGNATORY LETTERS
FFCS, AFCS, LFCS, MACS

THE INSTITUTE OF CHARTERED SECRETARIES AND ADMINISTRATORS

16 Park Crescent
London W1B 1AH
Tel: 020 7580 4741
Fax: 020 7323 1132
E-mail: studentsupport@icsaglobal.com
Website: www.icsaglobal.com

The Institute of Chartered Secretaries and Administrators is the international qualifying and membership body for the Chartered Secretary profession. With a global community of 37,000 members we provide Chartered Membership, training and a professional qualifying scheme to set you on the path to a diverse, challenging and rewarding career.

MEMBERSHIP
Affiliate
Graduate (GradICSA)
Associate (ACIS)
Fellow (FCIS)

QUALIFICATION/EXAMINATIONS
Chartered Secretaries Qualifying Scheme (CSQS)
Certificate in Offshore Finance and Administration
Diploma in Offshore Finance and Administration
Certificate in Company Secretarial Practice and Share Registration Practice
Certificate in Irish Company Secretarial Practice and Share Registration Practice
Certificate in Employee Share Plans
Postgraduate Certificate in Charity Management
ICSA Certificate in Further Education Governance

DESIGNATORY LETTERS
GradICSA, ACIS, FCIS

CATERING AND INSTITUTIONAL MANAGEMENT
Membership of Professional Institutions and Associations

BII

Wessex House
80 Park Street
Camberley
Surrey GU15 3PT
Tel: 01276 684449
E-mail: info@bii.org
Website: www.bii.org

Founded in 1981, BII is the professional body for the licensed retail sector with a remit to raise standards throughout the industry. BIIAB, the wholly owned awarding body of BII, does this through offering qualifications specifically tailored to, and designed in conjunction with, the industry.

MEMBERSHIP
There is a wide range of membership grades available, from those who have just started their careers in licensed retailing to those who have been in the industry for many years. The grade of membership awarded depends on both experience and qualifications and is determined by a points system. Member of the Hotel Catering and Management Association, HCIMA.

QUALIFICATION/EXAMINATIONS
Qualifications for licensing
Award for Designated Premises Supervisors (Level 2)
Award for Licensing Practitioners (Alcohol) (Level 2)
Award for Personal Licence Holders (Level 2)
Award for Upskilling Door Supervisors (Level 2)
Award for Upskilling Door Supervisors (Scotland)
Award in Door Supervision (Level 2)
Award in Door Supervision (Scotland)
Award in Door Supervision (Northern Ireland)
Award in CCTV Operations (Public Space Surveillance) (Scotland)
Award in Crime Scene Preservation (Level 2)
Award in Drug Awareness for Licensed Hospitality Staff (Level 2)
Award in Fire Safety (Level 2)
Scottish Certificate for Licensees (Drugs Awareness)
Award in Isle of Man Licensing Law
Award in Jersey Licensing Law
Qualifications for new licensed retail managers
Award in Licensed Retailing (Level 2)

Award in Beer and Cellar Quality (Cask and Keg) (Level 2)
Award in Beer and Cellar Quality (Keg) (Level 2)
Scottish Certificate in Licensed Retailing

Qualifications for staff development
Award in Kitchen Management (Level 3)
Award in Introduction to Employment in the Hospitality Industry (Level 1)
Professional Barperson's Qualification
Award in Conflict Management for Licensed Premises Staff (Level 2)
Award in Customer Service Excellence (Licensed Hospitality)
Award in Food Safety in Catering (Level 2)
Award in Health and Safety in the Workplace (Level 2)
Isle of Man Security Staff Qualification

Qualifications for management development

Award in Licensed Hospitality Operations (Level 2)
Certificate in Licensed Hospitality Operations (Level 2)
Certificate in Licensed Hospitality Skills (Level 2)
Award in Hospitality Business Management (Level 3)
Certificate in Hospitality Business Management (Level 3)
Certificate in Multiple Licensed Premises Management (Level 4)
Qualifications for personal and social responsibility

Award in Alcohol Awareness (Level 1)
Award in Assessment of Licensed Premises (Social Responsibility) (Level 2)
Award in Assessment of Licensed Premises (Social Responsibility) (Scotland)

GUILD OF INTERNATIONAL PROFESSIONAL TOASTMASTERS

Life President: Ivor Spencer
22 Great Mead
Denmead
Waterlooville
Hampshire PO7 6HH
Tel: 07802 250477
E-mail: info@guildoftoastmasters.co.uk
Website: www.guildoftoastmasters.co.uk

The Guild of Professional Toastmasters was established over 30 years ago to improve standards in the profession and support its members. A 5-day course is offered to prospective members, who may apply for membership upon successful completion of the course. Applications are considered by the Fellows of the Guild.

MEMBERSHIP
Fellow (FGIntPT)

DESIGNATORY LETTERS
FGIntPT

INSTITUTE OF HOSPITALITY

Trinity Court
34 West Street
Sutton
Surrey SM1 1SH
Tel: 020 8661 4900
Fax: 020 8661 4901
E-mail: awardingbody@instituteofhospitality.org
Website: www.instituteofhospitality.org

The Institute of Hospitality is the professional body for managers and aspiring managers in the hospitality, leisure and tourism industries and has a worldwide membership. We offer professional qualifications, accredit academic programmes of study, endorse training courses and provide a wide range of membership benefits to support career development.

MEMBERSHIP
Student Member
Affiliate
Associate (AIH)
Member (MIH)
Fellow (FIH)

DESIGNATORY LETTERS
AIH, MIH, FIH

CHEMISTRY
Membership of Professional Institutions and Associations

SOCIETY OF COSMETIC SCIENTISTS

Suite 5
Langham House West
Mill Street
Luton
Bedfordshire LU1 2NA
Tel: 01582 726661
Fax: 01582 405217
E-mail: gem.bektas@btconnect.com
Website: www.scs.org.uk

The main object of the Society, which was formed in 1948, is to advance the science of cosmetics. We endeavour to do this by attracting highly qualified scientists with both academic and industrial experience in cosmetics or a related science to our membership of around 900 members, and by means of our publications, educational programmes and scientific meetings.

MEMBERSHIP
Student
Affiliate
Associate Member
Member – B Grade
Member – A Grade
Honorary Member

QUALIFICATION/EXAMINATIONS
Certificate of Higher Education in Cosmetic Science

THE OIL AND COLOUR CHEMISTS' ASSOCIATION

The Oval
14 West Walk
Leicester LE1 7NA
Tel: 0116 257 5488
Fax: 0116 257 5499
E-mail: admin@occa.org.uk
Website: www.occa.org.uk

OCCA, founded in 1918, is a learned society comprising individual qualified persons employed in, or associated with, the worldwide surface coatings industries. Most of our members work in a technical capacity, but there are senior personnel from throughout the surface coating industries. The word 'oil' in our title refers to vegetable oils, which once formed a major part of surface coatings' formulations.

MEMBERSHIP
Student Member
Ordinary Member
Honorary Member
Licentiate (LTSC)
Associate (ATSC)
Fellow (FTSC)
Chartered Scientist (CSci)

DESIGNATORY LETTERS
LTSC, ATSC, FTSC, CSci

THE ROYAL SOCIETY OF CHEMISTRY

Thomas Graham House
Science Park
Milton Road
Cambridge CB4 0WF
Tel: 01223 420066
Fax: 01223 423623
E-mail: membership@rsc.org
Website: www.rsc.org

The RSC is the UK professional body for chemical scientists and an international learned society for advancing the chemical sciences. With over 46,000 members worldwide and an internationally acclaimed publishing business, our activities span education and training, conferences, science policy and the promotion of the chemical sciences to the public.

MEMBERSHIP
Affiliate
Associate Member (AMRSC)
Member (MRSC)
Fellow (FRSC)

QUALIFICATION/EXAMINATIONS
NVQ Analytical Chemistry (Level 5)
Registered Scientist and Registered Science Technician
MSc in Chemical Technology and Management
Mastership in Chemical Analysis (MChemA)
Chartered Chemist (CChem)
Chartered Scientist (CSci)

DESIGNATORY LETTERS
AMRSC, MRSC, FRSC, CChem

CHIROPODY
Membership of Professional Institutions and Associations

BRITISH CHIROPODY AND PODIATRY ASSOCIATION

The New Hall
149 Bath Road
Maidenhead
Berkshire SL6 4LA
Tel: 01628 632440
Fax: 01628 674483
E-mail: membership@bcha-uk.org
Website: www.bcha-uk.org

The BChA, formed in 1959, is the largest professional organization in the UK representing the interests of independent private chiropodists / podiatrists. Since 2005 we have added foothealth practitioners to include our 7,000 members, most of whom work mainly in private practice. Those who are registered with the Health Professions Council may work in the NHS or in education.

MEMBERSHIP
Member (MSSCh & MBChA) – Podiatrists

Fellow (FSSCh) – Podiatrist
Associate members are foothealth practitioners trained by The SMAE Institute.

QUALIFICATION/EXAMINATIONS
Diploma in Podiatric Medicine (DipPodMed)
Foothealth practitioners carry the qualification – MAFHP

DESIGNATORY LETTERS
MSSCh, MBChA, FSSCh and MAFHP

THE INSTITUTE OF CHIROPODISTS AND PODIATRISTS

150 Lord Street
Southport
Merseyside PR9 0NP
Tel: 01704 546141
E-mail: secretary@iocp.org.uk
Website: www.iocp.org.uk

The IOCP represents all levels of the profession and our CPD is open to both members and non-members, as by elevating professional standards we aim to improve public safety. We have branches throughout the UK and the Republic of Ireland, and members overseas, and hold lectures, seminars and workshops to enable members to keep up to date.

MEMBERSHIP
Full Member
Student
Associate

QUALIFICATION/EXAMINATIONS
MInstChP – Full Member

THE SOCIETY OF CHIROPODISTS AND PODIATRISTS

1 Fellmongers Path
Tower Bridge Road
London SE1 3LY
Tel: 020 7234 8620
E-mail: enq@scpod.org
Website: www.scpod.org

The SCP is the professional body and trade union for registered podiatrists. Membership is restricted to those qualified for registration and the Society represents around 10,000 NHS podiatrists, private practitioners and students. We monitor standards of undergraduate education and provide opportunities for CPD for our members.

MEMBERSHIP
Member (MChS)
Associate

DESIGNATORY LETTERS
MChS

CHIROPRACTIC
Membership of Professional Institutions and Associations

MCTIMONEY CHIROPRACTIC ASSOCIATION

Crowmarsh Gifford
Wallingford
Oxfordshire OX10 8DJ
Tel: 01491 829211
Fax: 01491 829492
E-mail: admin@mctimoney-chiropractic.org
Website: www.mctimoneychiropractic.org

The McTimoney Chiropractic Association is the professional association for McTimoney chiropractors, who in the UK are registered with the General Chiropractic Council.

MEMBERSHIP
Provisional Member
Full Member
Fellow

DESIGNATORY LETTERS
MMCA

SCOTTISH CHIROPRACTIC ASSOCIATION

1 Chisholm Avenue
Bishopton
Renfrewshire PA7 5JH
Tel: 0141 404 0260
E-mail: admin@sca-chiropractic.org
Website: www.sca-chiropractic.org

The SCA was formed in 1979 and now has more than 60 members practising in Scotland and over 120 associated members elsewhere in the UK and abroad. Our aims are to enhance the chiropractic profession in the UK, maintain high standards of professional practice, and provide advice and support to our members.

MEMBERSHIP
Member

UNITED CHIROPRACTIC ASSOCIATION

1st Floor
45 North Hill
Plymouth
Devon PL4 8EZ
Tel: 01752 658785
Fax: 01752 658786
E-mail: admin@united-chiropractic.org
Website: www.united-chiropractic.org

The UCA is a UK-based organization for qualified, professional, principal-based chiropractors, associates and students. Full membership is open to qualified, GCC-registered chiropractors from any recognized school of chiropractic.

MEMBERSHIP
Student
Associate
Affiliate
1st Year Graduate
2nd Year Graduate
Full Member
Overseas Member

THE CHURCHES
Membership of Professional Institutions and Associations

BAPTIST UNION OF SCOTLAND

48 Speirs Wharf
Glasgow G4 9TH
Tel: 0141 423 6169
Fax: 0141 424 1422
E-mail: admin@scottishbaptist.org.uk
Website: www.scottishbaptist.org.uk

The Baptist Union of Scotland was formed in 1869, when 51 churches with a total congregation of about 3,500 united. Today, with 164 churches and about 11,250 members, the Union strives for simplicity in organizational structure and promotes increasing contact between the local churches and the National Team, who function under the overall direction of the General Director.

QUALIFICATION/EXAMINATIONS
BD or BA in Theology
Graduate Diploma in Applied Theology through Work Based Learning
Graduate Diploma in Pastoral Studies
(awarded by the Scottish Baptist College, Paisley, and validated by the University of Paisley)

BRISTOL BAPTIST COLLEGE

The Promenade
Clifton Down
Clifton
Bristol BS8 3NJ
Tel: 0117 946 7050
Fax: 0117 946 7787
E-mail: reception@bristol-baptist.ac.uk
Website: www.bristol-baptist.ac.uk

The central aim of the College is to train men and women for ministry in the Church and in the world. We do this by enabling critical reflection upon the Bible and Christian theological tradition and on the contexts from which we come and within which we are placed.

QUALIFICATION/EXAMINATIONS
Certificate in Theological Studies
Diploma in Theological Studies
BA in Theological Studies
MA in Christian Theology
(all validated by the University of Bristol)

METHODIST CHURCH IN IRELAND

1 Fountainville Avenue
Belfast BT9 6AN
Tel: 028 9032 4554
Fax: 028 9023 9467
E-mail: secretary@irishmethodist.org
Website: www.irishmethodist.org

MEMBERSHIP
Candidates for training must normally have the standard of general education for university entrance. They must be accredited Local Preachers of the Methodist Church, and are examined by written papers in Biblical Studies and Theology and by oral aptitude and personality tests. After admission to training, candidates normally spend 3 years at Edgehill Theological College, Belfast, studying for a diploma or degree of Queen's University, Belfast, in New Testament Greek, Hebrew, the English Bible, Theology, Church History, Pastoral Psychology, or Homiletics. This is followed by 3 years as a probationer Minister working under a superintendent Minister. During probation the candidate continues study within a tutorial system and is examined by continuous assessment.

SCOTTISH EPISCOPAL INSTITUTE

Forbes House
21 Grosvenor Crescent
Edinburgh EH12 5EE
Tel: 0131 243 1347
E-mail: institute@scotland.anglican.org
Website: www.scotland.anglican.org

Candidates are trained for lay and ordained, stipendiary and non-stipendiary ministries in the Scottish Episcopal Church and the United Reformed Church.

The curriculum is delivered centrally through residential sessions and regionally through diocesan groups. The Diploma in Theology for Ministry course run by the Institute is validated by York St John's University. Some students undertake further studies through universities, leading to degree qualifications.

THE CHURCH IN WALES

St Michael's College
Llandaff
Cardiff CF5 2YJ
Tel: 029 205 63379
Fax: 029 208 38008
Website: www.stmichaels.ac.uk

The Church in Wales expects candidates for ordination and reader ministry to satisfy the requirements of recognized theological courses. University graduates usually spend at least 2 years full time (or its part time equivalent) at a theological college or course, and will be encouraged to study for a postgraduate degree.

Non-theological graduates are encouraged to study for a university degree, diploma or certificate in Theology, depending on their age and the ministry for which they are being trained. Non-graduate candidates must have at least 5 passes at GCSE and normally study for a university certificate or diploma in Theology or a degree in Theology if they have obtained the necessary grades at A level. These requirements may be modified in the case of older candidates.

THE CHURCH OF ENGLAND

Ministry Division of The Archbishops' Council
Church House
Great Smith Street
London SW1P 3AZ
Tel: 020 7898 1405
E-mail: david.way@churchofengland.org
Website: www.churchofengland.org/clergy-office-holders/ministry.aspx
www.archbishopofcanterbury.org/1027

The Church of England's Ministry Division oversees training for ordination and licensed lay ministry/Reader ministry including the Common Awards created by the Church and validated by Durham University.

In addition, The Archbishop's Examination in Theology offers means of study at three postgraduate levels.

QUALIFICATION/EXAMINATIONS
All awards are validated by Durham University:
Certificate of Higher Education in Theology, Ministry and Mission (120)
Certificate of Higher Education in Christian Ministry and Mission (180)
Diploma of Higher Education in Theology, Ministry and Mission
BA in Theology, Ministry and Mission
Graduate Certificate in Theology, Ministry and Mission
Graduate Diploma in Theology, Ministry and Mission
Postgraduate Certificate in Theology, Ministry and Mission
Postgraduate Diploma in Theology, Ministry and Mission
MA in Theology, Ministry and Mission
Archbishop's Examination:
PG Diploma of Student of Theology
Master of Philosophy
Doctor of Philosophy

THE CHURCH OF SCOTLAND

Church of Scotland Offices
121 George Street
Edinburgh EH2 4YN
Tel: 0131 225 5722
Website: www.churchofscotland.org.uk

The vision of The Church of Scotland is to be a church which seeks to inspire the people of Scotland and beyond with the Good News of Jesus Christ through enthusiastic worshipping, witnessing, nurturing and serving communities.

THE METHODIST CHURCH

Formation in Ministry Office (Initial Development of Ministries)
25 Marylebone Road
London NW1 5JR
Tel: 020 7486 5502
E-mail: helpdesk@methodistchurch.org.uk
Website: www.methodist.org.uk

Candidates for Diaconal or Presbyteral Ministry in the Methodist Church must have been members of the Methodist Church at least 2 years and are expected to offer at least 10 years of ministerial service. The first stage of preparation is Foundation Training, which requires 1 year (FT) or 2 years (PT) to complete, during which a person may apply to become a candidate for ordained ministry. The process of selection takes 6 months. To enter into training for Presbyteral Ministry, a candidate must be a trained Local Preacher, which involves taking the Methodist Local Preachers' Training Course, Faith &

Worship. Deacons become members of the Methodist Diaconal and are not required to be preachers. Accepted candidates for either order receive 1 or 2 years of further theological training, which in most cases leads to a degree or diploma in Theology or Ministry. Upon completion of training, a candidate serves as a Methodist Minister for 2 years on probation before ordination. For Presbyters, the appointment may be to an itinerant appointment (stipendiary) or to a local appointment (usually non-stipendiary) or as licensed to minister in secular employment. Deacons are always itinerant.

THE MORAVIAN CHURCH IN GREAT BRITAIN AND IRELAND

Moravian Church House
5–7 Muswell Hill
London N10 3TJ
Tel: 020 8883 3409
Fax: 020 8365 3371
E-mail: office@moravian.org.uk
Website: www.moravian.org.uk

Candidates for Moravian Church Service must be members of the Moravian Church and would normally have completed the Lay Training Course and have the support of their local church committee. They should make an initial application to the Provincial Board of the Moravian Church. Their qualifications are examined by the Church Service Advisory Board, which reports on them to the Provincial Board, with whom the final decision rests. Normally the standard of education required for the work of the Ministry is a university Divinity

degree or Certificate together with a thorough acquaintance with the history, principles and methods of the Moravian Church. Candidates receive guidance for the Ministry during a period of supervised service under the direction of experienced Ministers. A class of non-stipendiary Ministers has been established for those who wish to serve on a non-maintained basis. Training varies according to candidates' needs. In all cases applications should be made to the address given above.

THE PRESBYTERIAN CHURCH IN IRELAND

The Director of Ministerial Studies
Union Theological College
108 Botanic Avenue
Belfast BT7 1JT
Tel: 02890 205088
Fax: 02890 205099

Qualifications required: Under 30 – a non-theological degree; over 30 but under 40 (as reckoned on 1 October following application) – either a non-theological degree or 2 years, non-graduating Arts or 4 modules of PT BD study or 6 modules of PT study in Humanities acceptable to the Board of Studies; over 40 – not normally accepted, except in exceptional circumstances, where candidate is already possessed of good educational background and/or professional experience.

THE PRESBYTERIAN CHURCH OF WALES

Tabernacle Chapel
81 Merthyr Road
Whitchurch
Cardiff CF14 1DD
Tel: 02920 627465
Fax: 02920 616188
E-mail: swyddfa.office@ebcpcw.org.uk
Website: www.ebcpcw.org.uk

The Presbyterian Church of Wales (PCW) is a Protestant non-conformist denomination. Ordination is dependent on successful application through the local church and Presbytery to the Candidates and Training Department.

MEMBERSHIP
Ministers are ordained to the full-time, part-time or non-stipendiary ministry.

QUALIFICATION/EXAMINATIONS
Pastoral Studies course

THE ROMAN CATHOLIC CHURCH

Candidates for the priesthood in the RC Church attend a residential seminary course of at least 6 years. Among subjects studied are Philosophy, Psychology, Dogmatic and Moral Theology, Scripture, Church History, Canon Law, Liturgy, Catechetics, Communications and Pastoral Theology. Each college/seminary has its own arrangements for the university education of its students. Those who do not attend university take a final internal exam.

THE SALVATION ARMY

UK Headquarters
101 Newington Causeway
London SE1 6BN
Tel: 020 7367 4500
E-mail: info@salvationarmy.org.uk
Website: www.salvationarmy.org.uk

Salvation Army officers engaged in FT service are ordained ministers of religion, and are commissioned following a 2-year period of residential training at the William Booth College, Denmark Hill, London SE5 8BQ. This course – an HE Diploma in Salvation Army Officer Training – may now be undertaken by distance learning, or a mixture of residential and distance learning. Officers may be appointed to corps (church) work, to social services centres (for which additional professional qualifications are required) or to administrative posts.

THE SCOTTISH UNITED REFORMED AND CONGREGATIONAL COLLEGE

113 West Regent Street
Glasgow G2 2RU
Tel: 0141 248 5382
E-mail: Scottishcollege@urcscotland.org.uk
Website: www.scotland.urc.org.uk

The College is recognized as a resource centre for learning by the General Assembly of the United Reformed Church and is one of the institutions charged with responsibility for initial ministerial education.

QUALIFICATION/EXAMINATIONS
The College awards only its own certificate, which is part of the process of accreditation of ordinands as ministers of the United Reformed Church. Students, however, are normally concurrently matriculated for a degree, usually in Theology or Religious Studies, at a university.

THE UNITARIAN AND FREE CHRISTIAN CHURCHES

Essex Hall
London WC2R 3HY
Tel: 020 7240 2384
Fax: 020 7240 3089
E-mail: info@unitarian.org.uk
Website: www.unitarian.org.uk

Candidates accepted for training for the ministry in the Unitarian and Free Christian Churches take courses of training either at Manchester Academy & Harris College, Oxford (2 to 4 years' study for an Oxford degree in Theology/or Theology & Philosophy or an Oxford Certificate in Theology/Religious Studies), or at the Unitarian College (Luther King House, Brighton Grove, Rusholme, Manchester; an individually designed contextual theology course of the Partnership for Theological Education which may lead to a degree or other academic qualification validated by Chester or Manchester University). Alternative arrangements can be made for candidates wishing to study through the Welsh language. Placement work and Unitarian studies are also integral to ministerial preparation. Training normally takes 2 or more years.

THE UNITED REFORMED CHURCH

Church House
86 Tavistock Place
London WC1H 9RT
Tel: 020 7916 2020
Fax: 020 7916 2021
E-mail: urc@urc.org.uk
Website: www.urc.org.uk

Candidates for **Ministry of Word and Sacraments** must have been a member of the URC for at least 2 years. and complete a candidating process. Most then take a 3- or 4-year course of part-time or full-time academic study alongside a minimum of 800 hours of pastoral placements. The minimum required outcome is a Diploma of Higher Education, in Theology. **Church-related Community Workers** strengthen the local church's mission through community development. Candidates are required to obtain at least a Diploma in Theology and a Diploma in Community Work before being commissioned.

Lay Preacher's Certificate: The qualifying course for this takes 3 years in local groups, residential weekends, and practical work in churches.

THE WESLEYAN REFORM UNION

Wesleyan Reform Church House
123 Queen Street
Sheffield S1 2DU
Tel: 0114 272 1938
E-mail: gen.sec@thewru.co.uk
Website: www.thewru.com

The Wesleyan Reform Union has no training college of its own and encourages candidates for its Ministry to enter a Bible College for 2 or 3 years. All candidates are, however, under the personal supervision of a Union Tutor, who directs a Biblical Studies & Training Department offering fairly extensive courses. Candidates attend Headquarters once a year for an oral exam in Theology conducted by the Tutor in the presence of the Union Examination Committee; they also take written exams.

UNITED FREE CHURCH OF SCOTLAND

11 Newton Place
Glasgow G3 7PR
Tel: 01413 323435
Fax: 01413 331973
E-mail: office@ufcos.org.uk
Website: www.ufcos.org.uk

The United Free Church of Scotland is a small presbyterian denomination which came into being in 1929. Those seeking to become candidates for the ministry should normally have been members of the denomination for at least a year. They will require to undertake a degree course in Theology.

CINEMA, FILM AND TELEVISION
Membership of Professional Institutions and Associations

BRITISH KINEMATOGRAPH SOUND AND TELEVISION SOCIETY (BKSTS)

Pinewood Studios
Pinewood Road
Iver Heath
Buckinghamshire SL0 0NH
Tel: 01753 656656
E-mail: info@bksts.com
Website: www.bksts.com

The BKSTS was founded in 1931 to serve the growing film industry and today arranges meetings, presentations, seminars, international exhibitions and conferences, as well as organizing an extensive programme of training courses, lectures, workshops and special events. We ensure that our members remain up to date with the latest techniques through master classes and our print and electronic publications.

MEMBERSHIP
Student Member
Associate Member
Full Member (MBKS)
Retired Member
Fellow (FBKS)

DESIGNATORY LETTERS
MBKS, FBKS

THE LONDON FILM SCHOOL

24 Shelton Street
Covent Garden
London WC2H 9UB
Tel: 020 7836 9642
Fax: 020 7497 3718
E-mail: info@lfs.org.uk
Website: www.lfs.org.uk

The LFS is one of the foremost independent film schools in Europe and is recognized by Skillset as a Centre of Excellence. It is a registered charity and a non-profit-making company, limited by guarantee. Since 1956 we have trained thousands of directors, cinematographers, editors and other film professionals from around the world.

QUALIFICATION/EXAMINATIONS
MA in Filmmaking (validated by London Metropolitan University)
MA in Screenwriting (validated by London Metropolitan University)
MA International Film Business
PhD Film by Practice

THE NATIONAL FILM AND TELEVISION SCHOOL

Beaconsfield Studios
Station Road
Beaconsfield
Buckinghamshire HP9 1LG
Tel: 01494 671234
Fax: 01494 674042
E-mail: info@nfts.co.uk
Website: www.nfts.co.uk

Creative Skillset Film Academy, the UK's leading film and television school, offers full-time MA and Diploma courses in all the key film and television disciplines, from Animation to VFX. Purpose-built studios include two film stages, a large television studio, and post-production facilities rivalling those of many professional companies.

QUALIFICATION/EXAMINATIONS
Diploma (in 1 of 8 disciplines)
MA in Film and Television (specializing in 1 of 13 disciplines)

CLEANING, LAUNDRY AND DRY CLEANING
Membership of Professional Institutions and Associations

BRITISH INSTITUTE OF CLEANING SCIENCE

9 Premier Court
Boarden Close
Moulton Park
Northampton
Northants NN3 6LF
Tel: 01604 678710
Fax: 01604 645988
E-mail: info@bics.org.uk
Website: www.bics.org.uk

The BICSc is the largest independent professional and educational body within the cleaning industry. Our aim is to raise the status and standards of the cleaning industry through training and education. We offer our 5,000 members a range of assessment schemes and training courses, together with a telephone and e-mail helpline.

MEMBERSHIP
Student
Competent
Technical
Member with Diploma
Fellow

QUALIFICATION/EXAMINATIONS
Cleaning Professional Skills Suite (CPSS)
Qualifications and Credit Framework

THE GUILD OF CLEANERS AND LAUNDERERS

56 Maple Drive
Larkhall
South Lanarkshire ML9 2AR
Tel: 01698 322669
E-mail: enquiries@gcl.org.uk
Website: www.gcl.org.uk

The Guild, formed in 1949, is a technical and professional society whose aim is to further knowledge and skill in all branches of the industry. We keep our members up to date through lectures, seminars and written reports, exchange information of mutual benefit with other organizations in the industry, and voice our opinion in relevant forums.

MEMBERSHIP
Young Guilder

Member
Associate (AGCL)
Advanced Member (AdGCL)
Licentiate (LGCL)
Fellow (FGCL)
Guild Plus Member

DESIGNATORY LETTERS
AGCL, AdGCL, LGCL, FGCL

COLOUR TECHNOLOGY

Membership of Professional Institutions and Associations

PAINTING AND DECORATING ASSOCIATION

32 Coton Road
Nuneaton
Warwickshire CV11 5TW
Tel: 024 7635 3776
Fax: 024 7635 4513
E-mail: info@paintingdecoratingassociation.co.uk
Website: www.paintingdecoratingassociation.co.uk

The PDA is a registered trade and employers' organization, catering exclusively for the needs of professional painting and decorating trade employers. The Association conducts no examinations, but all membership applications are scrutinized at branch level to ensure that only bona fide firms that agree to abide by our code of conduct are admitted.

MEMBERSHIP
Full Member
Associate

THE SOCIETY OF DYERS AND COLOURISTS

Perkin House
82 Grattan Road
Bradford BD1 2LU
Tel: 01274 725138
Fax: 01274 392888
E-mail: members@sdc.org.uk
Website: www.sdc.org.uk

An educational charity, professional body and chartered society, serving globally all aspects of the coloration industries including the textile supply chain through the knowledgeable and enthusiastic involvement of its professional members and industry partners. Recognized as the authority for colour science and technology, delivering high-quality international qualifications and training programmes.

MEMBERSHIP
Individual Voting Member, Individual Non-voting Member, Individual Student Member, Graduate Member, College Member, Company Member

QUALIFICATION/EXAMINATIONS
Fellowship (FSDC), Associateship (ASDC), Licentiateship (LSDC), Chartered Colourist (CCol)

DESIGNATORY LETTERS
FSDC, ASDC, LSDC, CCol

COMMUNICATIONS AND MEDIA
Membership of Professional Institutions and Associations

THE PICTURE RESEARCH ASSOCIATION

c/o 10 Marrick House
Mortimer Crescent
London NW6 5NY
Tel: 0771403017
E-mail: chair@picture-research.org.uk
Website: www.picture-research.org.uk

The PRA, founded in 1977, is a professional organization for picture researchers, picture editors and anyone specifically involved in the research, management and supply of visual material to the media industry. Our aims are to provide information and give support to our members, and to promote their interests and specific skills to potential employers.

MEMBERSHIP
Introductory Member
Full Member
Sponsors

QUALIFICATION/EXAMINATIONS
To qualify as a member of the Association you need a minimum of 2 years experience as a qualified picture researcher/picture editor, eg you were involved in the online search of images, working to a specific brief or project. You would have supplied both digital or analogue files for reproduction. You would also be required to have knowledge and experience of fee negotiations, clearances, copyright and licensing of photographic images from a selection of photographic sources and collections.
Sponsors: A full- or part-time employee of a picture library, picture agency or image archive who are directly involved in the supply of images to the media in general.

COMPUTING AND INFORMATION TECHNOLOGY
Membership of Professional Institutions and Associations

ASSOCIATION OF COMPUTER PROFESSIONALS

ACP
Chilverbridge House
Arlington
East Sussex BN26 6SB
Tel: 01323 871874
Fax: 01323 871875
E-mail: admin@acpexamboard.com
Website: www.acpexamboard.com

The ACP is an independent professional examining body, founded in 1984 to set and maintain standards of education that reflect the constantly changing requirements of the computer industry, both in the UK and overseas. We do so through the provision of course syllabuses and examinations to our carefully vetted training centres around the world.

MEMBERSHIP
Student
Practitioner
Graduate (GradACP)

Licentiate (LACP)
Associate (AACP)
Member (MACP)
Fellow (FACP)

QUALIFICATION/EXAMINATIONS
Please see the ACP's website for details of certificates and diplomas.

DESIGNATORY LETTERS
GradACP, LACP, AACP, MACP, FACP

BRITISH COMPUTER SOCIETY

1st Floor, Block D
North Star House
North Star Avenue
Swindon
Wiltshire SN2 1FA
Tel: 01793 417417
Fax: 01793 417444
E-mail: customerservices@hq.bcs.org.uk
Website: www.bcs.org.uk

The BCS is the professional membership and accreditation body for IT and has more than 70,000 members, including practitioners, businesses, academics and students, in the UK and internationally. Our aim is to promote the academic study and professional practice of computing and to show the public that IT is about far more than simply using a PC.

MEMBERSHIP
Student
Affiliate

Associate Member (AMBCS)
Professional Fellow (FBCS)
Honorary Fellow
Distinguished Fellow
Incorporated Engineer (IEng)
Chartered Engineer (CEng)
Chartered IT Professional (MBCS CITP)
Chartered Fellow (FBCS CITP)
Chartered Scientist (CSci)
Education Affiliate (institutional member)

QUALIFICATION/EXAMINATIONS
Certificate in IT
Certificate in IT for Insurance Professionals (developed jointly with The Chartered Insurance Institute)

Diploma in IT
Professional GradDip in IT

See the BCS website for details of other qualifications.

INSTITUTE FOR THE MANAGEMENT OF INFORMATION SYSTEMS

Suite A (Part) 2nd Floor
3 White Oak Square
London Road
Swanley
Kent BR8 7AG
Tel: 0845 850 0006
Fax: 0845 850 0007
E-mail: imis@bcs.org
Website: www.imis.org.uk

IMIS is one of the leading professional associations in the IT sector. A registered charity, it plays a prominent role in fostering greater understanding of IS management, in working to enhance the status of those engaged in the profession, and in promoting higher standards through better education and training worldwide.

MEMBERSHIP
Student Member
Practitioner Member
Licentiate Member (LIMIS)

Associate Member (AIMIS)
Full Member (MIMIS)
Fellow (FIMIS)

QUALIFICATION/EXAMINATIONS
Foundation
Diploma
Higher Diploma

DESIGNATORY LETTERS
LIMIS, AIMIS, MIMIS, FIMIS

INSTITUTION OF ANALYSTS AND PROGRAMMERS

Boundary House
Boston Road
London W7 2QE
Tel: 020 8434 3685
E-mail: admin@iap.org.uk
Website: www.iap.org.uk

The IAP is a professional organization for people who work in the development, installation and testing of business systems and computer software. Our aim is to promote high standards of competence and conduct among our members, to encourage them to develop their skills and progress their career, and to facilitate the advancement and spreading of knowledge within the profession.

MEMBERSHIP
Licentiate
Graduate (GradIAP)
Associate Member (AIAP)
Member (MIAP)
Fellow (FIAP)

DESIGNATORY LETTERS
GradIAP, AIAP, MIAP, FIAP

COUNSELLING
Membership of Professional Institutions and Associations

COUNSELLING LTD

Registered Office
5 Pear Tree Walk
Wakefield
West Yorkshire WF2 0HW
E-mail: via website
Website: www.counselling.ltd.uk

Counselling, a registered charity founded in 1998, is a membership organization for counsellors and psychotherapists in the UK that has established a network of about 2,700 affiliated CCC-registered counsellors, many of whom are able to provide occasional free or discounted face-to-face counselling with clients on low incomes.

MEMBERSHIP
Affiliate

COUNSELLORS AND PSYCHOTHERAPISTS IN PRIMARY CARE

PO Box 3379
Littlehampton BN16 9HL
Tel: 01243 870701
E-mail: cpc@cpc-online.co.uk
Website: www.cpc-online.co.uk

CPC is a professional membership association for individual practitioners, whose names are entered in a Register of Members. The aims of the Association are to represent counsellors and psychotherapists working in an NHS setting and to lead the way in establishing national standards and guidelines for further development of professional and effective counselling throughout the NHS.

MEMBERSHIP
Student
Subscriber
Intermediate Member
Registered Member
Supervisor
Organizational Member

QUALIFICATION/EXAMINATIONS
PGDip in Supervision for the Primary Care Setting

CSCT COUNSELLING TRAINING

13 Coleshill Street
Sutton Coldfield
West Midlands B72 1SD
Tel: 0121 321 1396
Fax: 0121 355 5581
E-mail: info@counsellingtraining.com
Website: www.counsellingtraining.com

CSCT has been producing counselling training courses for over 25 years, during which time we have trained over 50,000 students. Our courses are offered PT via a network of colleges and private providers throughout the UK. Our training materials are written to the specifications of the appropriate awarding body and we provide 24-hour e-mail and telephone support from Client Services and the Academic Team.

QUALIFICATION/EXAMINATIONS
Please see the CSCT's website.

CREDIT MANAGEMENT
Membership of Professional Institutions and Associations

INSTITUTE OF CREDIT MANAGEMENT

The Water Mill
Station Road
South Luffenham
Oakham
Leicestershire LE15 8NB
Tel: 01780 722900
Fax: 01780 721333
E-mail: info@icm.org.uk
Website: www.icm.org.uk

The ICM is the largest professional credit management organization in Europe and the only one accredited by Ofqual as an awarding body. We represent the credit profession across trade, consumer and export credit, as well as in related activities such as collections, credit reporting, credit insurance and insolvency, promote excellence in credit management and raise awareness of its vital role in business and the community.

MEMBERSHIP
Affiliate
Associate Member (AICM)
Graduate Member (MICM(Grad))
Member (MICM)
Fellow (FICM)

Corporate Member

QUALIFICATION/EXAMINATIONS
Certificate in Credit Management
Diploma in Credit Management
Level 5 Diploma in Credit Management
Certificate in Debt Collection
Diploma in Debt Collection
Certificate in Money and Debt Advice
Diploma in Money and Debt Advice
Certificate in High Court Enforcement (Level 4)
Diploma in High Court Enforcement (Level 4)
Diploma in High Court Enforcement (Level 5)

DESIGNATORY LETTERS
AICM, MICM (Grad), MICM, FIFA

DANCING
Membership of Professional Institutions and Associations

BRITISH BALLET ORGANIZATION

Woolborough House
39 Lonsdale Road
Barnes
London SW13 9JP
Tel: 020 8748 1241
Fax: 020 8748 1301
E-mail: info@bbo.org.uk
Website: www.bbo.org.uk

The BBO, founded in 1930, is an awarding body offering teacher training and examinations in classical ballet, tap, modern dance and jazz. We have schools throughout the UK and in several other countries.

MEMBERSHIP
Student Member

Senior Student Member
Affiliated Member
Student Teacher Member
Teacher Member

QUALIFICATION/EXAMINATIONS
Please see the BBO website for details.

IMPERIAL SOCIETY OF TEACHERS OF DANCING

Imperial House
22/26 Paul Street
London EC2A 4QE
Tel: +44 (0)20 7377 1577
Fax: +44 (0)20 7247 8829
E-mail: via website
Website: www.istd.org

The ISTD is a registered educational charity and examinations board. We aim to promote knowledge of dance, to maintain and improve teaching standards, and to qualify (by examination) teachers of dancing. Our dance techniques cover more than 12 different genres and are taught by more than 7,500 members by our members worldwide.

MEMBERSHIP
A range of 9 categories from Student to Life Membership.

QUALIFICATION/EXAMINATIONS
Please see our website www.istd.org or www.dance-teachers.org

DESIGNATORY LETTERS
ISTD

INTERNATIONAL DANCE TEACHERS' ASSOCIATION LIMITED

International House
76 Bennett Road
Brighton BN2 5JL
Tel: 01273 685652
Fax: 01273 674388
E-mail: via website
Website: www.idta.co.uk

The IDTA is one of the world's largest dance examination boards, with more than 7,000 members in 55 countries. Our aims are to promote knowledge and foster the art of dance in all its forms, to maintain and improve dancing standards, and to offer a comprehensive range of professional qualifications in all dance genres.

MEMBERSHIP
Associate (AIDTA)
Licentiate (LIDTA)
Fellow (FIDTA)

DESIGNATORY LETTERS
AIDTA, LIDTA, FIDTA

THE BENESH INSTITUTE

36 Battersea Square
London SW11 3RA
Tel: 020 7326 8031
Fax: 020 7924 3129
E-mail: beneshinstitute@rad.org.uk
Website: www.benesh.org

The Benesh Institute is the international centre for Benesh Movement Notation (BMN) founded in 1962 to promote, develop and offer education in BMN. We also function as an examining body and professional centre, and are responsible for coordinating technical developments. Since 1997 The Benesh Institute has been incorporated within the Royal Academy of Dance.

QUALIFICATION/EXAMINATIONS
Certificate in Benesh Movement Notation (CBMN) (validated by the Royal Academy of Dance)
Diploma for Professional Benesh Movement Notators (DPBMN) (validated by the Royal Academy of Dance)
Associate of the Institute of Choreology (AI Chor)

DENTISTRY
Membership of Professional Institutions and Associations

BRITISH ASSOCIATION OF CLINICAL DENTAL TECHNOLOGY

44–46 Wollaton Road
Beeston
Nottingham N69 2NR
Tel: 0115 957 5370
Fax: 0115 925 4800
E-mail: info@bacdt.org.uk
Website: www.bacdt.org.uk

The CDTA provides political and educational representation for its members, who are registered with the General Dental Council and trained in designing, creating, constructing, repairing and rebasing removable appliances to ensure optimal fit, maximum comfort and general wellbeing of patients. We are committed to team dentistry and ensure that our members work to the highest professional standards.

MEMBERSHIP
Full Membership
In training Membership
Practice Membership
Multi Practice Membership

BRITISH ASSOCIATION OF DENTAL NURSES

PO Box 4, Room 200
Hillhouse International Business Centre
Thornton-Cleveleys
Lancashire FY5 4QD
Tel: 01253 338360
E-mail: admin@badn.org.uk
Website: www.badn.org.uk

The BADN represents dental nurses, whether qualified or unqualified, working in general practice, hospital, the community, the armed forces, industry, practice management or reception, and has representation on the National Examining Board, the Dental Nurses Standards and Training Advisory Board and its Registration Committee, the Joint Consultative Committee, and other bodies.

MEMBERSHIP
Associate Member
Full Member

BRITISH SOCIETY OF DENTAL HYGIENE AND THERAPY

3 Kestrel Court
Waterwells Business Park
Gloucester GL2 2AT
Tel: 01452 886365
Fax: 01452 886468
E-mail: enquiries@bsdht.org.uk
Website: www.bsdht.org.uk

The BSDHT is the only nationally recognized body that represents dental hygienists, dental hygienist-therapists and students of dental hygiene. We have a membership of more than 3,500 in the UK and beyond, and look after their interests through liaising with the Department of Health, General Dental Council, British Dental Association and other organizations.

MEMBERSHIP
Member

DENTAL TECHNOLOGISTS ASSOCIATION

3 Kestral Court
Waterwells Drive
Waterwells Business Park
Gloucester GL2 2AT
Tel: 01452 886366
E-mail: via website
Website: www.dta-uk.org

The DTA is an organization that supports the development of the dental technology profession by encouraging and promoting education, including CPD, and for the exchange of views between dental technicians. We advise, develop and support dental technicians and maintain links with the government, other dental organizations, service providers and the public.

MEMBERSHIP
Member

GENERAL DENTAL COUNCIL

37 Wimpole Street
London W1G 8DQ
Tel: 0845 222 4141
E-mail: information@gdc-uk.org
Website: www.gdc-uk.org

The GDC regulates dental professionals in the UK. All dentists, clinical dental technicians, dental hygienists, dental nurses, dental technicians, dental therapists and orthodontic therapists must be registered with the GDC in order to work in the UK.

THE BRITISH DENTAL ASSOCIATION

64 Wimpole Street
London W1G 8YS
Tel: 020 7935 0875
Fax: 020 7487 5232
E-mail: enquiries@bda.org
Website: www.bda.org

The BDA, which was founded in 1880, is the professional association and trade union for dentists in the UK. Our aims are to advance the science, arts and ethics of dentistry, improve the UK's oral health, and promote the interests of our members. Membership, which is voluntary, stands at around 23,000, mostly in general practice.

MEMBERSHIP
Essential
Extra
Expert

DIETETICS
Membership of Professional Institutions and Associations

THE BRITISH DIETETIC ASSOCIATION

5th Floor
Charles House
148–49 Great Charles Street Queensway
Birmingham B3 3HT
Tel: 0121 200 8080
Fax: 0121 200 8081
E-mail: info@bda.uk.com
Website: www.bda.uk.com

The BDA, established in 1936, is the UK's leading professional association and trade union for dietitians. Our aims are to advance the science and practice of dietetics and associated subjects, to promote education and training in the science and practice of dietetics and associated subjects, and to regulate relations between our 8,000+ members and their employers.

MEMBERSHIP
Full Member
Associate Member
Affiliate Member
Alliance Member
Student Member
International Member

DISTRIBUTION
Membership of Professional Institutions and Associations

THE CHARTERED INSTITUTE OF LOGISTICS AND TRANSPORT (UK)

Earlstrees Court
Earlstrees Road
Corby
Northamptonshire NN17 4AX
Tel: 01536 740104
Fax: 01536 740103
E-mail: membership@ciltuk.org.uk
Website: www.ciltuk.org.uk

The Chartered Institute of Logistics and Transport in the UK – CILT(UK) – is the independent professional body for transport, logistics, supply chain management and has more than 18,000 members in the industry. Our aim is to facilitate the development of personal and professional excellence.

MEMBERSHIP
Learner Affiliate
Full Time Student
Apprentice Affiliate
e-Member Affiliate
Corporate Affiliate
Affiliate
Corporate Affiliate
Member (MILT)
Chartered Member (CMILT)
Chartered Fellow (FCILT)

QUALIFICATION/EXAMINATIONS
Regulated Qualifications cover the Institute's eight professional sectors: Supply Chain, Transport Planning, Rail, Active Travel and Travel Planning, Bus and Coach, Ports Maritime and Waterways, Freight Forwarding and Aviation. CILT(UK) works in partnership with the Institute of Operations Management to develop and award regulated qualifications for the manufacturing and service sectors.

Level 1 – Award
Level 2 – Award, Certificate, Diploma
Level 3 – Award, Certificate
Level 5 – Award, Certificate, Diploma, Professional Diploma
Level 6 – Advanced Diploma

Accredited Qualifications
Humanitarian Logistics (3 programmes)
Supply Chain Practitioner Award (Foundation, Professional and Master programmes)
Certificate of Customs Competency
Certificate in Traffic and Transport

Partnerships
Certified European Logistician (Junior, Senior, Master programmes)
MSc in International Transport and Logistics or International Logistics and Supply Chain Management

DESIGNATORY LETTERS
MILT, CMILT, FCILT

DRAMATIC AND PERFORMING ARTS
Membership of Professional Institutions and Associations

DRAMA UK

Woburn House
20 Tavistock Square
London WC1H 9HB
Tel: 020 3393 6141
E-mail: info@dramauk.co.uk
Website: www.dramauk.co.uk

Drama UK was formed in 2012 following the merger of the National Council for Drama Training and the Conference of Drama Schools.

We act as an advocate for quality drama training; offer advice to students of all ages; and award a quality mark to the very best drama training available.

EQUITY

Guild House
Upper St Martins Lane
London WC2H 9EG
Tel: 020 7379 6000
E-mail: info@equity.org.uk
Website: www.equity.org.uk

Equity is the UK trade union representing professional performers and other creative workers from across the entertainment, creative and cultural industries. The main function of Equity is to negotiate minimum terms and conditions of employment for its members and to represent its members' interests to the government and other bodies.

MEMBERSHIP
Student Member
Graduate Member
Full Member

THE BRITISH (THEATRICAL) ARTS

12 Deveron Way
Rise Park
Romford
Essex RM1 4UL
Tel: 01708 756263
E-mail: sally.chennelle1@ntlworld.com
Website: www.britisharts.org

The British Arts is a non-profit-making organization dedicated to maintaining and where necessary raising the standard of the teaching of Performing Arts subjects. We work to encourage a strong technical foundation combined with an understanding of professional theatrical presentation and conduct exams in Dramatic Art, Classical & Stage Ballet, Mime, Tap, Musical Theatre and Modern Dance.

MEMBERSHIP
Student Member

Companion
Associate (Teaching and Non-teaching)
Member (Teaching and Non-teaching)
Advanced Teacher Member

Fellow

QUALIFICATION/EXAMINATIONS
Please see the British Arts website.

DRIVING INSTRUCTORS
Membership of Professional Institutions and Associations

REGISTER OF APPROVED DRIVING INSTRUCTORS

The Axis Building
112 Upper Parliament Street
Nottingham NG1 6LP
Tel: 0300 200 1122
E-mail: ADIReg@dsa.gsi.gov.uk

The Register of Approved Driving Instructors (ADI) and the licensing scheme for trainee instructors (PDI) are administered under the provisions of the Road Traffic Act 1988 by the Department for Transport (DfT). It is an offence for anyone to give professional instruction (that is instruction paid for by or in respect of the pupil) in driving a motor car unless: (a) his or her name is on the Register of Approved Driving Instructors; or (b) he or she holds a 'trainee's licence to give instruction' issued by the Registrar.

QUALIFICATION/EXAMINATIONS
Please see the GOV.UK website (www.gov.uk/apply-to-become-a-driving-instructor) for details of the qualifying examinations.

EMBALMING
Membership of Professional Institutions and Associations

INTERNATIONAL EXAMINATIONS BOARD OF EMBALMERS

146 Alexandra Road
Great Wakering
Essex SS3 0GW
Tel: 01702 218907
E-mail: admin@iebe.co.uk

The Board examines candidates who wish to become qualified members of the British Institute of Embalmers (qv), which is not itself an examining body but can provide information packs (also available from the above address) that contain lists of approved schools and accredited tutors.

THE BRITISH INSTITUTE OF EMBALMERS

Anubis House
21c Station Road
Knowle
Solihull
West Midlands B93 0HL
Tel: 01564 778991
Fax: 01564 770812
E-mail: info@bioe.co.uk
Website: www.bioe.co.uk

The BIE, founded in 1927, is an organization for professional embalmers. Its objectives include supporting and protecting the status, character and interests of embalmers, promoting the efficient tuition of persons seeking to become embalmers, and encouraging the study and practice of improved methods of embalming.

MEMBERSHIP
Member (MBIE)
Fellow (FBIE)

DESIGNATORY LETTERS
MBIE, FBIE

EMPLOYMENT AND CAREERS SERVICES
Membership of Professional Institutions and Associations

CAREER DEVELOPMENT INSTITUTE

Ground Floor
Copthall House
1 New Road
Stourbridge
West Midlands DY8 1PH
Tel: 01384 376464
E-mail: hq@thecdi.net
Website: www.thecdi.net

The CDI is the largest UK-wide professional association for career development professionals. Our aim is to support members and promote access to high-quality career development services, delivered by professionally qualified staff working within an appropriate ethical framework. Suitably qualified members can join the UK Register of Career Development Professionals.

MEMBERSHIP
Student Member

Full Member
Affiliate Organisation
School Affiliate

QUALIFICATION/EXAMINATIONS
 Qualification in Career Guidance (QCG)
Qualification in Career Guidance and Development (QCGD)
Certificate in Career Guidance Theory (CCGT)
Certificate in Careers Leadership (CCL)

RECRUITMENT AND EMPLOYMENT CONFEDERATION

Dorset House
First Floor
27–45 Stamford Street
London SE1 9NT
Tel: 020 7009 2100
E-mail: info@rec.uk.com
Website: www.rec.uk.com

The REC is the representative body for the UK's £27 billion private recruitment and staffing industry, with a membership of more than 8,000 Corporate Members comprising agencies and businesses from all sectors, and 6,000 members of the Institute of Recruitment Professionals (IRP) made up of recruitment consultants and other industry professionals.

MEMBERSHIP
Affiliate (AIRP)
Member (MIRP)
Fellow (FIRP)

QUALIFICATION/EXAMINATIONS
Certificate in Recruitment Practice (QCF)
Diploma in Recruitment Practice (QCF)
Diploma in Recruitment Management (QCF)

DESIGNATORY LETTERS
AIRP, MIRP, FIRP

ENGINEERING, AERONAUTICAL
Membership of Professional Institutions and Associations

ROYAL AERONAUTICAL SOCIETY

4 Hamilton Place
Hyde Park Corner
London W1J 7BQ
Tel: 020 7670 4300
Fax: 020 7670 4309
E-mail: raes@aerosociety.com
Website: www.aerosociety.com

The RAeS, founded in 1866 to further the science of aeronautics, is a multidisciplinary professional institution dedicated to the global aerospace community. We work on our members' behalf to promote the highest professional standards in all aerospace disciplines, to provide specialist information and act as a central forum for the exchange of ideas, and to play a leading role in influencing opinion on aviation matters.

MEMBERSHIP
Student Affiliate
Affiliate
Associate (ARAeS)
Associate Member (AMRAeS)
Member (MRAeS)
Companion (CRAeS)
Fellow (FRAeS)
Apprentice

ENGINEERING, AGRICULTURAL
Membership of Professional Institutions and Associations

BRITISH AGRICULTURAL AND GARDEN MACHINERY ASSOCIATION

Middleton House
2 Main Road
Middleton Cheney
Oxfordshire OX17 2TN
Tel: 01295 713344
Fax: 01295 711665
E-mail: info@bagma.com
Website: www.bagma.com

BAGMA is the trade association representing agricultural and garden machinery dealers in the UK. We have some 850 dealer members and 75 affiliated suppliers and allied industry companies. We offer a range of training and assessment courses through our online learning package and at approved Training and Assessment Centres.

QUALIFICATION/EXAMINATIONS
Please see the BAGMA website.

THE INSTITUTION OF AGRICULTURAL ENGINEERS

The Bullock Building
University Way
Cranfield
Bedford
Bedfordshire MK43 0GH
Tel: 01234 750876
Fax: 01234 751319
E-mail: secretary@iagre.org
Website: www.iagre.org

The IAgrE is the professional body for engineers, scientists, technologists and managers in agricultural and allied land-based industries, including forestry, food engineering and technology, amenity, renewable energy, horticulture and the environment. The IAgrE also administers the Landbased Engineering Technician Accreditation schemes (LTA) for the industry.

MEMBERSHIP
Student
Associate (AIAgrE)
Associate Member (AMIAgrE)
Member (MIAgrE)
Fellow (FIAgrE)
Honorary Fellow

QUALIFICATION/EXAMINATIONS
Chartered Engineer (CEng), Chartered Environmentalist (CEnv), Incorporated Engineer (IEng), Engineering Technician (EngTech)

DESIGNATORY LETTERS
AIAgrE, AMIAgrE, MIAgrE, FIAgrE

ENGINEERING, AUTOMOBILE
Membership of Professional Institutions and Associations

INSTITUTE OF AUTOMOTIVE ENGINEER ASSESSORS

The Firs
High Street
Whitchurch
Buckinghamshire HP22 4JU
Tel: 01296 642895
Fax: 01296 640044
E-mail: sally@theiaea.org
Website: www.iaea-online.org

The IAEA, a Professional Affiliate of the Engineering Council, was founded in 1932 and now represents more than 1,500 automotive engineer assessors responsible for activities such as vehicle damage assessment, accident reconstruction, investigation of mechanical failures, electrical failures and vehicle fires, providing expert witness testimony, repair assessment, car fleet surveys, and conciliation and arbitration.

MEMBERSHIP
Affiliate (AffInstAEA)
Associate (AInstAEA)
Member (MInstAEA)
Fellow (FInstAEA)

Honorary Fellow (HFInstAEA)

QUALIFICATION/EXAMINATIONS
Basic Principles of Maths & Physics Application to Accident Reconstruction
Motor Vehicle Legislation as related to Insurance Principles
Principles and Practice of Vehicle Damage Assessment
Motor Insurance
Automotive Technology

DESIGNATORY LETTERS
AffInstAEA, AInstAEA,MInstAEA, FInstAEA

THE INSTITUTE OF THE MOTOR INDUSTRY

Fanshaws
Brickendon
Hertford SG13 8PQ
Tel: 01992 511521
Fax: 01992 511548
E-mail: comms@theimi.org.uk
Website: www.motor.org.uk and www.automotivetechnician.org.uk

The IMI is the professional association for individuals working in the motor industry and exists to help individuals and employers improve professional standards and performance by qualifying, recognizing and developing people. We are the Sector Skills Council for the automotive retail industry, a Licensed Member of the Engineering Council and the governing body for Automotive Technician Accreditation (ATA) – the UK's first national voluntary assessment system for vehicle technicians.

MEMBERSHIP
Affiliate (AffIMI)
Licentiate (LIMI)
Associate (AMIMI)
Member (MIMI)
Fellow (FIMI)
For technicians only, there are two special IMI awards recognizing technical qualifications and experience:
AAE (Advanced Automotive Engineer)

CAE (Certificated Automotive Engineer)

DESIGNATORY LETTERS
AffIMI, LIMI, AMIMI, MIMI, FIMI, AAE, CAE

ENGINEERING, BUILDING SERVICES
Membership of Professional Institutions and Associations

THE CHARTERED INSTITUTION OF BUILDING SERVICES ENGINEERS

222 Balham High Road
London SW12 9BS
Tel: 020 8675 5211
Fax: 020 8675 5449
Website: www.cibse.org

CIBSE is the professional body for people involved in the design, construction, operation and maintenance of the engineering elements of a building other than its structure and enables it to operate efficiently by saving energy and contributing to a low carbon built environment. This includes heating, ventilation, air conditioning, electrical services, lighting etc.

MEMBERSHIP
Student Affiliate
Affiliate
Graduate
Companion
Licentiate (LCIBSE)
Associate (ACIBSE)
Member (MCIBSE)

Fellow (FCIBSE)
CIBSE is a licensed institution of the Engineering Council. This means that, as well as joining CIBSE, you will be Registered as a Chartered Engineer (CEng), Incorporated Engineer (IEng) or Engineering Technician (EngTech) when you have reached the appropriate level of qualification and professional skill.

QUALIFICATION/EXAMINATIONS
Please see the CIBSE website for more information www.cibse.org

DESIGNATORY LETTERS
LCIBSE, ACIBSE, MCIBSE, FCIBSE

ENGINEERING, CHEMICAL
Membership of Professional Institutions and Associations

THE INSTITUTION OF CHEMICAL ENGINEERS

Davis Building
Railway Terrace
Rugby
Warwickshire CV21 3HQ
Tel: 01788 578214
Fax: 01788 560833
E-mail: customerservices@icheme.org
Website: www.icheme.org

The IChemE, founded in 1922, is an international professional membership organization for chemical, biochemical and process engineers, and we have some 30,000 members in more than 113 countries. We promote competence and a commitment to sustainable development, advance the discipline for the benefit of society, and support the professional development of our members.

MEMBERSHIP
Student
Affiliate
Associate Member (AMIChemE)
Member (MIChemE)
Fellow (FIChemE)
Chartered Chemical Engineer (CEng MIChemE)
Chartered Engineer (CEng)

Chartered Scientist (CSci)
Chartered Environmentalist (CEnv)
Associate Fellow

DESIGNATORY LETTERS
AMIChemE, MIChemE, FIChemE, CEng MIChemE, CEng, CSci, CEnv

ENGINEERING, CIVIL
Membership of Professional Institutions and Associations

INSTITUTION OF CIVIL ENGINEERS

1 Great George Street
Westminster
London SW1P 3AA
Tel: 020 7222 7722
E-mail: membership@ice.org.uk
Website: www.ice.org.uk

The ICE is a UK-based international organization with 80,000 members that strives to promote and progress civil engineering around the world. Our purpose is to qualify professionals engaged in civil engineering, exchange knowledge and best practice, and support our members, and in the UK we liaise with government and publish reports on civil engineering issues.

MEMBERSHIP
Student
Graduate
Affiliate
Technician Member
Associate Member (AMICE)
Member (MICE)
Companion
Fellow (FICE)

ENGINEERING, ELECTRICAL, ELECTRONIC AND MANUFACTURING
Membership of Professional Institutions and Associations

INSTITUTION OF LIGHTING PROFESSIONALS

Regent House
Regent Place
Rugby
Warwickshire CV21 2PN
Tel: 01788 576492
E-mail: info@theilp.org.uk
Website: www.theilp.org.uk

The ILP is a professional lighting association with about 2,000 members, including lighting designers, consultants and engineers. We are dedicated to excellence in lighting and to raising awareness about the important contribution of lighting in road safety, crime prevention and the environment. We support members by providing technical advice and encourage their CPD through our monthly journal and by holding a wide range of conferences, regional meetings, seminars and courses.

MEMBERSHIP
Student
Affiliate
Associate Member (AMILP)
Member (MILP)
Fellow (FILP)

Corporate Member
Engineering Technician (EngTech)
Incorporated Engineer (IEng)
Chartered Engineer (CEng)

QUALIFICATION/EXAMINATIONS
Exterior Lighting Diploma
LET Diploma in Lighting

DESIGNATORY LETTERS
AMILP, MILP, FILP, EngTech, IEng, CEng

THE INSTITUTION OF ENGINEERING AND TECHNOLOGY

Michael Faraday House
Stevenage
Hertfordshire SG1 2AY
Tel: 01438 313311
Fax: 01438 765526
E-mail: postmaster@theiet.org
Website: www.theiet.org

The IET is working to engineer a better world through our mission to inspire, inform and influence the global engineering community, supporting technology innovation to meet the needs of society. The IET has over 163,000 members in 127 countries, with offices in Europe, North America, South Asia and Asia-Pacific.

MEMBERSHIP
Student
Associate

Member (MIET)
Fellow (FIET)
Honorary Fellow
ICT Technician (ICTTech)
Engineering Technician (EngTech)
Incorporated Engineer (IEng)
Chartered Engineer (CEng)

DESIGNATORY LETTERS
FIET, ICTTech, EngTech, IEng, CEng, MIET

ENGINEERING, ENERGY
Membership of Professional Institutions and Associations

ENERGY INSTITUTE

61 New Cavendish Street
London W1G 7AR
Tel: 020 7467 7100
Fax: 020 7255 1472
E-mail: info@energyinst.org
Website: www.energyinst.org

The EI is the chartered professional membership body for the energy industry, providing learning and networking opportunities, professional recognition and energy knowledge resources for individuals and companies worldwide. We offer professional qualifications including Chartered, Incorporated and Engineering Technician status for engineers, as well as

Chartered Scientist, Chartered Energy Manager and Chartered Environmentalist.

MEMBERSHIP
Student Member
Affiliate
Graduate Member (GradEI)
Member (MEI)
Fellow (FEI)
Engineering Technician (EngTech)

Incorporated Engineer (IEng)
Chartered Engineer (CEng)
Chartered Scientist (CSci)
Chartered Environmentalist (CEnv)
Chartered Energy Manager (exclusive EI title)
Chartered Energy Engineer (exclusive EI title)
Chartered Petroleum Engineer (exclusive EI title)

DESIGNATORY LETTERS
GradEI, MEI, FEI, EngTech, IEng, CEng, CEnv, CSci

ENGINEERING, ENVIRONMENTAL
Membership of Professional Institutions and Associations

INSTITUTE OF ENVIRONMENTAL MANAGEMENT AND ASSESSMENT

Saracen House
Lincoln LN6 7AS
Tel: 01522 540069
Fax: 01522 540090
E-mail: info@iema.net
Website: www.iema.net

The IEMA is a not-for-profit membership organization that provides recognition and support to environmental professionals and promotes sustainable development through improved environmental practice and performance. We have about 15,000 individual and corporate members in 87 countries, in the public, private and non-governmental sectors.

MEMBERSHIP
Student Member
Affiliate Member
Graduate Member
Associate (AIEMA)

Full Member (MIEMA)
Fellow (FIEMA)
Chartered Environmentalist (CEnv)
Corporate Member

QUALIFICATION/EXAMINATIONS
Foundation Certificate in Environmental Management
Associate Certificate in Environmental Management
Diploma

DESIGNATORY LETTERS
AIEMA, MIEMA, FIEMA, CEnv

THE CHARTERED INSTITUTION OF WATER AND ENVIRONMENTAL MANAGEMENT

15 John Street
London WC1N 2EB
Tel: 020 7831 3110
Fax: 020 7405 4967
E-mail: via website
Website: www.ciwem.org

Founded in 1895, CIWEM is an independent professional body and registered charity with 12,000 members that advances the science and practice of water and environmental management for a clean, green and sustainable world by promoting environmental excellence and professional development and training, supplying independent advice and evidence-based opinion, and providing a forum for debate through conferences, technical meetings and its publications.

MEMBERSHIP
Student

Associate ACIWEM
Graduate
Member MCIWEM C.WEM
Fellow FCIWEM C.WEM
Environmental Partner

Chartered Engineer (CEng)
Chartered Environmentalist (CEnv)
Chartered Scientist (CSci)

QUALIFICATION/EXAMINATIONS
Online training courses in partnership with Staffordshire University, accredited university courses at 12 leading institutions, CPD modules and Rural Environmental Management Programme

DESIGNATORY LETTERS
CEng, CEnv, CSi, C.WEM

THE SOCIETY OF ENVIRONMENTAL ENGINEERS

The Manor House
High Street
Buntingford
Hertfordshire SG9 9AB
Tel: 01763 271209
Fax: 01763 273255
E-mail: office@environmental.org.uk
Website: www.environmental.org.uk

The SEE, founded in 1959, is a professional society that promotes awareness of the discipline of environmental engineering (the measurement, modelling, control and simulation of all types of environment). We provide members with information, training and representation within this field and encourage communication and good practice in quality, reliability, and cost-effective product development and manufacture.

MEMBERSHIP
Student
Member
Corporate Member
Engineering Technician (EngTech)
Incorporated Engineer (IEng)
Chartered Engineer (CEng)

DESIGNATORY LETTERS
EngTech, IEng, CEng

ENGINEERING, FIRE
Membership of Professional Institutions and Associations

ASSOCIATION OF PRINCIPAL FIRE OFFICERS

9–11 Pebble Close
Amington
Tamworth
Staffordshire B77 4RD
Tel: 01827 302300
Fax: 01827 302399
E-mail: enquiries@apfo.org.uk
Website: www.apfo.org.uk

The APFO is the staff association of the most senior Fire Officers in the UK. Our objectives are: to represent and promote the interests of members in conditions of service and legal and employment matters; to negotiate and promote the settlement of disputes involving members; to provide assistance to members and their dependants in exceptional circumstances; and to provide support to members in matters concerning employment or a work-related injury.

MEMBERSHIP
Associate Member
Lifetime Past Member

CHIEF FIRE OFFICERS' ASSOCIATION

9–11 Pebble Close
Amington
Tamworth
Staffordshire B77 4RD
Tel: 01827 302300
Fax: 01827 302399
Website: www.cfoa.org.uk

The CFOA is a professional membership association of the most senior fire officers in the UK. We provide independent advice to the government, local authorities and others. Our aim is to reduce loss of life, personal injury and damage to property by improving the quality of fire fighting, rescue, fire protection and fire prevention in the UK.

MEMBERSHIP
Member

THE INSTITUTION OF FIRE ENGINEERS

IFE House
64–66 Cygnet Court
Timothy's Bridge Road
Stratford-upon-Avon CV37 9NW
Tel: 01789 261 463
Fax: 01789 296 426
E-mail: info@ife.org.uk
Website: www.ife.org.uk

The IFE, founded in 1918, is a non-profit-making professional body for fire professionals and has more than 12,000 members worldwide. Our aim is to encourage and improve the science and practice of fire extinction, fire prevention and fire engineering, to enhance technical networks, and to give advice and support to our members for the benefit of the community at large.

MEMBERSHIP
Student
Affiliate Member
Technician (TIFireE)
Graduate (GIFireE)
Associate (AIFireE)
Member (MIFireE)

Fellow (FIFireE)
Engineering Technician (EngTech)
Incorporated Engineer (IEng)
Chartered Engineer (CEng)
Affiliate Organization

QUALIFICATION/EXAMINATIONS
IFE Certificate in Fire Science, Operations and Safety (Level 2)
IFE Certificate in Fire Science, Operations, Fire Safety and Management (Level 3)
IFE Diploma in Fire Science and Fire Safety (Level 3)

DESIGNATORY LETTERS
TIFireE, GIFireE, AIFireE, MIFireE, FIFireE, EngTech, IEng, CEng

ENGINEERING, GAS
Membership of Professional Institutions and Associations

THE INSTITUTION OF GAS ENGINEERS AND MANAGERS

IGEM House
High Street
Kegworth
Derbyshire DE74 2DA
Tel: 0844 375 4436
Fax: 01509 678198
E-mail: general@igem.org.uk
Website: www.igem.org.uk

IGEM is licensed by EC(UK) and serves a wide range of professionals in the UK and international gas industry through membership and technical standards, having a diverse membership ranging from university students to qualified professionals. Anyone working or interested in the gas industry can form positive connections to enhance their career through IGEM.

MEMBERSHIP
Student Member
Associate (AIGEM)
Associate Member (AMIGEM)
Graduate Member (GradIGEM)
Member Manager (MIGEM)
Technician Member (Eng Tech (MIGEM))
Incorporated Member (I Eng (MIGEM))

Chartered Member (C Eng (MIGEM))	*DESIGNATORY LETTERS*
Fellow (C Eng (FIGEM))	MIGEM, Eng Tech (MIGEM), I Eng (MIGEM), C Eng
	(MIGEM), C Eng (FIGEM)

ENGINEERING, GENERAL
Membership of Professional Institutions and Associations

ASSOCIATION OF COST ENGINEERS

Lea House
Sandbach
Cheshire CW11 1XL
Tel: 01270 764798
Fax: 01270 766180
E-mail: enquiries@acoste.org.uk
Website: www.acoste.org.uk

The ACostE represents the professional interests of those with responsibility for the prediction, planning and control of resources for engineering, manufacturing and construction. As a Professional Affiliate of The Engineering Council, we can propose suitably qualified members for the award of the titles of Chartered Engineer (CEng) and Incorporated Engineer (IEng).

MEMBERSHIP
Student
Associate (AA Cost E)
Companion (Companion A Cost E)

Graduate (Grad A Cost E)
Member (MA Cost E)
Fellow (FA Cost E)
Honorary Fellow (Hon FA Cost E)
Certified Cost Engineer (CCE)
Engineering Technician (EngTech)
Incorporated Engineer (IEng)
Chartered Engineer (CEng)

DESIGNATORY LETTERS
AA Cost E, Companion A Cost E, Grad A Cost E, MA Cost E, FA Cost E, CCE, EngTech, IEng, CEng

INSTITUTE OF MEASUREMENT AND CONTROL

87 Gower Street
London WC1E 6AF
Tel: 020 7387 4949
Fax: 020 7388 8431
E-mail: membership@instmc.org.uk
Website: www.instmc.org.uk

The IMC is a multidisciplinary body that brings together thinkers and practitioners from the many disciplines that have a common interest in measurement and control. Our object is to promote for the public benefit, by all available means, the general advancement of the science and practice of measurement and control technology and its application.

MEMBERSHIP
Student Member
Affiliate Member
Associate Member
Member (MemInstMC)
Fellow (FInstMC)
Honorary Fellow (HonFInstMC)

SEMTA – THE SECTOR SKILLS COUNCIL FOR SCIENCE, ENGINEERING AND MANUFACTURING TECHNOLOGIES

14 Upton Road
Watford
Hertfordshire WD18 0JT
Tel: 0845 643 9001
E-mail: via website
Website: www.semta.org.uk

Semta is part of the Skills for Business network of 25 employer-led Sector Skills Councils in the UK and works with employers in the aerospace, automotive, electrical, electronics, marine, mechanical, metals and science & bioscience sectors to ascertain their current and future skills needs and provide short- and long-term solutions to meet those needs.

THE ENGINEERING COUNCIL

2nd Floor
246 High Holborn
London WC1V 7EX
Tel: 020 3206 0500
Fax: 020 3206 0501
Website: www.engc.org.uk

The Engineering Council holds the national registers of Engineering Technicians (EngTech), Incorporated Engineers (IEng), Chartered Engineers (CEng) and Information and Communications Technology Technicians (ICTTech). We set and maintain internationally recognised standards of competence and ethics, ensuring that employers, government and society can have confidence in registrants' skills and commitment.

DESIGNATORY LETTERS
EngTech, IEng, CEng, ICTTech

WOMEN'S ENGINEERING SOCIETY

Michael Faraday House
Six Hills Way
Stevenage
Herts SG1 2AY
Tel: 01438 765506
E-mail: info@wes.org.uk
Website: www.wes.org.uk

The WES, founded in 1919, is a professional, not-for-profit network of women engineers, scientists and technologists, who offer inspiration, support and professional development. Working in partnership, we campaign to encourage women to participate and achieve as engineers, scientists and as leaders.

MEMBERSHIP
Student Member

Associate
Full Member (MWES)
Fellow
Company Member

DESIGNATORY LETTERS
WES

ENGINEERING, MARINE
Membership of Professional Institutions and Associations

THE INSTITUTE OF MARINE ENGINEERING, SCIENCE AND TECHNOLOGY

33 Aldgate High Street
London EC3N 1EN
Tel: +44 (0)20 7382 2600
Fax: +44 (0)20 7382 2670
E-mail: via website
Website: www.imarest.org

The IMarEST, established in 1889, is the leading international membership body and learned society for marine professionals and has more than 15,000 members worldwide. We have a strong international presence, with a network of 50 international branches, affiliations with major marine societies around the world, representation on the key marine technical committees and non-governmental status at the International Maritime Organization.

MEMBERSHIP
Membership Categories

IMarEST membership is open to everyone with an interest in the marine world across scientific, engineering and technological disciplines and applications.

Categories of membership are available to those who are seeking professional recognition, those who are currently studying or just starting out in their careers, or those who simply have a general interest in the IMarEST and its activities. There are no academic requirements for Non-corporate Membership of the IMarEST. However, professionals seeking Corporate Membership will require certain academic qualifications according to the type of membership being sought.

Corporate Membership Categories
Fellow (FIMarEST)

Fellows are those who qualify for the category of Member and have demonstrated to the satisfaction of Council a level of knowledge and understanding, competence and commitment involving superior responsibility for the conceptual design, management or the execution of important work in a marine related profession, and have given a commitment to abide by the Institute's Code of Professional Conduct.

Member (MIMarEST)

Members are those who qualify for the category of Associate Member and have demonstrated to the satisfaction of Council that they have achieved a position of professional standing having normally been professionally engaged in the marine sector for a period of 5 years that includes significant responsibility and have given a commitment to abide by the Institute's Code of Professional Conduct.

Associate Member (AMIMarEST)

Associate Members are those demonstrating to the satisfaction of Council that they have achieved a position as a technician, or are professionally engaged in Initial Professional Development or occupy an occupational role in the marine sector, and have given a commitment to abide by the Institute's Code of Professional Conduct.

Non-corporate Membership Categories
Affiliate

Affiliates may either be those with an interest in, or who may contribute to, the activities of the Institute; or persons who, in the opinion of Council, can contribute to, or wish to have access to, the technical services of the Institute, being resident in a recognized overseas territory and also members of a professional society with which the Institute has a reciprocal arrangement.

Student (SIMarEST)

Student members are those enrolled on a programme of further or higher education accredited or recognized by the IMarEST.

Professional Registration

In addition to membership, the IMarEST is licensed to provide a range of registers covering the fields of engineering, science and technology. In addition, the IMarEST's Royal Charter empowers the Institute to offer registers designed to meet the specific needs of the marine profession. Corporate members can become registered (chartered) as follows:

Engineers
Chartered Engineer (CEng)
Chartered Marine Engineer (CMarEng)

Incorporated Engineer (IEng)
Incorporated Marine Engineer (IMarEng)
Engineering Technician (EngTech)
Marine Engineering Technician (MarEngTech)
Scientists
Chartered Scientist (CSci)
Chartered Marine Scientist (CMarSci)
Registered Marine Scientist (RMarSci)

Marine Technician (MarTech)
Technologists
Chartered Marine Technologist (CMarTech)
Registered Marine Technologist (RMarTech)
Marine Technician (MarTech)

DESIGNATORY LETTERS
SIMarEST, AMIMarEST, MIMarEST, FIMarEST

ENGINEERING, MECHANICAL
Membership of Professional Institutions and Associations

INSTITUTION OF MECHANICAL ENGINEERS

1 Birdcage Walk
Westminster
London SW1H 9JJ
Tel: 020 7222 7899
E-mail: enquiries@imeche.org
Website: www.imeche.org

The IMechE is a professional engineering body with about 80,000 members. Our aims are to promote sustainable energy and engineering sustainable supply, economic growth while mitigating and adapting to climate change and the depletion of natural resources, and safe, efficient transport systems to ensure less congestion and emissions, and to inspire, prepare and support tomorrow's engineers so we can respond to society's changes.

MEMBERSHIP
Affiliate

Associate Member (AMIMechE)
Member (MIMechE)
Fellow (FIMechE)
Engineering Technician (EngTech)
Incorporated Engineer (IEng)
Chartered Engineer (CEng)

DESIGNATORY LETTERS
AMIMechE, MIMechE, FIMechE, EngTech, IEng, CEng

ENGINEERING, MINING
Membership of Professional Institutions and Associations

INSTITUTE OF EXPLOSIVES ENGINEERS

Suite 3
7–8 Mill Street
Stafford ST16 2AJ
Tel: 01785 240154
Fax: 01785 240154
E-mail: secretariat@iexpe.org
Website: www.iexpe.org

The Institute of Explosives Engineers promotes the occupational competency, education and professional standing of those who work with explosives and provides consultative facilities for organizations and government departments within the explosives field.

Company
Company Affiliate

MEMBERSHIP
Student
Associate (AIExpE)
Member (MIExpE)
Fellow (FIExpE)

QUALIFICATION/EXAMINATIONS
CEng, IEng, Eng Tech

DESIGNATORY LETTERS
AIExpE, MIExpE, FIExpE

THE INSTITUTE OF MATERIALS, MINERALS AND MINING (IOM³)

1 Carlton House Terrace
London SW1Y 5DB
Tel: 020 7451 7300
Fax: 020 7839 1702
E-mail: via website
Website: www.iom3.org

IOM³ is a major UK engineering institution whose activities encompass the whole materials cycle, from exploration and extraction, through characterization, processing, forming, finishing and application, to product recycling and land reuse. We promote and develop all aspects of materials science and engineering, geology, mining and associated technologies, mineral and petroleum engineering and extraction metallurgy, as a leading authority in the worldwide materials and mining community.

MEMBERSHIP
Student
Graduate
Affiliate
Member (MIMMM)
Fellow (FIMMM)
Associate (AIMMM)
Technician (Eng Tech)

DESIGNATORY LETTERS
MIMMM, FIMMM, AIMMM, Eng Tech

THE INSTITUTE OF QUARRYING

McPherson House
8a Regan Way
Chetwynd Business Park
Chilwell
Nottingham NG9 6RZ
Tel: 0115 972 9995
E-mail: mail@quarrying.org
Website: www.quarrying.org

The Institute of Quarrying, which dates from 1917, is the international professional body for quarrying, construction materials and related extractive and processing industries, and has 6,000 members in some 50 countries. Our aim is to improve all aspects of operational performance through education and training at supervisory and management level.

MEMBERSHIP
Student

Associate
Technical Member (TMIQ)
Member (MIQ)
Fellow (FIQ)

QUALIFICATION/EXAMINATIONS
Diploma in Quarry Technology
Professional Examination

DESIGNATORY LETTERS
TMIQ, MIQ, FIQ

ENGINEERING, NUCLEAR
Membership of Professional Institutions and Associations

THE NUCLEAR INSTITUTE

CK International House
1–6 Yarmouth Place
London WJ1 7BU
Tel: 020 3475 4701
E-mail: admin@nuclearinst.com
Website: www.nuclearinst.com

The NI (a Nominated Body of the UK Engineering and Science Councils) is the only professional membership body for the Nuclear Sector. We organize lectures, seminars and events at a regional and national level, have a vibrant young generation network and provide opportunities for career development and networking.

MEMBERSHIP
Student Member
Learned Member
Graduate Member
Technician Member (TNucI)
Associate Member (AMNucI)
Member (MNucI)
Fellow (FNucI)

New Structure from Jan 2016:
Affiliate (formerly Student)
Associate (formerly Learned and Graduate Members)
Member (MNucI)(incorporating Member, Associate Member and Technician Member)
Fellows (FNucI)
*Member and Fellow Grades require interview to assess competency and professional standards against The Nuclear Deltaxxx

QUALIFICATION/EXAMINATIONS
The Nuclear Deltaxxx

DESIGNATORY LETTERS
MNucI, FNucI

ENGINEERING, PRODUCTION
Membership of Professional Institutions and Associations

THE INSTITUTE OF OPERATIONS MANAGEMENT

IOM
Earlstrees Court
Earlstrees Road
Corby
Northamptonshire NN17 4AX
Tel: 01536 740105
E-mail: info@iomnet.org.uk
Website: www.iomnet.org.uk

The Institute of Operations Management (IOM) is the UK professional body for operations management in manufacturing, service industries and the public sector. Our aim is to equip operations professionals with the skills and resources they need to maximise individual potential and organisational process.

MEMBERSHIP
Learner
Full Time Student
Apprentice Associate
e-Member
Corporate Associate
Associate

Corporate Associate
Member (MIOM)
Fellow (FIOM)
APICS Member

QUALIFICATION/EXAMINATIONS
IOM works in partnership with The Chartered Institute of Logistics and Transport to develop and award regulated operations management qualifications for the manufacturing and service sectors.
CILT(UK) – IOM Level 3 Certificate in Operations Management
CILT(UK) – IOM Level 5 Award in Supply Chain and Inventory Management

CILT(UK) – IOM Level 5 Certificate in Operations Management for the Service Environment
CILT(UK) – IOM Level 5 Diploma in Operations Management for the Service Environment
CILT(UK) – IOM Level 5 Diploma in Operations Management
CILT(UK) – IOM Level 6 Advanced Diploma in Operations Management
APICS – Certified in Production and Inventory Management (CPIM) and Certified Supply Chain Professional (CSCP) programmes.

DESIGNATORY LETTERS
MIOM, FIOM

ENGINEERING, REFRACTORIES
Membership of Professional Institutions and Associations

INSTITUTE OF REFRACTORIES ENGINEERING

575 Trentham Road
Burton
Stoke on Trent
Staffs ST3 3BN
Tel: 01782 310 234
Fax: 01782 310 234
E-mail: secretary@ireng.org
Website: www.ireng.org

The IRE is a non-profit-making organization dedicated to fostering the science, technology and skills of refractories engineering and to serving the needs of refractories engineers worldwide. Our members have a background in R&D, design, engineering, manufacturing and installation contracting in the iron & steel, cement, non-ferrous, glass, chemical/petrochemical incineration, power generation, ceramics/bricks and similar industries.

MEMBERSHIP
Student
Associate Member (AMI Ref Eng)
Member (MI Ref Eng)
Fellow (FI Ref Eng)

DESIGNATORY LETTERS
AMI Ref Eng, MI Ref Eng, FI Ref Eng

ENGINEERING, REFRIGERATION
Membership of Professional Institutions and Associations

THE INSTITUTE OF REFRIGERATION

Kelvin House
76 Mill Lane
Carshalton
Surrey SM5 2JR
Tel: 020 8647 7033
E-mail: ior@ior.org.uk
Website: www.ior.org.uk

The IOR is the professional body for the refrigeration and air conditioning industries. We promote the technical advancement and perfection of refrigeration, and the minimization of its effects on the environment, encourage the extension of refrigeration, air conditioning and heat pump services for the benefit of the community, and provide advice, CPD and support to our members.

MEMBERSHIP
Student

Technician Affiliate
Associate Member (AMInstR)
FellowMember (MInstR)
Service Engineering Section
Air Conditioning and Heat Pump Institute of the IOR

QUALIFICATION/EXAMINATIONS
REAL Zero CPD, REAL Skills Europe CPD

DESIGNATORY LETTERS
AMInstR, TMInstR, MInstR, FInstR

ENGINEERING, ROAD, RAIL AND TRANSPORT
Membership of Professional Institutions and Associations

INSTITUTE OF HIGHWAY ENGINEERS

De Morgan House
58 Russell Square
London WC1B 4HS
Tel: 020 7436 7487
Fax: 020 7436 7488
E-mail: secretary@theihe.org
Website: www.theihe.org

The IHE is the main professional body for highway and traffic professionals. We are run by engineers for engineers and technicians, and work to keep the standards of the profession high, to safeguard the interests of our members, and to ensure that their contribution is recognised.

MEMBERSHIP
Student Member
Associate Member (AMIHE)
Member (MIHE)
Fellow (FIHE)

Engineering Technician (EngTech)
Incorporated Engineer (IEng)
Chartered Engineer (CEng)

QUALIFICATION/EXAMINATIONS
Prof Cert in Traffic Sign Design
Prof Cert in Traffic Signal Control
Prof Cert in Transport Development Management

DESIGNATORY LETTERS
AMIHE, MIHE, FIHE, EngTech, IEng, CEng

INSTITUTION OF RAILWAY SIGNAL ENGINEERS

4th Floor
1 Birdcage Walk
Westminster
London SW1H 9JJ
Tel: 020 7808 1180
Fax: 020 7808 1196
E-mail: hq@irse.org
Website: www.irse.org

The Institution of Railway Signal Engineers, known more usually as the IRSE, is an international organization, active throughout the world. It is the professional institution for all those engaged or interested in railway signalling and telecommunications and allied disciplines. Membership is open to anyone engaged or interested in the management, planning, design, installation, telecommunications or associated equipment.

MEMBERSHIP
Student
Associate
Accredited Technician
Associate Member
Member
Fellow
Companion

QUALIFICATION/EXAMINATIONS
Professional Examination

DESIGNATORY LETTERS
AMIRSE, MIRSE, FIRSE, CompIRSE

SOCIETY OF OPERATIONS ENGINEERS

22 Greencoat Place
London SW1P 1PR
Tel: 020 7630 1111
Fax: 020 7630 6677
E-mail: soe@soe.org.uk
Website: www.soe.org.uk

SOE is a professional membership organisation representing more than 16,000 individuals and companies in the engineering industry. It was formed in 2000 by the merger of the Institute of Road Transport Engineers (IRTE) and the Institution of Plant Engineers (IPlantE). The Society's third Professional Sector, the Bureau of Engineer Surveyors (BES), joined in 2004.

MEMBERSHIP
Associate Member (AMSOE)
Member (MSOE)
Fellow (FSOE)
Engineering Technician (EngTech)
Incorporated Engineer (IEng)
Chartered Engineer (CEng)

THE CHARTERED INSTITUTION OF HIGHWAYS AND TRANSPORTATION

119 Britannia Walk
London N1 7JE
Tel: 020 7336 1555
Fax: 020 7336 1556
E-mail: info@ciht.org.uk
Website: www.ciht.org.uk

The CIHT is a learned society and membership organization concerned with the planning, design, construction, maintenance and operation of land-based transport systems and infrastructure. CIHT provides professional development and networking opportunities to members, with routes to qualifications, cutting-edge technical conferences and exciting social events.

MEMBERSHIP
Student

Associate Member (AMCIHT)
Member (MCIHT)
Fellow (FCIHT)

QUALIFICATION/EXAMINATIONS
Transport Planning Professional (TPP) status (awarded jointly with the Transport Planning Society (TPS))

DESIGNATORY LETTERS
AMCIHT, MCIHT, FCIHT

ENGINEERING, SHEET METAL
Membership of Professional Institutions and Associations

INSTITUTE OF SHEET METAL ENGINEERING

102 Richmond Drive
Perton
Wolverhampton
West Midlands WV6 7UQ
Tel: 07891 499146
E-mail: ismesec@googlemail.com
Website: www.isme.org.uk

The ISME is a learned body with individual membership open to those employed in the sheet metal and associated industries and corporate membership open to relevant companies. Our aims are to promote the science of working and using sheet metal by providing opportunities for the exchange of ideas and information, and to encourage the professional development of our members.

MEMBERSHIP
Student Member
Member (MISME)
Fellow (FISME)
Corporate Member

DESIGNATORY LETTERS
MISME, FISME

ENGINEERING, STRUCTURAL
Membership of Professional Institutions and Associations

THE INSTITUTION OF STRUCTURAL ENGINEERS

47–58 Bastwick Street
London EC1V 3PS
Tel: 020 7235 4535
Fax: 020 7235 4294
E-mail: membership@istructe.org
Website: www.istructe.org

The Institution of Structural Engineers, founded in 1908, is the world's largest membership organization dedicated to the art and science of structural engineering. Our aims include: maintaining professional standards for structural engineering; ensuring continued technical excellence; advancing safety, creativity and innovation; and promoting a sustainable approach to both the structural engineering profession and the built environment.

MEMBERSHIP
Student
Graduate
Technician (TIStructE)
Associate Member (AMIStructE)
Associate (AIStructE)
Chartered Member (MIStructE)
Fellow (FIStructE)

DESIGNATORY LETTERS
TIStructE, AMIStructE, AIStructE, MIStructE, FIStructE

ENGINEERING, WATER
Membership of Professional Institutions and Associations

INSTITUTE OF WATER

4 Carlton Court
Team Valley
Gateshead
Tyne and Wear NE11 0AZ
Tel: 0191 422 0088
Fax: 0191 422 0087
E-mail: info@instituteofwater.org.uk
Website: www.instituteofwater.org.uk

The IW is the only institute concerned with the UK water industry. Our aim is to promote high standards of integrity, conduct and ethics, and to provide our members with an opportunity for CPD and growth through sharing knowledge, experience and networking opportunities.

MEMBERSHIP
Student Member
Associate Member
Full Member
Fellow
Honorary Member
Engineering Technician (EngTech)
Incorporated Engineer (IEng)
Chartered Engineer (CEng)
Chartered Environmentalist (CEnv)
Company Member

DESIGNATORY LETTERS
EngTech, IEng, CEng, CEnv

ENGINEERING DESIGN
Membership of Professional Institutions and Associations

THE INSTITUTION OF ENGINEERING DESIGNERS

Courtleigh
Westbury Leigh
Westbury
Wiltshire BA13 3TA
Tel: 01373 822801
Fax: 01373 858085
E-mail: via website
Website: www.ied.org.uk

Established in 1945, the IED represents 4,000 members worldwide working in engineering design, product design and CAD. Benefits include a bimonthly journal, access to an extensive library, legal advice helpline, local branch activities, and guidance and support to registration with the EC(UK) for suitably qualified members.

MEMBERSHIP
IED membership has two divisions: Engineering Design, and Product Design and Technology.
Each division has a range of membership grades: Student Member (StudIED), Graduate/Diplomate Member (GradIED/DipIED), Competent Draughting Associate (CDAIED), Associate (AIED), Member (MIED), Fellow (FIED), Affiliate

QUALIFICATION/EXAMINATIONS
Registration with EC(UK) for suitably qualified members

DESIGNATORY LETTERS
AIED, MIED, FIED

ENVIRONMENTAL SCIENCES
Membership of Professional Institutions and Associations

CHARTERED INSTITUTE OF ECOLOGY AND ENVIRONMENTAL MANAGEMENT

43 Southgate Street
Winchester
Hampshire SO23 9EH
Tel: 01962 868626
E-mail: enquiries@cieem.net
Website: www.cieem.net

Founded in 1991 to advance the science, technology and practice of ecology, environmental management and sustainable development to further conservation and the enhancement of biodiversity through education, training, study and research. CIEEM now has more than 5,000 members drawn from local authorities, government agencies, industry, environmental consultancy, teaching/research and NGOs.

MEMBERSHIP
Supporter Member
Student Member
Qualifying Member
Graduate Member (Grad CIEEM)
Associate Member (ACIEEM)
Full Member (MCIEEM)
Fellow (FCIEEM)

DESIGNATORY LETTERS
Grad CIEEM, ACIEEM, MCIEEM, FCIEEM

EXPORT
Membership of Professional Institutions and Associations

THE INSTITUTE OF EXPORT

Export House
Minerva Business Park
Lynch Wood
Peterborough PE2 6FT
Tel: 01733 404400
E-mail: via website
Website: www.export.org.uk

Established since 1935 offering training and professional qualifications to those working within international trade. We are the only professional institute in the UK offering qualifications ranging from the new 14–19 Diploma up to a level 5 Diploma as well as standard and bespoke training courses for individuals and companies.

MEMBERSHIP
Affiliate
Student
Associate
Member MIEx (Grad)
Member MIEx
Fellow
Business

QUALIFICATION/EXAMINATIONS
Diploma in International Trade (DIT)
Certified International Trade Advisor (CIT)
Advanced Certificate in International Trade (ACIT)
Young International Trader (YIT)
Certificate in International Trade (CIT)
Foundation Degree (FdA)

FISHERIES MANAGEMENT
Membership of Professional Institutions and Associations

INSTITUTE OF FISHERIES MANAGEMENT

PO Box 679
Hull
East Yorkshire HU5 9AX
Tel: 0845 388 7012
E-mail: info@ifm.org.uk
Website: www.ifm.org.uk

The Institute of Fisheries Management is an international organization of persons sharing a common interest in the modern and sustainable management of recreational and commercial fisheries. It is a non-profit-making body and is a constituent body of the Society for the Environment.

MEMBERSHIP
Subscriber
Student Member
Associate Member (AMIFM)
Registered Member (MIFM)
Fellow (FIFM)
Honorary Fellow (Hon FIFM)
Corporate Member
Honorary Member (Hon MIFM)

QUALIFICATION/EXAMINATIONS
Certificate
Diploma (accredited by The Open University)

DESIGNATORY LETTERS
AMIFM, MIFM, FIFM, Hon FIFM, Hon MIFM

FLORISTRY
Membership of Professional Institutions and Associations

BRITISH FLORIST ASSOCIATION

PO Box 674
Wigan
Lancashire WN1 9LL
Tel: 0844 800 7299
E-mail: via website
Website: www.britishfloristassociation.org

The BFA, founded in 1951, is an awarding body that promotes the highest standards in professional floristry. We are responsible for preparing and setting the highest floristry qualifications and for designing programmes for the training of SOF judges and examiners. We provide help, advice and information to our more than 1,000 members, who include business owners, florists, training providers, and students.

MEMBERSHIP
Florist Individual
Student
Corporate
Associate
College Member
Honorary Member

FOOD SCIENCE AND NUTRITION
Membership of Professional Institutions and Associations

INSTITUTE OF FOOD SCIENCE AND TECHNOLOGY

5 Cambridge Court
210 Shepherd's Bush Road
London W6 7NJ
Tel: 020 7603 6316
E-mail: info@ifst.org
Website: www.ifst.org

IFST is the leading independent qualifying body for food professionals in Europe and the only professional body in the UK concerned with all aspects of food science and technology. As a registered charity we are independent of government, industry, lobby or special interest groups.

MEMBERSHIP
Associate

Member (MIFST)
Fellow (FIFST)
Chartered Scientist (CSci)
Registered Scientist (RSci)
Registered Science Technician (RSciTech)
Professional Food Sensory Group

DESIGNATORY LETTERS
MIFST, FIFST, CSci, RSci, RSciTech

FORESTRY AND ARBORICULTURE
Membership of Professional Institutions and Associations

INSTITUTE OF CHARTERED FORESTERS

59 George Street
Edinburgh EH2 2JG
Tel: 0131 240 1425
Fax: 0131 240 1424
E-mail: icf@charteredforesters.org
Website: www.charteredforesters.org

The ICF is the Royal Chartered body for foresters and arboriculturists in the UK. We have over 1,000 members, to whom we offer advice, guidance and support. We also strive to foster a greater public understanding and awareness of the profession, as the environment and its management become more relevant to everyone.

MEMBERSHIP
Student Member

Supporter
Associate Member
Professional Member (MICFor)
Fellow (FICFor)

QUALIFICATION/EXAMINATIONS
Professional Membership Entry (PME) exam

DESIGNATORY LETTERS
MICFor, FICFor

THE ARBORICULTURAL ASSOCIATION

The Malthouse
Stroud Green
Standish
Stonehouse
Gloucestershire GL10 3DL
Tel: 01242 522152
Fax: 01242 577766
E-mail: admin@trees.org.uk
Website: www.trees.org.uk

The Arboricultural Association, founded in 1964, is the leading body in the UK for the amenity tree care professional in either civic or commercial employment at craft, technical, supervisory, managerial or consultancy level. There are currently over 2,000 members of The Arboricultural Association in a variety of membership classes.

MEMBERSHIP
Student Member
Ordinary Member
Associate Member

Technician Member
Professional Member
Fellow
Fellow Retired
Corporate Member

QUALIFICATION/EXAMINATIONS
Arboricultural Association Approved Contractor
Arboricultural Association Registered Consultant

DESIGNATORY LETTERS
TechArborA, MArborA, FArborA

THE ROYAL FORESTRY SOCIETY

The Hay Barns
Home Farm Drive
Upton Estate
Banbury OX15 6HU
Tel: 01295 678588
Fax: 01295 670798
E-mail: rfshq@rfs.org.uk
Website: www.rfs.org.uk

The RFS was founded in 1882 and now has over 3,600 members. We are dedicated to promoting the wise management of trees and woodlands, and to increasing people's understanding of forestry. We publish a popular journal, the *Quarterly Journal of Forestry*, arrange outdoor meetings, organize woodland study tours in the UK and overseas, run courses in Forestry and arboriculture and manage model woodlands.

MEMBERSHIP
Member
Corporate Member
Full-time Student

QUALIFICATION/EXAMINATIONS
RFS Certificate in Arboriculture
RFS Certificate in Forestry
RFS Certificate in Silviculture

FOUNDRY TECHNOLOGY AND PATTERN MAKING
Membership of Professional Institutions and Associations

THE INSTITUTE OF CAST METALS ENGINEERS

National Metalforming Centre
47 Birmingham Road
West Bromwich
West Midlands B70 6PY
Tel: 01216 016979
Fax: 01216 016981
E-mail: info@icme.org.uk
Website: www.icme.org.uk

The ICME is the professional body for those in the castings and associated industry. It was formed in 1904, granted its first Royal Charter in 1921, a Third Supplemental Charter in 1994 and changed its name in 2001. The granting of the Third Supplemental Charter aligned its membership requirements with those of the EC(UK).

MEMBERSHIP
Student
Member (MICME)

Professional Member (Prof MICME)
Fellow (FICME)
Engineering Technician (EngTech)
Incorporated Engineer (IEng)
Chartered Engineer (CEng)
European Engineer (EurIng)

DESIGNATORY LETTERS
MICME, Prof MICME, FICME, EngTech, IEng, CEng, EurIng

FREIGHT FORWARDING
Membership of Professional Institutions and Associations

BRITISH INTERNATIONAL FREIGHT ASSOCIATION (BIFA)

Redfern House
Browells Lane
Feltham
Middlesex TW13 7EP
Tel: 020 8844 2266
Fax: 020 8890 5546
E-mail: bifa@bifa.org
Website: www.bifa.org/content/home

BIFA is the principal trade association providing representation, training and support to British companies engaged in the international movement of freight to and from the UK by air, rail, road and sea. It is a not-for-profit organisation. Members are encouraged to contribute to the running of the Association.

MEMBERSHIP
Associate Member
Trade Member

FUNDRAISING
Membership of Professional Institutions and Associations

INSTITUTE OF FUNDRAISING

Park Place
12 Lawn Lane
London SW8 1UD
Tel: 020 7840 1000
Fax: 020 7840 1001
E-mail: enquiries@institute-of-fundraising.org.uk
Website: www.institute-of-fundraising.org.uk

The Institute of Fundraising is the professional body for fundraisers in the UK, representing over 5,000 individual fundraisers and 340 organisations. We offer professional support, act as a voice for fundraisers and promote best practice. We offer professional qualifications and training, and the annual IoF National Convention is the largest fundraising conference of its type in Europe.

MEMBERSHIP
Associate
Full Member (MInstF)
Fully Certificated Member MInstF(Cert)
Diploma Qualified Member MInstF(Dip)
Organisational Member

QUALIFICATION/EXAMINATIONS
Introductory Certificate in Fundraising
Certificate in Fundraising
Diploma in Fundraising
Advanced Diploma in Fundraising (in development)
Certificate in Direct Marketing

DESIGNATORY LETTERS
MInstF, MInstF(Cert), MInstF(Dip), FInstF, FInstF(Cert), FInstF(Dip)

FUNERAL DIRECTING, BURIAL AND CREMATION ADMINISTRATION

Membership of Professional Institutions and Associations

NATIONAL ASSOCIATION OF FUNERAL DIRECTORS

618 Warwick Road
Solihull
West Midlands B91 1AA
Tel: 0845 230 1343
Fax: 0121 711 1351
E-mail: info@nafd.org.uk
Website: www.nafd.org.uk

The NAFD, founded in 1905, is an independent trade association whose members include more than 3,200 funeral homes throughout the UK, suppliers to the profession, and overseas funeral directing businesses. We provide support to our members and offer informed opinion to government.

MEMBERSHIP
Funeral Director (Category A) Member

Supplier (Category B) Member
Overseas Member

QUALIFICATION/EXAMINATIONS
Diploma in Funeral Arranging and Administration (Dip.FAA)
Diploma in Funeral Directing (Dip.FD)

NATIONAL ASSOCIATION OF MEMORIAL MASONS

1 Castle Mews
Rugby
Warwickshire CV21 2AL
Tel: 01788 542264
Fax: 01788 542276
E-mail: enquiries@namm.org.uk
Website: www.namm.org.uk

The NAMM was formed in 1907 to promote excellence and craftsmanship within the memorial masonry trade. Our services to members include training, business advice, technical advice, promotion, a legal helpline, a conciliation and arbitration service, trade exhibitions and a conference. We protect members' interests through representation to the British Standards Institution (BSI) and the Burial & Cemeteries Advisory Group (BCAG).

MEMBERSHIP
Individual Associate Member
Affiliate Member
Full Retail and Wholesale Members
Company Associate Member
Corporate Associate Member
Overseas Member
Overseas Affiliate Member

THE INSTITUTE OF BURIAL AND CREMATION AUTHORITIES

ICCM National Office & Training Centre
City of London Cemetery
Aldersbrook Road
Manor Park
London E12 5DQ
Tel: 020 8989 4661
Fax: 020 8989 6112
E-mail: iccmjulie@gmail.com
Website: www.iccm-uk.com

Accredited education and training opportunities for those working in cemeteries and crematori.

Best practice guidance and policy for burial and cremation authorities.

MEMBERSHIP
Member (MICCM)
Associate Member (AICCM)
Fellow (FICCM)
Corporate
Associate Corporate

QUALIFICATION/EXAMINATIONS
Diploma – Fully Accredited NHC in Cemetery & Crematorium Management and the Management of Natural Burial Grounds
Cemetery Operatives Training Scheme – A comprehensive suite of City & Guilds accredited qualifications
Crematorium Technicians Training Scheme – BTEC accredited qualifications for crematory staff

DESIGNATORY LETTERS
MICCM, AICCM, FICCM

FURNISHING AND FURNITURE
Membership of Professional Institutions and Associations

FLOORING INDUSTRY TRAINING ASSOCIATION

4c St Marys Place
The Lace Market
Nottingham NG1 1PH
Tel: 0115 9506836
E-mail: info@fita.co.uk
Website: www.fita.co.uk

FITA was set up and is fully supported by the CFA and the NICF to provide training for the floor-covering industry. We have a fully equipped training centre at Loughborough, where the majority of our courses are run. We also offer tailor-made courses to suit individual specifications and requirements.

QUALIFICATION/EXAMINATIONS
FITA Training Courses
The Flooring Industry Flooring Association was set up by, and is fully supported by the CFA and NICF to provide training.

FITA has a fully equipped training centre at Loughborough in Leicestershire where the majority of our standard courses are run. FITA also offers tailor-made courses to suit your specifications and requirements, quotations on request.

FITA instructors have all passed assessments and knowledge exams and are supported on courses by technicians with specialist knowledge from the trade.

FITA also enjoys the support of a considerable number of suppliers who freely donate materials, accessories and tools.

Fully trained staff are an asset to any company. The outlay for training courses far outweighs the initial cost.

Please be sure to book early to reserve your place on a course. Go to our Course Dates page for details of our latest courses and the training centres where they are being held.

Training courses considered suitable for Domestic Installers

Carpet Fitting – Basic

Carpet Fitting – Intermediate

Domestic Sheet Vinyl Fitting

Profitable Measuring and Quoting

Subfloor Preparation – Domestic

Training courses considered suitable for Commercial Installers

Commercial Vinyl Fitting – Advanced

Commercial Vinyl Fitting – Basic

Commercial Vinyl Fitting – Intermediate

Cost Effective Estimating and Planning

Linoleum Installation – Intermediate

Subfloor Preparation – Commercial

Training courses considered suitable for Domestic & Commercial Installers

Carpet Fitting – Advanced

Laminate and Wood Fitting – Basic

Linoleum Installation – Basic

Moisture – Preventing floor failures

Resilient / Luxury Vinyl Tile Fitting – Advanced

Resilient / Luxury Vinyl Tile Fitting – Basic

Wood Fitting – Advanced

Wood Fitting – Intermediate

Wood Sanding and Finishing

Assessments designed for FITA QA Accreditation

QA Card Adhered Carpet Assessment

QA Card Carpet Tile Assessment

QA Card Floating Timber Assessment

QA Card Resilient Sheet Assessment

QA Card Subfloor Preparation Assessment

QA Card Vinyl Tile Assessment

NATIONAL INSTITUTE OF CARPET AND FLOORLAYERS

4c St Marys Place
The Lace Market
Nottingham NG1 1PH
Tel: 0115 9583077
Fax: 0115 9412238
E-mail: info@nicfltd.org.uk
Website: www.nicfltd.org.uk

The NICF furthers the interests of its members by promoting excellence in the field of carpet and floorlaying and providing a range of benefits, products and services.

MEMBERSHIP

Master Fitter Member

Fitter Member

Trainee Fitter Member

Retailer Member

Associate Member

Patron Member

QUALIFICATION/EXAMINATIONS

Fitter qualification assessment

Master Fitter qualification assessment

GEMMOLOGY AND JEWELLERY
Membership of Professional Institutions and Associations

THE GEMMOLOGICAL ASSOCIATION OF GREAT BRITAIN

21 Ely Place
London EC1N 6TD
Tel: 020 7404 3334
Fax: 020 7404 8843
E-mail: information@gem-a.com
Website: www.gem-a.com

The Gemmological Association of Great Britain (Gem-A), a UK-registered charity, is the world's longest established provider of gem and jewellery education, our first diploma having been awarded in 1913. We are committed to promoting the study of gemmology and to providing CPD to our members – an international community of gem professionals and enthusiasts.

MEMBERSHIP
Member

Fellow (FGA)
Diamond Member (DGA)
Corporate Member

QUALIFICATION/EXAMINATIONS
Foundation Certificate in Gemmology
Diploma in Gemmology
Diamond Diploma

DESIGNATORY LETTERS
FGA, DGA

THE NATIONAL ASSOCIATION OF JEWELLERS

78A Luke Street
London EC2A 4XG
Tel: 020 7613 4445
E-mail: jet@jewellers-online.org
Website: www.nageducation.org

The NAJ serves and supports the jewellery industry of Great Britain and Ireland. We promote high professional standards among our members, who must adhere to a code of professional practice. In return, we offer them advice, support and learning and development in the form of distance learning courses and short courses.

MEMBERSHIP
Alumni Member
Allied Member

Affiliate Member
Ordinary Member

QUALIFICATION/EXAMINATIONS
Professional Jewellers' Diploma (JET 1 Certificate)
Professional Jewellers' Diploma (JET 2 Diploma)
Professional Jewellers' Management Diploma
Professional Jewellers' Business Development Diploma
Certificate of Appraisal Theory (CAT)

GENEALOGY
Membership of Professional Institutions and Associations

SOCIETY OF GENEALOGISTS

14 Charterhouse Buildings
Goswell Road
London EC1M 7BA
Tel: 020 7251 8799
Fax: 020 7250 1800
E-mail: info@sog.org.uk
Website: www.sog.org.uk

The Society (founded 1911) is the National Family History Centre. A registered educational charity, it was founded to encourage and foster the study, science and knowledge of genealogy. This it does chiefly through its library, publications and extensive education programme of courses and events. It currently does not hold exams.

MEMBERSHIP
Member
Fellow (FSG)
Honorary Fellow (FSG Hon)

DESIGNATORY LETTERS
FSG, FSG Hon

THE HERALDRY SOCIETY

53 Hitchin Street
Baldock
Herts SG7 6AQ
Tel: 01869 246188
E-mail: memsec@theheraldrysociety.com
Website: www.theheraldrysociety.com

The Heraldry Society is a registered charity that aims to encourage interest in heraldry through publications, lectures, visits and related activities. Members receive *The Heraldry Gazette*, which contains heraldic news and comments, and Society information quarterly. We maintain contact with heraldic societies in many parts of the UK and abroad.

MEMBERSHIP
Associate Member
Ordinary Member

Fellow (FHS)
Honorary Fellow (Hon FHS)

QUALIFICATION/EXAMINATIONS
Elementary Certificate
Intermediate Certificate
Advanced Certificate
Diploma (DipHS)

DESIGNATORY LETTERS
FHS, Hon FHS

THE INSTITUTE OF HERALDIC AND GENEALOGICAL STUDIES

79–82 Northgate
Canterbury
Kent CT1 1BA
Tel: 01227 768664
Fax: 01227 765617
E-mail: registrar@ihgs.ac.uk
Website: www.ihgs.ac.uk

The IHGS, founded in 1961, is an independent educational charitable trust that offers a wide range of courses on family history, heraldry and related historical subjects, and has an extensive library, archive and research facilities. We also offer a genealogical and heraldic research service.

MEMBERSHIP
Associate Member
Graduate Member

QUALIFICATION/EXAMINATIONS
Correspondence Course in Genealogy
Correspondence Course in Heraldry
Higher Certificate in Genealogy
Diploma in Genealogy
Online Course in Heraldry

DESIGNATORY LETTERS
Dip Gen, LHG, FHG

GEOGRAPHY
Membership of Professional Institutions and Associations

ROYAL GEOGRAPHICAL SOCIETY (WITH THE INSTITUTE OF BRITISH GEOGRAPHERS)

1 Kensington Gore
London SW7 2AR
Tel: 020 7591 3000
Fax: 020 7591 3001
E-mail: via website
Website: www.rgs.org

The RGS-IBG is the learned society and professional body for geography. We aim to foster an understanding and informed enjoyment of our world: developing, supporting and promoting geographical research, expeditions and fieldwork, education, public engagement, and providing geography input to policy.

MEMBERSHIP
Young Geographer

Member
Postgraduate Fellow
Fellow
Chartered Geographer (CGeog)
Corporate Member

DESIGNATORY LETTERS
FRGS, CGeog

GEOLOGY
Membership of Professional Institutions and Associations

THE GEOLOGICAL SOCIETY

Burlington House
Piccadilly
London W1J 0BG
Tel: 020 7434 9944
Fax: 020 7439 8975
E-mail: enquiries@geolsoc.org.uk
Website: www.geolsoc.org.uk

The Geological Society, founded in 1807, is the UK's national organization for professional Earth scientists. The normal grade of membership is Fellow. Students may become Candidate Fellows. Members of the public not eligible for any other status may join as Friends.

MEMBERSHIP
Friend
Candidate Fellow
Fellow
Chartered Geologist

DESIGNATORY LETTERS
FGS, CGeol

GLASS TECHNOLOGY
Membership of Professional Institutions and Associations

BRITISH SOCIETY OF SCIENTIFIC GLASSBLOWERS

Unit W1, MK2 Business Centre
Barton Road
Bletchley
Milton Keynes
Buckinghamshire MK2 3HU
Tel: 01908 821191
Fax: 01908 821195
E-mail: sales@biochemglass.co.uk
Website: www.bssg.co.uk

The Society was founded in 1960 for the benefit of those engaged in Scientific Glassblowing and its associated professions, and to uphold and further the status of Scientific Glassblowers. We welcome written submissions to our quarterly journal, which is circulated to members.

MEMBERSHIP
Associate
Student Member

Fellow
Full Member
Master
Honorary Member
Retired Member
Overseas Member

DESIGNATORY LETTERS
Master MBSSG, Fellow FBSSG

SOCIETY OF GLASS TECHNOLOGY

9 Churchill Way
Chapeltown
Sheffield
South Yorkshire S35 2PY
Tel: 0114 2634455
Fax: 0871 8754085
E-mail: info@sgt.org
Website: www.sgt.org

The objects of the Society of Glass Technology are to encourage and advance the study of the history, art, science, design, manufacture, after treatment, distribution and end use of glass of any and every kind.

MEMBERSHIP
Personal Member
Fellow (FSGT)
Fellow Emeritus
Honorary Fellow (HonFSGT)
Corporate Member

QUALIFICATION/EXAMINATIONS
Peer review by the Board of Fellows.
2016 is the SGT centenary and some Centenary Honorary Fellows will be created. These will be in addition to the limit of 12 for Honorary Fellows. Decided by the Board of Fellows as normal.

DESIGNATORY LETTERS
FSGT, HonFSGT

HAIRDRESSING

Membership of Professional Institutions and Associations

HABIA

Oxford House
Sixth Avenue
Sky Business Park, Robin Hood Airport
Doncaster
South Yorkshire DN9 3GG
Tel: 0845 6 123555
Fax: 01302 774949
E-mail: info@habia.org
Website: www.habia.org

Habia is the government-appointed standards-setting body for hair, beauty, nails, spa therapy, barbering and African-type hair, and creates the standards that form the basis of all qualifications, including NVQs, SVQs, apprenticeships, diplomas and foundation degrees, as well as industry codes of practice.

MEMBERSHIP
Habia offers a membership programme for training providers (Habia Members) and a wider, free membership for industry professionals and educators.

THE GUILD OF HAIRDRESSERS

Archway House
Barnsley S71 1AQ
Tel: 01226 786555
Fax: 01226 208300

The Guild of Hairdressers dates back to 1340, when it was part of the Guild of Barbers and Surgeons. Then in the late 16th century, when the surgeons split off, it became the Guild of Hairdressers, Wigmakers and Perfumers. Today it still exists for the benefit of its members, who adhere to a code of ethics and to whom it provides help and advice.

HEALTH AND HEALTH SERVICES
Membership of Professional Institutions and Associations

BRITISH OCCUPATIONAL HYGIENE SOCIETY – FACULTY OF OCCUPATIONAL HYGIENE

5/6 Melbourne Business Court
Millennium Way
Pride Park
Derby DE24 8LZ
Tel: 01332 298101
Fax: 01332 298099
E-mail: admin@bohs.org
Website: www.bohs.org

BOHS is a Chartered professional membership organisation and learned society, promoting public and professional awareness, good practice and high standards of occupational hygiene, to help reduce work-related ill-health. The Faculty is our professional arm and examining board, and administers examinations and awards qualifications in occupational hygiene and allied subjects.

MEMBERSHIP
Individual
Student
Affiliate (corporate)
Retired
Associate (AFOH)
Licentiate (LFOH)
Chartered Member (CMFOH)
Specialist Member (MFOH(S))
Chartered Fellow (CFFOH)

QUALIFICATION/EXAMINATIONS
A range of UK and international qualifications in occupational hygiene and related subjects, which include stand-alone modules covering general principles and practical applications at the technician level, through to BOHS's own professional level Certificate and Diploma qualifications.

The Occupational Hygiene Modules are aimed at those who want to gain a qualification in a particular topic of occupational hygiene to demonstrate technical expertise in that area or, grouped together, to gain exemption from the Faculty's professional level Certificate Core examination.

The International Occupational Hygiene Modules are based on the Occupational Hygiene Modules, without specific reference to UK or other legislation. The Proficiency Modules cover both theory and practical training in a specific subject, and are aimed at those needing to demonstrate a level of proficiency to carry out the area of work covered by the Module.

Our professional qualifications are as follows: The Certificate of Competence in an individual subject is for candidates wanting to establish their competence in a specific field, and follows on from successful completion of one of the Occupational Hygiene

Modules. This is an oral examination, supported by submission of a written report. The Certificate of Operational Competence in Occupational Hygiene is the qualification required to join the Faculty of Occupational Hygiene as a Licentiate, and demonstrates knowledge and competence in the broad principles and practice of occupational hygiene. This is a two-part written and oral examination. The Diploma of Professional Competence in Occupational Hygiene is the highest professional occupational hygiene qualification. Candidates must already hold the Certificate of Operational Competence, and be able to demonstrate 5 years' experience in the field of occupational hygiene. Award of the Diploma qualifies the holder to become a Member of the Faculty, and demonstrates knowledge of, and competence in, assessment of health hazards and the extent of risk in various workplace circumstances, and an ability to advise on suitable control procedures. This is also a two-part, written and oral, examination. Practising members who hold the Diploma are awarded the title of Chartered Occupational Hygienist.

For further information see www.bohs.org/education/examinations/

DESIGNATORY LETTERS
AFOH, LFOH, CMFOH, CFFOH, MFOH(S)

CHARTERED INSTITUTE OF ENVIRONMENTAL HEALTH

Chadwick Court
15 Hatfields
London SE1 8DJ
Tel: 020 7827 5800
Fax: 020 7806 0666
E-mail: via website
Website: www.cieh.org

The CIEH is an Awarding Organisation providing Ofqual regulated qualifications in Food Safety, Health & Safety, First Aid, Environmental Protection and Fire Safety.

MEMBERSHIP
Student Member
Associate
Accredited Associate
Graduate Member
Voting Member
Fellow
Chartered Environmental Health Practitioner

QUALIFICATION/EXAMINATIONS
The CIEH offers a range of Ofqual-regulated qualifications at four levels in health and safety, food safety, environmental protection, fire safety and education and training.

CHARTERED INSTITUTE OF ERGONOMICS & HUMAN FACTORS

Elms Court
Elms Grove
Loughborough
Leicestershire LE11 1RG
Tel: 07736 893350
E-mail: iehf@ergonomics.org.uk
Website: www.ergonomics.org.uk

Chartered Institute of Ergonomics & Human Factors, founded in 1949, is a UK-based professional society for ergonomists worldwide. We encourage and maintain high standards of professional practice through education, accreditation and development, promote the interests of our members across government, academia, business and industry, and raise awareness of ergonomics in general.

MEMBERSHIP
Student Member
Associate Member
Graduate Member

Registered Member
Fellow
Technical Member
Retired Member

INSTITUTE OF HEALTH PROMOTION AND EDUCATION

c/o Dawn Wills
20 Mardley Avenue
Welwyn
Hertfordshire AL6 0UD
Tel: c/o 01438 840040
E-mail: admin@ihpe.org.uk
Website: www.ihpe.org.uk

The IHPE was established 50 years ago to bring together professionals with a common interest in health education and promotion to share their experience, ideas and information. Our members come from a diverse range of backgrounds, including nursing, midwifery, health visiting, medicine, dentistry, public health, stress management, psychology and teaching.

MEMBERSHIP
Student Member
Associate Member (AIHPE)
Full Member (MIHPE)
Fellow (FIHPE)
Corporate Member

DESIGNATORY LETTERS
MIHPE, AIHPE, FIHPE

INSTITUTE OF HEALTH RECORDS AND INFORMATION MANAGEMENT

Marshall House
Heanor Gate Road
Heanor
Derbyshire DE75 7RG
Tel: 01773 713927
Fax: 01773 713927
E-mail: ihrim@zen.co.uk
Website: www.ihrim.co.uk

IHRIM was founded in 1948, primarily as an educational body, to provide qualifications as well as career and professional assistance to members. We encourage professionalism and high standards among our members who work in the fields of health records, information management, clinical coding and information governance.

MEMBERSHIP
Student
Affiliate
Licentiate
Certificated Member (CHRIM)
Accredited Clinical Coder (ACC)

Associate (AHRIM)
Fellow (FHRIM)
Corporate Affiliate

QUALIFICATION/EXAMINATIONS
Certificate of Technical Competence
Foundation exam
Certificate exam
Diploma exam
National Clinical Coding Qualification

DESIGNATORY LETTERS
CHRIM, ACC, AHRIM, FHRIM

INSTITUTE OF HEALTHCARE ENGINEERING AND ESTATE MANAGEMENT

2 Abingdon House
Cumberland Business Centre
Northumberland Road
Portsmouth PO5 1DS
Tel: 023 92 823186
Fax: 023 92 815927
E-mail: office@iheem.org.uk
Website: www.iheem.org.uk

The Institute of Healthcare Engineering and Estate Management (IHEEM) is a Professional Engineering Institute, a specialist institute for the Healthcare Estates Sector.

The Institute counts among its members employees of both public and private healthcare providers, as well as those employed in private sector engineering and consultancy firms and practices.

MEMBERSHIP
Graduate (GIHEEM)
Associate Member (AMIHEEM)
Technician (TIHEEM)
Member (MIHEEM)
Fellow (FIHEEM)

DESIGNATORY LETTERS
GIHEEM, AMIHEEM, TIHEEM, MIHEEM, FIHEEM

INSTITUTE OF HEALTHCARE MANAGEMENT

John Snow House
59 Mansell Street
London E1 8AN
Tel: 020 7265 7321
Fax: 020 7265 7301
E-mail: education@ihm.org.uk
Website: www.ihm.org.uk

The IHM is the professional organization for managers throughout healthcare, including the NHS, independent providers, healthcare consultants and the armed forces. Our focus is on improving patient/user care by publishing standards of management practice, promoting the IHM Code (which covers behavioural and ethical aspects of management practice) and establishing a CPD framework for our members.

MEMBERSHIP
Associate Member
Full Member (MIHM)

QUALIFICATION/EXAMINATIONS
Certificate in Health Management Studies (CertHMS)
Certificate in Health Services Management (CertHSM)
Certificate in Managing Health Services (CertMHS)
Certificate in Managing Health & Social Care (CertMHSC)
Diploma in Health Services Management (DipHSM)

DESIGNATORY LETTERS
MIHM, FIHM, CIHM

THE ROYAL SOCIETY FOR PUBLIC HEALTH

John Snow House
59 Mansell Street
London E1 8AN
Tel: 020 7265 7300
Fax: 020 7265 7301
E-mail: via website
Website: www.rsph.org.uk

The RSPH was formed in October 2008 by the merger of the Royal Society for the Promotion of Health (RSPH/RSH) and the Royal Institute of Public Health (RIPH). We offer a wide range of vocationally related qualifications in the fields of food safety and nutrition, hygiene, health and safety, pest control, health promotion and the built environment.

MEMBERSHIP
Associate (ARSPH)

Licentiate (LRSPH)
Member (MRSPH)
Fellow (FRSPH)
Student

QUALIFICATION/EXAMINATIONS
Please see the RSPH's website.

DESIGNATORY LETTERS
ARSPH, LRSPH, MRSPH, FRSPH

HORSES AND HORSE RIDING
Membership of Professional Institutions and Associations

EQUESTRIAN QUALIFICATIONS GB LTD

Equestrian Qualifications GB Ltd
Equestrian House
Abbey Park
Kenilworth
Warwickshire CV8 2XZ
Tel: 02476 840544
Fax: 02476 840501
E-mail: enquiry@equestrian-qualifications.org.uk
Website: www.equestrian-qualifications.org.uk

EQL offers vocational and work-based qualifications for the Equestrian Industry. We work in partnership with a variety of organisations to develop and award qualifications for grooms, stable managers and coaches. Our qualifications include UKCC qualifications, British Horse Society qualifications, Work Based Diplomas, Scottish Vocational Qualifications and Equestrian Tourism Qualifications.

QUALIFICATION/EXAMINATIONS
Our Awards include
BHS Horse Knowledge and Care Level 1 – Level 4
BHS Riding Exams Level 1 – Level 4

BHS Coaching and Teaching Exams Level 2 – Level 5
UKCC Certificates in Coaching (specialist routes)
Level 1 – Level 3
Work Based Diplomas
Scottish Vocational Qualifications

The BHS also offers higher level qualifications for BHS Instructor and Fellowship of the BHS, as well as those for the recreational horse owner.

EQL website: www.equestrian-qualifications.org.uk
BHS website: www.bhs.org.uk

HOUSING

Membership of Professional Institutions and Associations

THE CHARTERED INSTITUTE OF HOUSING

Octavia House
Westwood Way
Coventry CV4 8JP
Tel: 024 7685 1700
E-mail: membership.services@cih.org
Website: www.cih.org

The CIH is the professional body for people involved in housing and communities. We are a registered charity and not-for-profit organization. We have a diverse and growing membership of over 22,000 people – both in the public and private sectors – living and working in over 20 countries on five continents across the world.

MEMBERSHIP

Offering two grades of membership we look to support members at all stages of their career:
CIH Member
CIH Chartered Member
Visit www.cih.org/membership to find out more about CIH membership.

QUALIFICATION/EXAMINATIONS

Certificate Courses
The CIH offers a range of certificated courses at Levels 2, 3 and 4 delivered at various centres across the UK. They are also available by online learning.
Professional Qualifications
The CIH Professional Qualification can be achieved at either undergraduate or postgraduate level, FT or PT.
Please see the CIH's website for details.

DESIGNATORY LETTERS

CIH Members: CIH Member or CIHM, CIH Chartered Members: CIH Chartered Member or CIHCM (existing Fellows can continue to use FCIH and Honorary Members can use (Hon).

INDEXING

Membership of Professional Institutions and Associations

SOCIETY OF INDEXERS

Woodbourn Business Centre
10 Jessell Street
Sheffield S9 3HY
Tel: 01142 449561
E-mail: admin@indexers.org.uk
Website: www.indexers.org.uk

The Society of Indexers is the professional body for indexing in the UK and Ireland, and exists to promote indexing, the quality of indexes and the profession of indexing. We offer information to publishers and other organizations on commissioning indexes and our online directory 'Indexers Available' provides an up-to-date guide to indexers currently working in a wide range of fields.

MEMBERSHIP

Student Member
Member
Professional Member (MSocInd)
Advanced Professional Member (MSocInd(Adv))
Fellow (FSocInd)
Corporate Member

INDUSTRIAL SAFETY

Membership of Professional Institutions and Associations

BRITISH SAFETY COUNCIL

70 Chancellors Road
London W6 9RS
Tel: 020 8741 1231
Fax: 0844 583 4731
E-mail: info@britsafe.org
Website: www.britsafe.org

The BSC is one of the world's leading health and safety organizations. Our mission is to keep people healthy and safe at work. Our range of charitable initiatives, such as free health and safety qualifications for school children, is supported by a broad mix of commercial activities centred on membership, training, auditing and qualifications.

MEMBERSHIP
UK Member
International Member

QUALIFICATION/EXAMINATIONS
Award in COSHH Risk Assessment (Level 2)
Award in DSE Risk Assessment (Level 2)
Award in Fire Risk Assessment (Level 2)
Award in Manual Handling Risk Assessment (Level 2)
Award in Risk Assessment (Level 2)
Award in Supervising Staff Safely (Level 2)
Certificate in Occupational Health and Safety (Level 3)
Diploma in Occupational Health and Safety (Level 6)
International Certificate in Occupational Health and Safety
International Diploma in Occupational Health and Safety
Entry Level Award in Workplace Hazard Awareness
Award in Health and Safety at Work (Level 1)
Certificate in Fire Safety and Risk Management
National Certificate in Construction Health and Safety

HEALTH & SAFETY EXECUTIVE APPROVED MINING QUALIFICATIONS

Mining Qualifications, The Health & Safety Executive
2nd Floor, Foundry House
3 Millsands, Riverside Exchange
Sheffield
South Yorkshire S3 8NH
Tel: 0114 291 2394
Fax: 0114 291 2399
E-mail: sarah.johnson@hse.gsi.gov.uk
Website: www.hse.gov.uk/mining

The HSE issues First and Second Class Certificates of Qualification as required under the Management and Administration of Safety and Health at Mines Regulations (MASHAM) 1993 for the appointment of a manager and undermanager respectively, in mines of coal, shale and fireclay in the UK. It also issues certificates to Mining Mechanical and Mining Electrical Engineers, Mechanics and Electricians Class I and Class II, Mines Surveyor, and Mines Deputy. For details see: www.hse.gov.uk/mining

INTERNATIONAL INSTITUTE OF RISK AND SAFETY MANAGEMENT

Suite 7a
77 Fulham Palace Road
London W6 8JA
Tel: 020 8741 9100
Fax: 020 8741 1349
E-mail: info@iirsm.org
Website: www.iirsm.org

The IIRSM is a professional body for health & safety practitioners and specialists in associated professions. Our aim is to advance professional standards in accident prevention and occupational health throughout the world. We have more than 8,100 members, in the UK and over 70 other countries, to whom we provide support and offer advice via a technical helpline.

MEMBERSHIP
Student

Affiliate
Associate (AIIRSM)
Member (MIIRSM)
Specialist Member (SIIRSM)
Fellow (FIIRSM)
Specialist Fellow (SFIIRSM)

DESIGNATORY LETTERS
AIIRSM, MIIRSM, SIIRSM, FIIRSM, SFIIRSM

NEBOSH (THE NATIONAL EXAMINATION BOARD IN OCCUPATIONAL SAFETY AND HEALTH)

Dominus Way
Meridian Business Park
Leicester LE19 1QW
Tel: (+44) 116 263 4700
Fax: (+44) 116 282 4000
E-mail: info@nebosh.org.uk
Website: www.nebosh.org.uk

NEBOSH offers globally recognized qualifications designed to meet the health, safety, environmental and risk management needs of all places of work. Courses leading to NEBOSH qualifications attract over 50,000 candidates annually in over 120 countries around the world.

MEMBERSHIP
NEBOSH's National General Certificate, National Certificate in Fire Safety and Risk Management, National Certificate in Construction Health and Safety, and the International General Certificate are all accepted as meeting the academic requirements to apply for Technical Membership (Tech IOSH) of the Institution of Occupational Safety and Health (IOSH). In partnership with the Association for Project Safety (APS) the NEBOSH National and International Certificates in Construction Health and Safety meet the headline entrance criteria requirements for Construction Safety Associate membership (AaPS).

In addition holders of either the NEBOSH National or International Diploma in Occupational Health and Safety and either the NEBOSH National or International Certificate in Construction Health and Safety meet the headline qualification entrance criteria requirements for Registered Construction Safety Practitioner (RMaPS).

NEBOSH environmental management qualifications are now being accepted by CIWEM (The Chartered Institution of Water and Environmental Management) as meeting its membership requirements.

The NEBOSH Certificate in Environmental Management will be accepted for its new Technician Membership grade entitling the use of post-nominal designation (TechCIWEM).

The NEBOSH National Diploma in Environmental Management fulfils the qualification requirements for non-chartered Member of CIWEM (MCIWEM).

Progression on to chartered membership is a further opportunity.

NEBOSH's National Diploma and International Diploma are accepted as meeting the requirements to apply for Graduate Membership (Grad IOSH) of the Institution of Occupational Safety and Health (IOSH).

A NEBOSH Diploma provides a sound basis for progression to MSc level: a number of UK universities offer MSc programmes that accept the National Diploma as a full or partial entry requirement.

The new Masters of Research (MRes) Degree is open to holders of a NEBOSH Diploma who wish to further their career in Health and Safety and/or Environment. It will be delivered by distance learning through research directly relevant to the candidate's own work.

QUALIFICATION/EXAMINATIONS

NEBOSH Environmental Awareness at Work Qualification

NEBOSH Health and Safety at Work Qualification

NEBOSH Health, Safety and Environment in the Process Industries Qualification

NEBOSH National Certificate in Construction Health and Safety

NEBOSH Certificate in Environmental Management

NEBOSH National Certificate in Fire Safety and Risk Management

NEBOSH National General Certificate in Occupational Health and Safety

NEBOSH International General Certificate in Occupational Health and Safety

NEBOSH International Technical Certificate in Oil and Gas Operational Safety

NEBOSH National Certificate in the Management of Health and Well-being at Work

NEBOSH International Certificate in Construction Health and Safety

NEBOSH International Certificate in Fire Safety and Risk Management

NEBOSH National Diploma in Environmental Management

NEBOSH National Diploma in Occupational Health and Safety

NEBOSH International Diploma in Occupational Health and Safety

Masters programmes in partnership with the University of Hull

MRes in Occupational Health and Safety Management

MRes in Occupational Health, Safety and Environmental Management

MRes in Environmental Management

MSc in Occupational Health and Safety Management

MSc in Occupational Health, Safety and Environmental Management

MSc in Environmental Management

DESIGNATORY LETTERS
DipNEBOSH, EnvDipNEBOSH

THE INSTITUTION OF OCCUPATIONAL SAFETY AND HEALTH

The Grange
Highfield Drive
Wigston
Leicestershire LE18 1NN
Tel: 0116 257 3100
Fax: 0116 257 3101
E-mail: membership@iosh.co.uk
Website: www.iosh.co.uk

IOSH is the world's largest organization for health and safety professionals, with more than 44,000 members worldwide, including 13,000 Chartered Safety and Health Practitioners. The Institution was founded in 1945 and is an independent, not-for-profit organization that sets professional standards, supports and develops members, and provides authoritative advice and guidance on health and safety issues.

MEMBERSHIP
Affiliate Member
Associate Member
Technical Member (Tech IOSH)
Graduate Member (Grad IOSH)
Chartered Member (CMIOSH)
Chartered Fellow (CFIOSH)

DESIGNATORY LETTERS
AIOSH, Tech IOSH, Grad IOSH, CMIOSH, CFIOSH

INSURANCE AND ACTUARIAL WORK
Membership of Professional Institutions and Associations

ASSOCIATION OF AVERAGE ADJUSTERS

c/o RTI Ltd
2nd Floor, International House
1 St Katharine's Way
London E1W 1UN
Tel: 020 748 1250
E-mail: aaa@rtiForensics.com
Website: www.average-adjusters.com

The AAA was founded in 1869 to promote correct principles in the adjustment of marine insurance claims and general average, uniformity of practice among average adjusters and the maintenance of good professional conduct. It ensures the independence and impartiality of its members by imposing a strict code of conduct and has close links with other international associations and insurance markets.

MEMBERSHIP
Subscriber

Associate
Fellow

QUALIFICATION/EXAMINATIONS
The Association's examination consists of 6 modules. Passes in Modules A1 & A2 are required for Associateship, passes in Modules F3, F4, F5 and F6 for Fellowship. For details see the Association's website.

THE CHARTERED INSTITUTE OF LOSS ADJUSTERS

51–55 Gresham Street
London EC2V 7HQ
Tel: 020 7216 7580
E-mail: info@cila.co.uk
Website: www.cila.co.uk

The CILA, which was founded in 1941, is the professional body representing the claims specialists who investigate, negotiate and agree the conclusion of insurance and other claims on behalf of insurers and policyholders. We safeguard the interests of our members and maintain the high standards of the profession by requiring them to abide by our code of professional conduct.

MEMBERSHIP
Student Member

Ordinary Member
Certificate Member (Cert CILA)
Associate (ACILA)
Fellow (FCILA)
Honorary Member

QUALIFICATION/EXAMINATIONS
ACILA examination

DESIGNATORY LETTERS
Cert CILA, Dip CILA, ACILA, FCILA

THE CHARTERED INSURANCE INSTITUTE

42–48 High Road
South Woodford
London E18 2JP
Tel: 020 8989 8464
Fax: 020 8530 3052
E-mail: customer.serv@cii.co.uk
Website: www.cii.co.uk

The CII is the premier professional body for those working in the insurance and financial services industry. We are dedicated to promoting higher standards of competence and integrity through the provision of relevant qualifications for employees at all levels across all sectors of the industry.

MEMBERSHIP
Ordinary Member
Qualified Member
Associate Member (ACII)
Fellow (FCII)

QUALIFICATION/EXAMINATIONS
Award in Financial Planning
Certificate in Equity Release
Certificate in Financial Planning
Certificate in Insurance
Certificate in Life and Pensions
Certificate in Mortgage Advice
Diploma in Financial Planning
Diploma in Insurance
Advanced Diploma in Financial Planning

Advanced Diploma in Insurance
Award for the Foundation Insurance Test
Award in General Insurance
Award in London Market Insurance
Award in Customer Service Insurance
Award in Financial Administration
Award in Bancassurance
Award in Investment Planning
Certificate in Contract Wording
Certificate in Insurance and Financial Services
Certificate in London Market Insurance Specialisation
Certificate in Discretionary Investment Management
Certificate in Paraplanning
Certificate in Securities Advice and Dealing
Certificate in Investment Operations
Diploma in Regulated Financial Planning
Msc in Insurance and Risk Management
Msc in Wealth Management

DESIGNATORY LETTERS
ACII, FCII

THE FACULTY AND INSTITUTE OF ACTUARIES

Faculty of Actuaries
Maclaurin House
18 Dublin Street
Edinburgh EH1 3PP
Tel: 0131 240 1313
E-mail: faculty@actuaries.org.uk
Website: www.actuaries.org.uk

Institute of Actuaries
Staple Inn Hall
High Holborn
London WC1V 7QJ
Tel: 020 7632 2111
E-mail: institute@actuaries.org.uk

Napier House
4 Worcester Street
Oxford OX1 2AW
Tel: 01865 268211
E-mail: institute@actuaries.org.uk

Actuaries are experts in assessing the financial impact of tomorrow's uncertain events. They enable financial decisions to be made with more confidence by analysing the past, modelling the future, assessing the risks involved, and communicating what the results mean in financial terms.

MEMBERSHIP
Student Member
Affiliate Member

Associate (AFA or AIA)
Fellow (FFA or FIA)
Honorary Fellow

QUALIFICATION/EXAMINATIONS
Certificate in Financial Mathematics

DESIGNATORY LETTERS
AFA, AIA, FFA, FIA

JOURNALISM
Membership of Professional Institutions and Associations

NATIONAL COUNCIL FOR THE TRAINING OF JOURNALISTS

NCTJ Training Ltd
The New Granary
Newport
Saffron Walden
Essex CB11 3PL
Tel: 01799 544014
Fax: 01799 544015
E-mail: info@nctj.com
Website: www.nctj.com

The NCTJ provides a range of multimedia journalism training products and services in the UK, including: accredited courses; apprenticeships; qualifications and examinations; awards; careers information; distance learning; short courses and CPD; information and research; publications and events. We play an influential role in all areas of journalism education and training.

QUALIFICATION/EXAMINATIONS
Certificate in Foundation Journalism
Apprenticeship Standard for Junior Journalists
Diploma in Journalism
National Qualification in Journalism (NQJ)

THE CHARTERED INSTITUTE OF JOURNALISTS

2 Dock Offices
Surrey Quays Road
London SE16 2XU
Tel: 020 7252 1187
Fax: 020 7232 2302
E-mail: memberservices@cioj.co.uk
Website: www.cioj.co.uk

The CIoJ, which dates back to 1884, is a professional body and trade union for journalists. We expect our members to uphold high standards in the way they work and to adhere to a strict code of conduct, and in return we champion journalistic freedom, protect their interests in the workplace and campaign for better working conditions.

MEMBERSHIP
Student Member
Affiliate Member
Trainee Member
Full Member
International Member

DESIGNATORY LETTERS
MCIJ – Member, FCIJ – Fellow

LAND AND PROPERTY
Membership of Professional Institutions and Associations

RICS (ROYAL INSTITUTION OF CHARTERED SURVEYORS)

Parliament Square
London SW1P 3AD
Tel: 024 7686 8555
Fax: 020 7334 3811
E-mail: contactrics@rics.org
Website: www.rics.org/careers

RICS, an independent, not-for-profit organization, has around 100,000 qualified members and more than 50,000 students and trainees in some 140 countries, and provides the world's leading professional qualification in land, property, construction and associated environmental issues. We accredit over 600 courses at leading universities worldwide and provide impartial, authoritative advice on key issues for business, society and governments.

MEMBERSHIP
Student
Associate (AssocRICS)
Member (MRICS)
Fellow (FRICS)

DESIGNATORY LETTERS
AssocRICS, MRICS, FRICS

THE COLLEGE OF ESTATE MANAGEMENT

Whiteknights
Reading
Berkshire RG6 6AW
Tel: 0118 921 4696
Fax: 0118 921 4620
E-mail: enquiries@cem.ac.uk
Website: www.cem.ac.uk

The College of Estate Management is the leading provider of supported distance learning for real estate and construction professionals. We have been playing a key role in the property world for over 90 years. At any one time we have over 4,000 students based all over the world.

QUALIFICATION/EXAMINATIONS
BCSC Diploma in Shopping Centre Management
BSc(Hons) Building Surveying
BSc(Hons) Construction Management
BSc(Hons) Estate Management
BSc(Hons) Property Management
BSc(Hons) Quantity Surveying
Postgraduate Diploma/MSc Conservation of the Historic Environment
Postgraduate Diploma/MSc Surveying
MBA Real Estate and Construction Management
Postgraduate Diploma/MSc Facilities Management
Postgraduate Diploma/MSc Property Investment
RICS Professional Membership Graduate Route – Adaptation 1

THE INSTITUTE OF REVENUES, RATING AND VALUATION

Northumberland House
5th Floor
303–306 High Holborn
London WC1V 7JZ
Tel: 020 7831 3505
Fax: 020 7831 2048
E-mail: education@irrv.org.uk
Website: www.irrv.org.uk

The Institute offers professional and technical qualifications for all those whose professional work is concerned with local authority revenues and benefits, valuation for rating, property taxation and the appeals procedure. Our qualifications are widely recognized throughout the profession.

MEMBERSHIP
Student Member
Affiliate Member
Graduate Member
Technician Member (Tech IRRV)
Corporate Member (IRRV)
Diploma Member (IRRV Dip)
Honours Member (IRRV Hons)
Honorary Member
Fellow (FIRRV)

QUALIFICATION/EXAMINATIONS
Level 3 Certificate in Local Taxation and Benefits OR Business Rates
Level 3 Local Taxation & Benefits (QCF)
Professional Diploma in Local Taxation and Benefits Honours

DESIGNATORY LETTERS
Tech IRRV, IRRV, IRRV (Dip), IRRV (Hons), FIRRV

THE NATIONAL FEDERATION OF PROPERTY PROFESSIONALS AWARDING BODY

Arbon House
6 Tournament Court
Edgehill Drive
Warwick CV34 6LG
Tel: 0845 250 6008
Fax: 01926 417789
E-mail: quals@nfopp.co.uk
Website: www.nfopp-awardingbody.co.uk

The **NFOPP Awarding Body** is committed to raising standards within agency through the provision of accredited, nationally recognized qualifications. We are recognized by the Qualifications and Examinations Regulator (Ofqual) and Welsh Government and we have to follow strict guidelines and maintain quality standards in the provision of all our qualifications.

MEMBERSHIP
For membership details of the following organizations please refer to the relevant website:
APIP: www.apip.co.uk
ARLA: www.arla.co.uk
ICBA: www.icba.uk.com
NAEA: www.naea.co.uk
NAVA: www.nava.org.uk

QUALIFICATION/EXAMINATIONS
NFoPP **Level 2 Award** in Introduction to Residential Property Management Practice (QCF)
NFoPP **Level 3 Technical Award** in Commercial Property Agency (QCF)

NFoPP **Level 3 Technical Award** in Real Property Auctioneering (QCF)
NFoPP **Level 3 Technical Award** in Residential Letting and Property Management (QCF)
NFoPP **Level 3 Technical Award** in Residential Letting and Property Management Northern Ireland (QCF)
NFoPP **Level 3 Technical Award** in Sale of Residential Property (QCF)
NFoPP **Level 3 Technical Award** in Chattels Auctioneering (QCF)
NFoPP **Level 3 Technical Award** in Residential Inventory Management & Practice (QCF)
NFoPP **Level 4 Certificate** in Residential Letting & Property Management (QCF)
NFoPP **Level 4 Certificate** in Sale of Residential Property (QCF)
NFoPP **Level 4 Certificate** in Commercial Property Agency (QCF)
NFoPP **Level 6 Technical Award** in Sale of Residential Property Scotland (SCQF)
NFoPP **Level 6 Technical Award** in Residential Letting & Property Management Scotland (SCQF)

THE PROPERTY CONSULTANTS SOCIETY

Basement Office
Surrey Court
1 Surrey Street
Arundel
West Sussex BN18 9DT
Tel: 01903 883787
E-mail: info@propertyconsultantssociety.org
Website: www.propertyconsultantssociety.org

The Property Consultants Society is a non-profit-making organization that offers advice to qualified surveyors, architects, valuers, auctioneers, land and estate agents, master builders, construction engineers, accountants and members of the legal profession to help them to undertake their property consultancy in a competent, legitimate and publicly acceptable way.

MEMBERSHIP
Student (SPCS)
Licentiate (LPCS)
Associate (APCS)
Fellow (FPCS)

Honorary Member

DESIGNATORY LETTERS
SPCS, LPCS, APCS, FPCS

LANDSCAPE ARCHITECTURE
Membership of Professional Institutions and Associations

LANDSCAPE INSTITUTE

Charles Darwin House
107 Gray's Inn Road
London WC1X 8TZ
Tel: 020 7685 2640
E-mail: membership@landscapeinstitute.org
Website: www.landscapeinstitute.org

The LI is an educational charity and chartered body responsible for protecting, conserving and enhancing the natural and built environment for the benefit of the public. We champion well-designed and well-managed urban and rural landscape. Our 6,000 members include chartered landscape architects, academics and scientists working for local authorities, government agencies and in private practice, and students.

MEMBERSHIP
Student Member

Affiliate Member
Licentiate Member
Chartered Member (CMLI)
Fellow (FLI)
Academic

QUALIFICATION/EXAMINATIONS
Pathway to Chartership oral examination conferring chartered professional status (CMLI)

DESIGNATORY LETTERS
CMLI, FLI

LANGUAGES, LINGUISTICS AND TRANSLATION
Membership of Professional Institutions and Associations

INSTITUTE OF TRANSLATION & INTERPRETING

Milton Keynes Business Centre
Foxhunter Drive
Linford Wood
Milton Keynes MK14 6GD
Tel: 01908 325250
Fax: 01908 325259
E-mail: info@iti.org.uk
Website: www.iti.org.uk

The Institute of Translation & Interpreting is one of the primary sources of information on these services to government, industry, the media and the general public. We promote the highest standards, providing guidance to those entering the profession and advice to those who offer language services and to their customers.

MEMBERSHIP
Associate (AITI)
Student

Qualified Member (MITI)
Corporate Member
Fellow

QUALIFICATION/EXAMINATIONS
Applicants for qualified membership must take an exam (translators) or attend an interview (interpreters).

THE CHARTERED INSTITUTE OF LINGUISTS

Saxon House
48 Southwark Street
London SE1 1UN
Tel: 020 7940 3100
Fax: 020 7940 3101
E-mail: info@iol.org.uk
Website: www.iol.org.uk

The Chartered Institute of Linguistics, founded in 1910, is a respected language assessment and accredited awarding body, with about 6,500 members. Our aims include promoting the learning and use of modern languages, improving the status of all professional linguistics, and ensuring the maintenance of high professional standards through adherence to our code of conduct.

MEMBERSHIP
Registered Student
Associate Member (ACIL)

Member (MCIL)
Fellow (FCIL)
Chartered Linguist (CL)

QUALIFICATION/EXAMINATIONS
Certificate in Bilingual Skills (CBS)
Diploma in Public Service Interpreting (DPSI)
International Diploma in Bilingual Translation (IDBT)
Diploma in Translation (DipTrans)

DESIGNATORY LETTERS
ACIL, MCIL, FCIL, CL

THE GREEK INSTITUTE

29 Onslow Gardens
London N21 1DY
Tel: 020 8360 7968
Fax: 020 8360 7968
E-mail: info@greekinstitute.co.uk
Website: www.greekinstitute.co.uk

The Greek Institute, which was founded in 1969, is a non-profit-making cultural organization that promotes Modern Greek studies and culture through lectures, publications, literary competitions, Greek cultural evenings and the award of Certificates and a Diploma which are recognized by many UK universities as equivalent to GCSE and GCE A level Modern Greek.

MEMBERSHIP
Member
Associate (AGI)
Fellow (FGI)

QUALIFICATION/EXAMINATIONS
Certificate in Greek Conversation – Basic Stage: Levels 1 and 2
Certificate in Greek Conversation – Intermediate Stage: Levels 3 and 4
Certificate in Greek Conversation – Higher Stage: Levels 5 and 6
Preliminary Certificate
Intermediate Certificate
Advanced Certificate
Diploma in Greek Translation (DipGrTrans)

DESIGNATORY LETTERS
AGI, FGI

LAW

ENGLAND AND WALES

MAGISTRATES

The President of the Courts of England and Wales, The Lord Chief Justice, is head of the Judiciary. He is responsible for the welfare, training and deployment of magistrates, for approving the names of the candidates recommended for appointment and for disciplinary action, short of removal. He also has responsibility for the protection of judicial independence and for working to ensure that the magistracy reflects the diversity of society as a whole.

There are key qualities that a magistrate must possess: good character, understanding and effective communication, social awareness, maturity and a sense of fairness, sound judgement, commitment and reliability. Magistrates do not sit exams nor do they have to be legally qualified.

Before sitting in court, magistrates must undertake some basic training, which includes structured observations in court. This covers practice and procedure in court, structured decision making, sentencing, and so on. New magistrates are assigned a mentor for the first year or so. Core training also involves visits to penal institutions to equip magistrates with the key knowledge they need. Consolidation training takes place at the end of the first year; this is designed to help magistrates plan for their ongoing development and prepare for their first appraisal which takes place about 12 to 18 months after appointment. Magistrates only sit in adult courts when first appointed. Having got that experience they may apply to sit in youth courts and family courts and have to undertake more training before they can sit.

Ongoing training and development includes appraisals which take place every three years, continuation training which takes place once every three years, usually before appraisals, update training on new legislation and procedures and threshold training which accompanies each development in a magistrate's role.

JUDGES

All judicial office holders are Her Majesty's Judges and as such all appointments are made by the Queen or her Ministers. All candidates for judicial appointment in England and Wales have been selected by the independent Judicial Appointments Commission (JAC jac.judiciary.gov.uk), which passes its recommendations to the Lord Chancellor for approval. The key statutory responsibilities of the JAC are to select candidates solely on merit; to select only people of good character; to have regard to the need to encourage diversity in the range of people available for selection for appointments.

Once the JAC's selections have been received, the actual appointments are made in slightly different ways depending on the type of post. The Lord Chancellor himself appoints Deputy District Judges and most members of tribunals. He also appoints the 30,000 unpaid magistrates (who are selected by local Advisory Committees, not by the JAC). The Queen appoints High Court and Circuit Judges, Masters, Registrars and District Judges, District Judges (Magistrates' Courts) and Recorders on the advice of the Lord Chancellor. A special panel convened by the JAC appoints the Lord Chief Justice. The Queen appoints Heads of Division, Court of Appeal judges and senior judges with lengthy judicial experience, on the recommendation of a selection panel convened by the JAC. Scotland and Northern Ireland have their own separate court systems, with their own arrangements for appointing members of the judiciary.

The Supreme Court (http:/supremecourt.uk) has jurisdiction over the whole of the UK, so its Justices are not selected by the JAC, which is an England and Wales body. Rather, a special committee is set up, which is made up of the three judicial appointments bodies from around the UK (England and Wales, Scotland and Northern Ireland), who recommend a name to Ministers. The Queen appoints the Justices on the basis of advice from the Prime Minister.

Candidates for appointment as Justices of the Supreme Court must have held high judicial office for two years or must have been practising barristers or solicitors of the senior courts for at least 15 years (www.supremecourt.uk/faqs.html\1d). More information about judges can be found at the Courts and Tribunals Judiciary website: www.judiciary.gov.uk

OFFICERS OF THE COURT

Officers of the Court include judicial and administrative staff; the former include Masters and Registrars, the latter secretaries and clerks to the judges and the staff who administer the court service. Details are given in *The English Legal System*, 16th edition, 2014–5 (Routledge). Qualifications for the judicial offices vary somewhat, but most appointments are limited to established barristers and solicitors.

THE LEGAL PROFESSION

The legal profession consists of two branches. Each performs distinct duties, although there is a degree of overlap in some aspects of their work.

Solicitors undertake all ordinary legal business for their clients (with whom they are in direct contact). They may also appear on behalf of a client in the magistrates' and county courts and tribunals, and with specialist training are able to represent them in the higher courts (Crown Court, High Court and Court of Appeal). The website for the Law Society contains further information (www.lawsociety.org.uk).

Barristers (known collectively as the 'Bar' and collectively and individually as 'Counsel') advise on legal problems submitted by solicitors and conduct cases in court when instructed by a solicitor; only barristers or qualified solicitor advocates may represent clients in the higher courts. More information on barristers can be found on The Bar Council website (www.barcouncil.org.uk).

LEGAL EXECUTIVES

Both graduates and non-graduates can work in a legal office with the option of qualifying as a solicitor through further vocational training. Chartered Legal Executive lawyers are 'authorised persons' undertaking 'reserved legal activities' alongside, for example, solicitors and barristers. As a general rule, a Chartered Legal Executive lawyer is able to undertake all the same work that may be undertaken by a solicitor, with some conditions. The Chartered Institute of Legal Executives website has information on becoming a legal executive and the work they can undertake (www.cilex.org.uk).

CORONERS

Coroners must be barristers, solicitors or legally qualified medical practitioners of not less than five years' standing. They are appointed by local authorities. There are approximately 109 coroner areas in England and Wales; each area is locally funded and resourced by local authorities. Coroners are independent judicial officers. When not engaged in coronal duties, coroners (apart from 'whole-time' coroners) continue in their legal or medical practices. The Chief Coroner is head of the coroner system, assuming overall responsibilty and providing national leadership for coroners in England and Wales. He oversees the implementation of the Coroner and Justice Act 2009. Further information from the Coroners' Society of England and Wales, website: www.coronersociety.org.uk and the Crown Prosecution Service website: www.cps.gov.uk/legal/a_to_c/coroners/#a02.

BARRISTERS

Qualification as a barrister at the Bar of England and Wales

There are three stages that must be completed to qualify as a barrister. The academic stage consists of an undergraduate degree in law or in any other subject with a minimum of a 2:2. For those with an undergraduate degree in a subject other than law a one-year conversion course (CPE/GDL) must be completed.

Before commencing the vocational stage candidates must join one of the four Inns and then undertake the Bar Professional Training Course (BPTC), which is either one year full time or two years part time. The main skills taught on the BPTC are: casework skills, legal research, fact management, general written skills including opinion-writing (that is, giving written advice) and drafting, management and interpersonal skills including conference skills (interviewing clients), resolution of disputes out of court (ReDOC) and advocacy (court or tribunal appearances). The main areas of legal knowledge taught on the BPTC are: civil litigation, evidence and remedies, criminal litigation, evidence and sentencing, professional ethics, and two optional subjects or one double optional subject selected from a choice of at least six.

Three examinations are set by a Central Examinations Board comprised of experienced legal practitioners and academics appointed by the Bar Standards Board (BSB). The examinations are Civil Litigation, Evidence and Remedies, Criminal Litigation, Evidence and Sentencing and Professional Ethics. Applicants will also have to take the Bar Course Aptitude Test. It aims to test critical thinking and reasoning, but does not test legal knowledge. Practice tests are available on the BSB website. The Aptitude Test will ensure that those undertaking the BPTC have the required skills to succeed.

Once the BPTC has been successfully completed candidates are called to the Bar by their Inn. The Pupillage Stage consists of one year spent in an authorized pupillage training organization. Pupillage is divided into two parts: the non-practising six months (also known as 'the first six') and the practising six months (also known as 'the second six').

To find out more about all three stages of qualification as a barrister visit www.barcouncil.org. uk and www.barstandardsboard.org.uk

SOLICITORS

Qualification as a solicitor in England and Wales

To practise as a solicitor in England and Wales a person must have been admitted as a solicitor, his or her name having been entered on the Roll of Solicitors, and must hold a practising certificate issued by The Solicitors Regulation Authority (SRA) (Solicitors Regulation Authority, The Cube, 199 Wharfside Street, Birmingham B1 1RN; Tel: 0370 606 2555; www.sra.org.uk).

The SRA is the independent regulatory body of the Law Society of England and Wales. People will be admitted as solicitors only if they have passed the appropriate academic and vocational course and have completed a training contract and Professional Skills course, or have transferred from another jurisdiction or the Bar. The SRA controls the training of solicitors. Most solicitors become members of the Law Society, but membership is not compulsory. Intending solicitors other than Fellows of the Chartered Institute of Legal Executives (CILEx), Justices Clerk's Assistants and qualified lawyers from overseas, are required to serve a period of training with a practising solicitor after they have completed the legal practice course.

All new entrants to the profession are required to complete a Disclosure and Barring Service (DBS) standard disclosure prior to admission. Candidates wishing to start training must enrol as a student with the SRA and satisfy it that they have successfully completed the academic stage of training and there are no issues that may call their character and suitability into question.

It is not necessary for the first degree to be in law as about 20 per cent of solicitors qualify via the non-law graduate route. The key stages of this are:

- degree in any subject;
- Common Professional Examination/Graduate Diploma in Law;
- Legal Practice course;
- practice-based training incorporating the Professional Skills course;
- admission to the roll of solicitors.

THE COMMON PROFESSIONAL EXAMINATION (CPE) OR GRADUATE DIPLOMA IN LAW (GDL)

The seven taught modules are the foundation subjects prescribed by the Joint Academic Stage Board on behalf of the Law Society and General Council of the Bar: Criminal Law, Contract Law, the Law of Tort, Equity and Trusts, Public Law, European Union Law and Property Law. For an up-to-date list of course providers for the CPE, use the training provider search in the student section on the SRA website: www.sra.org.uk

THE LEGAL PRACTICE COURSE

Stage 1 covers core practice areas: Litigation, Property Law and Practice (PLP), Business Law and Practice (BLP); Course Skills: Research, Writing, Drafting, Interviewing and Advising, and Advocacy (these skills form an integral part of the compulsory and elective subjects) and also Professional Conduct and Regulation, Taxation and Wills and Administration of Estates; Solicitors Accounts and Professional Conduct and Regulation; Stage 2 covers three vocational electives chosen from a range of corporate client or private client topics (the range of electives available can differ from institution to institution). An up-to-date list of course providers for the LPC is available using the training provider search in the student section on the SRA website: www.sra.org.uk

TRAINING CONTRACT

The training contract to be served by all intending solicitors, other than Fellows of the Institute of Legal Executives and Justices Clerk's Assistants, is two years full time or a maximum of four years part time. The training contract can also be a part-time-study training contract that normally lasts between three and four years. During this period the trainee works and is studying the last two years of a part-time qualifying law degree, the part-time Common Professional Examination course and/or the part-time Legal Practice Course.

The law graduate who holds a qualifying law degree must complete the Legal Practice course at a recognized institution, and then serve under the training contract for two years. The non-law graduate must first pass the Common Professional Exam (CPE) or the Postgraduate Diploma in Law, having attended either a one-year full-time or two-year part-time preparatory course. He or she may then serve under the training contract for two years after completion of a Legal Practice Course. A Professional

Skills course must be attended and successfully completed during the training contract.

Fellows of the Institute of Chartered Legal Executives (CILEx) may obtain partial or full exemptions from the CPE and Justices Clerk's Assistants courses by virtue of similar subjects passed in their Fellowship exams or the Diploma in Magisterial Law. After passing or being exempted from the CPE, the Fellow/ Justices Clerk's Assistant may be exempt from serving under a training contract following successful completion of a Legal Practice Course. A Professional Skills course must be taken prior to application for admission.

THE PROFESSIONAL SKILLS COURSE

The aim of the Professional Skills course is to build on the foundations laid in the Legal Practice Course so as to develop a trainee's professional skills. Providers of the course, trainees and their employers are encouraged to regard the course as the first stage of a trainee's lifetime professional development.

Built upon the Legal Practice Course, the course provides training in three subject areas: financial and business skills; advocacy and communication skills; client care and professional standards. Elective topics will also be chosen, which fall within one or more of these three core areas. All trainees have to complete all sections of the course satisfactorily before being admitted. The course consists of face-to-face instruction on the core subjects, for a minimum of 18 hours each for financial and business skills and advocacy and communication skills, and a minimum of 12 hours for client care and professional standards. The elective topics require a minimum total of 24 hours, of which a minimum of 12 hours must be face-to-face. The instruction must be completed during the training contract. The PSC is offered by accredited external course providers.

QUALIFIED LAWYERS FROM OTHER JURISDICTIONS

UK and EU lawyers together with lawyers from certain foreign jurisdictions can apply for admission under the Qualified Lawyers Transfer Scheme Regulations 2011. They need to obtain a QLTS Certificate of Eligibility.

Under the European Communities Directive No 2005/36/EC, lawyers from EU jurisdictions may apply for admission if they can prove they have met the requirements of the Directive and implementing legislation. EU, Northern Irish and Scottish lawyers and barristers qualified in England and Wales follow a different transfer process and should get in touch with the SRA Contact Centre for further information. SRA Contact Centre Tel: 0370 606 2555 (International callers: +44(0)121 329 6800); Website: www.sra.org. uk/contact-us

All international applicants must satisfy the requirements and pass the QLTS Assessments. The Assessments are in two parts: Part 1 is a multiple choice test designed to test Part A of the SRA's Day One Outcomes, namely the knowledge of law expected of a newly qualified solicitor of England and Wales and consists of 180 questions; Part 2, is an Objective Structured Clinical Examination (OSCE). For the OSCE, candidates are examined in the three practice areas of:

- Business
- Property and probate
- Civil and criminal litigation

In each of these practice areas candidates do each of the following exercises once:

- Client interview and completion of attendance note/case analysis
- Advocacy/oral presentation
- Legal research
- Legal writing
- Legal drafting

In total therefore candidates undertake 15 assessed exercises: 5 in business, 5 in property and probate, and 5 in civil and criminal litigation.

The Solicitors Regulation Authority has appointed Kaplan QLTS as the assessment organization for the operation of the assessments (http://qlts.kaplan.co. uk).

EEA, Northern Irish and Scottish lawyers, and barristers qualified in England and Wales will be individually assessed against the Day One Outcomes. All transferees are required to prove their character and suitability to be a solicitor by taking the SRA Suitability Test. Candidates who have passed the LPC can get exemption from the Part 1 (MCT) assessment.

Prospective candidates wanting more information on QLTS can consult the website www.sra.org.uk/ solicitors/qlts/key-features.page for guidance, or contact the SRA on 0370 606 2555 (International callers: +44(0)121 329 6800); Website: www.sra.org.uk/contact-us..

SCOTLAND

The Court of Session, High Court of Justiciary, Sheriff Courts and Justice of the Peace Courts are administered by the Scottish Court service, an Executive Agency of the Scottish Government. For further information on Scottish Courts go to www.scotcourts.gov.uk

THE LEGAL PROFESSION

The profession consists of solicitors and advocates.

Qualification as a Solicitor in Scotland

Solicitors in Scotland have their names inserted in a Roll of Solicitors and are granted annual Certificates entitling them to practise by The Law Society of Scotland, contact details: 26 Drumsheugh Gardens, Edinburgh EH3 7YR; Tel: 0131 226 7411; Fax: 0131 225 2934; e-mail: lawscot@lawscot.org.uk; website: www.lawscot.org.uk; Education and Careers Helpline: Laura Gulliver; Tel: 0131 476 8203; careers@lawscot.org.uk; you can also use their new online chat facility to obtain career information. A Certificate is granted to candidates who have passed approved exams, completed a term of practical training and been admitted as solicitors.

THE QUALIFYING EXAMINATIONS

The standard route to qualification is the LLB (the Ordinary degree is a three-year course, the Honours is four years) followed by the Diploma in Professional Legal Practice (Professional Education and Training Stage 1: PEAT 1) and then the traineeship, the period of paid in-office training working towards the standard of the qualified solicitor (Professional Education and Training Stage 2: PEAT 2). Outcomes in professionalism, professional ethics and standards, 'professional communication' and 'business, commercial, financial and practice awareness' apply across both PEAT 1 and 2, linking them and providing real clarity across the two stages.

All trainees are required to undertake Trainee Continuing Professional Development (TCPD). All solicitors are required to undertake CPD for a minimum of 20 hours each year. To support solicitors in their CPD activities, the Society provides basic templates, which can be completed online, to assist with identifying training needs, recording CPD undertaken and evaluating the outcome of the training. A wide range of activities are acceptable as CPD, including structured and formalized one-to-one training, coaching and online training.

An alternate route to qualifying as a solicitor in Scotland is by a combination of the Law Society's own examinations and three years' pre-Diploma training. To be eligible to sit the Law Society's examinations, non-law graduates must find full-time employment as a pre-Diploma trainee with a qualified solicitor practising in Scotland. A pre-Diploma training contract lasts for three years. During the period of the training contract, a pre-Diploma trainee will study for the Law Society's examinations. European Law must be passed prior to admission as a solicitor, but can be obtained during post-Diploma training. The two routes to qualification (degree and Law Society exams) merge at this point as all intending solicitors are required to complete the Diploma in Professional Legal Practice. Upon successful completion of the Diploma the graduate will enter into a two-year post-Diploma training contract with a qualified solicitor practising in Scotland.

Qualification as an advocate in Scotland

Barristers in Scotland are called Advocates. Scottish Advocates are not only members of the Faculty of Advocates but also members of the College of Justice and officers of the Court. The procedure for the admission of 'Intrants' is subject in part to the control of the Court and in part to the control of the Faculty; the Court is responsible for most of the formal procedures and the Faculty for the exams and periods of professional training. To become an Intrant, applicants must produce evidence that they hold one of the following standard of degree: a degree with Honours, Second Class (Division 2) or above, in Scottish Law at a Scottish university, or a degree in Scottish Law at a Scottish university together with a degree with Honours, Second Class (Division 2) or above, in another subject at a UK university or an ordinary degree with distinction in Scottish Law at a Scottish university. A Diploma in Legal Practice from a Scottish University is also required, although in exceptional cases this requirement may be waived.

In order to go through the various stages of qualification and training, applicants must matriculate as intrants to the Faculty. Matriculation involves making an application to the Court of Session and to the Faculty. Further details can be obtained from the Clerk of Faculty (clerkoffaculty@advocates.org).

An Intrant must also comply with the professional training required by the Faculty, which consists of a period of 21 months' training in a solicitors' office (although the Faculty recommends a traineeship of

24 months). Subject-for-subject exemptions are granted to Intrants who have passed exams at this standard in the course of a curriculum for a law degree at a Scottish university. Every Intrant must pass or be exempted from exams in nine compulsory subjects and two optional subjects. The compulsory subjects include Roman Law of Property and Obligations, Jurisprudence, Constitutional and Administrative Law, Scottish Criminal Law, Scottish Private Law, Commercial Law and Business Institutions, Evidence, International Private Law and European Law and Institutions. In addition, and prior to the commencement of pupillage (also known as 'devilling') every Intrant must sit the Faculty's entrant examination in Evidence, Practice and Procedure. If successfully passed, the Intrant can then commence his or her pupillage.

During the first five or six weeks of pupillage pupils undertake the Foundation course. After about three months of work with their devil master, the pupils will participate in the February Skills course, comprising a series of performance workshops involving the use of documents in evidence, the conduct of a procedure roll discussion, workshops on judicial review, section 275 applications and working with expert evidence. Shortly before admission, the pupils attend the May Preparation for Practice course, covering workshops on vulnerable witnesses, longer motions, reclaiming motions, negotiation and mediation, as well as carrying out civil and criminal appeals before a serving judge.

Intrants who have passed all the necessary exams and undergone the necessary professional training as well as successfully completing their pupillage may apply to be admitted to membership of the Faculty and are admitted at a public meeting of the Faculty. Once admitted, Intrants are introduced to the Court by the Dean of Faculty, make a Declaration of Allegiance to the Sovereign in open Court and are then admitted by the Court to the public office of Advocate. For further information on becoming an advocate contact Dean's Secretariat, Faculty of Advocates, Parliament House, Edinburgh EH1 1RF; Tel: 0131 260 5795; e-mail: admissions@advocates.org.uk; website: www.advocates.org.uk

NORTHERN IRELAND

As in England and Wales, the superior courts are the Supreme Court, Court of Appeal, the High Court and the Crown Court. The latter is an exclusively criminal court. The Court of Appeal hears appeals on points of law in civil cases and criminal cases from all courts. Appeals lie from the Court of Appeal to the Supreme Court.

Inferior Courts: as in England and Wales, the county courts are principally civil courts, but in Northern Ireland they also hear appeals from conviction in the Magistrates' Courts for summary offences.

Magistrates' Courts: these deal principally with minor criminal offences (summary offences) and are presided over by Resident Magistrates (stipendiaries). Resident Magistrates are appointed by the Crown on the advice of the Lord Chancellor.

Coroners: coroners in Northern Ireland must be barristers or solicitors who have practised for not less than five years. They are appointed by the Lord Chancellor.

The legal profession

The legal profession in Northern Ireland consists of barristers and solicitors belonging to professional bodies organized on similar lines to those in England and Wales.

Qualification as a barrister in Northern Ireland

The path to becoming a barrister in Northern Ireland will differ depending on where you study, qualify and complete your pupillage training. There are different pathways for those who have trained as barristers in Northern Ireland, the Republic of Ireland or England and Wales. A different procedure exists for solicitors who wish to requalify as barristers or those who wish to transfer from European jurisdictions. Full information can be found at www.barofni.com/page/becoming-a-barrister

To qualify to practise as a barrister in Northern Ireland a candidate who has trained in Northern Ireland must have a recognized law degree of 2.1 honours standard or higher, or equivalent (the list of recognized law degrees for admission to the IPLS can be found at www.qub.ac.uk/schools/InstituteofProfessionalLegalStudies/Admissions/RecognisedLaw-Degrees). The candidate must then complete the Bar Post-Graduate Diploma in Professional Legal Studies at the Institute of Professional Legal Studies, Queen's University, Belfast (IPLS). Finally the candidate must call to the Bar of Northern Ireland and complete a 12-month pupillage. Enquiries about the Bar can be made to the Bar Council Office, The Bar Library, 91

Chichester Street, Belfast BT1 3JQ; Tel: 028 9024 1523; website: www.barofni.com).

To be called to the Bar of Northern Ireland the candidate needs to have obtained his or her Certificate of Professional Legal Studies or otherwise be qualified, to have completed and signed a Memorial and Undertaking, and to have submitted two certificates of good character.

Qualification as a solicitor in Northern Ireland

The solicitors' professional body in Northern Ireland is the Law Society of Northern Ireland (Law Society House, 96 Victoria Street, Belfast BT1 3GN; Tel: 028 9023 1614; website: www.lawsoc-ni.org). It has overall responsibility for education and admission to the profession.

Admission to training is generally dependent upon possession of a recognized law degree from a university. Details of the recognized law degrees are available on the website of the Institute of Professional Legal Studies (www.qub.ac.uk/schools/InstituteofProfessionalLegalStudies/Admissions/RecognisedLawDegrees/). Information is also available in the 'Information Booklet for Applicants', www.qub.ac.uk/schools/InstituteofProfessionalLegalStudies/Admissions. Law graduates must attend a two-year vocational apprenticeship course at the Institute of Professional Legal Studies, The Queen's University of Belfast, or the Graduate School of Professional Legal Education at the University of Ulster's Magee Campus. On completion of the two-year apprenticeship newly qualified solicitors receive restricted practising certificates, which means that although they are fully qualified they cannot practise on their own account or in partnership for at least two more years.

Non-law graduates must satisfy the Society that they possess an acceptable degree in a discipline other than law and have attained a satisfactory level of knowledge of the following subjects: Constitutional Law, Law of Tort, Law of Contract, Criminal Law, Equity, European Law, Land Law, Law of Evidence; that they have been offered a place in the Institute; and that they have obtained a Master (a solicitor with whom the applicant proposes to serve his or her apprenticeship).

Membership of Professional Institutions and Associations

CHARTERED INSTITUTE OF LEGAL EXECUTIVES (CILEX)

Kempston Manor
Kempston
Bedford MK42 7AB
Tel: 01234 841000
E-mail: membership@cilex.org.uk
Website: www.cilex.org.uk

The Chartered Institute of Legal Executives (CILEx) is the professional association which represents 20,000 Chartered Legal Executive lawyers, paralegals and other legal practitioners. Our role is to enhance the position and standing of Chartered Legal Executive lawyers in the legal profession. For more than 50 years, we have been offering unparalleled access to a flexible career in law. We work closely with Government and the Ministry of Justice and are recognised in England and Wales as one of the three core approved regulators of the legal profession alongside barristers and solicitors.

MEMBERSHIP
Student Member
Affiliate Member
Associate Member (ACILEx)

Graduate Member (GCILEx)
Chartered Legal Executive Lawyer (FCILEx)

QUALIFICATION/EXAMINATIONS
Level 1 Award/Certificate/Diploma in Legal Studies
Level 2 Award/Certificate/Diploma in Legal Studies
Level 2 Certificate/Diploma for Legal Secretaries
Level 3 Certificate/Diploma for Legal Secretaries
Level 3 Professional Diploma in Law and Practice
Level 3 Certificate in Law and Practice
Level 3 Certificate in Civil Litigation
Level 3 Certificate in Family Practice
Level 3 Certificate in Employment Practice
Level 3 Certificate in Private Client Practice
Level 3 Certificate in Property
Level 3 Diploma in Providing Legal Services
Level 4 Diploma in Commercial Litigation

Level 4 Diploma in Debt Recovery and Insolvency
Level 4 Diploma in Personal Injury Litigation
Level 4 Diploma in Providing Legal Services
Level 4 Extended Diploma in Personal Injury Litigation
Level 6 Certificate in Law

Level 6 Higher Diploma in Law and Practice
Graduate Fast-track Diploma (Level 6)

DESIGNATORY LETTERS
ACILEx, GCILEx, FCILEx

COUNCIL FOR LICENSED CONVEYANCERS

16 Glebe Road
Chelmsford
Essex CM1 1QG
Tel: 01245 349599
Fax: 01245 341300
E-mail: clc@clc-uk.org
Website: www.clc-uk.org

The CLC was established under the provisions of the Administration of Justice Act 1985 as the Regulatory Body for Licensed Conveyancers. Our purpose is to set entry standards and regulate the profession of Licensed Conveyancers effectively. CLC regulates Probate services provided by its licensed practitioners. CLC is an authorised regulator for ABS.

MEMBERSHIP
Student

Licensed Conveyancer
Probate Practitioner
ABS

QUALIFICATION/EXAMINATIONS
Foundation
Finals
Practical Training

THE ACADEMY OF EXPERTS

3 Gray's Inn Square
Gray's Inn
London WC1R 5AH
Tel: 020 7430 0333
Fax: 020 7430 0666
E-mail: admin@academy-experts.org
Website: www.academy-experts.org

The Academy of Experts, multidisciplinary body established in 1987 to establish and promote high objective standards for those acting as expert witnesses. We act as an accrediting and professional body, offering training, technical guidance and representation. In addition we promote cost-efficient dispute resolution, maintaining a register of qualified dispute resolvers.

MEMBERSHIP
Associate Member

Associate Member (AMAE)
Full Member (MAE)
Fellow (FAE)
Practising Corporate Member
Dispute Resolver Member

QUALIFICATION/EXAMINATIONS
There are examinations for upgrade.

DESIGNATORY LETTERS
AMAE, MAE, FAE, QDR

THE INSTITUTE OF LEGAL FINANCE AND MANAGEMENT (ILFM)

2nd Floor
Marlowe House
109 Station Road
Sidcup
Kent DA15 7ET
Tel: 020 8302 2867
Fax: 020 8302 7481
E-mail: kim.freeman@ilfm.org.uk
Website: www.ilfm.org.uk

The ILFM, which was founded in 1978, is a non-profit-making professional body dedicated to the education and support of specialist financial and administrative personnel working within the legal community. We encourage the development of our members' skills through educational courses, training workshops, seminars, conferences and our bimonthly magazine, *Legal Abacus*.

MEMBERSHIP
Ordinary Member
Diploma Member (ILFM (Dip))

Associate Member (AILFM)
Fellow Member (FILFM)
Affiliated Professional Member

QUALIFICATION/EXAMINATIONS
Diploma
Associate
Fellow

DESIGNATORY LETTERS
DILFM (Dip), AILFM, FILFM

THE LAW SOCIETY OF SCOTLAND

26 Drumsheugh Gardens
Edinburgh EH3 7YR
Tel: 0131 226 7411
Fax: 0131 225 2934
E-mail: lawscot@lawscot.org.uk
Website: www.lawscot.org.uk

The Law Society of Scotland is the membership organization of Scottish solicitors. We promote the interests of the profession and of the public in relation to the profession. Our services include providing initial career advice, overseeing legal education in Scotland, handling admissions to the profession, monitoring trainees, providing post-qualifying legal education, and administering courses and examinations for the Society of Law Accountants in Scotland.

MEMBERSHIP
All practising solicitors in Scotland must be members of the Society and must hold a current Practising Certificate which is issued by the Society.

QUALIFICATION/EXAMINATIONS
Please see the Law Society of Scotland's website.

LEISURE AND RECREATION MANAGEMENT
Membership of Professional Institutions and Associations

CHARTERED INSTITUTE FOR THE MANAGEMENT OF SPORT AND PHYSICAL ACTIVITY (CIMSPA)

Sportpark Loughborough University
3 Oakwood Drive
Loughborough
Leicestershire LE11 3QF
Tel: 01509 226474
Fax: 01509 226475
E-mail: info@cimspa.co.uk
Website: www.cimspa.co.uk

CIMSPA is the membership body for sport and physical activity professionals. We promote high standards and provide CPD as well as a wide range of training courses to our members in-house and at venues across the UK. We also work hard to influence government policy on behalf of our members.

MEMBERSHIP
Student Member
Affiliate Member
Associate Member
Member
Fellow
Companion
Chartered Member
Chartered Fellow
Retired Member

QUALIFICATION/EXAMINATIONS
National Pool Plant Operators Certificate
National Pool Plant Foundation Certificate
National Spa Pool Operators Certificate
Supervisory Management Certificate
Fitness Management Certificate
Health and Safety Management Certificate
Higher Professional Diploma in Sport and Recreation Management

Online Continuing Professional Development (CPD) (Entrance and Supervisory Level)
Online Continuing Professional Development (CPD) (Management Level)
Certificate in Leisure Operations (QCF) (1st4sport Level 2)
NVQ Award in Mechanical Ride Operation (QCF) (1st4sport Level 2)
NVQ Certificate in Active Leisure, Learning and Well-being Operational Services (QCF) (1st4sport Level 2)
Certificate in Leisure Management (QCF) (1st4sport Level 3)
NVQ Diploma in Leisure Management (QCF) (1st4sport Level 3)
NVQ Diploma in Sports Development (QCF) (1st4sport Level 3)
Award in Introductory Work in the Outdoors (QCF) (1st4sport Level 2)
NVQ Diploma in Outdoor Programmes (QCF) (1st4sport Level 3)
Award in Coordinating Sports Volunteers (QCF) (1st4sport Level 3)
Certificate in Managing Sports Volunteers (QCF) (1st4sport Level 3)

DESIGNATORY LETTERS
NPPO, RoPPPS, CPD, QCF

INSTITUTE OF GROUNDSMANSHIP

28 Stratford Office Village
Walker Avenue
Wolverton Mill East
Milton Keynes MK12 5TW
Tel: 01908 312511
Fax: 01908 311140
E-mail: iog@iog.org
Website: www.iog.org

The Institute of Groundsmanship is the only membership organisation supporting the whole of the grounds care industry. Serving the industry for more than 80 years, we provide a range of quality products, services and events including education, training and membership services, the national SALTEX exhibition, local information days, an annual conference and awards programme.

MEMBERSHIP
Student Member
Facility/Organisation Member
E-Member
Individual Member
Corporate and Corporate PLUS Member

QUALIFICATION/EXAMINATIONS
For details see: www.iog.org/training-training-courses.asp

LIBRARIANSHIP AND INFORMATION WORK
Membership of Professional Institutions and Associations

CHARTERED INSTITUTE OF LIBRARY AND INFORMATION PROFESSIONALS

7 Ridgmount Street
London WC1E 7AE
Tel: 020 7255 0500
Fax: 020 7255 0501
E-mail: memberservices@cilip.org.uk
Website: www.cilip.org.uk

CILIP is the professional body representing those working within libraries and the information profession in the UK.

MEMBERSHIP
Certified Affiliate (ACLIP)
Chartered Member (MCLIP)
Chartered Fellow (FCLIP)
Revalidated Chartered Member or Fellow
Student Membership

QUALIFICATION/EXAMINATIONS
Application for levels of professional registration is through the submission of a portfolio of evidence meeting published criteria. Please contact the Institute for further information.

DESIGNATORY LETTERS
ACLIP, MCLIP, FCLIP

MANAGEMENT
Membership of Professional Institutions and Associations

ASSOCIATION FOR PROJECT MANAGEMENT

Ibis House
Regent Park
Summerleys Road
Princes Risborough
Buckinghamshire HP27 9LE
Tel: 0845 458 1944
E-mail: via website
Website: www.apm.org.uk

The association is a registered charity with over 19,500 individual and 500 corporate members making it the largest professional body of its kind in Europe. APM's mission statement is 'to develop and promote the professional disciplines of project and programme management for the public benefit'.

MEMBERSHIP
Student Member
Associate Member
Full Member (MAPM)
Fellow (FAPM)
Corporate Member
Honorary Member/ Fellow (HonFAPM)

QUALIFICATION/EXAMINATIONS
Introductory Certificate in Project Management (IC)
APMP
APMP for PRINCE2 Practitioners
Practitioner Qualification (PQ)
Risk level 1
Risk level 2
Pan sector standard:
Registered Project Professional (RPP)
Higher Apprenticeship:
Higher Apprenticeship in Project Management

DESIGNATORY LETTERS
MAPM, FAPM, HonFAPM, RPP

ASSOCIATION OF CERTIFIED COMMERCIAL DIPLOMATS (ACCD)

Commercial Diplomats Regulation Authority
ACCD Global Headquarters
Central Administration Office
PO Box 50561, Canary Wharf
London E16 3WY
Tel: +44(0)8445 864249
E-mail: enquiries@chartereddiplomats.org.uk
Website: www.commercialdiplomats.org.uk

Association of Certified Commercial Diplomats is the first independent accreditation and regulation authority, and global professional awarding body for commercial diplomats. The umbrella of ACCD covers ambassadors, representatives of government, trade commissioners, advisors and negotiators, arbitrators, negotiators of IIAs, policy-makers & government officials involved in trade, commercial and/or investment issues, commercial counsellors, IIA experts, academia, private sector & NGO representatives, officials in government ministries, parastatals, corporations, academic, public and private institutions worldwide. Its principal objectives are to provide accreditation and regulation, and to advance the interests of its members as qualified, certified and competent commercial diplomats. As the global voice, ACCD has overall responsibility, including the setting of policy and guidelines, as well as the qualification and accreditation procedures for the commercial diplomatic profession. ACCD is nonpartisan, not-for-profit, independent of government, and uniquely the professional regulatory body for commercial diplomats, and institutions of higher learning providing advanced postgraduate, doctoral, and postdoctoral programmes on commercial diplomacy.

REGULATED FULL MEMBERSHIP
Associate
Member
Fellow

QUALIFICATION/EXAMINATIONS
ACCD REGULATED POSTGRADUATE EXAMINATIONS
Certificate of Competency
Advanced Certificate of Competency
Master Certificate of Competency
Advanced Master Certificate of Competency
ACCD REGULATED ACADEMIC QUALIFICATIONS
Master of Commercial Diplomacy
Doctor of Commercial Diplomacy
ACCD REGULATED ACCREDITATIONS
Qualified Policy Advocate (QA)
Qualified Certified Diplomat (QCD)
Chartered Diplomat (C. Dipl)

DESIGNATORY LETTERS
ACDipl, MCD, MCDipl, M.Arb, DCD, DCDipl, FCDipl, QA, QCD, C. Dipl

AUA

AUA National Office
University of Manchester
Sackville Street Building
Manchester M60 1QD
Tel: 0161 275 2063
Fax: 0161 275 2036
E-mail: aua@aua.ac.uk
Website: www.aua.ac.uk

As a member-led organization with over 3,500 members, AUA promotes best practice in higher education management and exists to advance and promote professional recognition and development of those who work in higher and further education by encouraging and fostering sound methods of leadership, management and administration, through a range of professional development initiatives.

AUA members are individually and collectively committed to:
- the continuous development of their own and others' professional knowledge, skills and practices;
- actively championing equality of educational and professional opportunity;
- the advancement of higher education through the robust application of professional knowledge, skills and practices;
- the highest standards of fair, ethical and transparent professional behaviours.

AUA is at the forefront of professional development in higher education and has developed a sector-wide framework to support the development of professional services colleagues. Through continuing professional development, individuals, teams and institutions can foster skills and behaviours associated with the profession. AUA also holds the largest professional development annual conference in the UK higher education calendar.

MEMBERSHIP
Member (MAUA)
Accredited Member (AAUA)
Fellow (FAUA)
Honorary Member (FAUA)
Student Member (MAUA)

QUALIFICATION/EXAMINATIONS
Postgraduate Certificate in Professional Practice (PG Cert)
This programme is validated by The Open University and credits from the course can be used on a number of MA courses.

BRITISH INSTITUTE OF FACILITIES MANAGEMENT

Number One Building
The Causeway
Bishop's Stortford
Hertfordshire CM23 2ER
Tel: 01279 712651
Fax: 01279 712669
E-mail: qualifications@bifm.org.uk
Website: www.bifm.org.uk

The BIFM is the professional body for facilities management (FM). Founded in 1993, the Institute provides information, education, training and networking services for over 16,500 members – both individual professionals and employers. The BIFM's mission is to advance the profession – to consolidate FM as a vital management discipline for the benefit of practitioners, the economy and society.

MEMBERSHIP
Affiliate
Associate (ABIFM)
Member (MBIFM)
Certified Member (CBIFM)
Fellow (FBIFM)
Corporate Member

QUALIFICATION/EXAMINATIONS
BIFM Level 2 Certificate in Facilities Services
BIFM Level 2 Certificate in Facilities Services Principles

BIFM Level 3 Award in Facilities Management
BIFM Level 3 Certificate in Facilities Management
BIFM Level 3 Certificate in Facilities Management Practice
BIFM Level 3 Diploma in Facilities Management
BIFM Level 4 Award in Facilities Management
BIFM Level 4 Certificate in Facilities Management
BIFM Level 4 Diploma in Facilities Management
BIFM Level 5 Award in Facilities Management
BIFM Level 5 Certificate in Facilities Management
BIFM Level 5 Diploma in Facilities Management
BIFM Level 6 Award in Facilities Management
BIFM Level 6 Certificate in Facilities Management
BIFM Level 6 Diploma in Facilities Management
BIFM Level 7 Certificate in Facilities Management
BIFM Level 7 Diploma in Facilities Management

DESIGNATORY LETTERS
ABIFM, MBIFM, CBIFM, FBIFM

BUSINESS MANAGEMENT ASSOCIATION

1 High Oak House
Collett Road
Ware
Hertfordshire SG12 7LY
Tel: 0871 231 1689
E-mail: enquiries@businessmanagement.org.uk
Website: www.businessmanagement.org.uk

The Business Management Association is a professional body for business owners and managers. We promote the aims and interests of the small business sector internationally, provide information and advice to our members, encourage networking between members, and seek to provide members with advanced knowledge, skill and qualifications in several aspects of management.

MEMBERSHIP
Affiliate (AffBMA)
Associate (ABMA)
Member (MBMA)
Fellow (FBMA)
Companion (CBMA)
Certified Manager (CertMgr)
Certified Master of Management (CMMgt)
Certified Master of Business Administration (CMBA)

Certified Doctor of Business Administration (CDBA)

QUALIFICATION/EXAMINATIONS
Entrepreneurs Award (EA)
Diploma In Business Management (DipBMA)

DESIGNATORY LETTERS
AffBMA, ABMA, MBMA, FBMA, CBMA, CertMgr,
CMMgt, CMBA, CDBA, MCBMA, FCBMA

DIPLOMATIC ACADEMY OF EUROPE AND THE ATLANTIC

Institution for the Training of Commercial Diplomats
ACCD Global Headquarters
PO Box 50561, Canary Wharf
Greater London E16 3WY

Diplomatic Academy of Europe and the Atlantic is an authoritative knowledge-based international professional diplomatic institution whose activities include advanced research, training and development, provision of postgraduate and post-qualification commercial diplomatic education, and contribution to responsible commercial diplomatic practice and service. It is a key independent extraterritorial diplomatic organization established for the advancement and development of greater knowledge and skills in commercial diplomacy. DAEA offers a complete portfolio of specialized mandatory postgraduate programmes on commercial diplomacy.

MEMBERSHIP
Fellow of the Diplomatic Academy (FDA)

QUALIFICATION/EXAMINATIONS
MANDATORY EXAMINATIONS
Qualified Policy Advocate
Qualified Certified Diplomat
Chartered Diplomat
QUALIFICATIONS
Advanced Certificate of Competency
Master Certificate of Competency
Master of Commercial Diplomacy

DESIGNATORY LETTERS
ACDipl, MCDipl, DCD, FCD

FACULTY OF PROFESSIONAL BUSINESS AND TECHNICAL MANAGEMENT

PO Box 93
Moreton-in-Marsh GL56 9WG
Tel: 01386 277973
E-mail: info@pbtm.org.uk
Website: www.pbtm.org.uk

FPBTM was founded in 1983 to forge the link between business and technology. We give professional recognition to the knowledge and skills of managers in business and technology, supporting lifelong learning to help members fulfil their career ambitions and develop their potential.

MEMBERSHIP
Student Member (SFPBTM)
Technician Member (TMFPBTM)
Associate Member (AMFPBTM)
Member (MFPBTM)
Fellow (FFPBTM)
Companion (CFPBTM)

INSTITUTE OF ADMINISTRATIVE MANAGEMENT

Coppice House
Halesfield 7
Telford
Shropshire TF7 4NA
Tel: 01952 585387
E-mail: info@instam.org
Website: www.instam.org

The IAM is the leading professional body and part of the IQ group who is a UK government-recognized awarding body for those involved in the administration and management of business.

MEMBERSHIP
Affiliate
Associate (AInstAM)
Member (MInstAM)
Fellow (FInstAM)
IAM Student
Non-IAM Student

QUALIFICATION/EXAMINATIONS
IQ IAM Level 2 Diploma in Team Leading
IQ IAM Level 2 Diploma in Business Administration
IQ IAM Level 3 Diploma in Business Administration
IQ IAM Level 3 Diploma in Management
IQ IAM Level 4 Award in Administration for Executive Assistants
IQ IAM Level 4 NVQ Diploma in Management

IQ IAM Level 4 Diploma in Business & Administrative Management
IQ IAM Level 4 NVQ Diploma in Business Administration
IQ IAM Level 5 Diploma in Business & Administrative Management
IQ IAM Level 5 NVQ Diploma in Management and Leadership
IQ IAM Level 6 Diploma in Business and Administrative Management
IQ IAM Level 6 Diploma in Business Management

IQ IAM Level 3 Certificate in Business and Administrative Management (VRQ)
IQ IAM Level 3 Certificate in Professional PA and Administration Skills (VRQ)
IQ IAM Level 4 Certificate in Office and Administration Management (VRQ)

DESIGNATORY LETTERS
AInstAM, MInstAM, FInstAM

INSTITUTE OF CONSULTING

4th Floor
2 Savoy Court
Strand
London WC2R 0EZ
Tel: 020 7497 0580
Fax: 020 7497 0463
E-mail: welcome@ibconsulting.org.uk
Website: www.iconsulting.org.uk

The Institute of Consulting was formed in 2007 by the merger of the Institute of Business Advisers and the Institute of Management Consultancy, and we are the professional body for business consultants and advisers. Our aim is to raise the standards of professional practice in support of better business performance.

MEMBERSHIP
Student
Affiliate
Associate (AIBC)
Member (MIBC)
Fellow (FIBC)
Certified Business Advisor (CBA)
Certified Management Consultant (CMC)

Practice Member (corporate membership)

QUALIFICATION/EXAMINATIONS
Award in Professional Consulting (Level 5) (QCF)
Certificate in Professional Consulting (Level 5) (QCF)
Diploma in Professional Consulting (Level 5) (QCF)
Award in Business Support (Level 5) (QCF)
Certificate in Business Support (Level 5) (QCF)
Diploma in Business Support (Level 5) (QCF)

Award in Professional Consulting (Level 7) (QCF)
Certificate in Professional Consulting (Level 7) (QCF)
Diploma in Professional Consulting (Level 7) (QCF)
Certified Management Consultant Award (CMC)
Certified Business Advisor Award (CBA)

DESIGNATORY LETTERS
AIBC, MIBC, FIBC

INSTITUTE OF DIRECTORS

116 Pall Mall
London SW1Y 5ED
Tel: 020 7766 2601
E-mail: professionaldev@iod.com
Website: www.iod.com/development

The IoD represents professional leaders, with individual members ranging from entrepreneurs of start-up companies to CEOs of multinational organizations. The Institute's principal objectives are to advance the interests of its members as company directors, and to provide them with business facilities and a variety of services.

MEMBERSHIP
Student
Associate Member

Member (MIoD)
Fellow (FIoD)
Chartered Director (C Dir)

QUALIFICATION/EXAMINATIONS
Certificate in Company Direction (CertIoD)
Diploma in Company Direction (DipIoD)
Chartered Director (C Dir)

DESIGNATORY LETTERS
MIoD, FIoD, C Dir

INSTITUTE OF LEADERSHIP & MANAGEMENT

Stowe House
Netherstowe
Lichfield
Staffordshire WS13 6TJ
Tel: 01543 266867
Fax: 01543 266893
E-mail: customer@i-l-m.com
Website: www.i-l-m.com

The ILM supports, develops and informs leaders and managers at every stage of their career. With our broad range of industry-leading qualifications, membership services and learning resources, the ILM provides flexible development solutions that can be blended to meet the specific needs of employers and learners.

MEMBERSHIP
Studying Member
Professional Member

QUALIFICATION/EXAMINATIONS
Management
Principles of Team Leading including Foundation
Award in Management Practice (Level 2)
Award, Certificate in Effective Team Member Skills (Level 2)

Award, Certificate in Leadership and Team Skills (Level 2)
NVQ Certificate in Team Leading (Level 2)
Certificate in Team Leading (Level 2)
NVQ Certificate in Management (Level 3)
Certificate in Effective Management (Level 3)
Certificate in Principles of Leadership and Management (Level 3)
Award, Certificate and Diploma in Leadership and Management (Level 4)
Diploma in Principles of Leadership and Management (Level 5)
NVQ Diploma in Management (Level 5)
Award in Management (Level 6)
NVQ Diploma in Management (Level 7)
Diploma in Strategic Leadership and Executive Management (Level 7)
Award, Certificate and Diploma in Executive Management (Level 7)
Leadership
Certificate in Leadership (Level 3)
Award in Leadership (Level 4)
Award, Certificate and Diploma in Strategic Leadership (Level 7)
Leadership and Management
Award, Certificate and Diploma in Leadership and Management (Level 3)
Award, Certificate and Diploma in Leadership and Management (Level 5)
Coaching and Mentoring
Certificate in Coaching and Mentoring (Level 3)
Certificate and Diploma in Coaching and Mentoring (Level 5)

Certificate and Diploma in Coaching Supervision (Level 7)
Certificate and Diploma in Executive Coaching and Leadership Mentoring (Level 7)
Specialist Management Qualifications
Environmental Management
Facilities Management
Equality and Diversity
Managing Volunteers
Sales Management
Waste Management
Business and Enterprise
Certificate in Enterprise (Level 2)
Award and Certificate in Enterprise and Entrepreneurship (Level 3)
Award in Management (Level 5)
Certificate and Diploma in Social Enterprise Support (Level 5)
Specialist Management Qualifications
Operational management
Service improvement
Waste management
Equality and diversity
Volunteer management
Management consultancy
Staff and organisational development
Quality improvement

Scottish Vocational Qualifications (SVQs)
SVQ 2 in Team Leading (Scottish Level 5)
SVQ 3 in Management (Scottish Level 7)
SVQ 4 in Management (Scottish Level 9)
SVQ 5 in Management (Scottish Level 11)

INSTITUTE OF MANAGEMENT SERVICES

Brooke House
Lichfield
Staffordshire WS13 6AA
Tel: 01543 266909
Fax: 01543 257848
E-mail: via website
Website: www.ims-productivity.com

DESIGNATORY LETTERS
AMS, MMS, FMS

INSTITUTE OF VALUE MANAGEMENT

PO Box 101
Ledbury
Herefordshire HR8 9JW
Tel: 01531 631444
E-mail: secretary@ivm.org.uk
Website: www.ivm.org.uk

The Institute aims to establish Value Management as an all-encompassing strategy for achieving value in every sector of the economy and to provide support in the innovative use of value management techniques.

MEMBERSHIP
Corporate Membership: Open to any company or organization practising or promoting value techniques. Each corporate member may nominate up to 10 members of their organization as representatives to the Institute. A member nominated by a corporate body can hold executive office and has full voting rights.
Ordinary Membership: Open to any professional person who has an interest in and can demonstrate an involvement in practising value techniques.
Student Membership: Open to students who have an interest in value management and who are registered FT students possessing a valid student card.
Fellow: Awarded to a member as a special honour for outstanding contribution to the field of value management.

QUALIFICATION/EXAMINATIONS
Certificate and Training: The Institute has worked closely with the Commission of the European Communities to establish a European Training System and Certification Procedure.
Roll of Practitioners: The Institute maintains an authorized list of value practitioners who are members of the Institute.
It launched its European Training and Certification System in 1998. This European Commission funded initiative offers, through the IVM's Certification Board, certification in the following categories: Qualified Value Associate (QVA); Professional in Value Management (PVM); Trainer in Value Management (TVM). The Certification Board also approves basic and advanced courses in value management that have been designed by trainers in value management. The Institute provides a list of trainers.

INTERNATIONAL PROFESSIONAL MANAGERS ASSOCIATION

5 Starnes Court
Union Street
Maidstone
Kent ME14 1EB
Tel: 01622 672867
Fax: 01622 755149
E-mail: admin@ipma.co.uk
Website: www.ipma.co.uk

The IPMA is an international examining, licensing and regulatory professional body, which, through its qualifying examinations, enables practising managers to participate in and be part of the process of improving managerial performance and effectiveness in all areas of business, industry and public administration.

MEMBERSHIP
Student Member
Graduate Member (GRD PMA)
Licentiate Member (LMPMA)
Certified Associate (AMPMA)
Certified Member (MPMA)
Certified Fellow (FPMA)

QUALIFICATION/EXAMINATIONS
Certified International Professional Manager (CIPM) examinations
Foundation: Economics, Legal Environment of Business, Information Communication and Technology, Business Management, Statistical Methods for Business, Principles of Finance
Intermediate: Business Marketing, Entrepreneurship, Corporate Law, Management Accounting, Advanced Management Practice, Managing People
Professional Level 1: Human Resource Management, Management Decision Making, Organisational Behaviour, Information Systems Management, Operations Management
Professional Level 2: Business Policy and Strategic Management, Corporate Finance and Risk Management, Organisation Change and Development, Multinational Business Management, Case Study and a Project

DESIGNATORY LETTERS
GRD PMA, LMPMA, AMPMA, MPMA, FPMA, CIPM

THE ASSOCIATION OF BUSINESS EXECUTIVES

5th Floor, CI Tower
St Georges Square
New Malden
Surrey KT3 4TE
Tel: 020 8329 2930
Fax: 020 8329 2945
E-mail: info@abeuk.com
Website: www.abeuk.com

ABE is a professional membership body and examination board. We develop business and management qualifications at Levels 4, 5, 6 & 7 on the QCF framework. ABE's range of OFQUAL accredited qualifications provide progression routes to degree and Master's programmes worldwide.

MEMBERSHIP
Affiliate Member
Student Member
Associate Member (AMABE)
Member (MABE)
Fellow (FABE)

QUALIFICATION/EXAMINATIONS
Diploma Levels 4, 5 and 6 in:
Business Management
Management of Information Systems (Pathway)
Financial Management (Pathway)
Human Resource Management
Marketing Management
Travel, Tourism and Hospitality Management
Diploma in Business Development (Level 7)
Diploma in Business Start-Up and Entrepreneurship (Level 4)

DESIGNATORY LETTERS
AMABE, MABE, FABE

THE CAMBRIDGE ACADEMY OF MANAGEMENT

Royal Arsenal Gatehouse
Beresford Square
Woolwich
London SE18 6AR
Tel: 0844 284 7190
E-mail: admin@camuk.org
Website: www.camuk.org.uk

The Cambridge Academy of Management (CAM) is a professional, autonomous, not-for-profit institution established to foster the concept of UK management education made available to all internationally. CAM is built on the foundation of promoting state-of-the-art knowledge and expertise in all facets of management education, training and development for the global educational arena.

MEMBERSHIP
Associate Category (ACAM)
Member Category (MCAM)
Fellowship Category (FCAM)

QUALIFICATION/EXAMINATIONS
All programmes offered by Cambridge Academy of Management are accredited by Quality Assurance Commission UK. Programmes offered:
CAM International Foundation Diploma
CAM International Certificate in Restaurant & Catering Management
CAM International Diploma in Business Management

CAM International Diploma in Business (Restaurant & Catering Management)
CAM International Diploma in Business (Tourism Management)
CAM International Advanced Diploma in Business Management
CAM International Advanced Diploma in Business (Restaurant & Catering Management)
CAM International Advanced Diploma in Business (Tourism Management)
CAM International Postgraduate Diploma in Hospitality Management
CAM International Postgraduate Diploma in Business
CAM International Postgraduate Diploma in Business with Specialization in: Marketing, Finance, Human Resource

THE CHARTERED MANAGEMENT INSTITUTE

Customer Service Department
Management House
Cottingham Road
Corby
Northants NN17 1TT
Tel: 01536 204222
Fax: 01536 201651
E-mail: enquiries@managers.org.uk
Website: www.managers.org.uk

CMI is the only chartered professional body in the UK dedicated to promoting the highest standards of management and leadership excellence. With a member community of over 100,000, CMI gives managers and leaders, and their organisations, the skills they need to improve their performance and create an impact.

MEMBERSHIP
Associate (ACMI)
Member (MCMI)
Fellow (FCMI)
Companion (CCMI)
Chartered Member (CMgr MCMI)
Chartered Fellow (CMgr FCMI)

QUALIFICATION/EXAMINATIONS
The breadth and depth of our management and leadership qualification portfolio is unmatched. We have over 80 individual qualifications ranging from team leading, strategic management to coaching and mentoring to name a few.

To support your development we have a wide range of online and hardcopy resources and materials, including ManagementDirect and Pathways Workbooks. With CMI Membership you can also enjoy benefits of CPD.

We have a network of more than 500 Centres delivering our qualifications so you can always find somewhere to study that's convenient for you.

DESIGNATORY LETTERS
ACMI, MCMI, FCMI, CCMI, CMgr MCMI, CMgr FCMI

THE INSTITUTE OF COMMERCIAL MANAGEMENT

ICM House
Castleman Way
Ringwood
Hampshire BH24 3BA
Tel: 01202 490555
E-mail: info@icm.education
Website: www.icm.education

Established in 1975, the Institute is the leading professional body for Commercial and Business Development Managers. It provides examining and assessment services for those undertaking business and management studies and offers in excess of 200 programmes. The Institute works with public and private sector education and training providers in more than 100 countries.

MEMBERSHIP
Student Membership

QUALIFICATION/EXAMINATIONS
ICM Awards cover the following areas: Accounting & Finance; Business Studies; Commercial Management; Hospitality Management; Human Resource Development; Journalism; Legal Studies; Management Studies; Maritime Management; Marketing Management; Sales Management; Travel & Tourism.

THE INSTITUTE OF MANAGEMENT SPECIALISTS

PO Box 93
Moreton-in-Marsh GL56 9WG
Tel: 01386 277973
E-mail: info@instituteofmanagementspecialists.org.uk
Website: www.instituteofmanagementspecialists.org.uk

The Institute of Management Specialists was founded in 1971 to give professional recognition to the knowledge and skills of managers and specialists. The Institute encourages management excellence and specialist expertise, and supports lifelong learning to help members fulfil their career ambitions.

Specialised Manager Awards are available in a range of specialised areas and IMS offers a CPD (Continuous Professional Development) programme leading to Certified Specialist Manager status.

MEMBERSHIP
Student Member (StudIMS)

Associate Member (AMIMS)
Member (MIMS)
Fellow (FIMS)
Companion (CompIMS)

QUALIFICATION/EXAMINATIONS
Diploma of Management
Executive Diploma in Business Leadership and Management
Professional Diploma in Project Management Development

THE SOCIETY OF BUSINESS PRACTITIONERS

PO Box 11
Sandbach
Cheshire CW11 3GE
Tel: 01270 526339
Fax: 01270 526339
E-mail: info@mamsasbp.org.uk
Website: www.mamsasbp.org.uk

SBP is an International Examination Board founded in 1956 by experienced educationalists and executives to fulfil a need to set standards in business practice achieved by examinations/assessments. Inexperienced and mature students should be able to follow careers in further education and/or be proficient in employment and receive the benefits of membership.

MEMBERSHIP
Student (StuSBP)
Member (MSBP)
Certified Professional Manager (CPMSBP)
Honorary Fellow
Professional Memberships *(Senior Professional Qualifications)*
Associateship (ASBP)
Licentiateship (LSBP)
Graduateship (GSBP)
Fellowship (FSBP)
These are certified competency-based Membership Awards open to persons occupied in business practice who are considered suitable by the Membership Committee.
CPD programmes are also offered for the Asia region.

QUALIFICATION/EXAMINATIONS
Diploma in Business Administration
Advanced Diploma in Business Administration
PGDip in Business Administration
PGDip in International Marketing
Diploma in Computer Studies
Advanced Diploma in Computer Studies
GradDip in IT & E-Commerce
GradDip in Entrepreneurship
Advanced Diploma in Accounting
Diploma & Advanced Diploma in Marketing Management (Joint Award with the Managing & Marketing Sales Association)

DESIGNATORY LETTERS
StuSBP, MSBP, CPMSBP, ASBP, LSBP, GSBP, FSBP

MANUFACTURING
Membership of Professional Institutions and Associations

THE INSTITUTE OF MANUFACTURING

PO Box 93
Moreton-in-Marsh GL56 9WG
Tel: 01386 277973
E-mail: info@instituteofmanufacturing.org.uk
Website: www.instituteofmanufacturing.org.uk

The Institute of Manufacturing was founded in 1978 to give professional recognition to the knowledge and skills of people in all aspects of manufacturing. The Institute supports lifelong learning to help members fulfil their career ambitions and develop their potential.

MEMBERSHIP
Student Member (StudIManf)
Associate Member (AMIManf)
Member (MIManf)
Fellow (FIManf)
Companion (CompIManf)

Associate Diploma in Manufacturing

Executive Diploma in Manufacturing
Certified Manufacturing Practitioner

MARKETING AND SALES
Membership of Professional Institutions and Associations

LONDON CENTRE OF MARKETING

Buckingham House West
Stanmore
London HA7 4EB
Tel: 020 8385 7766
Fax: 020 8385 7755
E-mail: info@lcmuk.com
Website: www.lcmuk.com

The London Centre of Marketing is an Ofqual accredited, non-political, Awarding Organisation based in London, which exists with the sole aim of providing internationally recognised professional qualifications in marketing and marketing management.

MEMBERSHIP
We offer 3 types of memberships:
1. Associate (ALCM)
2. Member (MLCM)
3. Fellow (FLCM)

QUALIFICATION/EXAMINATIONS
Diploma, Higher Diploma, Professional Diploma, Graduate Diploma and Postgraduate Dipolma in:
Business Management & Marketing
Human Resource Development & Marketing
Sales & Marketing Management
Travel & Tourism Marketing
Public Relations & Marketing
Entrepreneurship & Marketing

DESIGNATORY LETTERS
ALCM/MLCM/FLCM

MANAGING AND MARKETING SALES ASSOCIATION EXAMINATION BOARD

PO Box 11
Sandbach
Cheshire CW11 3GE
Tel: 01270 526339
Fax: 01270 526339
E-mail: info@mamsasbp.org.uk
Website: www.mamsasbp.org.uk

MAMSA is an international Examination Board offering qualifications in Sales, Marketing and Management and its senior specialist Diploma in Marketing Strategy Diploma. The importance of 'Customer Service' is emphasized throughout all the programmes.

MEMBERSHIP
Graduate (GradMAMSA)

Graduate Affiliate (GradAfMAMSA)
Professional (MMAMSA)
Fellow (FMAMSA)

QUALIFICATION/EXAMINATIONS
Standard Diploma in Salesmanship
Certificate in Sales Marketing
Higher Diploma in Marketing
Advanced Diploma in Sales Management

Certificate in Marketing Strategy

Diploma in Marketing Strategy & Management (Hypothesis/Thesis)

Diploma in Sales and Marketing Practices (Joint Award with the Society of Business Practitioners)

A CPD programme is also offered.

DESIGNATORY LETTERS

GradMAMSA, GradAfMAMSA, MMAMSA, FMAMSA

MRS (THE MARKET RESEARCH SOCIETY)

The Old Trading House
15 Northburgh Street
London EC1V 0JR
Tel: 020 7490 4911
Fax: 020 7490 0608
E-mail: profdevelopment@mrs.org.uk
Website: www.mrs.org.uk

With members in more than 50 countries, MRS is the world's leading authority on research and business intelligence. For those who need, use, generate or interpret the evidence essential to making good decisions for commercial and public policy. MRS is an awarding body for vocationally related qualifications in research.

MEMBERSHIP
Student Member
Member (MMRS)
Certified Member (CMRS)

Fellow (FMRS)
Honorary Fellow (Hon. FMRS)

QUALIFICATION/EXAMINATIONS
MRS Certificate in Market and Social Research
MRS Certificate in Interviewing Skills
MRS Advanced Certificate in Market and Social Research Practice
MRS Diploma in Market and Social Research Practice

DESIGNATORY LETTERS
MMRS, CMRS, FMRS, Hon. FMRS

THE CHARTERED INSTITUTE OF MARKETING

Moor Hall
Maidenhead
Berkshire SL6 9QH
Tel: 01628 427120
Fax: 01628 427158
E-mail: qualifications@cim.co.uk
Website: www.cim.co.uk/learningzone

The Chartered Institute of Marketing is the leading international professional marketing body, with 47,000 members worldwide. We aim to improve the skills of marketing practitioners, enabling them to deliver exceptional results for their organization. Qualifications from Introductory to Chartered postgraduate level are offered to anyone wanting to develop their career in marketing.

MEMBERSHIP
Affiliate (Studying/Professional)
Associate (ACIM)

Member (MCIM)
Fellow (FCIM)
Chartered Marketer

QUALIFICATION/EXAMINATIONS
Professional Certificate in Marketing
Professional Diploma in Marketing
Chartered Postgraduate Diploma in Marketing
Diploma in Marketing Communications
Diploma in Digital Marketing
Professional Diploma in Marketing for Business Services and Solutions

Diploma in Digital Marketing (Mobile)
Diploma in Digital Marketing (Metrics and Analytics)
Diploma in Digital Marketing (Media and Branding)
Certificate in Professional Sales Practice
Advanced Certificate in Professional Sales Management Practice

Advanced Certificate in Account Management Practice
Intensive Diploma on Strategic Sales Practice

DESIGNATORY LETTERS
ACIM, MCIM, FCIM

THE INSTITUTE OF DIRECT AND DIGITAL MARKETING

1 Park Road
Teddington
Middlesex TW11 0AR
Tel: 020 8164 0277
E-mail: enquiries@theidm.com
Website: www.theidm.com

The Institute of Direct and Digital Marketing is the UK's only government-approved Institute for the professional development of direct and digital marketers, offering a broad range of practitioner-taught training courses and professional marketing qualifications. It is also a membership organisation, providing status, knowledge and networking opportunities to senior marketers.

MEMBERSHIP
Affiliate Member
Associate Member
Member
Fellow
Corporate Member

QUALIFICATION/EXAMINATIONS
MSc in Digital Marketing

MSc in Marketing Management
Postgraduate Diploma in Digital Marketing
Postgraduate Diploma in Digital Marketing with B2B
Postgraduate Diploma in Direct and Digital Marketing
Postgraduate Diploma in Direct and Digital Marketing with B2B
Professional Diploma in Digital Marketing
Professional Diploma in Direct and Digital Marketing
Certificate in Social Media
Certificate in Email Marketing
Certificate in Search Marketing
Award in Digital Copywriting
Award in Data Management
Award in Direct and Digital Marketing
Award in Mobile Marketing

THE INSTITUTE OF SALES AND MARKETING MANAGEMENT (ISMM)

Basepoint Business & Innovation Centre
Unit 22A, 110 Butterfield
Great Marlings
Luton
Bedfordshire LU2 8DL
Tel: 01582 840001
E-mail: education@ismm.co.uk
Website: www.ismm.co.uk

Founded in 1911, the ISMM is the worldwide representative body for sales people. To help members improve their skills set the ISMM provide qualifications, approved by Ofqual, the UK Government's regulatory body for education. Written by qualified and experienced sales professionals they cover the salesperson's career right up to sales director level.

MEMBERSHIP
Affiliate
Associate (AInstSMM)
Member (MInstSMM)
Fellow (FInstSMM)
Companion (CInstSMM)

QUALIFICATION/EXAMINATIONS
Level 1 Award in Selling Lawfully and Ethically
Level 1 Award in Understanding the Sales Cycle
Level 1 Award in Understanding Marketing
Level 1 Award in Communication Skills in Sales
Level 1 Award in Sales and Marketing
Level 2 Award in Understanding Laws and Ethics of Selling
Level 2 Award in Understanding Marketing
Level 2 Award in Understanding Buyer Behaviour
Level 2 Award in Sales Targets
Level 2 Award in Selling to Customers
Level 2 Award in Understanding Selling to Customers
Level 2 Award in Telesales
Level 2 Certificate in Sales and Marketing
Level 3 Award in Preparing and Delivering a Sales Presentation
Level 3 Award in Handling Objections, Negotiating and Closing Deals
Level 3 Award in Understanding Influences on Buyer Behaviour
Level 3 Award in Understanding customer segmentation and profiling
Level 3 Award in Understanding sales and marketing in organisations
Level 3 Award in Using market information for sales
Level 3 Award in Time and territory management for sales people
Level 3 Award in Planning for professional development
Level 3 Award in Prospecting for new business
Level 3 Award in Sales pipeline management
Level 3 Certificate in Sales and Marketing
Level 3 Diploma in Sales and Marketing
Level 4 Award in Managing responsible selling
Level 4 Award in Understanding segmentation, targeting and positioning
Level 4 Award in Managing a sales team
Level 4 Award in Operational sales planning
Level 4 Award in Sales negotiations

Level 4 Award in Analysing the marketing environment
Level 4 Award in Finance for sales managers
Level 4 Award in Writing and delivering a sales proposal
Level 4 Certificate in Sales and Marketing Management
Level 4 Diploma in Sales and Marketing Management
Level 5 Award in Understanding and developing customer accounts
Level 5 Award in Understanding the integrated functions of sales and marketing
Level 5 Award in Sales forecasts and target setting
Level 5 Award in Leading a team
Level 5 Award in Motivation and compensation for sales teams
Level 5 Award in Coaching and mentoring
Level 5 Award in Designing, planning and managing sales territories
Level 5 Award in Analysing the financial potential and performance of customer accounts
Level 5 Award in Relationship management for account managers
Level 5 Award in Bid and tender management for account managers
Level 5 Award in Developing a product portfolio
Level 5 Certificate in Sales and Account Management
Level 5 Diploma in Sales and Account Management
Level 6 Award in Leading a culture for responsible selling
Level 6 Award in Leadership and management in sales
Level 6 Award in Planning and implementing sales and marketing strategy
Level 6 Award in Salesforce organisation
Level 6 Award in Sales forecasting and budgeting
Level 6 Award in Developing strategic relationships with major customers
Level 6 Award in Managing sales-related change
Level 6 Award in Developing and using customer insight
Level 6 Certificate in Strategic Sales Management
Level 6 Diploma in Strategic Sales Management

DESIGNATORY LETTERS
AInstSMM, MInstSMM, FInstSMM

MARTIAL ARTS
Membership of Professional Institutions and Associations

INSTITUTE OF MARTIAL ARTS AND SCIENCES

1 Henrietta Street
Bolton
Lancashire BL3 4HL
Tel: 07792 214993
E-mail: admin@instituteofmartialartsandsciences.com
Website: www.instituteofmartialartsandsciences.com

The IMAS is a professional institute for martial artists, dedicated to education and research in the martial arts and offering memberships, accredited training and qualifications, and university degrees in martial arts studies. IMAS has a quarterly, peer reviewed journal, and an annual yearbook containing its research articles.

MEMBERSHIP
Affiliate
Student
Associate (AIMAS)
Member (MIMAS)

Fellow (FIMAS)

QUALIFICATION/EXAMINATIONS
Accredited instructor training
Specialist courses for police/security professionals
Higher Educational opportunities include: Graduate of the Institute of Martial Arts and Sciences (Grad. IMAS); BA (Hons); Masters by Research (MRes); Doctoral studies (PhD) available through our associated university in the UK

DESIGNATORY LETTERS
Grad.IMAS, BA (Hons), MRes, PhD

MASSAGE AND ALLIED THERAPIES
Membership of Professional Institutions and Associations

BRITISH MEDICAL ACUPUNCTURE SOCIETY

BMAS House
3 Winnington Court
Winnington Street
Northwich
Cheshire CW8 1AQ
Tel: 01606 786782
Fax: 01606 786783
E-mail: admin@medical-acupuncture.co.uk
Website: www.medical-acupuncture.co.uk

The BMAS was formed in 1980 as an association of medical practitioners interested in acupuncture and we now have a membership of more than 2,500 registered doctors and allied health professionals who practise acupuncture alongside more conventional techniques. We believe that acupuncture has an important role to play in healthcare and promote its use as a therapy following orthodox medical diagnosis by suitably trained practitioners. We run training programmes in the UK for doctors, dentists and other healthcare professionals.

MEMBERSHIP
Member
Accredited Member
Dental/Veterinary Member
Retired Member
Affiliated

Overseas Member

Diploma of Medical Acupuncture (DipMedAc)

QUALIFICATION/EXAMINATIONS
Certificate of Basic Competence (CoBC)

LCSP REGISTER OF REMEDIAL MASSEURS AND MANIPULATIVE THERAPISTS

38A High Street
Lowestoft
Suffolk NR32 1HY
Tel: 01502 563344
Fax: 01502 582220
E-mail: admin@lcsp.uk.com
Website: www.lcsp.uk.com

The Register accepts practitioners who currently work in Massage, Sports / Remedial Massage or Manipulative Therapy. Applicants must have completed a course of education at an establishment whose training meets or exceeds the National Occupational Standards. The Register offers heavily discounted comprehensive medical malpractice insurance, business support, regular communications and CPD.

MEMBERSHIP
Student Member
Associate Member (LCSP (Assoc))
Full Member (LCSP (Phys))
Affiliate
Fellow (FLCSP)
Honorary Member

DESIGNATORY LETTERS
LCSP (Assoc), LCSP (Phys), FLCSP

NORTHERN INSTITUTE OF MASSAGE LTD

14–16 St Mary's Place
Bury
Greater Manchester BL9 0DZ
Tel: 0161 797 1800
E-mail: information@nim.co.uk
Website: www.nim.co.uk

The NIM was founded in 1924 and offers professional training in Remedial Massage, Advanced Remedial Massage, and Manipulative Therapy. We also offer a number of CPD seminars and short courses to supplement our main training programme. Research is carried out mostly by therapists on patients from their own clinics or by students completing university courses.

QUALIFICATION/EXAMINATIONS
Advanced Remedial Massage Diploma
Manipulative Therapy Diploma

SOCIETY OF HOMEOPATHS

11 Brookfield Duncan Close
Moulton Park
Northampton NN3 6WL
Tel: 01604 817890
Fax: 01604 648848
E-mail: info@homeopathy-soh.org
Website: www.homeopathy-soh.org

The Society of Homeopaths was established in 1978 and is now the largest organization registering professional homeopaths in Europe. Our vision is 'homeopathy for all' and we aim to achieve this both by supporting our members and by raising the profile of homeopathy in general.

MEMBERSHIP
Subscriber
Student Member
Student Clinical Member
Registered Member (RSHom)

DESIGNATORY LETTERS
RSHom

MATHEMATICS
Membership of Professional Institutions and Associations

EDINBURGH MATHEMATICAL SOCIETY

School of Mathematics, Edinburgh University
James Clerk Maxwell Building
Mayfield Road
Edinburgh EH9 3JZ
Tel: 01316 505060
Fax: 01316 506553
E-mail: queries@maths.ed.ac.uk
Website: www.maths.ed.ac.uk

The EMS, founded in 1883, is the principal mathematical society for the academic community in Scotland as well as mathematicians in industry and commerce. We organize meetings, publish a journal and support mathematical activities through various funds.

MEMBERSHIP
Ordinary Member
Reciprocal Member
Honorary Member

THE INSTITUTE OF MATHEMATICS AND ITS APPLICATIONS

Catherine Richards House
16 Nelson Street
Southend-on-Sea
Essex SS1 1EF
Tel: 01702 354020
Fax: 01702 354111
E-mail: post@ima.org.uk
Website: www.ima.org.uk

The IMA, founded in 1964, is the UK's learned society for mathematics and its applications. We promote mathematical research, education and careers, and the use of mathematics in business, industry and commerce. In 1990 the Institute was incorporated by Royal Charter and subsequently granted the right to award the status of Chartered Mathematician, Chartered Scientist and Chartered Mathematics Teacher.

MEMBERSHIP
Student

Affiliate
Associate Member (AMIMA)
Member (MIMA)
Fellow (FIMA)
Chartered Mathematician (CMath)
Chartered Mathematics Teacher (CMathTeach)
Chartered Scientist (CSci)

DESIGNATORY LETTERS
AMIMA, MIMA, FIMA, CMath, CMathTeach, CSci

THE MATHEMATICAL ASSOCIATION

259 London Road
Leicester LE2 3BE
Tel: 01162 210013
Fax: 01162 122835
E-mail: office@m-a.org.uk
Website: www.m-a.org.uk

The MA dates from 1871 and supports and improves the teaching and learning of mathematics and its applications, and provides opportunities for communication and collaboration between teachers and students of mathematics. We publish a number of books, journals and magazines, hold an annual conference and regional meetings, and organize CPD events for our members. We also confer with government re the curriculum and assessment.

MEMBERSHIP
Student Member
Personal Member
Institutional Member

MEDICAL HERBALISM
Membership of Professional Institutions and Associations

THE NATIONAL INSTITUTE OF MEDICAL HERBALISTS

Clover House
James Court
South Street
Exeter
Devon EX1 1EE
Tel: 01392 426022
Fax: 01392 498963
E-mail: info@nimh.org.uk
Website: www.nimh.org.uk

The NIMH is the UK's leading professional organization of qualified medical herbal practitioners. We maintain high standards of practice and patient care, and work to promote the benefits of western herbal medicine. We provide codes of conduct, ethics and practice, and represent the profession, patients and the public through participation in external processes.

MEMBERSHIP
Member (MNIMH) Membership is open to graduates holding a BSc(Hons) degree in Herbal Medicine from Lincoln College or University of Westminster. There is also a student affiliate membership scheme for those who are undergraduates of either of the above schools.

QUALIFICATION/EXAMINATIONS
The NIMH has historically managed its own accreditation process, with universities currently offering a BSc(Hons) degree in Herbal Medicine at Lincoln College and University of Westminster.
From 2011 accreditation of the above courses transferred to The European Herbal and Traditional Medicine Practitioners Association (EHTPA), as an umbrella body of Professional Herbal Medicine Associations, although graduates will continue to be eligible to apply for NIMH membership.

DESIGNATORY LETTERS
MNIMH, FNIMH

MEDICAL SECRETARIES
Membership of Professional Institutions and Associations

ASSOCIATION OF MEDICAL SECRETARIES, PRACTICE MANAGERS, ADMINISTRATORS AND RECEPTIONISTS

Tavistock House North
Tavistock Square
London WC1H 9LN
Tel: 020 7387 6005
Fax: 020 7388 2648
E-mail: info@amspar.co.uk
Website: www.amspar.com

AMSPAR is a professional membership and educational organization. We work with City & Guilds to provide non-clinical qualifications for health administration within the UK qualification frameworks. We aim to promote quality and coherence in the delivery of qualifications, and encourage and support standards of excellence in the pursuit of continuous professional development and lifelong learning.

MEMBERSHIP
Associate Member (AAMS)
Member (MAMS)
Fellow (FAMS)

QUALIFICATION/EXAMINATIONS
The Level 5 Diploma in Primary Care & Health Management
The Level 5 Certificate in Primary Care & Health Management
The Level 3 Diploma for Medical Secretaries
The Level 3 Certificate in Medical Administration
The Level 3 Certificate in Medical Terminology

The Level 3 Award in Legal Aspects of Medical Administration
The Level 3 Award in Medical Principles for the Administrator
The Level 3 Award in Medical Word Processing
The Level 3 Award in Production of Medical Documents from Recorded Speech
The Level 2 Diploma in Medical Administration
The Level 2 Certificate in Medical Administration
The Level 2 Award in Medical Terminology
The Level 2 Award in Working in the NHS
The Level 2 Award in Medical Word Processing
The Level 2 Award in Production of Medical Documents from Recorded Speech

DESIGNATORY LETTERS
AAMS, MAMS, FAMS

MEDICINE

A student who wishes to qualify as a doctor in the UK must first obtain a primary qualification. Medical students in the UK typically study for five years to receive their medical degrees or for four years on a graduate-entry accelerated course. There are also courses offered for candidates with non-science subjects to offer at A level (or equivalent) that include the pre-medical year. The pre-medical year is a preliminary course in chemistry, physics and biology and lasts normally 30 weeks. Each medical school sets its own entry requirements, and may require applicants to complete clinical aptitude tests.

After graduation, a trainee doctor will enter the two-year Foundation Programme. There is a national application process for entry to the F1 year, but trainees successfully completing this year move into F2 without having to compete for a place. The trainee is provisionally registered with a licence to practise with the General Medical Council (GMC) while completing the first year and full registration is awarded upon completion of year one.

The F1 year aims to provide experience in a broad range of settings prior to full GMC registration. Regular work based assessments take place, and trainees must maintain a national learning portfolio in order to progress.

The F2 year usually consists of four varied three-month placements giving trainees the opportunity to try a number of different specialities before making a decision about which specialty training programme they would like to pursue. More information can be found at www.nhscareers.nhs.uk

The GMC is charged with the responsibility under the Medical Act 1983 of keeping a register of all duly qualified medical practitioners. General Medical Council, Regent's Place, 350 Euston Road, London NW1 3JN; Tel: 0161 923 6602; e-mail: gmc@gmc-uk.org; website: www.gmc-uk.org. For information on how to apply to join the register, see www.gmc-uk.org/doctors/applications.asp

PRIMARY QUALIFICATIONS

The GMC decides which universities are entitled to issue medical degrees. Qualifying examinations are examinations held for the granting of one or more primary medical qualifications (PMQs) by any one of the bodies or combinations of bodies in the United Kingdom that are included in a list maintained by the GMC and published on the GMC's website (www.gmc-uk.org/education/undergraduate/awarding_bodies.asp). Primary United Kingdom qualifications means any of the following qualifications:
- the degree of bachelor of medicine or bachelor of surgery granted by a body or combination of bodies included in the GMC list;
- licentiate of the Royal College of Physicians of London or the Royal College of Surgeons of

England or the Royal College of Physicians of Edinburgh or the Royal College of Surgeons of Edinburgh or the Royal College (formerly Royal Faculty) of Physicians and Surgeons of Glasgow;
- membership of the Royal College of Surgeons of England granted before the coming into force of section 1 of the Medical Qualifications (Amendment) Act 1991;
- licentiate in medicine and surgery of the Society of Apothecaries of London.

LICENSING AND REVALIDATION

Doctors must be registered with a licence to practise with the General Medical Council (GMC) and hold a licence to practise medicine in the UK. The licence to practise gives a doctor the legal authority to undertake certain activities in the UK, for example prescribing, signing death or cremation certificates and holding certain medical posts (such as working as a doctor in the NHS). Any person whose fitness to practise is not impaired and who a) holds one or more primary United Kingdom qualifications and has satisfactorily completed an acceptable programme for provisionally registered doctors; or b) being a national of any relevant European State, holds one or more primary European qualifications, is entitled to be registered as a fully registered medical practitioner. Doctors who do not work in the UK, or who do not undertake any activities for which a licence is required, do not need to hold a licence to practise an can continue to be registered without a licence.

Revalidation ensures that all licensed doctors demonstrate on an ongoing basis that they are up to date and fit to practise in their chosen field and able to provide a good level of care. Licensed doctors have to revalidate, usually every five years, by having regular appraisals based on the GMC's core guidance for doctors, *Good Medical Practice*. It is planned that the majority of licensed doctors will be revalidated for the first time by the end of March 2016.

Membership of Professional Institutions and Associations

COLLEGE OF OPERATING DEPARTMENT PRACTITIONERS

130 Euston Road
London NW1 2AY
Tel: 0870 121 5414
E-mail: office@codp.org
Website: www.codp.org.uk

The CODP is the professional body for Operating Department Practitioners. It is a membership, not-for-profit organization that sets standards of education for the pre-registration aspect of the profession and promotes the enhancement of knowledge and skills, in the context of the multidisciplinary team, through regional, national and international networks.

MEMBERSHIP
Student Member
Association Member
Full College Member

ROYAL COLLEGE OF GENERAL PRACTITIONERS

30 Euston Square
London NW1 2FB
Tel: 020 3188 7400
Fax: 020 3188 7401
E-mail: info@rcgp.org.uk
Website: www.rcgp.org.uk

The aims of the College are to encourage, foster and maintain the highest possible standards in general medical practice. Full entry to the College is by exam undertaken whilst in training for General Practice, or assessment as a qualified GP.

MEMBERSHIP
Associate in Training
Associate
Member (MRCGP)
Fellow (FRCGP)

International Member (MRCGP[INT])
Undergraduate medical students and Foundation programme students may register with the College's Student Forum, which exposes the students to life in general practice.

QUALIFICATION/EXAMINATIONS
Assessment for Membership of the RCGP (MRCGP)

DESIGNATORY LETTERS
MRCGP, FRCGP

ROYAL COLLEGE OF OBSTETRICIANS AND GYNAECOLOGISTS

27 Sussex Place
London NW1 4RG
Tel: 020 7772 6200
E-mail: library@rcog.org.uk
Website: www.rcog.org.uk

The RCOG encourages the study and advancement of the science and practice of obstetrics and gynae-cology. We do this through postgraduate medical education and training development, and the pub-lication of clinical guidelines and reports on aspects of the specialty and service provision. The RCOG International Office works with other international organizations to help lower maternal morbidity and mortality in under-resourced countries.

MEMBERSHIP
Affiliate
Associate
Diplomate

Trainee – pre-membership
Member without Examination (MRCOG)
Member (MRCOG)
Fellow (FRCOG)
Fellow *honoris causa*
Fellow *ad eumdem* (FRCOG)
Honorary Fellow (FRCOG)

QUALIFICATION/EXAMINATIONS
MRCOG (Membership Exam)
FRCOG (Diploma)

DESIGNATORY LETTERS
MRCOG, FRCOG

ROYAL SOCIETY OF MEDICINE

1 Wimpole Street
London W1G 0AE
Tel: 020 7290 2900
Fax: 020 7290 2992
E-mail: membership@rsm.ac.uk
Website: www.rsm.ac.uk

The RSM, founded in 1805, is a medical charity that promotes the exchange of information and ideas in medical science. We provide a broad range of educational activities and opportunities for doctors, dentists, veterinary surgeons, students of these disciplines and allied healthcare professionals, organize conferences, and publish books and journals through our publishing division, RSM Press.

MEMBERSHIP
Student

Associate
Fellow
Corporate

QUALIFICATION/EXAMINATIONS
NONE

DESIGNATORY LETTERS
N/A

THE FEDERATION OF ROYAL COLLEGES OF PHYSICIANS OF THE UNITED KINGDOM

MRCP(UK)
11 St Andrews Place
Regent's Park
London NW1 4LE
Tel: +44 (0)20 3075 1248
E-mail: policy.officer@mrcpuk.org
Website: www.mrcpuk.org

The Federation is a partnership between the Royal College of Physicians of Edinburgh, the Royal College of Physicians and Surgeons of Glasgow and the Royal College of Physicians of London. Working together, the colleges develop and deliver membership and specialty examinations that are recognized around the world as quality benchmarks.

MEMBERSHIP
Membership of the Royal Colleges of Physicians (MRCP(UK)): Once candidates have successfully completed their final Part of the examination they must then submit and complete the Form of Faith as a testimonial for election to membership.

QUALIFICATION/EXAMINATIONS
The Federation is responsible for a portfolio of examinations: MRCP(UK) Diploma (Membership of the Royal Colleges of Physicians of the United Kingdom): Candidates for the MRCP(UK) Diploma

may enter through the Royal College of Physicians of Edinburgh, the Royal College of Physicians and Surgeons of Glasgow, the Royal College of Physicians of London, or through the online application system. There are three components to the MRCP(UK) Diploma. The part 1 examination has a two-paper format. Each paper is 3 hours in duration and contains 100 multiple choice questions in one from five (best of five) format, where a candidate chooses the best answer from five possible answers. The part 2 written examination has a three-paper format. All papers in the MRCP(UK) part 2 written examination are 3 hours in duration and contain up to 100 multiple choice questions. The questions will usually have a clinical scenario, may include the results of investigations and may be illustrated. The part 2 clinical examination (PACES) consists of five clinical stations, each assessed by two independent examiners. Candidates will start at any one of the five stations, and then move round the carousel of stations at 20-minute intervals until they have completed the cycle. There is a 5-minute period between each station. Candidates may apply to sit the MRCP(UK) part 1 examination provided they graduated at least 12 months in advance of the examinations date (and have had at least 12 months' experience in medical employment). Candidates who have passed the part 1 examination can proceed to complete the remaining components. The MRCP(UK) Examination provides valid, reliable evidence of attainment in knowledge, clinical skills and behaviour, and is a mandatory component of assessment for Core Medical Training (CMT). The Specialty Certificate Examinations (SCEs): The Federation of Royal Colleges of Physicians of the UK, in association with the Specialist Societies, has developed a programme to deliver Specialty Certificate Examinations within the new specialist training structure. The aim of these national assessments is to ensure that trainees have sufficient knowledge of their specialty to practise safely and competently as consultants. The Specialty Certificate Examination is delivered in computer-based format (referred to as CBT) at a Pearson VUE test centre. Each paper is based on the MRCP(UK) written paper format and contains 100 multiple choice questions in 'best of five' format. A Specialty Certificate Examination is a compulsory component of assessment for Certificate of Completion of Training (CCT) for all UK trainees whose specialist training began in or after August 2007 and is in one of the following specialties: Dermatology; Endocrinology and Diabetes; Gastroenterology; Geriatric Medicine; Infectious Diseases; Medical Oncology; Nephrology; Neurology; Palliative Medicine; Respiratory Medicine and Rheumatology.

DESIGNATORY LETTERS
MRCP(UK)

THE INSTITUTE OF CLINICAL RESEARCH

10 Cedar Court
Grove Park
White Waltham Road
Maidenhead
Tel: 0845 521 0056
E-mail: info@icr-global.org
Website: www.icr-global.org

The ICR was founded in 1978 and is now the largest professional clinical research body in Europe and India. Our aim is to promote knowledge and understanding by engaging with the healthcare community and the general public, to support and facilitate communication between our members, and to provide opportunities for learning and development to enhance professional competence.

MEMBERSHIP
Affiliate

Registered Member (RICR)
Professional Member (MICR)
Fellow (FICR)
Honorary Fellow (Hon FICR)

QUALIFICATION/EXAMINATIONS
Please see the ICR's website.

DESIGNATORY LETTERS
RICR, MICR, FICR, HonFICR

THE ROYAL COLLEGE OF ANAESTHETISTS

Churchill House
35 Red Lion Square
London WC1R 4SG
Tel: 020 7092 1500
Fax: 020 7092 1730
E-mail: info@rcoa.ac.uk
Website: www.rcoa.ac.uk

The RCoA, which dates from 1948, is the professional body responsible for the specialty of anaesthesia throughout the UK. Our principal responsibility is to ensure the quality of patient care through the maintenance of standards in anaesthesia, pain medicine and critical care. We set and run examinations, and provide CPD for all practising anaesthetists.

MEMBERSHIP
Trainee
Affiliate
Associate Member
Member (MRCA)
Associate Fellow
Fellow *ad eundem* (FRCA)
Fellow (FRCA)
Honorary Fellow (FRCA)

QUALIFICATION/EXAMINATIONS
FRCA Examinations (FRCA)

DESIGNATORY LETTERS
MRCA, FRCA

THE ROYAL COLLEGE OF PATHOLOGISTS

2 Carlton House Terrace
London SW1Y 5AF
Tel: 020 7451 6700
E-mail: info@rcpath.org
Website: www.rcpath.org

The College aims to advance the science and practice of pathology, to provide public education, to promote research in pathology and to disseminate the results.

MEMBERSHIP
Affiliate Member
Associate
Diplomate Member (DipRCPath)
Fellow (FRCPath)

QUALIFICATION/EXAMINATIONS
Training programmes are approved for all pathology specialities and sub-specialities. The exact examination arrangements vary for each speciality but they will all involve a Part 1 and a Part 2 which include, inter alia, written, practical and oral components. In addition the College offers a Diploma in Cytopathology, a Diploma in Dermatopathology and a Diploma in Forensic Pathology. Further details may be obtained from the Examinations Department or the College's website.

DESIGNATORY LETTERS
DipRCPath, FRCPath

THE ROYAL COLLEGE OF PHYSICIANS AND SURGEONS OF GLASGOW

232–242 St Vincent Street
Glasgow G2 5RJ
Tel: 0141 2216072
Fax: 0141 2211804
E-mail: exams@rcpsg.ac.uk
Website: www.rcpsg.ac.uk

The Royal College of Physicians and Surgeons of Glasgow (RCPSG) welcomes professionals from a diverse range of disciplines. At present, our collegiate body includes Physicians, Surgeons, professionals in Dentistry, Travel Medicine, Podiatric Medicine and other professions allied to medicine. The College aims to provide career support to our membership through education, training, professional development, examinations and assessment, whilst acting as a charity and leading voice on health issues in order to set the highest standards of health care.

MEMBERSHIP

Member MRCPS(Glasg)/ MFDS RCPS(Glasg)/ MRCS(Glasg)/ MRCS(ENT)(Glasg)/ MFTM RCPS(Glasg)/ MFPM RCPS(Glasg)
Fellow FRCP(Glasg)/ FRCS(Glasg)/ FDS RCPS(Glasg)/ FFTM RCPS(Glasg)/ FFPM RCPS(Glasg)
Associate Member
Affiliate Member
Associate in Training
Introductory Member

QUALIFICATION/EXAMINATIONS

Diploma in Dermatology (Dip Derm)
Diploma in Otolaryngology – Head and Neck Surgery (DOHNS)
Diploma in Travel Medicine (DipTravMed)
Diploma in Expedition and Wilderness Medicine
Postgraduate Diploma in Clinical Education
Diploma of Membership of the Royal Colleges of Physicians of the United Kingdom (MRCP(UK))
Diploma of Membership of the Royal College of Surgeons (MRCS(Glasg))
Diploma of Membership of the Royal College of Surgeons (MRCS(ENT)(Glasg))
Diploma of Membership of the Faculty of Dental Surgery (MFDS RCPS(Glasg))
Diploma of Membership in (dental specialty) (M(dental specialty) RCPS(Glasg)
Diploma of Membership of the Faculty of Travel Medicine (MFTM RCPS(Glasg))
Diploma of Membership of the Faculty of Podiatric Medicine (MFPM RCPS(Glasg))
Diploma of Fellowship of the Royal College of Physicians and Surgeons of Glasgow in Ophthalmology (FRCS(Glasg))
Diploma of Fellowship of the Royal College of Physicians and Surgeons of Glasgow (FDS (dental specialty)RCPS(Glasg))
Diploma of Fellowship of the Royal College of Physicians and Surgeons of Glasgow (FRCSGlasg (surgical specialty))
Diploma of Fellowship of the Faculty of Travel Medicine (FFTM RCPS(Glasg))
Diploma of Fellowship of the Faculty of Podiatric Medicine (FFPM RCPS(Glasg))

DESIGNATORY LETTERS

MFDS RCPS(Glasg), MFTM RCPS(Glasg), MRCP(UK), MRCS(Glasg), MRCS(ENT)(Glasg), MRCPS(Glasg), MFPM RCPS(Glasg), M(dental specialty) RCPS(Glasg)/ FRCP(Glasg)/ FRCS(Glasg)/ FRCSGlasg(surgical specialty)/ FDS RCPS(Glasg)/ FRCS(Urol)(Glasg), FFTM RCPS(Glasg)

THE ROYAL COLLEGE OF PHYSICIANS OF EDINBURGH

9 Queen Street
Edinburgh EH2 1JQ
Tel: 01312 257324
E-mail: l.tedford@rcpe.ac.uk
Website: www.rcpe.ac.uk

The RCPE promotes the highest standards in internal medicine in the UK and internationally. Along with our sister Colleges in Glasgow and London we oversee the membership examination of the Royal Colleges of Physicians, MRCP(UK), enabling doctors to enter higher specialist training, leading eventually to a Certificate of Completion of Specialist Training (CCST).

MEMBERSHIP
Student + Foundation
Associate
Collegiate Member (MRCPE)
Fellow (FRCPE)

QUALIFICATION/EXAMINATIONS
MRCP(UK)
Specialty Certificate Examinations

DESIGNATORY LETTERS
MRCPE, FRCPE

THE ROYAL COLLEGE OF PHYSICIANS OF LONDON

11 St Andrews Place
Regent's Park
London NW1 4LE
Tel: +44 (0)20 3075 1649
E-mail: via website
Website: www.rcplondon.ac.uk

The Royal College of Physicians of London offers a Diploma in Geriatric Medicine (DGM) Examination and a Diploma in Tropical Medicine and Hygiene, run in conjunction with the London School of Tropical Medicine and Hygiene.

MEMBERSHIP
The Royal College of Physicians of London runs the MRCP(UK) Examination which is the MRCP(UK) membership examination. As the examination is run in conjunction with two other Royal Colleges of Physicians, this examination and the membership qualification MRCP(UK) are listed in this directory under *The Federation of Royal Colleges of Physicians*

QUALIFICATION/EXAMINATIONS
Diploma in Geriatric Medicine The Diploma in Geriatric Medicine is designed to give recognition of competence in the provision of care of older people to General Practitioner vocational trainees, staff physicians and others working in non-consultant career posts in Departments of Geriatric Medicine, and

other doctors with interests in or responsibilities for the care of older people.

The Diploma in Geriatric Medicine is available to all registered doctors. It is not primarily directed towards career geriatricians, but is generally to family doctors, psycho-geriatricians and indeed any doctor involved in the care of older people.

The Diploma in Geriatric Medicine is in two parts, the first of which is a written examination of multiple choice (best of 5) questions, lasting 2 hours and 30 minutes normally held twice a year at the Royal College of Physicians of London.

The second part is a Clinical Examination also held twice a year at various clinical centres in England and Wales. The clinical examination is a four-station standardized examination similar to an Objective Standard Clinical Examination (OSCE).

Diploma in Tropical Medicine and Hygiene The Diploma in Tropical Medicine and Hygiene is intended to test the knowledge required of physicians who wish to practise medicine effectively in developing countries.

Candidates for the Diploma in Tropical Medicine & Hygiene must hold a primary medical qualification recognized by the Royal College of Physicians of London.

The Royal College of Physicians of London will accept applications from candidates who are in the process of completing, or have completed within the last 5 years, the Tropical Medicine courses in London, Liverpool, Sheffield and Glasgow, which are recognized as appropriate training centres for the examination. The examination is held once a year over 2 days (unless required for a viva) and is conducted in the following sections: A **Practical Section** lasting 2 hours and 30 minutes consists of a mixture of microscopy specimens, including 20 'spot' questions that are set up on a microscope for identification. Other specimens require the candidate to use the microscopes themself. They are mainly parasitological and may include faecal, blood and haematological preparations together with some entomological specimens. A **Written Section** (3 hours and 20 minutes in total) consists of three papers. The **Clinical Paper** (1 hour) contains 18 compulsory questions. The first 16 are based on clinical pictures – usually of patients with abnormal physical signs; but occasionally laboratory slides, X-rays, or epidemiological data may be shown. There will be 2 or 3 questions on each, asking (for example) identification, diagnosis, further investigation, treatment etc. Each of these 16 questions is worth a maximum of 5 marks. The last 2 questions (17 and 18) are brief clinical cases, with 2 or 3 questions (again concentrating on diagnosis or differential diagnosis, investigation and treatment). The **Multiple Choice Question Paper** (1 hour and 20 minutes) consists of 40 multiple choice questions designed to test the knowledge of tropical medicine and hygiene over a wide area. The **Preventative Medicine Paper** (1 hour including 5 minutes reading time) consists of 10 questions of which the candidate must choose 5. Each question may have several parts, covering all aspects of preventative medicine and international community health in a tropical context.

There is also an **Oral ('Viva') Examination** for borderline candidates. The examination is conducted by two examiners. The first part of the examination (10 minutes) is a discussion of an illustrated clinical case history, which candidates are allowed to study for 10 minutes before the examination. The second part of the examination (10 minutes) consists of more general questions.

THE ROYAL COLLEGE OF PSYCHIATRISTS

21 Prescot Street
London E1 8BB
Tel: 020 7235 2351
Fax: 020 3701 2761
E-mail: reception@rcpsych.ac.uk
Website: www.rcpsych.ac.uk

The RCPsych is the professional and educational body for psychiatrists in the UK and Ireland. We are committed to improving the understanding of psychiatry and mental health, and are at the forefront in setting and achieving the highest standards through education, training and research. We actively promote psychiatry as a career, and provide guidance and support to our members and associates.

MEMBERSHIP
Pre-Membership Psychiatric Trainee
New Associate
Affiliate
Specialist Associate
Member (MRCPsych)

Fellow (FRCPsych)
Honorary Fellow
International Associate

QUALIFICATION/EXAMINATIONS
MRCPsych qualifying exams
Paper A – The Scientific and Theoretical Basis of Psychiatry
Paper B – Critical Review and the Clinical Topics in Psychiatry
CASC – Clinical Assessment of Skills and Competencies

DESIGNATORY LETTERS
MRCPsych, FRCPsych

THE ROYAL COLLEGE OF RADIOLOGISTS

63 Lincoln's Inn Fields
London WC2A 3JW
Tel: 020 7405 1282
E-mail: enquiries@rcr.ac.uk
Website: www.rcr.ac.uk

The Royal College of Radiologists (RCR) leads, supports and educates in medical imaging and cancer treatment. RCR sets and maintains the standards for entry to, and practice in, the specialties of clinical oncology and clinical radiology and shapes their future development for the benefit of patients. The College works to advance the science and practice of radiology and oncology. It furthers public awareness and education, and promotes study and research through setting professional standards of practice. It also sets the curriculum for the two specialties ensuring that high educational standards are met in the interests of safe and responsible practice.

MEMBERSHIP
Junior Member
Associate
Trainee
Member
Fellow (FRCR)
Honorary Member/Fellow (Hon MRCR/Hon FRCR)

QUALIFICATION/EXAMINATIONS
First FRCR Examination
Final FRCR Examination
Diploma in Dental and Maxillofacial Radiology (DDMFR)

DESIGNATORY LETTERS
FRCR, Hon MRCR, Hon FRCR

THE ROYAL COLLEGE OF SURGEONS OF EDINBURGH

Nicolson Street
Edinburgh EH8 9DW
Tel: 0131 527 1600
Fax: 0131 557 6406
E-mail: mail@rcsed.ac.uk
Website: www.rcsed.ac.uk

The Royal College of Surgeons of Edinburgh, which dates from 1505, is dedicated to the maintenance and promotion of the highest standards of surgical practice, through education, training and rigorous examination, and its liaison with external medical bodies. Today, with more than 20,000 Fellows and Members, we pride ourselves also on our innovation and adaptability.

MEMBERSHIP
Affiliate

Associate
Member (MRCSEd)
Fellow (FRCSEd)

QUALIFICATION/EXAMINATIONS
Please see the Royal College of Surgeons of Edinburgh website.

DESIGNATORY LETTERS
MRCSEd, FRCSEd

THE ROYAL COLLEGE OF SURGEONS OF ENGLAND

35–43 Lincoln's Inn Fields
London WC2A 3PE
Tel: 020 7405 3474
E-mail: membership@rcseng.ac.uk
Website: www.rcseng.ac.uk

The Royal College of Surgeons of England is committed to enabling surgeons to achieve and maintain the highest standards of surgical practice and patient care. We examine trainees, supervise the training of and provide support and advice for surgeons, promote and support surgical research in the UK, and liaise with the DoH, health authorities, Trusts and hospitals in the UK and other medical and academic organizations worldwide.

MEMBERSHIP
Affiliate
Associate
Fellow *ad eundem*
Membership *ad eundem*
Specialty Membership

QUALIFICATION/EXAMINATIONS
Please see the Royal College of Surgeons of England website.

THE WORSHIPFUL SOCIETY OF APOTHECARIES OF LONDON

Apothecaries' Hall
Black Friars Lane
London EC4V 6EJ
Tel: 020 7236 1180
Fax: 020 7329 3177
E-mail: via website
Website: www.apothecaries.org

The Society of Apothecaries of London was incorporated by Royal Charter in 1617 and allowed to prepare and sell drugs for medicinal purposes, laying the foundations of the British pharmaceutical industry. Later, apothecaries were permitted to prescribe and dispense medicines, becoming the forerunners of today's GPs. Now the Society is primarily an examining body.

QUALIFICATION/EXAMINATIONS
PGDip in Forensic Medical Sciences (DFMS)
PGDip in Genitourinary Medicine (Dip GU Med)
PGDip in the History of Medicine (DHMSA)
PGDip in HIV Medicine (Dip HIV Med)
PGDip in the Medical Care of Catastrophes (DMCC)
PGDip in Medical Jurisprudence (Pathology) (DMJ[Path])
PGDip in the Philosophy of Medicine (DPMSA)

METALLURGY
Membership of Professional Institutions and Associations

INSTITUTE OF CORROSION

The Newton Building
St George's Avenue
Northampton NN2 6JB
Tel: 01604 893883
Fax: 01604 893878
E-mail: admin@icorr.org
Website: www.icorr.org

The Institute of Corrosion has since 1959 been serving the corrosion science, technology and engineering community in the fight against corrosion, which costs the UK around 4 per cent of GNP per annum. We promote the establishment and promotion of sound corrosion management practice, the advancement of cost-effective corrosion control measures, and a sustained effort to raise corrosion awareness at all stages of design, fabrication and operation.

MEMBERSHIP
Student Member
Ordinary Member
Technical Member (TICorr)
Professional Member (MICorr)

Engineering Technician (EngTech)
Incorporated Engineer (IEng)
Chartered Engineer (CEng)
Chartered Scientist (CSci)

QUALIFICATION/EXAMINATIONS
Cathodic Protection Technician (Level 1)
Senior Cathodic Protection Technician (Level 2)
Senior Cathodic Protection Engineer (Level 3)
Painting Inspector (ICorr Levels 1, 2 and 3)
Coating Inspector (ICorr Levels 1 and 2)

DESIGNATORY LETTERS
TICorr, MICorr, EngTech, IEng, CEng

THE INSTITUTE OF METAL FINISHING

Exeter House
48 Holloway Head
Birmingham B1 1NQ
Tel: 01216 227387
Fax: 01216 666316
E-mail: exeterhouse@instituteofmetalfinishing.org
Website: www.uk-finishing.org.uk

The IMF, founded in 1925, provides a focus for surface engineering and finishing activities worldwide through the fulfilment of technical, educational and professional needs at all levels for individuals and companies involved in the coatings industry. We promote R&D within the industry and CPD for our members, cooperate with other institutes, and liaise with legislative bodies to influence decision making.

MEMBERSHIP
Student
Affiliate

Associate (AssocIMF)
Technician (TechIMF)
Licentiate (LIMF)
Member (MIMF)
Fellow (FIMF)
Engineering Technician (EngTech)
Sustaining Member (company)

QUALIFICATION/EXAMINATIONS
Foundation Certificate
Technician Certificate
Advanced Technician Certificate

DESIGNATORY LETTERS
AssocIMF, TechIMF, LIMF, MIMF, FIMF, EngTech

METEOROLOGY AND CLIMATOLOGY
Membership of Professional Institutions and Associations

MET OFFICE COLLEGE

Met Office
Fitzroy Road
Exeter
Devon EX1 3PB
Tel: 01392 885680
Fax: 01392 885681
E-mail: enquiries@metoffice.gov.uk
Website: www.metoffice.gov.uk

The Meteorological Office College is part of the Met Office and is located in Exeter, Devon. We provide meteorological training for our own staff and to meteorological services worldwide, as places become available on a fee-paying basis.

QUALIFICATION/EXAMINATIONS
Level 3 Diploma in Meteorological Observing (QCF)

Level 4 Certificate for a Meteorological Forecasting Technician (QCF)
Level 5 Diploma in Meteorological Forecasting (QCF)
Level 5 Award in Meteorological Briefing (QCF)
Level 5 Certificate in Meteorological Broadcasting (QCF)
Level 6 Diploma in Flood Forecasting (QCF)

ROYAL METEOROLOGICAL SOCIETY

104 Oxford Road
Reading RG1 7LL
Tel: 0118 956 8500
Fax: 0118 956 8571
E-mail: info@rmets.org
Website: www.rmets.org

The RMetS is the learned and professional society for anyone whose profession or interests are connected with weather and climate. It administers the NVQs of the profession and is the accreditation body for the status of Chartered Meteorologist. Its principal aim is the advancement of the understanding of weather and climate for the benefit of everyone.

MEMBERSHIP
Student

Associate Fellow
Fellow (FRMetS)
Honorary Member
Chartered Meteorologist (CMet)
School Member
Corporate Member

DESIGNATORY LETTERS
FRMetS, CMet

MICROSCOPY
Membership of Professional Institutions and Associations

THE ROYAL MICROSCOPICAL SOCIETY

37/38 St Clements
Oxford OX4 1AJ
Tel: 01865 254760
Fax: 01865 791237
E-mail: info@rms.org.uk
Website: www.rms.org.uk

The RMS, which dates from 1839, is an international scientific society dedicated to advancing the science of microscopy and the interests of its 1,400 members, who range from individuals interested in microscopy to scientists and company members representing manufacturers and suppliers of microscopes, other equipment and services.

MEMBERSHIP
Ordinary Member
Fellow (FRMS)
Corporate Member

DESIGNATORY LETTERS
FRMS

MUSEUM AND RELATED WORK
Membership of Professional Institutions and Associations

MUSEUMS ASSOCIATION

42 Clerkenwell Close
London EC1R 0AZ
Tel: 020 7566 7800
E-mail: info@museumsassociation.org
Website: www.museumsassociation.org

The MA is the oldest museums association in the world, set up in 1889 to guard the interests of museums and galleries. Today, we have 5,200 individual members, 600 institutional members and 250 corporate members. Our aim is to enhance the value of museums to society by sharing knowledge, developing skills, inspiring innovation and providing leadership.

MEMBERSHIP
Student
Volunteer
Professional Member
Associate (AMA)
Corporate Member
Institutional Member

DESIGNATORY LETTERS
AMA

MUSIC

Membership of Professional Institutions and Associations

ABRSM (ASSOCIATED BOARD OF THE ROYAL SCHOOLS OF MUSIC)

24 Portland Place
London W1B 1LU
Tel: 020 7636 5400
Fax: 020 7637 0234
E-mail: abrsm@abrsm.org
Website: www.abrsm.org

ABRSM's mission is to motivate musical achievement. We aim to support the development of learners and teachers in music education worldwide and to celebrate their achievements. We do this through authoritative and internationally recognized assessments, publications and professional development support for teachers, and through charitable donations.

MEMBERSHIP
Licentiate (LRSM)
Fellow (FRSM)

QUALIFICATION/EXAMINATIONS
Certificate of Teaching (CT ABRSM)
Diploma in Instrumental/Vocal Teaching (DipABRSM)
Diploma in Music Direction (DipABRSM)
Diploma in Music Performance (DipABRSM)

Please see the ABRSM website for details of other examinations and awards.

DESIGNATORY LETTERS
CT ABRSM, DipABRSM, LRSM, FRSM

INCORPORATED SOCIETY OF MUSICIANS

10 Stratford Place
London WIC 1AA
Tel: 020 7629 4413
Fax: 020 7408 1538
E-mail: membership@ism.org
Website: www.ism.org

The ISM, a non-profit-making organization founded in 1882, is the UK's professional body for musicians. We promote the art of music and the interests of musicians through campaigns, support and practical advice. Members also receive our monthly in-house magazine, *Music Journal*, which includes news and information on CPD.

MEMBERSHIP
Student Member
Associate Member
Full Member
Corporate Member
Graduate Member

MUSICAL INSTRUMENT TECHNOLOGY
Membership of Professional Institutions and Associations

PIANOFORTE TUNERS' ASSOCIATION

PO Box 230
Hailsham
East Sussex BN27 9EA
Tel: 0845 602 8796
E-mail: secretary@pianotuner.org.uk
Website: www.pianotuner.org.uk

The PTA is a professional body committed to improving standards, and applicants for membership must pass a theoretical and practical examination to prove their ability as a qualified piano tuner or technician. We publish a regular newsletter and hold an Annual Convention and General Meeting in different towns around Britain, to which members and aspiring non-members are invited.

MEMBERSHIP
Student
Patron
Associate
Technician Member
Member
Subscriber

THE INCORPORATED SOCIETY OF ORGAN BUILDERS

The Tower
7 Lower Port View
SALTASH
Cornwall PL12 4BY
Tel: 01752-842027
Fax: 01752-842027
E-mail: secretary@isob.co.uk
Website: www.isob.co.uk

The ISOB was founded in 1947 to advance the science and practice of organ building, to provide a central organization for organ builders, and to provide for the better definition and protection of the profession by a system of examinations and the issue of certificates and distinctions. We hold regular meetings and conferences around the UK and overseas.

MEMBERSHIP
Student Member

Ordinary Member (MISOB)
Associate Member (AISOB)
Fellow (FISOB)
Counsellor (CISOB)
Companion

DESIGNATORY LETTERS
MISOB, AISOB, FISOB, CISOB

NAVAL ARCHITECTURE
Membership of Professional Institutions and Associations

THE ROYAL INSTITUTION OF NAVAL ARCHITECTS

8–9 Northumberland Street
London WC2N 5DA
Tel: 020 7235 4622
Fax: 020 7259 5912
E-mail: membership@rina.org.uk
Website: www.rina.org.uk

The RINA is an internationally renowned professional institution whose members are involved at all levels in the design, construction, maintenance and operation of marine vessels and structures. Our members are widely represented in industry, universities and colleges, and maritime organizations in over 90 countries.

MEMBERSHIP
Student Member
Associate (AssocRINA)
Associate Member (AMRINA)
Member (MRINA)
Fellow (FRINA)

DESIGNATORY LETTERS
AssocRINA, AMRINA, MRINA, FRINA

NAVIGATION, SEAMANSHIP AND MARINE QUALIFICATIONS
Membership of Professional Institutions and Associations

THE NAUTICAL INSTITUTE

202 Lambeth Road
London SE1 7LQ
Tel: 020 7928 1351
Fax: 020 7401 2817
E-mail: sec@nautinst.org
Website: www.nautinst.org

The Nautical Institute is the international representative body for maritime professionals involved in the control of sea-going ships with an interest in nautical matters. It provides a wide range of services to enhance the professional standing and knowledge of members who are drawn from all sectors of the maritime world.

MEMBERSHIP
Honorary Fellow
Fellow (FNI)
Associate Fellow (AFNI)

Member (MNI)
Associate Member (AMNI)

QUALIFICATION/EXAMINATIONS
Harbour Master's Certificate
Pilotage Certificate
Command Diploma
International Sail Endorsement Scheme

DESIGNATORY LETTERS
FNI, AFNI, MNI, AMNI

THE ROYAL INSTITUTE OF NAVIGATION

1 Kensington Gore
London SW7 2AT
Tel: 020 7591 3134
Fax: 020 7591 3131
E-mail: admin@rin.org.uk
Website: www.rin.org.uk

The RIN is a learned society with charitable status. Our aims are: to unite those with a professional or personal interest in any aspect of navigation in one unique body; to further the development of navigation in every sphere; and to increase public awareness of both the art and science of navigation, how it has shaped the past, how it impacts our world today, and how it will affect the future.

MEMBERSHIP
Junior Associate Member
Student

Associate
Member (MRIN)
Associate Fellow (AFRIN)
Fellow (FRIN)
Affiliate Club
Affiliate College or University
Corporate Member
Small Business

DESIGNATORY LETTERS
MRIN, AFRIN, FRIN

NON-DESTRUCTIVE TESTING
Membership of Professional Institutions and Associations

THE BRITISH INSTITUTE OF NON-DESTRUCTIVE TESTING

Newton Building
St George's Avenue
Northampton NN2 6JB
Tel: 01604 89 3811
Fax: 01604 89 3861
E-mail: info@bindt.org
Website: www.bindt.org

The BINDT was formed in 1976 from the merger of the Society of Non-Destructive Examination (SONDE) and the Society of Industrial Radiology and Allied Methods of Non-Destructive Testing, later renamed the NDT Society of Great Britain (NDTS), both formed in 1954. Our aim is to promote and advance the science and practice of non-destructive testing, condition monitoring, diagnostic engineering and all other materials and quality testing disciplines.

MEMBERSHIP
Student Member
Affiliate

Practitioner Member (PInstNDT)
Graduate Member (GInstNDT)
Member (MInstNDT)
Fellow (FInstNDT)
Engineering Technician (EngTech)
Incorporated Engineer (IEng)
Chartered Engineer (CEng)
Licensed Engineering Practitioner
Associate Member (corporate)

DESIGNATORY LETTERS
PInstNDT, GInstNDT, MInstNDT, FInstNDT, EngTech, IEng, CEng

NURSERY NURSING
Membership of Professional Institutions and Associations

COUNCIL FOR AWARDS IN CHILDREN'S CARE AND EDUCATION

Apex House
81 Camp Road
St Albans
Hertfordshire AL1 5GB
Tel: 0845 347 2123
Fax: 01727 818618
E-mail: info@cache.org.uk
Website: www.cache.org.uk

CACHE is an Awarding Body that designs courses and qualifications in the care and education of children and young people. Our courses, which are widely available, range from entry level to advanced qualifications for sector professionals. We regularly lobby the government and other agencies to raise the quality and professionalism of child care.

QUALIFICATION/EXAMINATIONS
Please see the CACHE website.

THE SOCIETY OF NURSERY NURSING PRACTITIONERS

40 Archdale Road
East Dulwich
London SE22 9HJ
Tel: 0208 693 0555
Fax: 0208 693 0555
E-mail: info@snnp.org.uk
Website: www.snnp.org.uk

The Society is the only professional examining body in the field. Incorporated in 1991, it caters for the interests and aspirations of childminders, nursery nurses and all those who look after children and young people from birth to age 5. It also exists to raise the flagging professional image of nursery nurses.

MEMBERSHIP
Graduate (GSNNP)
Associate (ASNNP)
Fellow (FSNNP)

QUALIFICATION/EXAMINATIONS
The examinations in Early Childhood Studies are in three stages: Certificate, Advanced Certificate and Diploma. The subjects for all the examinations are the same but the questions are set and marked at the appropriate level. The subjects are:
Care of the sick child and special needs
Data investigation and interpretation
Early childhood play and learning
First aid and safety
Legal aspects of child care, health and community care
Management in the Early Years (Diploma level)
Managing self evaluation reflection
Observation, assessment and the young child
Overview of growth and development
Practice in service in child care
Pregnancy, birth and child development
Preparing for employment with young children
Protecting children from abuse
Social and psychological development
Working with parents and young children
Course work on a topic selected by the student

DESIGNATORY LETTERS
GSNNP, ASNNP, FSNNP

NURSING AND MIDWIFERY

Membership of Professional Institutions and Associations

THE NURSING & MIDWIFERY COUNCIL

23 Portland Place
London W1B 1PZ
Tel: 020 7333 9333
E-mail: UKenquiries@nmc-uk.org
Website: www.nmc-uk.org

We are the nursing and midwifery regulator for England, Wales, Scotland, Northern Ireland and the Islands. We exist to safeguard the health and well-being of the public.

OCCUPATIONAL THERAPY

Membership of Professional Institutions and Associations

BRITISH ASSOCIATION OF OCCUPATIONAL THERAPISTS

106–114 Borough High Street
Southwark
London SE1 1LB
Tel: 020 7357 6480
Fax: 020 7450 2299
E-mail: membership@cot.co.uk
Website: www.cot.org.uk

The British Association and College of Occupational Therapists is the professional body for occupational therapy in the UK. The College has over 30,000 members and represents the profession nationally and internationally. COT accredits pre-registration occupational therapy degree programmes in 31 UK Universities.

MEMBERSHIP
Student Member
Associate
Discounted Associate
Professional Member
Discounted Professional Member
Self-employed Member
Retired Member
Overseas Member

QUALIFICATION/EXAMINATIONS
BA (Hons)
PG Dip
MSc

DESIGNATORY LETTERS
MBAOT

OPTICIANS (DISPENSING)

Dispensing opticians must be registered with the General Optical Council (GOC, 41 Harley Street, London W1G 8DJ; Tel: 020 7580 3898; e-mail: goc@optical.org; website: www.optical.org). The GOC publishes registers of all optometrists, dispensing opticians, student opticians and optical businesses that are qualified and fit to practise, train or carry on business.

Qualification takes three years in total, and can be completed by combining a distance learning course or day release while working as a trainee under the supervision of a qualified and GOC-registered optician. Alternatively students can do a two-year full-time course followed by one year of supervised practice with a qualified and registered optician. The GOC has approved training courses in dispensing optics at the following institutions in the UK: Anglia Ruskin University, Association of British Dispensing Opticians (ABDO) College (Distance Learning Institute), Bradford College, City and Islington College, City University and Glasgow Caledonian University. All routes are assessed by final ABDO examinations. On successful completion of training you must register with the GOC in order to practise in the UK. Once qualified, you will need to undertake a minimum amount of continuing education and training to remain on the register. All registered dispensing opticians have to renew their registration each year: this is called 'retention'.

The approved training course for the contact lens specialty is run by ABDO College and City and Islington College. For further information contact the ABDO Education department on education@optical.org or 0207 307 9488.

If you qualify as a dispensing optician and have worked in practice as a qualified dispensing optician for at least two years, the University of Bradford offers a career progression course that enables you to graduate with a degree in optometry in one calendar year (Tel: 01274 236296; email: do-optom@bradford.ac.uk).

Continuing education and training is statutory requirement for all fully-qualified dispensing opticians. The CET scheme is a points-based scheme that runs over a three-year cycle. All full registrants must earn a minimum number of CET points by the end of each cycle to stay on the registers.

Nationals of EU/EEA countries who have gained optical quailfications in an EU/EEA country can apply to another EU/EEA country to have their qualifications recognised.

ENTRY REQUIREMENTS

Requirements vary according to the college or university, but typically five GCSEs at Grade C or above, to include Mathematics, English and Science and one A Level at a minimum of a Grade D or equivalent are required. Relevant work experience will also be considered.

For further details contact the admissions tutor or check the website of the university you wish to apply to.

Membership of Professional Institutions and Associations

ASSOCIATION OF BRITISH DISPENSING OPTICIANS

199 Gloucester Terrace
London W2 6LD
Tel: 020 7298 5100
E-mail: general@abdolondon.org.uk
Website: www.abdo.org.uk

The ABDO is the qualifying body for dispensing opticians in the UK. Our aims are to advance the science and art of dispensing optics, to further the education and training of dispensing opticians, and to support and promote the interests of the profession.

MEMBERSHIP
Student Member
Associate Member
Full Member
Fellow (FBDO)

Elder

QUALIFICATION/EXAMINATIONS
Certificate in Contact Lens Practice (Level 6)
Diploma in The Assessment & Management of Low Vision (Level 6)
Diploma in Ophthalmic Dispensing (Level 6)
Diploma in Advanced Contact Lens Practice (Level 7)
Diploma in Spectacle Lens Design (Level 7)

DESIGNATORY LETTERS
FBDO

ASSOCIATION OF CONTACT LENS MANUFACTURERS

PO Box 735
Devizes
Wiltshire SN10 3TQ
Tel: 01380 860418
Fax: 01380 860863
E-mail: secgen@aclm.org.uk
Website: www.aclm.org.uk

The ACLM was founded in 1962 to publicize the work of UK contact lens manufacturers, to develop new products and to raise standards. Today we represent the manufacturers of the vast majority of prescription contact lenses and lens care products sold in the UK, and provide a cohesive voice for our members.

MEMBERSHIP
Member

OPTOMETRY

Careers in optometry are overseen by the General Optical Council (41 Harley Street, London W1G 8DJ; Tel: 020 7580 3898; e-mail: goc@optical.org; website: www.optical.org). You can study for an undergraduate optometry degree from one of nine GOC-approved institutions in the UK: Anglia Ruskin University, Aston University, the University of Bradford, Cardiff University, City University, Glasgow Caledonian University, Plymouth University, the University of Manchester and the University of Ulster.

LENGTH OF COURSE
Usually four years in total (five in Scotland): a full-time three-year (four-year in Scotland) degree course, followed by one year's salaried pre-registration training with a practice under the guidance of an optometrist member of the College of Optometrists, or a supervisor approved by the University of Manchester. This includes a series of assessments, set by the College of Optometry, or the University of Manchester, throughout the placement. Trainees must have gained a degree in Optometry at 2:2 or above from an institution recognized by the GOC and have a valid Certificate of Clinical Competency in order to enter a pre-registration placement.

ENTRY REQUIREMENTS
You will normally need five GCSEs (or equivalent) at grade C or above, one of which should be English; often maths and physics or double science are also required. You will normally be required to have three A Level passes/approximately 320 UCAS tariff points from the following subjects: physics, biology, chemistry or mathematics. Requirements vary between universities, so be sure to check the university's prospectus and/or consult the relevant admission tutors.

REGISTRATION
On successful completion of the pre-registration period of training, which includes work-based assessment and a final assessment on the Stage 2 core competencies for optometry, the qualified optometrist must register with the GOC in order to practise.

Nationals of EU/EEA countries who have gained optical qualifications in an EU/EEA country can apply to another EU/EEA country to have their qualifications recognised. For people who gained their qualification outside the EU/EEA the requirements for registration as an optometrist in the UK are detailed on the GOC website.

Membership of Professional Institutions and Associations

ASSOCIATION OF OPTOMETRISTS

2 Woodbridge Street
London EC1R 0DG
Tel: 020 7549 2000
Fax: 020 7251 8315
E-mail: postbox@aop.org.uk
Website: www.aop.org.uk

The AOP serves its members by promoting and protecting them, providing them with relevant services, representing and supporting them, enhancing their professional and business effectiveness, and expanding the role of optometry in primary and secondary eyecare.

MEMBERSHIP
Student Member
Honorary Member
Dispensing Associate
Full Member

ORTHOPTICS
Membership of Professional Institutions and Associations

BRITISH AND IRISH ORTHOPTIC SOCIETY

Salisbury House
Station Road
Cambridge CB1 2LA
Tel: 01353 66 55 41
E-mail: bios@orthoptics.org.uk
Website: www.orthoptics.org.uk

Orthoptists diagnose and treat problems with visual development and binocular vision (how the eyes work together as a pair), and eye movement disorders. They are experts in childhood vision screening. Most orthoptists in the UK work in the Ophthalmology Clinics of acute hospitals, treating patients with stroke, glaucoma, reading difficulties, neurological disorders, low vision and other conditions.

MEMBERSHIP
Student, Full, Associate

QUALIFICATION/EXAMINATIONS
Degrees in orthoptics are offered by Liverpool University (www.liv.ac.uk), Sheffield University (www.sheffield.ac.uk) and Glasgow Caledonian University (www.gcu.ac.uk)

OSTEOPATHY AND NATUROPATHY

Membership of Professional Institutions and Associations

BRITISH OSTEOPATHIC ASSOCIATION

3 Park Terrace
Manor Road
Luton
Bedfordshire LU1 3HN
Tel: 01582 488455
Fax: 01582 481533
E-mail: boa@osteopathy.org
Website: www.osteopathy.org

The BOA was formed in 1998 as a result of the merger of the British Osteopathic Association, the Osteopathic Association of Great Britain and the Guild of Osteopaths. We provide opportunities for individual and professional development in osteopathic practice and promote the highest standards of osteopathic education and research.

MEMBERSHIP
Student Member
1st/2nd/3rd/4th Year Graduate Member
Full Member
Overseas Member

PATENT AGENCY

Membership of Professional Institutions and Associations

THE CHARTERED INSTITUTE OF PATENT ATTORNEYS

95 Chancery Lane
London WC2A 1DT
Tel: 020 7405 9450
Fax: 020 7430 0471
E-mail: mail@cipa.org.uk
Website: www.cipa.org.uk

CIPA is the professional, training and examining body for patent attorneys in the UK. From 2010 the IP Regulation Board, an independent body within the CIPA, sets the standards for regulation of the profession. Trainees, all technical graduates, also study for the qualification to practise before the European Patent Office.

MEMBERSHIP
Student Member
Associate

Fellow
British Overseas Member
Foreign Member

QUALIFICATION/EXAMINATIONS
Qualifying examination for registration as a Patent Attorney

DESIGNATORY LETTERS
RPA, CPA

PENSION MANAGEMENT
Membership of Professional Institutions and Associations

THE PENSIONS MANAGEMENT INSTITUTE

PMI House
4–10 Artillery Lane
London E1 7LS
Tel: 020 7247 1452
Fax: 020 7375 0603
E-mail: via website
Website: www.pensions-pmi.org.uk

The Pensions Management Institute is the professional body that promotes standards of excellence and lifetime learning for pensions professionals and trustees through its qualifications, membership and ongoing support services. For further details please visit our website.

MEMBERSHIP
Student Membership
Certificate Membership
Diploma Membership
Associate Membership
Fellowship
Affiliate Membership
Trustee Group Membership

QUALIFICATION/EXAMINATIONS
Award in Pensions Essentials (APE)

Certificate in Pensions Essentials (CPE)
Certificate in Pension Calculations (CPC)
Certificate in Pensions Administration (CPA)
Diploma in Pensions Administration (DPA)
Retirement Provision Certificate (RPC)
Certificate in Pensions Automatic Enrolment (CPAE)
Diploma in Retirement Provision (DRP)
Diploma in Employee Benefits and Retirement Savings (DEBRS)
Diploma in International Employee Benefits (DipIEB)
Diploma in Regulated Retirement Advice (DRRA)
Advanced Diploma in Retirement Provision (ADRP)
Awards in Pensions Trusteeship (APT)

DESIGNATORY LETTERS
CertPMI, DipPMI, APMI, FPMI

PERSONNEL MANAGEMENT
Membership of Professional Institutions and Associations

CHARTERED INSTITUTE OF PERSONNEL AND DEVELOPMENT

151 The Broadway
Wimbledon
London SW19 1JQ
Tel: +44(0)20 8612 6208
Fax: +44(0)20 8612 6201
E-mail: membershipenquiry@cipd.co.uk
Website: www.cipd.co.uk

The CIPD is the world's largest Chartered HR and development professional body. With 135,000 members across 120 countries it supports and develops those responsible for the management and development of people within organisations.

MEMBERSHIP
Affiliate Member
Student Member
Associate Member (Assoc CIPD)
Chartered Member (MCIPD)

Chartered Fellow (FCIPD)
Academic Member
For further information see: www.cipd.co.uk/membership

QUALIFICATION/EXAMINATIONS
CIPD qualifications are available at three levels:
Level 3 Foundation
Level 5 Intermediate
Level 7 Advanced
In three different sizes:

Awards
Certificates
Diplomas
For more information and to find out where to study CIPD qualifications visit: www.cipd.co.uk/qualifications

DESIGNATORY LETTERS
Assoc CIPD, Chartered MCIPD, Chartered FCIPD, CCIPD

THE INSTITUTE OF CONTINUING PROFESSIONAL DEVELOPMENT

Royal Institute of Chartered Surveyors
Parliament Square
London SW1P 3AD
Tel: 020 7695 1673
E-mail: info@cpdinstitute.org
Website: www.cpdinstitute.org

The Institute of Continuing Professional Development is part of the Continuing Professional Development Foundation, an educational charitable trust providing high-quality and broad-ranging CPD since 1981. We serve the public interest by helping to raise the effectiveness of professionals through the promotion of CPD as an important and integral element of lifelong learning.

MEMBERSHIP
Member (MInstCPD)
Fellow (FInstCPD)

DESIGNATORY LETTERS
MInstCPD, FInstCPD

UK EMPLOYEE ASSISTANCE PROFESSIONALS ASSOCIATION

PO Box 7966
Wilson
Derby DE1 0XP
E-mail: info@eapa.org.uk
Website: www.eapa.org.uk

The UK Employee Assistance Professionals Association represents the interests of professionals concerned with employee assistance, psychological health and wellbeing in the UK. Members include external and internal EAP providers, purchasers, counsellors, consultants and trainers.

MEMBERSHIP
◆ Registered Internal Provider: £1,200 per annum

◆ Registered External Provider: £1,200 per annum
◆ Non Registered Provider: £500 per annum
◆ Consultant Associate Member: £300 per annum
◆ Associate Member: £150 per annum
◆ Individual Member: £50 per annum
◆ Student Member: £25 per annum

PHARMACY

Membership of Professional Institutions and Associations

GENERAL PHARMACEUTICAL COUNCIL

1 Lambeth High Street
London SE1 7JN
Tel: 020 7735 9141
Fax: 020 7735 7629
E-mail: enquiries@rpsgb.org
Website: www.pharmacyregulation.org

The RPSGB, which dates from 1841, is the professional body for pharmacists and pharmacy technicians in England, Scotland and Wales. Our primary objectives are to lead, regulate, develop and represent the profession. We promote advancement of the science and practice of pharmacy, and pharmaceutical education and knowledge, and liaise with government and other bodies in the interests of our members.

MEMBERSHIP
Pharmacy Technician
Pharmacist
Student

DESIGNATORY LETTERS
MRPharmS, FRPharmS

THE PHARMACEUTICAL SOCIETY OF NORTHERN IRELAND

73 University Street
Belfast BT7 1HL
Tel: 028 9032 6927
Fax: 028 9043 9919
E-mail: info@psni.org.uk
Website: www.psni.org.uk

The Pharmaceutical Society of Northern Ireland, founded in 1925, is the regulatory and professional body for pharmacists in Northern Ireland. It maintains a register of more than 2,000 pharmacists and over 500 pharmacy premises, and sets and promotes the standards for pharmacists' admission to and remaining on the register, thereby protecting public safety.

MEMBERSHIP
Trainee
Member

QUALIFICATION/EXAMINATIONS
Registration Examination

PHOTOGRAPHY
Membership of Professional Institutions and Associations

ASSOCIATION OF PHOTOGRAPHERS (AOP)

21 Downham Road
London N1 5AA
Tel: 020 7739 6669
E-mail: info@aophoto.co.uk
Website: www.the-aop.org

The AOP was founded in 1968 to promote the highest standards throughout the industry and to improve the rights of all professional photographers based in the UK. Our membership currently comprises 1,800 photographers and photographic assistants, and we are supported by photographers' agents, printers, and manufacturers and suppliers of photographic equipment.

MEMBERSHIP
Student Member
Assistant Member
Photographer (full) Member
Agent Member
College Member
Affiliated Company

BRITISH INSTITUTE OF PROFESSIONAL PHOTOGRAPHY

The Coach House
The Firs, High Street
Whitchurch
Aylesbury
Buckinghamshire HP22 4SJ
Tel: 01296 642020
Fax: 01296 641553
E-mail: info@bipp.com
Website: www.bipp.com

The BIPP is the qualifying body for professional photographers in the UK. We provide support, training and qualifications for photographers across all types of photography, and organize a number of regional activities and events. A not-for-profit organization, we ensure that professional standards are met and maintained.

MEMBERSHIP
Open to full- or part-time professional photographers. Join as a Provisional member (maximum of 1 year) and work towards gaining a professional qualification. Friends' & Student membership is also available.

QUALIFICATION/EXAMINATIONS
Three tiers of qualification:
Licentiateship (LBIPP)
Associateship (ABIPP)
Fellowship (FBIPP)
BIPP is also aligned with the BA Hons in Photography through the OCA. Full details of the qualifications criteria can be found at www.bipp.com

DESIGNATORY LETTERS
LBIPP, ABIPP, FBIPP

MASTER PHOTOGRAPHERS ASSOCIATION

Jubilee House
1 Chancery Lane
Darlington
Co Durham DL1 5QP
Tel: 01325 356555
Fax: 01325 357813
E-mail: general@mpauk.com
Website: www.mpauk.com

The MPA was founded in 1952 and is now the UK's only organization for FT, qualified professional photographers. We have more than 2,000 members, who enjoy a range of benefits, including education, qualifications, informative regional meetings, business building promotions and marketing support, and abide by the Association's Code of Conduct.

MEMBERSHIP
Licentiate (LMPA)
Associate (AMPA)
Fellow (FMPA)

QUALIFICATION/EXAMINATIONS
The Diploma in Photographic Practice (DipPP) is recognized by SkillSet, as a benchmark competence mapped to the Photo Imaging National Standards: it is available to all qualified members and is an assessment process of professional photographic business and personal skills.

DESIGNATORY LETTERS
LMPA, AMPA, FMPA, DipPP

THE ROYAL PHOTOGRAPHIC SOCIETY

Fenton House
122 Wells Road
Bath
Somerset BA2 3AH
Tel: 01225 325733
E-mail: reception@rps.org
Website: www.rps.org

The RPS was founded in 1853. It is an educational charity and membership organisaton with the aim of promoting photography and supporting photographers. It realises these through exhibitions, workshops and courses and a distinctions and qualifications programme. It lobbies on behalf of photographers and photography. Membership is open to anyone.

MEMBERSHIP
Member
Family
Student
65 and over
25 and under
Disabled
Overseas

QUALIFICATION/EXAMINATIONS
Licentiate (LRPS)
Associate (ARPS)
Fellowship (FRPS)
Qualified Imaging Scientist and Licentiate (QIS LRPS)
Graduate Imaging Scientist and Associate (GIS ARPS)
Accredited Imaging Scientist and Associate (AIS ARPS)
Accredited Senior Imaging Scientist and Fellow (ASIS FRPS)
Qualified in Imaging in the Creative Industries (QICI & LRPS)
Graduate in Imaging in the Creative Industries (GICI & ARPS)

Accredited in Imaging in the Creative Industries (AICI & ARPS)
Accredited Senior in Imaging in the Creative Industries (ASICI FRPS)

DESIGNATORY LETTERS
LRPS, ARPS, FRPS

PHYSICS
Membership of Professional Institutions and Associations

INSTITUTE OF PHYSICS AND ENGINEERING IN MEDICINE

Fairmount House
230 Tadcaster Road
York YO24 1ES
Tel: 01904 610821
Fax: 01904 612279
E-mail: office@ipem.org.uk
Website: www.ipem.ac.uk

The IPEM is dedicated to bringing together physical science, engineering and clinical professionals in academia, healthcare services and industry to share knowledge, advance science and technology, and inform and educate the public, with the purpose of improving the understanding, detection and treatment of disease and the management of patients.

Affiliate
Associate
Medical Member (MedMIPEM)
Medical Fellow (MedFIPEM)
Corporate Member (MIPEM)
Fellow (FIPEM)
International

MEMBERSHIP
Student Member

DESIGNATORY LETTERS
MedMIPEM, MedFIPEM, IIPEM, MIPEM, FIPEM

THE INSTITUTE OF PHYSICS

76 Portland Place
London W1B 1NT
Tel: 020 7470 4800
Fax: 020 7470 4848
E-mail: physics@iop.org
Website: www.iop.org

The IOP is a scientific charity devoted to increasing the practice, understanding and application of physics. We have a worldwide membership of over 36,000 and are a leading communicator of physics-related science to all audiences, from specialists through to government and the general public. Our publishing company, IOP Publishing, is a world leader in scientific publishing and the electronic dissemination of physics.

MEMBERSHIP
Student Member
Affiliate
Associate Member (AMInstP)
Member (MInstP)
Fellow (FInstP)
Chartered Physicist (CPhys)
IOPi Member

DESIGNATORY LETTERS
AMInstP, MInstP, FInstP, CPhys

PHYSIOTHERAPY
Membership of Professional Institutions and Associations

THE CHARTERED SOCIETY OF PHYSIOTHERAPY

14 Bedford Row
London WC1R 4ED
Tel: 0207 306 6666
E-mail: via website
Website: www.csp.org.uk

The CSP is the professional, educational and trade union body for the UK's 52,000 chartered physiotherapists, physiotherapy students and assistants. In order to become a member of the CSP it is necessary to have undertaken a qualification recognized by the Health and Care Professions Council (HCPC) – see: www.hcpc-uk.org

MEMBERSHIP
Student Member
Associate
Member (MCSP)
Fellow (FCSP)

DESIGNATORY LETTERS
MCSP, FCSP

PLUMBING
Membership of Professional Institutions and Associations

CHARTERED INSTITUTE OF PLUMBING AND HEATING ENGINEERING

64 Station Lane
Hornchurch
Essex RM12 6NB
Tel: 01708 472791
Fax: 01708 448987
E-mail: info@ciphe.org.uk
Website: www.ciphe.org.uk

The CIPHE, founded in 1906, is the professional body for the UK plumbing and heating industry. Our membership of around 12,000 is made up of individuals from a wide range of backgrounds and includes consultants, specifiers, designers, public health engineers, lecturers, trainers, trainees and practitioners, as well as manufacturers and distributors.

MEMBERSHIP
Trainee
Affiliate
Companion (CompCIPHE)
Associate (ACIPHE)
Member (MCIPHE)
Fellow (FCIPHE)

QUALIFICATION/EXAMINATIONS
Apprentice, Journeyman and Master Plumber Certificate (awarded jointly with the Worshipful Company of Plumbers and the City & Guilds of London Institute)

DESIGNATORY LETTERS
CompCIPHE, ACIPHE, MCIPHE, FCIPHE

PRINTING

Membership of Professional Institutions and Associations

PROSKILLS UK

Unit 24 East Central
127 Olympic Avenue
Milton Park
Abingdon
Oxfordshire OX14 4SA
Tel: 01235 833844
E-mail: info@proskills.co.uk
Website: www.proskills.co.uk

Proskills UK is the bridge between employers and government on skills and training. Employer-led representing key industries including: Building Products, Coatings, Furniture, Furnishings & Interiors, Glass & Related Industries, Health and Safety Paper, Printing and Wood industries, which make up a third of the UK manufacturing sector. We help to raise the profile of the sector, set the skills standards and qualifications and ensure that the skills and funding system delivers against the current and future needs of the industries.

QUALIFICATION/EXAMINATIONS
Please see the Proskills UK website.

THE INSTITUTE OF PAPER, PRINTING AND PUBLISHING (IP3)

Claremont House
70–72 Alma Road
Windsor
Berks SL4 3EZ
Tel: 0870 330 8625
Fax: 0870 330 8615
E-mail: info@ip3.org.uk
Website: www.ip3.org.uk

IP3 is the professional body representing the interests of individuals within the paper, printing and publishing sector. It was formed in 2005 from the merger of the Institute of Paper, the Institute of Printing and the Institute of Publishing, and brought together more than 2,000 members and a wealth of knowledge.

MEMBERSHIP
Student

Associate (AIP3)
Member (MIP3)
Fellow (FIP3)

QUALIFICATION/EXAMINATIONS
Certificate

DESIGNATORY LETTERS
AIP3, MIP3, FIP3

PROFESSIONAL INVESTIGATION
Membership of Professional Institutions and Associations

THE INSTITUTE OF PROFESSIONAL INVESTIGATORS

Claremont House
70–72 Alma Road
Windsor
Berkshire SL4 3EZ
Tel: 0870 330 8622
Fax: 0870 330 8612
E-mail: admin@ipi.org.uk
Website: www.ipi.org.uk

The IPI was founded in 1976 as a professional body, catering primarily for the work and educational needs of professional investigators of all types and all specializations. We encourage members' CPD and require them to adhere to the Institute's strict code of ethics, and we promote the recognition of professional investigation as a profession by government, legislative bodies and the public.

MEMBERSHIP
Associate
Member (MIPI)
Student

Fellow (FIPI)

QUALIFICATION/EXAMINATIONS
The Institute provides an interactive online Foundation Course for students and others interested in becoming part of the investigative industry; this course also provides a refresher course for those who need to update their specialization and/or interest in other areas of investigative work.

DESIGNATORY LETTERS
MIPI, FIPI

PSYCHOANALYSIS
Membership of Professional Institutions and Associations

THE BRITISH PSYCHOANALYTICAL SOCIETY

Byron House
112a Shirland Road
London W9 2EQ
Tel: 020 7563 5000
Fax: 020 7563 5001
E-mail: admin@iopa.org.uk
Website: www.psychoanalysis.org.uk

The British Psychoanalytical Society has c500 members and c50 candidates for membership. Our aims include: to support the development of psychoanalytical knowledge as a general theory of mind, to further the clinical and scientific standards of psychoanalysis, and to train high-quality psychoanalytical professionals in sufficient numbers to develop the profession.

MEMBERSHIP
Associate Member
Full Member
Fellow

PSYCHOLOGY
Membership of Professional Institutions and Associations

BRITISH PSYCHOLOGICAL SOCIETY

St Andrews House
48 Princess Road East
Leicester LE1 7DR
Tel: 0116 254 9568
Fax: 0116 227 1314
E-mail: enquiries@bps.org.uk
Website: www.bps.org.uk

Psychology is the scientific study of people, the mind and behaviour. The British Psychological Society is the representative body for psychology and psychologists in the UK. We are responsible for the development, promotion and application of psychology for the public good.

MEMBERSHIP
Student Member
Graduate Member (MBPsS)
Associate Fellow (AFBPsS)
Fellow (FBPsS)
Honorary Fellow (HonFBPsS)
Affiliate
Chartered Membership (CPsychol)
Subscriber
e-Subscriber

QUALIFICATION/EXAMINATIONS
Statement of Equivalence in Clinical Psychology (SoE)
Qualification in Educational Psychology (Scotland) (Stage 2)
Qualification in Forensic Psychology (Stage 2) (QFP)
Qualification in Clinical Neuropsychology (QiCN)
Qualification in Counselling Psychology (QCoP)
Qualification in Health Psychology (Stage 2)
Qualification in Occupational Psychology (QOccPsych)
Qualification in Sport & Exercise Psychology (QSEP)

DESIGNATORY LETTERS
MBPsS, AFBPsS, FBPsS, CPsychol, HonMBPsS, HonFBPsS, SoE

PSYCHOTHERAPY
Membership of Professional Institutions and Associations

ASSOCIATION OF CHILD PSYCHOTHERAPISTS

Unit 7, 19–23 Wedmore Street
London N19 4RU
Tel: 020 7281 8479
E-mail: admin@childpsychotherapy.org.uk
Website: www.childpsychotherapy.org.uk

The ACP is the main professional body for psychoanalytic child and adolescent psychotherapists in the UK. Our members work with children and young people as well as their parents, families and wider networks, treating a wide range of difficulties ranging from problems with sleeping and bedwetting to eating disorders, self-harm, depression and anxiety.

MEMBERSHIP
Member

BRITISH ASSOCIATION FOR COUNSELLING AND PSYCHOTHERAPY

BACP House
15 St John's Business Park
Lutterworth
Leicestershire LE17 4HB
Tel: 01455 883300
Fax: 01455 550243
E-mail: bacp@bacp.co.uk
Website: www.bacp.co.uk

BACP is the largest and broadest body within the sector and participates in the development of counselling and psychotherapy at an international level. Our work with large and small organizations ranges from advising schools on how to set up a counselling service to assisting the NHS on service provision, working with voluntary agencies and supporting independent practitioners.

MEMBERSHIP
Individual Member
Registered Member (MBACP)
Senior Accredited Member (Snr Accred)
Student Member
Affiliate Member
Associate Member
Member (MBACP)
Accredited Member (MBACP Accred)
Fellow (FBACP)

QUALIFICATION/EXAMINATIONS
We run workshops for members and accredit individual counsellors/psychotherapists, supervisors, counselling services and training courses. For details see our website.

DESIGNATORY LETTERS
MBACP, MBACP (Accred), FBACP, Snr Accred

BRITISH ASSOCIATION FOR THE PERSON CENTRED APPROACH

BAPCA
PO Box 143
Ross-on-Wye
Herefordshire HR9 9AH
Tel: 01989 763863
E-mail: via website
Website: www.bapca.org.uk

The BAPCA was founded in 1989 as a non-religious, non-profit-making organization with the aim of advancing education in Client-Centred Psychotherapy and Counselling and the Person-Centred Approach through its publications and website, and cooperation with other national and international organizations with similar goals.

MEMBERSHIP
Individual Member
Joint Member
International Member
Institutional Member

BRITISH PSYCHOTHERAPY FOUNDATION

37 Mapesbury Road
London NW2 4HJ
Tel: 020 8452 9823
E-mail: mail@bap-psychotherapy.org
Website: www.bap-psychotherapy.org

The BAP is one of the longest established and largest independent providers of Jungian analytic and psychoanalytic psychotherapy for adults and children in the UK. We have been training psychoanalytic and Jungian psychotherapists for nearly 60 years, and our members work in the NHS, the corporate and voluntary sectors and as private practitioners.

MEMBERSHIP
Member

QUALIFICATION/EXAMINATIONS
Certificate/Diploma/MSc in Psychodynamics of Human Development (jointly with Birkbeck College, University of London)
DPsych in Child and Adolescent Psychotherapy (jointly with Birkbeck College, University of London)

CAMBRIDGE COLLEGE OF HYPNOTHERAPY

7 Bold Street
Warrington WA1 1DN
Tel: 01925 659303
E-mail: info@thecch.com
Website: www.hypnotherapytraining.org.uk

The CCH offers training to become a professional hypnotherapist. The course is accredited by the NCH, HA, APHP, NGH and NRAH. No formal qualifications are required to enrol on the course. What is required is a willingness to learn, a sense of humour and a genuine compassion and liking for people from all paths in life. This can be a very rewarding new or second career or a supplement to your current work / lifestyle. In addition to the College Diploma, it is possible to gain the HPD (Hypnotherapy Practitioner Diploma) which is awarded by ncfe and also possible to gain a Diploma awarded by the National Guild of Hypnotists in the USA. The HPD is at NVQ level 4/5 and has transferable credits of 45 for a first year degree with the Open University.

QUALIFICATION/EXAMINATIONS
Intermediate Practitioner Certificate
Diploma in Therapeutic Hypnosis (DipTHP)

DESIGNATORY LETTERS
DipTHP

NATIONAL COLLEGE OF HYPNOSIS AND PSYCHOTHERAPY

PO Box 5779
Loughborough
Leicestershire LE12 5ZF
Tel: 0845 257 8735
E-mail: enquiries@nchp.org.uk
Website: www.hypnotherapyuk.net

The NCHP is a not-for-profit organization founded in 1977 and now offers accredited hypnotherapy training, hypnosis training and psychotherapy training at weekends in Leicester, London, Manchester and Oxford. We also provide a programme of 1- and 2-day workshops and seminars, and (where appropriate) distance-learning courses.

MEMBERSHIP
United Kingdom Council for Psychotherapy
European Association for Psychotherapy
European Association for Hypno-Psychotherapy

QUALIFICATION/EXAMINATIONS
Foundation Course

Certificate in Hypno-Psychotherapy (CHP(NC))
Diploma in Hypno-Psychotherapy (DHP(NC))
Advanced Diploma in Hypno-Psychotherapy (ADHP(NC))

NATIONAL COUNCIL OF PSYCHOTHERAPISTS

PO Box 541
Keighley BD21 9DS
Tel: 0800 170 1250
E-mail: info@thencp.org
Website: www.ncphq.co.uk

The National Council is a registering and accrediting body for psychotherapists, counsellors and coaches within the UK and also, through the International Council, the rest of the world.

Members can join the Council regardless of which discipline and where they completed their training.

MEMBERSHIP
Accredited Member (MNCP Accred)
Member (MNCP)
Fellow (FNCP)

DESIGNATORY LETTERS
ANCP, LNCP, MNCP, FNCP

THE FOUNDATION FOR PSYCHOTHERAPY AND COUNSELLING

5 Maidstone Buildings Mews
72–76 Borough High Street
London SE1 1GN
Tel: 0207 378 7392
E-mail: membership@thefpc.org.uk
Website: www.thefoundation-uk.org

The Foundation for Psychotherapy and Counselling was formed during the 1970s as the graduate body of WPF Therapy (the largest charitable provider of counselling and psychotherapy in England) and now has some 700 fully trained and qualified members, most of whom are in private practice.

MEMBERSHIP
Member

THE NATIONAL REGISTER OF HYPNOTHERAPISTS AND PSYCHOTHERAPISTS

1st Floor
18 Carr Road
Nelson
Lancashire BB9 7JS
Tel: 01282 716839
E-mail: admin@nrhp.co.uk
Website: www.nrhp.co.uk

NRHP (est 1985) – a professional association of qualified hypno-psychotherapists who trained with a UKCP-accredited training organisation. Members are required to adhere to a code of ethics and carry appropriate insurance. We publish a Directory of Practitioners and offer a public referral service via our website and office. Member of the UKCP.

MEMBERSHIP
Student
Associate 1 (NRHP(Assoc 1))
Associate 2 (NRHP(Assoc 2))
Associate 3 (NRHP(Assoc 3))
Full Member (MNRHP)
Fellow (FNRHP)

DESIGNATORY LETTERS
NRHP(Assoc 1), NRHP(Assoc 2), NRHP(Assoc 3), MNRHP, FNRHP

UK COUNCIL FOR PSYCHOTHERAPY (UKCP)

2nd Floor Edward House
2 Wakley Street
London EC1V 7LT
Tel: 020 7014 9955
Fax: 020 7014 9977
E-mail: info@ukcp.org.uk
Website: www.psychotherapy.org.uk

UKCP is the leading professional body for the education, training, accreditation and regulation of psychotherapists and psychotherapeutic counsellors. Our register is accredited by the government's Professional Standards Authority. As part of our commitment to protecting the public, we work to improve access to psychotherapy, to support and disseminate research, to improve standards and to respond effectively to complaints against our members.

PURCHASING AND SUPPLY
Membership of Professional Institutions and Associations

THE CHARTERED INSTITUTE OF PURCHASING & SUPPLY

Easton House
Easton on the Hill
Stamford
Lincolnshire PE9 3NZ
Tel: 01780 756777
Fax: 01780 751610
E-mail: press@cips.org
Website: www.cips.org

The Chartered Institute of Purchasing & Supply (CIPS) is the world's largest procurement and supply professional organisation. It is the worldwide centre of excellence on purchasing and supply management issues. CIPS has a global community of 106,000 in 150 different countries, including senior business people, high-ranking civil servants and leading academics. The activities of purchasing and supply chain professionals have a major impact on the profitability and efficiency of all types of organisation and CIPS offers corporate solutions packages to improve business profitability.

MEMBERSHIP
Student Member

Affiliate
Certificate Member
Diploma Member
Associate Member
Full Member (MCIPS)
Fellow (FCIPS)
We hope Chartered Status will be available by end 2014

QUALIFICATION/EXAMINATIONS
Please see website: www.cips.org

DESIGNATORY LETTERS
MCIPS, FCIPS, Chartered Procurement and Supply Management Professional

QUALITY ASSURANCE
Membership of Professional Institutions and Associations

THE CHARTERED QUALITY INSTITUTE

2nd Floor North
Chancery Exchange
10 Furnival Street
London EC4A 1AB
Tel: 020 7245 6722
Fax: 020 7245 6788
E-mail: membership@thecqi.org
Website: www.thecqi.org

The CQI is the chartered body for quality management professionals. Established in 1919, we gained a Royal Charter in 2006 and became the CQI shortly afterwards. Our vision is to place quality at the heart of every organization; we promote the benefits of quality management to industry, disseminate quality knowledge and resources, provide qualifications and training, and assess quality competence.

MEMBERSHIP
Student
Associate Member (ACQI)

Practitioner (PCQI)

Member, Chartered Quality Professional (MCQI, CQP)

Fellow, Chartered Quality Professional (FCQI, CQP)

QUALIFICATION/EXAMINATIONS

Level 3 Certificate in Quality Management (QCF)

Level 5 Certificate in Systems Management (QCF)

Level 5 Certificate in Assuring Service & Product Quality (QCF)

Level 5 Certificate in Managing Supply Chain Quality (QCF)

Level 5 Certificate in Quality Improvement for Business (QCF)

Level 5 Certificate in Quality Management Systems Audit (QCF)

Level 5 Diploma in Quality Management (QCF)

DESIGNATORY LETTERS

MCQI, CQP; FCQI, CQP

RADIOGRAPHY

Membership of Professional Institutions and Associations

THE SOCIETY OF RADIOGRAPHERS

207 Providence Square
Mill Street
London SE1 2EW
Tel: 020 7740 7200
Fax: 020 7740 7233
E-mail: via website
Website: www.sor.org

The Society of Radiographers, founded in 1920, represents diagnostic and therapeutic radiographers in the UK. Associated professionals working in medical imaging, radiation therapy and oncology are also welcome. It is responsible for their professional, educational, public and workplace interests. Together with the College of Radiographers, our charitable subsidiary, our efforts are directed towards education, research and other activities in support of the science and practice of radiography.

MEMBERSHIP

We have a range of membership options, including student, associate professional, healthcare support worker and assistant practitioner, retired and international membership options.

RETAIL

Membership of Professional Institutions and Associations

FOOD AND DRINK TRAINING AND EDUCATION COUNCIL LTD (FTC)

Icon Business Centre
4100 Park Approach
Leeds
West Yorkshire LS15 8GB
Tel: 0113 3970 398
E-mail: ftc@foodtraining.org.uk
Website: www.foodtraining.org.uk

Food and drink training and education council (ftc) formerly known as Meat Training Council (MTC). Ftc is a food industry skills-focused charity, dedicated to working collaboratively to build a world class food industry in the UK. We are involved in a range of practical and impactful charitable work to help support our industry in competing with the greatest nations in the world. We are the parent company of FDQ, a specialist food industry awarding organisation.

INSTITUTE OF MASTERS OF WINE

24 Fitzroy Square
London W1T 6EP
Tel: 020 7383 9130
Fax: 020 7383 9139
E-mail: peter@mastersofwine.org
Website: www.mastersofwine.org

The Institute of Masters of Wine is a membership body that represents the interests of its members (Masters of Wine), administers the MW Examination, and runs an education programme in preparation for the examination. We also hold a number of events throughout the year, including seminars and tastings, master classes, discussions and, every 4 years, a symposium, most of which are open to the public.

MEMBERSHIP
Master of Wine (MW)

QUALIFICATION/EXAMINATIONS
Master of Wine Examination

DESIGNATORY LETTERS
MW

THE BRITISH ANTIQUE DEALERS' ASSOCIATION

20 Rutland Gate
London SW7 1BD
Tel: 020 7589 4128
Fax: 020 7581 9083
E-mail: info@bada.org
Website: www.bada.org

BADA, which was founded in 1918, is the trade association for antique dealers in Britain. Our vetted members are elected for their high business standards and expertise, and adhere to a strict code of practice; we provide safeguards for members of the public who deal with our members, including independent arbitration if a dispute arises.

MEMBERSHIP
Member

THE GUILD OF ARCHITECTURAL IRONMONGERS

BPF House
6 Bath Place
Rivington Street
London EC2A 3JE
Tel: 0207 033 2480
Fax: 0207 033 2486
E-mail: info@gai.org.uk
Website: www.gai.org.uk

The GAI represents the interests of architectural ironmongers and manufacturers of architectural ironmongery. We develop, promote and protect standards of integrity and excellence, and encourage academic study relating to the industry, operating an Institute for individual members to facilitate their continuous professional development. We liaise with various bodies on matters affecting the industry.

MEMBERSHIP
Affiliate Member
Associate Member
Full Member
Registered Architectural Ironmonger (Reg AI)

QUALIFICATION/EXAMINATIONS
The GAI provides a 3-year incremental training programme. Students are examined each year and must pass each year in turn before progressing to the next. A Certificate is awarded to successful students each year, culminating in the GAI Diploma (Dip GAI) on successful completion of year 3.

DESIGNATORY LETTERS
Reg AI

THE INSTITUTE OF BUILDERS MERCHANTS

1180 Elliot Court
Coventry Business Park
Herald Avenue
Coventry CV5 6UB
Tel: 01767 650662
E-mail: admin@iobm.co.uk
Website: www.iobm.co.uk

To improve through seminars and website articles, the technical and general knowledge of persons engaged in builders' merchants; to verify management training courses with providers; to acknowledge personal achievements and award diplomas, certificates and other distinctions; to encourage the need for knowledge, integrity and efficiency in the builders' merchants industry.

MEMBERSHIP
Student
Associate
Member
Fellow
Corporate Supporter

QUALIFICATION/EXAMINATIONS
University Degree
The Institute of Builders Merchants Business Studies Course
The Builders Merchants Federation Diploma in Merchanting
Higher National Certificate (HNC) in Business Studies
Higher National Diploma (HND) in Business Studies
NVQ Level 4
Company management programmes as approved by the Board of Governors

THE SOCIETY OF SHOE FITTERS

c/o The Anchorage
28 Admirals Walk
Hingham
Norfolk NR9 4JL
Tel: 01953 851171
Fax: 01953 851190
E-mail: secretary@shoefitters-uk.org
Website: www.shoefitters-uk.org

The Society of Shoe Fitters, a non-profit organisation since 1959. Freely assists public and industry with footwear/fitting/foothealth enquiries via website, help-line and leaflets. Teaches professional shoe fitting via five–month course, also instore training and application for experienced shoe fitters. Provides

National Shoe Fitting Week and lobbies government for better health education.

MEMBERSHIP
Student Member
Associate Member
Member (MSSF)
Fellow (FSSF)
Associate Member (corporate membership)

QUALIFICATION/EXAMINATIONS
One-day on-site courses – certificate only
Five-month course leading to membership qualification
Entrance Examination and Entrance Application for experienced shoe fitters leading to qualification

DESIGNATORY LETTERS
MSSF, FSSF

SECURITY
Membership of Professional Institutions and Associations

THE SECURITY INSTITUTE

1 The Courtyard
Caldecote
Warwickshire CV10 0AS
E-mail: info@security-institute.org
Website: www.security-institute.org

The Security Institute promotes professionalism in the security world and encourages a proper understanding of the value of the security function by management. The Institute operates the Register of Chartered Security Professionals – the ultimate standard for practitioners. Institute membership is recognized as an employment prerequisite by many companies and government departments.

MEMBERSHIP
Affiliate/Student
Graduate

Associate (ASyI)
Member (MSyI)
Fellow (FSyI)
Chartered Security Professional (CSyP)

QUALIFICATION/EXAMINATIONS
Certificate in Security Management (Level 3)
Diploma in Security Management (Level 5)
Advanced Diploma in Security Management (Level 7)

DESIGNATORY LETTERS
ASyI, MSyI, FSyI, CSyP

SOCIAL WORK AND PROBATION

SOCIAL WORK
Social work is a career for people who like people and much of a social worker's time is spent working in the community, helping support and protect people who are vulnerable and at risk. They work with people who are experiencing social and emotional problems and their families if they are affected. They may help people who use services to claim benefits, plan budgets, obtain legal advice or deal with other local authority departments. Social workers undertake assessment in relation to childcare, mental health and criminal justice. Depending on individual needs, a social worker may arrange services such as home care assistance or hospital treatment.

HEALTH AND CARE PROFESSIONS COUNCIL
The role of the Health and Care Professions Council (HCPC) is to protect the public. It does this by developing and monitoring strategy and policy for the HCPC, and ensuring that the organization fulfils its functions under the Health and Social Work Professions Order 2001. The Council has 12 members made up of 6 registrant and 6 lay members. The HCPC also runs committees to help the Council with its work. Four statutory committees have been set up to establish and monitor standards of education and

training and to deal with fitness to practise issues. In addition, the Council has established two non-statutory committees to provide it with advice and guidance on specific issues.

The HCPC is a regulator and keeps a register of health and care professionals who meet their standards for their training, professional skills, behaviour and health. It is an offence for someone to claim they are registered with the HCPC when they are not or to use a protected title they are not entitled to use. Each of the professions regulated by the HCPC have at least one professional title that must be registered.

The HCPC accredits universities that offer social work qualifications at both qualifying and post-qualifying levels, and quality-assures all social work courses.

EDUCATION AND TRAINING

Social workers need a breadth of skills, as they will act as an adviser, advoate, counsellor and listener. There are various routes to becoming a social worker, but you will need to gain a professional qualification in social work (usually at degree level) either on a full-time or part-time basis. This is offered at under-graduate and postgraduate masters level. It is also possible to take a degree course combining social work with mental health or learning disability nursing. To find HCPC-approved degree courses visit www.hcpc-uk.org/education/programmes/register

Students following a social work course may be eligible for a bursary from the Department of Health.

For further information visit the NHS Business Authority website: www.nhsbsa.nhs.uk/837.aspx and the Gov.UK website: www.gov.uk/social-work-bursaries/overview.

REGISTRAION

Social work regulation in the UK is covered by the HCPC in England, The Care Council for Wales in Wales, the Scottish Social Services Council (SSSC) in Scotland and the Northern Ireland Social Care Council (NISCC) in Northern Ireland. It is possible to register with more than one regulator.

For further details, contact The Health and Care Professions Council, Park House, 184 Kennington Park Road, London SE11 4BU; Tel: 0845 300 6184; Fax: 020 7820 9684; e-mail: registrations@hcpc-uk.org; website: www.hcpc-uk.org

For information about social work training and registration in Scotland, contact Scottish Social Services Council, Compass House, 11 Riverside Drive, Dundee DD1 4NY; Tel: 0345 6030 891; website: www.sssc.uk.com (online contact form).

For information about social work training and registration in Wales, contact Care Council for Wales, South Gate House, Wood Street, Cardiff CF10 1EW; Tel: 0300 3033 444; e-mail: info@ccwales.org.uk; website: www.ccwales.org.uk

For information about social work training and registration in Northern Ireland, contact Northern Ireland Social Care Council, 7th Floor, Millennium House, 19--25 Great Victoria Street, Belfast BT2 7AQ; Tel: 028 9536 2600; e-mail: info@niscc.hscni.net; website: www.niscc.info

Membership of Professional Institutions and Associations

THE BRITISH ASSOCIATION OF SOCIAL WORKERS

16 Kent Street
Birmingham B5 6RD
Tel: 0121 6223911
Fax: 0121 6224860
E-mail: membership@basw.co.uk
Website: www.basw.co.uk

The BASW is the largest professional association representing social work and social workers in the UK. Whether you are qualified or not, experienced or just entering the profession, we are here to help, support, advise and campaign on your behalf.

MEMBERSHIP
Student Member
Affiliate
Member (4 categories)
Retired Member
Overseas Member

SOCIOLOGY
Membership of Professional Institutions and Associations

BRITISH SOCIOLOGICAL ASSOCIATION

Bailey Suite, Palatine House
Belmont Business Park
Belmont
Durham DH1 1TW
Tel: 0191 383 0839
Fax: 0191 383 0782
E-mail: enquiries@britsoc.org.uk
Website: www.britsoc.co.uk

The BSA was founded in 1951 to promote sociology in the UK. Our members include researchers, teachers, students and practitioners in a variety of fields. We provide a network of communication to all who are concerned with the promotion and use of sociology and sociological research.

SPEECH AND LANGUAGE THERAPY
Membership of Professional Institutions and Associations

ROYAL COLLEGE OF SPEECH AND LANGUAGE THERAPISTS

2 White Hart Yard
London SE1 1NX
Tel: 020 7378 1200
E-mail: info@rcslt.org
Website: www.rcslt.org

The RCSLT is the professional body for speech and language therapists and support workers. We set, promote and maintain high standards in education, clinical practice and ethical conduct. Our national campaigning work aims to improve services for people with speech, language, communication and swallowing needs and to influence health, education and social care policies.

MEMBERSHIP
Student Member
Newly Qualified Member
Full Member
Fellow (FRCSLT)
Honorary Fellow (Hon FRCSLT)

DESIGNATORY LETTERS
FRCSLT, Hon FRCSLT

SPORTS SCIENCE
Membership of Professional Institutions and Associations

LONDON SCHOOL OF SPORTS MASSAGE

28 Station Parade
Willesden Green
London NW2 4NX
Tel: 020 8452 8855
Fax: 020 8452 4524
E-mail: via website
Website: www.lssm.com

The LSSM, founded in 1989, was the first to provide specialist training in Sport & Remedial Massage. We offer vocational training for those who want to develop a professional career in massage therapy and were instrumental in setting up the Institute of Sport & Remedial Massage (ISRM), which is the professional body promoting our needs and aspirations as clinical therapists.

MEMBERSHIP
Member

QUALIFICATION/EXAMINATIONS
Introductory Massage Workshop
Professional Diploma in Clinical Sport & Remedial Massage Therapy (BTEC Level 5)

STATISTICS
Membership of Professional Institutions and Associations

THE ROYAL STATISTICAL SOCIETY

12 Errol Street
London EC1Y 8LX
Tel: 020 7638 8998
E-mail: rss@rss.org.uk
Website: www.rss.org.uk

The RSS is the learned society and professional body for statistics and statisticians in the UK. We have over 7,000 members worldwide, and are active in a wide range of areas both directly and indirectly relating to the study and application of statistics.

MEMBERSHIP
Student Member
Fellow

Affiliate
Graduate Statistician (GradStat)
Chartered Statistician (CStat)

QUALIFICATION/EXAMINATIONS
Ordinary Certificate in Statistics
Higher Certificate in Statistics
Graduate Diploma in Statistics

DESIGNATORY LETTERS
GradStat, CStat

STOCKBROKING AND SECURITIES
Membership of Professional Institutions and Associations

CFA SOCIETY OF THE UK

2nd Floor
135 Canon Street
London EC4N 5BP
Tel: 020 7280 9620
Fax: 020 7280 9636
E-mail: info@cfauk.org
Website: www.cfauk.org

The CFA Society of the UK was formerly the UK Society of Investment Professionals (UKSIP) and was renamed in 2007. Our aim is to promote the development of the investment profession in the UK through the promotion of the highest standards of ethical behaviour and the provision of education, professional development, information, career support and advocacy to our members.

MEMBERSHIP
IMC Member
Candidate Member
Affiliate Member
Regular Member

QUALIFICATION/EXAMINATIONS
Investment Management Certificate (IMC)

THE CHARTERED INSTITUTE FOR SECURITIES & INVESTMENT

8 Eastcheap
London EC3M 1AE
Tel: 020 7645 0600
E-mail: customersupport@cisi.org
Website: www.cisi.org.uk

The Chartered Institute for Securities & Investment is the largest professional body for practitioners in stockbroking, derivatives markets, investment management, corporate finance, operations and related activities, having over 44,000 members.

MEMBERSHIP
Student Member
Affiliate
Associate (ACSI)
Member (MCSI)
Chartered Member (Ch. MCSI)
Fellow (FCSI)
Chartered Fellow (Ch. FCSI)

QUALIFICATION/EXAMINATIONS
Introduction to Investment
Islamic Finance Qualification
IT in Investment Operations
Risk in Financial Services
Combating Financial Crime

Global Financial Compliance
Investment Operations Certificate (IOC) also known as Investment Administration Qualification (IAQ)
Certificate in Corporate Finance
Certificate in Investments
Certificate in Private Client Investment Advice & Management
International Certificate in Wealth Management
Investment Advice Diploma
Advanced Certificate in Global Securities Operations
Advanced Certificate in Operational Risk
Diploma in Investment Compliance
Diploma in Investment Operations
CISI Diploma
CISI Masters in Wealth Management
Fundamentals of Financial Services
International Introduction to Investment
Diploma in Finance, Risk & Investment
Certificate in Finance Risk & Decision Making

Certificate for Introduction to Securities & Investment

Level 3 Certificate in Investment Management

Level 3 International Certificate in Investment Management

Level 4 Certificate in Investment Management

DESIGNATORY LETTERS
ACSI, MCSI, Ch. MCSI, FCSI, Ch.FCSI

SURGICAL, DENTAL AND CARDIOLOGICAL TECHNICIANS
Membership of Professional Institutions and Associations

THE BRITISH INSTITUTE OF DENTAL AND SURGICAL TECHNOLOGISTS

4 Thompson Green
Shipley
West Yorkshire BD17 7PR
Tel: 0115 9683 182
E-mail: via website
Website: www.bidst.org

The BIDST has been established for over 70 years and exists to provide a vehicle for the continuing education of technicians within the spheres of dental and surgical technology. It is our aim to make membership of the Institute an aspiration for all technicians, raising standards and portraying an image of professionalism which professional technicians deserve.

MEMBERSHIP
Affiliate (Overseas)
Affiliate (DCP)
Affiliate (Student)
Associate
Member
Fellow
Corporate Member

DESIGNATORY LETTERS
LBIDST, FBIDST

SURVEYING
Membership of Professional Institutions and Associations

CHARTERED ASSOCIATION OF BUILDING ENGINEERS

Lutyens House
Billing Brook Road
Weston Favell
Northampton
Northamptonshire NN3 8NW
Tel: 44 (0)1604 404 121
E-mail: info@cbuilde.com
Website: www.cbuilde.com

The ABE is the professional body for those specializing in the technology of building and the management processes by which buildings are designed, constructed, renewed and maintained. Our objectives are to promote and advance the planning, design, construction, maintenance and repair of the built environment; to maintain a high standard of professional practice; and to encourage cooperation between professionals.

MEMBERSHIP
Student
Technician
Training Affiliate
Academic Affiliate
Associate Member (ABEng)
Graduate Member (GradBEng)
Corporate Member (MBEng)
Corporate Fellow (FBEng)
Honorary Fellow (HonFBEng)

QUALIFICATION/EXAMINATIONS
ABBE Level 3 NVQ Diploma in Town Planning
Technical Support (QCF)
ABBE Level 3 NVQ Diploma in Conservation
Technical Support (QCF)
ABBE Level 3 NVQ Diploma in Building Control
Technical Support (QCF)
ABBE Level 6 NVQ Diploma in Building Control
(QCF)

ABBE Level 6 NVQ Diploma in Town Planning
(QCF)
Edexcel Level 3 NVQ Diploma in Construction Site
Supervision (Construction) (QCF)
Edexcel Level 3 NVQ Diploma in Construction
Contracting Operations (QCF)
Edexcel Level 6 NVQ Diploma in Construction
Contracting Operations (QCF)
Edexcel Level 6 NVQ Diploma in Construction Site
Management (Construction) (QCF)
Edexcel Level 6 NVQ Diploma in Senior Site
Inspection (QCF)
Edexcel Level 6 NVQ Diploma in Built Environment
Design Management (QCF)
Edexcel Level 7 NVQ Diploma in Built Environment
Design and Consultancy Practice (QCF)
Edexcel Level 7 NVQ Diploma in Construction
Senior Management (QCF)

DESIGNATORY LETTERS
ABEng, GradBEng, MBEng, FBEng

SWIMMING INSTRUCTION
Membership of Professional Institutions and Associations

THE SWIMMING TEACHERS' ASSOCIATION

Anchor House
Birch Street
Walsall
West Midlands WS2 8HZ
Tel: 01922 645097
Fax: 01922 720628
E-mail: sta@sta.co.uk
Website: www.sta.co.uk

The STA is dedicated to the preservation of human life by the teaching of swimming, lifesaving and survival techniques to as many people as possible, both in the UK and internationally. We offer a range of specialist training programmes and qualifications, which are used in more than 25 countries worldwide, and liaise with other organizations concerned with swimming teaching and water safety.

MEMBERSHIP
Junior Member
Associate Member (ASTA)
Qualified Member (MSTA)
Corporate Member

QUALIFICATION/EXAMINATIONS
STA Level 2 Award in Swimming Teaching (QCF)
STA Level 2 Certificate in Swimming Teaching (QCF)
STA Level 1 Award for Pool to Open Water Swimming Coaching (QCF)
STA Level 2 Award for Open Water Swimming Coaching (QCF)
STA Level 2 Award in Aquatic Teaching – People with Disabilities (QCF)
STA Level 2 Award in Aquatic Teaching – Baby & Pre-School (QCF)
STA Level 1 Award in Pool Emergency Procedures (QCF)
STA Level 2 Award for Pool Responder (QCF)
STA Level 2 Award for Pool Lifeguard (QCF)

STA Level 2 Award in Emergency First Aid at Work (QCF)

STA Level 2 Award in Paediatric First Aid (QCF)

STA Level 2 Award in Activity First Aid (QCF)

STA Level 2 Award in Swimming Pool Water Testing (QCF)

STA Level 2 Award in Swimming Pool Water Treatment (QCF)

STA Level 3 Award in Pool Plant Operations (QCF)

STA Level 3 Award in Preparing to Teach in the Lifelong Learning Sector (QCF)

STA Level 4 Award in Preparing to Teach in the Lifelong Learning Sector (QCF)

STA Professional Award in Teaching Swimming at SCQF Level 6

STA Professional Certificate in Teaching Swimming

STA Professional Award in Aquatic Teaching – Baby and Pre-School at SCQF Level 6

STA Professional Award in Pool Emergency Procedures at SCQF Level 6

STA Professional Award for Pool Responder at SCQF Level 7

STA Professional Award for Pool Lifeguard at SCQF Level 7

STA Award in Emergency First Aid at Work at SCQF Level 5

STA Award in First Aid at Work at SCQF Level 6

DESIGNATORY LETTERS
ASTA, MSTA

TAXATION

Membership of Professional Institutions and Associations

SOCIETY OF TRUST & ESTATE PRACTITIONERS

Artillery House (South)
11–19 Artillery Row
London SW1P 1RT
Tel: +44 (0)20 7340 0500
Fax: +44 (0)20 7340 0501
E-mail: step@step.org
Website: www.step.org

The Society of Trust and Estate Practitioners (STEP) is the worldwide professional association for practitioners dealing with family inheritance and succession planning. The Society helps to improve public understanding of the issues families face in this area and promotes education and high professional standards among its members.

MEMBERSHIP
Full members of STEP are the most experienced and senior practitioners in the field of trusts and estates.

QUALIFICATION/EXAMINATIONS
STEP Diplomas and Certificates are recognised as essential qualifications and TEPs are sought after by employers. A portfolio of courses has been designed to enhance your career, including the STEP Diploma for England & Wales (Trusts and Estates), STEP Diploma for Ireland, STEP Diploma for Scotland, STEP Diploma in International Trust Management and the STEP Diploma for Accountants & Tax Practitioners. The Certificate series includes the STEP Advanced Certificate in Family Business Advising, the STEP Certificate for Financial Services (Trusts and Estate Planning) and many more.

DESIGNATORY LETTERS
STEP

THE ASSOCIATION OF TAXATION TECHNICIANS

1st Floor
Artillery House
11–19 Artillery Row
London SW1P 1RT
Tel: 020 7340 0551
E-mail: info@att.org.uk
Website: www.att.org.uk

The ATT was founded in 1989 in recognition of the increasing demand for tax services and the development of tax practice as a professional activity in its own right. Our primary aim is to provide an appropriate qualification for individuals who undertake such work, and we now have more than 10,500 members, affiliates and registered students.

MEMBERSHIP
Member

QUALIFICATION/EXAMINATIONS
Certificate of Competency

DESIGNATORY LETTERS
ATT

THE CHARTERED INSTITUTE OF TAXATION

First Floor
11–19 Artillery Row
London SW1P 1RT
Tel: 020 7340 0550
E-mail: via website
Website: www.tax.org.uk

The CIOT, which dates from 1930, is the professional body for Chartered Tax Advisers and has 14,300 members. Our aims are to promote education in and the study of the administration and practice of taxation, and to achieve a better, more efficient, tax system for all affected by it – taxpayers, advisers and the authorities.

MEMBERSHIP
Member (CTA)

QUALIFICATION/EXAMINATIONS
Chartered Tax Adviser (CTA) examination
Advanced Diploma in International Taxation (ADIT)
VAT Compliance Diploma (VCD) (offered by the Institute of Indirect Taxation)

DESIGNATORY LETTERS
CTA, ATII, FTII

TAXI DRIVERS
Membership of Professional Institutions and Associations

TAXI DRIVERS (LONDON)

Cab drivers and cab proprietors in the Metropolitan Police District and City of London are licensed by an Assistant Commissioner of the Metropolitan Police, through the Public Carriage Office at 15 Penton Street, Islington N1 9PU. A cab driver's licence is valid for 3 years and a cab proprietor's licence for 1 year.

TEACHING/EDUCATION

Initial qualifications in the UK

Qualified Teacher Status

To obtain a teaching appointment as a qualified teacher in maintained schools and non-maintained special schools in England and Wales, it is necessary to have Qualified Teacher Status (QTS). To be qualified, teachers must have satisfactorily completed an approved course of initial teacher training (ITT), and to be able to teach in maintained schools in England must have successfully completed their induction period (there are similar arrangements for teaching in Scotland, Wales and Northern Ireland). The National College for Teaching and Leadership (NCTL), an executive agency of the Department for Education, is the awarding body for QTS.

Qualified Teacher Learning and Skills

Qualified Teacher Learning and Skills (QTLS) status is recognised in law as equal to QTS for teaching in schools. The Society for Education and Training (SET) provides QTLS which you can gain by successfully completing professional formation -- a process that enables you to demonstrate the ability to use effectively the skills and knowledge acquired whilst training to be a teacher and also the application of the occupational standards required of a teacher.

To apply for QTLS, you need an initial teacher training qualification at Level 5, for example, equivalent to the Diploma to Teach in the Lifelong Learning Sector (DTLLS) or Diploma in Education and Training (DET). You are also required to demonstrate numeracy and literacy qualifications at (or above) Level 2.

The Society for Education and Training also offers a recognition route to QTLS for members with substantial teaching experience but who do not hold a recognised teaching qualification. Visit the SET website for more information: https://set.et-foundation.co.uk. The Society for Education and Training, 157--197 Buckingham Palace Road, London, SW1W 9SP; telephone: 0800 093 9111 (free) or 020 3092 5001 (local call); email: membership.enquiries@etfoundation.co.uk.

Teacher training courses

Initial teacher training courses in England and Wales are provided by accredited training providers mainly through university departments of education. Courses available include Bachelor of Arts or Bachelor of Science with QTS, Bachelor of Education (BEd) for undergraduates, and Postgraduate Certificates of Education (PGCEs) for graduates.

Undergraduate training courses generally take three or four years full time, or four to six years part time. However, if you have undergraduate credits from previous study you may be able to complete a course in two years. A PGCE generally lasts one year full time, or up to two years part time.

There are also some employment-based routes into teaching. The School Direct Programme allows schools to recruit trainees with the expectation that they will go on to work in the school or group of schools in which they have been trained, though there is no guarantee of employment. There are more than 100 schools offering places. Courses generally last for one year full time.

School Direct offers two separate training options: the School Direct Training Programme and the School Direct Training Programme (salaried). The School Direct Training Programme (salaried) is open to graduates with three or more years' career experience (there may be exceptions for some subjects). Trainees will be employed as unqualified teachers with a salary subsidized by The National College for Teaching and Leadership. Trainees on a School Direct Training Programme will have to pay tuition fees to cover the cost of the course, but home and EU trainees will be eligible for a tuition fee loan to cover these costs and you might be eligible for funding through training bursaries or scholarships. For more information, see The National College for Teaching and Leadership, School Direct (www.education.gov.uk). WIth School Direct, you are selected for training by a school or group of schools in partnership with a university or SCITT.

School-centred initial teacher training (SCITT) is training in a school environment for those with a UK degree or an equivalent qualification. SCITT programmes are designed and delivered by groups of neighbouring schools and colleges; they are usually full time for one year. Taught by experienced, practising teachers, and often tailored towards local teaching needs, all SCITT courses lead to QTS. Many, though not all, will also award you a PGCE validated by a higher education institution. There are consortia of schools and colleges running SCITT courses all over England. These groups provide all kinds of SCITT, covering primary, middle years and the full range of secondary subjects. Application for SCITT courses is usually through UCAS (www.ucas.com/ucas/teacher-training).

Teach First offers a two-year Leadership Development Programme for those interested in an employment-based route into teaching. Teach First enables graduates with a 2:1 or a First to spend two years working in secondary and primary schools in low-income communities while earning a full-time salary. It offers the programme in different regions in the UK; during the application process you will be able to state your local area preference but they recommend that you be open minded about local area and understand that they will prioritise the needs of the schools and their children over the preferences of applicants. A PGCE is awarded on completion of the course. Candidates have to demonstrate a high proficiency in eight core competencies throughout this process to ensure they can achieve real impact for pupils: Humility, respect and empathy, interaction, leadership, planning and organising, problem solving, resilience, self-evaluation, and knowledge of Teach First and their academic subjects. Visit the Teach First website for further information: www. teachfirst.org.uk.

There are also other ways into teaching, including Troops to Teachers, Researchers in Schools and Assessment Only. Further details can be found at https://getintoteaching.education.gov.uk/explore-my-options.

The qualification of Professional Graduate Diploma in Education (PGDE) is a one-year postgraduate degree course leading to registration as a primary or secondary school teacher in Scotland (see www.teachinscotland.org). Alternatively it is possible to undertake a four-year undergraduate degree course in education. In Scotland there are seven universities that offer teacher training courses: University of Aberdeen, University of Dundee, University of Edinburgh, University of Stirling, University of Glasgow, University of Strathclyde and University of the West of Scotland. For more information on how to apply for a teaching course in Scotland contact the Universities and Colleges Admissions System (UCAS), Tel: 0371 468 0469, www.ucas.com/ucas/teacher-training. The General Teaching Council for Scotland is also a useful source of information: www.gtcs.org.uk.

The Education Workforce Council (EWC) is the independent regulator in Wales for teachers in maintained schools, Further Education teachers and learning support staff in both school and FE settings. Contact details: EWC 9th Floor Eastgate House, 35--43 Newport Road, Cardiff, CF24 0AB; Tel: 029 20460099; Fax: 029 20475850; e-mail: information@ewc.wales; website: www.ewc.wales. EWC is responsible for the administering the award of Qualified Teacher Status (QTS) in Wales, on behalf of the Welsh Government. The main ways to gain QTS in Wales are completion of a course of teacher training at an accredited institution in Wales (see www.teachertrainingcymru.org/home) or completion of employment-based training under the Graduate Teacher Programme (GTP). GTP programmes in Wales are managed and delivered by three regional centres of teacher training and education on behalf of the Welsh Government. Their contact details can be found at www.teacher trainingcymru.org/node/4

Initial Teacher Education (ITE) in Northern Ireland consists of the Postgraduate Certificate of Education course, approved by the Department of Education Northern Ireland, or a four-year BEd (Hons) course, leads to recognition as a schoolteacher in Northern Ireland (see www.deni.gov.uk).

Qualifications for admission to training

Higher education institutions offering undergraduate ITT or ITE courses will set admissions criteria, typically two good A levels (or equivalent qualifications). Entrants to PGCE and other graduate training courses will require a relevant UK Bachelor's degree or a recognized equivalent and be expected to demonstrate a standard equivalent to GCSE grade C in English and mathematics, and additionally a standard equivalent to GCSE grade C in a science subject for those wishing to train to teach primary school children. Trainees who have undertaken their initial teacher training in England must pass professional skills tests in numeracy and literacy before starting the course. These tests cover core skills that teachers need in their jobs and QTS cannot be awarded until they are passed. If you are undertaking initial teacher training in Wales, you are not required to complete the skills tests in order to be awarded QTS.

There are various funding options available to support you throughout your teacher training. These include tax-free scholarships and bursaries. Your eligibility for financial support, and the amount you can expect to receive, generally depends on the subject you choose to teach, the class of your degree, and sometimes other qualifications and experience are taken into account too.

The National College for Teaching and Leadership
The National College for Teaching and Leadership is the executive agency of the Department for Education (DfE). It is the body responsible for ITT in England and the award of QTS. It has two key aims:

improving the quality of the education workforce; and helping schools to help each other to improve. NCTL works with schools to develop an education system supported locally by partnerships and led by the best head teachers. For information about the College, visit www.gov.uk/government/organisa-tions/national-college-for-teaching-and-leadership.

Visit https://getintoteaching.education.gov.uk for queries relating to becoming a teacher, initial teacher training, recruitment opportunities or provision of relevant training.

General Teaching Councils

General Teaching Councils exist in Wales (EWC), Scotland (GTCS) and Northern Ireland (GTCNI). These councils hold registers of qualified teachers and also act as disciplinary bodies. You can find out more from their respective websites: EWC: www.ewc.wales; GTCS: www.gtcs.org.uk; GTCNI: www.gtcni.org.uk

Applications

Applications for undergraduate and postgraduate courses are made through UCAS. For courses in Northern Ireland visit the Department for Education on Northern Ireland's website (www.deni.gov.uk). You can find out more about training to teach from the following websites: UCAS: www.ucas.ac.uk; The National College for Teaching and Leadership: www.gov.uk/government/organisations/national-college-for-teaching-and-leadership. Get Into Teaching: https://getintoteaching.education.gov.uk

Membership of Professional Institutions and Associations

TECHNICAL COMMUNICATIONS
Membership of Professional Institutions and Associations

THE INSTITUTE OF SCIENTIFIC AND TECHNICAL COMMUNICATORS (ISTC LTD)

Airport House
Purley Way
Croydon CR0 0XZ
Tel: 020 8253 4506
Fax: 020 8253 4510
E-mail: istc@istc.org.uk
Website: www.istc.org.uk

The ISTC is a non-profit-making organization and the largest UK body representing professional communicators and information designers. Our aims include improving standards of scientific and technical communication, promoting scientific and technical communication as a career, supporting our members, and consulting, cooperating and collaborating with other bodies that share our ideals.

MEMBERSHIP
Student
Associate
Junior
Member (MISTC)
Fellow (FISTC)
Business Affiliate

DESIGNATORY LETTERS
MISTC, FISTC

TEXTILES
Membership of Professional Institutions and Associations

THE TEXTILE INSTITUTE

1st Floor St James' Buildings
79 Oxford Street
Manchester M1 6FQ
Tel: 0161 2371188
Fax: 0161 2361991
E-mail: tiihq@textileinst.org.uk
Website: www.textileinstitute.org

The Textile Institute covers all disciplines – from technology and production to design, development and marketing – relating to fibres, fabrics, clothing, footwear, and interior and technical textiles.

MEMBERSHIP
Student
Individual
Licentiate (LTI)

Associate (CText ATI)
Fellow (CText FTI)
Companion
Honorary Fellow
Corporate

DESIGNATORY LETTERS
LTI, CText ATI, CText FTI

TIMBER TECHNOLOGY
Membership of Professional Institutions and Associations

WOOD TECHNOLOGY SOCIETY

The Boilerhouse
Springfield Business Park
Caunt Road
Grantham
Lincs NG31 7FZ
Tel: 01476 513880
Fax: 01476 513899
E-mail: emily.drury@iom3.org
Website: www.iom3.org/content/wood-technology

The Wood Technology Society (IWSc – a Division of the Institute of Materials, Minerals and Mining), formerly the Institute of Wood Science, is the professional body for the timber and allied industries. We promote and encourage a better understanding of timber, wood-based materials and associated timber processes, and are the UK examining body, awarding qualifications at Foundation, Certificate and Diploma level.

MEMBERSHIP
Student Member

Affiliate Member
Technician (EngTech)
Fellow (FIMMM)
Professional Member (MIMMM)
Graduate (Grad IMMM)
Corporate Member

QUALIFICATION/EXAMINATIONS
Level 2 Award in Timber and Panel Products (QCF)
Certificate
Diploma

DESIGNATORY LETTERS
TIWSc, LIWSc, MIWSc, FIWSc

TOWN AND COUNTRY PLANNING

Membership of Professional Institutions and Associations

ROYAL TOWN PLANNING INSTITUTE

41 Botolph Lane
London EC3R 8DL
Tel: 020 7929 9494
E-mail: education@rtpi.org.uk
Website: www.rtpi.org.uk

The RTPI is the largest professional institute for planners in Europe, with over 23,000 members. As well as promoting spatial planning, we develop and shape policy affecting the built environment, work to raise professional standards and support members through continuous education, training and development.

MEMBERSHIP
Student Member
Licentiate Member
Associate Member
Legal Associate Member (LARTPI)
Technical Member (TechRTPI)
Retired Member
Chartered Member (MRTPI)

QUALIFICATION/EXAMINATIONS
Please see www.rtpi.org.uk/education-and-careers/find-a-course for a list of accredited training providers

DESIGNATORY LETTERS
LARTPI, TechRTPI, HonMRTPI, MRTPI, FRTPI

TRADING STANDARDS

Membership of Professional Institutions and Associations

THE CHARTERED TRADING STANDARDS INSTITUTE

1 Sylvan Court
Sylvan Way
Southfields Business Park
Basildon
Essex SS15 6TH
Tel: 01268 582200
Fax: 01268 582225
E-mail: institute@tsi.org.uk
Website: www.tradingstandards.uk

The CTSI, formed in 1881, is a not-for-profit membership association representing trading standards professionals in both the public and private sectors in the UK and overseas. CTSI encourages honest enterprise and business, and helps safeguard the economic, environmental, health and social well-being of consumers.

MEMBERSHIP
Student Member
Affiliate Member
Associate Member (ACTSI)
Full Member (MCTSI)
Chartered Trading Standards Practitioner (CTSP)
Fellow (FCTSI)

Corporate Affiliate
International

QUALIFICATION/EXAMINATIONS
The Trading Standards Qualifications Framework consists of:
Certificate of Competence
Core Skills in Consumer Affairs and Trading Standards

Module Certificate in Consumer Affairs and Trading Standards
Diploma in Consumer Affairs and Trading Standards
Higher Diploma in Consumer Affairs and Trading Standards

DESIGNATORY LETTERS
ACTSI, MCTSI, CTSP, FCTSI

TRANSPORT
Membership of Professional Institutions and Associations

INSTITUTE OF TRANSPORT ADMINISTRATION

The Old Studio
25 Greenfield Road
Westoning
Bedfordshire MK45 5JD
Tel: 01525 634940
Fax: 01525 750016
E-mail: director@iota.org.uk
Website: www.iota.org.uk

The primary aim of IoTA is to broaden and improve the knowledge, skills and experience of its members in the practice of efficient road, rail, air and sea transport. We are one of the few professional bodies still recognized within the terms of the Road Traffic 1968 (Statutory Instrument 78), wherein it is permitted to proffer qualified opinion as to the professional competence of its members. Established in 1944, the Institute continues to set new benchmark standards for the industry; promoting a policy of Experience Teaches.

MEMBERSHIP
Student (StInstTA)
Associate (AInstTA)
Honorary Member
Associate Member (AMInstTA)
Member (MInstTA)
Fellow (FInstTA)
Patron Scheme for Companies

DESIGNATORY LETTERS
StInstTA, AInstTA, AMInstTA, MInstTA, FInstTA

THE INSTITUTE OF TRAFFIC ACCIDENT INVESTIGATORS

Column House
London Road
Shrewsbury
Shropshire SY2 6NN
Tel: 08456 212066
Fax: 08456 212077
E-mail: gensec@itai.org
Website: www.itai.org

The Institute provides a means of communication, education, representation and regulation in the field of Traffic Accident Investigation. Our main aim is to provide a forum for spreading knowledge and enhancing expertise among those engaged in the discipline. Members include police officers, lecturers in higher education and private practitioners.

MEMBERSHIP
Affiliate

Associate (AITAI)
Member (MITAI)

DESIGNATORY LETTERS
AITAI, MITAI

TRAVEL AND TOURISM
Membership of Professional Institutions and Associations

CONFEDERATION OF TOURISM AND HOSPITALITY

37 Duke Street
London W1U 1LN
Tel: 020 7258 9850
Fax: 020 7258 9869
E-mail: info@cthawards.com
Website: www.cthawards.com

The Confederation of Tourism and Hospitality is an awarding body approved by Ofqual, and registered on the QCA's National Qualifications Framework. We were established in 1982 to provide recognized standards of management and vocational training appropriate to the needs of the hotel and travel industries, via our syllabuses, examinations and awards.

MEMBERSHIP
Student Member
Professional Member (MCTH)
Honorary Fellow (FCTH)

QUALIFICATION/EXAMINATIONS
Level 2 Diploma in English Communication Skills (QCF)

Level 3 Diploma in Communication and Research Skills (QCF)
Level 3 Diploma in Tourism and Hospitality (QCF)
Level 4 Diploma in Hospitality Management (QCF)
Level 4 Diploma in Tourism Management (QCF)
Level 5 Diploma in Hospitality Management (QCF)
Level 5 Diploma in Tourism Management (QCF)
Level 6 Diploma in Hospitality and Tourism Management (QCF)
Level 7 Diploma in Hospitality and Tourism Management (QCF)

DESIGNATORY LETTERS
MCTH, FCTH

INSTITUTE OF TRAVEL AND TOURISM

PO Box 217
Ware
Hertfordshire SG12 8WY
Tel: 0844 4995 653
Fax: 0844 4995 654
E-mail: enquiries@itt.co.uk
Website: www.itt.co.uk

The ITT, founded in 1956, is a professional membership body for individuals employed in the travel and tourism industry. We provide support and guidance for our members throughout their career and offer

them CPD and training to maintain standards for the benefit of the industry as a whole.

MEMBERSHIP
Student Member

Introductory Member
Affiliate Member
Member
Member (MInstTT)
Fellow
Fellow (FInstTT)
University/College Member

Group Member
Corporate Member
Retired Member

DESIGNATORY LETTERS
MInstTT, FInstTT

THE TOURISM MANAGEMENT INSTITUTE

c/o Hon Secretary, Dr Cathy Guthrie, FTMI, FTS
18 Cuninghill Avenue
Inverurie
Aberdeenshire AB51 3TZ
Tel: 01467 620769
E-mail: secretary@tmi.org.uk
Website: www.tmi.org.uk

TMI is the professional body for tourism destination managers. Its network of 250+ members shares information via website, conferences, e-mails and newsletters. The TMI CPD programme aims to support destination management professionals throughout their career. TMI HE Course Recognition gives students & lecturers assurance of industry engagement, relevance and employability.

MEMBERSHIP
Student
Associate (ATMI)
Member (MTMI)
Fellow (FTMI)

DESIGNATORY LETTERS
ATMI, MTMI, FTMI

THE TOURISM SOCIETY

Queens House
55–56 Lincoln's Inn Fields
London WC2A 3BH
Tel: 020 7269 9693
Fax: 020 7404 2465
E-mail: admin@tourismsociety.org
Website: www.tourismsociety.org

The Tourism Society, founded in 1977, is the professional membership body for people working in all sectors of tourism. We strive to drive up standards of professionalism and act as an advocate of tourism to the government and the public and private sectors, and liaise with other tourism professionals worldwide. We also provide advice, support and networking opportunities to our 1,200 or so members.

MEMBERSHIP
Student
Full Member (MTS)
Fellow (FTS)
Overseas/Retired Member
Group Member
Corporate Member
Graduate

DESIGNATORY LETTERS
MTS, FTS

VETERINARY SCIENCE
Membership of Professional Institutions and Associations

BRITISH VETERINARY ASSOCIATION

7 Mansfield Street
London W1G 9NQ
Tel: 020 7636 6541
Fax: 020 7908 6349
E-mail: bvahq@bva.co.uk
Website: www.bva.co.uk

The BVA is the representative body for the veterinary profession in the UK and has more than 11,500 members. We promote and support the interests of our members and the animals under their care, liaise with the government and are the leading provider of veterinary information to the media and general public.

MEMBERSHIP
Student Member
Associate Member
Full Member
Overseas Member

SOCIETY OF PRACTISING VETERINARY SURGEONS

The Governor's House
Cape Road
Warwick CV34 5DJ
Tel: 01926 410454
Fax: 01926 411350
E-mail: office@spvs.org.uk
Website: www.spvs.org.uk

The SPVS was founded in 1933 with the aim of promoting the interests of veterinary surgeons in private practice. We are a non-territorial division of the British Veterinary Association. Our remit is to advise on all aspects of managing the business of a clinical veterinary practice, and we hold one-day, weekend and week-long courses and an annual congress.

MEMBERSHIP
Student Member
Graduate Member
Practice Member
Retired Member

THE ROYAL COLLEGE OF VETERINARY SURGEONS

Belgravia House
62–64 Horseferry Road
London SW1P 2AF
Tel: 020 7222 2001
Fax: 020 7222 2004
E-mail: info@rcvs.org.uk
Website: www.rcvs.org.uk

The RCVS is the regulatory body for veterinary surgeons and veterinary nurses in the UK. We aim to enhance society through improved animal health and welfare. We do this by setting, upholding and advancing the educational, ethical and clinical standards of veterinary surgeons and veterinary nurses.

MEMBERSHIP
Member (MRCVS)
Fellow (FRCVS)
Registered veterinary nurse (RVN)

QUALIFICATION/EXAMINATIONS
Certificate in Advanced Veterinary Practice (CertAVP)
RCVS Advanced Practitioner
RCVS Specialist
Diploma in Advanced Veterinary Nursing
RCVS Diploma
Diploma of Fellowship (FRCVS)

DESIGNATORY LETTERS
MRCVS, FRCVS

WASTES MANAGEMENT
Membership of Professional Institutions and Associations

CHARTERED INSTITUTION OF WASTES MANAGEMENT

9 Saxon Court
St Peter's Gardens
Marefair
Northampton NN1 1SX
Tel: 01604 620426
Fax: 01604 621339
E-mail: membership@ciwm.co.uk
Website: www.ciwm.co.uk

The CIWM represents more than 6,000 waste management professionals – predominantly in the UK but also overseas. We promote education, training and research in the scientific, technical and practical aspects of waste management for the safeguarding of the environment, and set and strive to maintain high standards for individuals working in the waste management industry.

MEMBERSHIP
Student Member
Technician Member (TechMCIWM)
Associate Member (AssocMCIWM)
Graduate Member (GradMCIWM)

Licentiate (LCIWM)
Member (MCIWM)
Fellow (FCIWM)
Affiliated Organization

QUALIFICATION/EXAMINATIONS
CIWM Training Services specializes in developing and providing waste management training for individuals and organizations. Each year we organize more than 70 courses. For details see the website.

DESIGNATORY LETTERS
TechMCIWM, AssocMCIWM, GradMCIWM, LCIWM, MCIWM, FCIWM

WATCH AND CLOCK MAKING AND REPAIRING
Membership of Professional Institutions and Associations

THE BRITISH HOROLOGICAL INSTITUTE LIMITED

Upton Hall
Upton
Newark
Nottinghamshire NG23 5TE
Tel: 01636 813795
Fax: 01636 812258
E-mail: via website
Website: www.bhi.co.uk

The BHI, which was formed in 1858 to promote horology, is a professional body with about 3,000 members worldwide. We provide education and specialist training, set recognized standards of excellence in workmanship and professional conduct, and support our members in their work, making, repairing and servicing clocks and watches.

MEMBERSHIP
Associate
Member (MBHI)

Fellow (FBHI)

QUALIFICATION/EXAMINATIONS
Diploma in Clock and Watch Servicing (Level 3)
Diploma in the Servicing and Repair of Clocks / Watches (Level 4)
Diploma in the Repair, Restoration and Conservation of Clocks / Watches (Level 5)

DESIGNATORY LETTERS
MBHI, FBHI

WELDING
Membership of Professional Institutions and Associations

THE WELDING INSTITUTE

Granta Park
Great Abington
Cambridge CB21 6AL
Tel: 01223 899000
E-mail: professional@twi.co.uk
Website: www.theweldinginstitute.com

The Welding Institute is the engineering institution for welding and joining professionals. We are committed to promoting the importance of welding/materials joining technology, given its importance as a key industrial technology governing the reliability and safety of many products, and to the advancement of education, training and CPD for our members.

MEMBERSHIP
Associate (AWeldI)

Technician (TechWeldI)
Member (MWeldI)
Fellow (FWeldI)
Engineering Technician (EngTech)
Incorporated Engineer (IEng)
Chartered Engineer (CEng)

DESIGNATORY LETTERS
AWeldI, TechWeldI, MWeldI, FWeldI, EngTech, IEng, CEng

WELFARE

Membership of Professional Institutions and Associations

INSTITUTE OF WELFARE

PO Box 5570
Stourbridge DY8 9BA
Tel: 0800 0 32 37 25
E-mail: info@instituteofwelfare.co.uk
Website: www.instituteofwelfare.co.uk

The Institute of Welfare was founded in 1945 and exists to promote the highest possible standards in the delivery of welfare to those who need it. We make representations to government, undertake research on welfare issues, encourage and facilitate the exchange of information, and provide opportunities for those engaged in welfare work to pursue CPD.

MEMBERSHIP
Affiliate Member
Member (MIW)
Fellow (FIW)
Companion (CIW)

DESIGNATORY LETTERS
MIW, FIW, CIW

Part 6

Bodies Accrediting Independent Institutions

THE BRITISH ACCREDITATION COUNCIL FOR INDEPENDENT FURTHER AND HIGHER EDUCATION (BAC)

BAC is a registered charity that was established in 1984 to act as the national accrediting body for independent further and higher education. It is independent of both government and of the colleges it accredits.

A college that is accredited by BAC undergoes a thorough inspection every three or four years, with an interim visit in the middle of the accreditation cycle. BAC accreditation is not only available to colleges in the United Kingdom, there are now accredited colleges in 11 countries around the world. At present BAC accredits or approves 241 colleges in the United Kingdom and 23 overseas. Lists of accredited colleges are published each year; full details can be viewed on the BAC website.

BAC has a close relationship with the accreditation scheme operated by Accreditation UK (in the field of English as a Foreign Language) and is an affiliate of ENQA, the European Association for Quality Assurance in Higher Education. It maintains close links with The British Council, UK Council for International Student Affairs (UKCISA), Study UK and the Federation of Awarding Bodies (FAB). In 2015 it was admitted onto the European Quality Assurance Register for Higher Education (EQAR).

Accreditation by BAC is recognized by the UK Visas and Immigration (UKVI) department of the Home Office as a qualifying requirement for institutions to enrol visa students.

Further details of the work of the BAC and a current list of accredited institutions may be obtained from The Chief Executive, BAC, Fleet House, 5th Floor, 8–12 New Bridge Street, London EC4V 6AL; Tel: 0300 330 1400; Fax: 0300 330 1401; e-mail: info@the-bac.org; website: www.the-bac.org

THE BRITISH COUNCIL

The British Council runs the Accreditation UK scheme in partnership with English UK for the inspection and accreditation of organizations that provide courses in English as a Foreign Language (EFL) in Britain. The British Council aims to make quality language materials available to learners and teachers all over the world, and they offer over three million UK examinations worldwide, helping people gain access to trusted qualifications to support their career and study prospects.

Under the terms of the scheme, institutions are inspected rigorously every four years in the areas of management, resources and environment, teaching and learning, and welfare and student services. The scheme also includes a system of random spot-checking. The management and policy of the scheme are conducted by an independent board while a separate independent committee reviews inspectors' reports.

The majority of recognized schools are also members of English UK, which insists on British Council accreditation as a criterion for membership. In addition, all English UK members, of which there are around 470, are required to abide by the Association's Code of Practice and Regulations. English UK exists to raise the high standards of its members even further through conferences, training courses and publications. The association also represents the interests of members and students to government bodies, and promotes international student mobility.

Further information on the Accreditation UK scheme may be obtained from the Accreditation Unit, British Council, Bridgewater House, 58 Whitworth Street, Manchester M1 6BB; Tel: 0161 957 7692; e-mail: accreditation.unit@britishcouncil.org; website: http://www.britishcouncil.org/education/accreditation

Further information on English UK may be obtained from English UK, 219 St John Street, London EC1V 4LY; Tel: 020 7608 7960; Fax: 020 7608 7961; e-mail: info@englishuk.com; website: www.englishuk.com

THE OPEN AND DISTANCE LEARNING QUALITY COUNCIL (ODLQC)

ODLQC was established in 1968 as the Council for the Accreditation of Correspondence Colleges, a joint initiative of the then Labour government and representatives of the sector. It is the principal accrediting body for a wide variety of providers of open and distance learning (ODL) in the UK, from commercial colleges to professional and public-sector institutions. Now independent, it nevertheless continues to have the informal support of government. ODLQC promotes quality by:

- establishing standards of education and training in ODL;
- recognizing good quality provision, wherever it occurs;
- supporting and protecting the interests of learners;
- encouraging the improvement of existing methods and the development of new ones;
- linking ODL with other forms of education and training;
- promoting wider recognition of the value of ODL.

Accreditation includes a rigorous assessment of educational provision, covering materials, tutorial support, publicity, contractual arrangements with learners and general administrative procedures, each of which is measured against the Council's published benchmark standards. If accredited, the provider is monitored on a regular basis and reassessed at least once every three years.

The Council promotes those colleges that it accredits, which are by definition quality providers of ODL, and acts as honest broker in matching accredited colleges to potential markets. A list of accredited providers is included on the Council's website: www.odlqc.org.uk. The Council also seeks to protect the interests of learners by promoting the importance of accreditation, and by offering advice and support directly to learners. At the same time, knowledge of good practice is disseminated more widely, and quality encouraged wherever ODL occurs.

The Council consists of members drawn from professional and public bodies involved in education, as well as representatives of accredited providers, and has strong links with other bodies in the sector, both in the UK and abroad.

All enquiries should be through the contact form on the website: www.odlqc.org.uk

THE COUNCIL FOR INDEPENDENT EDUCATION (CIFE)

CIFE was founded in 1973 to promote strict adherence by independent sixth-form and tutorial colleges to the highest standards of academic and professional integrity and to provide an inspection service for these colleges. All member colleges must be accredited by the British Accreditation

Council for Independent Further and Higher Education (BAC), and/or the Independent Schools Inspectorate (ISI). CIFE colleges all undergo regular inspection by the Department for Education. They are also inspected either by the British Accreditation Council, the Independent Schools Inspectorate, or both. Ofsted (Office for Standards in Education) check college-provided accommodation and student welfare. Candidate membership is available for up to three years for colleges that are seeking BAC or ISI accreditation and otherwise satisfy CIFE's exacting membership criteria. All colleges must also abide by stringent codes of conduct and practice; the character and presentation of their published exam results are subject to regulation, and the accuracy of the information must be validated by BAC as academic auditor to CIFE. Full members are subject to reinspection by their accrediting bodies. There are 19 colleges in full or candidate membership of CIFE at present, spread throughout England but with concentrations in London and Oxford.

CIFE colleges offer a wide range of GCSE, A and AS level courses. In addition, some CIFE colleges offer English language tuition for students from overseas, and degree-level tuition. Most colleges also provide A level and GCSE revision courses during the Easter holidays. Further information on CIFE may be obtained from the CIFE website: www.cife.org.uk; Tel: 020 8767 8666; e-mail: enquiries@cife.org.uk

Part 7

Study Associations and the 'Learned Societies'

Study associations consist of people who wish to increase their knowledge of a particular subject or range of subjects; they may be professionals or amateurs. Some associations consist almost entirely of specialists (e.g. the Royal Statistical Society); others (e.g. the Royal Geographical Society and the Zoological Society of London) have a more general membership. The learned societies usually have two grades of membership: fellows and members. Some also admit group members (such as schools or libraries), known as corporate members, and junior associate, corresponding and overseas members, who pay lower subscriptions. Some also elect honorary fellows or members. The members of some societies may use designatory letters, but this does not mean that the holder is 'qualified' in the same sense as a doctor or a chartered accountant.

Membership of some learned societies is by election, and is commonly accepted as distinguishing the candidate by admission to an exclusive group. Candidates may be selected in respect of pre-eminence in their subject or in the public service. The chief associations of this type are the Royal Society (founded in 1660 and granted Royal Charters in 1662 and 1663), the Royal Academy of Arts (founded in 1768) and the British Academy (granted the Royal Charter in 1902).

The Royal Society (www.royalsociety.org) was established to improve 'natural knowledge' and is mainly concerned with pure and applied science and technology. Election to Fellowship (FRS) is regarded as one of the highest distinctions. The society elects Fellows, Foreign Members, Royal Fellows, Statute 12 Fellows and Honorary Fellows. The Royal Academy (www.royalacademy. org.uk) was established to cultivate and improve the arts of painting, sculpture and architecture. There are two main grades of membership: Academicians (RA), including Senior Academicians, Honorary Fellows and Honorary Members. The British Academy (www.britac.ac.uk) is the UK's national academy for the humanities and the social sciences. It is the counterpart to the Royal Society that exists to serve the natural sciences. The Academy has Fellows (FBA), Corresponding Fellows and a small number of Honorary Fellows.

A list of learned societies and study associations can be found below.

OCCUPATIONAL ASSOCIATIONS

The occupational associations do not qualify practitioners but organize them. Some coordinate the activities of specialists and others promote the individual and collective interests of professionals working in a wider area. Both types also seek to safeguard the public interest and to offer an educational service to their members. The latter type of association is especially numerous among teachers (e.g. the National Union of Teachers (NUT), the Educational Institute of Scotland (EIS), NASWUT (the National Association of Schoolmasters/Union of Women Teachers) and the National Association of Head Teachers (NAHT)), and is represented in the medical profession by the British Medical Association.

LIST OF STUDY ASSOCIATIONS AND LEARNED SOCIETIES

This list largely excludes qualifying bodies, which are covered in Part 5. The date on the left is that of foundation or adoption of title.

Agriculture and related subjects

1926	Agricultural Economics Society
1952	British Agricultural History Society
1945	British Grassland Society
1944	British Society of Animal Science
1947	British Society of Soil Science
1921	Commonwealth Forestry Association
1927	Herb Society of Great Britain
1925	Institute of Chartered Foresters
1938	Institution of Agricultural Engineers
1947	International Fertiliser Society

1839	Royal Agricultural Society of England (now part of Innovation for Agriculture)
1882	Royal Forestry Society of England, Wales and N Ireland
1784	Royal Highland and Agricultural Society of Scotland
1804	Royal Horticultural Society
1854	Royal Scottish Forestry Society
1904	Royal Welsh Agricultural Society
1943	Society of Dairy Technology
1945	The Soil Association

Anthropology and related subjects

1963	African Studies Association of the UK
1979	Association for the Study of Modern and Contemporary France
1982	Association for the Study of Modern Italy
1946	Association of Social Anthropologists of the UK and Commonwealth
1985	British Association for Irish Studies
1974	British Association for Japanese Studies
1972	British Association for South Asian Studies
1961	British Institute of Persian Studies
1973	British Society for Middle Eastern Studies
1981	European Association for Jewish Studies
1878	Folklore Society
1943	Hispanic and Luso Brazilian Council (Canning House)
1974	International Association for the Study of German Politics

1972	Japan Foundation
1891	Japan Society
1843	Royal Anthropological Institute of Great Britain and Ireland
1823	Royal Asiatic Society of Great Britain and Ireland
1868	Royal Commonwealth Society
1901	Royal Society for Asian Affairs
1936	Saltire Society
1977	Society for Caribbean Studies
1964	Society for Latin American Studies
1969	Society for Libyan Studies
1983	Society for the Promotion of Byzantine Studies
1879	Society for the Promotion of Hellenic Studies
1910	Society for the Promotion of Roman Studies
1969	University Association for Contemporary European Studies
1892	Viking Society for Northern Research

Archaeology and related subjects

1924	Ancient Monuments Society
1979	Association for Environmental Archaeology
1843	British Archaeological Association
1996	British Epigraphy Society
1948	British Institute at Ankara
1846	Cambrian Archaeological Association
1944	Council for British Archaeology
1838	Ecclesiological Society

1882	Egypt Exploration Society
1855	London and Middlesex Archaeological Society
1865	Palestine Exploration Fund
1908	Prehistoric Society
1843	Royal Archaeological Institute
1967	Society for Post-Medieval Archaeology

Art and Design

1974	Association of Art Historians	1754	Royal Society for the Encouragement of Arts, Manufactures and Commerce
1910	Contemporary Art Society		
1915	Design and Industries Association		
1950	International Institute for Conservation of Historic and Artistic Works	1904	Royal Society of British Sculptors
		1904	Royal Society of Marine Artists
		1895	Royal Society of Miniature Painters, Sculptors and Gravers
1888	National Society for Education in Art and Design	1884	Royal Society of Painter-Printmakers
1898	Pastel Society	1891	Royal Society of Portrait Painters
1768	Royal Academy of Arts	1804	Royal Watercolour Society
1814	Royal Birmingham Society of Artists	1919	Society of Graphic Fine Art
1883	Royal Institute of Oil-Painters	1952	Society of Portrait Sculptors
1831	Royal Institute of Painters in Watercolours	1952	United Society of Artists
		1955	William Morris Society
1826	Royal Scottish Academy of Art and Architecture		

Biology and related subjects

1936	Association for the Study of Animal Behaviour	1931	Society for Applied Microbiology
		1911	The Biochemical Society
1904	Association of Applied Biologists	1913	The British Ecological Society
1968	Biomedical Engineering Society	1896	The British Mycological Society
1836	Botanical Society of Scotland	1858	The British Ornithologists' Union
1836	Botanical Society of the British Isles	1959	The British Society for Cell Biology
1896	British Bryological Society	1933	The British Trust for Ornithology
1929	Freshwater Biological Association	1937	The Systematics Association
1889	Marine Biological Association	1826	Zoological Society of London
1833	Royal Entomological Society		

Chemistry

1918	Oil and Colour Chemists' Association	1897	Society of Leather Technologists and Chemists
1980	Royal Society of Chemistry		
1881	Society of Chemical Industry		

Economics, Statistics and related subjects

1992	Chartered Association of Business Schools	1902	Royal Economic Society
		1834	Royal Statistical Society
1927	Economic History Society	1897	Scottish Economic Society
1955	Institute of Economic Affairs		

Engineering and related subjects

1997	Chartered Institute of Ergonomics and Human Factors	1997	Faculty of Party Wall Surveyors
		1978	Institute of Concrete Technology
1966	Concrete Society	2006	Institution of Engineering and Technology
1946	Forum for the Built Environment (formerly the Faculty of Building)	1976	Royal Academy of Engineering

1866	Royal Aeronautical Society	1958	Society of Environmental Engineers
1916	Royal Incorporation of Architects in Scotland	2003	The Energy Institute
1860	Royal Institution of Naval Architects	1899	Town and Country Planning Association
1916	Society of Automotive Engineers		

Geography, Geology and related subjects

1963	British Cartographic Society	1846	Hakluyt Society
1949	British Geotechnical Society	1971	Institution of Environmental Sciences
1940	British Society of Rheology	1876	Mineralogical Society of Great Britain and Ireland
1923	English Place-Name Society		
1931	Gemmological Association of Great Britain	1847	Palaeontographical Society
		1957	Paleontological Association
1893	Geographical Association	1830	Royal Geographical Society
1807	Geological Society of London	1997	Royal Institute of Navigation
1858	Geologists' Association	1884	Royal Scottish Geographical Society

History and related subjects

1902	British Academy	1921	Oriental Ceramic Society
1952	British Agricultural History Society	1868	Royal Historical Society
1888	British Record Society	1836	Royal Numismatic Society
1932	British Records Association	1869	Royal Philatelic Society, London
1947	British Society for the History of Science	1953	Scottish Genealogy Society
		1886	Scottish History Society
1988	Centre for Metropolitan History	1897	Scottish Record Society
1864	Early English Texts Society	1976	Social History Society
1964	Furniture History Society	1921	Society for Army Historical Research
1869	Harleian Society	1910	Society for Nautical Research
1885	Huguenot Society of Great Britain and Ireland	1967	Society for Renaissance Studies
		1970	Society for the Social History of Medicine
1961	Institute of Heraldic and Genealogical Studies	1707	Society of Antiquaries of London
1921	Institute of Historical Research	1780	Society of Antiquaries of Scotland
1893	Jewish Historical Society of England	1956	Society of Architectural Historians in Great Britain
1964	London Record Society		
1920	Newcomen Society for the Study of the History of Engineering and Technology	1911	Society of Genealogists
		1906	The Historical Association
		1958	Victorian Society

Languages

1883	Alliance Française	1910	Chartered Institute of Linguists
1891	An Comunn Gaidhealach	1991	Instituto Cervantes
1981	Association for French Language Studies	1964	National Association for the Teaching of English
1932	Association for German Studies in Great Britain and Ireland	1993	University Council of Modern Languages
1990	Association for Language Learning	1988	Women in German Studies

Law

1958	British Institute of International and Comparative Law	1920	Royal Institute of International Affairs (Chatham House)
1972	Intellectual Property Bar Association	1965	Scottish Law Commission
1922	Law Society of Northern Ireland	1887	Selden Society
1949	Law Society of Scotland		

Literature and Arts

1959	Yr Academi Gymreig (The Welsh Academy)	1906	English Association
1973	Alliance of Literary Societies	1886	Francis Bacon Society Inc
1969	Art Libraries Society	1960	H. G. Wells Society
1970	Association for Scottish Literary Studies	1997	Historical Novel Society
		1973	Joseph Conrad Society
1989	Association of Independent Libraries	1997	Leeds Philosophical and Literary Society
1892	Bibliographical Society	1906	Malone Society
1992	British Association for Information and Library Education and Research	1781	Manchester Literary and Philosophical Society
1975	British Comparative Literature Association	1995	Philip Larkin Society
		1842	Philological Society
		1909	Poetry Society
1933	British Film Institute	1820	Royal Society of Literature
1960	British Society of Aesthetics	1884	Society of Authors
1893	Bronte Society	2004	Society of College, National and University Libraries
1949	Cambridge Bibliographical Society		
1935	Charles Lamb Society	2009	Deans and leaders of Arts, Social Sciences and Humanities (DASSH-UK)
1904	Classical Association		
1902	Dickens Fellowship		
1890	Edinburgh Bibliographical Society	1968	Thomas Hardy Society

Management

1986	British Academy of Management

Mathematics and Physics

1924	Astronomical Society of Edinburgh	1933	British Interplanetary Society
1890	British Astronomical Association	1871	Mathematical Association
1966	British Biophysical Society	1820	Royal Astronomical Society
1927	British Institute of Radiology	1850	Royal Meteorological Society

Medicine (including Psychology)

1887	Anatomical Society of GB and Ireland	1932	Association of Anaesthetists of GB and Ireland
1957	Association for Child and Adolescent Mental Health	1933	Association of British Neurologists
1957	Association for the Study of Medical Education	1953	Association of Clinical Biochemistry and Laboratory Medicine

1927	Association of Clinical Pathologists
1920	Association of Surgeons of GB and Ireland
1959	British Academy for Forensic Science
2003	British Association for Sexual Health and HIV
1977	British Association of Clinical Anatomists
1950	British Association of Forensic Medicine
1962	British Association of Oral Surgeons
1943	British Association of Otolaryngologists (ENT)
1954	British Association of Paediatric Surgeons
1971	BASO – The Association for Cancer Surgery
1945	British Association of Urological Surgeons
1934	Diabetes UK
1948	British Geriatrics Society
1832	British Medical Association
1950	British Neuropathological Society
1953	British Occupational Hygiene Society
1965	British Orthodontic Society
1918	British Orthopaedic Association
2014	Institute of Osteopathy
1924	Institute of Psychoanalysis
1901	British Psychological Society
1948	British Society for Allergy and Clinical Immunology
2011	British Association for Cytopathology

1937	British Society of Gastroenterology
1960	British Society for Haematology
1947	British Society for Research on Ageing
1945	British Thoracic Society
2014	Chartered Institute of Ergonomics and Human Factors
1946	Experimental Psychology Society
1950	Faculty of Homeopathy
1959	Chartered Society of Forensic Sciences
1819	Hunterian Society
1969	Institute of Occupational Medicine
1964	Institute of Pharmacy Management
1773	Medical Society of London
1901	Medico-Legal Society
1941	Nutrition Society
1906	Pathological Society of Great Britain and Ireland
1875	Royal Environmental Health Institute of Scotland
1734	Royal Medical Society
1931	Royal Pharmaceutical Society of Great Britain
2008	Royal Society for Public Health
1805	Royal Society of Medicine
1907	Royal Society of Tropical Medicine and Hygiene
1946	Society for Endocrinology
1950	Society for Reproduction and Fertility
1884	Society for the Study of Addiction
1926	Society of British Neurological Surgeons

Music

1977	Alkan Society
1979	British Music Society
1971	Chopin Society
1932	English Folk Dance and Song Society

1882	Incorporated Society of Musicians
1888	Plainsong and Medieval Music Society
1874	Royal Musical Association
1955	Welsh Music Guild

Philosophy

1880	Aristotelian Society
1984	British Society for the History of Philosophy
1819	Cambridge Philosophical Society
1990	Friedrich Nietzsche Society
1979	Hegel Society of Great Britain

1781	Manchester Literary and Philosophical Society
1913	Philosophical Society of England
1925	Royal Institute of Philosophy
1802	Royal Philosophical Society of Glasgow

Politics

1975	British International Studies Association	1987	Institute of Welsh Affairs
1951	David Davies Memorial Institute of International Studies	1974	International Association for the Study of German Politics
		1950	Political Studies Association
1884	Electoral Reform Society	1868	Royal Commonwealth Society
1945	Federal Trust for Education and Research	1920	Royal Institute of International Affairs (Chatham House)

Science general

1924	Association for Informational Management	1960	British Society for the Philosophy of Science
1831	British Science Association	1799	Royal Institution of Great Britain
1947	British Society for the History of Science	1660	Royal Society
		1783	Royal Society of Edinburgh

Theology and Religious Studies

1908	Baptist Historical Society	1981	European Association for Jewish Studies
1954	British Association for the Study of Religions	1903	Friends Historical Society
1904	Canterbury and York Society	1972	United Reformed Church History Society
1904	Catholic Record Society	1893	Wesley Historical Society
1961	Ecclesiastical History Society		

General Index

Note: In addition to the abbreviations listed at the beginning of the book, the following are used throughout the index; FE – Further Education; HE – Higher Education. Universities are listed under locations eg: Aberdeen, University of